Computer Architecture
and Organization

McGraw-Hill
Computer Science Series

Edward A. Feigenbaum
Stanford University

Richard W. Hamming
Naval Post Graduate School

Computer Architecture and Organization

John P. Hayes

University of Southern California

McGraw-Hill Book Company

New York   St. Louis   San Francisco   Auckland   Bogotá
Düsseldorf   Johannesburg   London   Madrid
Mexico   Montreal   New Delhi   Panama   Paris
São Paulo   Singapore   Sydney   Tokyo   Toronto

Computer Architecture and Organization

1112 HDHD 898765

This book was set in Times Roman by A Graphic Method Inc.
The editors were Peter D. Nalle and J. W. Maisel; the production supervisor was
Dennis J. Conroy. The drawings were done by ANCO/BOSTON.

Hayes, John P

    Computer architecture and organization.

    (McGraw-Hill computer science series)
    Includes bibliographies and index.
    1. Computer architecture. 2. Electronic
digital computers—Design and construction.
I. Title.
QA76.9.A73H39   621.3819'52   77-18898
ISBN 0-07-027363-4

To my father
Patrick J. Hayes
(1910–1968)
IN
MEMORIAM

CONTENTS

PREFACE

Computer architecture can be loosely defined as the study of the structure, behavior, and design of computers. It has emerged as a separate discipline in recent years mainly as a result of the proliferation of computers and advances in computer technology. The development of medium- and large-scale integrated circuits in the 1970s has provided a variety of powerful but inexpensive components for computer design. Perhaps the most significant of these developments is the appearance of microprocessors and microcomputers, devices that in a remarkably short time have resulted in the use of computer systems in many applications that previously used special-purpose logic circuits. Consequently, the concepts of computer architecture have become increasingly relevant to a large number of engineers and scientists.

This book is intended primarily as a text for electrical engineering and computer science courses in computer architecture and organization at the advanced undergraduate and beginning graduate levels. Its emphasis is on computer hardware, but the relevant aspects of software are also treated. The book assumes that the reader has a good understanding of computer programming and is familiar with the workings of at least one simple computer. Some familiarity with logic design is also assumed. There are no special mathematical prerequisites; however, occasional use is made of elementary calculus and probability theory.

The aim of the book is to provide a comprehensive and self-contained view of computer architecture. The topics covered are broadly consistent with the recommendations of the IEEE Computer Society Task Force on Computer Architecture.[1] Underlying design principles and performance evaluation are stressed; and an attempt has been made to use a uniform terminology and notation throughout. About a hundred problems are included to provide the student

---

[1]G. E. Rossmann, et al.: "A Course of Study in Computer Hardware Architecture," *Computer*, vol. 8. no. 12, pp. 44–63, December 1975.

with meaningful exercises in computer analysis and design. A solutions manual containing complete answers to all the problems can be obtained by course instructors from the publisher.

The book is divided into six chapters. Chapter 1 traces the evolution of computers from a historical viewpoint and introduces most of the notation and terminology used throughout the book. Chapter 2 deals with design methodology and examines register- and processor-level design in detail. Performance evaluation using elementary queueing theory and simulation is also introduced. The next two chapters are concerned with the design of instruction set processors. Chapter 3 covers instruction sets, arithmetic unit design, and parallel processing. Control-unit design is the topic of Chapter 4. Hardwired control is examined briefly; and a thorough discussion of microprogramming is presented. Chapter 5 examines memory technology and organization including virtual memories, associative memories, and caches. The final chapter is concerned with system structure and communications. Input-output systems, multiprocessors, fault-tolerant computers, and computer networks are discussed. Many actual computer systems are used as examples in the book, including von Neumann's IAS machine, the IBM System/360-370 series, the Intel 8080 and 8748, the Control Data STAR-100, the Hewlett-Packard 21MX, ILLIAC IV, the Bell No. 1 ESS, and the ARPANET computer network.

The material of this book has been used in the introductory graduate course on computer system architecture at the University of Southern California for several years. Somewhat more topics are included in the book than can be covered comfortably in a one-semester course, which should allow an instructor some leeway in choosing topics to emphasize. Much of the background material in Chapters 1 and 2, e.g., the review of logic design in Section 2.1, can be omitted or made into reading assignments if students are suitably prepared. Some of the more specialized topics, e.g., Section 4.3.2 on "Minimizing Microinstruction Size," Section 5.3.3 on "Associative Memories," or Section 6.3.2 on "Fault-Tolerant Computers," can also be omitted, if desired, without loss of continuity.

I wish to thank my colleagues and students at the University of Southern California, particularly P. Vahdat and A. Zygielbaum for their suggestions. The comments of G. Miller of Berkeley are also gratefully acknowledged. I owe a special thanks to my wife Terre who reviewed and proofread the book at all its many stages.

John P. Hayes

Computer Architecture and Organization

ONE

THE EVOLUTION OF COMPUTERS

This chapter traces the historical development of digital computers. It provides a broad overview of computer architecture and introduces most of the concepts that are examined in depth in later chapters. Detailed descriptions of a number of representative computers are presented.

1.1 THE NATURE OF COMPUTERS

Throughout most of history human beings have relied mainly on their brains to perform calculations; in other words, they were the computer. A variety of computational aids such as the abacus and the slide rule were invented; they simplified but did not replace manual computation. As the size and complexity of the calculations being carried out increased, two serious limitations of manual computation became apparent.

1. The speed at which a human computer can work is limited. A typical elementary operation such as addition or multiplication takes several seconds or minutes. Problems requiring billions of such operations are now routinely tackled and quickly solved using computing machines. Such problems could never be solved manually in a reasonable period of time or at reasonable cost.
2. Human beings are notoriously prone to error, so that complex calculations performed by hand are generally unreliable unless the most elaborate

1

precautions are taken to eliminate errors. Since machines are not affected by the usual sources of human error (distractions, carelessness, fatigue, etc.), they can provide results that are, within very broad limits, free of error.

The following example was frequently cited by Charles Babbage (1792–1871) to justify the construction of his first computing machine, the Difference Engine [20]. In 1794 a project was begun by the French government under the direction of G. F. Prony to compute entirely by hand an enormous set of mathematical tables. Among the tables constructed were the logarithms of the natural numbers from 1 to 200,000 calculated to 19 decimal places. Comparable tables were constructed for the natural sines and tangents, their logarithms, and the logarithms of the ratios of the sines and tangents to their arcs. The entire project took about 2 years to complete and employed from 70 to 100 people. The mathematical abilities of most of the people involved were limited to addition and subtraction. A small group of skilled mathematicians provided them with their instructions. To minimize errors, each number was calculated twice by two independent human calculators and the results were compared. The final set of tables occupied 17 large folio volumes (which were never published, however). The table of logarithms of the natural numbers alone was estimated to contain about 8 million digits.

1.1.1 Requirements for Computation

It can be useful as a starting point to analyze the processes involved in a manual calculation using pencil and paper. The primary purpose of the paper is *information storage*. The information stored on paper may include a list of instructions—i.e., an *algorithm*, or *program*—to be followed in carrying out the calculation, as well as the *data* (numbers) to be used. During the calculation, intermediate results and, ultimately, the final results, are recorded on the paper. The computational processes needed take place in the brain, which can be called the *processor*. Two major functions performed by the brain can be distinguished: a control function, which interprets the instructions and ensures that they are performed in the correct sequence; and an execution function, which carries out specific calculations such as addition, subtraction, multiplication, and division. In the execution function, the human brain is aided nowadays by the ubiquitous electronic pocket calculator. Figure 1.1*a* illustrates this view of human computation.

The major components of a computing machine are similar; these are illustrated in Fig. 1.1*b*. The *memory unit* corresponds to the paper used by the human calculator; its purpose is to store both instructions and data. The *program control unit* interprets and sequences instructions. The *arithmetic-logic unit* executes instructions. It is so called in recognition of the fact that instructions either involve numerical operations (arithmetic) or nonnumerical operations, such as program branching and symbolic processing. A convenient, if not

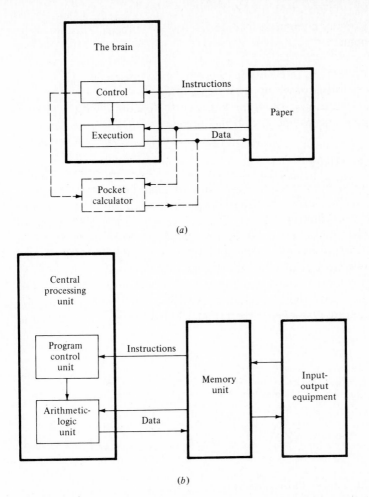

Figure 1.1 The main components of (*a*) human computation and (*b*) machine computation.

very expressive, term for the latter is logical operations. The program control and arithmetic-logic units together form the *central processing unit* (CPU), which corresponds roughly to the brain in human computations. A significant difference between the human and the machine lies in the way in which they represent information, i.e., instructions and data. Humans employ natural languages with a wide range of symbols and usually represent numbers in decimal (base 10) form. In modern computing machines, however, information is stored and processed in binary form, i.e., using two symbols conventionally denoted by 0 and 1. To provide for communication between the machine and its human users, a means of converting information from machine language to human language is thus needed. This is a major function of the box labeled *input-output (IO) equipment* in Fig. 1.1*b*.

Consequently, every computer, whether human or artificial, must have the following components.

1. A processor capable of interpreting and executing programs.
2. A memory for storing programs and data.
3. A means of transferring information between the memory and the processor, and between the computer and the outside world.

1.1.2 An Abstract Model

A *computation* can be viewed as the evaluation of some function $f(X)$, where X is the given input data and $Z = f(X)$ is the desired output data. X, Z, and f can be given very broad interpretations. X and Z can represent numbers, word statements, information files, etc. f can be a numerical calculation, the proof of a theorem, a file updating procedure, etc. In order to evaluate $f(X)$ using a particular computer, we must be able to express f as a sequence of functions $f_1, f_2, \ldots, f_n$ that can be specified using the computer's *instruction set*, i.e., the set of elementary functions that the computer can perform. $f_1, f_2, \ldots, f_n$ can be viewed as a program to evaluate $f(X)$, and the sequence of elementary operations

$$Y_1 = f_1(X)$$
$$Y_2 = f_2(Y_1)$$
$$\cdots\cdots\cdots$$
$$Y_{n-1} = f_{n-1}(Y_{n-2})$$
$$Z = f_n(Y_{n-1})$$

can be taken as a formal definition of the computation.

A question that should naturally precede any study of computer design is: Are there computations that no "reasonable" computing machine can perform? If there are, then it is clearly desirable to be aware of them, lest we attempt to build machines to carry out impossible tasks. Two very broad notions of reasonableness are generally accepted.

1. The machine should not store the answers to all possible problems.
2. It should process information (execute instructions) at a finite speed.

Such a machine is considered to be capable of performing a particular computation only if it can generate the answer in a finite number of steps, i.e., in a finite amount of time.

An abstract model of a computer that satisfies the foregoing criteria of reasonableness was introduced by the English mathematician Alan Turing (1912–1954) in 1936 [26]. This model is now called a *Turing machine*. Figure

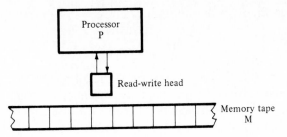

Figure 1.2 A Turing machine.

1.2 shows the components of a Turing machine. As noted in the preceding section, two essential elements of any computer are a memory and a processor. The memory of a Turing machine is a tape M of unbounded length divided lengthwise into squares. Each square may be blank or contain one of a finite set of symbols. The processor is a digital machine with a finite number of states. It has a read-write head capable of reading the contents of any one square on the tape, changing the contents of that square, and moving the tape one square to the left or right of its current position.

A Turing machine can be viewed as having a finite set of instructions with the following format:

$$s_h \quad t_i \quad o_j \quad s_k$$

meaning if the control processor P is in state s_h and the symbol t_i is currently under the read-write head, then perform the operation o_j and change the state of P to s_k. The operation o_j can be any one of the following four.

1. $o_j = t_j$, meaning write the symbol t_j on the tape (this replaces the previous symbol t_i).
2. $o_j = R$, meaning position the read-write head over the square to the right of the current square, i.e., move the tape to the left.
3. $o_j = L$, meaning position the read-write head over the square to the left of the current square, i.e., move the tape to the right.
4. $o_j = H$, meaning halt the computation.

The instruction set is essentially all possible state transitions of P. The information in the instructions can also be obtained from a state table description of P.

A computation $Z = f(X)$ is performed by a Turing machine in the following way. First the input data X is placed in suitably coded form on an otherwise blank tape. Then the Turing machine is started, causing the sequence of operations $f_1, f_2, \ldots, f_n$ to be performed. At the conclusion of the nth operation, the machine should halt, and the tape should contain the result Z.

Example 1.1: A Turing machine that can add two natural numbers Any natural number n can be represented in unary form by a sequence of n 1s. The tape symbol alphabet need only consist of the two symbols, 1 and b, where b denotes a blank. The two numbers n_1 and n_2 to be added are initially written on the tape in the following format:

$$b \underbrace{1\ 1 \ldots 1}_{n_1}\ b\ \underbrace{1\ 1 \ldots 1}_{n_2} b$$

and the read-write head is positioned over the blank to the left of the leftmost 1. The machine computes $n_1 + n_2$ by the simple expedient of replacing the blank that separates n_1 and n_2 by the symbol 1, and then deleting the leftmost 1. The resulting pattern

$$b\ b \underbrace{1\ 1 \ldots 1\ 1\ 1 \ldots 1}_{n_1 + n_2} b$$

appearing on the tape is the required answer in the same unary format as the input data. The behavior (program) of a six-state Turing machine that carries out this computation is shown in Fig. 1.3.

One of Turing's most remarkable results was a proof that there exists a *"universal" Turing machine* capable of performing every computation that can be done by any Turing machine. A universal Turing machine is essentially a simulator of Turing machines. If supplied with a description dM of another machine M, e.g., a listing of its instruction set, the universal machine proceeds to simulate the operations performed by M. It has also been shown that a universal Turing machine need only have t tape symbols and an s-state processor where $ts < 30$. Such a machine has a very small instruction set, but it is nevertheless believed to be capable of executing all the computations that can be performed by the most powerful "reasonable" computer. (This claim, often referred to as Church's thesis after the American mathematician Alonzo Church, cannot be rigorously proven because the notion of a reasonable computer is intuitive.)

1.1.3 Limitations of Computers

Unsolvable problems Since Turing machines appear to be capable of performing all possible computations, we can define the concept of a computable func-

Instruction			Comments
s_0	b	R	s_0	
s_0	1	R	s_1	Move read-write head to right across n_1.
s_1	1	R	s_1	
s_1	b	1	s_2	Replace blank between n_1 and n_2 by 1.
s_2	1	L	s_3	Move read-write head to left.
s_3	1	L	s_3	
s_3	b	R	s_4	End of 1s reached, backspace.
s_4	1	b	s_5	Delete leftmost 1.
s_5	1	H	s_0	$n_1 + n_2$ now on tape.

Figure 1.3 A Turing machine program to add two unary numbers.

tion in terms of Turing machines. A function f is (*effectively*) *computable* if $f(X)$ can be evaluated for any specified X in a finite number of steps by a Turing machine. Surprisingly, there are reasonable functions that are not computable in this sense, a fact first demonstrated by Kurt Gödel in his celebrated 1931 paper [10].

Let (M,X) denote a Turing machine M with input tape X, that is, X is the initial information on its tape. We will say that (M,X) halts if M, when started with input tape X, halts after a finite number of steps. Let $f_H(M,X)$ be a function defined for all Turing machines and input tapes as follows.

$$f_H(M,X) = 1 \qquad \text{if } (M,X) \text{ halts}$$

$$f_H(M,X) = 0 \qquad \text{if } (M,X) \text{ never halts}$$

It can be shown that the function f_H is not computable [19]. This implies that the problem of devising a general method to determine if (M,X) halts, where (M,X) is any Turing machine and input tape pair, is *unsolvable* (also called *undecidable*). This particular problem is known as the Turing machine halting problem. A large number of related problems are also known to be unsolvable.

The existence of unsolvable problems has some important implications. A common and often costly error made by inexperienced computer programmers is to write programs that contain infinite loops and therefore fail to halt under certain input conditions. It would be useful to have a universal debugging program or machine that could determine whether any given program halts. The unsolvability of the Turing machine halting problem immediately implies that no such debugging tool can be designed. It is important to note that this assertion is only true when applied to the class of *all* possible programs. For any specific program or set of programs, it may be possible to devise a solution to the halting problem. Hence the limitations imposed by the existence of unsolvable problems can be ignored in most practical design situations.

Intractable problems The Turing machine model of digital computers discussed in the preceding section has at least one unrealistic, if not unreasonable, aspect: the number of tape states is unbounded. A Turing machine can be called an infinite-state computer [19]. Real computers have a finite amount of memory and are therefore *finite-state machines*. This means that there are certain computations which can be performed by Turing machines but cannot, in principle, be performed by finite-state machines. For example, a finite-state machine cannot multiply two arbitrarily large binary numbers, but a Turing machine can. The number of states of a typical computer is extremely large, so the limitation has no significant practical impact. For example, the main memory of a large computer typically has 10^6 or more binary storage cells. The number of possible states is therefore $2^{10^6} \approx 10^{300,000}$. The binary numbers that cannot be multiplied by this machine would have to contain about $10^{300,000}$ bits!

Many computational problems can, in principle, be solved to an acceptable degree of accuracy by real finite-state computers. There is, however, a large class of "difficult" problems, some of great practical importance, that are solvable by real machines but require such an excessively large amount of memory space or computation time that no reasonable computer, no matter how fast, can ever be expected to solve them.

Suppose that an algorithm A is to be executed by a computer. Two questions can be raised concerning the difficulty of the algorithm.

1. How much memory space is needed to execute it? *space complexity*
2. How much time is needed to execute it? *time complexity*

The answers to these questions are termed the *space complexity* and the *time complexity* of A, respectively [1]. These quantities are generally difficult to measure, and they depend on the particular input data to which A is applied. The limitations imposed by time seem to be much more restrictive than those imposed by memory space. We will therefore confine our discussion to time complexity. An algorithm is said to have *time complexity* $O(f(n))$ if the number of steps it needs to process data of "size" n is $cf(n)$, where $f(n)$ is some function of n and c is a constant. The *size* of the input data is typically defined as the number of independent input parameters. The time complexity of the algorithm provides an approximate indication of the time required to execute it on some computer, e.g., a Turing machine.

It is common to regard a problem as *tractable* if and only if there is an algorithm to solve it that has time complexity $O(p(n))$, where $p(n)$ is a polynomial function of the input size n. A problem, all of whose algorithms have time complexity $O(k^n)$, that is, which have an execution time that grows exponentially with n, is intractable. There are many important problems for which no algorithm of time complexity $O(p(n))$ is known. These are therefore considered to be intractable.

Example 1.2: Finding the minimum disjunctive (sum-of-products) form of an n-variable Boolean function $f(x_1, x_2, \ldots, x_n)$ This is a classic problem in switching theory [25]. Most algorithms for solving it involve the following two steps:

Step 1 Compute all prime implicants of f.
Step 2 Select a minimal set of prime implicants that covers all the minterms of f.

The maximum number of minterms of f is 2^n, while the maximum number of prime implicants lies between 2^{n-1} and 3^{n-1}. Thus step 1 can easily require more than 2^n operations to generate the prime implicants (and also a memory space that is of the order of 2^n if all the prime implicants are to be stored). Step 2 requires selection of one of the 2^p possible subsets of the p prime implicants of f. Clearly, in the worst case, this algorithm has a complexity that is exponential in the input size n.

Technology	Date	Number of operations per second
Mechanical	1930	1
Electromechanical	1940	10
Vacuum tube	1945	10^3
Discrete semiconductor	1960	10^6
Integrated semiconductor	1970	10^8

Figure 1.4 The influence of technology on computing speed.

The fact that a problem is intractable generally means that it can be solved exactly in a reasonable amount of time only when the input size is below some maximum value m. The value of m depends on the speed (number of operations per second) of the computer used to solve the problem. It might be expected that computer speeds could be increased to make m any desired value. We now present some arguments which indicate that this is most unlikely.

Speed limitations The speed at which computers operate, as measured by the number of basic operations performed per second, has undergone rapid and continual improvement. This has been mainly due to improvements in the technology of switching circuits and memory devices. Figure 1.4 shows the influence of the major technologies introduced during the past 50 years on computer speed [4]. It can be concluded that computer speed has increased linearly by a factor of about 100 per decade since 1930. Let us suppose that computer speeds continue to increase at a steady linear rate.

Consider four algorithms A_1, A_2, A_3, and A_4 with time complexity $O(n)$, $O(n^2)$, $O(n^{100})$, and $O(2^n)$, respectively. Suppose that all four are run on a computer M having a speed of s operations per second. Let m_i denote the input size of the largest problem that can be solved by algorithm A_i in a fixed time period t seconds. Let m_i' denote the input size of the largest problem that can be solved by A_i in t seconds on a new computer M' with a computing speed of $100s$ operations per second. Figure 1.5 shows the values of m_i' for the four algorithms. In the case of the intractable algorithm A_4, the increase in the size of the problem that can be handled on moving from M to M' is insignificant. This is also true of A_3, even though it does not fall within the strict definition of intractable given above. In order to increase the maximum problem sizes that can be processed by A_3 and A_4 in the given time period by a factor of 100, i. e., from m_i to $100 \, m_i$, we would need computers with speeds of $10^{200} s$ and $10^{30m_4} s$,

Algorithm	Time complexity	Maximum problem input size	
		Computer M	Computer M'
A_1	$O(n)$	m_1	$100m_1$
A_2	$O(n^2)$	m_2	$10m_2$
A_3	$O(n^{100})$	m_3	$1.047m_3$
A_4	$O(2^n)$	m_4	$m_4 + 6.644$

Figure 1.5 Effect of computer speedup by a factor of 100 on maximum problem input size for four algorithms.

respectively! It is reasonable to suppose that problems of these magnitudes can never be solved using the given algorithms.

Because so many important problems are intractable, inexact or non-algorithmic methods have been devised to solve them. Two major techniques can be identified.

1. The intractable problem Q is replaced by a tractable problem Q' whose solution approximates that of Q.
2. A relatively small set of possible solutions to Q is examined using reasonable, intuitive, but often poorly understood selection criteria. The "best" of these potential solutions is taken as the solution to Q. Methods such as this which are designed to produce acceptable, if not optimal, answers using a reasonable amount of computation time are sometimes called *heuristic procedures*.

It is widely believed that the rate of increase in computer speed due to technology improvements is diminishing, which suggests that significant increases in speed can come only from improved algorithms or heuristics, although the intractable problems may not permit such improvement. An important way of increasing the overall operating speed of a computer is to introduce *parallel processing*. Most conventional computers perform their basic operations in strict sequence; only one operation may take place at any time. This is termed *sequential (serial) processing*. The parallel processing approach attempts to replace a computation requiring n steps by m independent subcomputations that can be carried out simultaneously, i.e., in parallel. This often results in a substantial reduction in overall computation time. Not all problems are amenable to this technique, since many algorithms are inherently sequential in nature; step $i + 1$ cannot begin until step i computes its results.

In conclusion, it might be asked: What are the ultimate physical limitations on computing speed? Using arguments based on quantum mechanics, Bremermann has conjectured that no computer system, either living or artificial, can process more than 2×10^{47} bits of information per gram of its mass per second [6]. If true, a computer the size of the earth (6×10^{27} g) operating continuously for a period equal to the estimated age of the earth (10^{10} years) could then process fewer than 10^{93} bits! This is far fewer than the number of possible states $10^{300,000}$ of the computer with 10^6 storage cells cited earlier. It is also less than the number of possible sequences of moves in chess, which has been estimated at 10^{120}.

1.2 THE MECHANICAL ERA: 1623 to 1945

1.2.1 The First Calculators

Machines capable of automatically performing the four arithmetic operations (addition, subtraction, multiplication, and division) first appeared in Europe in the early seventeenth century. The earliest such machine seems to have been designed and built in 1623 by Wilhelm Schickhard (1592–1635), who was a professor at the University of Tübingen. Schickhard's machine was little known in his day. Far more influential was the machine built by the great French philosopher and scientist Blaise Pascal (1623–1662) in 1642 [12, 24]. This was essentially a mechanical counter for performing addition and subtraction "automatically." It contained two sets of six dials, or "counter wheels," for representing decimal numbers. (Two additional dials were used for calculations involving the nondecimal currency then used in France; for simplicity, we ignore them.) Each dial had the 10 decimal numerals engraved on it, separated by equal intervals. The position of the dial indicated the decimal value being stored. One set of dials $W = w_5 w_4 w_3 w_2 w_1 w_0$ acted as a six-digit accumulator register; the other set $W' = w_5' w_4' w_3' w_2' w_1' w_0'$ was used to enter a number to be added (or subtracted) from the accumulator. W and W' were connected by gears so that when w_i' was rotated k units, w_i also rotated k units to indicate the number $w_i \pm k$. Pascal's main technical innovation was a ratchet device for automatically transferring a carry from w_i to w_{i+1} whenever w_i passed from 9 to 0. Negative numbers were handled by a complements representation, so that the same mechanical motion could perform both subtraction and addition.

Around 1671 the German philosopher and mathematician Gottfried Leibniz (1646–1716) constructed a calculator that could perform multiplication and division automatically. It consisted of two parts: an adding-subtracting machine that, in Leibniz's words "coincides completely with the calculating box of Pascal" [24]. Two additional sets of wheels were provided to represent a multiplier and a multiplicand. Multiplication was implemented by means of chains and pulleys. (An extremely clear account of the machine by Leibniz can be found in Ref. 24.) Leibniz's machine was the forerunner of many machines that are now called four-function calculators. They remained academic curiosities until the nineteenth century, when the commercial production of mechanical calculators was begun.

1.2.2 Babbage's Computers

One of the most remarkable figures in the history of computing machines is the Englishman Charles Babbage [20]. He designed two computers: the Difference Engine (begun in 1823) and the Analytical Engine (conceived in 1834), both of which represented fundamental advances. For a variety of reasons, neither machine was ever completed.

The Difference Engine The objective of the Difference Engine was automatic computation of mathematical tables. Babbage was greatly impressed by the number of errors in tables that were computed manually. His machine was intended to calculate the entries of a table automatically and transfer them via steel punches to an engraver's plate, from which the tables could be printed. The only arithmetic operation performed was addition. However, using only addition, a large number of useful functions can be calculated by a technique called the *method of finite differences*.

Let

$$f(x) = \sum_{j=0}^{n} a_j x^j$$

be an nth degree polynomial with constant coefficients, which is defined for some sequence $x_1, x_2, x_3, \ldots$ of values of x separated by equal intervals Δx. Let $y_j = f(x_j)$. The ith *difference* of y_j, denoted $\Delta^i y_j$, is defined recursively as follows:

$$\Delta^0 y_j = y_j$$
$$\Delta^i y_j = \Delta^{i-1} y_{j+1} - \Delta^{i-1} y_j \qquad \text{for } i \geq 1 \qquad (1.1)$$

It can easily be shown that $\Delta^n y_j = $ constant and $\Delta^i y_j = 0$ for $i > n$. Suppose that the values of the first $n + 1$ nonzero differences of y_j are known. Then we can calculate the corresponding differences for y_{j+1} from Eq. (1.1); thus

$$\Delta^i y_{j+1} = \Delta^i y_j + \Delta^{i+1} y_j \qquad (1.2)$$

In this way, starting from y_0, we can compute successive values of y_j. It will be observed that the only operation in Eq. (1.2) is addition. Any continuous function can be approximated as closely as desired by a polynomial; the method of finite differences can hence be used to evaluate such functions.

Example 1.3:   Computation of sin x over the range $0.0 \leq x \leq 0.5$ at intervals of 0.1 rad by the method of finite differences The sine function can be expressed as a power series:

$$\sin x = x - \frac{x^3}{3!} + \frac{x^5}{5!} - \frac{x^7}{7!} + \ldots$$

We can therefore employ the polynomial

$$y = x - \frac{x^3}{3!}$$

to approximate $\sin x$ for small values of x. Four differences (including $\Delta^0 y = y$) must be computed using the following equations:

$$y_{j+1} = y_j + \Delta^1 y_j$$
$$\Delta^1 y_{j+1} = \Delta^1 y_j + \Delta^2 y_j$$
$$\Delta^2 y_{j+1} = \Delta^2 y_j + \Delta^3 y_j$$
$$\Delta^3 y_{j+1} = \Delta^3 y_j$$

In order to start the computation we need the initial values y_0, $\Delta^1 y_0$, $\Delta^2 y_0$, and $\Delta^3 y_0$. These values can be found by computing y_0, y_1, y_2, and y_3 direct-

x_j	$y_j \approx \sin x_j$	$\Delta^1 y_j$	$\Delta^2 y_j$	$\Delta^3 y_j$
0.0	0.00000	0.09983	-0.00100	-0.00100
0.1	0.09983	0.09883	-0.00200	-0.00100
0.2	0.19866	0.09683	-0.00300	-0.00100
0.3	0.29549	0.09383	-0.00400	-0.00100
0.4	0.38932	0.08983	-0.00500	-0.00100
0.5	0.47915	0.08483	-0.00600	-0.00100

Figure 1.6 Computation of sin x by the method of finite differences.

ly from the defining polynomial $x - x^3/3!$ and using the following relations implied by Eq. (1.1).

$$y_0 = 0.0$$

$$\Delta^1 y_0 = y_1 - y_0$$

$$\Delta^2 y_0 = y_2 - 2y_1 + y_0$$

$$\Delta^3 y_0 = y_3 - 3y_2 + 3y_1 - y_0$$

Figure 1.6 contains a table for computing y to five decimal places using the method of finite differences.

Figure 1.7 shows the logical structure of a Difference Engine. It contains a set of mechanical registers (counter wheels) to store the differences $\Delta^0 y_i$, $\Delta^1 y_i, \ldots, \Delta^n y_i$. Each pair of adjacent registers is connected by an adding mechanism similar in principle to Pascal's to implement Eq. (1.2). Once initial values

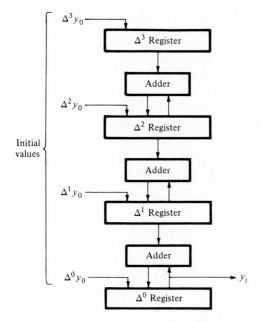

Figure 1.7 Structure of Babbage's Difference Engine.

are assigned to each register, the Difference Engine can, if driven by a suitable motor (presumably a steam engine), automatically "crank out" successive values of y.

Babbage proposed to build a Difference Engine that would accommodate sixth-degree polynomials and 20-digit numbers. The project was begun in 1823 and abandoned in 1842, despite a grant of £17,000 from the British government. One reason for Babbage's failure to complete his engine was the inadequacy of the mechanical technology then available. A second reason was Babbage's loss of interest in the Difference Engine when he conceived of a much more powerful and ambitious machine he called the Analytical Engine. Several modest difference engines were successfully completed, notably that of the Swede Georg Scheutz (1785–1873) which was built during the period 1837 to 1853. The Scheutz machine could handle third-degree polynomials and 15-digit numbers.

The Analytical Engine Unlike the Difference Engine, the Analytical Engine was intended to perform any mathematical operation automatically. Figure 1.8 shows the general structure of the final design proposed by Babbage. It consists of two main parts: *the store*, a memory unit comprising sets of counter wheels, and *the mill*, which corresponds to a modern arithmetic-logic unit. The mill was to be capable of performing the four basic arithmetic operations. In order to control the sequence of operations of the machine, Babbage proposed to use punched cards of the type developed for the Jacquard loom. The cards, which constituted a program, were divided into two groups.

1. *Operation cards*, used to control the operation of the mill. Each operation card selected one of the four possible operations (+, −, ×, ÷) to be performed at each step in the program.
2. *Variable cards*, intended to select the memory locations to be used by a particular operation, i.e., the source of the operands and the destination of the results.

Provision was also made for supplying numerical information (constants) either

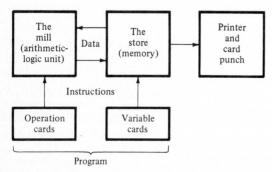

Figure 1.8 Structure of Babbage's Analytical Engine.

by punched cards or by manually setting counter wheels. It was intended to have output data either printed or punched on cards.

Example 1.4: A program for the Analytical Engine to solve the simultaneous equations

$$a_{11}x_1 + a_{12}x_2 = b_1$$
$$a_{21}x_1 + a_{22}x_2 = b_2$$

This hypothetical program was devised by L. F. Menebrea, a contemporary of Babbage's [20]. The variables x_1 and x_2 are to be evaluated using the relations

$$x_1 = \frac{a_{22}b_1 - a_{12}b_2}{a_{11}a_{22} - a_{12}a_{21}}$$

$$x_2 = \frac{a_{11}b_2 - a_{21}b_1}{a_{11}a_{22} - a_{12}a_{21}}$$

Let W_0, W_1, ... denote the number locations (sets of counter wheels) in the store. The constants of the problem are assigned to the store as follows: $W_0 = a_{11}$, $W_1 = a_{12}$, $W_2 = b_1$, $W_3 = a_{21}$, $W_4 = a_{22}$, $W_5 = b_2$. Figure 1.9 shows the sequence of operation and variable cards needed to calculate x_1. A similar sequence can be used to calculate x_2.

One of Babbage's most significant contributions was a mechanism for enabling a program to alter the sequences of its operations automatically. In modern terms, he conceived of conditional branch instructions. They were to be implemented by testing the sign of a number; one course of action was to be taken if the sign were positive; another, if negative. He also proposed a mechanism for both advancing and reversing the control cards to permit branching to any desired instruction.

The design of the Analytical Engine embodied all the features essential to a general-purpose automatic computing machine. Again Babbage proposed to

	Program		
	Variable cards		
Operation cards	Source	Destination	Comments
$\times$	W_2, W_4	W_8	$W_8 \leftarrow a_{22}b_1$
$\times$	W_1, W_5	W_9	$W_9 \leftarrow a_{12}b_2$
$\times$	W_0, W_4	W_{10}	$W_{10} \leftarrow a_{11}a_{22}$
$\times$	W_1, W_3	W_{11}	$W_{11} \leftarrow a_{12}a_{21}$
$-$	W_8, W_9	W_{12}	$W_{12} \leftarrow a_{22}b_1 - a_{12}b_2$
$-$	W_{10}, W_{11}	W_{13}	$W_{13} \leftarrow a_{11}a_{22} - a_{12}a_{21}$
$\div$	W_{12}, W_{13}	W_{14}	$W_{14} \leftarrow W_{12} \div W_{13}$

Figure 1.9 Part of a program for the Analytical Engine.

build it on a grand scale. The store was to have a capacity of 1000 50-digit decimal numbers. He estimated that the addition of two numbers would take a second, and multiplication, a minute. It is very unlikely that a mechanical computer of this size could ever be successfully built. Babbage spent much of the latter half of his life refining the design of the Analytical Engine. Only a small part of the machine was actually constructed.

1.2.3 Later Developments

Commercial calculators A number of improvements in the design of four-function mechanical calculators were made in the nineteenth century which lead to their widespread use. The first to achieve commercial success was the Arithmomètre designed in France about 1820. The Comptometer, designed by the American inventor D. E. Felt (1862–1930) in 1885, was one of the earliest calculators to use depressible keys for entering data and commands; and it also printed its results on paper. A later innovation was the use of electric motors to drive the mechanical components and thus increase the speed of operation.

Another important development in the late nineteenth century was the commercial application of punched-card equipment for sorting and tabulating large amounts of data. The inventor of the punched-card tabulating machine was the American Herman Hollerith (1860–1929). The first major application of Hollerith's system was to process the data collected in the 1890 United States census. Hollerith's punched cards, like those of Babbage, were based on the cards used in the Jacquard loom. The various characteristics of the population were indicated by holes punched in specific locations on the cards. These holes were then sensed by an electrical mechanism and counted (tabulated) mechanically. In 1896 Hollerith formed the Tabulating Machine Company to manufacture his equipment. In 1911 his company merged with several others to form the Computing-Tabulating-Recording Company, which was renamed the International Business Machines Corporation (IBM) in 1924.

Electromechanical computers No significant attempts to build general-purpose digital computers were made after Babbage's death until the 1930s when, independently, such computers were constructed in Germany and the United States. In Germany in 1938, Konrad Zuse built a mechanical computer, the Z1, apparently unaware of Babbage's work. The Z1, unlike previous mechanical computers, used binary instead of decimal arithmetic. A subsequent machine, the Z3, completed in 1941, is believed to have been the first operational general-purpose program-controlled computer. The arithmetic unit of the Z3 was constructed from relays (electromechanical binary switches) and employed floating-point number representation. Zuse's work was interrupted by the Second World War and had very little influence on the subsequent development of computers. A number of special-purpose relay computers were also built around this time in the United States, notably at Bell Telephone Laboratories [21].

Howard Aiken (1900–1973), a physicist at Harvard University, proposed the design of a general-purpose electromechanical computer in 1937. Unlike Zuse, Aiken was apparently aware of the work of Babbage and earlier pioneers. An arrangement was made to have IBM construct the machine according to Aiken's basic design. Work was begun on the computer, originally called the Automatic Sequence Controlled Calculator and later the Harvard Mark I, in 1939, and it became operational in 1944. Like Babbage's machines, the Harvard Mark I employed decimal counter wheels for its working memory. It had a storage capacity of 72 23-digit decimal numbers. The machine was controlled (programmed) by means of a punched paper tape which combined the functions of Babbage's operation cards and variable cards. Each instruction had the format

$$A_1 \quad A_2 \quad OP$$

where OP was an operation to be performed, e.g., multiplication, A_1 and A_2 were the registers storing the operands to be used, and A_2 was also the destination of the result.

Figure 1.10 summarizes the major steps in the development of mechanical computers.

1.3 THE FIRST GENERATION: 1946 to 1954

Mechanical computers suffer from two serious drawbacks:

1. Computing speed is limited by the inertia of the moving parts.

Date	Inventor: machine	Capability	Technical innovations
1642	Pascal	Addition, subtraction	Automatic carry transfer; complements number representation
1671	Leibniz	Addition, subtraction multiplication, division	"Stepped reckoner" mechanism for multiplication and division
1827	Babbage: Difference Engine	Polynomial evaluation by method of finite differences	Automatic multistep operation
1834	Babbage: Analytical Engine (never completed)	General-purpose computation	Automatic sequence control mechanism (program)
1941 1944	Zuse: Z3 Aiken: Harvard Mark I	General-purpose computation	The first operational general-purpose computers

Figure 1.10 Milestones in the development of mechanical computers.

2. The transmission of information by mechanical means (gears, levers, etc.) is cumbersome and unreliable.

For electronic computers, on the other hand, the "moving parts" are electrons. Information can be transmitted by electric currents at speeds approaching the speed of light (300,000 km/s). The triode vacuum tube invented by Lee de Forest (1873–1961) in 1906 permits the switching of electrical signals at speeds far exceeding those of any mechanical device. Vacuum tubes can also be used to construct very fast binary storage devices.

1.3.1 Electronic Computers

The first attempt to construct an electronic computer using vacuum tubes appears to have been made by John Atanasoff in the late 1930s at Iowa State University. This was a special-purpose machine for solving simultaneous linear equations. The first general-purpose electronic computer was probably the ENIAC (*E*lectronic *N*umerical *I*ntegrator *a*nd *C*alculator) built at the University of Pennsylvania under the direction of John Mauchly and J. Presper Eckert. Like Babbage's Difference Engine, part of the motivation for the ENIAC was the need to construct tables automatically—in this case, ballistics tables for the U.S. Army Ordnance Department which funded the project. Work on the ENIAC began in 1943 and it was completed in 1946. It was an enormous machine weighing 30 tons and containing over 18,000 vacuum tubes. It was also substantially faster than any previous computer. Thus, while the Harvard Mark I required about 3 s to perform a 10-digit multiplication, the ENIAC required only 3 ms.

The ENIAC had a working memory comprising 20 electronic accumulators, each of which could accommodate a signed 10-digit decimal number. A decimal digit was stored in a ring counter consisting of 10 vacuum-tube flip-flops connected in a closed loop. Digit i was stored by setting flip-flop i to the 1 state and the remaining nine flip-flops to the 0 state. Thus the ring counter was the electronic equivalent of the mechanical counter wheel. The ENIAC was basically a decimal rather than a binary computer. The accumulators in the ENIAC combined the functions of storage and addition and subtraction as do counter wheels. Additional units were included for multiplication, division, and extraction of square roots.

Figure 1.11 shows the architecture of the ENIAC. It was programmed manually by setting switches and plugging and unplugging cables. Thus, for example, to add the contents of accumulator A_1 to accumulator A_2, a data path from A_1 to A_2 had to be established manually. A "master programmer" unit (which was also set manually) could be used to cause multistep or iterative operations to take place automatically. Data was entered via a "constant transmitter" (usually a punched-card reader). Special memories, called "function tables," were used for storing tables of constants. Results could be punched on cards or printed on an electric typewriter.

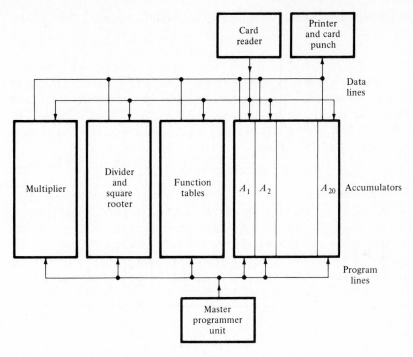

Figure 1.11 Structure of the ENIAC.

1.3.2 Stored-Program Computers

In the Analytical Engine and its modern successors the Harvard Mark I and the ENIAC, programs and data were stored in separate memories. Entering or altering programs was an extremely tedious task. The idea of storing programs and data in the same memory unit, the *stored-program concept*, is usually attributed to the ENIAC designers, most notably the Hungarian-born mathematician John von Neumann (1903–1957), who was a consultant on the ENIAC project. It was first published in a 1945 proposal by von Neumann for a new computer, the EDVAC (*E*lectronic *D*iscrete *V*ariable *C*omputer). Besides facilitating the programming process, the stored-prcgram concept makes it possible for a program to modify its own instructions.

As well as being a stored-program computer, the EDVAC differed from its predecessors in several important respects. It had a much larger store, provided by a mercury-delay-line main memory with a capacity of 1024 or 1K words (numbers or instructions); and a secondary, slower, magnetic-wire memory with a capacity of about 20K words. Unlike earlier machines, binary rather than decimal number representation was used. Because access to the main delay-line memory was serial (bit by bit) rather than parallel (word by word) the EDVAC used serial binary arithmetic-logic circuits.

Before a program could be executed by EDVAC, all instructions and data were placed in its main memory. Arithmetic instructions had the following format

$$A_1 \quad A_2 \quad A_3 \quad A_4 \quad OP$$

meaning perform the operation OP (addition, subtraction, multiplication, or division) on the contents of the main-memory locations with addresses A_1 and A_2 and place the results in memory location A_3. The fourth address A_4 specified the location of the next instruction to be executed. Conditional branch instructions had the format

$$A_1 \quad A_2 \quad A_3 \quad A_4 \quad C$$

meaning if the number in A_1 is not less than the number in A_2, take the next instruction from A_3; otherwise take the next instruction from A_4. Finally, a pair of input-output instructions were provided for transferring information between the main and secondary memories. In these instructions, the second address field was split into two components, an operation modifier m, indicating the direction of the data transfer, and a number n, which represented the address of the particular secondary storage wire to be used. The instruction format was

$$A_1 \quad m, n \quad A_3 \quad A_4 \quad W$$

meaning

1. If $m = 1$, transfer to wire n the sequence of words stored in locations A_1, $A_1 + 1$, $A_1 + 2, \ldots, A_3$.
2. If $m = 2$, transfer from wire n a sequence of words to main-memory locations A_1, $A_1 + 1$, $A_1 + 2, \ldots, A_3$.

Again A_4 was the address of the next instruction to be used. The input-output equipment of the EDVAC consisted of a typewriterlike device, which transferred information directly to magnetic wires, and a printer, which reversed this process. The EDVAC became operational in 1951.

In 1946, von Neumann and his colleagues began the design of a new stored-program computer, now referred to as the IAS computer, at the Princeton Institute for Advanced Studies. This machine employed a random-access cathode-ray-tube main memory, which permitted an entire word to be accessed in one operation. Unlike the EDVAC, parallel binary circuits were employed. Each instruction contained only one memory address and had the format

$$OP \quad A$$

The central processing unit (CPU) contained several high-speed (vacuum-tube) registers used as implicit storage locations for operands and results. Although its input-output facilities were limited, the IAS machine was quite modern in its conception. It can be regarded as the prototype of all subsequent general-purpose computers. Several reports describing its design were published and had a far-reaching influence on the development of computers. Because of its importance, the IAS machine is described in detail in Sec. 1.3.3.

Figure 1.12 shows the architecture typical of general-purpose computers in the late 1940s and early 1950s. It is common to refer to machines of this period as *first-generation computers* which exhibits a somewhat short-sighted view of computer history. The control of the computer was centralized in a single CPU; all operations in the system, e.g., the transfer of a single word of information between an IO device and main memory, required direct intervention by the CPU. This is suggested in Fig. 1.12 by broken arrows which represent control lines.

In the late 1940s and early 1950s, the number of computers being built grew very rapidly. Besides those already mentioned, notable early machines include the Whirlwind I constructed at Massachusetts Institute of Technology (MIT) and a series of machines culminating with the ATLAS computer that were designed at Manchester University. Whirlwind I was the first computer to have a ferrite-core main memory, while the Manchester machines introduced the concepts of one-level storage (now called virtual memory) and B registers (now called index registers).

In 1947 Eckert and Mauchly formed a company, the Eckert-Mauchly Computer Corporation, to manufacture computers commercially. Their first

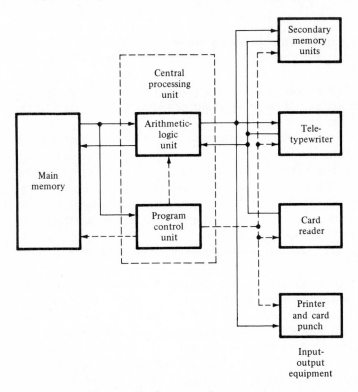

Figure 1.12 Architecture of a first-generation computer.

successful machine was the UNIVAC (*Uni*ve*rsal* *A*utomatic *C*omputer), delivered in 1951. It employed a mercury delay-line main memory of the type used in EDVAC and had a magnetic-tape secondary memory. The Eckert-Mauchly Computer Corporation eventually became part of the UNIVAC Division of Sperry-Rand Corporation. IBM, which had helped build the Harvard Mark I and was then the major manufacturer of punched-card processing equipment, delivered its first electronic stored-program computer, the 701, in 1953. The 701 employed an electrostatic (cathode-ray-tube) main memory, and magnetic-drum and -tape secondary memories. The 701 was the first of the long 700 series of IBM machines.

The earliest computer programs were written in the binary code, or *machine language*, used to represent the instructions in memory. Thus the binary string

$$0011 \quad 1011 \quad 0000 \quad 0000 \quad 0111$$

might represent the instruction add the contents of memory location 7 to the accumulator. Machine-language instructions are tedious to write and difficult to recognize. A substantial improvement is obtained by allowing operations and addresses to be specified in symbolic mnemonic form. The above instruction might then be written as

$$\text{ADD} \quad \text{X1.}$$

This type of programming, which came into use in the early 1950s, was called *symbolic programming*; it is now called *assembly-language* programming. Assembly language is obviously much easier to use than machine language. It does, however, require a special systems program, called an *assembler*, to translate a user's program from assembly language to machine language before the user's program is to be executed.

First-generation computers had very little system software compared with modern machines. Programs had to be written in machine or assembly languages which varied from computer to computer. Usually only one programmer could have access to the computer at any time. This meant that the CPU was frequently idle, e.g., while slow IO data transfers were taking place or while control of the machine was being transferred to a new programmer.

1.3.3 A First-Generation Computer

This section is based on a classic series of reports by A. W. Burks, H. H. Goldstine, and J. von Neumann written from 1946 to 1948 that described the logic design and programming of the IAS computer [7,11]. We have changed the authors' terminology and notation to conform more closely with current usage. The structure of the IAS computer is shown in Fig. 1.13, including the main registers, processing circuits, and information paths within the central processing unit. This computer can be taken as representative of what are now called first-generation computers.

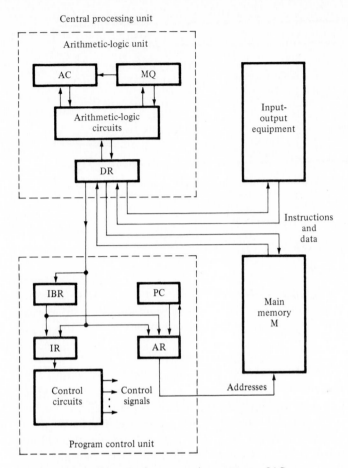

Central processing unit

Figure 1.13 Structure of a first-generation computer: IAS.

Information formats The basic quantity of information in the IAS machine is a 40-bit "word," which is usually defined as the amount of information that can be transferred between the main memory M and the CPU in one step. The memory M has a capacity of $2^{12} = 4096$ words. A word stored in M can represent either instructions or data. The basic data item is a fixed-point binary number having the format shown in Fig. 1.14. The leftmost bit (bit 0) represents the sign of the number. The coding used is twos complement, which permits an adder to be used for both addition and subtraction. The binary point is assumed to be between bits 0 and 1; hence only numbers lying between -1 and 1 are dealt with directly. All numbers used in calculations must be adjusted by some suitable scaling to be within this range. Each instruction requires 20 bits, so that two instructions can be stored in each memory location, as shown in Fig. 1.14. The rightmost 12 bits of each instruction are used to contain the *address* of a location in M; the remaining 8 bits, called the *opcode*, specify an operation to be performed.

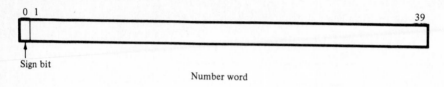

Number word

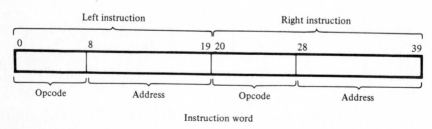

Instruction word

Figure 1.14 Information formats of the IAS computer.

Note that while each EDVAC instruction contained four memory addresses, the IAS instruction allows only one. This results in a substantial reduction in word length. Two aspects of the IAS organization make this possible.

1. Fixed registers in the CPU are used to store operands and results. The IAS instructions automatically make use of these registers as required. In other words, CPU register addresses are implicit in the opcode.
2. The instructions of a program are stored in main memory in approximately the sequence in which they are to be executed. Hence the address of the next instruction is the address of the current instruction plus one. The need for a next instruction address in the instruction format is eliminated. Special branch instructions are included to permit the instruction execution sequence to be varied.

CPU organization The CPU of the IAS computer contains a set of high-speed registers used for temporary storage of instructions, memory addresses, and data. Data processing is performed by the arithmetic-logic circuits. The control circuits decode the instructions, route information correctly through the system, and provide proper timing signals for all actions. A clock is used to synchronize the operation of the system.

The main memory M is used for storing programs and data. A word transfer can take place between the 40-bit *data register* DR of the CPU and any location M(X) with address X in M. The address X to be used is stored in a 12-bit *address register* AR. The DR may be used to store an operand during the execution of an instruction. Two additional registers for the temporary storage of operands and results are included: the *accumulator* AC and the *multiplier-quotient* register MQ. Two instructions are fetched simultaneously from

M and transferred to the program control unit. The instruction that is not to be executed immediately is placed in an *instruction buffer register* IBR. The opcode of the other instruction is placed in the *instruction register* IR where it is decoded. The address field of the current instruction is transferred to the memory address register. Another address register called the *instruction address register* or the *program counter* PC is used to store the address of the next instruction to be executed.

Instruction set It is assumed that consecutive instructions of a program are stored in consecutive locations in M. Unless a branch instruction is encountered, the address of the next instruction is the address of the current instruction plus one. The program counter is therefore incremented by one to determine the address of the next instruction.

Following Burks et al., we use a formal notation, called a description language, or *register transfer language*, as a shorthand way of describing instructions and microoperations within the computer. The description language approximates an assembly language used to prepare programs for the computer. The use of computer description languages can be traced to Babbage [20]. The one introduced here and used throughout this book is representative and largely self-explanatory. Storage locations (in the CPU or M) are referred to by acronym. The transfer of information is denoted by an arrow; thus $A \leftarrow B$ means transfer the contents of storage location B to A. Elements of storage arrays are indicated by subscripts or by appending a list of indices in parentheses to the array name. Thus M is considered to be 4096×40 array so that M(X,0:19) denotes bits 0 through 19 of word X in M.

Figure 1.15 illustrates the use of our descriptive notation in a simple IAS program that adds two numbers. The numbers to be added are stored in memory locations 100 and 101. The sum is stored in location 102. Note the central role played by the accumulator AC in this program.

The complete set of instructions defined for the IAS computer in [7] is given in Fig. 1.16. We have divided them into five groups: data transfer, unconditional branch, conditional branch, arithmetic, and address modify instructions. The data-transfer instructions cause data to be transferred unchanged (except possibly in sign) among CPU registers and main-memory locations. There are two unconditional branch instructions (also called "jump" or "go to" instructions) which cause the next instruction to be taken from either the left or

Instruction	Comments
$AC \leftarrow M(100)$	Transfer contents of memory location 100 to the accumulator
$AC \leftarrow AC + M(101)$	Add the contents of memory location 101 to the contents of the accumulator and place the result in the accumulator
$M(102) \leftarrow AC$	Store the contents of the accumulator in memory location 102

Figure 1.15 An IAS program to add two numbers.

Instruction type	Shorthand notation	Description
Data transfer	AC ← MQ	Transfer contents of register MQ to the accumulator AC
	MQ ← M(X)	Transfer contents of memory location X to MQ
	M(X) ← AC	Transfer contents of accumulator to memory location X
	AC ← M(X)	Transfer M(X) to the accumulator
	AC ← −M(X)	Transfer −M(X) to the accumulator
	AC ← |M(X)|	Transfer absolute value of M(X) to the accumulator
	AC ← −|M(X)|	Transfer −|M(X)| to the accumulator
Unconditonal branch	**go to** M(X, 0:19)	Take next instruction from left half of M(X)
	go to M(X, 20:39)	Take next instruction from right half of M(X)
Conditional branch	**if** AC ≥ 0 **then go to** M(X, 0:19)	If number in the accumulator is nonnegative, take next instruction from left half of M(X)
	if AC ≥ 0 **then go to** M(X, 20:39)	If number in the accumulator is nonnegative, take next instruction from right half of M(X)
Arithmetic	AC ← AC + M(X)	Add M(X) to AC; put the result in AC
	AC ← AC + |M(X)|	Add |M(X)| to AC; put the result in AC
	AC ← AC − M(X)	Subtract M(X) from AC; put the result in AC
	AC ← AC − |M(X)|	Subtract |M(X)| from AC; put the result in AC
	AC, MQ ← MQ × M(X)	Multiply M(X) by MQ; put most significant bits of result in AC, put least significant bits in MQ
	MQ, AC ← AC ÷ M(X)	Divide AC by M(X); put the quotient in MQ and the remainder in AC
	AC ← AC × 2	Multiply accumulator by 2, i.e., shift left one bit position
	AC ← AC ÷ 2	Divide accumulator by 2, i.e., shift right one bit position
Address modify	M(X, 8:19) ← AC(28:39)	Replace left address field at M(X) by 12 rightmost bits of AC
	M(X,28:39) ← AC(28:39)	Replace right address field at M(X) by 12 rightmost bits of AC

Figure 1.16 Instruction set of the IAS computer.

the right half of M(X). The conditional branch instructions permit a jump to take place if and only if the accumulator contains a nonnegative number. These instructions allow the results of a computation to alter the instruction execution sequence; they are of great importance. The arithmetic instructions provide the basic data-processing commands of the computer. The last two, which we call address modify instructions, permit addresses to be computed in the arithmetic-logic unit and then inserted into instructions stored in main memory. The address modify feature allows a program to alter its own instructions, an important characteristic of stored-program machines.

Method of operation Instructions are fetched and executed in two separate consecutive steps called the *fetch cycle* and the *execution cycle*. Together they form the *instruction cycle*. Figure 1.17 shows the principal actions carried out in each cycle. The fetch cycle is common to all instructions. Since two instructions are obtained simultaneously from M, the next instruction may be in the instruction buffer register. If not, the contents of the program counter are transferred to the address register and a READ request is sent to M. The required data at memory location X is then transferred to the data register DR. The opcode of the required instruction (which is in either the left or right half of the fetched word) is sent to the instruction register and decoded. The address part

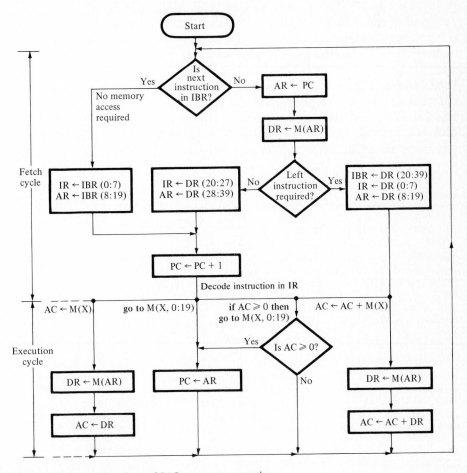

Figure 1.17 Partial flowchart of IAS computer operation.

of the instruction goes to the address register, while the second instruction may be transferred to the instruction buffer register IBR. The program counter PC is incremented whenever the next instruction is not in IBR.

The computer now enters the execution cycle, and its subsequent actions depend on the particular instruction being executed. Figure 1.17 shows the execution cycles of four representative instructions. Note that each instruction is executed by a sequence of microoperations. Each microoperation typically involves a single register transfer operation of the form $S \leftarrow f(S_1, S_2, \ldots, S_k)$, where $S_1, S_2, \ldots, S_k$ are the storage locations of the operands, f is a logical or arithmetic operation, and S is where the result is stored. Thus the ADD instruction $AC \leftarrow AC + M(X)$ is implemented by two microoperations, as shown in Fig. 1.17. First the contents of the memory location $M(AR)$ specified by the address register AR are transferred to the data register DR. Then the contents of the data register and the accumulator are added and the result is placed in the accumulator. Certain instructions such as multiply were implemented by a much larger number of microoperations. A multiplication algorithm requiring 39 addition and shift microoperations was used. The intrinsic capabilities of the arithmetic-logic circuits are limited to addition, subtraction, and simple operations such as shifting and complementing.

Programming Figure 1.18 shows an IAS version of Menabrea's program to compute $x_1 = (a_{22}b_1 - a_{12}b_2)/(a_{11}a_{22} - a_{12}a_{21})$ using the Analytical Engine (cf. Fig. 1.9). The input data are assigned to main memory as follows: $M(0) = a_{11}$, $M(1) = a_{12}$, $M(2) = b_1$, $M(3) = a_{21}$, $M(4) = a_{22}$, $M(5) = b_2$. For simplicity, all constants are assumed to be decimal integers and the problem of scaling

Instruction	Comments
$MQ \leftarrow M(1)$	Transfer a_{12} to MQ
$AC, MQ \leftarrow MQ \times M(3)$	Compute $a_{12}a_{21}$
$M(11) \leftarrow AC$	Transfer $a_{12}a_{21}$ to $M(11)$
$MQ \leftarrow M(0)$	Transfer a_{11} to MQ
$AC, MQ \leftarrow MQ \times M(4)$	Compute $a_{11}a_{22}$
$AC \leftarrow AC - M(11)$	Compute $a_{11}a_{22} - a_{12}a_{21}$
$M(13) \leftarrow AC$	Transfer $a_{11}a_{22} - a_{12}a_{21}$ to $M(13)$
$MQ \leftarrow M(1)$	Transfer a_{12} to MQ
$AC, MQ \leftarrow MQ \times M(5)$	Compute $a_{12}b_2$
$M(9) \leftarrow AC$	Transfer $a_{12}b_2$ to $M(9)$
$MQ \leftarrow M(4)$	Transfer a_{22} to MQ
$AC, MQ \leftarrow MQ \times M(2)$	Compute $a_{22}b_1$
$AC \leftarrow AC - M(9)$	Compute $a_{22}b_1 - a_{12}b_2$
$MQ, AC \leftarrow AC \div M(13)$	Compute x_1
$M(14) \leftarrow AC$	Transfer remainder of x_1 to $M(14)$
$AC \leftarrow MQ$	Transfer quotient of x_1 to AC
$M(15) \leftarrow AC$	Transfer quotient of x_1 to $M(15)$

Figure 1.18 IAS version of Menabrea's program.

numerical quantities is ignored. The characteristics of the component technologies used in the IAS, and indeed in most computers, are such that the time
required to access information in M is much greater (by a factor of perhaps 10)
than the time required to access information in CPU registers. Hence it is
desirable to use the CPU data registers (AC and MQ) for storage of intermediate results as often as possible. The steps of Menabrea's program have been
reordered with this objective in view. It should be noted that the IAS program
is the longer of the two, since it is a *one-address* machine, permitting only one
main-memory address per instruction. The Analytical Engine program permits
three addresses per instruction. We now consider a more complex IAS
programming problem.

Example 1.5: An IAS program to perform vector addition Let A = A(1),
A(2), . . . , A(1000) and B = B(1), B(2), . . . , B(1000) be two vectors (one-
dimensional arrays) comprising 1000 numbers each that must be added.
The result C is computed by 1000 additions of the form C(I) = A(I) + B(I),
where I = 1, 2, . . . , 1000. Using the IAS instruction set, each addition can
be implemented by three instructions thus:

$$AC \leftarrow A(I)$$

$$AC \leftarrow AC + B(I)$$

$$C(I) \leftarrow AC$$

Clearly, a straight-line program with 1000 copies of these three instructions, each with a different value of the index I, would perform the desired
vector addition. Such a program, besides being extremely inconvenient to
write, would not fit in M with the 3000 words needed to store A, B, C.
Some type of loop or iterative program structure is thus needed.

Figure 1.19 shows such a program. The data A, B, and C are stored
sequentially, beginning in locations 1001, 2001, and 3001, respectively.
The symbol to the left of each instruction in Fig. 1.19 is its location in M;
thus 2L(2R) denotes the left (right) half of M(2). M(0) is used to store a
count N and is initally set to 999. N is systematically decremented by one;
when it reaches -1, the program halts. The address modify instructions in
locations 8L, 9L, and 10L are used to decrement the address fields of the
three instructions in locations 3L, 3R, and 4L, respectively. Thus the program is continuously modifying itself during execution. Figure 1.19 shows
the program before execution commences. At the end of the computation,
the first three instructions will have changed to the following:

$$3L \quad AC \leftarrow M(1001)$$

$$3R \quad AC \leftarrow AC + M(2001)$$

$$4L \quad M(3001) \leftarrow AC$$

Location	Instruction	Comments
0	999	Count N
1	1	Constant
2	1000	Constant
3L	AC ← M(2000)	Transfer A(I) to AC
3R	AC ← AC + M(3000)	Compute A(I) + B(I)
4L	M(4000) ← AC	Transfer sum to C(I)
4R	AC ← M(0)	Load count N
5L	AC ← AC − M(1)	Decrement N by 1
5R	**if** AC ≥ 0 **then go to** M(6, 20:39)	Test N
6L	**go to** M(6, 0:19)	Halt
6R	M(0) ← AC	Update N
7L	AC ← AC + M(1)	Increment AC by 1
7R	AC ← AC + M(2)	
8L	M(3, 8:19) ← AC(28:39)	Modify address in 3L
8R	AC ← AC + M(2)	
9L	M(3, 28:39) ← AC(28:39)	Modify address in 3R
9R	AC ← AC + M(2)	
10L	M(4, 8:19) ← AC(28:39)	Modify address in 4L
10R	**go to** M(3, 0:19)	

Figure 1.19 An IAS program for vector addition.

Critique In the more than 30 years that have elapsed since the IAS computer was designed, many refinements in computer organization have appeared. Thus, with hindsight, some of the shortcomings of its design can be pointed out.

1. The address modification scheme (indexing) used in Example 1.5 was awkward and inefficient. To restart a program, the original unmodified program must be reloaded into main memory. By providing special addressable CPU registers, called index registers, the indexing operation can be made simpler and faster, and the need to modify instructions stored in main memory can be eliminated.
2. No facilities for linking programs were provided, such as instructions for calling subroutines which automatically save the return address of the calling program.
3. Floating-point arithmetic was not implemented mainly due to the cost of the hardware needed. Special subroutines had to be written for this purpose.
4. The storing of two instructions in each word added to the complexity of the program control unit and the instruction set. This feature was dropped from most later computers. However, it had the advantage of reducing the time spent fetching instructions from main memory by a factor of about $\frac{1}{2}$.
5. The instruction set was heavily oriented towards numerical computation, so that programming logical and nonnumerical problems was difficult.
6. Input-output instructions were considered of minor importance. In fact no mention of them is made in Ref. 7 beyond the observation that they are

needed. IAS was implemented with two basic IO instruction types INPUT and OUTPUT [9]. INPUT(X, N) caused N words to be transferred from a punched-card reader to the CPU and thence to N consecutive main-memory locations starting at address X. OUTPUT(X, N) transferred N consecutive words from the main-memory region with starting address X to an output device, again via the CPU. A similar pair of IO instructions transferred blocks of information between main memory and a magnetic-drum unit used for secondary storage. Since the IO devices in IAS were electromechanical, they operated at much slower speeds than the electronic CPU and main memory. Hence the CPU was largely idle while executing an IO instruction. This rather inefficient way of controlling IO operations was frequently responsible for poor overall system performance.

1.4 THE SECOND GENERATION: 1955 to 1964

1.4.1 General Characteristics

The so-called second-generation computers can be taken to be those produced during the second decade of the electronic computer era (1955 to 1964); there is no general agreement about the exact period involved.[1] It is mainly characterized by the change from vacuum tube to transistor technology; however, several other important developments also occurred which are summarized below.

1. The transistor, which had been invented in 1948 at Bell Telephone Laboratories, gradually replaced vacuum tubes in the design of switching circuits.
2. Cathode-ray-tube memories and delay-line memories were replaced by ferrite cores and magnetic drums as the technologies used in main memories.
3. The use of index registers and floating-point arithmetic hardware became widespread.
4. Machine-independent "high-level" programming languages such as ALGOL, COBOL, and FORTRAN were introduced to simplify programming.
5. Special processors (IO processors) were introduced to supervise input-output operations, thus freeing the CPU from many time-consuming housekeeping functions.
6. Computer manufacturers began to provide systems software such as compilers, subroutine libraries, and batch monitors.

The earliest transistor computer appears to have been an experimental

---

[1]Denning [8] defines 1950 to 1960 as the second-generation period, while Bell and Newell [4] suggest 1958 to 1966.

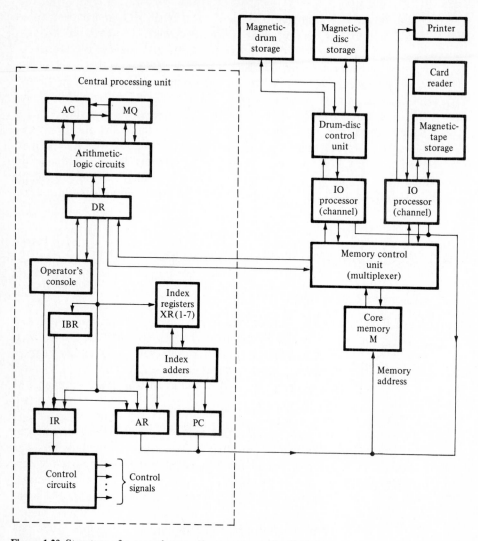

Figure 1.20 Structure of a second-generation computer: the IBM 7094.

machine, the TX-0, built at the Lincoln Laboratory of MIT, which was operational in 1953. Many of the improvements associated with second-generation computers actually first appeared in vacuum tube or hybrid machines. The IBM 704, a vacuum-tube computer produced in 1955 had index registers and floating-point hardware. It was also the first commercial machine with a "control program," which was a rudimentary operating system. Later models of the 704 and its successor, the 709, had *input-output processors* (called "data synchronizers" and later "channels"), which were special-purpose processors used exclusively to control input-output operations. In early machines such as the

IAS computer, all IO operations were controlled directly by the CPU; this is now termed *programmed IO*. The IBM 7090 and 7094 were essentially transistorized versions of the 709 and were very successful commercially.

With the second generation it became necessary to talk about computer *systems*, since the number of memory units, processors, IO devices, and other system components could vary between different installations, even though the same basic computer was used.

1.4.2 A Second-Generation Computer

Figure 1.20 shows the structure (slightly simplified) of the IBM 7094 system, which is a representative large-scale scientific machine of the second generation [4, 16]. The CPU differs from that of the IAS computer mainly in the addition of a set of index registers, and arithmetic circuits that can handle both floating-point and fixed-point operations. All input-output operations are controlled by a set of IO processors which have direct access to the main memory M. A control unit is used to switch the memory between the CPU and the various IOPs. In the following description of the 7094, only those aspects that are significantly different from the IAS machine are discussed.

Figure 1.21 shows the basic information formats of the 7094. A 36-bit word is used which may represent a fixed-point number, a floating-point number, or an instruction. A floating-point number is composed of an exponent E and a mantissa M and represents a number of the form $M \times 2^E$. Each instruction contains a 15-bit address, allowing $2^{15} = 32K$ memory locations to be addressed.

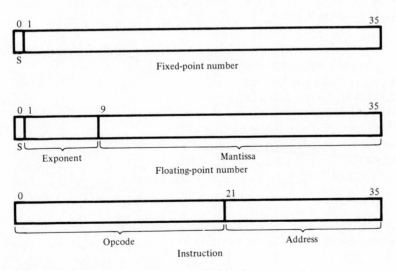

Figure 1.21 Information formats of the IBM 7094.

Most of the CPU registers are similar to those in the IAS computer and have been assigned the same names.[2] During the instruction cycle, the CPU fetches two successive instructions from memory; the second instruction is stored in the instruction buffer register IBR. The memory unit is partitioned into two modules: one accommodates even addresses; the other has only odd addresses assigned to it. Each module can be accessed simultaneously, hence the memory unit can supply two successive words to the CPU in one memory cycle period. The distribution of addresses among several independent memory modules is called *interleaving*.

The 7094 has no less than seven index registers, each of which can store a 15-bit address. A 3-bit "tag" subfield of the opcode of an instruction is used to indicate if indexing is required and which index register is to be used. If index register XR(I) is indicated, then the address field currently in the address register AR has the contents of XR(I) subtracted from it using a special set of index adders to form an *effective address*, AR-XR(I). The effective address is used to access main memory. Figure 1.22 shows a 7094 program to implement the vector addition problem of Example 1.5. It is written in the assembly language designed for this machine. The operation, tag, and decrement are possible components of the 21-bit opcode. Unlike the IAS vector-addition program of Fig. 1.19, this program does not alter its own instructions, since the address modification operations are carried out in the CPU and not in main memory.

Another useful feature of this machine is *indirect addressing*. If this is specified in an instruction, then the effective address is computed in the normal manner and the specified word is fetched. This word is then used to compute a *second* effective address and the specified operation is executed using this second address.

The instruction repertoire of the 7094 has more than 200 instructions. They can be classified as follows:

1. Data-transfer instructions for transferring a word of information between the CPU and memory or between two CPU registers.
2. Fixed-point arithmetic instructions.
3. Floating-point arithmetic instructions.
4. Logical (nonnumerical) instructions.
5. Instructions for modifying index registers.
6. Conditional and unconditional branching, and related control instructions.
7. Input-output operations for transferring data between IO devices and main memory. (Some of these are executed by the CPU, but most are executed by the IOPs.)

An important feature of second-generation machines is the provision of special branch instructions to facilitate the transfer of control between different programs, e.g., calling subroutines. In the 7094 an instruction TSX (*transfer*

---

[2]See Sec. 1.3.3 for the definitions of AC, AR, DR, IBR, IR, MQ, PC.

Location	Operation	Address, tag, decrement	Comments
	AXT	0, 2	Load zero into index register XR(2)
START	CLA	2000, 2	Clear accumulator and add M(2000-XR(2)) to it
	ADD	3000, 2	Add M(3000-XR(2)) to accumulator
	STO	4000, 2	Store accumulator contents in M(4000-XR(2))
	TXI	TEST, 2, 1	Increment XR(2) by 1 then go to instruction TEST
TEST	TXL	START, 2, 999	If XR(2) ≤ 999, go to START
	HPR		Halt

Figure 1.22 An IBM 7094 assembly-language program for vector addition.

and *s*et inde*x*) is available for this purpose. Suppose execution of a subroutine that begins in location SUB is desired. Then the instruction

$$\text{LINK} \quad \text{TSX} \quad \text{SUB, 4}$$

causes its own address (LINK) to be placed in the designated index register XR(4), and the next instruction is taken from the memory location SUB. In order to return control to the calling program, the subroutine must terminate with an instruction such as

$$\text{TRA} \quad 1, 4$$

meaning: go (*tra*nsfer) to the address $1 + \text{XR}(4)$ which contains the next instruction after LINK in the main program.

1.4.3 Input-Output Processing

IO processors, such as those of the 7094, supervise the flow of information between main storage and IO devices. They do so by executing special *IO programs*, which are composed of IO instructions and are stored in main memory. An IOP begins execution of an IO program only when an initiation instruction is sent to the IOP by the CPU. This instruction typically contains the address of the first instruction in the IO program to be executed. The IOP can then execute the program without reference to the CPU. The CPU can, however, monitor IO operations by means of instructions that obtain status information from the IOPs. An IOP may also be able to communicate with the CPU to indicate unusual conditions, such as the end of an IO operation, by means of special control signals called *interrupts*.

The structure of an IOP based on that of the IBM 7094 computer system is presented in Fig. 1.23. Data is transferred between the IOP and main memory a word (36 bits) at a time, but transfer between the IOP and IO devices, e.g., magnetic tapes, is by character (6 bits). The IOP therefore has circuits for as-

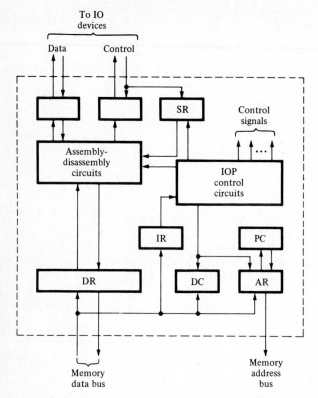

Figure 1.23 Structure of an input-output processor.

sembling characters into words and disassembling words into characters. The main data register DR stores one word and is connected to the memory data bus. Its role is that of a buffer register. A 5-bit instruction register IR stores the opcode part of the current IO instruction, while the address register AR holds a 15-bit memory address. The number of words to be transferred during data-transfer operations is stored in a data count register DC. A program counter register PC stores the address of the next IO instruction to be executed by the IOP. Finally, the status of the current IO operation is maintained in a status register SR in the IOP. This register may be used to store abnormal or error condition information and can be examined by the CPU.

IO operations typically proceed in the following way:

1. The CPU initiates the operation when it encounters an IO instruction while executing some program. This instruction specifies that IO device d connected to IOP c is to be selected for an input (read) or output (write) operation. It (or a subsequent instruction) also specifies the address a in main memory of the first instruction in the IO program to be executed by the designated IOP.

2. The CPU transfers the IO device name d and the IO program starting address a to IOP c.

3. IOP c then proceeds to execute the IO program in question. When the IO

operation terminates, either normally or abnormally, the status register SR is set accordingly, and an interrupt signal may be sent to the CPU.

The IOP instruction set is considerably simpler than that of the CPU. For example, it has negligible arithmetic capabilities. IOP instructions fall into three groups.

1. *IO device-control instructions.* These are transmitted from the IOP to the active IO device and are peculiar to the device in question. Some examples are rewind magnetic tape, skip a line on a printer, and position a magnetic-disk storage read-write head.
2. *Data-transfer instructions.* These have the form: transfer n words between the active IO device and main storage. Each such instruction contains the data count n, which is stored in the IOP data count register DC, and the initial address of the main-memory-data area to be used, which is placed in the address register AR. The IOP then proceeds to carry out the data transfer. Each time a word is transmitted through the IOP, DC is decremented by 1 and AR is incremented by 1. When DC reaches zero, i.e., all n words have been transferred, the IOP can proceed to the next instruction whose address is in its program counter PC.
3. *IOP control instructions.* These are mainly conditional and unconditional branch instructions not unlike those executed by the CPU.

IOPs and the CPU share a common access path to main memory, usually via a *memory control unit*, which may be part of the CPU. The function of this unit is to schedule memory-access requests from the various processors. Since IO operations are typically very slow compared with CPU speeds, most of the memory-access requests can be expected to come from the CPU. When a memory access is requested by an IOP, it may cause a CPU request to be delayed one memory cycle period. This type of IO data transfer is therefore called *cycle stealing*.

The CPU and the IOPs operate independently and asynchronously; however, control over system operation is retained by the CPU. The CPU can supervise the IOPs by periodically requesting status information from them. It is much more efficient to provide special control lines from the IOPs to the CPU which permit an IOP to inform the CPU of an infrequent condition, e.g., the end of an IO operation, when the condition occurs. This type of communication from an IOP to the CPU is called an interrupt. Interrupt facilities, introduced in some second-generation machines, enable the CPU to respond rapidly to changes in IO activity and greatly improve its overall efficiency.

1.4.4 Software and Other Developments

Programming languages While assembly languages are much easier to use than machine languages, they are quite different from a typical user's problem specification language. Furthermore, different computers have different assembly languages, hence an assembly language program for one machine cannot be used on a different machine. An important development of the mid-1950s was the introduction of automatic programming languages, now called *high-level languages*, which permit a program to be written in a form closer to the user's problem specification than to the machine instruction set [23]. Such languages are intended to be usable on many different computers. They require programs, called *compilers*, to translate the high-level language into the machine language of the particular computer being used.

The first widely used high-level language was FORTRAN (*For*mula *Tran*slation), developed by an IBM group under the direction of John Backus from 1954 to 1957. FORTRAN permits the specification of algebraic operations in a form approximating normal algebraic notation. Thus the vector addition programs of Figs. 1.19 and 1.22 can be replaced by the following two-line FORTRAN program:

$$\text{DO } 10 \text{ I} = 1, \ 1000$$

$$10 \quad \text{C(I)} = \text{A(I)} + \text{B(I)}$$

FORTRAN was the forerunner of several important programming languages, notably ALGOL (*Algo*rithmic *L*anguage) and APL (*A P*rogramming *L*anguage), intended mainly for scientific applications.

High-level programming languages were also developed for business applications. These are characterized by instructions that resemble statements in English and operate primarily on alphanumeric information files. One of the earliest such languages was the now obsolete FLOW-MATIC developed in the UNIVAC organization by Grace Hopper and her staff from 1955 to 1958. FLOW-MATIC was one of several languages that influenced the design of the very important COBOL language (*Co*mmon *B*usiness *O*riented *L*anguage) [23]. COBOL was specified in 1959 by the CODASYL (*Co*nference *o*n *D*ata *S*ystems *L*anguages) committee, a group representing users and manufacturers, and sponsored by the U.S. Department of Defense.

Batch processing In the early days each user's program, or job, was run separately, and the computer had to be halted and prepared manually for each new program. With the improvements in IO equipment that came with second-generation computers, it became feasible to prepare a batch of jobs in advance, store them on magnetic tape, and then have the computer process them in one continuous sequence, placing all results on another magnetic tape. This mode of operation is termed *batch processing*. It was common to use a small auxiliary computer to process the input and output magnetic tapes off-line. Batch-processing requires the use of a supervisory program, or *monitor*, which is permanently resident in main memory, so that a relatively large memory is needed.

Addressing methods and stacks A source of controversy during the early days of computers was the number of memory addresses to include in each machine-language instruction. The IAS and 7094 computers were one-address machines, while the EDVAC had four addresses per instruction. Two-address and three-address machines were also common. As noted earlier, fewer addresses means a reduction in the memory space occupied by an individual instruction. However, this is balanced by the fact that more instructions are required. Thus the FORTRAN addition statement

$$C = A + B$$

can be implemented very naturally by a single instruction in a three-address machine. In a one-address machine, three instructions are required, as in the IAS program of Fig. 1.15.

A number of companies developed machines that permit so-called zero-address instructions. These make use of a special memory organization, called a *stack*. Two of the earliest stack-oriented computers were the English Electric KDF-9 and the Burroughs B5000, both of which were first delivered in 1963. The B5000 was the first of a continuing line of stack computers from Burroughs Corp. The arithmetic registers of the B5000 are organized as a last-in first-out (LIFO) or pushdown stack. The top two words of the stack are fast CPU registers, while the rest of the stack is in main memory. All instructions take their operands from the top of the stack and place their results in the stack; hence in most cases, no address has to be specified. Thus the instruction

ADD

causes the top two numbers stored in the stack to be removed from the stack and added; the resulting sum is placed in the top of the stack. Two instructions characteristic of stack processing are PUSH X and POP X, which cause the contents of memory location X to be transferred to the stack or from the stack, respectively. Stack processors have two advantages:

1. They simplify the programming of certain types of arithmetic operations by reducing the need for operand address specification.
2. They greatly facilitate the transfer of control between programs, particularly when recursion is involved (a recursive program can call itself). Successive return addresses can be pushed into the stack and later removed (popped) from the stack in the correct (LIFO) sequence.

Large computer systems Because of their small size, transistors made it possible to design extremely large and extremely fast computers, popularly termed *supercomputers*. Such computers are of particular value in areas such as nuclear physics where problems requiring a vast number of computations must be solved. Two of the earliest machines of this type, begun in the mid-1950s, were the LARC (*L*ivermore *A*tomic *R*esearch *C*omputer) designed by UNIVAC and the Stretch (also called the 7030) designed by IBM. These machines introduced a number of techniques for increasing the effective computation speed of a computer system, including various ways of increasing the number of operations that could be performed concurrently. The most notable of these techniques, often collectively referred to as *parallel-processing* techniques, were the following:

1. Overlapping the fetching and execution of individual instructions within a single program. This is primarily achieved by special hardware facilities, such as multiple arithmetic-logic units, instruction buffers, interleaved memories, and the like.
2. Overlapping the execution of different programs. This can be done in several ways. The system can be designed with a single CPU capable of concurrent execution of more than one program. This is called *multiprogramming*. It is accomplished by enabling the CPU to temporarily suspend execution of a program, begin execution of another program and then return to the interrupted program later. Multiprogramming systems that allow many user programs to be executed concurrently in an interactive real-time manner are called *timesharing* systems. The concurrent execution of several programs can also be achieved by designing computers with more than one CPU; these are termed *multiprocessor* systems. Multiprogramming and multiprocessing require complex supervisory programs.

Both the LARC and the Stretch computers were commercial failures. They are important, however, because they had considerable influence on the design of the next generation of computers. They also influenced some late second-generation machines such as the IBM 7094.

1.5 RECENT DEVELOPMENTS

1.5.1 The Third Generation

1965 may be considered as marking the beginning of the third computer generation, but the distinction between the second and third generations is not very clear-cut. The following developments are frequently singled out:

1. Integrated circuits (ICs) began to replace the discrete transistor circuits used in second-generation machines, resulting in a substantial reduction in physical size and cost.
2. Semiconductor (IC) memories began to augment, and ultimately replace, ferrite cores in main-memory designs.
3. A technique called microprogramming came into widespread use to simplify the design of processors and increase their flexibility.
4. A variety of techniques for concurrent or parallel processing were introduced such as pipelining, multiprogramming, and multiprocessing. These had the objective of increasing the effective speed at which a set of programs could be executed.

5. Methods for automatic sharing of the facilities or resources of a computer system, e.g., its processors and memory space, were developed. These were intended to improve resource utilization, particularly the use of memory space.

The existence of many concurrent processes in a computer system requires the presence of an entity that exercises overall control, supervises the allocation of system resources, schedules operations, prevents interference between different programs, etc. This is termed an executive, a master control program (Burroughs), or more commonly, an *operating system*. The operating system of a large computer is generally a complex program, although some of its functions may be implemented in hardware. The widespread use of operating systems is an important characteristic of third-generation computers. The development of operating systems can be traced to the batch-processing monitors designed in the 1950s. Manchester University's ATLAS computer, which became operational around 1961, had one of the first operating systems. The design of timesharing systems to allow many users simultaneous access to a computer in an interactive, or "conversational," manner must also be mentioned. CTSS (*C*ompatible *T*ime-*S*haring *S*ystem), developed at MIT in the early 1960s, had considerable influence on the design of subsequent timesharing and operating systems.

The number of different third-generation computers is very great. Probably the most influential computer introduced in the mid-1960s was IBM's System/360 series. This is a family of computers (distinguished by model numbers) intended to cover a wide range of computing performance. The various models are largely compatible in that a program written for one model should be capable of being executed by any other model in the series; only the execution time and, perhaps, the memory space requirements should be affected. The S/360 was announced by IBM in 1964 and first delivered in 1965. Many of its features have become standard in the computer industry. The architecture of this family of machines is discussed in detail in Sec. 1.5.2.

The design of large powerful computers that began with the LARC and the Stretch was continued. The Control Data Corporation (CDC) produced a series of large machines beginning with the CDC 6600 in 1964 and continuing with the 7600 delivered in 1969, and the subsequent CYBER series. These machines are characterized by the inclusion of many IOPs (called peripheral processors) with a high degree of autonomy. In addition, each CPU is subdivided into a number of independent processing units which can be operated simultaneously. A CPU organization called pipelining is used to achieve very fast processing in several computers such as the CDC STAR-100 (*S*tring *A*rray computer) and the Texas Instruments ASC (*A*dvanced *S*cientific *C*omputer). Another notable supercomputer is ILLIAC IV (*Illi*nois *A*utomatic *C*omputer), designed at the University of Illinois. ILLIAC IV can be considered to have 64 separate arithmetic-logic units (called processing elements) all supervised by a common control unit and all capable of operating simultaneously.

A contrasting development of the mid-1960s was the mass production of small low-cost computers called *minicomputers*. The origins of minicomputers can be traced to the LINC (*L*aboratory *I*nstrument *C*omputer) developed at MIT in 1963. The LINC greatly influenced the design of the PDP (*Pro-grammed Data Processor*) series of small computers produced by Digital Equipment Corporation (DEC), which did much to establish the minicomputer market. The first commercial minicomputer was the DEC PDP-5 produced in 1963. It was superceded in 1965 by the very successful PDP-8. Minicomputers are characterized by short word lengths (8 to 32 bits), limited hardware and software facilities, and small physical size. Their low cost, however, makes them suitable for a wide variety of applications such as industrial control, where a *dedicated* computer, i.e., a computer which is permanently assigned to one application, is needed. In recent years, improvements in device technology have resulted in minicomputers which are comparable in performance to large second-generation machines and which greatly exceed the performance of most first-generation machines.

Microprogramming Microprogramming is a technique for implementing the control function of a processor in a systematic and flexible manner. The concept was first enunciated by Maurice V. Wilkes in 1951 [28]. It was implemented in several first- and second-generation machines. However, it was not until the mid-1960s, with its appearance in some models of the IBM S/360 series, that the use of microprogramming became widespread [13].

Microprogramming may be considered as an alternative to *hardwired control* circuits. A hardwired control circuit for a processor is typically a sequential circuit with the general structure shown in Fig. 1.24. A microprogrammed processor control circuit has the structure shown in Fig. 1.25. Each instruction of the processor being controlled causes a sequence of microinstructions, called a *microprogram*, to be fetched from a special random access memory, called a *control memory*. The microinstructions specify the sequence of microoperations or register transfer operations needed to interpret and execute the main instruction. Each instruction fetch from main memory thus initiates a sequence of microinstruction fetches from control memory.

Microprogramming provides a systematic way of designing control circuits. It greatly increases the flexibility of a computer. The instruction set of a microprogrammed machine can be changed merely by replacing the contents of the control memory. This makes it possible for a microprogrammed computer

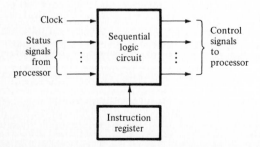

Figure 1.24 A hardwired control circuit.

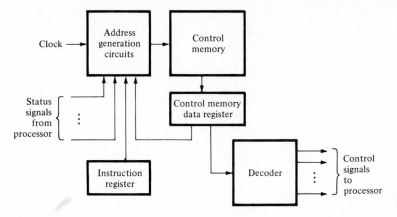

Figure 1.25 A microprogrammed control circuit.

to execute directly programs written in the machine language of a different computer, a process called *emulation.* Microprogrammed control units tend to be more costly and slower than hardwired units. Because of the close interaction of software and hardware in microprogrammed systems, microprograms are sometimes referred to as *firmware.*

Parallel processing The increased level of parallel processing characteristic of the third generation was achieved in part by the use of multiple processors with a high degree of autonomy and flexible intrasystem communication facilities. This is illustrated in Fig. 1.26, which shows a possible configuration of the Burroughs B5000 and its successor the B5500. The main memory is partitioned

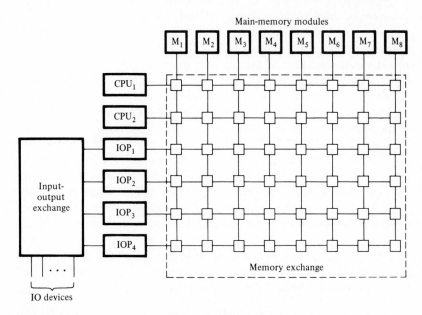

Figure 1.26 Organization of a multiprocessor: the Burroughs B5000.

into eight independently accessible modules $M_1:M_8$. These are connected via the memory exchange to two CPUs and four IOPs. The memory exchange, which is a crossbar switching network, permits simultaneous access by the six processors to main memory provided that they each access different modules. A similar switching network, the IO exchange, connects the IOPs to up to 32 input-output devices. This organization permits many operations to take place simultaneously.

Parallelism can also be introduced on a lower level by overlapping the fetching and/or the execution of individual instructions by a single CPU. Two distinct methods of achieving this have evolved.

1. More than one unit can be provided to carry out a particular operation, e.g., addition. By employing n independent adders, n additions can be performed simultaneously. This type of structure permits array operations (cf. Example 1.5) to be performed very rapidly.
2. A processing unit can be designed in the form of a *pipeline*.

Figure 1.27 shows how a floating-point adder can be implemented in pipeline form. The addition operation is broken into four independent sequential steps, each of which is carried out in a separate subunit, or *segment*, of the pipeline. The intermediate results produced by each segment are transferred to the next segment. The segments are isolated so that at any time each segment can be executing a different add instruction. The pipeline can therefore overlap the execution of four separate additions. The throughput of an n-segment pipeline is comparable to that of a system comprising n identical units performing the same function as the pipeline.

Memory management Multiprogramming and multiprocessing usually involve a number of concurrently executing programs sharing the same main memory. Because main-memory capacity is limited by cost considerations, it is generally impossible to store all executing programs and their data sets in main memory simultaneously. Thus it becomes necessary to allocate memory space dynamically among different competing programs and move or "swap" information back and forth between main and secondary memory as required. A major function of an operating system is to perform these memory management operations automatically.

The programmer's task is greatly simplified if he can view the computer as having a single addressable memory of essentially unlimited size to which he alone has access. This is the *virtual-memory* concept, which is considered an attribute of third-generation computers, even though it originated with the one-level-store concept implemented in the Manchester University machines of the late 1940s. To understand virtual-memory systems, we must distinguish between the set of (symbolic) addresses appearing in a program, called the *logical address space* L, and the set of actual addresses in memory, called the *physical address space* P. L may be larger than the P—hence the term virtual. During

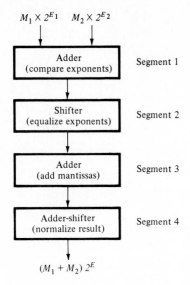

$$M_1 \times 2^{E_1} \quad M_2 \times 2^{E_2}$$

Adder
(compare exponents) — Segment 1

Shifter
(equalize exponents) — Segment 2

Adder
(add mantissas) — Segment 3

Adder-shifter
(normalize result) — Segment 4

$$(M_1 + M_2) \, 2^E$$

Figure 1.27 A pipelined floating-point adder.

execution of the program, each logical address in L is translated into a physical address in P. Thus an *address mapping mechanism* is needed which implements a function f: L $\rightarrow$ P. If it is determined that the specified item is not in main memory, execution of the program is suspended while the relevant item is transferred from secondary to main memory.

It is convenient when implementing a virtual memory system to divide main memory into fixed-size contiguous areas, called *page frames*, and to divide programs into pieces of the same size, called *pages*. In a paging system, all swapping and reallocation of stored information is by pages. Figure 1.28 contains a flowchart of a typical *demand paging algorithm*. A page swap takes place only when the page containing a word required by the CPU is not currently stored in main memory. When this condition, called a *page fault*, occurs, the execution of the program in question is suspended until the required page is brought into main memory. In a multiprogramming environment, the CPU can switch to another program while the page swap takes place. Since page swapping is basically an IO operation, it can proceed independently under control of an IOP.

A simple mechanism for dynamically allocating memory space is a *base register*. This is a CPU register, which is controlled by the operating system. Every memory address generated by a program then has the contents of a base register, called a base address, added to it. The operating system can change all addresses in a program during execution by the simple expedient of changing the contents of the program's base register. In a memory management system using paging, it is convenient to store page addresses in the base registers, in which case they may be called *page registers*.

Parallel processing by the CPU implies a need to be able to transfer several words simultaneously between the CPU and main memory. This can be satis-

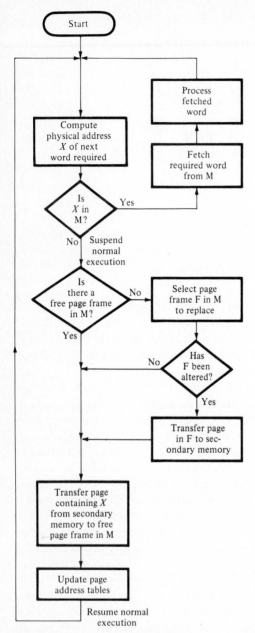

Figure 1.28 Operation of a demand paging system.

fied by providing multiple memory modules with address interleaving, and by including buffer storage registers in the CPU. Both these features exist in rudimentary form in the IBM 7094. The development of semiconductor IC memory technology made it feasible to provide relatively large high-speed buffer memories to act as an intermediate store between the CPU and main memory. These memories are now usually called *cache* memories and are used for storing both instructions and data.

1.5.2 A Third-Generation Computer Family

In this section we examine the architecture of the series of computers that began with the announcement of the System/360 by IBM in 1964. The Spectra 70 series also announced by Radio Corporation of America (RCA) in 1964 is largely compatible with the 360. A new series, the System/370 announced by IBM in 1970, has the same basic architecture as the 360 but contains a number of performance improvements, or "enhancements." Amdahl Corporation's 470 and Itel Corporation's AS (*A*dvanced *S*ystem) series, introduced in the mid-1970s, are members of the same family.

Design objectives The major design goals of S/360 have been well documented [3, 5].

1. The members of the series were to be equally suited for business and scientific application. The required generality was achieved in part by including many data types and providing both binary and decimal (i.e., binary coded decimal or BCD) arithmetic instructions.
2. The different models were to be program compatible, so that users starting with a small model could move with ease to larger models as their computing needs increased. All models were required to be able to execute a common instruction set, despite differences in physical implementation. The smaller, slower members of the S/360-370 series were designed with microprogrammed CPUs, whereas the larger, faster models have hardwired CPUs.
3. The design was intended to be open-ended in the sense that new or additional units such as processors or I/O devices could be easily attached to the system. This objective greatly influenced the design of the IO subsystem, which included several types of IOPs ("channels") and a standard IO interface connecting IOPs to IO devices.
4. The system was to be capable of supporting both multiprogramming and multiprocessing. To this end, a very large and complex operating system OS/360 was designed.

Figure 1.29 shows some original design parameters for two S/360 models, the small Model 30 and the large Model 70 (the latter was withdrawn shortly after its announcement and apparently replaced by the Model 75). These parameters indicate the wide performance range desired.

System structure Figure 1.30 shows the general structure of a typical S/360-370 series computer. It bears a strong resemblance to that of the IBM 7094, cf. Fig. 1.20. Two types of IOPs are used: multiplexer[3] channels and selector channels. Multiplexer channels can interleave (multiplex) data transmission between main memory and several IO devices, whereas only one IO device connected to a selector channel can transmit or receive information at a

---

[3]Also spelled "multiplexor" in earlier IBM literature.

Subsystem	Design parameter	Model 30	Model 70
	Memory cycle time	2 μs	1 μs
Main	Memory bus width	8 bits	64 bits
memory	Number of interleaved modules	1	2
	Maximum data-transfer rate	4×10^6 bits/s	128×10^6 bits/s
	Nominal delay per gate	30 ns	6 ns
	CPU cycle time	1 μs	0.2 μs
CPU	Working register technology	Ferrite core	Semiconductor
	CPU internal bus width	8 bits	64 bits
	Relative computing speed	1	50

Figure 1.29 Design parameters of two models in the IBM S/360 series.

given time. Selector channels are intended for use with very high speed IO devices, e.g., magnetic disks, while multiplexer channels are intended for controlling a number of low-speed devices, e.g., printers, card readers, and card punches. Each IOP is connected to a bus, called the I/O interface, which is composed of a standard set of data and control lines. The IO interface bus is shared by all devices attached to a given IOP. An IO device, or a group of IO devices of the same type, is supervised locally by a control unit which is peculiar to the type of IO device in question. An S/360-370 IOP is generally

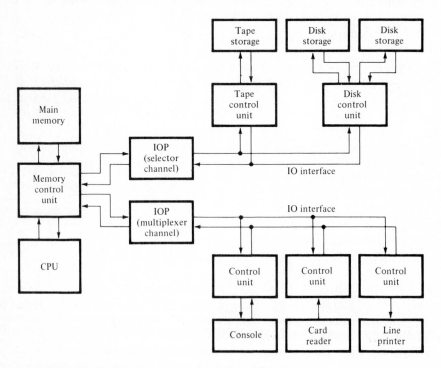

Figure 1.30 Structure of an S/360-370 series computer.

similar to the channel used in the IBM 7094 computer, which was discussed in detail in Sec. 1.4.3.

Data formats The basic unit of storage employed is the *byte*, or 8 bits; a byte is capable of representing up to 256 different symbols. Every byte location in main memory can be accessed directly. The term "word" is used for a group of 4 bytes. Numerical data can be represented in four ways: zoned decimal, packed decimal, fixed-point binary, and floating-point binary, as illustrated in Fig. 1.31.

The decimal formats are intended for business applications and can be processed directly by decimal arithmetic circuits. The numbers are fixed-point integers and can be of variable length. The "zone" halfbytes are unused, except for the low-order zone which represents the sign of the number. In the packed format (which makes far more efficient use of storage), the low-order halfbyte represents the sign. The 10 decimal digits are encoded in standard 4-bit BCD form. The binary number formats are intended primarily for scientific applications. The fixed-point format represents an integer in twos-complement code, and can be a half word (short form) or a full word (long form) in length. The

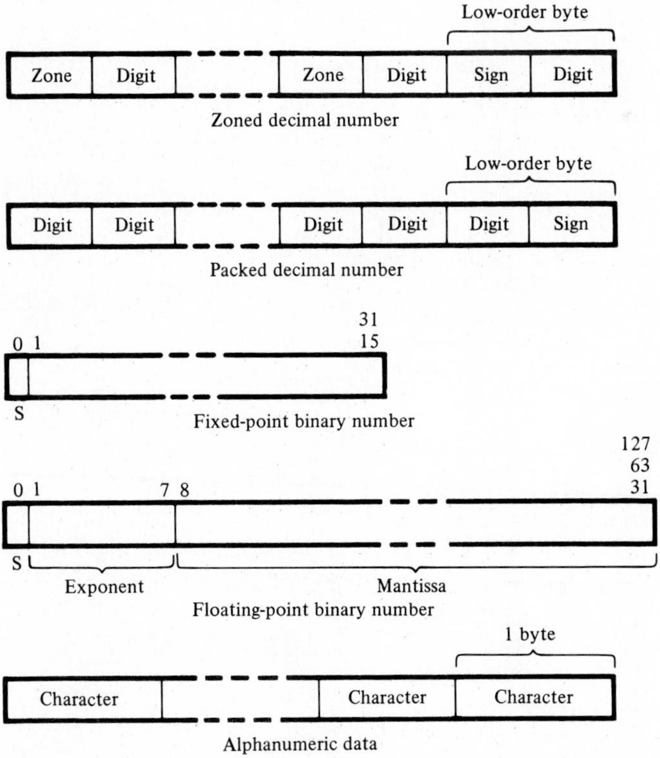

Figure 1.31 S/360-370 data formats.

floating-point format consists of a mantissa, which is a fraction that is usually, but not always, normalized by eliminating leading zeros, and a 7-bit exponent in excess 64 code, which represents a power of 16. Bit 0 is the sign of the mantissa. Floating-point numbers may be one, two, or four words long. Alphanumeric data is represented by a variable sequence of bytes, where each byte represents a character in some code such as EBCDIC (*E*xtended *B*inary *C*oded *D*ecimal *I*nterchange *C*ode).

CPU organization The CPU structure common to many S/360-370 models is depicted in Fig. 1.32. The arithmetic-logic unit is divided into three subunits with the following functions.

1. Fixed-point operations, including integer arithmetic and effective address computation
2. Floating-point operations
3. Variable-length operations, including decimal arithmetic and character string operations

Two sets of independent addressable registers are used for data and address storage. The 16 general registers can be used to store operands and results and

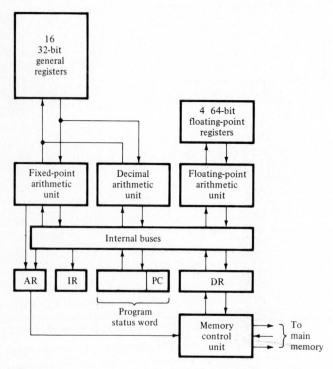

Figure 1.32 CPU structure of S/360-370 series computers.

can also be used as index registers. Four floating-point registers are used in floating-point arithmetic. The general and floating-point registers augment the accumulator and multiplier-quotient registers of earlier computers. The data register DR, the address register AR, and the instruction register IR are standard. A *program status word* PSW (actually two words), stored in a special register, indicates program status, interruptions ("interrupts") that the CPU may respond to, and the address of the next instruction to be executed. The PSW is primarily intended for processing interrupts. The CPU responds to an interrupt by storing the current PSW in main memory and fetching a new PSW. This PSW specifies the program to be executed to process the interrupt. After the interrupt program has been executed, the CPU can retrieve the old PSW from main memory and resume execution of the interrupted program.

The CPU is at any time in one of several control states. When it is executing a routine from the operating system, i.e., the operating system has explicit control of the CPU, it is said to be in the *supervisor state*. Certain instructions can be executed by the CPU in this state only. The CPU is normally in the *problem state* when executing user programs. The state of the CPU at any time is specified by its PSW.

The PSW register also contains a key used for *memory protection*. Main memory is divided into blocks of 2K bytes, each of which is assigned a storage key. The storage key specifies the type of access allowed (read only, read and write, neither read nor write). An operation that involves accessing information in a particular 2K block B is executed only if B's storage key matches the current key in the PSW register.

Instruction set Instructions in S/360-370 computers consist of 2, 4, or 6 bytes and can contain up to three addresses. Five different formats are used depending on the location of the various operands required; they are illustrated in Fig. 1.33.

1. RR (register-register) instructions. The operands R_1 and R_2 are CPU general registers. The result is placed in R_1.
2. RX (register-index) instructions. One operand is in R_1, the other is in main memory. The effective memory address is $X_2 + B_2 + D_2$, where X_2 and B_2 denote the contents of general registers being used as index and base registers respectively, and D_2 is the 12-bit relative address or "displacement" contained in the instruction. The result may be placed in R_1.
3. RS (register-storage) instructions. Two operands are in general registers, a third is in main memory.
4. SI (storage-immediate) instructions. One operand is in main memory, the other is in bits 8:15 of the instruction itself. This is an immediate operand, as opposed to the usual operand address.
5. SS (storage-storage) instructions. Both operands are in main memory. The addresses specified by the instructions are typically the initial addresses of two operand fields, whose length is L bytes.

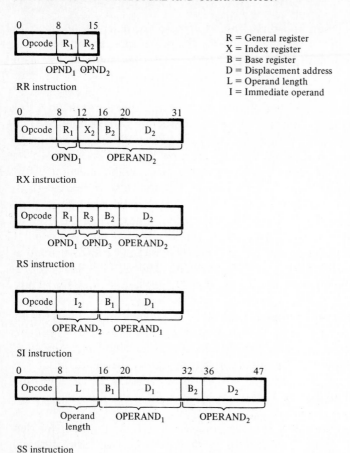

R = General register
X = Index register
B = Base register
D = Displacement address
L = Operand length
I = Immediate operand

Figure 1.33 S/360-370 instruction formats.

The CPU instruction set of the S/360-370 family includes all the major types discussed previously: data transfer, arithmetic, branch, and IO instructions. The number of distinct opcodes available is close to 200. This is due mainly to the profusion of different data types. Figure 1.34 lists some of the instructions available for performing addition. We only mention here some instructions that differ significantly from those encountered earlier in this chapter; a complete listing of the S/360-370 instruction set can be found in the Refs. 4, 17, and 18.

The SS instruction MOVE is used to transfer a block of information of specified length from one part of main memory to another. The execution time of this instruction depends on the amount of information to be moved. A variety of instructions exist, as might be expected, for changing data formats, e.g., convert packed decimal to fixed-point binary. Boolean operations such as AND and OR can also be specified. A set of control instructions exist which are called *privileged* instructions, since they can be executed only when the

Mnemonic	Instruction type	Operand type
A	RX	Long fixed-point
AR	RR	Long fixed-point
AH	RX	Short fixed-point
AP	SS	Packed decimal
AD	RX	Long floating-point (normalized)
ADR	RR	Long floating-point (normalized)
AE	RX	Short floating-point (normalized)
AW	RX	Long floating-point (unnormalized)
AU	RX	Short floating-point (unnormalized)

Figure 1.34 Some S/360-370 addition instructions.

CPU is in the supervisor state. These are used to modify the PSW, alter storage protection keys, and the like. The IO instructions executed by the CPU are similar to those of the 7094; they allow the CPU to initiate, terminate, and monitor the execution of an IO program by an IOP. A large number of IO instructions (called *commands* to distinguish them from CPU instructions) exist which are executed by the IOPs.

1.5.3 Microprocessors and Microcomputers

Integrated circuits Since the late 1960s the dominant technology for manufacturing computer components has been integrated-circuit technology. An *integrated circuit* (IC) is formed by fabricating a logic circuit from a single tiny piece of semiconductor material (usually silicon). The resulting IC "chip" is then mounted in a package that facilitates the interconnection of ICs. A typical IC package, called a *dual in-line package* (DIP), is illustrated in Fig. 1.35. The external connections, or pins, of the DIP are organized in two parallel rows—hence its name. A 16-pin DIP is shown, but DIPs with as many as 64 pins are available.

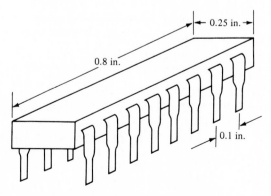

Figure 1.35 An integrated circuit (IC) housed in a 16-pin dual in-line package (DIP).

Within IC technology, many subtechnologies exist that are distinguished by the manufacturing processes employed and the physical behavior of the resulting circuits. Two of the more important of these technologies are *bipolar* and *MOS*. They both use transistors as the basic switching elements; they differ, however, in the polarities of the charges associated with the primary carriers of electric current within the IC chips. Bipolar circuits use both negative carriers (electrons) and positive carriers (holes). MOS circuits use field-effect transistors in which there is only one type of charge carrier: positive in the case of *P*-type MOS, and negative in the case of *N*-type MOS. The term MOS (metal oxide semiconductor) describes the materials from which MOS circuits are typically formed; the term unipolar might be more appropriate, but it is not used. MOS ICs are generally smaller and consume less power than the corresponding bipolar circuits. On the other hand, bipolar ICs generally have faster switching speeds.

Integrated circuits can also be roughly classified on the basis of the number of logic gates per chip, i.e., the *gate density*. Small-scale integration (SSI) implies about one to ten gates per chip. Medium-scale integration (MSI) implies up to a hundred gates per chip. Large-scale integration (LSI) allows hundreds or thousands of gates to be manufactured on a single IC chip. The gate density achievable has increased steadily with improvements in IC manufacturing techniques. LSI circuits began to be produced in large quantities around 1970 for computer main memories and for pocket calculators. Because IC manufacture is almost entirely automated (in many respects it resembles a printing process), the cost of making an LSI chip is very small, provided that a high production volume is maintained.

LSI technology has made it possible to fabricate a CPU or even an entire computer (excluding IO devices which cannot be minaturized) on a single IC. A CPU or similar programmable processor on a single IC or, occasionally, several ICs, is called a *microprocessor*.[4] A one-chip computer, or a computer assembled from a few LSI circuits including a microprocessor, memory, and IO interface circuits, is called a *microcomputer*. Because the cost of a LSI chip is very low when large numbers of chips are produced, microprocessors and microcomputers, despite their complexity, are very inexpensive. At the time of writing, one-chip microcomputers are available to high-volume users at prices as low as $5 each.

Microprocessors The first commercially available microprocessor was the Intel Corporation's 4004, which appeared in 1971. It is called a 4-bit microprocessor since it processes 4 bits in parallel, i.e., the CPU word size is 4 bits. It has a repertoire of 45 instructions. Since 1971, microprocessors have been produced by many manufacturers. The small word size reflects limitations on chip gate density and the number of external pins available. These limitations appear to be temporary, however. Already 8-bit and 16-bit microprocessors are avail-

---

[4]The prefix *micro* refers to physical size only. It has nothing to do with whether or not microprogrammed control is used in the microprocessor.

able, and their performance/cost ratio is increasing steadily. It can be expected that all the features of large computers (IOPs, operating systems, and the like) will eventually appear in microcomputers. The distinctions frequently made between large, mini, and micro computer systems have become so vague that they are now of questionable value.

Figure 1.36 shows the structure of a representative 8-bit microprocessor, the Intel 8080 [14]. This influential machine, which was introduced in 1973, is the forerunner of several compatible microprocessors, including the Intel 8085 and Zilog Corporation's Z80. The 8080 is housed in a dual-in-line package with 40 external pin connections. It can address up to $2^{16} = 64K$ 8-bit words of memory; hence 16 address lines are provided. All CPU operations use 8-bit operands, and internal communication is organized around an 8-bit bus. Eight bidirectional data lines are used for input and output of data and instructions. The arithmetic circuits can perform addition and subtraction on both binary and decimal fixed-point numbers. Multiplication, division, and floating-point operations must be programmed, however.

The 8080 contains a register array which can be used for storing data and memory addresses. There are six 8-bit registers designated B, C, D, E, H, and L which, in addition to the accumulator AC, can be used as addressable general-purpose or scratch-pad registers. The pairs (B, C), (D, E), and (H, L) can also be treated as single 16-bit registers for storing memory addresses. The 8080 is designed to maintain a pushdown stack (see Sec. 1.4.4) anywhere in memory. The stack is intended to facilitate interrupt handling and subroutine calls. A 16-bit stack pointer register in the 8080 stores the address of the next available location at the top of the stack.

The 8080 has 72 different instructions. Instruction length ranges from one

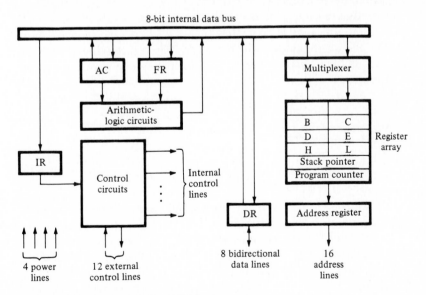

Figure 1.36 Structure of the Intel 8080 microprocessor.

to three bytes. Three bytes allow an opcode and one 16-bit memory address to be specified. All the common types of instructions are represented in its instruction set. A variety of stack operations (variations of PUSH and POP) are also included to simplify the transfer of program control. IO operations are handled directly by the 8080. An IO device is connected via an addressable buffer register to the address and data buses of the 8080. Two instructions, IN and OUT, cause a byte of information to be transferred between this IO buffer and the accumulator AC. This constitutes a simple form of programmed IO.

A flag register FR comprising five flip-flops is used to store certain information on the result of an operation, e.g., its sign, or a carry bit indicating accumulator overflow. The flag bits can be tested by conditional branch instructions in the usual manner. They are also used to simplify the programming of operations involving multiple-byte operands. For example, besides the conventional addition instruction

$$\text{ADD M}$$

which performs the operation $AC \leftarrow AC + M(H, L)$, there is another instruction called add with carry specified by

$$\text{ADC M}$$

which performs the operation $AC \leftarrow AC + M(H, L) + FR(C)$, where $FR(C)$ is the flag used to indicate an overflow (carry) bit.

The arithmetic operations (basically addition and subtraction) act on 8-bit operands which can represent either 8-bit binary numbers or two-digit decimal (BCD) numbers. The same arithmetic instruction, e.g., ADD, are used in each case. These instructions perform binary arithmetic and produce the correct answer if the operands are binary. If decimal numbers are involved, however, then the result is incorrect. It is corrected by applying a special instruction DAA (*decimal adjust accumulator*) which converts the result in the accumulator to proper decimal form. Thus while binary addition can be implemented by the single instruction

$$\text{ADD M}$$

decimal addition requires the two instructions

$$\text{ADD M}$$

$$\text{DAA}$$

Example 1.6: An 8080 program to add two 16-digit decimal numbers Figure 1.37 shows the required program written in 8080 assembly language. The numbers to be added are stored in eight consecutive 1-byte memory locations beginning at N1 and N2. The sum is stored in the eight consecutive locations beginning at N1, and thus replaces an input operand. The required addition is done by a sequence of eight 1-byte additions. The

Location	Operation	Operands	Comments
	LXI	D, N1	Load immediate operand N1 into registers D and E
	LXI	H, N2	Load immediate operand N2 into registers H and L
	MVI	C, 8	Load immediate operand 8 into register C
	XRA	A	Clear carry flag by executing $AC \leftarrow AC \oplus AC$
LOOP:	LDAX	D	Load M(D, E) into accumulator
	ADC	M	Add M(H, L) to accumulator including carry
	DAA		Decimal adjustment to accumulator
	STAX	D	Store accumulator contents in M(D, E)
	INX	D	Increment register (D, E)
	INX	H	Increment register (H, L)
	DCR	C	Decrement C
	JNZ	LOOP	If C $\neq$ 0, go to LOOP
	HLT		Halt

Figure 1.37 An Intel 8080 assembly-language program for decimal addition.

ADC instruction is used so that carry bits can effectively propagate across all 16 digits. The register pairs (D, E) and (H, L) are used as memory address registers. After each 1-byte addition, (D, E) and (H, L) are incremented, and register C, which is used as a counter, is decremented. The addition is complete when C reaches zero. This rather complicated addressing procedure reflects the fact that the 8080 lacks index registers, a deficiency it shares with many microprocessors. (The Motorola 6800 is the most notable early microprocessor that allows indexed addressing.) The advantages of index registers can be clearly seen by comparing this 8080 program to a similar IBM 7094 program with indexing, which appears in Fig. 1.22.

Microcomputers The one-chip microcomputer is a landmark development in LSI technology, in that it reduces an entire computer to one inexpensive and easily replaceable design component. Figure 1.38 shows the structure of a typical one-chip microcomputer, the Intel 8748, one of several one-chip implementations of the Intel MCS-48 system, introduced in 1976 [15]. It bears a strong family resemblance to the 8080 microprocessor described earlier (see Fig. 1.36). In addition to having an 8-bit ALU and program control unit similar to the 8080's, the 8748 contains over a thousand words of memory and several ports for the direct connection of IO devices to the chip. The 8748 main memory consists of a 1024-word electrically programmable read-only memory (EPROM) intended for program storage and a 64-word read-write memory intended for data-storage purposes. This separation of program and data memories (which implies that the 8748 is not a stored-program computer) is common

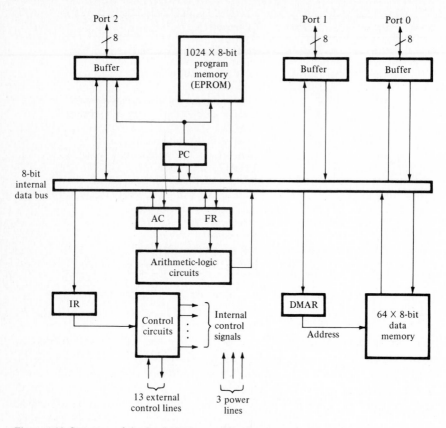

Figure 1.38 Structure of the Intel 8748 one-chip microcomputer.

in microcomputers. The program counter PC is the address register for the program memory, while a separate address register DMAR is used by the data memory. The 8748 has three sets of external pins which function as bidirectional external ports. They allow IO devices to be connected directly to the microcomputer. They also allow additional IO ports and memory chips to be attached to the system.

Suppose, for example, that a particular application requires a larger program memory than the 1K memory included in the 8748. The program memory can be expanded to a maximum of 4K words in the manner illustrated in Fig. 1.39. Because the 8748, like the 8080, is housed in a standard 40-pin package, there are insufficient pins available for separate data and address buses to the external memory. Thus one set of pins (port 1) is used for both data and address transmission. As shown in Fig. 1.39, port 1 of the 8748 is connected directly to the 8-bit data port of the external program memory. A 12-bit address is transmitted to the external memory via port 1 and four lines of port 2. An address

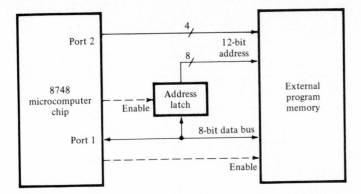

Figure 1.39 Expanding the program memory of the 8748 microcomputer.

latch is used to store temporarily the part of the address transmitted from port 1, so that port 1 can subsequently be used to transmit or receive a word of data. An external memory access is therefore performed in two steps: the memory address is transmitted and then the data. The 8748 data memory and the number of addressable IO ports can be expanded in much the same way as the program memory.

Design using microprocessors The small size and low cost of microprocessors have made it feasible to use microcomputers in many applications which previously employed special-purpose logic circuits, e.g., a traffic-light controller for a single intersection, or a domestic washing machine. The microcomputer is tailored to a particular application by means of programs which are frequently stored in read-only memory (ROM) chips. Changes are made merely by replacing the ROM programs. Hence the task of designing special-purpose logic circuits can be replaced, often at substantial cost savings, by programming a standard microcomputer system. Logic designers must therefore be programmers and, to some extent, computer architects, since they must determine the microcomputer organization that best suits the application.

Figure 1.40 shows one of the earliest microprocessor applications: point-of-sale (POS) terminals to replace cash registers in retail stores. The computer architecture is based around a single bus comprising data, address, and control lines to which are attached the microprocessor (the CPU), one or more ROM chips for program storage, and one or more read-write random-access memory (RAM) chips for data and working storage. All IO devices are also connected to the main bus using standard IO buffer or interface chips. The IO devices involved are the POS keyboard, printer, visual display, and a credit-card reader. The latter is used for credit authorization and requires a connection to the outside telephone system. Finally, there is a link to a central computer that can be used to obtain pricing information, perform inventory control, etc.

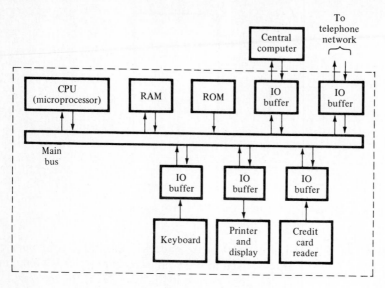

Figure 1.40 A microprocessor-controlled point-of-sale terminal.

1.6 SUMMARY

The design of computers has evolved gradually over a long period of time. Calculators to perform the basic arithmetic operations were invented in the seventeenth century. The concept of a general-purpose program-controlled computer was conceived by Charles Babbage in the nineteenth century. Such a machine was not completed until the 1940s. Since then, progress has been rapid. The first major step was the abandonment of mechanical technology in favor of electronic. Four generations of electronic computers have been distinguished; their major characteristics are summarized in Fig. 1.41. Note that this classification by generation, while useful, is based on rather vague criteria.

The evolution of computers has been strongly influenced by improvements in component technology. Often a design innovation must await the arrival of a suitable technology before it can be implemented. Babbage's vain attempts to realize his ideas provide a graphic illustration of this. Market forces also play an important part in the evolutionary process. The adoption of a particular design feature by an influential manufacturer can result in the appearance of that feature (which may be an old concept) throughout the computer industry.

Despite rapid technological advances, the logical structure of computers has changed rather slowly. The following observation perhaps explains why this is so: "A frequent reason for a given (design) choice is that it is the same as, or the logical next step to a choice that was made once before" [2]. Thus in the ENIAC one finds a rather inefficient decimal representation of numbers; this representation is, however, essentially the same as that used in the ENIAC's

Generation	Technologies	Hardware features	Software features	Representative computers
First (1946–54)	Vacuum tubes; acoustic memories; CRT memories	Fixed-point arithmetic	Machine language; assembly language	IAS; UNIVAC
Second (1955–64)	Discrete transistors; ferrite cores; magnetic disks	Floating-point arithmetic; index registers; IO processors	High-level languages; subroutine libraries; batch monitors	IBM 7094; CDC 1604
Third (1965–74)	Integrated circuits (SSI and MSI)	Microprogramming; pipelining; cache memory	Multiprogramming; multiprocessing; operating systems; virtual memory	IBM S/360; DEC PDP-8
Fourth? (1975–	LSI circuits; semiconductor memories			Amdahl 470 Intel 8748

Figure 1.41 Milestones in the development of electronic computers.

mechanical predecessors. A particularly conservative influence on computer development is the high cost of writing programs. Once the software of a particular computer becomes widely used, there is a marked reluctance on the part of users to switch to computers requiring radically different software.

A new technology may introduce new hardware and software problems but may also lead to the resurrection of old and perhaps discarded approaches. Microcomputers are a case in point. Many of the characteristics of a simple microcomputer system; e.g., the absence of floating-point arithmetic, the need to program in assembly language, and the limited IO facilities available make it comparable from a logical and functional point of view to a first-generation machine. The inclusion of hardware and software features of the second and third generations in microcomputer systems appears to be the next logical step. All of which suggests that a familiarity with the history of computers is very relevant to the understanding of present-day machines.

PROBLEMS

1.1 Design a Turing machine that divides a unary natural number n by 2. n is stored on an otherwise blank tape in the following format

$$\ldots b\, b\, A\, \underbrace{1\ 1 \ldots 1\ 1\ 1}_{n\ ones}\, B\, b\, b\, \ldots$$

where b denotes blank and A and B are delimiter symbols. The machine should compute $\lfloor n/2 \rfloor$, which is the integer part of $n/2$, and write the result in the format shown above. The only tape symbols allowed are b, A, B, and 1. Describe your machine by a state diagram or a "program listing," with comments similar to those in Example 1.1.

1.2 (*a*) Prove that a finite-state machine can be used to add two arbitrarily large binary numbers. Give a logic design for such a machine.

(*b*) Can a finite-state machine multiply two arbitrarily large binary numbers? Prove your answer.

1.3 Two instructions I_1 and I_2 in a computer program are "parallel" if the order of their execution does not affect the final results of the program for all input data sets. This means that I_1 and I_2 can be executed in parallel by independent processors. The identification of parallel instructions is very important in the design of systems for high-speed parallel processing. Prove that the problem of determining if any two instructions are parallel is unsolvable for arbitrary programs. (Hint: Prove that solving this problem is equivalent to solving the halting problem for Turing machines.)

1.4 Let A_1, A_2, A_3 be three algorithms that can be used to solve the same problem $Q(n)$ with input size n on a given computer. Let the exact time complexities of A_1, A_2, and A_3 be $100n$, $10^{-3}n^{10}$, and 2^n, respectively.

(*a*) Assuming that n is a positive integer, find the range of values of n for which each algorithm is best suited.

(*b*) Which algorithms provide the fastest solutions to $Q(1)$, $Q(10)$, and $Q(100)$?

1.5 Using the method of finite differences embodied in Babbage's Difference Engine, compute $x^2 - x + 41$ for all integer values of x in the range $0 \le x \le 9$.

1.6 Describe how a Difference Engine could be used to compute e^x where e is the base of the natural logarithms. e^x is to be calculated for values of x in the range $0 \le x \le 0.1$ at intervals of 0.01. The values computed should have an error not exceeding ± 0.0001.

1.7 Consider the problem of computing a table of the natural logarithms of the integers from 1 to 200,000 to 19 decimal places, a task carried out manually by the Prony group around 1795. Select any modern commercially available computer system with which you are familiar and estimate the total time it would require to compute and print this table. Define all the parameters used in your estimation.

1.8 Discuss the advantages and disadvantages of storing programs and data in the same memory (the stored program concept). Under what circumstances is it desirable to store programs and data in separate memories?

1.9 Consider the set S of 11 data transfer and branch instructions for IAS given in Fig. 1.16. Identify all the instructions in S that are "redundant" in the following sense: I is redundant if all the operations performed by I can be performed by a program that may contain any instructions from S except I.

1.10 Suppose that a vector of 10 nonnegative numbers is stored in consecutive locations beginning in location 100 in the memory of the IAS computer. Using the instruction set of Fig. 1.16, write a program that computes the address of the largest number in this array. If several locations contain the largest number, the smallest of their addresses should be specified.

1.11 Write an essay outlining the evolution of CPU register organization from the ENIAC to the IBM System/360.

1.12 Discuss the significance of index registers. List as many applications of index registers as you can.

1.13 Explain the following statement: "In the early years all computers were crippled by their input and output devices" (M. V. Wilkes, 1972).

1.14 Discuss the impact of developments in computer device technology on the evolution of each of the following:

(*a*) The logical complexity of the smallest replaceable components
(*b*) The operating speed of the smallest replaceable components
(*c*) The formats used for data and instruction representation

1.15 Analyze the influence of pin limitations, i.e., the fact that the number of external connections to an IC package is limited, on the architecture of one-chip microprocessors and microcomputers.

REFERENCES

1. Aho, A. V., J. E. Hopcroft, and J. D. Ullman: *The Design and Analysis of Algorithms*, Addison-Wesley, Reading, Mass., 1974.
2. Alonso, R. L., H. Blair-Smith, and A. L. Hopkins: "Some Aspects of a Control Computer: A Case Study," *IEEE Trans. Electron. Comput.*, vol. EC-12, pp. 687–697, December 1963. (Reprinted in Ref. 4, pp. 146–156.)
3. Amdahl, G. M., G. A. Blaauw, and F. P. Brooks: "Architecture of the IBM System/360," *IBM J. Res. Develop.*, vol. 8, pp. 86–101, April 1964.
4. Bell, C. G., and A. Newell: *Computer Structures: Readings and Examples*, McGraw-Hill, New York, 1971.
5. Blaauw, G. A., et al.: "The Structure of the System/360," *IBM Syst. J.*, vol. 3, pp. 119–195, April 1964 (5 papers).
6. Bremermann, H. J.: "Optimization through Evolution and Recombination," in M. C. Yovits et al. (eds.): *Self-organizing Systems*, pp. 93–106, Spartan Books, Washington, D.C., 1962.
7. Burks, A. W., H. H. Goldstine and J. von Neumann: "Preliminary Discussion of the Logical Design of an Electronic Computing Instrument," Report prepared for U.S. Army Ordnance Department, 1946. (Reprinted in Ref. 27, vol. 5, pp. 34–79, in Ref. 4, pp. 92–119, and Ref. 25, pp. 221–259.)
8. Denning, P.: "Third Generation Computer Systems," *Comput. Surv.*, vol. 3, pp. 176–210, December 1971.
9. Estrin, G.: "The Electronic Computer at the Institute for Advanced Studies," *Mathematical Tables and Other Aids to Computation*, vol. 7, pp. 108–114, April 1953.
10. Gödel, K.: "Uber formal unentscheidbare Sätze der Principia Mathematica und vervandter Systeme I," *Monatsh. Math. Phys.*, vol. 38, pp. 173–198, 1931. (English translation in M. Davis (ed.): *The Undecidable*, pp. 4–38, Raven Press, Hewlett, N.Y., 1965.)
11. Goldstine, H. H., and J. von Neumann: "Planning and Coding Problems for an Electronic Computing Instrument," part II, vols. 1 to 3. Three reports prepared for U.S. Army Ordnance Department, 1947–1948. (Reprinted in Ref. 27, vol. 5, pp. 80–235.)
12. Goldstine, H. H.: *The Computer from Pascal to von Neumann*, Princeton University Press, Princeton, N.J., 1972.
13. Husson, S. S.: *Microprogramming: Principles and Practices*, Prentice-Hall, Englewood Cliffs, N.J., 1970.
14. Intel Corp.: *8080 Microcomputer Systems User's Manual*, Santa Clara, Calif., 1975.
15. Intel Corp.: *MCS-48 Microcomputer User's Manual*, Santa Clara, Calif., 1976.
16. International Business Machines Corp.: *Reference Manual IBM 7094 Data Processing System*, publ. A22-6703, White Plains, N.Y., 1962.
17. International Business Machines Corp.: *IBM System/370 Principles of Operation*, publ. A22-6821-3, White Plains, N.Y., 1974.
18. Katzan, H.: *Computer Organization and the System/370*, Van Nostrand, New York, 1971.
19. Minsky, M.: *Computation: Finite and Infinite Machines*, Prentice-Hall, Englewood Cliffs, N.J., 1967.
20. Morrison, P., and E. Morrison (eds.): *Charles Babbage and His Calculating Engines*, Dover, New York, 1961.
21. Randell, B. (ed.): *The Origins of Digital Computers: Selected Papers*, Springer-Verlag, Berlin, 1973.
22. Rosen, S.: "Electronic Computers: A Historical Survey," *Comput. Surv.*, vol. 1, pp. 7–36, March 1969.
23. Samet, J. E.: *Programming Languages: History and Fundamentals*, Prentice-Hall, Englewood Cliffs, N.J., 1969.
24. Smith, D. E.: *A Source Book in Mathematics*, McGraw-Hill, New York, 1929.
25. Swartzlander, E. E. (ed.): *Computer Design Development: Principal Papers*, Hayden Rochelle Park, N.J., 1976.

26. Turing, A. M.: "On Computable Numbers with an Application to the Entscheidungsproblem," *Proc. Lond. Math. Soc.*, ser. 2, vol. 42, pp. 230–265, 1936.
27. von Neumann, J.: *Collected Works* (ed. A. H. Taub), 6 vols., Pergamon, New York, 1963; vol. 5: *Design of Computers, Theory of Automata and Numerical Analysis.*
28. Wilkes, M. V.: "The Best Way to Design an Automatic Calculating Machine," Rept. of the Manchester University Computer Inaugural Conf., Manchester University, Electrical Engineering Department, pp. 16–18, 1951. (Reprinted in Ref. 25, pp. 266–270.)

TWO

DESIGN METHODOLOGY

The computer design process is the topic of this chapter. It is viewed as having three major levels of complexity: the gate, register, and processor levels. Gate-level design is reviewed briefly, while register- and processor-level design are discussed in detail. An introduction to performance evaluation using queueing theory and simulation is also presented.

2.1 INTRODUCTION

A complex object such as a digital computer is an example of a system. A *system* may be defined informally as a collection of objects, called components, connected to form a coherent entity with a well-defined function or purpose. The function performed by the system is determined by those performed by its components and by the manner in which the components are interconnected.

We are interested in information-processing systems whose function is to transform a set A of input information items, e.g., a program and its data sets, into output information B, e.g., the results computed by the program acting on the data sets. The transformation may be expressed formally by a mapping or mathematical function f from A into B denoted $f: A \rightarrow B$. If f maps $a \in A$ onto $b \in B$, we write $b = f(a)$ or $b \leftarrow f(a)$. We restrict membership of A and B to digital or discrete quantities defined only at discrete points of time.

2.1.1 System Modeling

A natural and very useful way of modeling a system is a graph. A (directed) *graph* consists of a set of objects V called nodes or vertices, and a set of edges

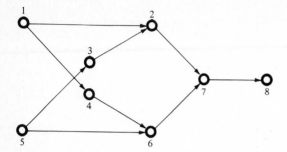

Figure 2.1 A graph with eight nodes and nine edges.

E whose members are (ordered) pairs of nodes from V, that is, $E \subseteq V \times V$.*
The edge (v_i, v_j) is said to join node v_i to node v_j. A graph is often defined by a
diagram in which nodes are represented by circles or dots and edges are
represented by lines; the diagram is taken to be synonymous with the graph
(see Fig. 2.1). Note that the ordering implied by (v_i, v_j) is denoted by an arrow-
head pointing from v_i to v_j.

We can view a system as comprising two classes of objects: a set of information-processing components C and a set of signals S that carry information
between components. In modeling the system by a graph G, we can associate C
with the nodes of G and S with the edges of G; the resulting graph is generally
called a *block diagram*. This term stems from the fact that it is convenient to
draw each node (component) as a block or box in which its name and/or its
function can be written. Thus the various diagrams of computer structures
presented in Chap. 1 are block diagrams. Figure 2.2 shows a block diagram representing a simple logic circuit, an EXCLUSIVE-OR or modulo-2 adder. It
can be seen that this circuit has the same general form as the abstract graph of
Fig. 2.1. (It is convenient in this case to include nodes representing the external
signal sources and destinations.) Several other graphical representations of systems are also possible. If the components are interpreted as edges and the signals as nodes, a *signal-flow graph* model is obtained. Signal-flow graphs are
mainly of value for modeling linear analog systems and will therefore not be
considered further.

Structure and behavior Two central properties of any system are its structure
and behavior. These very general concepts are not always defined precisely,
and they are frequently confused with each other. We define the *structure* of a
system as the abstract graph consisting of its block diagram with no functional
information. Thus Fig. 2.1 shows the structure of the simple system of Fig. 2.2.
A structural description merely names components and defines their interconnection. A behavioral description, on the other hand, enables one to determine
for any given input signal a to the system the corresponding output $f(a)$. We
define the function f to be the *behavior* of the system. The behavior f may be

---

*$P \times Q$ denotes the cartesian product of the sets P and Q, that is, the set of all ordered pairs
(p_i, q_j) where $p_i \in P$ and $q_j \in Q$.

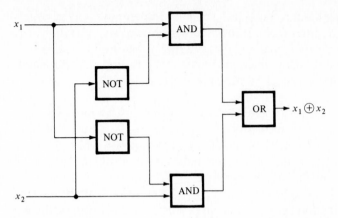

Figure 2.2 A block diagram representation of an EXCLUSIVE-OR logic circuit.

represented in many different ways. Figure 2.3 shows a specific behavioral description (a truth table) for the logic circuit of Fig. 2.2. Note that the structural and behavioral descriptions embodied in Figs. 2.1 and 2.3 are independent; neither can be derived from the other. The block diagram of Fig. 2.2 serves as both a structural and behavioral description for the logic circuit in question, since from it we can derive Figs. 2.1 and 2.3.

In general, a block diagram is used to convey structure rather than behavior. For example, in many of the block diagrams of computers in Chap. 1, blocks are identified as being arithmetic-logic circuits or control circuits. Such functional descriptions do not completely describe the behavior of the components in question; therefore, the behavior of the system as a whole cannot be deduced from the block diagram. If a more precise description of system behavior is needed, it is generally supplied separately. The description can be a narrative or a more formal description such as a state table or a flowchart.

The design problem Having distinguished structure and behavior, we can now define in very general terms the problem facing the computer designer (or indeed any systems designer). Given a desired range of behavior and a set of available components, determine a structure formed from these components that achieves the desired behavior at an acceptable cost, e.g., a minimum cost. The complexity of computer systems is such that the design problem must usually be broken down into many smaller problems involving various classes

Input a		Output
x_1	x_2	$f(a)$
0	0	0
0	1	1
1	0	1
1	1	0

Figure 2.3 Truth table for the logic circuit of Fig. 2.2.

of components. Although interrelated, the smaller problems are solved largely independently of one another. As a result, the behavior of the overall system may deviate from the desired behavior. The determination of the actual behavior of a newly designed system, which falls under the heading of performance evaluation, is an important aspect of computer-system design.

Data and control It can be very useful to divide a digital system into two parts, a data processing unit and a control unit. For example, in the simple computer model shown in Fig. 1.1b, the CPU is the data processing part, while the memory, which contains the programs to be executed, is the control part (we are ignoring the IO equipment for simplicity). The CPU is neatly divided into an arithmetic-logic unit (the data processing part) and a program control unit (the control part). The distinction between data and control units is based on the implicit recognition of a subset of the information processed by the machine as its data. The components and connections (data paths) traversed by the data constitute the data processing unit. The rest of the machine is the control unit. The paths to be traversed by the data and the operations to be performed at each point of time by the data processing unit are specified by the control unit.

The distinction between control and data can be modeled using our functional definition $f : A \rightarrow B$ of machine behavior by decomposing f, A, and B into control and data parts indicated by the subscripts c and d, respectively. Letting $A \subseteq A_c \times A_d$ and $B \subseteq B_c \times B_d$, we can view f as consisting of a control function $f_c : A_c \rightarrow B_c$ and a data function $f_d : (A_d \times A_c) \rightarrow B_d$. If we implement the control and data functions separately, then the two-block diagram of Fig. 2.4 represents the system structure. This diagram clearly indicates the causal relationship implicit in the distinction between data and control; the control inputs A_c affect the behavior of the data processing unit, but the data inputs do not affect the control unit.

In practice the distinction between data and control is usually less clear-cut than that given above. Often the data processing part of a network is permitted to influence the control unit. For example, an arithmetic operation within a CPU can result in overflow or underflow, and this fact may be used to alter the behavior of the program control unit. Thus f_c becomes dependent on both A_c and A_d, as indicated in Fig. 2.5. This blurring of the causal relationship between

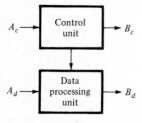

Figure 2.4 Idealized partition of a system into control and data processing units.

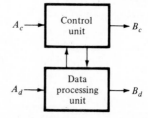

Figure 2.5 Usual partition of a system into control and data processing units.

the two components makes the boundary separating them somewhat arbitrary and subjective [29]. The same signals may be viewed as control signals at certain times in the design process and as data signals at other times.

Suppose that a system is specified by a block diagram. If each block is divided into control and data processing parts, the resulting diagram can be viewed as containing two subdiagrams: one consisting of control units only, the other consisting of data -processing units. It is then not difficult to visualize the system as comprising two distinct but interconnected subsystems: one for processing data, the other for processing control information. This division is important because control and data processing units are generally designed separately. Furthermore, systems may be classified by the way in which their (major) control function is implemented. If the control unit consists of fixed logic circuits so that f_c is essentially permanent, then the system is said to be *hardwired*. If f_c is implemented by storing control information in a memory, i.e., the control function resides in software rather than hardware, then the system is said to be *programmable*. The problems of designing control circuits are examined in Chap. 4.

There is no standard notation for distinguishing data units and signals from control units and signals. It is not uncommon to use broken lines to indicate control signals and solid lines to indicate data signals, as shown in Fig. 2.6. The functions of the controls lines are usually indicated by labeling the lines themselves rather than the block they control.

Descriptive methods A component or block in a block diagram has the general form shown in Fig. 2.7. It is a proverbial black box in that its internal structure is not specified. Only its behavior is defined either wholly or in part. The components of interest here are finite-state machines; their behavior is thus state-determined. The total input states A of a machine which determine its behavior can be divided into two parts: the primary input signals X applied by an external source, and the internal states Y, which comprise the information stored internally in the machine. Similarly, the total output states B of the machine consist of a primary output part Z and a new internal state part Y. Thus the mapping f which describes the function of the component in question has the general form $f: X \times Y \rightarrow Y \times Z$. If f maps $(x, y) \in X \times Y$ onto $(y', z) \in Y \times Z$, we write $y', z \leftarrow f(x, y)$. This mapping is represented explicitly by a function table

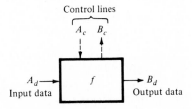

Figure 2.6 A block with distinguished control and data lines.

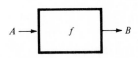

Figure 2.7 A block representing a component in a block diagram.

called a *state table* whose rows and columns represent Y and X, respectively, and whose entries are the total output states $Y \times Z$.

It is also common to represent the information in the state table by means of a graph, called a *state diagram*. The nodes of a state diagram represent internal states, and the edges, transitions between states. Unlike a block diagram, a state diagram contains no structural information; it is strictly a behavioral description. Another way to represent state behavior is by means of a set of *state transitions* or equations of the form

$$y_1, z_1 \leftarrow f(x_0, y_0)$$

$$y_2, z_2 \leftarrow f(x_0, y_1) \tag{2.1}$$

$$\cdots \cdots \cdots \cdots$$

$$y_p, z_q \leftarrow f(x_r, y_s)$$

(cf. the Turing machine description of Fig. 1.3). Each transition can be viewed as a statement about the machine which, in grammatical terms, can be interpreted as either indicative (a statement of what the machine does) or imperative (a statement of what the machine should do). In the latter case, the state transitions are viewed as orders or instructions. A sequence of transitions of this type that specifies a certain desired behavior is, of course, a program. Such programlike descriptions of digital systems have become popular in recent years; and a variety of special languages, known variously as *design languages*, (*hardware*) *description languages*, and *register transfer languages*, have been developed [2, 11, 25, 26]. Their characteristics are discussed further in Sec. 2.2.2.

2.1.2 Design Levels

Three major levels The design of a complex system such as a computer can be viewed on many different levels, depending on the components recognized as primitive or indivisible. At least three major levels can be identified in digital computer design: the *processor* level, the *register* level (also called the register transfer level), and the *gate* level. Figure 2.8 lists the typical components recognized at each level. The boundaries between the levels are not clear-cut, so it is quite common to encounter descriptions which include components from more than one level.

The processor level can be regarded as the computer-center manager's view of a computer system. The register level is approximately the level seen by an assembly-language programmer. The gate level, which is the subject of classical switching theory, is primarily the concern of the logic designer. The three design levels also correspond roughly to the major subdivisions of integrated-circuit technology into LSI, MSI, and SSI components.

Figure 2.8 shows some further distinctions between the design levels. The type of information processed increases in complexity as one progresses from

Design level	Components	Information units	Time units
Processor	CPUs, IOPs, memories, IO devices	Blocks of words	10^{-3}–10^3 s
Register	Registers, combinational circuits, simple sequential circuits	Words	10^{-9}–10^{-6} s
Gate	Logic gates, flip-flops	Bits	10^{-10}–10^{-8} s

Figure 2.8 The major computer design levels.

the gate to the processor level. At the gate level, individual or "random" bits are processed. At the register level, information is organized into words or vectors, usually of a small number of standard types. Such words represent numbers, instructions, character strings, and the like. At the processor level, the units of information are blocks of words, e.g., programs and data sets. Another important difference can be found in the time required for an elementary operation; successive levels typically differ by several orders of magnitude in this parameter. At the gate level, elementary operations such as gate switching are typically measured in nanoseconds. At the processor level, an elementary operation might be the execution of a program with the execution time measured in seconds or minutes.

Hierarchical design It is customary to refer to design levels as high or low, depending on component complexity; the more complex the components, the higher the level. In this book we are primarily concerned with the two highest levels, the processor and register levels, which embrace what is generally regarded as computer architecture. The ordering of the levels suggested by the terms high and low is in fact quite strong. A component in any level L_i is equivalent to a network of components taken from the level L_{i-1} beneath it. This is illustrated in Fig. 2.9. Formally speaking, there is a one-to-one mapping h_i between components in L_i and disjoint subsystems in level L_{i-1}; a system with levels of this type is called a *hierarchical system*. Thus in Fig. 2.9, the subsystem composed of blocks 1, 3, and 4 in the low-level description maps onto block A in the high-level description.

Complex systems, both natural and artificial, tend to have a hierarchical organization; a profound explanation of this phenomenon has been given by Simon [28]. The components of a hierarchical system at each level are self-contained and stable entities. The evolution of systems from simple to complex organizations is greatly facilitated by, and perhaps requires, the existence of stable intermediate structures. Hierarchical organization also has important implications in the design of computer systems. It is perhaps most natural to proceed from higher to lower design levels because this corresponds to a progression to successively greater levels of details. Thus, if a complex system

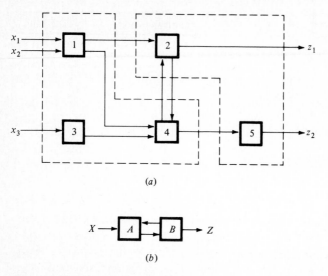

(a)

(b)

Figure 2.9 Two descriptions of a hierarchical system: (a) low-level; (b) high-level.

is to be designed using SSI circuits, the design process might consist of the following three steps.

Step 1. Specify the processor-level structure of the system.
Step 2. Specify the register-level structure of each distinct component identified in step 1.
Step 3. Specify the gate-level structure of each distinct component identified in step 2.

This design approach has been termed "top down," or "structured," design; it has been most aggressively promoted in recent years by the proponents of structured programming [10].

A good hierarchical design may be defined as one in which the most appropriate components are chosen at each level. The following characteristics are desirable.

1. The components should be as independent as possible. This permits each component to be designed or analyzed, e.g., to verify its correctness, largely independently of the other components. A corollary of this is that the interfaces between components should be simple and involve relatively little information transfer.

2. The component boundaries should correspond to physical boundaries dictated by the current device technologies. Generally speaking, each design component should be a physically replaceable component such as an integrated circuit, a printed circuit board, or an entire cabinet. This is to facilitate the manufacture of the system and its subsequent modification or maintenance.

Design techniques As might be expected, the design problems arising at each design level are quite different. Only in the case of gate-level design is there a substantial theoretical basis (switching theory). Register- and processor-level design is largely an art, so it is highly dependent on the designer's skill and experience. Computer architecture must therefore be treated mainly in descriptive terms at the present time. The need to establish a theoretical basis for computer architecture has been widely recognized [1].

In Secs. 2.1.3 and 2.1.4 the elements of switching theory and gate-level design are reviewed; it is assumed that the reader is already familiar with the subject. A knowledge of gate-level design is essential to the understanding of register-level design, which is the topic of Sec. 2.2. Our discussion will emphasize the design methodology employed at the gate level, since this may serve as a model for high-level design theories which have yet to be developed.

2.1.3 Combinational Circuit Design

Combinational circuits Switching theory deals with binary variables $\{x_i\}$ whose two values are represented by the bits (binary digits) 0 and 1. A *combinational (switching) function* is a mapping $z: B^n \rightarrow B$, where $B = \{0, 1\}$ and B^n denotes the set of 2^n binary n-tuples. Any combinational function can, in principle, be defined by a truth table which specifies for every input combination $(x_1, x_2, \ldots, x_n)$ the corresponding output value $z(x_1, x_2, \ldots, x_n)$. A physical realization of a combinational function is called a *combinational circuit*. Combinational circuits are constructed from standard components called *gates* which themselves realize very simple combinational functions. The most important gate types are listed in Fig. 2.10. The function performed by each gate is defined by a truth table. Each gate will be represented in logic diagrams by the special logic symbols shown in Fig. 2.10. The symbols conform with several widely used standards and replace the more general block symbols used in Fig. 2.2. All the gate definitions except NOT can easily be generalized to allow any number of input lines k. Practical considerations limit k, which is called the gate *fan-in*, to a maximum value of 8 or so. Note that the NOT gate, or inverter, can also be regarded as a one-input NAND or NOR.

A set G of gate types is said to be *complete* if any combinational function can be realized by a circuit that contains gates from G only. Examples of complete sets of gates are {NAND}, {NOR}, {AND, NOT}, {OR, NOT}, {AND, OR, NOT}. NANDs and NORs are particularly important in logic design because they are easily manufactured using most semiconductor technologies and are the only gate types that are complete by themselves.

Combinational circuits are formed by connecting gates according to certain rules. A *well-formed (wf) combinational circuit* is defined recursively as follows [7].

1. A single line or gate is a wf circuit.
2. The juxtaposition of two wf circuits is wf.

Name	Circuit symbol	Truth table	Equation
AND	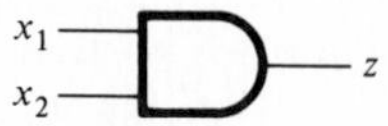	x_1 x_2 | z 0 0 | 0 0 1 | 0 1 0 | 0 1 1 | 1	$z = x_1 x_2$ or $z = x_1 \wedge x_2$
OR	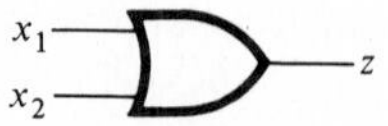	x_1 x_2 | z 0 0 | 0 0 1 | 1 1 0 | 1 1 1 | 1	$z = x_1 + x_2$ or $z = x_1 \vee x_2$
NOT		x | z 0 | 1 1 | 0	$z = \bar{x}$
NAND		x_1 x_2 | z 0 0 | 1 0 1 | 1 1 0 | 1 1 1 | 0	$z = \overline{x_1 x_2}$
NOR	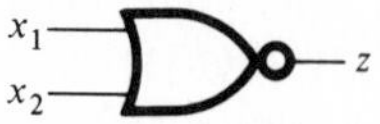	x_1 x_2 | z 0 0 | 1 0 1 | 0 1 0 | 0 1 1 | 0	$z = \overline{x_1 + x_2}$
EXCLUSIVE- OR		x_1 x_2 | z 0 0 | 0 0 1 | 1 1 0 | 1 1 1 | 0	$z = x_1 \oplus x_2$

Figure 2.10 The major gate types.

3. Let C_1 and C_2 be disjoint wf circuits. The circuit obtained by connecting a set of output lines of C_1 to a distinct set of input lines of C_2 is wf.
4. If x_i and x_j are primary inputs to a wf circuit, the circuit obtained by connecting x_i and x_j to form a single primary input line x is wf.

The theory of combinational circuits, which has been extensively developed, deals almost exclusively with wf circuits.

Well-formed combinational circuits have several important properties. They are *acyclic*, i.e., they contain no closed loops or feedback. In a wf circuit the output lines of two gates may not be joined together as in Fig. 2.11a; such a structure implies a logical contradiction if the two gates generate different output signals. With certain logic device technologies, however, it may be possible to connect the outputs z_1 and z_2 of two *physical* gates to a common line z so that the signal on z is always well-defined. In such cases, the junction of the wires

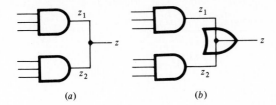

Figure 2.11 Two representations of a wired OR: (*a*) implicit; (*b*) explicit.

behaves like a logic gate defining a function

$$z = f(z_1, z_2)$$

Connections of this kind are referred to as *wired logic*. If the function f realized by the connector junction is AND or OR, it is called a wired AND or wired OR, respectively. Frequently, a wired gate is indicated on a logic diagram by joining gate outputs as in Fig. 2.11*a*. It is generally better to make the logical function explicit as in Fig. 2.11*b*, which shows a common representation of a wired OR.

Boolean algebra   The behavior of any combinational circuit can be derived by constructing the truth table for the entire circuit from the truth tables of its constituent gates. Since the truth table for an n-variable function contains 2^n rows, computation using truth tables is very unwieldy, even for moderate values of n. An alternative approach is to represent the circuit by algebraic expressions in which the variables represent binary logic signals and the operators of the algebra represent gate functions. The algebra which models combinational circuits is a type of Boolean algebra which originated with the work of George Boole (1815–1864), a contemporary of Babbage [4].

  Boolean algebra, like any algebra, is defined by a set of elements K, a set of operators P over K, and a set of axioms or laws defining the properties of P and K. It is convenient to let $P = \{\textbf{and}, \textbf{or}, \textbf{not}\}$, where **and** and **or** are binary operations represented by juxtaposition and $+$, respectively, and **not** is a unary operation represented by an overbar. The more common and useful laws of Boolean algebra involving these operations are summarized in Fig. 2.12. Every Boolean algebra contains two special elements denoted 0 and 1; hence the simplest such algebra is two-valued, with $K = \{0, 1\}$. The operators **and** and **or** are closed, which means that if a and b are in K, $a + b$ and ab are also in K. This closure property and laws 1 through 4 of Fig. 2.12 form a complete set of axioms called *Huntington's postulates* for a Boolean algebra.

  The significance of Boolean algebra in logic design derives from the fact that the set of all 2^{2^n} combinational switching functions of up to n variables is a Boolean algebra, where $P = \{\text{AND}, \text{OR}, \text{NOT}\}$ and AND, OR, and NOT are the standard gate operators. Switching functions can also be defined using other operators such as NAND which correspond to the gate types actually being used. However, when analyzing or designing a circuit, it is generally convenient to use only the operators AND, OR, and NOT. This is because AND and

No.	Statement of axiom	Name
1	There exist elements $0, 1 \in K$ such that $$a + 0 = a$$ $$a1 = a$$	Existence of identity elements
2	$$a + b = b + a$$ $$ab = ba$$	Commutative laws
3	$$a(b + c) = ab + ac$$ $$a + (bc) = (a + b)(a + c)$$	Distributive laws
4	For every $a \in K$, there exists $\bar{a} \in K$ such that $$a\bar{a} = 0$$ $$a + \bar{a} = 1$$	Existence of inverse
5	$$a + (b + c) = (a + b) + c$$ $$a(bc) = (ab)c$$	Associative laws
6	$$a + a = a$$ $$aa = a$$	Idempotent laws
7	$$\overline{a + b} = \bar{a}\bar{b}$$ $$\overline{ab} = \bar{a} + \bar{b}$$	De Morgan's laws
8	$$\bar{\bar{a}} = a$$	Involution

Figure 2.12 The basic laws of Boolean algebra (a, b, and c are arbitrary elements of K).

OR obey many of the same laws as addition and multiplication in the ordinary algebra of real numbers. Indeed, the notation + for OR and juxtaposition for AND derives from this similarity. For example, the associative laws

$$a + (b + c) = (a + b) + c$$

$$a(bc) = (ab)c$$

are equally true for Boolean and numerical algebras, permitting the parentheses to be omitted without ambiguity.

Design techniques The fundamental design problem for combinational circuits may be expressed as follows. Design a logic circuit to realize a given set of combinational functions using the minimum number of gates. Additional constraints are often imposed on the circuit structure, such as

1. The number of logic levels (which determines the circuit operating speed) should not exceed some number l
2. The fan-in (number of input lines) and fan-out (number of gate inputs to which the gate output line is connected) of any gate should not exceed specified values. Fan-in and fan-out are mainly limited by circuit power requirements.

The classic Quine-McCluskey minimization procedure and its many variations solve the design problem for $l = 2$ with no fan-in or fan-out constraints

[21]. The technique is based on the correspondence between two-level combinational circuits and Boolean equations of the form

$$f(x_1, x_2, \ldots, x_n) = \sum_i \dot{x}_{i1} \dot{x}_{i2} \ldots \dot{x}_{in_i} \tag{2.2}$$

and

$$f(x_1, x_2, \ldots, x_n) = \prod_i (\dot{x}_{i1} + \dot{x}_{i2} + \ldots + \dot{x}_{in_i}) \tag{2.3}$$

where Σ and Π denote the logical sum (OR) and product (AND) operations, and the *literal* $\dot{x}_{ij}$ denotes either x_{ij} or $\bar{x}_{ij}$. For example, the sum-of-products expression

$$f(x_1, x_2, x_3) = x_1 x_2 + x_1 x_3 + \bar{x}_1 \bar{x}_2 \bar{x}_3 \tag{2.4}$$

corresponds to the two-level circuit in Fig. 2.13. An unambiguous mapping between (2.4) and this circuit is easily defined. Boolean algebra therefore yields a precise hardware description language of the type discussed in Sec. 2.2.2.

Expressions like (2.2) and (2.3) can also be used as standard or *canonical forms* for combinational functions if each sum or product term is required to contain n distinct literals. A product (sum) term containing n distinct literals is called a *minterm* (*maxterm*) of the corresponding function. The canonical sum-of-minterms form for the function defined by (2.4) is

$$f = \bar{x}_1 \bar{x}_2 \bar{x}_3 + x_1 \bar{x}_2 x_3 + x_1 x_2 \bar{x}_3 + x_1 x_2 x_3$$

while the canonical product-of-maxterms expression is

$$f = (x_1 + x_2 + \bar{x}_3)(x_1 + \bar{x}_2 + x_3)(x_1 + \bar{x}_2 + \bar{x}_3)(\bar{x}_1 + x_2 + x_3)$$

A minimal sum-of-products expression such as (2.4) is one which corresponds to a two-level AND-OR circuit with the fewest gates and (a secondary consideration) the fewest gate inputs. Each product term is then a *prime implicant* of the function being realized. Similarly, a minimal product-of-sums expression defines the simplest two-level OR-AND realization of the function; each sum term in such an expression is a *prime implicate* of the function being realized.

Although many approaches to the general multilevel-circuit gate-minimization problem have been explored, notably decomposition theory [9], they have not seen much practical application due to their computational complexity. Even the relatively simple two-level gate minimization problem mentioned

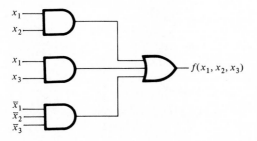

Figure 2.13 A two-level combinational circuit represented by the Boolean equation $f(x_1, x_2, x_3) = x_1 x_2 + x_1 x_3 + \bar{x}_1 \bar{x}_2 \bar{x}_3$.

above is intractable in the sense discussed in Sec. 1.1.3; its use is limited to problems in which the number of variables is relatively small. Improvements in device technology have greatly reduced the cost of manufacturing a gate, a fact which has tended to decrease the importance of gate minimization in logic design. In practice, a nonminimal circuit derived using heuristic or ad hoc techniques is often acceptable. Other design objectives, e.g., minimizing the test requirements of the circuit, may be more important than gate minimization [16]. Unfortunately, very little is known about such problems.

2.1.4 Sequential Circuit Design

Sequential circuits may be defined as switching circuits whose present outputs depend on past inputs. Unlike combinational circuits, they are capable of storing or remembering information; sequential switching functions are therefore time-dependent. The gates of Fig. 2.10 are abstract models of physical gates in which the signal-propagation delay is ignored. A more accurate (but still idealized) gate model is shown in Fig. 2.14. A pure delay element characterized by the equation

$$z(t + \Delta) = y(t)$$

is placed in the gate-output line. The delay element has the property that it stores the signal on its input line for Δ time units before transferring it to its output line; the delay element is therefore a simple storage device. The behavior of the circuit of Fig. 2.14 is described by the time-dependent or *sequential Boolean equation*

$$z(t + \Delta) = x_1(t)\bar{x}_2(t)$$

The information stored in this gate may be defined as the value of the variable y, which is termed the internal state variable.

A simple delay element has only a finite memory span; the stored information y is lost after Δ time units. In order to obtain a logic circuit capable of storing information indefinitely, it is necessary to introduce feedback or cycles. The simplest useful circuit of this type is a device called a *flip-flop* comprising two cross-connected NAND or NOR gates. Figure 2.15 shows a set-reset, or SR,

Figure 2.14 A more accurate model of a physical AND gate.

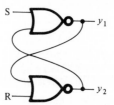

Figure 2.15 A simple SR (set-reset) flip-flop.

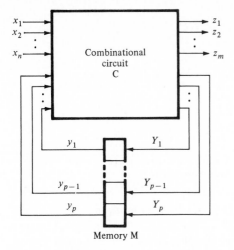

Figure 2.16 Huffman model of a sequential circuit.

flip-flop consisting of two NOR gates. Note that it is customary to omit delay elements in logic diagrams of sequential circuits, although these delays must be taken into account in analyzing circuit behavior.

A useful sequential-circuit model was proposed by Huffman [18]. The circuit is viewed as consisting of two parts, a combinational circuit C and a set of memory elements M interconnected as shown in Fig. 2.16. The internal state of the circuit is defined by information stored in M only. The advantage of this model is that the design problem can be reduced to two major steps.

Step 1. Identify the states of M and the state transitions required.
Step 2. Design the combinational circuit C to produce the desired internal state transitions and primary output signals.

A well-formed sequential circuit may be defined as one with the structure of Fig. 2.16, where C is a well-formed combinational circuit.

Timing considerations The sequential behavior of any circuit constructed from elementary gates can, in principle, be analyzed if the delays associated with all the gates are known. In practice, however, these delays are not known with any accuracy; deviations from the "nominal" (average) gate delay by as much as 50 percent are not uncommon. Thus, the times at which the output signals of a combinational circuit change in response to a known change in its input signals cannot be predicted exactly. In order to eliminate this uncertainty, special timing signals, called *clock signals*, are used to synchronize the signal changes within the circuit. Figure 2.17 shows a basic way in which this is done. A set of AND gates connected to a common clock is inserted in the lines to be synchronized. While the output signals of circuit C_1 are changing in response to an input change, the clock is inactive or disabled (CLOCK = 0). This holds the inputs of C_2 at the "neutral" all-zero value. When the output values of C_1

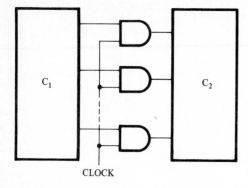

CLOCK

Figure 2.17 Introduction of a clock signal for synchronization.

have stabilized, they are made available to C_2 by activating or enabling the clock signal (CLOCK = 1). The period during which the clock is inactive must be at least as long as the worst-case signal propagation delay in C_1. Circuits which use clock signals in this way are called *synchronous* circuits. Most sequential switching circuits are synchronous. *Asynchronous* sequential circuits although necessary in certain applications are much more difficult to design [30].

The clock circuit of Fig. 2.17 may be included in either C_1 or C_2 or both. It is particularly useful to include clock circuits in flip-flops, so that the time at which a state transition takes place is governed by a clock. In general, a clock signal has the effect of quantizing time, so that successive events of interest (primarily state changes) take place at discrete times $t, t + 1, t + 2, \ldots, t + n$, where $t + n$ denotes n clock periods after the reference point of time t. A quantum of time is therefore a clock period. The signal values that determine circuit behavior are those that exist when the clock is active.

Flip-flops A variety of flip-flop types may be derived from the basic (asynchronous) circuit of Fig. 2.15 by the addition of clock circuits and control inputs. Figure 2.18 defines the more common flip-flop types. Each device has two stable states and two complementary outputs. Besides the clock input CLOCK, there are two additional inputs, preset P and clear C, which can be used to force the flip-flop into its 1 state ($y = 1$) or 0 state ($y = 0$), respectively. P and C are primarily intended for state initialization; they are therefore omitted from the state tables and equations of Fig. 2.18.

The SR flip-flop has the disadvantage that the input combination S = R = 1 results in indeterminate behavior and so is forbidden. The JK flip-flop was designed to overcome this limitation; J = K = 1 is an acceptable input which results in a change of state. In both the SR and JK flip-flops, the all-zero input combination has no effect on the state of the flip-flop. The other two flip-flops have only one data input. The trigger, or T, flip-flop changes state when T = 1. The state of the delay or D flip-flop changes to 1(0) whenever D = 1(0); the D flip-flop therefore behaves like a clocked delay element.

The memory part of a Huffman-type sequential circuit is realized by a set

Name	Circuit symbol	State table	Equation
SR	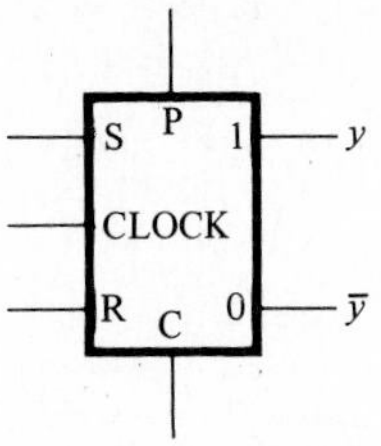	**Input SR** 00 01 10 State 0 | 0 0 1 y 1 | 1 0 1 Note: SR = 11 is forbidden.	$y(t+1) = S(t) + \bar{R}(t)y(t)$ where $S(t)R(t) = 0$
JK	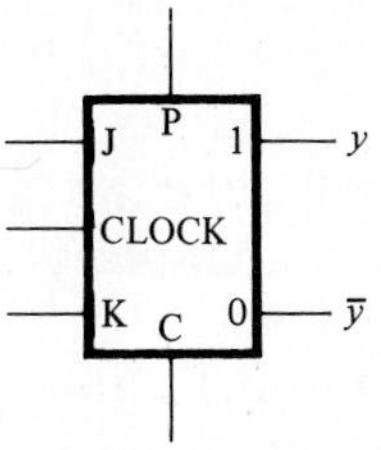	**Input JK** 00 01 10 11 State 0 | 0 0 1 1 y 1 | 1 0 1 0	$y(t+1) = J(t)\bar{y}(t) + \bar{K}(t)y(t)$
T !	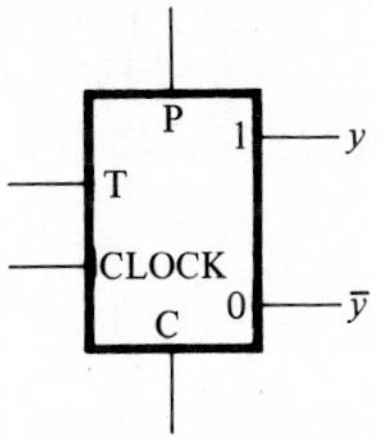	**Input T** 0 1 State 0 | 0 1 y 1 | 1 0	$y(t+1) = T(t) \oplus y(t)$
D	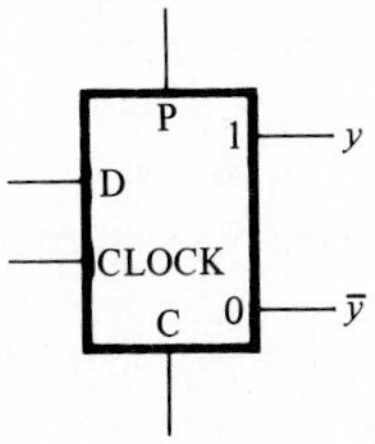	**Input D** 0 1 State 0 | 0 1 y 1 | 0 1	$y(t+1) = D(t)$

Figure 2.18 The major flip-flop types.

of flip-flops connected to a common clock signal. The clock must be enabled (on) sufficiently long for each flip-flop to respond to its new input signals. While the clock is enabled, the flip-flop inputs should be stable. If the flip-flop outputs change while the clock is on, these changes can propagate through the circuit back to the flip-flop inputs and cause them to change also. To prevent this from happening, a *master-slave flip-flop* may be used. This is basically two simple flip-flops connected in series, as in Fig. 2.19. The primary input signals are applied to the first flip-flop (the master) when the clock is on; at the same time the second flip-flop (the slave), from which the primary outputs are derived, is disabled. When the clock signal returns to 0, the slave is enabled and assumes

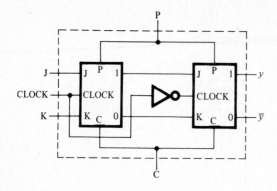

Figure 2.19 A JK master-slave flip-flop.

the state of the master flip-flop. The primary outputs change after the clock signal goes to 0. Thus a master-slave flip-flop has the important property that its state can be read and altered simultaneously.

Many different versions of the flip-flops listed in Fig. 2.18 are available from circuit manufacturers. Their main differences lie in the methods used for timing the input and output signals of the flip-flops; see Ref. 15 for a clear discussion of these issues. The term flip-flop and the symbolism of Fig. 2.18 are sometimes restricted to storage devices such as the master-slave flip-flop of Fig. 2.19 in which the timing of input and output changes is precisely controlled. Simple flip-flops, such as that depicted in Fig. 2.15, are often called *latches*.

Design techniques A well-defined design methodology exists for gate-level sequential circuits which may be summarized as follows:

Step 1. Construct a state table from the given behavioral specifications.
Step 2. Reduce the state table to its minimal form using the well-known state-minimization techniques.
Step 3. Determine the binary code used to represent the internal states (the state assignment problem).
Step 4. Construct a transition table using the given flip-flop types. This is, in effect, a truth table for the primary output functions $\{z_i\}$ and the flip-flop inputs or excitation signals $\{Y_i\}$. The transition table therefore defines the behavior of the circuit C of Fig. 2.16.
Step 5. Design C using any appropriate technique, e.g., the Quine-McCluskey algorithm or the Karnaugh map method [21].

The foregoing approach is strictly limited to small sequential circuits involving very few states. It is applicable to the design of simple data processing circuits, e.g., a serial adder, and also to the design of small control units. Minimizing the number of gates or other cost parameters in sequential circuits is very difficult. For example, the number of gates needed is affected by the choice of flip-flops and the state assignment, in addition to the combinational design techniques used in step 5. As noted already, the importance of component minimization in gate-level circuits has diminished with the development of integrated-circuit technology.

2.2 THE REGISTER LEVEL

2.2.1 General Characteristics

The register level is a natural choice as the next highest level after the gate level in the computer design hierarchy. Related bits of information are grouped into ordered sets called *words* or *vectors*. Words may be further classified as data or control words, e.g., numbers and instructions. The physical lines or wires carrying the bits of a word may be referred to collectively as a *bus* and may be represented by a single line in a block diagram. The components at the register level can be subdivided into combinational and sequential circuits, where registers form the main sequential components. The combinational circuits are word processing elements, just as gates can be viewed as bit processing elements. Similarly, registers are word-storage elements just as flip-flops are bit-storage elements.

Component types The most important types of components used by the register-level designer may be classified into the following groups.

Combinational components

1. Word gates
2. Multiplexers
3. Decoders and encoders
4. General-purpose logic arrays
5. Arithmetic elements

Sequential components

6. Registers (including shift registers)
7. Counters

These circuits have been found to be generally useful in digital system design. It might be asked if they can be identified a priori based on some property analogous to the completeness property of gate-level Boolean operations. The answer appears to be no. For example, we will show that any combinational function can be realized by a network of multiplexers. This completeness property is incidental to their main application, which is signal selection or path switching. Similarly, a type of logic-array element, called a programmable logic array (PLA), is functionally complete. Either of these components in combination with registers (which are simply sets of flip-flops) could be used to realize any sequential machine according to the Huffman model of Fig. 2.16.

Circuit symbols There are no widely accepted circuit symbols for the above components. They are generally represented in block diagrams by blocks containing an appropriate written description of their behavior, as in Fig. 2.20. Similar to the format of Fig. 2.6, there is frequently an explicit or implicit separation of the input-output lines into data and control lines. Each such line may represent a bus transmitting $m \geq 1$ bits of information in parallel; m may be indicated in the block diagram by placing a slash (/) in the line and writing m next to it, as is done in Fig. 2.20.

Each m-bit line in a register-level block diagram is given a name which identifies the data transmitted over the line or, in the case of a control line, indicates the function initiated by the control line when it is in its "active" state. The active state of a line is usually that which exists when all the binary signals it transmits assume the logical 1 value. A small circle (representing logical inversion) placed at an input or output of a block indicates that the corresponding lines are active in the 0 state and inactive in the 1 state.

The control input lines associated with a block may be divided into two broad categories:

1. Select lines, which specify one of several possible operations that the circuit is to perform
2. Enable lines, which specify the time at which a previously selected operation is to be performed

Thus, in Fig. 2.20, to perform the operation F_1, first activate the F_1 SELECT line by applying a logical 1 and then activate F_1 ENABLE by applying a logical 0. Enable lines are frequently connected directly to timing signals (clocks), as in Fig. 2.17. The output control signals, if any, from a component generally in-

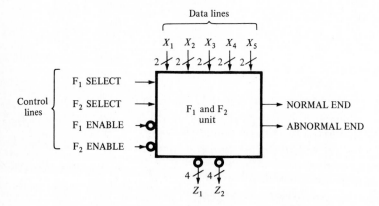

Figure 2.20 Typical block representation of a register-level component.

dicate the time that the component completes its processing or the completion state (normal or abnormal end). These control signals can then be used to select the next operation to be performed.

Word-based Boolean algebra The two-valued Boolean algebra that forms the basis of switching theory has as its elements combinational functions of the form $z: B^n \rightarrow B$, where $B = \{0, 1\}$. We can extend this algebra in a straightforward way to a 2^m-valued Boolean algebra whose elements are word- or vector-based combinational functions that perform the mapping $z: (B^m)^n \rightarrow B^m$. Let $z(x_0, x_1, \ldots, x_{n-1})$ be any two-valued Boolean function. Let $X_0, X_1, \ldots, X_{n-1}$ denote m-bit binary words, i.e., members of B^m, having the form

$$X_i = (x_{i,0}, x_{i,1}, \ldots, x_{i,m-1})$$

for $i = 0, 1, \ldots, n - 1$. We define $z: (B^m)^n \rightarrow B^m$ as follows:

$$z(X_0, X_1, \ldots, X_{n-1}) = [z(x_{0,0}, x_{1,0}, \ldots, x_{n-1,0}),$$

$$z(x_{0,1}, x_{1,1}, \ldots, x_{n-1,1}),$$

$$\cdots\cdots\cdots\cdots$$

$$z(x_{0,m-1}, x_{1,m-1}, \ldots, x_{n-1,m-1})]$$

Using this definition, we can immediately extend the usual gate operations, AND, OR, NOT, NAND, etc., to word-gate operations. It is easily shown that the set K_n^m of all $2^{2^{mn}}$ combinational functions of up to n m-bit words is a Boolean algebra with respect to the m-bit word-gate operations {AND, OR, NOT}.

The extension of z to apply to m-bit vectors is achieved by operating on components of the vector with the same index. This is analogous to the extension of the algebra of real numbers to real vectors. Pursuing this analogy, we can regard one-bit words as "scalars" and define scalar logical multiplication and addition by

$$yX = (yx_0, yx_1, \ldots, yx_{m-1})$$

and

$$y + X = (y + x_0, y + x_1, \ldots, y + x_{m-1})$$

respectively.

Although a word-based Boolean algebra is useful in analyzing certain aspects of register-level design, it does not by itself provide an adequate design theory. This may be attributed to several causes.

1. The operations performed by some of the basic components are numerical rather than logical and are not easily incorporated within the framework of a Boolean algebra.

2. Many of the logical operations associated with the basic components are complex and do not have the properties of the gate functions (associativity, commutativity, etc.) which simplify gate-level design.
3. Although a standard word length w is defined in many systems, based on the width of some important buses or registers, many lines carry signals with a different number of bits. For example, the outcome of a logical test on a set S of w-bit words (does S have property P?) is 1 bit rather than w. The lack of a uniform word size for all signals makes it difficult to define a useful algebra to describe operations on these signals.

Another perspective on the design problem may be obtained by noting that hardware design at the register level is analogous to the design of a program using an assembly language (a somewhat weaker analogy can be made with high-level language programming). In each case, the designer is concerned with processing words using a fixed set of elementary logical and arithmetic operations. Although assembly-language programming has been practiced for 30 years or so and has been the subject of intensive study, it remains more an art than a science. Lacking an adequate general theory, the useful goal of optimizing program design is, in practice, attacked mainly by heuristic and intuitive methods. The status of register-level hardware design is essentially the same.

Component expandability Since many different word sizes are encountered in register-level design, it is desirable to be able to use k-input components of a given type to construct K-input components of the same type where $k \neq K$. The case where $K < k$ is usually relatively simple. A single k-input component is taken and the superfluous inputs are deactivated by connecting them to appropriate logical constant values. In many device technologies it suffices to leave superfluous inputs unconnected, or "floating." When $K > k$, a circuit constructed from several copies of the basic k-input components, and possibly other types of components as well, is required. Register-level components are designed so that increasing the number of inputs is relatively easy. It will be seen in Sec. 2.2.3 that the control lines often play an important role in component expandability.

2.2.2 Description Languages

Although block diagrams, state tables, and their many variations are, in principle, quite sufficient to describe the structure and behavior of any system, other descriptive methods have been developed which strive for the precision and conciseness of a set of equations or a computer program. The construction of such description languages can be traced back at least as far as Babbage [24]. Babbage's notation, of which he was very proud, centered around the use of various arrow symbols such as $\rightarrow$ to represent the transfer of mechanical motion. In modern times, the introduction of Boolean algebra as a descriptive method for logic circuits is due mainly to Shannon [27]. The use of symbolic descriptions for high-level computer design was pioneered by Reed [26]. These efforts are distinguished from developments in programming languages in that the objective is to describe the structure or behavior of a computer; they are not concerned with applications of the computer. Since a large number of description languages have been proposed in recent years [2,11], we will therefore consider their relevance to computer design. As the common name "register transfer language" implies, these languages are primarily intended for describing computer systems at the register level.

Essential features The essential element of all computer description languages is the *register transfer statement*. This has the general form

$$Z \leftarrow f(X_1, X_2, \ldots, X_n) \tag{2.5}$$

where $Z, X_1, X_2, \ldots, X_n$ denote registers or their contents, and f denotes a function, usually Boolean or numerical. Statement (2.5) has the following behavioral interpretation: compute the function f using the contents of registers $X_1, X_2, \ldots, X_n$ as inputs, and place the result in register Z. It therefore specifies a (partial) state transition for the machine [cf. (2.1)]. It is frequently useful to separate the data and control functions by explicitly naming the control conditions necessary for the register transfer to take place. Thus

$$c: \quad Z \leftarrow f(X_1, X_2, \ldots, X_n) \tag{2.6}$$

might be used to mean: when the Boolean expression c is 1, that is, when the control condition c is satisfied, perform the indicated transfer. Frequently, the format of a conditional statement in a programming language such as ALGOL is adopted. An alternate notation for (2.6) might be

$$\textbf{if } c = 1 \textbf{ then } Z \leftarrow f(X_1, X_2, \ldots, X_n)$$

A natural starting point in developing a description language is an existing high-level programming language. Indeed, programming languages may be used directly to describe the behavior of a complex system; see, for example, the APL description of the IBM System/360, which represents one of the earliest and most ambitious efforts of this type [12]. Difficulties arise, however, when such languages are used to describe the hardware of the system in question. For this to be possible, it is necessary to provide a hardware interpretation for the language, i.e., to specify a correspondence between elements of the language and hardware components and signals. For example, the statement

$$c: \quad A \leftarrow A + B$$

could be used to describe the circuit of Fig. 2.21. In this interpretation, $+$ represents the parallel adder. The input connections to the adder from registers A and B are inferred from the fact that A and B are the arguments of $+$, while the output connection from the adder to register A may be inferred from $A \leftarrow$. The role of the control signal c is unclear without further information.

High-level programming languages are, by definition, machine-indepen-

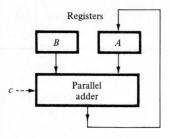

Figure 2.21 Hardware represented by the statement c: $A \leftarrow A + B$.

dent. This implies that they are not necessarily capable of describing machine hardware. One finds, therefore, that most description languages are programming languages augmented by constructs that describe hardware features such as component types, signal-propagation times, and the like. Unfortunately, in many instances an adequate hardware interpretation is lacking, resulting in descriptions that may be ambiguous from a structural point of view. However, such languages are very suitable for behavioral or functional descriptions. They are particularly useful in two areas of system design: describing control unit behavior and simulation. In cases where the control function is implemented by programs, as in a microprogrammed control unit, the control programs themselves may constitute the most useful description of the control unit's behavior. The programming language used is then the natural description language. The second application of formal description languages has to do with defining the input to simulation programs used for design verification and performance evaluation. This application is considered further in Sec. 2.3.5. Many potential applications exist in the area of design automation of digital systems [5]; however, these are limited by our lack of understanding of the design process itself.

A description language In this book use is made of the simple description language introduced in Sec. 1.3.3 to describe the IAS instruction set. The language is mainly employed in conjunction with flowcharts as a short-hand notation for describing system behavior; block diagrams are used for describing structure. It is intended to be self-explanatory, and it is used in a relatively informal way. (No formal syntax or hardware interpretation is provided.) The following example defines the language and illustrates its use as a descriptive tool.

> **Example 2.1: Description of a fixed-point binary multiplier** Figure 2.22 shows the structure of the multiplier. It is designed to multiply two numbers X and Y which are in sign-magnitude form. Each number is an 8-bit word. The leftmost bit is the sign bit, while the remaining 7 bits represent the magnitude of the number. The magnitude part is assumed to be a fraction with the binary point on the left of the most significant bit. For simplicity, the straightforward circuitry to process the sign bits is omitted. Multiplication is performed by repeated addition and shifting in a way analogous to "long" manual multiplication. There are three main registers in the multiplier. The 8-bit M register stores the multiplicand Y throughout the

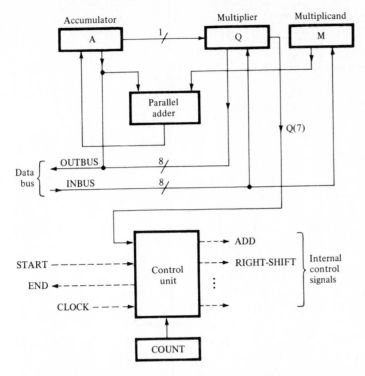

Figure 2.22 Block diagram of a fixed-point binary multiplier.

multiplication process. The 8-bit register Q, called the multiplier register, has the multiplier X placed in it at the start of multiplication. The 8-bit accumulator A is used as a working register in combination with the Q register for storing intermediate results. The most significant half of the final result is stored in A, from which it may be transferred to the output data bus. The A and Q registers are physically connected to form a single shift register A, Q which, on receiving the RIGHT-SHIFT control signal from the control unit, shifts its contents one position to the right.

The multiplier is viewed as having an external controller, e.g., the program control unit of the CPU containing the multiplier, which is the source of the input data and which issues a START control signal to initiate the multiplication process. The multiplier's local control unit then controls the seven add-shift iterations required for the multiplication. In each iteration the control unit examines the rightmost bit Q(7) of the multiplier register. If Q(7) = 1, the rightmost 7 bits of A and M, denoted by A(1:7) and M(1:7), respectively, are added and the result is placed in A (note that an 8-bit result may be obtained). If Q(7) = 0, the addition step is skipped. In either case, the combined A, Q register is right-shifted, bringing a new multiplier bit into the Q(7) position. The process continues through seven iterations, at which point the multiplier has been destroyed and the double-length prod-

```
              Declare registers A[8], M[8], Q[8], COUNT[3];
              Declare buses INBUS[8], OUTBUS[8];
START:        A ← 0, COUNT ← 0, M ← INBUS;
              Q ← INBUS;
TEST:         if Q(7) = 0 then go to RSHIFT;
ADD:          A ← A(1:7) + M(1:7);
RSHIFT:       A,Q ← RIGHTSHIFT (A,Q);
              if COUNT = 6 then go to FINISH;
              COUNT ← COUNT + 1;
              go to TEST;
FINISH:       OUTBUS ← A;
              OUTBUS ← Q;
              STOP;
```

Figure 2.23 A formal language description of the multiplier of Fig. 2.22.

uct is in A, Q. The control unit then inserts the product sign bit in A(0) and the product can be transferred to the output data bus. The control unit keeps track of the iterations by means of a 3-bit register called COUNT.

Figure 2.23 contains a description of the multiplier behavior using our illustrative description language. It consists of a collection of statements representing register transfer operations. Operations which take place simultaneously are separated by commas. A semicolon separates sets of operations that occur in sequence. The description is organized into (compound) statements separated by semicolons. The sequence in which these statements are written defines the sequence in which the actions they specify should occur. Deviations from the normal sequence implied by the statement order are specified by conditional and unconditional **go to** statements and the use of statement labels. The labels, which are delimited by colons, correspond loosely to control signals in the circuit being described.

By way of contrast, a flowchart description of the same machine is shown in Fig. 2.24. Conceptually, it is not too different from the formal language description of Fig. 2.23. A set of concurrent operations is represented by a list of register transfer statements enclosed in a rectangular box. Consecutive operations are indicated by arrows between the boxes. Conditional branching is represented by diamond-shaped decision boxes in which the condition to be tested is written. The flowchart has the advantage that, like a state diagram, it can show explicitly "structural" aspects of machine behavior such as loops. Loops are less clearly seen in the one-dimensional format of the formal description language.

2.2.3 Combinational Components

Word gates Let $X = (x_0, x_1, \ldots, x_{m-1})$ and $Y = (y_0, y_1, \ldots, y_{m-1})$ be two m-bit binary words. It is often useful to perform gate operations (AND, OR, etc.) on X and Y to obtain another m-bit vector Z. We coin the term *word-gate operations* for functions of this type. More formally, if

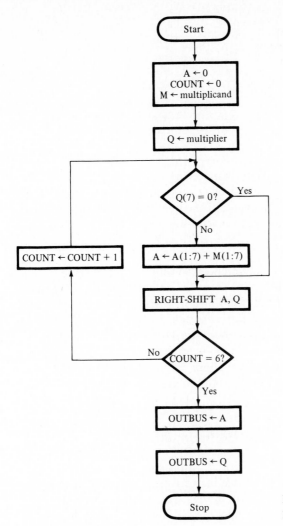

Figure 2.24 A flowchart for the multiplier of Fig. 2.22.

$f \in \{ \text{AND, OR, NOT, NAND, NOR, EXCLUSIVE-OR} \}$, then we write $Z = f(X, Y)$ if $z_i = f(x_i, y_i)$ for $i = 0, 1, \ldots, m - 1$. As mentioned in Sec. 2.2.1, this represents an extension of the two-valued Boolean algebra used for gate-level design to a 2^m-valued Boolean algebra; it is therefore natural to use the same notation. Thus, $Z = \overline{XY}$ denotes the m-bit NAND operation defined by

$$(z_0, z_1, \ldots, z_{m-1}) = (\overline{x_0 y_0}, \overline{x_1 y_1}, \ldots, \overline{x_{m-1} y_{m-1}})$$

This generalized NAND operation is realized by the circuit in Fig. 2.25a. We may represent this circuit by a single two-input NAND symbol, as shown in Fig. 2.25b, in register-level diagrams. It is also useful to represent scalar operations on words by a single gate. Thus the operation $y + X$ is realized by the circuit of Fig. 2.26a and will be represented by the OR gate of Fig. 2.26b.

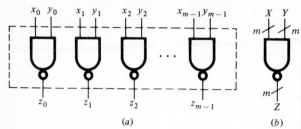

Figure 2.25 A two-input m-bit word NAND gate: (a) logic diagram; (b) symbol.

Word gates are universal design components, i.e., they are logically complete, and word-gate circuits can be analyzed using Boolean algebra. In practice, their usefulness is limited because of the relatively simple or low-level operations they perform and because of the variability in word size, which was discussed in Sec. 2.2.1.

Multiplexers A multiplexer is a device intended to route data from one of several sources to a common destination; the source is determined by applying appropriate control (select) signals to the multiplexer. If the maximum number of data sources is k and each IO data line carries m bits, the multiplexer is referred to as a *k-input m-bit multiplexer* and may be represented by the symbol shown in Fig. 2.27. It is convenient to make $k = 2^p$, so that source selection is determined by an encoded pattern or address of p bits. Let $a_i = 1$ when input X_i is to be selected. Then the operation of the multiplexer can be defined by the Boolean equations

$$z_j = \sum_{i=0}^{k-1} x_{i,j} a_i e \qquad \text{for } j = 0, 1, \ldots, m-1 \qquad (2.7)$$

Figure 2.28 shows a realization of a two-input 4-bit multiplexer.

k-input multiplexers can be used to route more than k data paths by connecting them in the treelike fashion shown in Fig. 2.29. A q-level tree circuit of this type forms a k^q-input multiplexer. A distinct set of select lines is associated with each level of the tree and is connected to all k-input multiplexers in that level. Thus each level performs a partial selection of the input line X_i to be connected to the output Z.

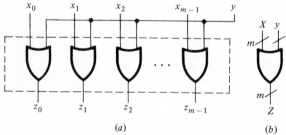

Figure 2.26 A word OR gate implementing scalar logical addition: (a) logic diagram; (b) symbol.

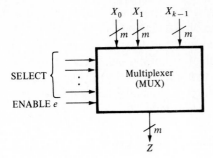

Figure 2.27 A k-input m-bit multiplexer.

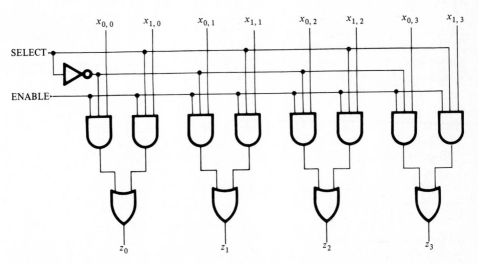

Figure 2.28 Realization of a two-input 4-bit multiplexer.

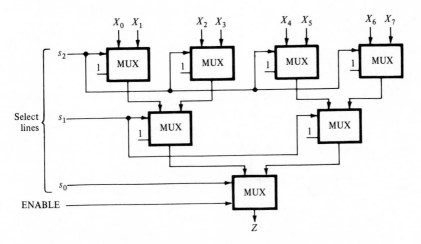

Figure 2.29 An eight-input multiplexer constructed from two-input multiplexers.

Multiplexers have the interesting property that they can be used to generate any combinational function and can therefore be viewed as a type of universal logic module. Specifically, any n-variable function z can be generated by a 2^n-input 1-bit multiplexer. This is accomplished by connecting the n input variables $(s_0, s_1, \ldots, s_{n-1})$ to the n select control lines of the multiplexer. If x_i denotes the ith data input line, then the output z which is defined by (2.7) becomes

$$z = \sum_{i=0}^{2^n-1} x_i a_i e \qquad (2.8)$$

The term a_i, which is 1 when x_i is selected, constitutes the ith minterm with respect to the select variables $s_0, s_1, \ldots, s_{n-1}$. By setting $e = 1$ and $x_i = 1(0)$ if a_i is a minterm (maxterm) of $z(s_0, s_1, \ldots, s_{n-1})$, (2.8) becomes a canonical sum-of-minterms expression for z. Hence by connecting each input data line to the appropriate constant logic value 0 or 1, any of the 2^{2^n} functions of n variables can be realized. In fact, a 2^n-input 1-bit multiplexer can be used to realize any $(n + 1)$-variable function (see Prob. 2.4).

Decoders A 1-out-of-2^n or $1/2^n$ *decoder* is a combinational circuit with n input data lines and 2^n output data lines such that each of the 2^n possible input combinations X_i activates (sets to 1) exactly one of the output lines z_i. Figure 2.30 shows a 1/4 decoder.

The primary application of a decoder is that of addressing, where the n-bit input X is interpreted as an address used to select one of 2^n output lines. $1/2^n$ decoders can be used to decode more than n lines by connecting them in a tree circuit analogous to the multiplexer tree of Fig. 2.29. Another common application of decoders is that of routing data from a common source to one of several destinations. A circuit of this kind is called a *demultiplexer*, since it is, in effect, the inverse of a multiplexer. In this application the enable (control) input of the

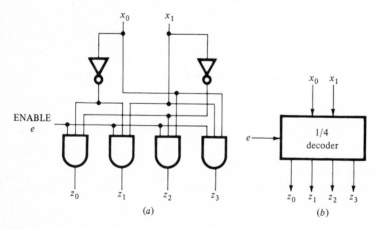

Figure 2.30 A 1/4 decoder: (*a*) logic diagram; (*b*) symbol.

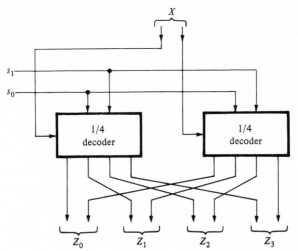

Figure 2.31 A four-output 2-bit demultiplexer.

decoder is viewed as a 1-bit "data source" to be routed to one of 2^n destinations as determined by the address applied to the decoder. Thus a $1/2^n$ decoder is a 2^n-output 1-bit demultiplexer. A k-output m-bit demultiplexer can be constructed from a network of decoders. Figure 2.31 shows a four-output 2-bit demultiplexer that employs two 1/4 decoders of the type in Fig. 2.30.

Encoders An *encoder* is a circuit used to generate the address or name of an active input line; it is therefore the inverse of a decoder. A typical encoder has 2^k input data lines and k output address lines. An additional output control line may be used to indicate the presence or absence of an active input line. Figure 2.32 shows a simple 8-bit encoder of this type. Note that the control output is necessary to distinguish the input x_0 active and no input active states. A disadvantage of this type of encoder is that if more than one input line is active, an invalid address is generated. For example, if $x_1 = x_2 = 1$ in the circuit of Fig. 2.32, the output $Z = (0, 1, 1)$ is produced which normally indicates that x_3 is active. To avoid this ambiguity, it is useful to assign priorities to the input lines and design the encoder so that the output address is always that of the active input line with the highest priority; a circuit of this type is called a *priority encoder*. A fixed priority is assigned to each input line, for example, x_i has higher priority than x_j if $i > j$. The logic design of a priority encoder is left as an exercise (Prob. 2.6).

Array logic elements There are many applications, especially in the design of control logic, where a set of combinational functions must be implemented that are essentially random, i.e., which cannot easily be classified. A number of general-purpose logic elements have been developed which permit efficient realization of complex random combinational functions. In general, such components have to meet the following requirements.

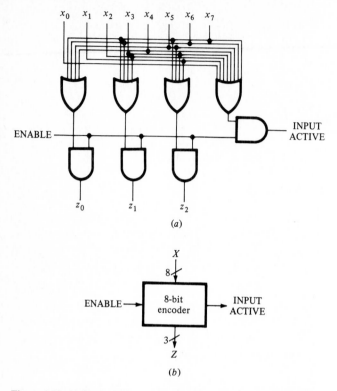

Figure 2.32 A simple 8-bit encoder: (*a*) logic diagram; (*b*) symbol.

1. Each component should have a uniform underlying structure permitting efficient mass production using modern integrated-circuit techniques.
2. It should be possible to modify the basic structure during manufacture to implement the specific functions required by a designer.

These objectives can be achieved by a class of integrated circuits whose physical structure is that of a two-dimensional array of simple switching elements. We will discuss one representative type of array logic element here, the so-called programmable logic array. Another important array element is the read-only memory (see Prob. 2.8).

Programmable logic arrays A programmable logic array is a device that realizes a set of combinational functions by means of a two-level circuit corresponding to the sum-of-products form given by Eq. (2.2). The physical structure of a PLA typically has the form of a grid of conductors arranged as p rows and q columns, with a coupling element such as a diode connecting the horizontal and vertical wires at each grid point. Figure 2.33a shows such an array. A subset of $2n$ columns are chosen as inputs; each of the n input variables and their complements are applied to these lines. The remaining $q - 2n$ columns may be used as output lines to realize a set of $q - 2n$ n-variable combinational

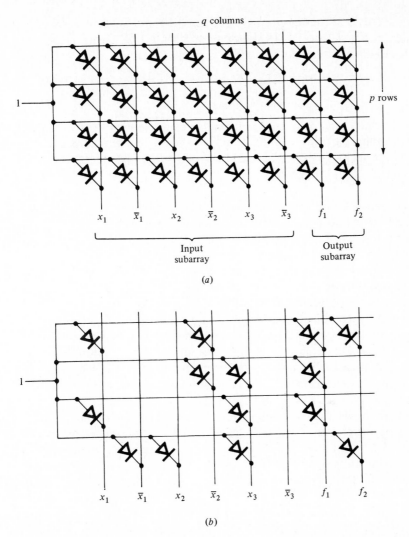

Figure 2.33 A 4 × 8 programmable logic array: (*a*) before and (*b*) after modification to realize a pair of three-variable functions f_1, f_2.

functions. The functions to be realized are determined by breaking the connections to certain diodes. This may be done by either customizing the connector grid layout or else eliminating unwanted diodes during manufacture of the PLA.

The diodes in the $p \times 2n$ subarray connected to the input variables act as AND gates. Each row of this subarray generates a product term. These product terms are input to the $p \times (q - 2n)$ subarray connected to the output lines. The diodes in this output subarray act as OR gates so that the function on each output line is the logical sum of the product terms on the rows to which it is connected. In general, a $p \times q$ PLA can realize a set of $q - 2n$ functions of n-

variables provided the functions can collectively be expressed as sums of at most p product terms. Figure 2.33b shows a 4×8 array that has been specialized (programmed) to realize the two three-variable functions:

$$f_1 = x_1\bar{x}_2 + \bar{x}_2x_3 + x_1x_3 \qquad (2.9)$$

$$f_2 = x_1\bar{x}_2 + \bar{x}_1x_2x_3 \qquad (2.10)$$

The interested reader can easily deduce from this example the rules for removing diodes to implement any given function. The classical combinational function minimization techniques can be used to obtain sum-of-product forms that are simple enough to fit in a given PLA.

Arithmetic elements A number of standard components have been developed to process numerical information. Computer number formats fall into two main groups, fixed-point and floating-point, representative examples of which were presented in Chap. 1. A further distinction may be based on the codes used for the numbers. Among the more important codes are the "binary" codes sign-magnitude and twos-complement, and the "decimal" code BCD. Many arithmetic operations, e.g., addition of floating-point numbers, are too complex to be implemented by combinational circuits. The operations of addition, subtraction, and to a lesser extent, multiplication and division can be efficiently implemented by combinational circuits in the case of fixed-point numbers (fixed-point multiplication involving long numbers is often implemented by sequential circuits as in Example 2.1). The methods used for designing arithmetic circuits are examined in detail in Chap. 3.

Figure 2.34 shows a basic arithmetic component, a fixed-point *parallel adder*. The two control lines are used for carry signals and permit simple extension of the circuit to add numbers of arbitrary size; the addition time is usually proportional to the number length. If twos-complement number representation is used, the basic adder can easily be modified to perform subtraction as well as addition.

Another useful circuit is a *comparator* whose function is to compare the magnitudes of two numbers. Figure 2.35 shows our symbol for a 4-bit comparator. Comparators are relatively complex circuits requiring either many gates or many logic levels. (Readers may convince themselves of this by deriving a logic circuit for the 4-bit comparator of Figure 2.35.) When large numbers are in-

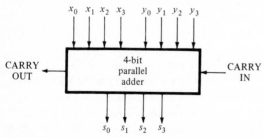

Figure 2.34 Symbol for a 4-bit parallel adder.

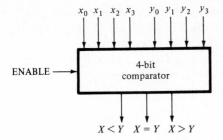

$$x_0 \quad x_1 \quad x_2 \quad x_3 \qquad y_0 \quad y_1 \quad y_2 \quad y_3$$

ENABLE →

4-bit
comparator

$X < Y \quad X = Y \quad X > Y$

Figure 2.35 Symbol for a 4-bit comparator.

volved, it may be more efficient to implement the comparison operation by subtracting one number from the other and testing the sign of their difference.

2.2.4 Sequential Components

Registers An *m-bit register* is an ordered set of m flip-flops used to store an m-bit word $(z_0, z_1, \ldots, z_{m-1})$. Each bit of the word is stored in a separate flip-flop. Unless otherwise specified, the data lines of the flip-flops are assumed to be independent. Data may be transferred to or from all flip-flops simultaneously; this mode of operation is called *parallel input-output*. Since the stored information is treated as a single entity, common control signals (clock, preset, clear) are used for all flip-flops in the register. Registers can be constructed from any of the flip-flop types defined in Sec. 2.1.4. Master-slave configurations are often employed so that no restrictions have to be placed on feedback from the register's outputs to its inputs. Figure 2.36*a* shows a 4-bit register con-

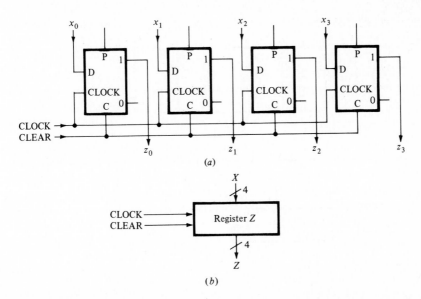

Figure 2.36 A 4-bit register with parallel input-output: (*a*) logic diagram; (*b*) symbol.

structed from D flip-flops. Figure 2.36b shows a representative circuit symbol for this register. The register and its output signal (which also represents the register state, or contents) are frequently assigned the same name.

There are many situations in computer design where it is useful to be able to shift the contents of a register to the left or the right. A right-shift operation changes the register state as follows

$$(0, z_0, z_1, \ldots, z_{m-2}) \leftarrow (z_0, z_1, \ldots, z_{m-1})$$

while a left shift performs the transformation

$$(z_1, z_2, \ldots, z_{m-1}, 0) \leftarrow (z_0, z_1, \ldots, z_{m-1})$$

A register organized to allow left- or right-shift operations of this kind is called a *shift register*. In its simplest form, an m-bit shift register consists of m master-slave flip-flops each of which is connected to its left or right neighbor. Data may be entered 1 bit at a time at one end of the register and may be removed (read) 1 bit at a time from the other end; this is called *serial input-output*. Figure 2.37 shows a simple 4-bit shift register using D flip-flops. A right shift is accomplished by activating the shift enable control line connected to the clock input of each flip-flop. It may also be useful to provide direct access to the internal flip-flops in an m-bit shift register. In addition to the serial data lines, m input or output lines may be provided to permit parallel data transfers to or from the shift register. Additional control lines are required to select the serial or parallel input modes. A further refinement is to permit both left- and right-shift operations as in Fig. 2.38.

Shift registers are useful design components in a number of applications.

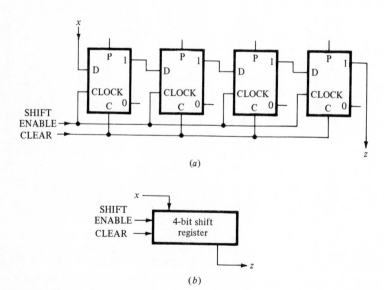

(a)

(b)

Figure 2.37 A 4-bit right-shift register: (a) logic diagram; (b) symbol.

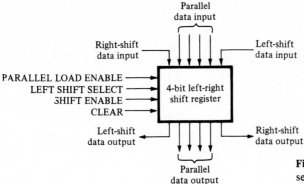

Figure 2.38 A 4-bit register with serial and parallel input-output and left- and right-shift capability.

These applications include:

1. Storage of serial data
2. Serial-to-parallel and parallel-to-serial data conversion
3. Performing arithmetic operations; left- (right-) shifting a binary number is equivalent to multiplication (division) by two

Shift operations are included in the instruction sets of most computers. A useful related operation is called *rotation*. A left rotation performs the transformation

$$(z_1, z_2, \ldots, z_{m-1}, z_0) \leftarrow (z_0, z_1, \ldots, z_{m-2}, z_{m-1})$$

while a right rotation is defined by

$$(z_{m-1}, z_0, \ldots, z_{m-3}, z_{m-2}) \leftarrow (z_0, z_1, \ldots, z_{m-2}, z_{m-1}).$$

Rotation is easily implemented by connecting the serial output of a shift register to the corresponding serial input.

Counters A counter is a simple sequential machine designed to cycle through a predetermined sequence of k distinct states $S_0, S_1, \ldots, S_{k-1}$ in response to pulses on an input line. The k states usually represent k consecutive numbers; the state transitions can thus be described by the expression

$$S_{i+1} \leftarrow S_i + 1 \,(\text{modulo } k)$$

Each input pulse increments the state by one; the machine can therefore be viewed as counting the input pulses. Counters come in many different varieties depending on the number codes used, the modulus k, and the timing mode (synchronous or asynchronous).

The simplest counters can be obtained by minor modifications of an ordinary register or a shift register. Figure 2.39 shows a modulo-16 binary counter composed of four (master-slave) JK flip-flops. This circuit counts pulses on the count enable line. The output count is a 4-bit standard binary number. Note

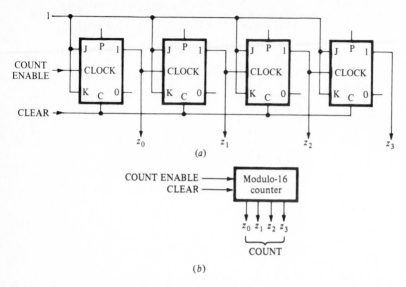

Figure 2.39 An asynchronous modulo-16 ripple counter: (a) logic diagram; (b) symbol.

that the output of each flip-flop may alter the state of its right neighbor, so that "carry" signals ripple through the counter from left to right. This type of counter is therefore called a *ripple counter*. Its mode of operation is asynchronous, and its operating speed is proportional to the number of stages (flip-flops) present. It has the advantage that it is easily expandable without additional logic elements.

A counter is basically a serial-input parallel-output device. As in the case of shift registers, it can be useful to have a parallel load capability. (Consider, for example, the input modes required in the program counter of a processor.) Another refinement that is occasionally useful is to permit the counter to be decremented as well as incremented. A counter with this capability is called an *up-down counter*. Counters are also available whose modulus can be altered by means of modulus select control lines; such counters are frequently termed *programmable*. Figure 2.40 shows a programmable counter having all these features.

Counters have two major applications in computer design.

1. Storing the state of a control unit, e.g., a program counter. Incrementing the counter provides a convenient means of generating a sequence of control states.
2. Generating timing signals. Suppose that the count enable input is connected to a source of clock pulses. Then pulses appear on the output lines of the counter with frequencies which are directly related to the clock frequency. For example, if the modulo-16 counter of Fig. 2.39 is used, the pulses appearing on output z_0 have half the frequency of the clock source, the pulses on z_1 have one-quarter of the clock frequency, and so on. In this role, the counter is acting as a *frequency divider*. In general, if

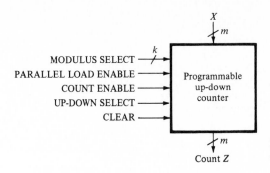

Figure 2.40 A programmable up-down counter.

the period of the clock source is one time unit, then using a counter and, perhaps, some additional logic, pulses with a period of k time units can be obtained for any $k \geq 1$. Counters can therefore be used to introduce precise and controlled time delays into a system.

Buses A *bus* is a set of connectors (wires) designed to transfer all bits of a w-bit word from a specified source to a specified destination; the source and destination are typically registers. A bus may be unidirectional, i. e., capable of transmitting data in one direction only, or it may be bidirectional. A *dedicated bus* is one with a unique source and destination. If n units must be interconnected by buses in all possible ways, then the number of dedicated buses required is $n(n-1)$. Although buses perform no logical functions, there is a significant cost associated with them, since they usually comprise some switching elements for control purposes as well as signal amplification circuits (bus drivers and receivers). If the buses are long, the cost of the wires or cables used must also be taken into account. Also the pin requirements and gate density of an integrated circuit increase rapidly with the number of external buses connected to the circuit. Because of these costs, it is common to use *shared buses* which can connect one of several sources to one of several destinations. This results in fewer buses but requires more complex bus-control mechanisms. Figure 2.41*a* shows the use of dedicated buses to connect four units in all possible ways; a total of twelve buses are required. Figure 2.41*b* shows how the same units can be connected using a single shared bus. While shared buses are cheaper, they do not permit simultaneous transfers between different pairs of devices which is possible with dedicated buses. Sharing buses, therefore, can result in a loss of performance. Bus structures are explored further in Chap. 6.

A bus frequently has some of the attributes of a register. It may store data temporarily, possibly in buffer registers associated with the bus. It may be assigned a name and be addressed by instructions in the same manner as a register or memory location. The transfer of information between two registers via a bus is often broken down into a sequence of two "register" transfers thus:

$$c_1: \quad \text{DATABUS} \leftarrow \text{REGISTER A}$$

$$c_2: \quad \text{REGISTER B} \leftarrow \text{DATABUS}$$

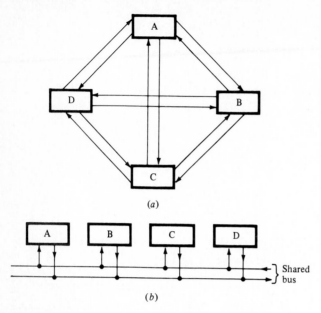

(a)

(b)

Figure 2.41 Interconnection of four units via (a) dedicated buses and (b) a single shared bus.

2.2.5 Design Methods

Introduction The behavior of a register-level machine is defined by a finite set of operations or functions $F_1, F_2, \ldots, F_n$ to be performed on various types of words. Each operation is implemented by a sequence of elementary register transfer operations of the form

$$Z \leftarrow f(X_1, X_2, \ldots, X_K)$$

where f is an operation such as addition performed by one of the components of the machine. The sequence of register transfers that implements F_i constitutes the algorithm for F_i. The particular operation to be performed by the machine may be selected by an external control signal. The register-level machine of Fig. 2.22 performs only one operation, multiplication, so that no function selection is required. When multiple functions are involved, the function-selection signals are frequently organized into words called instructions; in such cases the machine is then referred to as an *instruction set processor*. The central processing units (CPUs) and input-output processors (IOPs) introduced in Chap. 1 are examples of instruction set processors.

It is usually convenient to partition a register-level design into a data processing unit and a control unit. In the case of instruction set processors, the division between the two is relatively clear. The control unit is responsible for the interpretation of instructions and is often called the program control unit or the instruction unit. The data processing part performs the actions specified by the control unit and is generally called the arithmetic-logic unit or the execution unit. The program control unit may be further divided into a data and control part, in which case the second level of control corresponds to microprogramming. Further subdivisions are possible yielding a hierarchy of levels of control. Control concepts for instruction set processors are the topic of Chap. 4. In the case of simple machines such as the multiplier of Example 2.1, the control unit is usually a special-purpose hard-wired sequential circuit that can be designed using standard gate-level-design techniques. In more complex cases, both the data processing and control units must be treated as register-level machines.

Circuit structure A register-level circuit is a network of register-level components. It is typically viewed as a set of registers interconnected by combinational circuits. A design may be called well-formed if all combinational circuits it contains are well-formed in the sense defined in Sec. 2.1.3. This requires all feedback paths to pass through registers.

The simplest view of machine structure may be given by a block diagram that shows only the registers and functional components of the data processing part of the machine (see Fig. 2.42*a* for an example). The lines of such a diagram

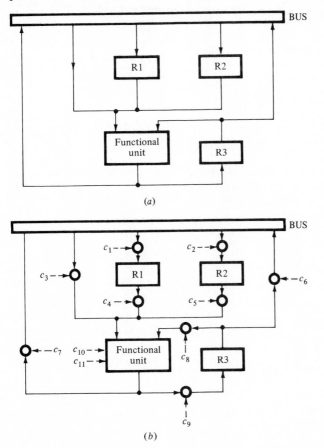

(*a*)

(*b*)

Figure 2.42 A register-level block diagram: (*a*) data paths and (*b*) data paths and control points.

are called the *data paths* of the machine. Often the data paths shown are logical rather than physical. When several data paths enter or leave a component, control circuits must be introduced to select one of the available data paths. This is indicated schematically in Fig. 2.42b, where control circuits, called control points, indicated by circles have been inserted. A *control point* is a data path switch which, when activated by a control signal, allows data to be transferred over the data path. When inactive, the data path is effectively blocked. A control point is primarily a conceptual device to aid in circuit design and description. Control points are implemented by logic circuits whose nature depends on the characteristics of the devices connected by the data paths in question. For example, Fig. 2.43 shows how the input data paths to the "functional unit" of Fig. 2.42 might be controlled. A four-input multiplexer is used to select one of the three data paths that can be connected to the left input of the unit. Since the select inputs of the multiplexer are assumed to be encoded, an encoder may also be required to encode the control signals. The right input to the functional unit is connected to R3 only; hence an AND word gate may suffice to implement control point c_8. The control signals that activate the data path control points are generated by the control unit of the machine.

Circuit behavior The behavior required of a register-level circuit can be described formally by the following methods, possibly used in some combination:

1. Flowcharts
2. Description languages
3. State tables

Examples of flowchart and description-language usage were given in Sec. 2.2.2. If state tables are to be used, then the states chosen must be high-level to keep

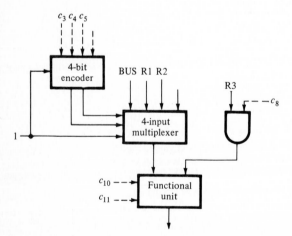

Figure 2.43 Implementation of some representative control points in the circuit of Fig. 2.42b.

their number at manageable levels. Note that an m-bit register has 2^m distinct states. If m is large, then the 2^m possible states must be merged into a much smaller number of equivalent states in order for the state-table approach to be feasible.

Design techniques The design problem for register-level circuits may be stated as follows. Given a set of algorithms or instructions, design a circuit using a specified set of register-level components which implements the desired functions while satisfying certain cost and performance criteria. No ways are known for imposing useful mathematical structures on the circuit behavior or structure corresponding to, say, Boolean algebra and the two-level constraint in gate-level design. Lacking appropriate mathematical tools, register-level-design methods tend to be ad hoc and depend heavily on the designer's experience. It is possible, however, to identify some general approaches to the design problem, which we will now outline.

A heuristic design procedure

Step 1. Define the desired behavior by a set S of sequences of register transfer operations, such that each operation can be implemented directly using the available design components.

Step 2. Analyze S to determine the types of components and the number of each type required for the data processing unit.

Step 3. Construct a block diagram D for the data processing unit using the components identified in step 2. Choose the interconnections between the components so that

1. All data paths implied by S are present
2. The given performance and cost constraints are satisfied

Step 4. Analyze S and D to identify the control points and control signals needed. Introduce the necessary logic to implement the control points.

Step 5. Design the control unit for the machine so that the required control signals are generated in the order specified by S.

Step 6. Consolidate the design to eliminate duplication and simplify the circuit where possible.

The first step in the foregoing procedure involves a translation process analogous to writing an assembly-language program to implement the given set of algorithms. S therefore reflects the skill of the designer. The identification of data processing components in step 2 is straightforward. A statement such as

$$c: \qquad A \leftarrow A + B;$$

implies the existence of two registers to store A and B and an adder to which A and B must be connected via data paths. Complications arise when the possibility of sharing components exists. For example, the statement

$$c: \quad A \leftarrow A + B, C \leftarrow C + D;$$

defines two addition operations. Since the additions do not involve the same operands, they can be carried out in parallel if two independent adders are provided. However, the cost of the circuit can probably be lowered by sharing a single adder and performing the two additons sequentially:

$$c(t_0): \quad A \leftarrow A + B;$$
$$c(t_0 + 1): \quad C \leftarrow C + D;$$

This is a typical example of a cost-performance tradeoff. The identification of parallelism inherent in an algorithm can be exceedingly difficult.

The construction of the block diagram in step 3 requires defining an appropriate data bus structure. The performance of the machine in executing a particular algorithm A in S is proportional to the total delays of all the data paths and components traversed during the execution of A. The cost of the circuit may be taken to be $\sum_i n_i c_i$, where c_i is the cost of components of type i, and n_i is the number of such components used. If a particular design does not meet a required performance criterion, e.g., some algorithm is executed too slowly, or if some maximum component cost is exceeded, it may be necessary to return to step 1 and redesign S. This points out the fact that the various design steps interact with one another, so that it may be necessary to modify repeatedly decisions made in earlier steps.

The design issues involved in step 4 are illustrated by Figs. 2.42 and 2.43. The design of the control unit (step 5) requires careful timing analysis of the algorithms in S.

The final step recognizes that the heuristic nature of the design procedure can result in certain inefficiencies, some of which can be removed by minor modifications to the design. In practice, such improvements are made in every step of the design.

Example 2.2: Design of a fixed-point binary multiplier for twos-complement numbers. To illustrate some of the foregoing ideas, we now consider the design of a simple sequential multiplier. Essentially the same approach (repeated addition and shifting) as that of Example 2.1 is used with certain modifications to handle twos-complement instead of sign-magnitude numbers. As in Example 2.1, 8-bit fractions are assumed with the leftmost bit representing the sign (0 for plus and 1 for minus). For instance, the 8-bit word $X = 00100101$ represents the number $+0.2890625_{10}$. The sign-magnitude and twos-complement representations of positive numbers are identical. $-X$ in twos-complement form is 11011011. $-X$ can be obtained from X using the following rules.

1. Complement every bit of X to form $\bar{X}$.
2. Add 1 to the least significant bit of $\bar{X}$.

The term twos-complement derives from the fact that $-X$ can also be obtained by subtracting X from 2:

$$
\begin{aligned}
2 &= 10.0000000 \\
X &= 0.0100101 \\
\hline
2 - (X) = -X &= 1.1011011
\end{aligned}
$$

Note that the sign bit is treated like any other bit in this calculation, a common stratagem in twos-complement arithmetic.

The particular multiplication algorithm we intend to use is described in Fig. 2.44. Let $X = x_0 x_1 x_2 x_3 x_4 x_5 x_6 x_7$ denote the multiplier and $Y = y_0 y_1 y_2 y_3 y_4 y_5 y_6 y_7$ the multiplicand. There are four possible cases depending on the signs of X and Y.

1. $x_0 = y_0 = 0$, that is, both X and Y are positive. The computation in this case is identical to that of Example 2.1. The product P is computed by

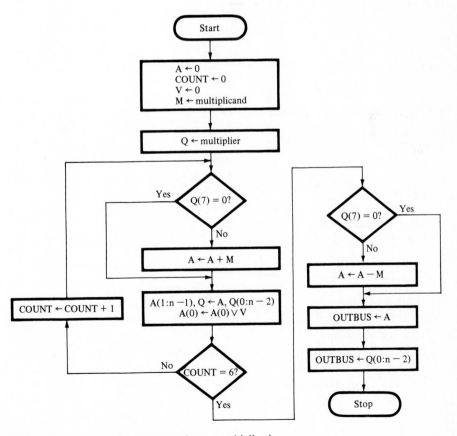

Figure 2.44 Flowchart for twos-complement multiplication.

repeatedly adding the accumulator and the multiplicand (this addition is modulo 2) and right-shifting the accumulator.

2. $x_0 = 0$, $y_0 = 1$, that is, X is positive but Y is negative. The foregoing procedure is again used, except that when the accumulator containing a negative partial product is right-shifted, a 1 rather than a 0 is entered into the leftmost accumulator cell $A(0)$. This is necessitated by the fact that a negative fraction in twos-complement code contains leading 1s rather than leading 0s in front of the most significant bit.

3. $x_0 = 1$, $y_0 = 0$, that is, X is negative and Y is positive. First, the two numbers are treated as if they were positive and multiplied as in case 1. The result is

$$P' = (1 + X)Y$$

where the addition of 1 to X (this addition is modulo 2) has the same effect as changing the sign of X. Then P' is "corrected" to give the true product P by adding to it the number $-Y$, thus,

$$P = (1 + X)Y + (-Y) = XY$$

4. $x_0 = y_0 = 1$, that is, both X and Y are negative. The procedure of case 2 is again followed, introducing leading 1s rather than leading 0s into the accumulator during shifting. As in case 3, the result obtained must be corrected by subtracting the multiplicand.

Thus the changes from the sign-magnitude multiplication algorithm are special treatment of the accumulator sign bit for proper representation of negative partial products and a final correction step when the multiplier is negative. Addition of the accumulator and multiplicand is modulo 2, so an overflow bit from the accumulator can be ignored. However, the overflow bit can be used in determining the new value of $A(0)$ during each right shift; here it will be stored in an overflow flip-flop V. It can readily be shown that when a leading 1 must be entered into $A(0)$, either $A(0)$ or V has been set to 1 by a preceding addition. When 0 is to be entered into $A(0)$, both $A(0)$ and V are zero. Hence, in all four cases listed above, the transfer

$$A(0) \leftarrow A(0) \lor V$$

suffices to set $A(0)$ to the correct value during each right shift.

Having established the circuit behavior in terms of register transfer sequences, we may now apply the design procedure described in Sec. 2.2.5. Three 8-bit registers A, Q, and M are obviously needed. Since the contents of A and Q must be right-shifted, A and Q should be shift registers. Speed considerations imply that all three registers should have parallel input-output capability. The statement $A \leftarrow A + M$ requires an adder for its implementation, an 8-bit parallel adder being most suitable. The subtraction specified by the statement $A \leftarrow A - M$ will be implemented by forming the twos-complement of M and then executing the register transfer

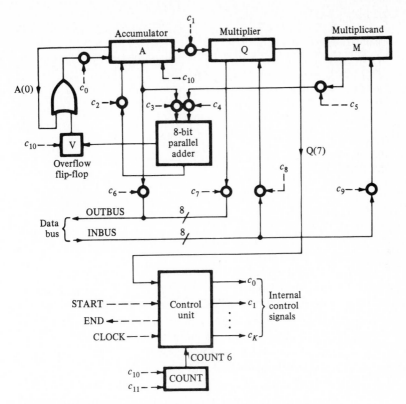

Figure 2.45 Block diagram of twos-complement fixed-point multiplier.

$A \leftarrow A + (-M)$. The data paths required by the algorithm are easily identified from the flowchart. For example, the statement $A \leftarrow A + M$ requires both A and M to be connected via 8-bit data paths to the adder inputs; another data path routes the adder output into register A. Figure 2.45 shows the structure of the resulting machine. Symbolic control points have been introduced into the various data paths. The set of signals $\{c_i\}$ that activate these control points are described in Fig. 2.46. To complete the design of the data processing part of the multiplier, it is only necessary to implement the control points, a straightforward logic design problem. Figure 2.47 shows how the control points in the data paths from the accumulator A and the multiplicand register M to the adder might be implemented. The EXCLUSIVE-OR word gate is used to change M from M to $\overline{M}$ when c_5 changes from 0 to 1; c_5 is also applied to the carry in terminal of the adder effectively adding 1 to the sum. Thus when $c_3c_4c_5 = 1$, the addition $A + \overline{M} + 1$ is carried out which is, of course, the same as $A - M$. When $c_3c_4 = 1$ and $c_5 = 0$, the addition $A + M$ is performed. The design of the control unit for this multiplier is discussed in Chap. 4.

The foregoing design represents only one possible implementation of

Control signal	Operation controlled
c_0	$A(0) \leftarrow A(0) \lor V$
c_1	$A(1{:}n-1), Q \leftarrow A,Q(0{:}n-2)$. (right shift)
c_2	Transfer adder output to A
c_3	Transfer A to left input of adder
c_4	Transfer $\pm M$ to right input of adder
c_5	Transform the output of M to $-M$
c_6	OUTBUS $\leftarrow A$
c_7	OUTBUS $\leftarrow Q(0{:}n-2)$
c_8	$Q \leftarrow$ INBUS
c_9	$M \leftarrow$ INBUS
c_{10}	$A \leftarrow 0$, COUNT $\leftarrow 0$, $V \leftarrow 0$. (reset)
c_{11}	Increment COUNT

Figure 2.46 Control signals for the twos-complement multiplier.

twos-complement multiplication. Its performance as measured by its multiplication speed could be increased, for example, by incrementing the counter COUNT at the same time the register pair A, Q is right-shifted, instead of performing these operations in sequence, as shown in Fig. 2.44. Corresponding modifications to the termination test performed on COUNT would then be needed. Little reduction in hardware cost is possible within the framework of the selected multiplication technique. The circuit of Fig. 2.45 makes relatively efficient use of the available hardware, for example, by storing both the multiplier and the low-order half of the product in the Q register. Other approaches to the design of twos-complement multipliers are studied in Sec. 3.3.2.

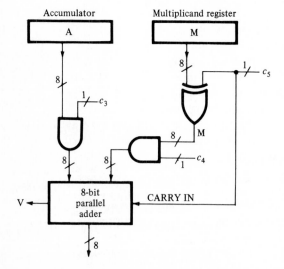

Figure 2.47 Implementation of some of the control points of Fig. 2.45.

2.3 THE PROCESSOR LEVEL

2.3.1 Introduction

A system viewed at the register level transforms individual words; at the processor level, it transforms sequences or blocks of words. As always, the information being processed can be subdivided into data and control information. Sequences of data words are called variously data sets, records, or data files. Sequences of control words, i.e., instructions, are called programs. At the highest level, a computer system can be viewed as a single component whose inputs are programs and data sets and whose outputs are the results obtained by executing the programs with the given data sets; this is suggested by Fig. 2.48.

The component types recognized at the processor level fall into four main groups:

1. (Instruction set) processors
2. Memories
3. Input-output devices
4. Switching networks

For obvious reasons, information is transferred between the components in words or small groups of words. Thus the "signals" observable in a processor-level block diagram at any time are words rather than programs or data sets. However, the problems of interest at this level deal with the processing of programs and data sets. Typical questions of interest are

1. What is the time required to execute a given set of programs?
2. How much storage space is needed for a given set of programs or data sets?
3. To what extent are the various components of the system utilized?

The answers to the foregoing questions cannot be supplied easily, since no simple characterization of the programs or data sets processed by general-purpose systems exists. Often the best we can do is determine the properties of an average program. A better characterization is provided by determining the probability that a program of a given type has a given property. The behavior of

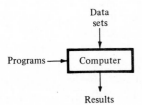

Figure 2.48 A computer system viewed as a single component.

a class of programs with respect to this property can then be represented by an appropriate probablilty distribution. For example, it might be determined experimentally that the probability $p(t)$ of a processor executing a program in time t or less is approximated by the exponential function

$$p(t) = 1 - e^{-t/T}$$

where T is an average execution time. This probability distribution function therefore characterizes one aspect of program performance with respect to the processor. Probabilistic or statistical parameters of this kind are often used in the analysis and synthesis of processor-level systems. As a result, there is inherent uncertainty in the behavior of the system components. There may be even more uncertainty in the behavior of the entire system. Although it may have been designed with a certain type of behavior as an objective, the exact behavior of the system must often be determined *after* a design has been completed, a process called *performance evaluation*. Performance evaluation is clearly important to the prospective user of a new computer; it is equally important to the computer designer.

Performance evaluation The goal of performance evaluation is to determine functions of the form $\varphi(x_1, x_2, \ldots, x_n) = \varphi(X)$, where X is a set of design parameters (including input data characteristics) and φ is a performance measure such as processing time, waiting time, or resource utilization. It is generally desirable to be able to write φ as an algebraic expression involving X; such an expression is said to be an *analytic model* of φ. Tractable analytic models have been developed for certain aspects of computer performance evaluation, but accurate models of this kind are, in general, quite rare.

The difficulties of purely analytical approaches to performance evaluation arise from the fact that the components of a system can interact in complex ways. Communication between processor-level components is asynchronous, and contention for shared system resources frequently results. In cases where φ cannot be expressed in a tractable algebraic form, it may be possible to compute $\varphi(X)$ systematically for specific (numerical) values of X. Such approaches may be termed numerical or experimental and fall into two main groups: computer-based simulation and performance measurement on an actual system. Only simulation is considered in detail here (in Sec. 2.3.5), since it is more applicable to the design process than measurement techniques.

The mathematical discipline that appears to be most appropriate for performance evaluation at the processor level is queueing theory [17, 19]. *Queueing theory* is a branch of applied probability theory concerned with processes that involve sharing limited resources; the resource limitations result in waiting lines or queues forming at the resources. The origins of queueing theory are usually traced to the analysis of congestion in telephone systems made by the Danish engineer A. K. Erlang (1878–1929) in 1909. A queueing system is a collection of queues which are waiting for service by a set of "servers." The manner in which the queues are formed and serviced is

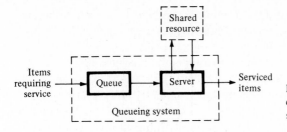

Figure 2.49 A simple queueing model consisting of a single queue and a single server.

determined by suitable probability distributions. Figure 2.49 shows the simplest queueing system consisting of a single queue and a single server. The appropriateness of queueing theory for computer performance evaluation stems from the fact that a computer system consists of a set of limited resources such as memory space, IO channel capacity, and CPU time, which must be shared among competing programs. Unfortunately, the analysis of queueing systems is extremely difficult unless rather restrictive assumptions are made.

Frequently, a useful mathematical model of a computer can be constructed whose behavior cannot be determined analytically, but can be determined numerically by using simulation. Figure 2.50 shows the structure of a typical simulation system. A computer program S called a *simulator* is used to mimic the behavior of the system C whose performance is to be evaluated. S is supplied with a description of C, a set of input data for C, and a set of instructions concerning the performance parameters to be computed and reported. S is then executed on an appropriate host computer C'. During this execution, S computes all the relevant actions taken by C and prints a report on the performance of C. The value of this performance analysis depends on the accuracy of both the model used for C and the input data created for C. Accurate simulation may require elaborate modeling and extensive simulation runs. The cost of designing the model and the cost of the host computer time may be significant. These costs are usually primary limitations on the use of simulation in the

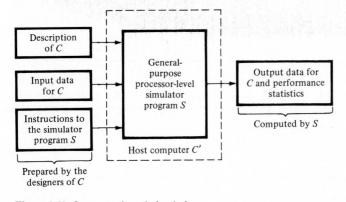

Figure 2.50 Computer-based simulation.

design process. The great advantage of simulation is that minor modifications to the model C can easily and quickly be made and their effects evaluated. Simulation may also be of value at the register and gate level.

Another approach to performance evaluation is to construct a physical prototype of the target system, run it under representative working conditions, and monitor its performance. The prototype system may be a "breadboard" version of the final system so that minor design changes can be evaluated. This can be considered to be physical simulation, in contrast with the computer simulation discussed in the preceding paragraph. Performance information is obtained by physical measurement of the parameters of interest in real time. For example, a timer may be used to determine program execution times, and a counter may be used to determine the frequency of occurrence of an event of interest. These measuring techniques may be software-implemented by inserting appropriate timing or counting instructions into the programs being executed. Such accounting routines are commonly used by computer centers to provide users with performance statistics for their programs. An alternative technique is to attach special hardware to the machine for measurement purposes. The main advantage of performance measurement via a prototype machine is that actual programs for the target machine can be executed. It is not necessary to design artificial models for these programs as is usually the case when computer simulation or analytic methods are employed.

2.3.2 Components

CPUs We define a central processing unit to be a general-purpose instruction set processor. Most computer systems have one such processor which is assigned overall responsibility for program interpretation and execution. The qualifier general-purpose distinguishes CPUs from other instruction set processors such as input-output processors whose functions are in some way restricted or special-purpose. An instruction set processor is characterized by the fact that it operates on word-organized instructions and data which are obtained by the processor from an external memory; results computed by the processor are also stored in this memory. Generally only one CPU is present in a computer installation. A computer with one CPU is called a uniprocessor; a computer with more than one CPU is called a multiprocessor.

CPUs generally exhibit a clear-cut division into data processing and control parts; the former is called the arithmetic-logic unit (ALU) or execution unit; the latter is called the program control unit or instruction unit. CPUs are undoubtedly the most complex processor-level components and can be classified in many ways. The more important design considerations appear to be the following:

1. The types of instructions forming the CPU's instruction set and their execution times
2. The register-level organization of the ALU

3. The register-level organization of the program control unit
4. The manner in which the CPU communicates with external devices

CPU design problems are examined in detail in Chaps. 3 and 4. The evolution of CPU structure from the single accumulator organization of the IAS machine to the complex multiple-register organizations of modern CPUs is outlined in Chap. 1.

Figure 2.51 shows the simple block symbol used here to represent a CPU. A one-word data bus is the main path by which information is transferred to and from the CPU. Note that the data bus is used to transfer both instructions and data words to the CPU. A second bus is generally, but not always, provided for transferring addresses from the CPU to main memory and, possibly, to IO devices. Finally, some control lines are present which are used by the CPU to control the other components of the system and synchronize their operations with those of the CPU.

Until LSI manufacturing techniques made it possible to mass-produce inexpensive single-chip CPUs (microprocessors), CPUs were treated as design components only by a handful of computer architects employed by computer manufacturers. Microprocessors have vastly increased the number of situations where it is economically feasible to use CPUs. This expansion can be expected to result in changes in CPU architecture, so that CPUs can be used more easily by designers who are not themselves computer architects. For example, in certain applications it may be desirable to have CPUs capable of operating on data words of nonstandard length. The introduction of CPUs that are expandable so that they can operate on words of any required length is a natural development; this can be accomplished by a technique called bit-slicing, which is discussed in Chap. 3.

Memories CPUs and other instruction set processors are designed to operate in conjunction with external memory devices that store the programs and data required by the processors. Many different memory technologies are used which vary greatly in cost and performance. Generally the cost of a memory device increases rapidly with the speed of operation required. The memory part of a computer system can be divided into two major subsystems:

1. Main memory, consisting of relatively fast storage devices connected directly to and controlled by the CPU
2. Secondary memory, consisting of slower and less expensive devices that communicate indirectly with the CPU via main memory

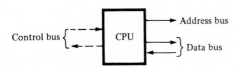

Figure 2.51 A central processing unit.

Secondary memory devices such as magnetic tape and disk units are used for storing large amounts of information needed relatively infrequently by the CPU. They are often controlled directly by special-purpose processors (memory control units or IOPs). Secondary memory devices are considered to be part of a computer's input-output system.

Main memory is, in most cases, a word-organized addressable random-access memory (RAM). This means that information can be accessed (read from or written into the memory) one word at a time. Each word storage location has associated with it an address that uniquely identifies it. To access a particular word in main memory, the CPU sends its address and appropriate control signals (read or write commands) to the memory. In a write operation, the CPU also places the word to be written into memory on the main memory data bus, from which it is transferred into the addressed location. In a read operation, the contents of the addressed location are transferred to the memory data bus and thence to the CPU. The term random access stems from the fact that the access time for every location is the same. Random access is contrasted with serial access, where access times vary with the location being accessed. Serial access memories are generally slower and less expensive than RAMs; most secondary memory devices use serial access. Because of their lower operating speeds and serial access modes, the manner in which the stored information is organized in secondary memories is more complex than the simple word organization of main memory. Memory technologies and the organization of stored information are covered in Chap. 5. Figure 2.52 shows the symbol used for a memory unit.

LSI manufacturing technologies have had as profound an impact on memories as they have had on processors. Inexpensive RAM chips are available with capacities of many thousands of bits. They are particularly simple design components, because both the number of words and the word size can easily be expanded. The most common serial access devices are electromechanical, but several LSI-based technologies are likely to at least partly replace the relatively unreliable electromechanical devices in the near future.

IO devices Input-output devices are the means by which a computer communicates with the outside world. The primary function of most IO devices is to act as transducers, i.e., to convert information from one physical representation to another. Unlike processors, IO devices do not alter the information content or meaning of the data on which they act. Since data is transferred and processed within a computer system in the form of digital electrical signals, input (output) devices transform other forms of information to (from) digital

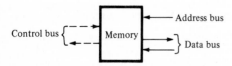

Control bus { Memory — Address bus } Data bus

Figure 2.52 A memory unit.

electrical signals. Figure 2.53 lists some typical IO devices and the information media they employ. Note that many of these devices make use of electromechanical technologies, hence their speed of operation is slow compared with processor and main-memory speeds. An IO device can be controlled directly by the CPU, but it is often under the immediate control of a special-purpose processor or control unit which directs the flow of information between the processor and main memory. The design of IO systems is examined in Chap. 6.

Switching networks Processor-level components communicate by word-oriented buses. In systems with many components, this communication may be controlled by one or more devices which we call switching networks (terms such as switching exchange, communications controller, and bus controller are also used in this context). The primary function of a switching network is to establish dynamic communication paths between the components under its control. For cost reasons, buses are frequently shared. This can result in contention for access to a bus. The switching network resolves such contention by selecting one of the requesting devices (on some priority basis) and connecting it to the desired bus. The other requesting devices may be placed in a queue by the switching network. Simultaneous requests for access to a given device or bus result from the fact that communication between processor-level components is generally asynchronous. This can be attributed to several causes.

IO device	Type		Medium to/from which IO device transforms digital electrical signals
	Input	Output	
Card reader	✔		Characters on punched cards
Card punch		✔	Characters on punched cards
Document reader	✔		Characters on paper
Line printer		✔	Characters on paper
Teletype	✔	✔	Characters on paper
Line plotter		✔	Visual images on paper
TV scanner	✔		Visual images
CRT (TV) display		✔	Visual images on screen
Light pen	✔		Visual images on screen
Keyboard	✔		Characters on keyboard
Seven-segment digital display		✔	Characters on screen
Magnetic-tape unit	✔	✔	Characters on magnetic tape
Magnetic-disk unit	✔	✔	Characters on magnetic disk
Analog-digital converter	✔	✔	Analog (continuous) electrical signals
Modem (modulator-demodulator)	✔	✔	Frequency-modulated electrical signals
Voice synthesizer		✔	Spoken words

Figure 2.53 Representative IO devices.

1. A high degree of independence exists among the components. For example, CPUs and IOPs execute different types of programs and interact relatively infrequently and at unpredictable times.
2. Component operating speeds vary over a wide range. For example, CPUs typically operate from 1 to 10 times faster than main-memory devices, while main-memory speeds may be many orders of magnitude faster than IO-device speeds.
3. The physical distance separating the components may be too large to permit synchronous transmission of information between them.

Asynchronous communication is frequently implemented by using interlocked control signals, a technique referred to as "handshaking." Suppose that a data word is to be transferred from device *A* to device *B*. *A* places the word in question on the data bus from *A* to *B* and then sends a control signal, often called a *ready* signal, to *B* to indicate the presence of the data on the data bus. When *B* recognizes the ready signal, it transfers the data from the data bus to a register within *B* and then activates an *acknowledge* control line to *A*. On receiving the acknowledge signal, *A* begins transmission of the next word. Thus a sequence of ready/acknowledge signals accompanies the data transfer, making it largely independent of the operating speeds of the two devices. The data and control lines connected to a device and the signal sequences required to communicate with the device constitute the device's *interface*. Clearly the more similar their interfaces, the more readily two devices can communicate. By using a standard interface throughout a system, the ease with which it can be expanded or otherwise modified is greatly increased.

Bus control is often one of the functions of a processor such as a CPU or an IOP. For example, in the IBM S/360 system discussed in Sec. 1.5.2, an IOP controls a common IO bus to which many IO devices are connected. The IOP is responsible for selecting the device to be connected to the IO bus and from there to main memory. It also acts as a buffer between the relatively slow IO devices and the relatively fast main memory. Special processors whose sole function is to supervise data transfers over shared buses can be found in many large systems. Thus in the Burroughs B5000 system depicted in Fig. 1.26 a switching network called the memory exchange controls data transfers between the main-memory modules and the main processors. Another switching network, the IO exchange, connects the IOPs to the IO devices.

More difficult communications problems are encountered when a number of computers must be connected over long distances to form a computer network. Data transmission in such cases may be via shared telephone lines. In computer networks such as the ARPANET, each main, or host, computer is connected to the network via a small computer (called an interface message processor, IMP, in the ARPANET) whose function is to supervise the transmission of blocks of data (messages) to and from its host computer. Communications controllers of this type are often regarded as special-purpose IO devices or IOPs.

2.3.3 Design Techniques

Introduction Processor-level design is even less amenable to formal analysis than design at the register level. This is mainly due to the difficulty of giving a sufficiently precise description of the desired system behavior. To say that the computer should execute efficiently all programs supplied to it is of little help to the designer. The usual approach to design at this level is to take a *prototype design* of known performance and modify it where necessary to accommodate new technologies or specific performance requirements. Performance specifications usually take the following form:

1. The computer should be capable of executing *a* instructions of type *b* per second.
2. The computer should be able to support *c* IO devices of type *d*.
3. The computer should be hardware and/or software compatible with computers of type *e*.
4. The total cost of the system should not exceed *f*.

Even when a new computer is closely based on a known design, it may not be possible to predict its performance accurately. This is due to our lack of understanding of the relation between the structure of a computer and its performance. Performance evaluation must generally be done experimentally, either by computer simulation or by measurement of the performance of a copy of the machine under actual working conditions. Thus we can view the design process as involving two major steps.

Step 1. Select a prototype design and adapt it to satisfy the given performance constraints.

Step 2. Determine the performance of the proposed system. If unsatisfactory, modify the design and repeat this step. Continue until an acceptable design is obtained.

This conservative approach to computer design has been widely followed and accounts in part for the relatively slow evolution of computer architecture. It is rare to find a computer structure that deviates substantially from the norm. The adherence to proven designs is also influenced by the need to remain compatible with existing hardware and software standards. Computer users are understandably reluctant to spend money retraining computer operators and programmers and replacing old software.

Prototype computer structures The prototype structures of interest here are all universal machines, i.e., general-purpose computers. They differ primarily in the number of components used and their autonomy. The variety of interconnection or communication structures used is surprisingly small. Figure 2.54 shows the simplest computer structure which is typical of first-genera-

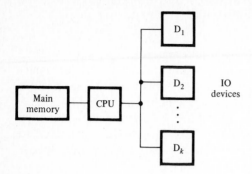

Figure 2.54 The simplest computer structure.

tion machines and many modern microprocessor-based systems. The addition of special-purpose IO processors typical of the second and subsequent generations is shown in Fig. 2.55. Here S denotes the switching network that controls memory-processor communication. Figure 2.56 shows one of the most general single-computer prototype structures employing multiple CPUs (it is therefore a multiprocessor) and multiple main-memory banks. The preceding two uniprocessor systems are special cases of this general configuration.

More complex structures, called multicomputer systems or computer networks, may be obtained by connecting several copies of the foregoing prototype computer structures. The connection between the different computers is made via special IO devices that act as intercomputer communication controllers. Dedicated small computers are often used for this purpose. The computers are considered to be loosely coupled since their processors and memories are not directly connected. Figure 2.57 shows an example of two computers with the structure of Fig. 2.55 which have been connected to form a

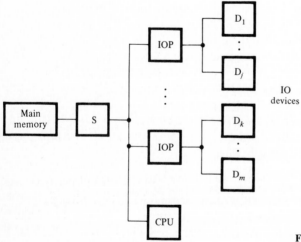

Figure 2.55 Computer with IOPs.

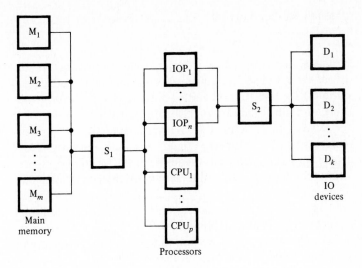

Figure 2.56 General computer structure.

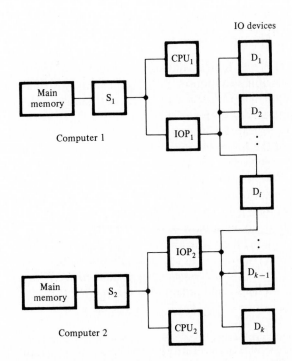

Figure 2.57 A multicomputer system similar to the IBM ASP organization.

single system. This system has essentially the same structure as IBM's ASP organization.[1]

Simple performance measures Several widely used performance parameters for a computer system are based on the performance of its major components, e.g., the main memory and the CPU. Two representative parameters of this type are main-memory bandwidth and CPU instruction execution speed.

The *main-memory bandwidth* is defined as the maximum rate in bits per second at which information can be transferred to or from main memory. This clearly imposes a basic limitation on the computer's performance, since processing speed is ultimately determined by the rate at which instructions and data can be fetched from memory.

Many performance measures are based on CPU behavior. The time required to execute an instruction is one such parameter. Since execution times vary from one instruction to another, the execution time of an instruction common to most processers, e.g., fixed-point addition, may be chosen as representative. A better measure is obtained by taking an average of all CPU instruction execution times weighted by their frequency of use. Let $I_1, I_2, \ldots, I_n$ be a set of representative instruction types. Let t_i denote the average execution time of an instruction of type I_i and let p_i denote the probability of occurrence of type I_i instructions in representative programs. Then the *average instruction execution time* t_E is given by

$$t_E = \sum_{i=1}^{n} p_i t_i$$

The set of instruction types selected and their frequency of occurrence constitute an *instruction mix*. A number of instruction mixes have been proposed as being representative of various system workloads. One of the best known is the *Gibson mix* [14], which is summarized in Fig. 2.58. An equivalent performance measure is $1/t_E$, the CPU *instruction execution rate*.

The most serious limitation of the foregoing parameters is that they do not measure the performance of the system as a whole. In particular, the influence of IO operations is ignored. Perhaps the most satisfactory performance measure is the cost of executing a set of representative programs. This cost is typically the total execution time but may also include the use made of the various system components. A set of actual programs taken by a user to be representative of his computing environment may be chosen as the representative programs for performance evaluation. Such programs are called *benchmarks*, and are run by the user on a copy of the machine being evaluated. It is occasionally useful to devise an artificial benchmark, or *synthetic program*,

---

[1]In the ASP (attached support processor) configuration, one computer acts as the main processor and overall system supervisor. The other computer manages input-output processing and other supporting tasks. The device D_i that couples the two computers is called a channel-to-channel adapter.

Instruction type	Probability of occurrence
Transfers to and from main memory	0.31
Indexing	0.18
Branching	0.17
Floating-point arithmetic	0.12
Fixed-point arithmetic	0.07
Shifting	0.04
Miscellaneous	0.11

Figure 2.58 Summary of the Gibson instruction mix.

whose sole purpose is to exercise the machine and provide data for performance evaluation.

Descriptive methods Block diagrams supplemented by narrative descriptions are the most common ways of describing systems at the processor level. Most formal description languages that have been proposed are suitable for lower-level descriptions only (see Sec. 2.2.2). Bell and Newell have developed a concise descriptive system called PMS (*processors memories switches*) that can be used for representing systems at the processor level [2]. They identify seven basic components, which are listed in Fig. 2.59. Each component is denoted by a distinct symbol (a capital letter). These symbols may be qualified by appending additional (small) letters. For example, M denotes a memory and Mp denotes a primary memory, i.e., main memory. Further component information may be added in the form of a list of attributes in parentheses, e.g., Mp (technology: semiconductor; access time: 100 ns). A computer system is represented by a graph called a PMS diagram whose nodes are PMS component symbols and whose edges are connections such as data and control buses (control buses are distinguished by using broken lines as edges). Figure 2.60 shows the PMS diagram for the computer of Fig. 2.55. The symbol X denotes the external environment of the computer. It can be concluded from this example that a PMS diagram is essentially the same as a block diagram. It is mainly useful for

Component name	Symbol	Examples
Processor	P	CPU, IOP
Control	K	Program control unit
Data operation	D	Arithmetic-logic unit
Memory	M	Main memory, secondary memory
Transducer	T	IO devices
Link	L	IO port
Switch	S	Multiplexer, crossbar switch

Figure 2.59 Basic components of Bell and Newell's PMS representation.

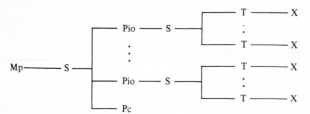

Figure 2.60 PMS diagram equivalent to Fig. 2.55.

structural descriptions since only a limited amount of behavioral information can reasonably be included among the component attributes.

Another class of formal description languages for processor-level designs can be found in the input languages for system simulators. They are intended for describing behavior only and do not, in general, allow precise description of system structure. An example of such a language, ASPOL, is discussed in detail in Sec. 2.3.5.

2.3.4 Queueing Models

In order to give the reader some flavor of analytic models of computer systems, we will consider a simple queueing model. Our treatment is relatively informal; the interested reader is referred to the Refs. 17 and 19 for further mathematical details.

Single-queue single-server model The simplest queueing system is the single-queue single-server case depicted in Fig. 2.49. The parameters that define the behavior of this system are the rate at which items requiring service arrive and the rate at which items are serviced. It is assumed that items in the queue are serviced on a first-come first-served basis. The mean arrival and service rates are commonly denoted by λ and μ, respectively. The actual arrival and service rates vary randomly around these average values and are therefore characterized by probability distributions.

The way in which items arrive at the queueing system (the arrival process) is often modeled by a *Poisson probability distribution* function which has the form

$$p_P(n, t) = \frac{(\lambda t)^n}{n!} e^{-\lambda t} \tag{2.11}$$

where $p_P(n, t)$ is the probability of exactly n items arriving in a time period of length t. If items are not removed from the queue, $p_P(n, t)$ represents the probability that the queue length increases by n in time t. Figure 2.61 shows a plot of $p_P(n, t)$ as a function of t for fixed values of n and λ; this bell-shaped curve typifies the Poisson distribution. Many physical arrival processes, e.g., the arrival of calls at a telephone exchange, can be quite accurately modeled by a Poisson distribution.

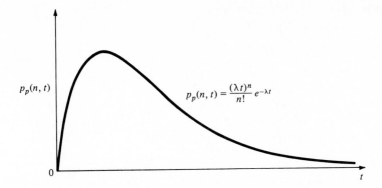

$$p_P(n, t) = \frac{(\lambda t)^n}{n!} e^{-\lambda t}$$

Figure 2.61 Poisson distribution for fixed n and λ.

Another important characteristic of an arrival process is the distribution of the time periods between two consecutive arriving items. The *interarrival time distribution* $p_I(t)$ is defined to be the probability that at least one item arrives during a period of length t. Clearly, for a Poisson arrival process

$$p_I(t) = 1 - p_P(0, t) \qquad (2.12)$$

Therefore, on setting $n = 0$ in (2.11) and substituting into (2.12), we obtain

$$p_I(t) = 1 - e^{-\lambda t} \qquad (2.13)$$

This is the (negative) *exponential distribution*, which has the form shown in Fig. 2.62. Hence the interarrival times of a Poisson arrival process are characterized by the exponential distribution (2.13). The probability density function corresponding to (2.13) is $\lambda e^{-\lambda t}$, while its mean value is $1/\lambda$. Exponential distributions are particularly simple and convenient to use in analytic models. It is therefore common to model the behavior of the server (the service process) by an exponential distribution also. Let $p_S(t)$ be the probability that the service required by an item is completed in time t or less after its removal from the queue. Then the service process is often characterized by the expression

$$p_S(t) = 1 - e^{-\mu t}$$

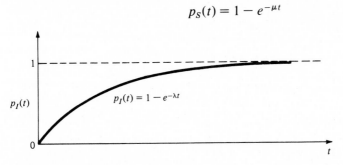

Figure 2.62 Exponential distribution for fixed λ.

Performance evaluation The performance of a queueing system can be measured by the following parameters:

1. The average number of items waiting in the system, including the items waiting for service and those actually being served. The parameter is called the *mean queue length* and is denoted by l_Q.
2. The average time that arriving items spend in the system, both waiting for service and being served. This is called the *mean waiting time* and is denoted by t_Q. t_Q is sometimes called the system delay or response time.

We now consider the problem of calculating l_Q and t_Q for a single-queue single-server system in which the arrival distribution is Poisson (or, equivalently, the interarrival time distribution is exponential) and the service-time distribution is exponential.[2] The state of the queue can be specified by $p_Q(n, t)$, which is the probability that at time t there are exactly n items in the queue awaiting service. When the system has been in operation for some time, the queue can be expected to reach a state of equilibrium in which $p_Q(n, t)$ can be assumed to be independent of t, so we write $p_Q(n, t) = p_Q(n)$. It can be shown[3] [17, 19] that under these conditions,

$$p_Q(n) = \left(\frac{\lambda}{\mu}\right)^n \left(1 - \frac{\lambda}{\mu}\right) \qquad (2.14)$$

provided $\lambda < \mu$. If $\lambda > \mu$, then the queue grows indefinitely. Equation (2.14) is called the *steady-state* or *balance* equation for the queuing system. Note that it is based on the assumption of exponential interarrival and service-time distributions. The quantity $\rho = \lambda/\mu$ is the mean utilization of the server. ρ is often called the *traffic intensity*. Equation (2.14) can be rewritten in terms of ρ; thus,

$$p_Q(n) = \rho^n(1 - \rho) \qquad (2.15)$$

The mean queue length l_Q can be immediately expressed in terms of $p_Q(n)$ as follows:

$$l_Q = \sum_{n \geq 1} n p_Q(n)$$

Substituting from (2.15) we obtain

$$l_Q = (1 - \rho) \sum_{n \geq 1} n\rho^n$$

$$= \rho(1 - \rho) \frac{d}{d\rho} \left[\sum_{n \geq 1} \rho^n\right]$$

[2]This is also called the M/M/1 queueing model, where the two Ms denote that the arrivals and service processes are Markov processes (essentially the same as Poisson processes) while the 1 denotes the number of servers.
[3]See also Prob. 6.13.

The summation in this last expression is an infinite geometric progression equal to $\rho/(1-\rho)$. Hence

$$l_Q = \rho(1-\rho)\frac{d}{d\rho}\frac{\rho}{1-\rho}$$

Using the formula

$$\frac{d}{dx}\frac{u}{v} = \frac{1}{v}\frac{du}{dx} - \frac{u}{v^2}\frac{dv}{dx}$$

we obtain

$$\frac{d}{d\rho}\frac{\rho}{1-\rho} = \frac{1}{1-\rho} + \frac{\rho}{(1-\rho)^2}$$
$$= \frac{1}{(1-\rho)^2}$$

whence

$$l_Q = \frac{\rho}{1-\rho} \qquad (2.16)$$

which defines the mean queue length.

Finally, we turn to the parameter t_Q, which is the mean time items spend in the queueing system. t_Q and l_Q may be related intuitively as follows [19]. An average item X passing through the system should encounter the same number of waiting items l_Q when it enters as it leaves behind when it departs from the system. The number left behind is λt_Q, which is the number of items that enter the system at rate λ during the period t_Q when X is present. Hence we conclude that $l_Q = \lambda t_Q$, that is,

$$t_Q = \frac{l_Q}{\lambda} \qquad (2.17)$$

Equation (2.17) is known as *Little's equation*. It is valid for all queueing systems, not just the M/M/1 model used here. Combining (2.16) and (2.17) yields the desired expression for t_Q:

$$t_Q = \frac{1}{\mu - \lambda} \qquad (2.18)$$

General queueing models A queueing model for a system is a network of queues and servers. Each major shared resource such as main memory, CPUs, and IO channels is represented by a set of $n_q \geq 0$ servers as suggested by Fig. 2.63. The number of queues and servers reflects the degree of parallelism in the resources being modeled. Note that the queueing network of Fig. 2.63 is intended to model processor-level behavior only; the structure of the actual system cannot be deduced from this model. Queues are generally software entities

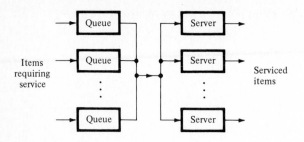

Figure **2.63** General queueing model of a shared resource.

created and maintained by the operating system in main memory. Each queue-server component is defined by three factors:

1. The rate at which items enter the queue
2. The rate at which items are processed by the server
3. The order in which the items are selected from the queue by the server, called the queuing or scheduling discipline

The arrival and processing rates are generally defined by probability distributions. Unfortunately, only a handful of useful probability distributions exist that result in models amenable to analytic solution. In many cases, the only feasible approach is to obtain numerical solutions by Monte Carlo simulation using a computer.

2.3.5 Simulation

As noted in the preceding sections, many models for computer systems such as queueing models are amenable to analytic solution in special cases only. If analytic solutions cannot be found, the best recourse is often simulation, which within the time and cost limitation of the simulation operation itself, allows complex models to be studied numerically. A variety of general-purpose simulators for processor-level systems, usually called "system" simulators, have been developed and are available commercially. One such simulator, ASPOL, will be illustrated in a later example.

Processes The behavior of a computer system can be described as a set of asynchronous, concurrent, and interacting processes, where a *process* is loosely defined as an identifiable sequence of related actions. (The terms "job," "task," and "operation" are frequently used in the same general sense as process is used here.) A process is identified with a computation or a single execution of a program. A process can be in one of three major states:

1. Busy or executing
2. Idle but ready to begin execution
3. Idle while execution is temporarily suspended

Much of the interaction between processes in a computer results from sharing system resources. Execution of a process is suspended if a resource it requires has been preempted by other processes. Figure 2.64 shows the behavior of a typical process. Many systems simulators are classified as *process-oriented*, since they require the system being modeled to be defined as a set of processes similar to that of Fig. 2.64.

A process executes by performing operations on certain data. When simulating a system, we typically want to know how the system performs when each process is supplied with a set of representative data. The data is usually characterized by a set of stochastic variables with appropriate probability distributions. In the process of Fig. 2.64, for example, the data variables chosen are the process initiation time t_I, the number of resources needed n_R, the queue waiting time t_W, the execution time t_E, and the idle period t_S.

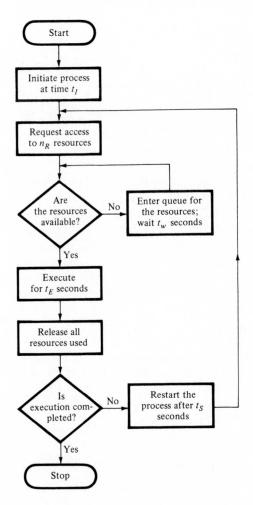

Figure 2.64 Flowchart of a general process.

Process-oriented simulation A process-oriented simulator provides a language for describing implicitly or explicitly the various operations specified in the flowchart of Fig. 2.64. Thus **request** (resource), **queue**, and **release** (resource) are typical keywords in such a language. By means of random-number generators, values can be assigned to the data variables according to various probability distributions. For example, suppose that it is desired to make n_R a random integer between 2 and 6. This can be accomplished by the statement

$$n_R = \textbf{irandom } (2,6);$$

Each time this statement is encountered during simulation, an integer within the desired range is pseudo-randomly generated by the simulator and assigned to the variable n_R. Certain widely used distributions such as the Poisson, Erlang[4], and exponential distributions can also be expected to be incorporated in the simulator. The execution operations of a process are viewed as simply waiting periods or time delays. Thus, in the ASPOL system, the execution block of Fig. 2.64 might be modeled by

$$t_E = \textbf{expntl } (12.);$$

$$\textbf{hold } (t_E);$$

The first statement causes t_E to be selected from an exponential distribution with mean 12. The **hold** statement instructs the simulator to suspend the simulated process for t_E seconds, after which time the actions required by the statement following **hold** should take place. The simulator does this by adding the specified **hold** period t_E to the current simulation time t and scheduling interpretation of the next statement for the time $t + t_E$.

Figure 2.50 shows the elements of a simulation system. Once the model of the target system C has been prepared, it is supplied to the simulator S which constructs a program P_C that represents C and can be run on the host computer. P_C is then executed. This execution generates a sequence of events which occur at well-defined points along the artificial time scale used by the simulator. A typical event is the initiation or termination of a process. Events are represented by variables having two states, occurred and not occurred. Events allow communication between distinct processes. For example, the ASPOL statement

$$\textbf{wait } (x)$$

causes the process in which it appears to be suspended until the event x occurs. If x is appropriately defined, its state may be set by other processes. Certain simulators such as SIMSCRIPT are called *event-oriented*, since they require models to be organized as a set of event-processing routines [23].

The purpose of a simulation run is to gather performance data for the sys-

---

[4]The Erlang distribution has the density function $f(x) = [(a^k x^{k-1} e^{-ax})/(k-1)!]$ with mean k/a and variance k/a^2. When $k = 1$, $f(x)$ reduces to ae^{-ax}, which is the density function of the exponential distribution.

tem being modeled. This is done by instructing the simulator to monitor quantities of interest and, at the end of the run, create a report with a statistical summary of the quantities being monitored. For example, the process execution period t_E in Fig. 2.64 might be monitored and its mean value, its distribution (in the form of a table or histogram), and other pertinent information might be included in the simulation report.

An outline of ASPOL We now sketch the main features of ASPOL (*a Simulation Process-Oriented Language*), a commercially available simulator. Our purpose is not to provide a comprehensive description of ASPOL — the interested reader may find it in the Refs. 8 and 23 — but rather to provide enough information for understanding some examples of its use.

An ASPOL description bears a strong resemblance to an ALGOL or PASCAL program. It is organized into procedures and blocks delimited by **begin** and **end**. The familiar control statements **goto, if. . . then. . . else,** and **while. . . do** are permitted. A process is described in a manner similar to a procedure or subroutine. A process description is identified by the declaration **process** and terminated by **end process**. A special process called **sim** plays the role of main program in an ASPOL description. Execution of a process p is started by the statement **initiate** p and terminates when **end process** is encountered. A process may be suspended for t seconds by the statement **hold** (t).

Variables are declared and assigned types in ASPOL in the usual way. In addition to the standard number types *integer* and *real*, ASPOL includes the following data types peculiar to processor-level simulation.

1. *Event*: An event can have the two values occurred (set) or not occurred (clear). The statements **set** (x) and **clear** (x) cause the event x to be assigned the values set and clear, respectively. The statements **wait** (x) and **queue** (x) cause a process to suspend execution until the event x is set.
2. *Facility*: A facility is any system resource except memory, such as a processor or an IO device, which may have one of two states, busy and nonbusy (available). A facility f is set to the busy state by the statements **reserve** (f) and **preempt** (f), and restored to the nonbusy state by **release** (f). If a process attempts to reserve or preempt a busy facility, it is automatically placed in a queue for that facility. Queues are serviced on a priority basis; processes with the same priority gain access to the facility on a first-come first-served basis. A process is assigned priority x by the statement **priority** $= x$.
3. *Storage*: Memories are defined by the **storage** declaration. They are treated differently from other facilities since each memory has an attribute *size*, which is its maximum storage capacity. A specific amount s of storage space can be reserved or released by the statements **allocate** (s) and **deallocate** (s). A memory appears busy only if a process requests more space than is currently available, in which case the process is placed in a queue for the memory.

ASPOL provides a number of library functions which generate pseudo-random numbers according to various distributions such as the Poisson, Erlang, and exponential distributions. These are invoked by expressions such as **poisson** (m), **erlang** (m, v), and **expntl** (m), where m and v denote the parameters mean and variance. **random** (a, b) generates a random real number from a uniform distribution with the range a to b; **irandom** (a, b) produces a random integer from the same distribution.

The ASPOL simulator automatically computes and reports usage statistics for all declared facilities and storage units. For each facility it lists its utilization (the fraction of time it spent in the busy state), the mean length of each busy period, and the number of requests made for access to the facility. In the case of a *storage* facility, the mean and maximum number of jobs occupying the storage unit are also reported. Statistics on the queue associated with facility x are requested by the statement **monitor** (x). The simulator then reports such data as the mean and maximum queue length and waiting time in the queue. Additional control features in ASPOL allow tables of performance data to be listed or printed as histograms.

Example 2.3: Simulation model of CPU behavior We conclude with a simple ASPOL program that simulates the behavior of a single CPU executing a sequence of programs. The programs are assumed to generate requests for CPU service according to a Poisson distribution with a mean rate of $\lambda = 5$ programs/min. The programs form a queue at the CPU and are executed on a first-come first-served basis. The execution times are exponentially distributed with a mean value of 10 s; hence the mean service time μ is 6 programs/min. The CPU is modeled as a single-queue single-server system of the type shown in Fig. 2.65.

Figure 2.66 contains an ASPOL model for Monte Carlo simulation of this system. It consists of two processes: the main process **sim**, which simulates the program arrivals, and a second process **execution**, which models the server. When a program arrives at the CPU, it immediately requests execution via the **initiate** statement. This requires access to the CPU, which is requested by the statement **reserve** (cpu). If the cpu is busy, the requesting program is automatically placed in a queue. The program is serviced when it reaches the head of the queue and the **release** (cpu) statement is processed for the preceding program.

A more complex ASPOL model for a multiprocessor system is described in Sec. 6.3.1.

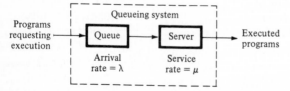

Figure 2.65 Queueing model of CPU behavior.

ASPOL statement	Comments
sim uniprocessor;	
real tarrival;	tarrival = program interarrival time
facility cpu;	
monitor cpu;	Requests report on CPU queue statistics
while (time .le. 10. *60.) **do**	Requests termination after 10 min simulation time
begin	
initiate execution;	Calls the process "execution"
tarrival = **expntl**(12.);	Selects random value for tarrival
hold(tarrival);	Waits tarrival seconds before next execution request
end;	
end sim;	
process execution;	
real tservice;	tservice = program execution time
reserve(cpu);	Requests access to CPU
tservice = **expntl**(10.);	Selects random value for execution time
hold(tservice);	Waits tservice seconds
release(cpu);	Releases CPU
end process;	

Figure 2.66 ASPOL model of CPU behavior.

2.4 SUMMARY

The central problem facing the digital-systems designer is to devise structures that use available components and perform a specified range of operations at minimum cost. Abstractly, this means transforming a given behavioral description into an appropriate structural description. A variety of descriptive methods exist. Block diagrams are used primarily to describe structure, while flowcharts and formal languages are used to describe behavior. A system is frequently divided into two parts for both design and descriptive purposes, a control unit and a data processing unit. Computer systems can also be viewed at various levels of detail. Each level is determined by the primitive components and information units recognized at that level. Three levels have been identified here: the gate, register, and processor levels. The components at these levels are bit-, word-, and block-processing elements, respectively. Computer architecture deals with the register and processor levels. The gate level, which is the level of classical logic design, is characterized by a well-developed theory (switching theory) based on Boolean algebra. No equivalent theory exists at the register or processor level; hence heuristic design techniques must normally be used.

Register-level components include combinational devices such as word gates, multiplexers, decoders, and adders, as well as sequential devices such as (parallel) registers, shift registers, and counters. These components can be easily expanded to accommodate additional inputs. The behavior of register-level circuits can be described by register transfer languages, many of which have been proposed. The fundamental element of such languages is the register transfer statement

$$c: \quad Z \leftarrow f(X_1, X_2, \ldots, X_n)$$

where c denotes a control expression and $Z \leftarrow f(X_1, X_2, \ldots, X_n)$ denotes the transfer of data from registers $X_1, X_2, \ldots, X_n$ to register Z via a combinational processing circuit f. The first step in register-level design is to construct a formal description of the desired behavior. From this the required components and connections (data paths) for the data processing part can be determined and a block diagram constructed. The necessary control signals and control points are then identified. Finally, a control unit is designed to generate the required control signals in the correct sequence.

The primitive components identified at the processor level include processors, memories, and IO devices. The behavior of processor level systems is complex and must often be specified in probabilistic terms. Performance evaluation is an important part of the design process. Queueing models of system behavior are particularly useful. Relatively few performance models can be solved analytically. Instead, experimental approaches using computer-based simulation, or performance measurements on an actual system may be used. Processor-level design is frequently based on the use of prototype structures. A prototype structure is selected and modified if necessary to meet the given performance specifications. The actual performance of the system is then evaluated, and the design is further modified until a satisfactory performance level is achieved.

PROBLEMS

2.1 A gate-level combinational circuit is said to be well-behaved if the logical value (state) of every line at time t can be determined from the circuit structure and the logical values of all its primary input lines at time t.

    (a) Prove that every well-formed circuit is well-behaved.

    (b) Prove that some well-behaved circuits are not well-formed.

2.2 Let $|$, the Sheffer stroke symbol, denote the binary NAND operation, that is, $a | b = \overline{ab}$. Determine whether or not $|$ obeys the commutative, associative, and idempotent laws of Boolean algebra.

2.3 The complexity of the functions that can be performed by a single IC is, in part, limited by the number of pins on the IC package. More effective use of the available pins could be made if multivalued logic circuits, i.e., circuits allowing more than two logic values per line or pin, were employed in place of the usual two-valued or binary logic. Explain why, despite this apparent advantage, multivalued logic is rarely employed in digital circuit design.

2.4 (a) Prove that if the input variables are available in both true and complemented form (double-rail logic), a 2^n-input 1-bit multiplexer can be used to realize any $(n + 1)$-variable combinational function.

    (b) Show how a four-input 2-bit multiplexer can be used to realize a full adder circuit.

2.5 Describe how a $1/k^2$ decoder circuit can be constructed using $1/k$ decoders only.

2.6 Modify the logic diagram of the 8-bit nonpriority encoder given in Fig. 2.32 to obtain an 8-bit priority encoder.

2.7 Design a 16-bit priority encoder using two copies of an 8-bit priority encoder. Additional gates may also be used if needed.

2.8 A general-purpose logic element similar in concept to a PLA is a read-only memory (ROM). A ROM is used to generate a set of combinational functions $F(X)$ in the following way. X is treated as the ROM address and $F(X)$ is stored as data in the ROM location with address X. When X is applied to the ROM input (address) lines and the read operation is enabled, $F(X)$ appears at the ROM output (data) lines. The ROM thus stores a direct physical representation of the truth table for $F(X)$. ROMs are particularly useful in applications like code conversion where there is no simple logical relationship between the input and output variables.

(*a*) Describe how a $p \times q$ diode array of the type shown in Fig. 2.33 can be used as a ROM for generating combinational functions. Explain how address decoding can be performed wholly or in part by the diode array.

(*b*) Using the 4×8 array of Fig. 2.33, obtain an ROM realization of the functions f_1 and f_2 defined by Eq. (2.9) and (2.10).

(*c*) Write a short note comparing the efficiency of the PLA and ROM organizations when the array dimensions p and q are fixed.

2.9 Design a comparator for two 10-bit numbers using only 4-bit comparators of the kind shown in Fig. 2.35.

2.10 Design a modulo-16 binary counter similar to that of Fig. 2.39 which operates synchronously, i.e., which allows all flip-flops to change state simultaneously.

2.11 The following listing describes a familiar combinational circuit in an APL-based hardware description language. The variable names and identifiers have been chosen so that they do not provide mnemonic clues to circuit function.

1. SUBROUTINE WHATSIT (A, B)
2. X, Y ← 19ρ0, 18ρ0
3. X_{18} ← 0
4. i ← 17
5. X_i ← F(B_i, A_i, X_{i+1})
6. Y_i ← G(B_i, A_i, X_{i+1}, F)
7. i ← i − 1
8. i: 0 ($\geq$, $<$) → (5, 9)
9. c ← ($X_0 \oplus$ d)
10. WHATSIT (A, B) ← c, Y
11. RETURN

Draw a block diagram for the circuit described by this listing. Comment on any difficulties you encounter in interpreting the description. (Note: X ← 19ρ0 means X is a 19-bit word that is initialized to zero. Statement 8 means if $i \geq 0$, go to statement 5, otherwise go to statement 9.)

2.12 Figure 2.67 shows an algorithm for multiplication that is used in low-speed systems. It is implemented using three up-down counters CQ, CM, and CP, which store the multiplier, multiplicand, and product, respectively. Although the algorithm is slow (the product p is formed by incrementing counter CP a total of p times), only very simple logic is required to implement it, and different number codes can easily be accommodated.

Consider the design of a multiplier that implements this algorithm. The numbers to be multiplied are four-digit integers in sign-magnitude BCD code. For example, the number -1709 is represented by the bit sequence

$$1 \quad 0001 \quad 0111 \quad 0000 \quad 1001$$

CQ, CM, and CP are to be constructed from modulo-10 up-down counters with parallel input-output capability. Carry out the logic design of this multiplier at the register transfer level.

2.13 (*a*) Draw the flowchart of a counting algorithm similar to that of Fig. 2.67 which performs integer division.

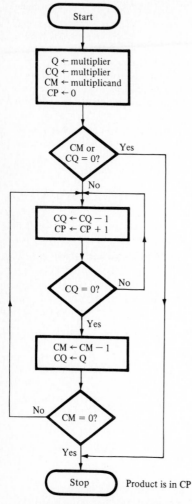

Figure 2.67 A multiplication algorithm using counters.

(b) Carry out the register-level logic design of a machine that performs both multiplication and division on four-digit BCD integers using the counting algorithm approach. A single control signal should select the function (multiplication or division) to be performed.

2.14 Suppose that jobs arrive randomly at a processor with the following distribution properties:

1. The number of arrivals during any period of length T is λT, where λ is a constant.
2. In a small interval of length Δt, the probability of one arrival is $\lambda \Delta t$, while the probability of more than one arrival is negligible.

Let $p_0(t)$ be the probability that there are no arrivals during a period of length t or less.
  (a) Prove that $p_0(t) = e^{-\lambda t}$.
  (b) Prove that the interarrival time has the probability distribution $1 - e^{-\lambda t}$.
(Properties 1 and 2 also imply that the arrivals have a Poisson distribution.)

2.15 The quantities l_Q and t_Q defined by Eqs. (2.16) and (2.18) refer to items that are either waiting for access to the server or are actually being served. Let l_w denote the mean number of items waiting in the queue excluding those being served, and let t_w denote the mean waiting time in the queue excluding service time. Derive expressions for l_w and t_w in terms of λ and μ.

2.16 Suppose that CPU behavior in a multiprogramming system can be analyzed using the single-queue single-server model. Programs are sent to the CPU for execution at a mean rate of 8 programs/min and are executed on a first-come first-served basis. The average program requires 6 s of CPU execution time.

(a) What is the mean time between program arrivals at the CPU?

(b) What is the mean number of programs waiting for CPU execution to be completed?

(c) What is the mean time a program must wait for its execution to be completed?

2.17 A Monte Carlo simulation program is to be written in a high-level programming language, e.g., FORTRAN. As part of that program, it is desired to generate a sequence of numbers $T = t_1, t_2, t_3, \ldots$, which represent consecutive interarrival times for a Poisson process. The available program library contains only one random number generating function, RANDOM (A, B), which produces a real number that is uniformly distributed between A and B. Describe how you would use RANDOM (A, B) to generate the sequence T.

2.18 A program is to be written in an ordinary high-level programming language that simulates the behavior of the single-queue single-server model depicted in Fig. 2.65. The program should be able to calculate the performance measures l_Q and t_Q under steady-state conditions for any given values of λ and μ.

(a) Draw a flowchart for the simulation program.

(b) Code your program and execute it for several sample queueing systems using any available computer. Explain any discrepancies observed between the simulated and analytic values of l_Q and t_Q.

REFERENCES

1. Auerbach, I. L.: "Need for an Information Systems Theory," in H. Zemanek (ed.), *The Skyline of Information Processing*, pp. 9–21, North-Holland, Amsterdam, 1972.
2. Bell, C. G., and A. Newell: *Computer Structures: Readings and Examples,* McGraw-Hill, New York, 1971.
3. Blakeslee, T. R.: *Digital Design with Standard MSI and LSI*, Wiley, New York, 1975.
4. Boole, G.: *The Laws of Thought*, MacMillan, London, 1854. (Reprinted by Dover, New York, 1958.)
5. Breuer, M. A. (ed.): *Digital System Design Automation: Languages, Simulation and Data Base*, Computer Science Press, Woodland Hills, Calif., 1975.
6. Brinch Hansen, P.: *Operating System Principles*, Prentice-Hall, Englewood Cliffs, N.J., 1973.
7. Burks, A. W., and J. B. Wright: "Theory of Logical Nets," *Proc. IRE*, vol. 41, pp. 1357–1365, October 1953.
8. Control Data Corp.: *A Simulation Process-oriented Language (ASPOL) Reference Manual*, Sunnyvale, Calif., 1972.
9. Curtis, H. A.: *A New Approach to the Design of Switching Circuits*, Van Nostrand, Princeton, N.J., 1962.
10. Dahl, O. J., E. W. Dijkstra, and C. A. R. Hoare: *Structured Programming*, Academic, New York, 1972.
11. Dietmeyer, D. L., and J. R. Duley: "Register Transfer Languages and their Simulation," in Ref. 5, pp. 117–218.
12. Falkoff, A. D., K. E. Iverson, and E. H. Sussenguth: "A Formal Description of SYSTEM/360" *IBM Syst. J.*, vol. 3, pp. 198–263, 1964.
13. Friedman, T. D., and S. C. Yang: "Methods Used in an Automatic Logic Design Generator (ALERT)," *IEEE Trans. Comput.*, vol. C-18, pp. 593–614, July 1969.
14. Gibson, J. C.: "The Gibson Mix," IBM Rep. TR00.2043, IBM Corp., Poughkeepsie, N.Y., June 1970.
15. Gschwind, H. W., and E. J. McCluskey: *Design of Digital Computers*, 2d ed., Springer-Verlag, New York, 1975.

16. Hayes, J. P.: "On Realizations of Boolean Functions Requiring a Minimal or Near Minimal Number of Tests," *IEEE Trans. Comput.*, vol. C-20, pp. 1506–1513, December 1971.
17. Hellerman, H., and T. E. Conroy: *Computer System Performance*, McGraw-Hill, New York, 1975.
18. Huffman, D. A.: "The Synthesis of Sequential Switching Circuits," *J. Franklin Inst.*, vol. 257, pp. 161–190 and pp. 275–303, 1954.
19. Kleinrock, L.: *Queueing Systems*, vol. 1: *Theory*, Wiley, New York, 1975.
20. Lucas, H. C.: "Performance Evaluation and Monitoring," *Comput. Surv.*, vol. 3, pp. 79–91, September 1971.
21. McCluskey, E. J.: *Introduction to the Theory of Switching Circuits*, McGraw-Hill, New York, 1965.
22. MacDougall, M. H.: "Computer System Simulation: An Introduction," *Comput. Surv.*, vol. 2, pp. 191–209, September 1970.
23. MacDougall, M. H.: "System Level Simulation," in Ref. 5, pp. 1–115.
24. Morrison, P., and E. Morrison (eds.): *Charles Babbage and his Calculating Engines*, Dover, New York, 1961.
25. Parnas, D. L., and J. A. Darringer: "SODAS and a Methodology for System Design," *AFIPS Conf. Proc.*, vol. 31, pp. 449–474, 1967.
26. Reed, I. S.: "Symbolic Design Techniques Applied to a Generalized Computer," MIT Lincoln Lab. Tech. Rep. TR-141, January 1956. (Reprinted with revisions in *Computer*, vol. 5, pp. 47–52, May/June 1972.)
27. Shannon, C. E.: "A Symbolic Analysis of Relay and Switching Circuits," *Trans. AIEE*, vol. 57, pp. 713–723, 1938.
28. Simon, H. A.: "The Architecture of Complexity," *Proc. Amer. Phil. Soc.*, vol. 106, pp. 467–482, December 1962. (Reprinted in H. A. Simon: *The Sciences of the Artificial*, pp. 84–118, M.I.T. Press, Cambridge, Mass., 1969.)
29. Stabler, E.: "Microprogram Transformations," *IEEE Trans. Comput.* vol. C-19, pp. 906–916, October 1970.
30. Unger, S. H.: *Asynchronous Sequential Switching Circuits*, Wiley, New York, 1969.

PROCESSOR DESIGN

This chapter examines the data processing function of computers; the selection and implementation of instruction sets, with emphasis on arithmetic instructions; and parallel-processing techniques for improving performance.

3.1 INTRODUCTION

3.1.1 Processor Organization

The primary function of an instruction set processor, as exemplified by the central processing unit (CPU) of a computer, is to execute sequences of instructions stored in a memory (main memory), which is external to the CPU. The CPU must first fetch an instruction from this memory before it can be executed. The sequence of operations involved in processing an instruction constitutes an *instruction cycle*, which can be subdivided into two major phases: the *fetch cycle* and the *execution cycle*.The instruction is obtained from main memory during the fetch cycle. The execution cycle typically includes decoding the instruction, fetching any required operands, and performing the operation specified by the instruction's opcode. The behavior of the CPU during an instruction cycle may be defined by a sequence of *microoperations*, each of which involves a register transfer. The time t_{CPU} required for the shortest well-defined CPU microoperation is defined to be the *CPU cycle time* and is the basic unit of time for measuring all CPU actions. The reciprocal of t_{CPU} is the CPU *clock rate*, generally measured in megahertz. The clock rate depends directly on the device technology used to fabricate the CPU.

In addition to executing programs, the CPU supervises the other system components, usually via special control lines. For example, the CPU directly or indirectly controls IO operations such as data transfers between IO devices and main memory. These operations require the CPU's attention relatively infrequently; it is therefore more efficient to allow the CPU to ignore IO devices and the like until they actively request service from the CPU. Such a request is called an *interrupt*. In the event of an interrupt, the CPU suspends execution of the program that it is executing and transfers to an appropriate interrupt handling program. Interrupts, particularly IO interrupts, frequently require a rapid response by the CPU. A test for the presence of interrupt signals is thus normally carried out at the end of each instruction cycle. The major functions of the CPU are summarized in the flowchart in Fig. 3.1, which is equivalent to a state diagram of CPU behavior at a very high level.

Interaction with main memory Despite the great improvements in device technology over the past 30 years, almost all CPU designs have been based on the following two premises.

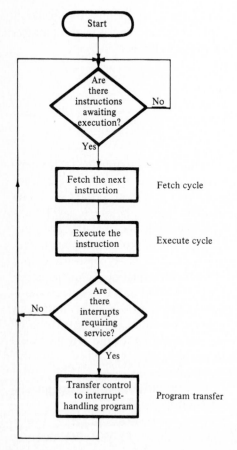

Figure 3.1 Overview of CPU behavior.

1. The CPU should be as fast (measured by its cycle time t_{CPU}) as the available technology permits. Since cost invariably increases with speed, the number of components in the CPU must be kept relatively small.
2. A main memory of relatively large capacity is needed to store the programs and data required by the CPU. Because of the size of the main memory, it must be constructed using less expensive and therefore slower technology than that of the CPU.

Main-memory speed may be measured by *memory cycle time* t_M, which is the minimum time that must elapse between two successive read or write operations. The ratio t_M/t_{CPU} typically ranges from 1 to 10. The CPU contains a small number of storage devices called *registers*, used for temporary storage of instructions and operands. The transfer of information among these registers can proceed at a rate approximately t_M/t_{CPU} times that of a transfer between the CPU and main memory. Instructions whose operands are in fast CPU registers can be executed more rapidly than instructions whose operands are in main memory. Program execution is therefore frequently implemented as follows.

1. Transfer the required operands from main memory to CPU registers.
2. Compute the desired results in the CPU.
3. Transfer the results from the CPU to main memory.

There is a discernible trend, albeit a slow one, toward blurring the distinction between CPU registers and main memory. In particular, the use of the same semiconductor technologies for both CPU and main memory has increased markedly in recent years. making t_M approach t_{CPU}. For example, a CPU and a small main memory can be fabricated on a single integrated circuit chip forming a one-chip microcomputer. If $t_M = t_{CPU}$, then the CPU registers can be at least partially incorporated into main memory without diminishing overall system performance. This is done in the memory-to-memory architecture of the Texas Instruments 900 computer series [28].

Basic CPU organization The design proposed by von Neumann and his colleagues for the IAS computer is the basis for almost all CPUs designed since then. It comprises a minimal set of registers and the necessary circuits to execute a small single-address instruction set. One of the CPU registers, called the *accumulator*,[1] plays a central role, being used to store an input or an output operand (result) in the execution of most instructions.

[1]The term "accumulator" originally meant a device that combined the functions of number storage and addition. Any quantity transferred to an accumulator was automatically added to its previous contents. The counter wheel memories of early mechanical computers had accumulators of this type.

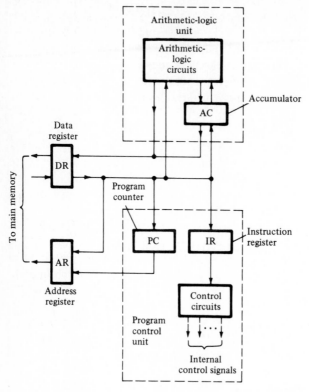

Figure 3.2 A simple accumulator-based CPU.

Figure 3.2 shows the essential structure of an accumulator-oriented CPU. This architecture is typical of first-generation machines such as IAS (cf. Fig. 1.13) and many modern computers in the mini and micro classes. The accumulator AC is the main operand register of the arithmetic-logic unit. The data register DR acts as a buffer between the CPU and main memory. It is used as an input operand register with the accumulator so that operations of the form $AC \leftarrow f(AC, DR)$ can be performed. The other major registers are the program counter PC, which stores the address of the next instruction; the instruction register IR, which holds the opcode of the current instruction; and the memory address register AR.

Figure 3.3 shows the sequence of microoperations involved in fetching and executing some typical instructions in a machine with the foregoing architecture. The program counter PC is automatically incremented after an instruction has been fetched, under the assumption that instructions are normally executed in the sequence in which they are stored. PC may be subsequently modified during the instruction cycle by a jump instruction, as illustrated in Fig. 3.3.

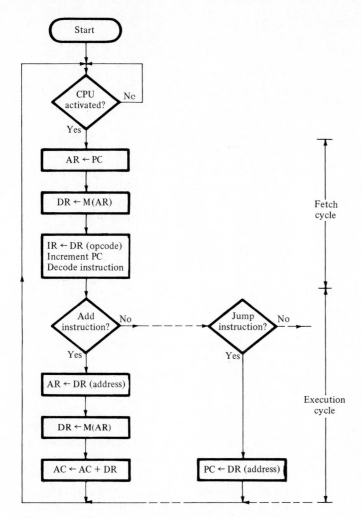

Figure 3.3 Operation of the CPU of Fig. 3.2

Extensions to the basic organization There are several ways in which the basic configuration of Fig. 3.2 can be made more powerful.

1. Additional addressable registers can be provided for storing operands and addresses; this can be viewed as replacing the single accumulator by a set of registers. If the registers are multipurpose, the resulting machine is said to have the *general register organization* exemplified by the IBM System 360/370 (see Fig. 1.32). A set of general registers is sometimes referred to as a *"scratch-pad"* memory. A major function of these registers is to store operands needed for memory address construction. Sometimes special address registers, e.g., index or base registers, are provided for this purpose.

2. The capabilities of the arithmetic-logic circuits, particularly their arithmetic capabilities, can be extended. Many microprocessors, for example, can perform only addition and subtraction on fixed-point numbers. Relatively little extra circuitry is required for fixed-point multiplication and division. A substantial increase in hardware is required to implement floating-point arithmetic, however. Arithmetic function implementation is the topic of Sec. 3.3.

3. Additional registers can be provided for storing instructions. This is particularly useful if t_M is long compared with the average instruction execution time. Several instructions can be fetched simultaneously by appropriate partitioning of main memory and replication of the memory addressing circuits. A sequence of instructions can then be stored in an *instruction buffer* in the CPU where the instructions can be accessed immediately.

4. Special control circuitry can be included to facilitate the temporary transfer of control between programs required when calling subroutines or processing interrupts. A mechanism must be introduced for saving the status of the interrupted program and subsequently returning control to that program. Many machines employ special *status registers* for this purpose which record the state of the currently executing program. When an interrupt occurs, the status register contents and any other essential information stored in the CPU are transferred to a predetermined memory area from which they can subsequently be retrieved.

   A particularly efficient way of storing and retrieving this status information is to use a pushdown *stack*. The primary advantage of the stack is the ease with which it can be controlled. A special address register, called the *stack pointer*, is all that is needed. The stack pointer always indicates the address of the topmost filled location of the stack. It is automatically incremented (decremented) after each transfer of a word to (from) the top of the stack. Stacks may also be used to replace the accumulator or general registers as temporary operand stores during instruction execution. (This point of view has been particularly exploited by Burroughs in many of their computers.) Stack processing of this kind largely eliminates the need for explicit address specification in instructions, resulting in so-called zero-address machines. Program control methods are examined further in Sec. 4.1.

5. Facilities can be provided for *parallel processing*, which may be defined as the simultaneous processing of two or more distinct instructions. As noted above, several instructions or operands can be fetched simultaneously by extending the memory addressing circuits and adding sufficient buffer storage to the CPU. The execution of several instructions can also be overlapped in several ways. The ALU can be divided into k parts or replicated k times to permit up to k instructions to be executed at once. An ALU or a portion thereof can be organized as a pipeline permitting several distinct operand sets to be processed simultaneously. Parallel-processing techniques are considered in detail in Sec. 3.4.

3.1.2 Information Representation

Words and characters Information is represented in a computer by means of binary sequences which are usually organized into words. A *word* is a unit of information of fixed length n, where n is primarily determined by hardware cost considerations. A word may be viewed as a sequence of binary coded characters. Early computers such as the IBM 7094 used 6-bit character codes, since 6 is the minimum number of bits needed to encode the 26 letters of the English alphabet and the 10 decimal digits. Moreover, 6 bits also allow a reasonable number (28) of special characters such as punctuation marks and mathematical symbols to be represented. In recent years the use of 8-bit binary sequences, called *bytes*, for character representation has become widespread. As well as allowing additional characters, e.g., both uppercase and lowercase alphabets, 8-bit characters permit efficient representation of BCD numbers. Two BCD digits can be stored in an 8-bit field with no wasted space. Only one BCD digit can be stored in a 6-bit field, thus wasting 2 bits. Most current computers have word sizes which are multiples of 8; 8, 16, 32, and 64-bit words are common choices. Two standard 8-bit character codes are widely used: EBCDIC (*ex*tended *b*inary *c*oded *d*ecimal *i*nterchange *c*ode) developed by IBM, and ASCII (*a*merican *s*tandards *c*ommittee on *i*nformation *i*nterchange).

Information types Figure 3.4 shows the basic types of information represented in a computer. There is a fundamental division into instructions (control information) and data. Data may be further subdivided into numerical and nonnumerical. In view of the importance of numerical computation, a great deal of attention has been given to the development of number codes. Two major formats have evolved, fixed-point and floating-point. The fixed-point format is of the form

$$b_0 b_1 b_2 \ldots b_{n-1}$$

where $b_i \in \{0, 1\}$ and a binary or decimal point separating the integer and fraction parts is in some fixed but implicit position. A floating-point number, on

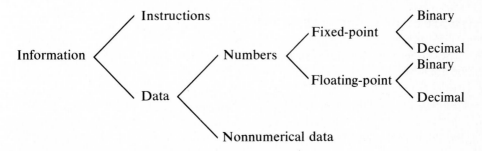

Figure 3.4 Some basic information types.

the other hand, consists of a pair of fixed-point numbers

$$M, E$$

which represent the number $M \times B^E$, where B is a predetermined base. Floating-point corresponds to the so-called scientific notation. A variety of codes are used to represent fixed-point numbers. These codes may be classified as binary, e.g., twos-complement, or decimal, e.g., BCD. Large computers frequently employ several different fixed-point and floating-point number formats. Number codes are discussed further in Sec. 3.2.2. Nonnumerical data usually takes the form of variable-length character strings encoded in ASCII or EBCDIC.

Tags In stored-program computers, instructions and data are stored together in main memory. In the classic stored-program machine, often referred to as a *von Neumann machine*, instructions and data words stored in main memory are indistinguishable from one another. In other words, a word chosen at random from memory cannot be identified as an instruction or a data word. Different data types such as fixed-point and floating-point numbers also cannot be distinguished. The meaning of the word is determined by the way a processor interprets it. Indeed the same word can be treated as an instruction and data at different times, e.g., the word X in the instruction sequence

$$X \leftarrow X + Y$$

go to X

Clearly it is the programmer's responsibility to ensure that data are not interpreted as instructions, and vice versa.

The reason for this deliberate indistinguishability of data and instructions can be clearly seen in the design of the first-generation IAS computer (see Sec. 1.3.3). The address modify instructions alter stored instructions in main memory. The ability to modify instructions in this way—in effect, treating them as data—is useful when processing indexed variables, as illustrated in Example 1.5. However, this type of instruction modification in main memory became largely obsolete with the introduction of indexing hardware. Most programmers, particularly those using high-level languages, have no need for programs that modify themselves; indeed it appears to be difficult to write a high-level language program that modifies itself in a useful way.

A number of computer designers have argued that the major information types should be assigned representations that identify them [12, 19]. This can be done by associating with each basic information unit a group of bits, called a *tag*, that identifies its type. The tag may be considered as a physical implementation of the *type* declaration found in many high-level programming languages. One of the first machines to use tags was the Burroughs B5000. It uses a single tag bit (called a flag) to distinguish two types of words called operands and descriptors. Its successors, the B6500 and B7500, employ a 3-bit tag field in every word, so that eight word types can be distinguished [9]. The 52-bit word format of the B6500/7500 is shown in Fig. 3.5.

The advantage of tagged information is that instruction sets and therefore the programming task can be simplified. In conventional von Neumann machines an instruction must specify the type of data on which it operates. It is therefore necessary to provide distinct instructions for each data type; see, for example, the list of different addition instructions for the S360/370 given in Fig. 1.34. If the operand types are identified by tags, a single addition instruction suffices. The processor merely has to inspect the operand tags to determine the specific type of operation to be performed, e.g., a fixed-point double-precision addition. Furthermore, the tag inspection permits the hardware to check for software errors, such as an attempt to add operands whose types are incompatible. The disadvantage of tags is that they increase memory size and therefore add to the system hardware costs without increasing computing performance, which has restricted the use of tagged architecture in the past. However, hardware costs have been decreasing while software costs have been increasing, so that the advantages of tagged architecture may well outweigh this disadvantage in some applications.

Error detection and correction A variety of factors such as faulty components and inadequate design tolerances can result in errors appearing in the information being processed by a computer. Such errors frequently occur in information that is being transmitted between two relatively distant points within the system, or in information stored in a memory device. A bit x that is being transmitted from A to B may, due to "noise" in the communication channel, be corrupted so that $\bar{x}$ instead of x is received at the destination B. In order to guard against errors of this type, the information can be coded in such a way that the errors can be detected, and possibly even corrected, by special logic circuits. A general approach to this is to append check bits to each word which can be used to detect or locate errors in the word.

One of the simplest and most widely used techniques for error control is the use of a single check bit, called a *parity check*. Let $X = (x_0, x_1, \ldots x_{n-1})$ be an n-bit word. A check bit c is defined by

$$c = x_0 \oplus x_1 \oplus \ldots \oplus x_{n-1} \tag{3.1}$$

where $\oplus$ denotes EXCLUSIVE-OR. Equation (3.1) defines an *odd parity* check, since $c = 1$ if X contains an odd number of ones. An *even parity* check is

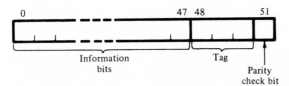

Information bits · Tag · Parity check bit

Figure 3.5 Word format of the Burroughs B6500/7500 computer series.

defined by

$$\bar{c} = x_0 \oplus x_1 \oplus \ldots \oplus x_{n-1}$$

Suppose that a word X is to be transmitted from A to B. At the source point A, the check bit c is computed using, say, (3.1), and $(x_0, x_1, \ldots, x_{n-1}, c)$ is transmitted to B. Suppose that $X = (x'_0, x'_1, \ldots, x'_{n-1}, c')$ is actually received at B. The bit

$$c^* = x'_0 \oplus x'_1 \oplus \ldots \oplus x'_{n-1}$$

is then computed and c' *and* c^* are compared. If $c' \neq c^*$, it can be concluded that the received information contains an error. In particular, if exactly one bit of $(x_0, x_1, \ldots, x_{n-1}, c)$ is changed to its complement, this error results in $c' \neq c^*$. If $c' = c^*$, it can be concluded that no single error has occurred, but the possibility of two or more erroneous bits exists. The parity check bit c therefore provides *single-error detection*. It does not allow detection of all multiple errors, nor does it identify the erroneous information.

A number of third-generation computers such as the IBM S/370 and the Data General ECLIPSE use parity check codes for detecting and correcting errors in main memory. These codes are capable of detecting all errors involving one or two incorrect bits, and they can also determine the location of the erroneous bit in the event of a single error. A set of check bits is appended to every memory word. Each check bit specifies the parity of a subfield of the word being protected. By appropriately overlapping these subfields, the correctness of every bit can be determined. Note that single-error correction assumes that no double errors are present, hence single-error correction and double-error detection cannot be performed simultaneously. Consider, for example, the ECLIPSE computer which uses a single-error correcting Hamming code for memory protection. When a word $X = (x_0, x_1, \ldots, x_{15})$ is written into memory, five check bits $(c_0, c_1, c_2, c_3, c_4)$ are computed and stored with X. The check bits are specified by the following parity equations.

$$
\begin{aligned}
\bar{c}_0 &= \qquad\qquad x_2 \qquad\qquad \oplus x_5 \qquad\qquad\qquad \oplus x_{10} \oplus x_{11} \oplus x_{12} \oplus x_{13} \oplus x_{14} \oplus x_{15} \\
c_1 &= \qquad\qquad\qquad\qquad x_4 \oplus x_5 \oplus x_6 \oplus x_7 \oplus x_8 \oplus x_9 \oplus x_{10} \qquad\qquad\qquad\qquad\qquad \oplus x_{15} \\
\bar{c}_2 &= \qquad x_1 \oplus x_2 \oplus x_3 \qquad\qquad \oplus x_7 \oplus x_8 \oplus x_9 \qquad\qquad\qquad\qquad \oplus x_{14} \oplus x_{15} \\
c_3 &= x_0 \qquad \oplus x_2 \oplus x_3 \qquad \oplus x_5 \oplus x_6 \qquad\qquad \oplus x_9 \qquad\qquad \oplus x_{12} \oplus x_{13} \\
\bar{c}_4 &= x_0 \oplus x_1 \qquad \oplus x_3 \oplus x_4 \qquad \oplus x_6 \qquad \oplus x_8 \qquad\qquad \oplus x_{11} \qquad \oplus x_{13}
\end{aligned}
$$

When the word is subsequently read from memory, it may have been altered by errors to $(x'_0, x'_1, \ldots, x'_{15}, c'_0, c'_1, c'_2, c'_3, c'_4)$. A new set of check bits $(c^*_0, c^*_1, c^*_2, c^*_3, c^*_4)$ is then derived from $(x'_0, x'_1, \ldots, x'_{15})$ and the error vector

$$E = (c'_0 \oplus c^*_0, \; c'_1 \oplus c^*_1, \; c'_2 \oplus c^*_2, \; c'_3 \oplus c^*_3, \; c'_4 \oplus c^*_4)$$

is computed. If $E = 0$, then no detectable error has occurred. Every single and double error results in $E \neq 0$. Furthermore, each single error results in a distinct value of E, so that by including appropriate logic circuits, E can be used to complement, and therefore correct, the erroneous bit. For example, the fault causing x_0 to become $\bar{x}_0$ is detected by c_3 and c_4 and results in $E = (0, 0, 0, 1, 1)$. It can be seen from the parity check equations that no other single fault is detected by c_3 and c_4 only; hence this value of E always indicates the presence of an error in bit x_0.

Many methods of designing error-detecting and error-correcting codes are known [22]. Any desired level of protection against errors can be obtained by using sufficient check bits. If single-error correction is required for n-bit words, k check bits must be added that can indicate $n + k$ errors as well as the error-free condition. Hence k must be such that $2^k \geq n + k + 1$, from which it follows that $k > \log_2 n$. The cost increases rapidly with the level of protection required due to the added memory costs for storing the check bits and also the cost of the error detection or correction logic. Figure 3.6 shows the structure of a typical error-detection and -correction scheme.

3.1.3 Number Formats

In selecting a number representation to be used in a computer the following factors should be taken into account.

1. The types of numbers to be represented, e. g., integers, real numbers, complex numbers
2. The range of values likely to be encountered
3. The precision of the number, which refers to the maximum accuracy of the representation
4. The cost of the hardware required to store and process the numbers

The two principal number formats are fixed-point and floating-point. In general, fixed-point formats allow a limited range of values and have relatively simple hardware requirements. Floating-point numbers, on the other hand, allow a much larger range of values but require more costly processing hardware.

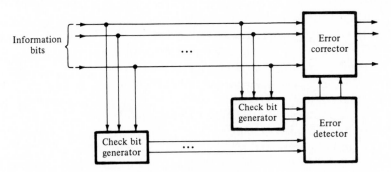

Figure 3.6 Errror-detection and -correction logic.

Fixed-point numbers The fixed-point format is derived directly from the ordinary (decimal) representation of a number as a sequence of digits separated by a decimal point. The digits to the left of the decimal point represent an integer; the digits to the right represent a fraction. This is a *positional notation* in which each digit has a fixed weight according to its position relative to the decimal point. If $i \geq 1$, the ith digit to the left (right) of the decimal point has weight 10^{i-1} (10^{-i}). Thus the five-digit decimal number 192.73 is equivalent to

$$1 \times 10^2 + 9 \times 10^1 + 2 \times 10^0 + 7 \times 10^{-1} + 3 \times 10^{-2}$$

More generally, we can assign weights of the form r^i to each digit where r is the *radix* or *base* of the number system. The most fundamental number representation used in computers employs a positional notation with 2 as the radix. A binary sequence of the form

$$b_N \ldots b_3 b_2 b_1 b_0 \cdot b_{-1} b_{-2} b_{-3} b_{-4} \ldots b_M \qquad (3.2)$$

represents the number

$$\sum_{i=M}^{N} b_i 2^i$$

This is an example of a fixed-point binary number. The format of (3.2) is generally used for representing positive numbers. Several distinct methods used for representing negative numbers are discussed later.

Suppose that an n-bit word is to be used to contain a fixed-point number. A bit is reserved to represent the sign of the number. The remaining bits indicate its magnitude. To permit uniform processing of all n bits, the sign is placed in the leftmost position and the values 0 and 1 are used to denote plus and minus, respectively. Thus we obtain the format

$$\underset{\uparrow}{x_0} \underbrace{x_1 x_2 \cdots x_{n-2} x_{n-1}} \qquad (3.3)$$
$$\text{Sign} \qquad \text{Magnitude}$$

The precision allowed by this format is $n - 1$ bits, which is equivalent to $(n - 1)/\log_2 10$ decimal digits. The binary point is not explicitly represented; it is implicitly assigned to a fixed location within the word. The position of the binary point is not particularly important from the point of view of design. In many situations the numbers being processed are integers, so the binary point is assumed to lie immediately to the right of the least significant bit x_{n-1}. Monetary quantities are often expressed as integers, e. g., $54.30 might be expressed as 5430 cents. Using an n-bit integer format, we can represent all integers N with magnitudes in the range $0 \leq |N| \leq 2^n-1$. The other most widely used format treats (3.3) as a fraction with the binary point lying between x_0 and x_1. The fraction format permits numbers with magnitudes in the range $0 \leq |N| \leq 1-2^{-n}$ to be represented.

Negative number representation Suppose that fixed-point binary numbers are to be represented by an n-bit word $X = x_0 x_1 x_2 \cdots x_{n-1}$. The simplest and most common way of representing positive numbers is to use the format of (3.3) with the standard positional notation for the magnitude part. This means that each magnitude bit x_i has a fixed weight of the form 2^{k-i}, where k depends on the position of the binary point. Perhaps the most natural way to represent negative numbers is to employ the same positional notation for the magnitude and simply change the sign bit x_0 to 1 to indicate minus. This number code is called *sign-magnitude*. Certain operations, notably subtraction, cannot be most efficiently implemented using sign-magnitude representation.

Several number codes have been devised which use the same representation for positive numbers as the sign-magnitude code but represent negative numbers differently. Suppose that X is an n-bit fraction. In the *ones-complement* code, $-X$ is defined as $\bar{X}$, the bitwise logical complement of X. In the *twos-complement* code, $-X$ is defined as $\bar{X} + 1$ (modulo 2). In each of these codes, x_0 retains its role as the sign bit, but the remaining bits no longer form a simple positional code when the number is negative. The primary advantage of these codes is that subtraction can be performed by logical complementation and addition only. Consider, for example, the twos-complement code. To subtract X from Y, compute $\bar{X} + Y + 1$ (modulo 2). The requirement that addition be modulo 2 means that carry bits from the sign position are ignored. Furthermore, all bits including the sign bit are processed uniformly.

Multiplication and division are somewhat more difficult to implement if twos-complement code is used rather than sign magnitude. (Compare the multiplication algorithms in Figs. 2.24 and 2.44.) The addition of ones-complement numbers is complicated by the fact that a carry bit from the most significant magnitude bit x_1 must be added to the least significant bit position x_{n-1}. Otherwise ones-complement codes have very similar properties to twos-complement codes and so will not be considered further.

Figure 3.7 illustrates how integers are represented using each of the three codes discussed above when $n = 4$. These are called binary codes to distinguish them from the so-called decimal codes discussed later. Note that in all cases, 0000 represents zero. Only in the case of twos-complement is the numerical complement of 0000 also 0000, which is an advantage in implementing instructions that test for zero.

Binary arithmetic The rules for carrying out the basic arithmetic operations can easily be derived for each of the binary number codes. They are treated in detail in most logic design texts, so they will not be discussed here. If the result of an arithmetic operation involving n-bit numbers is too large (small) to be represented by n bits, *overflow* (*underflow*) is said to occur. It is generally necessary to detect overflow and underflow since they are frequently an indication of a programming error.

Consider, for example, the addition operation

$$z_0 z_1 \cdots z_{n-1} \leftarrow x_0 x_1 \cdots x_{n-1} + y_0 y_1 \cdots y_{n-1}$$

using n-bit twos-complement operands. Assume that bitwise addition is per-

Decimal representation	Binary code		
	Sign magnitude	Ones complement	Twos complement
+7	0111	0111	0111
+6	0110	0110	0110
+5	0101	0101	0101
+4	0100	0100	0100
+3	0011	0011	0011
+2	0010	0010	0010
+1	0001	0001	0001
+0	0000	0000	0000
−0	1000	1111	0000
−1	1001	1110	1111
−2	1010	1101	1110
−3	1011	1100	1101
−4	1100	1011	1100
−5	1101	1010	1011
−6	1110	1001	1010
−7	1111	1000	1001

Figure 3.7 Comparison of three 4-bit binary number codes.

formed with a carry bit c_i generated by the addition of x_i, y_i, and c_{i+1}. z_i and c_i for $1 \leq i \leq n - 1$ can be computed according to the usual full adder equations

$$z_i = x_i \oplus y_i \oplus c_{i+1}$$

$$c_i = x_i y_i + x_i c_{i+1} + y_i c_{i+1}$$

Let v be a binary variable indicating overflow or underflow when $v = 1$. Figure 3.8 shows how the sign bit z_0 and v are determined as functions of the sign bits x_0, y_0 and the carry bit c_1. The overflow-underflow indicator v is defined by the logic equation

$$v = \bar{x}_0 \bar{y}_0 c_1 + x_0 y_0 \bar{c}_1$$

If the combinations $(x_0, y_0, c_1) = (0, 0, 1)$ and $(1, 1, 0)$, which set v to 1, are re-

Input			Output	
x_0	y_0	c_1	z_0	v
0	0	0	0	0
0	0	1	0	1
0	1	0	1	0
0	1	1	0	0
1	0	0	1	0
1	0	1	0	0
1	1	0	1	1
1	1	1	1	0

Figure 3.8 Computation of the sign bit z_0 and the overflow-underflow indicator v in twos-complement addition.

moved from the truth table of Fig. 3.8, it can then be seen that z_0 is defined correctly for all the remaining combinations by the equation

$$z_0 = x_0 \oplus y_0 \oplus c_1$$

This has the important consequence that during twos-complement addition, the sign bits of the operands can be treated in much the same way as the remaining (magnitude) bits.

Another important factor in machine arithmetic is *roundoff error*, which results from the fact that every number must be represented by a limited number of bits. Frequently, an operation involving n-bit numbers produces a result of more than n bits. For example, the product of two n-bit numbers contains up to $2n$ bits, all but n of which must normally be discarded. Retaining the n most significant bits of the result without modification is called *truncation*. Clearly the resulting number is in error by the amount of the discarded digits. This error can be reduced by a process called *rounding*. One way of doing this is to add $r^j/2$ to the number before truncation, where r^j is the weight of the least significant retained digit. For instance, to round 0.346712 to three decimal places, add 0.0005 to obtain 0.347212 and then take the three most significant digits 0.347. Simple truncation yields the less accurate value 0.346. Successive computations can cause roundoff errors to build up unless countermeasures are taken. The number formats provided in a computer should have sufficient precision that roundoff errors are of no consequence to most users. It is also desirable to provide facilities for performing arithmetic to a higher degree of precision if required. Such high precision is usually achieved by using several words to represent a single number and writing special subroutines to perform multiword, or "multiple precision," arithmetic.

Decimal numbers Since individuals today normally use decimal arithmetic, numbers being entered into a computer must first be converted from decimal to some binary representation. Similarly, binary-to-decimal conversion is a normal part of the computer's output processes. In certain applications the number of decimal-binary conversions forms a large fraction of the total number of elementary operations performed by the computer. It is therefore important that number conversion be carried out rapidly. The various binary number codes discussed above do not lend themselves to rapid conversion. For example, to convert a binary number $x_0 x_1 x_2 \ldots x_{n-1}$ to decimal, a polynomial of the form

$$\sum_{i=1}^{n-1} x_i 2^{k-i}$$

must be evaluated.

Several number codes are used which allow very rapid binary-decimal conversion. This is achieved by encoding each decimal digit separately by a sequence of bits. Codes of this kind are called *decimal codes*. They should properly be called binary coded decimal, but the term is reserved for one of the most widely used decimal codes, the *binary coded decimal*, or BCD, code. In

Decimal digit	Decimal code				
	BCD	EBCDIC	ASCII	Excess-three	Two-out-of-five
0	0000	1111 0000	0011 0000	0011	11000
1	0001	1111 0001	0011 0001	0100	00011
2	0010	1111 0010	0011 0010	0101	00101
3	0011	1111 0011	0011 0011	0110	00110
4	0100	1111 0100	0011 0100	0111	01001
5	0101	1111 0101	0011 0101	1000	01010
6	0110	1111 0110	0011 0110	1001	01100
7	0111	1111 0111	0011 0111	1010	10001
8	1000	1111 1000	0011 1000	1011	10010
9	1001	1111 1001	0011 1001	1100	10100

Figure 3.9 Some important decimal number codes.

the BCD representation of a decimal number, each digit d_i is represented by its 4-bit equivalent $b_{i,3}b_{i,2}b_{i,1}b_{i,0}$ in standard binary form. Thus the BCD number representing 971 is 100101110001. BCD is a weighted number code, since $b_{i,j}$ has the weight $10^i 2^j$. BCD numbers are generally in sign-magnitude form. The 8-bit EBCDIC and ASCII codes represent the 10 decimal digits in a 4-bit field in the same way as BCD. The remaining 4 bits (the "zone" field) are essentially unused.

Two other decimal codes of moderate importance are shown in Fig. 3.9. The *excess-three* code can be formed by adding 0011 to the corresponding BCD number—hence its name. Excess-three code has the advantage that it may be processed using the same logic used for binary codes. If two excess-three numbers are added like binary numbers, the required decimal carry is automatically generated from the high-order bits. The sum must be corrected by adding ± 3. For example, consider the addition $5 + 9 = 14$ using excess-three code.

$$
\begin{array}{r}
1000 = 5 \\
+\ 1100 = 9 \\
\hline
\text{Carry } 1 \leftarrow \quad 0100 \quad \text{Binary sum} \\
+\ 0011 \quad \text{Correction} \\
\hline
0111 \quad \text{Excess-three sum}
\end{array}
$$

Binary addition of the BCD representations of 5 and 9 results in 1101 and no-carry generation.[2] Some arithmetic operations are difficult to implement using excess-three code, mainly because it is a *nonweighted* code, that is, each bit position in an excess-three number does not have a fixed weight.

The final decimal code shown in Fig. 3.9 is the *two-out-of-five* code. Each

---

[2]The binary sum of two BCD numbers can also be corrected to give the proper BCD sum as described later in Sec. 3.3.1.

decimal digit is represented by a 5-bit sequence containing two 1s and three 0s; there are exactly 10 distinct sequences of this type. The particular merit of the two-out-of-five code is that it is single-error detecting, since changing any one bit results in a sequence that does not correspond to any valid codeword. Its disadvantages are that it is a nonweighted code and uses 5 rather than 4 bits per decimal digit.

The main advantage of the decimal codes is ease of conversion between the internal computer representation that allows only the symbols 0, 1 and external representations using the 10 decimal symbols $0, 1, 2, \ldots, 9$. Decimal codes have two disadvantages.

1. They use more bits to represent a number than the binary codes. Decimal codes therefore require more memory space. An n-bit word can represent 2^n numbers using binary codes; approximately $10^{n/4} = 2^{0.830n}$ numbers can be represented if a 4-bit decimal code such as BCD or excess-three is used.
2. The circuitry required to perform arithmetic using decimal operands is more complex than that needed for binary arithmetic. For example, in adding BCD numbers bit by bit, a uniform method of propagating carries between adjacent positions is not possible since the weights w_i and w_{i+1} of adjacent bits do not differ by a constant factor.

Floating-point numbers The range of numbers that can be represented by a fixed-point number code is insufficient for many applications, particularly scientific computations where very large and very small numbers are frequently encountered. Scientific notation permits such numbers to be represented using relatively few digits. For example, it is easier to write a quintillion in the form

$$1.0 \times 10^{18} \tag{3.4}$$

than as the fixed-point integer

$$1\ 000\ 000\ 000\ 000\ 000\ 000$$

The floating-point codes used in digital processors are essentially binary versions of (3.4).

Three numbers are associated with a floating-point number, the *mantissa* M, the *exponent* E, and the *base* B. These three components together represent the number $M \times B^E$. For example, in (3.4), 1.0 is the mantissa, 18 is the exponent, and 10 is the base. For machine implementation the mantissa and exponent are encoded as fixed-point numbers with radix r, where r is usually 2 or 10. The base B is invariably some power of r for reasons that will be obvious later. Since the base is a constant, it need not be included in the number code; it can simply be built into the circuits that process the numbers. A floating-point number is therefore stored as a pair of fixed-point numbers—a mantissa M, which is usually a fraction or an integer; and an exponent E, which is an integer.

The precision of $M \times B^E$ is determined primarily by the number of bits used to represent M. The range is determined by B and E. Floating-point formats are used to represent real numbers over some continuous interval $\pm R$.

Since only a finite set of numbers can be represented (at most 2^n, where n is the floating-point word size), these numbers are sparsely distributed over the interval $\pm R$. Increasing B greatly increases the range of the numbers that can be represented but results in a sparser distribution of numbers over that range.

Normalization Floating-point number representation is inherently redundant in the sense that the same number can be represented in more than one way. For example, 1.0×10^{18}, 0.1×10^{19}, 1000000×10^{12}, and 0.000001×10^{24} are possible floating-point forms of a quintillion. It is generally desirable to specify a unique normal form for floating-point numbers in a computer implementation. Consider the case where the mantissa is a sign-magnitude fraction and a base of 2 is used. The mantissa is said to be *normalized* if the digit to the right of the binary point is not 0, that is, there are no leading 0s in the magnitude part of the number. Thus, for example, 0.1×10^{19} is the unique normal form of a quintillion using base 10 and decimal mantissa and exponent. A binary fraction in twos-complement code is normalized when the sign bit x_0 differs from the bit x_1 to its right. This implies that there are no leading 1s in negative numbers. Normalization restricts the magnitude $|M|$ of a fractional mantissa to the range

$$1/2 \leq |M| < 1$$

Normal forms can be defined similarly for other number codes. An unnormalized floating-point number is easily normalized by shifting the mantissa to the right or left and appropriately incrementing or decrementing the exponent.

The representation of zero poses some special problems. The mantissa must, of course, be zero, but the exponent may have any value since $0 \times B^E = 0$ for all values of E. Often in attempting to compute zero, roundoff errors and the like result in a mantissa that is very small but not exactly zero. In order for the entire floating-point number to be close to zero, its exponent must be a very large negative number. This suggests that the exponent used for representing zero should be the negative number with the largest magnitude that can be contained in the exponent field of the number format. If k bits are allowed for the exponent (including its sign), then all numbers between -2^{k-1} and $+2^{k-1} - 1$ can be represented. The exponent -2^{k-1} would therefore be used in the normal format for zero. A second complication arises from the fact that it is desirable that zero be represented by a sequence of 0 bits only, primarily to facilitate implementation of instructions that test for zero. The exponent consisting of a sequence of 0s must then be assigned the value -2^{k-1}. This suggests that the exponents be encoded to an excess-2^{k-1} code similar to the excess-three code discussed earlier, where the exponent field contains the actual exponent value plus 2^{k-1}. The quantity 2^{k-1} is called the *bias*, and an exponent encoded in this manner is called a *biased exponent* or *characteristic*. Figure 3.10 shows all values of a 4-bit exponent with bias 8.

Example 3.1: The 32-bit floating-point format of the IBM S/360-370 series. This format, which is typical of many processors, is shown in Fig.

Exponent	Number represented
1111	+7
1110	+6
1101	+5
1100	+4
1011	+3
1010	+2
1001	+1
1000	0
0111	−1
0110	−2
0101	−3
0100	−4
0011	−5
0010	−6
0001	−7
0000	−8

Figure 3.10 A 4-bit biased exponent code (excess-eight code).

3.11. The leftmost bit is the sign of the mantissa which is also the sign of the number being represented. This is the usual sign position for fixed-point binary numbers; it is clearly advantageous to use it for floating-point numbers as well. The 24-bit mantissa occupies bits 8 through 31, and with bit 0 forms a fraction in sign-magnitude code. The mantissa field is viewed as containing six hexadecimal digits giving a precision of approximately seven decimal digits. The base B used is 16, so that a change of one in the exponent is equivalent to a 4-bit shift of the mantissa. The 7-bit exponent is biased by $2^6 = 64$ and is therefore in excess-64 code. This format allows numbers with magnitudes from zero to $(1 - 2^{-24}) \times 16^{63}$ (approximately 0.7×10^{76}) to be represented. In contrast, the 32-bit fixed-point number format used in the S/360-370 can only represent integers with magnitudes from zero to 2^{31} (approximately 0.2×10^{10}). The positive number 0.125×16^5 has the floating-point representation

$$0\ 1000101\ 001000000000000000000000$$

Note that the leftmost 4 bits of the mantissa represent the nonzero hexadecimal digit 2; hence the mantissa is normalized. The negative number -0.125×16^{-5} has the representation

$$1\ 0111011\ 001000000000000000000000$$

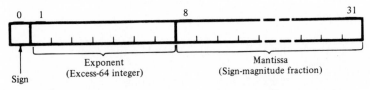

Figure 3.11 32-bit floating-point number format of the IBM S/360-370.

The exponent 0111011 represents +59 in sign-magnitude code; hence its value in excess-64 code is $59 - 64 = -5$.

3.2 INSTRUCTION SETS

3.2.1 Instruction Formats

The purpose of an instruction is to specify an operation to be carried out and the set of operands or data to be used. Operands include the input data or arguments of the operation and the results that are produced. The operation and operands are usually described by specific "fields" of the instruction word. The operation field is normally called the *opcode* (*operation code*). The operand fields often contain the *addresses* of storage locations in main memory or in the processor. The format of Fig. 3.12, comprising an opcode and a set of n operand addresses, is typical of processor instructions.

Most instructions specify a register transfer operation of the form

$$X_1 \leftarrow f(X_1, X_2, \ldots, X_n)$$

which involves n operands. The natural representation for this is the n-operand format of Fig. 3.12. To reduce instruction size and thereby reduce program storage space, it is common to specify only $m < n$ operands explicitly in the instruction; the remaining operands are implicit. If m is the maximum number of explicit operand addresses allowed in any processor instruction, the processor is called an *m-address machine*. Implicit operands must be placed in locations known to the processor before the instruction that refers to them is executed.

Operand specification Every operand field of an instruction is associated with some piece of data X. In order to execute the instruction, the processor requires the current value of X. This value can be specified in several ways. If X is a constant, then its value can be placed in the instruction operand field, in which case X is called an *immediate operand*. More often, the quantity of interest is a variable, and the corresponding operand field contains the address X of the storage location containing the required value. This value can then be varied without modifying any instruction addresses. Operand specification of this type is called *direct addressing*. It is frequently useful to change the location (as opposed to the value) of X without changing the address fields of any instructions that refer to X. This may be accomplished by *indirect addressing*, whereby the instruction contains the address W of a storage location which in turn contains the address X of the desired operand. By changing the contents of

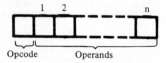

Opcode   Operands

Figure 3.12 Basic instruction format.

W, the address of the operand value required by the instruction is effectively changed. While direct addressing requires only one fetch operation to obtain an operand value, indirect addressing requires two. Figure 3.13 illustrates these different ways of specifying operands in the case of three load instructions which transfer the number 999 to the processor register AC.

Address formation *Absolute addressing*, the simplest mode of address specification, requires the complete operand address to appear in the instruction operand field. This address is used without further modification to access the desired data item. Frequently, only partial addressing information is included in the instruction, so the complete (absolute) operand address must be constructed by the processor. One of the commonest techniques is *relative addressing*, in which the operand field contains a relative address or displacement D. The instruction also implicitly or explicitly identifies other storage locations $R_1, R_2, \ldots, R_K$ (usually processor registers) containing additional addressing information. The absolute address A is then some function $f(D, R_1, R_2, \ldots, R_K)$. For example, in many processors a single register R is designated for address

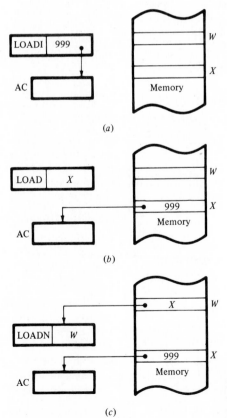

Figure **3.13** Three ways of operand specification (*a*) immediate, (*b*) direct addressing, and (*c*) indirect addressing.

construction, and the absolute address is the arithmetic sum of the contents of R and the displacement D, that is,

$$A = R + D$$

It may be useful to view R as containing a modifier for the instruction address D.

There are several important reasons for using relative addressing.

1. Since all the address information need not be included in the instructions, instruction length is reduced.
2. By changing the contents of R, the processor can change the absolute addresses referred to by a block of instructions B. This permits the processor to move (relocate) the entire block B from one region of main memory to another without invalidating the addresses in B. When used in this way, R is referred to as a *base register* and its contents as a base address.
3. R can be used for storing indices to facilitate the processing of indexed data. In this role, R is called an *index register*. The indexed items $X(0)$, $X(1), \ldots, X(k)$ are stored in consecutive addresses in main memory. The instruction address field D contains the address of the first item $X(0)$, while the index register R contains the index i. The address of item $X(i)$ is $D + R$. By changing the contents of the index register, a single instruction can be made to refer to any item $X(i)$ in the given data list. The main disadvantages of relative addressing lie in the extra logic circuits and extra processing time required for address computation.

So far we have assumed that each operand is a single memory word and can therefore be specified by a single address. If variable-length data consisting of many words are to be processed by an instruction, each operand field is usually divided into two parts: an address field, which points to the location of the first word of the operand; and a length field, which indicates the number of words in the operand. The instruction address field is automatically incremented by the processor as successive words of the operand are accessed. The access is complete when a number of words equal to the contents of the length field have been accessed.

The instruction formats used in the IBM S/360-370 series are shown in Fig. 1.33. All aspects of relative addressing mentioned here are included. Some instructions require both an index register and a base register to construct an absolute operand address.

Number of addresses A source of some controversy since the early days of the first-generation computers is the question of how many explicit operand addresses to include in instructions. Clearly the fewer the addresses, the shorter the instruction. However, limiting the number of addresses also limits the range of functions each instruction can perform. Roughly speaking, fewer addresses mean more primitive instructions, and longer programs are therefore required to perform any given task. While the storage requirements of shorter instructions and longer programs tend to balance, larger programs require longer execution times. On the other hand, long instructions with multiple addresses usually require more complex decoding and processing circuits.

As noted earlier, processors are often classified by the maximum number of address fields in their instructions. Computers generally have instructions of several different lengths containing varying numbers of addresses. Most instructions require no more than three operands. For example, the fundamental arithmetic operations—addition, subtraction, multiplication, and division—require three operands: two input and one output operand. In a three-address machine such as the CDC 6600, all three operands can be specified. For example, addition may be defined by an assembly-language instruction with the format

$$ADD \; Z, X, Y$$

meaning add the contents of memory locations X and Y and place the results in location Z, that is, $Z \leftarrow X + Y$. The add instruction in a one-address machine typically has the format

$$ADD \; X$$

The unspecified operands are assumed to be stored in fixed locations, commonly in a processor register called the accumulator AC. The ADD instruction in this case results in the operation $AC \leftarrow AC + X$ being performed. In the case of a two-address machine, the accumulator may be used to store the result (the sum) only. Thus

$$ADD \; X, Y$$

could be given the interpretation $AC \leftarrow X + Y$. An alternative implementation is to use one address, say X, to store both the addend X and the sum as follows: $X \leftarrow X + Y$. In the latter case the addition operation destroys the addend.

To illustrate the influence of the number of addresses on program length, we consider the execution of a high-level language arithmetic statement

$$X = A \times B + C \times C$$

where $\times$ denotes multiplication. Let M_1, M_2, and M_3 denote one-address, two-address and three-address processors, respectively. Figure 3.14 shows typical assembly-language programs that implement the arithmetic statement above. Besides the obvious tradeoffs between instruction length and program size, certain other performance factors should be considered when comparing these machines. In particular, instruction execution time may be very dependent on the location of the operands. Operands stored in processor registers can generally be obtained much faster than those stored in the external main memory. But without further details on the way in which the three machines are implemented, we cannot really compare the execution time of the three programs appearing in Fig. 3.14.

Instruction	Comments
LOAD A	Transfer A to accumulator AC
MULTIPLY B	$AC \leftarrow AC \times B$
STORE T	Transfer AC to memory location T
LOAD C	Transfer C to accumulator AC
MULTIPLY C	$AC \leftarrow AC \times C$
ADD T	$AC \leftarrow AC + T$
STORE X	Transfer result to memory location X

(a) One-address machine M_1

Instruction	Comments
MOVE T, A	$T \leftarrow A$
MULTIPLY T, B	$T \leftarrow T \times B$
MOVE X, C	$X \leftarrow C$
MULTIPLY X, C	$X \leftarrow X \times C$
ADD X, T	$X \leftarrow X + T$

(b) Two-address machine M_2

Instruction	Comments
MULTIPLY T, A, B	$T \leftarrow A \times B$
MULTIPLY X, C, C	$X \leftarrow C \times C$
ADD X, X, T	$X \leftarrow X + T$

(c) Three-address machine M_3

Figure 3.14 Programs to execute the statement $X = A \times B + C \times C$ in one-address, two-address and three-address processors.

Zero-address instructions Some computers have been designed so that most instructions contain no explicit addresses; they are therefore termed zero-address machines. Addresses are eliminated by storing operands in a pushdown stack. All operands used by a zero-address instruction are required to be in the top positions in the stack. For example, addition is invoked by an instruction such as

ADD

which causes the top two operands X and Y to be removed from the stack and added. The resulting sum $X + Y$ is placed at the top of the stack. Control of stacks is automatic using a special address register called a stack pointer to indicate the current position of the topmost filled location in the stack. In order to transfer data to and from the stack, two special instructions with the generic names PUSH and POP are needed. PUSH X causes the contents of X to be placed at the top of the stack. POP X causes the topmost word in the stack to be transferred to location X. Note that PUSH and POP are not themselves

Instruction	Comments
PUSH A	Transfer A to top of stack
PUSH B	Transfer B to top of stack
MULTIPLY	Remove A, B from stack and replace by $A \times B$
PUSH C	Transfer C to top of stack
PUSH C	Transfer second copy of C to top of stack
MULTIPLY	Remove C, C from stack and replace by $C \times C$
ADD	Remove $C \times C$, $A \times B$ from stack and replace by their sum.
POP X	Transfer result from top of stack to X

Figure 3.15 Program to execute the statement $X = A \times B + C \times C$ in a stack-based zero-address processor.

zero-address instructions. Figure 3.15 shows how a program to evaluate the arithmetic statement $X = A \times B + C \times C$ considered earlier might be written for a zero-address machine.

The order in which an arithmetic expression is evaluated in a stack machine corresponds to the order in the *Polish notation* for the expression, so-called after the Polish logician Jan Łukasiewicz (1878–1956), who first introduced it. The basic idea is to write a binary operation $X * Y$ either in the form $*XY$ (prefix notation) or $XY*$ (suffix or reverse Polish notation). The suffix Polish notation for the expression $A \times B + C \times C$ is thus $AB \times CC \times +$. Comparing this expression to the program of Fig. 3.10, we can see that every appearance of a variable X corresponds to PUSH X in the program, while every operator appears in the same position as the corresponding instruction in the program. Compilers for stack machines therefore convert ordinary infix arithmetic expressions into Polish form for execution in a stack. An important advantage of Polish notation is that no parentheses are needed. Thus while parenthesis are essential in the infix expression $X(Y + Z)$, they are not required in the corresponding (suffix) Polish expression $XYZ + \times$.

Opcodes In most computers, the opcode is a fixed-length field of k bits within each instruction permitting up to 2^k distinct operations to be specified. In computers with small word size, additional operations may be specified by using all or part of the operand fields as an extension to the opcode. Consider, for example, the 12-bit instruction formats used in the DEC PDP-8 minicomputer [11]. Figure 3.16a shows the basic one-address format used for instructions that refer to main memory. Bits 0, 1, and 2 form the opcode, bit 3 indicates whether or not indirect addressing is to be used, and the remaining 8 bits specify a relative address in main memory. Only six of the eight possible patterns in the opcode field are used for memory reference instructions. The remaining two patterns indicate that the opcode is augmented by bits 3 through 11. The format of Fig. 3.16b is used to specify a variety of "operate" instructions, which act on the main CPU registers (the accumulator AC and the multiplier-quotient register MQ) and hence do not require explicit addresses. Examples of

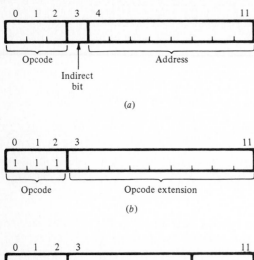

(a)

(b)

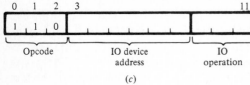

(c)

Figure **3.16** Instruction formats of the DEC PDP-8 computer. (a) Memory reference instruction; (b) operate instruction; (c) input-output instruction.

operate instructions are: clear AC, transfer contents of MQ to AC, skip the next instruction if AC = 0. A further class of instructions, called input-output transfer instructions, have the format shown in Fig. 3.16c. Bits 3 through 8 contain an IO device address and are used for IO device selection. The remaining 3 bits specify an IO operation to be performed using the designated IO device.

Instruction lengths Since programs occupy a considerable amount of valuable storage space, it is desirable to reduce their length as much as possible. One way of doing so that is primarily of theoretical interest is to assign the shortest formats to the most frequently used instructions and the longest formats to the least frequently used. This is a common technique for encoding information. For example, in the Morse code, the shortest code, ·, is assigned to the most common letter in English (e), while the longest codes are assigned to the least frequently occurring letters. The frequency with which operand addresses occur cannot be reasonably determined; all may be assumed to have equal probability. The frequency with which specific instruction types (determined by their opcodes) occur can be determined, however; it is the basis for instruction mixes such as the Gibson mix (see Fig. 2.58). One can therefore attempt to base opcode lengths on their probability of occurrence. This has been done in at least one computer, the Burroughs B1700 [33].

Consider, for example the hypothetical set of five instructions shown with their probabilities of occurrence in Fig. 3.17. If fixed-length opcodes are used, 3 bits are needed for every opcode. With the variable-length opcodes shown,

Instruction	Probability of occurrence p_i	Opcode c_i
I_1	0.5	1
I_2	0.3	00
I_3	0.1	011
I_4	0.05	0100
I_5	0.05	01010

Figure 3.17 Variable-length opcodes based on instruction occurrence probabilities.

the average number of opcode bits per instruction is

$$\sum_{i=1}^{5} p_i |c_i| = 1.85$$

which implies a reduction of 38 percent in the memory space needed to store opcodes. If variable-length opcodes are used, they must be carefully chosen so that each opcode can be uniquely decoded. The opcodes in Fig. 3.17 can be decoded by scanning any given instruction from left to right, since no opcode is a prefix of any other opcode. Thus an instruction beginning 0001 . . . . must be of type I_2. It would be impossible to uniquely identify this instruction if 0 were a valid opcode, since 0 is a prefix of 00. A systematic method of constructing codes of this type is due to Huffman [17]. Despite their inefficient storage utilization, fixed-length opcodes are generally preferred because of the ease with which they can be decoded.

Many computers, e.g., the IBM S/360-370 series, use instructions of several different lengths. The length of an instruction is determined mainly by the number or types of operands it contains. It is generally desirable to restrict instruction lengths to multiples or submultiples of w, where w is the main-memory word size, i.e., the number of bits accessed in one memory cycle. This allows some saving in address bits by requiring instructions to begin at predetermined (sub) word boundaries in the memory address space. It also permits efficient transfer and processing of the instructions, since all buses and registers involved can be tailored to the memory word size. In the DEC PDP-8 computer, for example, all instructions are one word (12 bits) long. In the IBM S/360-370 series, instructions may have length $w/2$, w, or $3w/2$, where $w = 32$ bits is the standard word size. (The actual number of bits accessed during a memory cycle depends on the S/360-370 model.) Several adjacent short instructions may be fetched simultaneously, which has the advantage of reducing the average instruction time. More than one memory cycle may be required to fetch long instructions.

3.2.2 Instruction Types

We turn now to the question: What types of instructions should be included in a general-purpose processor's instruction set? We are concerned here with the instructions that are in the processor's machine language. For simplicity we will represent these in the symbolic form of assembly-language instructions, or in our register transfer notation. Almost all processors have a well-defined machine language. Some implement lower-level languages, called micro-programming languages, which are discussed in Chap. 4. Few successful attempts have been made to construct computers whose basic machine language directly implements a high-level programming language such as ALGOL or FOR-TRAN [8].

The requirements to be satisfied by an instruction set can be stated in the following general but rather imprecise terms.

1. They should be complete in the sense that one should be able to write an assembly-language program to evaluate any function that is computable using the available memory space.
2. They should be efficient in the sense that commonly required functions can be implemented using relatively few instructions.
3. To simplify both the hardware design of the processor and its subsequent programming, the instruction types should be similar to those that have been widely adopted by computer manufacturers.

The conservative influence of 3 is quite marked. Almost all instruction sets bear a strong family resemblance and can be traced back directly to the IAS computer whose instruction set is described in Chap. 1.

Completeness A function $f(x)$ is defined to be computable if it can be evaluated in a finite number of steps by a Turing machine (see Sec. 1.1.2). While real computers differ from Turing machines in having only a finite amount of memory, they can, in practice, be used to evaluate any computable function, at least to a reasonable degree of approximation. When viewed as instruction set processors, Turing machines require a very simple instruction set. In the discussion of Turing machines in Sec. 1.1.2, four basic instruction types were defined (write, move tape one square to the left, move tape one square to the right, and halt). It follows that complete instruction sets can be constructed for finite-state machines using equally simple instruction types. Van der Poel has designed a simple one-address computer that has only one instruction [31]. While simple instruction sets require simple and therefore inexpensive logic circuits to implement them, they can lead to excessively complex programs. There is therefore a fundamental tradeoff between processor simplicity and programming complexity.

Instructions are conveniently divided into the following five major types.

1. *Data-transfer* instructions, which cause information to be copied from one location to another either in the processor's internal memory or in the external main memory
2. *Arithmetic* instructions, which perform operations on numerical data

3. *Logical* instructions, which include Boolean and other nonnumerical operations
4. *Program control* instructions, such as branch instructions, which change the sequence in which programs are executed
5. *Input-output* (IO) instructions, which cause information to be transferred between the processor or its main memory and external IO devices

These types are not always mutually exclusive. For example, the arithmetic operation $A \leftarrow B + C$ includes a data transfer. If $C = 0$, then it can be used to implement the simple data transfer $A \leftarrow B$.

The completeness of an instruction set can be demonstrated informally by showing that certain basic operations in each of these five groups can be programmed. It must be possible to transfer a word between the processor and any main-memory location. It must be possible to add two numbers, so an addition instruction is therefore included in most instruction sets. Other arithmetic operations can readily be programmed using addition. As shown in Sec. 3.1.3, subtraction of twos-complement numbers requires addition and logical complementation (NOT) only. More complex arithmetic operations such as multiplication, division, exponentiation, etc., can be programmed using addition and subtraction. If any complete set of Boolean operations such as AND and NOT are in the instruction set, then any other Boolean operation, e.g., EXCLUSIVE-OR, can be programmed. To implement branching, at least one conditional branch instruction is required which tests some stored quantity and alters the instruction execution sequence based on the test outcome. An unconditional branch can easily be realized using a conditional branch instruction.

Clearly an instruction set that is limited to one or two instructions is quite impractical. There is no agreement about what constitutes a suitable number of instructions. For example, the Scientific Micro Systems Microcontroller and the Texas Instruments TMS 9900 are roughly comparable microprocessors. The TMS 9900 has about 70 basic instruction types, whereas the Microcontroller has only 8. Some large computers have several hundred instructions. A reasonable indication of the efficiency or power of an instruction set is its subset of arithmetic instruction types. Figure 3.18 shows the range of arithmetic instructions that can be found. Note that instruction execution times must be taken into account in any comparisons between instruction sets. Many pocket calculators implement all the scalar operations of Fig. 3.18, but their execution times are usually extremely long compared with that of most computers. Furthermore, complex operations such as multiplication, although invoked by a single keystroke, may in fact be programmed (in read-only memory), so they cannot be considered as part of the instruction set of the calculator's internal processor.

Catalog of common instruction types We conclude this section with a brief survey of the machine instruction types that have been implemented in computers over the years. Our list has been compiled from the instruction sets of a number

Scalar arithmetic			Vector arithmetic (floating-point $+, -, \times, \div$)	Representative machine
Fixed-point		Floating-point $(+, -, \times, \div)$		
$+, -$	$\times, \div$			
✔				PDP-8
✔	✔			TMS 9900
✔	✔	✔		S/360-370
✔	✔	✔	✔	STAR-100

Figure 3.18 Arithmetic operations included in the instruction sets of some representative computers.

of representative machines, but it is by no means exhaustive. We are concerned only with the basic operations performed; variations due to operand format, length, or location are not considered. As noted earlier, the large size of many instruction sets is primarily a result of the presence of many (untagged) data types each requiring its own version of every applicable instruction type.

Figure 3.19 lists the most widely used instruction types. It is assumed that each instruction cycle involves the following standard sequence of operations.

1. The instruction is fetched.
2. The program counter PC is incremented.
3. The instruction is decoded and executed.

Note that only program-control instructions can change PC during the instruction execution phase. Instructions are frequently encountered which are simple combinations of the instructions included in Fig. 3.19. For example, the IAS instruction set includes combinations of ABSOLUTE and NEGATE with MOVE and certain arithmetic operations (see Fig. 1.16).

The complexity of the IO instructions depends on the extent to which the processor delegates control over IO operations to other parts of the computer system. Most IO operations involve fairly simple data transfers. Special control instructions for IO devices such as REWIND TAPE, PRINT LINE, and the like are treated as data by the IO control processors and are only interpreted as instructions by the IO devices to which they are transferred.

3.2.3 Implementation

The design of circuits to implement an instruction set is primarily an exercise in register-level logic design. First it is necessary to devise an algorithm in terms of appropriate register transfers or microoperations for each instruction. The particular component technology used to implement the processor determines the microoperations that can be used. The algorithms should be designed to provide an acceptable compromise between circuit cost and instruction execution speed. It is also common to choose algorithms that permit circuits used by different instructions to be shared.

Of the five major instruction types defined earlier (data transfer, arithmetic, logical, program control, and input-output), all but arithmetic and input-output are relatively easy to implement. Data-transfer instructions require only the creation of a data path from the source to the destination. A Boolean operation can be implemented by connecting the input operands to an appropriate word gate. Consider the implementation of the four logical operations AND, OR, EXCLUSIVE-OR, and NOT using n-bit operands. The inputs are stored in registers X and Y and the output is to be placed in register Z. The particular operation to be performed is specified by two control signals c_1 and c_2. It is easily seen that the logic circuit required to implement the four instructions is defined by the Boolean equation

$$Z = \bar{c}_1 \bar{c}_2 XY + \bar{c}_1 c_2 (X + Y) + c_1 \bar{c}_2 (X \oplus Y) + c_1 c_2 \bar{X}$$

where $c_1 c_2 = 00$ specifies AND, $c_1 c_2 = 01$ specifies OR, etc. This equation may be rewritten in the following sum-of-products form

$$Z = \bar{c}_1 \bar{c}_2 XY + \bar{c}_1 c_2 X + \bar{c}_1 c_2 Y + c_1 \bar{c}_2 \bar{X}Y + c_1 \bar{c}_2 X\bar{Y} + c_1 c_2 \bar{X}$$

and implemented using the two-level NAND circuit of Fig. 3.20. Other common nonnumerical instructions such as shift and rotate are equally easy to implement. Branch instructions also present no serious difficulties. Figure 3.21 shows a possible implementation of two representative conditional branch instructions: SZA (skip on zero accumulator) and SNA (skip on nonzero accumulator), which are used in the PDP-8 computer [11].

Arithmetic and IO instructions require relatively complex circuits. The design of arithmetic circuits, a large and well-developed field, is discussed in Sec. 3.3. The implementation of IO instructions is discussed in Chap. 6. Unlike the others, IO instructions involve more components of a computer system than its CPU and main memory.

3.3 ARITHMETIC OPERATIONS

3.3.1 Fixed-Point Addition and Subtraction

The most basic arithmetic operations which are included in the instruction set of every computer are fixed-point addition and subtraction. Adder-subtracters are frequently used to implement multiplication and division, as in Examples 2.1 and 2.2. As discussed in Chap. 2, the fixed-point addition time of a computer is often used as a simple measure of its processing speed. For these reasons, considerable effort, beginning with Babbage, has been devoted to the design of

Type	Operation name(s)	Description
DATA TRANSFER	MOVE (TRANSFER)	Transfer word or block from source to destination
	STORE	Transfer word from processor to external memory
	LOAD (FETCH)	Transfer word from external memory to processor
	EXCHANGE	Swap contents of source and destination
	CLEAR (RESET)	Transfer word of 0s to destination
	SET	Transfer word of 1s to destination
	PUSH	Transfer word from source to top of stack
	POP (PULL)	Transfer word from top of stack to destination
ARITHMETIC	ADD	Compute sum of two operands
	SUBTRACT	Compute difference of two operands
	MULTIPLY	Compute product of two operands
	DIVIDE	Compute quotient of two operands
	ABSOLUTE	Replace operand by its absolute value
	NEGATE	Change sign of operand
	INCREMENT	Add 1 to operand
	DECREMENT	Subtract 1 from operand
LOGICAL	AND	
	OR	
	NOT (COMPLEMENT)	Perform the specified logical operation bitwise
	EXCLUSIVE-OR	
	EQUIVALENCE	
	SHIFT	Left- (right-) shift operand introducing constants at end
	ROTATE	Left- (right-) shift operand around closed path
	CONVERT (EDIT)	Change data format, e.g., from binary to decimal

	JUMP (BRANCH)	Unconditional transfer; load PC with specified address
	JUMP CONDITIONAL	Test specified condition; depending on condition, either load PC with specified address or else do nothing
	JUMP TO SUBROUTINE (CALL, BRANCH-AND-LINK)	Place current program control information (PC, status register, etc.) in known location, e.g., in top of stack; jump to specified address
	RETURN	Replace contents of PC, status register, etc. with information from known location, e.g., from top of stack
	EXECUTE	Fetch operand from specified location and execute as instruction; note that PC is not modified
PROGRAM CONTROL	SKIP	Increment PC to skip the next instruction
	SKIP CONDITIONAL	Test specified condition; depending on outcome, either increment PC or else do nothing
	TEST	Test specified condition; set flag(s) based on outcome
	COMPARE	Make logical or arithmetic comparison of two or more operands; set flag(s) based on outcome
	SET CONTROL VARIABLES	Large class of instructions to set controls for protection purposes, interrupt handling, timer control, etc. (often privileged instructions.)
	HALT	Stop program execution
	WAIT (HOLD)	Stop program execution; test a specified condition continuously; when the condition is satisfied, resume execution
	NO OPERATION	No operation is performed, but program execution continues
INPUT-OUTPUT	INPUT (READ)	Transfer data from specified IO port or device to destination, e.g., main memory or processor register
	OUTPUT (WRITE)	Transfer data from specified source to IO port or device
	START IO	Transfer instructions to IOP to initiate IO operation
	TEST IO	Transfer status information from IO system to specified destination
	HALT IO	Transfer instructions to IOP to terminate IO operation

Figure 3.19 List of common instruction types.

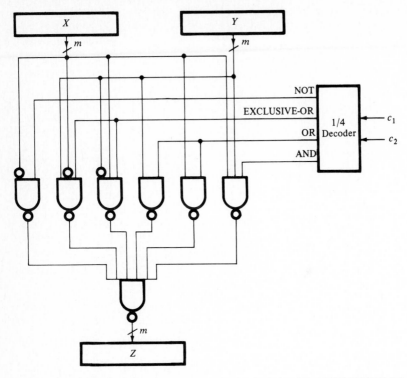

Figure 3.20 Implementation of 4 logical instructions AND, OR, EXCLUSIVE-OR, and NOT.

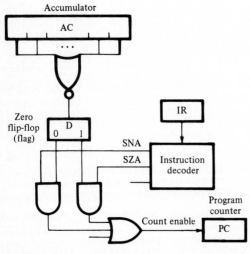

Figure 3.21 Implementation of two conditional branch instructions SZA (skip on zero accumulator) and SNA (skip on nonzero accumulator).

high-speed addition and subtraction circuits. The complexity of an arithmetic circuit is determined in part by the number codes used. Twos-complement is perhaps the most widely used code for fixed-point binary numbers, since both addition and subtraction are easily implemented by a positive-number adder with an input complementer, as shown in Fig. 2.47. We will therefore restrict our discussion mainly to the structure of adders for positive binary numbers. (Recall that most number codes use identical representations for positive numbers.)

Basic binary adders The fastest n-bit binary adder is, in principle, a two-level combinational circuit in which each of the n sum bits is expressed as a (logical) sum of products or product of sums of the input variables. In practice, such a circuit is feasible for very small values of n only, as it requires $c(n)$ gates with fan-in $f(n)$ where both $c(n)$ and $f(n)$ grow exponentially with n. Practical adders take the form of multilevel combinational circuits or, occasionally, sequential circuits. They therefore sacrifice operating speed for a reduction in circuit complexity as measured by the number and size of the components used. In general, the addition of two n-bit numbers X and Y is performed by subdividing the numbers into segments X_i and Y_i of length n_i, where $n \geq n_i \geq 1$. X_i and Y_i are added separately and the resulting partial sums are combined to form the total sum. The formation of the total sum usually involves assimilation of carry bits generated by the partial additions.

A simple binary adder which computes the sum of 1-bit numbers is defined by the logic equations

$$z_i = x_i \oplus y_i \oplus c_{i+1}$$

$$c_i = x_i y_i + x_i c_{i+1} + y_i c_{i+1}$$

Two output bits are generated: a sum bit z_i and a carry bit c_i. Provision is made to include a carry bit c_{i+1} as an input, where c_{i+1} may be the carry generated by some other segment of a larger addition operation. A circuit implementing these equations is called a *full adder*. Figure 3.22 shows a two-level realization of a full adder.[3]

A simple circuit for adding binary numbers of arbitrary length is the *serial adder* shown in Fig. 3.23. Corresponding bits x_i and y_i of the two numbers to be added are applied to the inputs of the adder, beginning with the least significant bits. The carry generated by each 1-bit addition is stored in the flip-flop and applied as an input during the following 1-bit addition . If d and D denote the delays associated with the full adder and the flip-flop, respectively, then the

[3]The term *half adder* is used for a circuit realizing the pair of functions

$$z_i = x_i \oplus y_i$$

$$c_i = x_i y_i$$

A half adder does not accommodate an input carry bit. It is easily shown that a full adder can be constructed using two half adders.

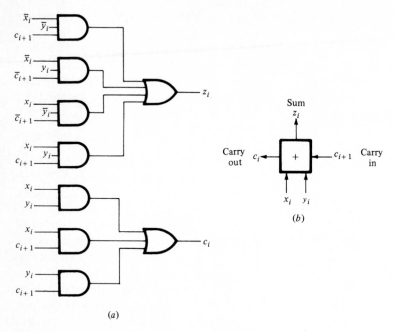

Figure 3.22 A full adder: (*a*) two-level logic circuit; (*b*) symbol.

time required to perform an *n*-bit addition is $n(d + D)$. Note, however, that the amount of circuitry needed is independent of *n*.

Circuits which add all *n* pairs of bits simultaneously are called *parallel adders*. A simple parallel adder can be formed by connecting *n* full adders in the cascade arrangement of Fig. 3.24. Each full-adder stage supplies a carry bit to the stage on its left. A carry appearing on the input of a full adder may cause it to generate a carry signal on its output carry line; thus carry signals can propagate serially through the adder from right to left giving rise to the name *ripple carry adder*. In the worst case, carries may ripple through all *n* stages of the

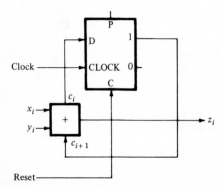

Figure 3.23 A serial binary adder.

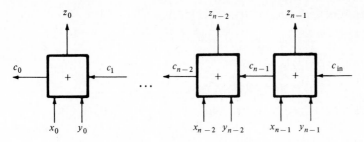

Figure 3.24 An n-bit ripple carry adder.

adder; the maximum delay (which in synchronous circuit design determines the operating speed) is thus nd, where d is the delay of a full-adder stage. Note that unlike a serial adder, the amount of hardware required by a ripple carry adder increases linearly with n.

It is occasionally useful to construct subtracters for numbers in sign-magnitude format. The basic element used is a *full subtracter*, which is defined by the logic equations

$$z_i = x_i \oplus y_i \oplus b_{i+1}$$

$$b_i = \bar{x}_i y_i + \bar{x}_i b_{i+1} + y_i b_{i+1}$$

z_i is the difference bit, while b_{i+1} and b_i are the borrow-in and borrow-out bits, respectively. n-bit serial or parallel binary subtracters are constructed in essentially the same way as the corresponding adders. Subtracters are of relatively minor interest compared with adders, since an adder suffices for both addition and subtraction when ones-complement or twos-complement number codes are used.

High-speed binary adders The general strategy in designing fast adders is to reduce the time associated with carry propagation. One way of doing this is to generate the input carry bit of stage i directly from the inputs to the preceding stages $i + 1, i + 2, \ldots, i + k$ rather than allow carries to ripple from stage to stage. Adders designed using this principle are called *carry-lookahead adders*. An n-bit carry-lookahead adder can be formed from k stages, each of which is a full adder modified by replacing its carry output line c_i by two carry generate and propagate signals g_i and p_i defined by the logic equations

$$g_i = x_i y_i$$

$$p_i = x_i \oplus y_i$$

The carry signal to be transmitted to stage $i - 1$ is then defined by the logic equation

$$c_i = g_i + p_i c_{i+1} \tag{3.5}$$

Similarly, c_{i+1} can be expressed in terms of g_{i+1}, p_{i+1}, and c_{i+2}:

$$c_{i+1} = g_{i+1} + p_{i+1}c_{i+2} \tag{3.6}$$

On substituting (3.6) into (3.5) we obtain

$$c_i = g_i + p_i g_{i+1} + p_i p_{i+1} c_{i+2}$$

Continuing in this way, c_i can be expressed as a sum-of-products function of the p and g outputs of the preceding k stages. For example, the carries in a four-stage carry-lookahead adder are defined by

$$c_3 = g_3 + p_3 c_{in}$$

$$c_2 = g_2 + p_2 g_3 + p_2 p_3 c_{in}$$

$$c_1 = g_1 + p_1 g_2 + p_1 p_2 g_3 + p_1 p_2 p_3 c_{in}$$

$$c_0 = g_0 + p_0 g_1 + p_0 p_1 g_2 + p_0 p_1 p_2 g_3 + p_0 p_1 p_2 p_3 c_{in}$$

Figure 3.25 shows the corresponding circuit. The lookahead circuit is a two-level logic circuit that generates c_0, c_1, c_2, c_3 according to the equations above. If d is the propagation delay of a two-level circuit, then the total delay of a carry-lookahead adder is $3d$. Since the complexity of the carry-generation equations increases with the number of stages, practical considerations limit the number of carry-lookahead stages to $k \leq 8$ or so.

The carry-lookahead principle can be extended to handle mk bits by performing carry-lookahead addition on groups of k adjacent bits and transferring the output carry bit of each group to the carry input of its left neighbor. Thus carries ripple through the m groups. Figure 3.26 shows a 12-bit adder designed in this way using three 4-bit carry-lookahead adders of the type given in Fig. 3.25. In this kind of adder, each group can generate an output carry d time units (where d is the two-level delay) after it receives its input carry. Hence if there are m groups, the total addition time is $(m + 2)d$. The 12-bit adder of Fig. 3.26 has a delay of $5d$ compared with $12d$ for a simple ripple carry adder.

Decimal adders Adders that handle numbers in decimal codes such as BCD or excess-three are, as might be expected, more complex than binary adders. Dec-

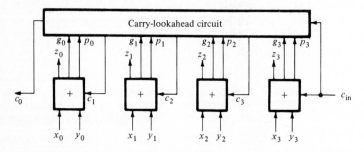

Figure 3.25 A 4-bit carry-lookahead adder.

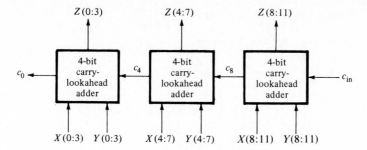

Figure 3.26 A 12-bit adder with group carry-lookahead and ripple carry between groups.

imal adders can often be regarded as binary adders with appropriate "correction" logic added to transform the sum to the required decimal format. As an example, we consider the design of a simple n-digit ripple carry BCD adder analogous to the binary adder of Fig. 3.24. Speedup methods such as carry lookahead can readily be extended from the binary to the decimal case.

The general structure of an n-digit BCD ripple carry adder is illustrated in Fig. 3.27. There are n stages, each of which adds a pair of 4-bit BCD digits and is connected via 1-bit carry lines to its neighbors. As a first approximation, one might attempt to implement each stage by a 4-bit binary adder and add X_i and Y_i as if they were binary numbers. Let Z_i^* denote the resulting 4-bit binary sum and let c_i^* be the output carry. Let Z_i be the correct BCD sum and let c_i be the correct carry. If $X_i + Y_i + c_{i+1} < 10$, $Z_i^* = Z_i$, otherwise $Z_i^* \neq Z_i$ and Z_i^* must be "corrected" to change it to Z_i. As the reader can readily verify, this correction can be made by adding 6 to Z_i^*, since the low-order 4 bits of $Z_i^* + 6$ are equal to Z_i whenever $X_i + Y_i + c_{i+1} \geq 10$. The output carry c_i is 1 whenever $c_i^* = 1$ or $Z_i^* \geq 10$. Figure 3.28 shows a logic circuit for a BCD adder stage that implements these concepts. A 4-bit ripple carry binary adder computes the sum Z_i^*. Z_i^* then passes through a second binary adder, which adds either 0 or 6 to it to form Z_i. Note that the correction by adding 6 is required only when $c_i = 1$, so c_i is used to generate the required correction factor 0 or 6.

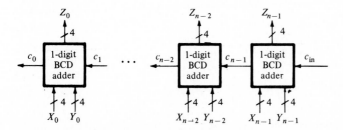

Figure 3.27 An n-digit ripple carry BCD adder.

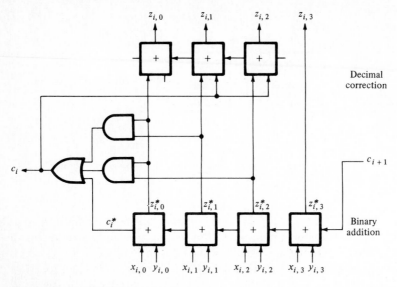

Figure 3.28 A 1-digit BCD adder stage.

3.3.2 Fixed-Point Multiplication

Multiplication requires substantially more hardware than addition and, as a result, may not be included in the instruction sets of some small or inexpensive processors, e.g., microprocessors. However, it is an operation that is useful in almost all types of computations. Multiplication is usually implemented by some form of repeated addition. One of the simplest but slowest methods is to add the multiplicand M to itself Q times, where Q is the multiplier. An implementation of this technique using counters is discussed in Prob. 2.12. More commonly, multiplication is implemented by multiplying M by Q k bits at a time and adding the resulting terms. Figure 3.29 shows how this is done in pencil-and-paper calculations with $k = 1$. The operations involved are shifting and addition. (Subtraction may be used to handle negative twos-complement numbers, but this presents no difficulty because an adder can be used for both addition and subtraction). The algorithm of Fig. 3.29 is inefficient in that the 1-bit products $x_j 2^i Y$ must be stored until the final addition step is completed. In

$$
\begin{array}{ll}
1010 & \text{Multiplicand } Y \\
\underline{1101} & \text{Multiplier } X = x_0 x_1 x_2 x_3 \\
1010 & x_3 Y \\
0000 & x_2 2Y \\
1010 & x_1 2^2 Y \\
\underline{1010} & x_0 2^3 Y \\
10000010 & \text{Product } P = \displaystyle\sum_{j=0}^{3} x_j 2^{3-j} Y
\end{array}
$$

Figure 3.29 Typical pencil-and-paper method for multiplication of positive numbers.

$$
\begin{array}{ll}
\quad 1010 & Y \\
\quad 1101 & X \\
\hline
00000000 & P_0 = 0 \\
\quad 1010 \\
\hline
00001010 & P_1 = P_0 + x_3 Y \\
\quad 0000 \\
\hline
00001010 & P_2 = P_1 + x_2 2Y \\
\quad 1010 \\
\hline
00110010 & P_3 = P_2 + x_1 2^2 Y \\
\quad 1010 \\
\hline
10000010 & P_4 = P_3 + x_0 2^3 Y = P
\end{array}
$$

Figure 3.30 The multiplication of Fig. 3.29 modified for machine implementation.

machine implementations, it is desirable to add each $x_j 2^i Y$ term as it is generated to the sum of the preceding terms to form a number P_{i+1} called the partial product. Figure 3.30 shows the calculation in Fig. 3.29 implemented in this way. The computation involved in processing one multiplier bit x_j can be described by a register transfer statement of the form

$$
P_{i+1} \leftarrow P_i + x_j 2^i Y
$$

where $2^i Y$ is equivalent to Y shifted i positions to the left. Multiplication circuits using this technique are discussed in detail in Examples 2.1 and 2.2.

High-speed multiplication In certain applications such as real-time signal processing, very fast multiplication is desirable. There are several ways in which multiplication speed can be increased.

1. *High-speed addition.* This may be achieved by a variety of methods, such as carry lookahead (see Sec. 3.3.2), which reduce carry propagation time. Another speedup method made possible by the fact that multiplication requires a sequence of addition steps is *carry save multiplication.* The carry bits produced during an addition step are not assimilated immediately but are stored and gradually assimilated in subsequent additions. An example of this is presented later.

2. *High-speed shifting.* In many steps of an add-shift multiplication algorithm, shifting alone takes place, for example, when a run of k 0s or 1s is encountered. Special circuitry may be introduced to identify this situation and perform a variable-length k-bit shift operation very rapidly.

3. *Simultaneous multiplication by several multiplier bits.* Instead of multiplying the multiplicand by one multiplier bit during each cycle, multiply by $k > 1$ adjacent bits of the multiplier. This corresponds to increasing the radix of the number system from 2 to 2^k. It is then necessary to construct logic to multiply by any of 2^k numbers instead of just 0 and 1. However, the total number of add-shift steps is reduced by a factor of k.

Booth's multiplication algorithm The multiplication technique for twos-complement numbers used in Example 2.2 (see Fig. 2.44) is complicated by the correction step needed when the multiplier is negative. An interesting multiplication algorithm for twos-complement numbers was developed by Booth [5]. It treats positive and negative numbers uniformly and thereby eliminates the need for correcting the result. Furthermore, runs of 0s or 1s in the multiplier are skipped over without any addition or subtraction being performed, thereby making possible faster multiplication.

Suppose that $Y = y_0 y_1 \ldots y_{n-1}$ is to be multiplied by $X = x_0 x_1 \ldots x_{n-1}$, where X and Y are twos-complement fractions. As in the basic multiplication algorithms discussed earlier, the multiplier X is scanned sequentially from right

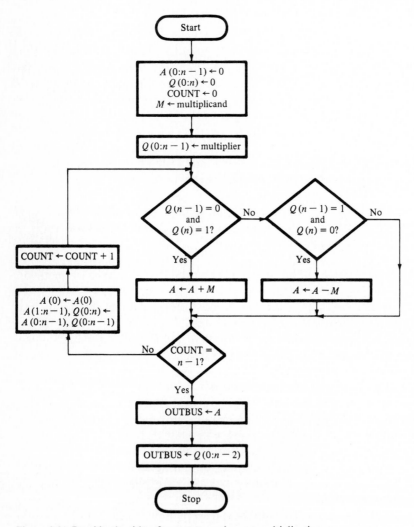

Figure 3.31 Booth's algorithm for twos-complement multiplication.

to left. In this case, however, two adjacent bits, x_i and x_{i+1}, are examined during each step i of the procedure. If $x_i x_{i+1} = 01(10)$, the multiplicand Y is added to (subtracted from) the accumulated partial product term P_i and the latter is then shifted. If $x_i = x_{i+1}$, only the shift operation takes place. Figure 3.31 shows a version of this algorithm to multiply two n-bit fractions using essentially the same logic circuit as Example 2.2 (see Fig. 2.45). As in that example, intermediate results are stored in the accumulator-multiplier register pair A, Q. An extra cell $Q(n)$ is appended to the right end of Q to facilitate the double-bit inspection process. Figure 3.32 illustrates this algorithm for a negative multiplier and a positive multiplicand with $n = 4$.

Correctness proof for Booth's algorithm X and Y are numbers of the form $r_0 r_1 r_2 \ldots r_{n-1}$, where r_0 is the sign bit and the remaining bits form a fraction. First consider the case where X and Y are both positive, that is, $x_0 = y_0 = 0$. Let X^* be any subsequence of the multiplier X consisting of a sequence of 1s preceded and followed by 0s.

M	A	Q	Comments
0.010	0.000	10110	
	0.010		Subtract M
	1.110	10110	
	1.111	01011	Shift A, Q
			No addition or subtraction
	1.111	10101	Shift A, Q
	0.010		Add M
	0.001	10101	
	0.000	11010	Shift A, Q
	0.010		Subtract M
	1.110	11010	

Product P

Figure 3.32 Example of twos-complement multiplication using Booth's algorithm.

$$X^* = x_i x_{i+1} x_{i+2} \ldots x_{i+k-1} x_{i+k} x_{i+k+1}$$

$$= 011 \ldots 110$$

Using conventional multiplication, Y is multiplied by each bit of X^* and the results are added so that the contribution of X^* to the product XY is

$$Y \sum_{j=i+1}^{i+k} 2^{-j}.$$

(Note that since X represents a fraction, each bit x_j of X has weight 2^{-j}.) Using Booth's algorithm, an addition is performed when bit x_i is inspected, while a subtraction is performed at bit x_{i+k}. Hence the contribution of X^* to the final product is $Y2^{-i} - Y2^{-(i+k)}$. However,

$$Y2^{-i} - Y2^{-(i+k)} = Y2^{-(i+k)}(2^k - 1)$$

$$= Y2^{-(i+k)} \sum_{m=0}^{k-1} 2^m$$

$$= Y \sum_{m=0}^{k-1} 2^{m-i-k}$$

$$= Y \sum_{j=i+1}^{i+k} 2^{-j}$$

Hence the contribution X^*Y of X^* to the product using Booth's algorithm is the same as that obtained by conventional bit-by-bit multiplication. If the multiplier contains k disjoint runs of 1s, then it can be expressed as the sum

$$\sum_k X_k^*$$

where X_k^* has the same form as X^*. For example, $011010 = 011000 + 000010$. Thus the algorithm computes

$$\sum_k X_k^*Y$$

which equals the desired result XY.

The foregoing analysis shows that when X and Y are positive, the result generated by Booth's algorithm corresponds directly to the expression

$$\sum_{j=1}^{n-1} x_j 2^{-j} Y$$

When X is positive and Y is negative, the same sequence of operations is performed, and the result again can be expressed in the form

$$\sum_{j=1}^{n-1} x_j f_j(Y)$$

where $f_j(Y)$ represents the contribution of the negative multiplicand Y in the jth step. It can readily be seen that $f_j(Y) = 2 - 2^{-j} \tilde{Y}$, where $\tilde{Y}$ is the twos-complement of Y, that is, $Y = 2 - \tilde{Y}$. The term $2 - 2^{-j} \tilde{Y}$ represents Y shifted j positions to the right with leading 1s instead of leading 0s entered at the left. The result therefore is equivalent to

$$\sum_{j=1}^{n-1} x_j(2 - 2^{-j} \tilde{Y})$$

where the summation is modulo 2. Now

$$\sum_{j=1}^{n-1} x_j(2 - 2^{-j}\tilde{Y}) = 2\sum_{j=1}^{n-1} x_j - \tilde{Y}\sum_{j=1}^{n-1} x_j 2^{-j} \qquad \text{modulo } 2$$

$$= 2\sum_{j=1}^{n-1} x_j - \tilde{Y}X \qquad \text{modulo } 2$$

$$= 2 - \tilde{Y}X \qquad \text{modulo } 2$$

$$= XY$$

Next let Y be positive but X be negative. The twos-complement fraction format implies that

$$X = 1 + |X| \qquad \text{modulo } 2 \tag{3.7}$$

Let P_{n-1} be the accumulated partial product after multiplication by $x_1 x_2 \dots x_{n-1}$. Since X is negative, x_0 is 1. x_1 may be either 0 or 1.

Case 1 $x_1 = 0$. Since $x_0 x_1 = 10$, Booth's algorithm requires a subtraction in the last step so that

$$P_n = P_{n-1} - Y \qquad \text{modulo } 2 \tag{3.8}$$

Now if x_0 is changed to 0, the computation up to the last step is unaffected. This changes X to $|X|$ and we conclude that $P_{n-1} = |X|Y$ independent of the value of x_0. Hence (3.8) can be rewritten as

$$P_n = |X|Y - Y \qquad \text{modulo } 2 \tag{3.9}$$

Case 2 $x_1 = 1$. No subtraction or addition is performed in the last step; therefore, $P_n = P_{n-1}$. If x_0 is again changed to 0, P_n becomes $|X|Y$ and an addition is performed in the last step. This implies that

$$|X|Y = P_{n-1} + Y \qquad \text{modulo } 2$$

This is valid for $x_0 = 1$; hence substituting P_n for P_{n-1}, we again obtain (3.9). Thus in all cases, the result computed by Booth's algorithm when Y is positive and X is negative is $|X|Y - Y$, modulo 2. But

$$|X|Y - Y = (|X| - 1)Y = (|X| + 1)Y \qquad \text{modulo } 2$$

which by (3.7) is the required result XY. A similar argument holds when X and Y are both negative.

It will be observed that in Booth's algorithm, addition or subtraction occurs only when a 0-to-1 or 1-to-0 transition is encountered in the multiplier. Runs of 0s or 1s are effectively ignored. By arranging the logic so that such runs can be skipped over rapidly, one can reduce the average multiplication time.

Multiplier recoding The process of inspecting the multiplier bits required by the Booth algorithm can be viewed as encoding the multiplier using three digits $0, 1, \bar{1}$, where 0 means shift the multiplicand relative to the accumulator, while $1(\bar{1})$ means add (subtract) the multiplicand before shifting. Thus the number

$$X = 0111\ 1011\ 0010\ 0011 \tag{3.10}$$

which represents +31,523, can be replaced by

$$X^* = 1000\ \bar{1}10\bar{1}\ 01\bar{1}0\ 010\bar{1} \tag{3.11}$$

where each $1(\bar{1})$ in X^* indicates that an addition (subtraction) should be performed. X^* is an example of a *signed digit* number. It is a variation of the usual positional notation which allows a bit to have weight -2^i (indicated by $\bar{1}$ in that bit position) as well as the usual values of 0 and 2^i. The process of converting a multiplier X to signed digit form to simplify the multiplication process is called *multiplier recoding*.

The number of add-subtract operations needed using the Booth algorithm is determined by the number of runs of 1s in the multiplier. Two such operations, one subtraction and one addition, are required for every run of $k \geq 1$ 1s, instead of the k additions required in the earlier multiplication schemes. If, however, $k = 1$, that is, we have a single 1 preceded and followed by 0s, we are replacing one addition by an addition and a subtraction. Clearly the algorithm can be improved if isolated 1s are identified and only a single addition is performed. A similar improvement can be obtained at an isolated 0 such as

$$x_{i-1}x_ix_{i+1}$$

$$\cdots\ 1 \quad 0 \quad 1\ \cdots$$

by noting that the contribution of this subsequence computed by the basic Booth algorithm is $(2^{-i} - 2^{-(i-1)})Y = -2^{-i}Y$. Hence it suffices to perform a single subtraction at the isolated 0 position.

Figure 3.33 gives the rules for a multiplier recoding scheme that takes isolated 0s and 1s into account [15]. Called *canonical signed digit* recoding, it can easily be incorporated into the Booth multiplication algorithm described above. First $x_{-1} = 0$ is appended to the left end of the input number $x_0x_1 \ldots x_{n-1}$ to form $X = x_{-1}x_0x_1 \ldots x_{n-1}$. X is then scanned from right to left and the pair of bits $x_{i-1}x_i$ is used to determine bit x_i^* of the output number X^*. A marker m, which is initially 0, is set to 1(0) while a run of 1s (0s) is being traversed. Note that m is not altered when an isolated 1(0) is encountered in a sum of 0s (1s). Applying these rules to the number X defined by equation (3.10) yields the canonical signed digit form

$$X^* = 1000\ 0\bar{1}0\bar{1}\ 0010\ 010\bar{1}$$

which contains more 0s than (3.11). On the average, an n-bit twos-complement number contains $n/2$ 0s. The canonical signed digit representation, however, contains an average of $2n/3$ 0s, indicating that one-third fewer add-subtract operations are required.

Input			Output		Comments
x_{i-1}	x_i	m	x_i^*	m	
0	0	0	0	0	
0	1	0	1	0	x_i is an isolated 1
1	0	0	0	0	
1	1	0	$\bar{1}$	1	x_i begins a run of 1s
0	0	1	1	0	x_i begins a run of 0s
0	1	1	0	1	
1	0	1	$\bar{1}$	1	x_i is an isolated 0
1	1	1	0	1	

Figure 3.33 Rules for forming the canonical signed-digit representation of a number.

Combinational array multipliers For moderate values of n, for example, $n \leq 16$, it is feasible to perform multiplication using combinational logic [23]. For simplicity, only unsigned positive integers will be considered. Suppose that $X = x_0 x_1 \ldots x_{n-1}$ and $Y = y_0 y_1 \ldots y_{n-1}$ are to be multiplied. Their product can be expressed as

$$P = \sum_{i=0}^{n-1} x_i 2^{n-1-i} Y \qquad (3.12)$$

corresponding to the usual bit-by-bit multiplication (cf. Fig. 3.29). Now (3.12) can be rewritten as

$$P = \sum_{i=0}^{n-1} 2^{n-1-i} \left(\sum_{j=0}^{n-1} x_i y_j 2^{n-1-j} \right) \qquad (3.13)$$

Each of the n^2 1-bit products $x_i y_j$ in (3.13) may be computed by a two-input AND gate. (Note that the arithmetic and logical products coincide in the 1-bit case.) Hence an $n \times n$ array of two-input ANDs of the type shown in Fig. 3.34

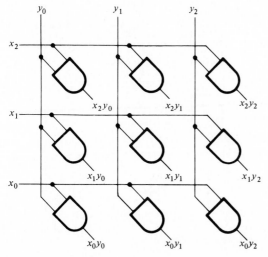

Figure 3.34 AND array for a 3-bit combinational multiplier.

can compute the $x_i y_j$ terms. The summation of these terms is accomplished according to (3.13) by an array of $n(n-1)$ full adders, as illustrated in Fig. 3.35. The shifts implied by the 2^{n-1-i} and 2^{n-1-j} factors in (3.13) are implemented by the spatial displacement of the full adders.

The full adder array is essentially a two-dimensional ripple carry adder. The multiplication time is clearly determined by the worst-case carry propagation and can be expressed as

$$2(n-1)d + d'$$

where d and d' are the propagation delays of a full adder and an AND gate, respectively. Note that the component cost of this multiplier increases as the square of n. However, the array organization makes it very suitable for manufacture using modern integrated circuits.

The functions of the AND gates and full adders may be combined in a single cell, as shown in Fig. 3.36. This cell can be viewed as evaluating the arithmetic expression

$$ac + b + d$$

n^2 cells of this type can easily be used to construct an array multiplier of uniform structure. Other multiplication schemes, such as Booth's algorithm, can also be implemented by combinational arrays, but the cells required are more complex (see Prob. 3.10).

Carry-save multiplication An n-bit carry-save adder consists of n disjoint full adders. Its input is three n-bit numbers to be added, while the output consists of the n sum bits forming a word S and the n carry bits forming a word C. Unlike the adders discussed so far, there is no carry propagation within the adder. S and C may be fed into another n-bit carry-save adder where, as shown in Fig.

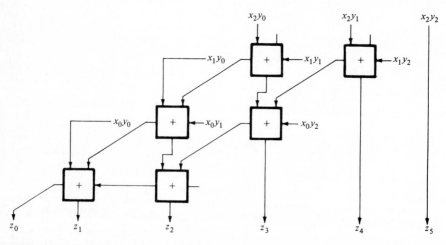

Figure 3.35 Full adder array for a 3-bit combinational multiplier.

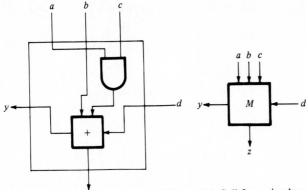

Figure 3.36 Cell for a simple array multiplier.

3.37, they may be added to a third n-bit number W. Note that the carry connections are shifted to the left to correspond to normal carry propagation. In general, m numbers can be added by a treelike network of carry-save adders to produce a result in the form (S, C). To obtain the final sum, S and C must be added by a conventional adder with carry propagation.

Multiplication can be performed using a multistage carry-save adder circuit of the type shown in Fig. 3.38. The inputs to the carry-save adder tree are n

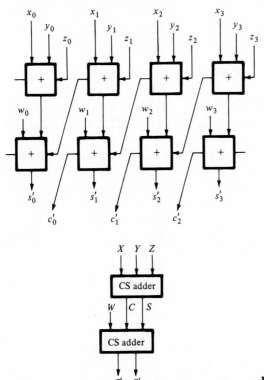

Figure 3.37 A two-stage carry-save adder.

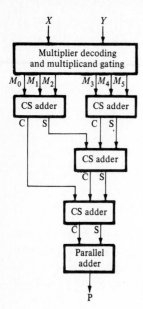

Figure 3.38 A carry-save multiplier.

terms of the form $M_i = x_i Y 2^{k-i}$. M_i represents the multiplicand Y multiplied by the ith multiplier bit weighted by the appropriate power of 2. For simplicity, assume that M_i is represented by $2n$ bits and that the full double-length product is required. The desired product P is given by

$$\sum_{i=0}^{n-1} M_i$$

This sum is computed by the carry-save adder tree, which produces a $2n$-bit sum and a $2n$-bit carry. The final carry assimilation is performed by a parallel adder with carry propagation.

The strictly combinational multiplier of Fig. 3.38 is practical for small n. For large n, the number of carry-save adders required may become excessive. Carry-save techniques may still be used if the multiplier is partitioned into k m-bit segments. Only m terms M_i are generated and added via the carry-save adder circuit. The process is repeated k times and the resulting sums are accumulated. The product is therefore obtained after k iterations. Carry-save multiplication appears to have first been used in the Whirlwind computer in the late 1940s. It is also particularly suitable for pipelined implementation and is used in some modern pipelined computers [16]. Carry-save multiplication is discussed further in Sec. 3.4.2 in the context of pipelining.

3.3.3 Fixed-Point Division

In fixed-point division two numbers, a divisor V and a dividend D, are given. The object is to compute a third number Q, called the quotient, such that $Q \times V$

equals or is close to D. For example, if integer formats are being used, Q is computed so that

$$D = Q \times V + R$$

where R, the remainder, is required to be of smaller magnitude than V, that is, $0 \leq |R| < V$. If fraction formats are used, the number of bits in the quotient is not necessarily bounded a priori. For example $0.2000 \div 0.3000 = 0.66666\ldots$, a repeating fraction. It is necessary, therefore, to limit the number of quotient bits generated by the division process. Division of 0.2000 by 0.3000 might thus be required to yield a four-digit quotient Q with truncation or rounding determining the final digit of Q. Division circuits are usually designed to yield quotients of some specified length. In most cases only the quotient Q is required, and the remainder R, which is generated as a by-product of the division, is discarded. R may be used to generate additional quotient digits if required via a second division operation $R \div V$. In this way successive fixed-length division instructions can be used to generate a more accurate quotient.

The relationship $D \approx Q \times V$ suggests that there is a close correspondence between division and multiplication, specifically that the dividend, quotient, and divisor correspond to the product, multiplicand, and multiplier, respectively. This correspondence means that similar algorithms and circuits can be used for multiplication and division. In multiplication the shifted multiplicand is added to yield the product. In division the shifted divisor is subtracted from the dividend to yield the quotient.

One of the simplest division methods is the sequential digit-by-digit algorithm similar to that used in pencil-and-paper methods. Figure 3.39 illustrates this approach. Suppose that the divisor V and dividend D are positive integers. The quotient $Q = q_0 q_1 q_2 \ldots$ is computed 1 bit at a time. At each step i, $2^{-i}V$, which represents the divisor shifted i bits to the right, is compared with the current partial remainder[4] R_i. The quotient bit q_i is set to $0(1)$ if $2^{-i}V$ is less (greater) than R_i; and a new partial remainder R_{i+1} is computed according to the relation

$$R_{i+1} \leftarrow R_i - q_i 2^{-i} V \qquad (3.14)$$

In machine implementations it is usually more convenient to shift the partial remainder to the left relative to a fixed divisor, in which case (3.14) is equivalent to

$$R_{i+1} \leftarrow 2R_i - q_i V$$

Figure 3.40 shows the calculation of Fig. 3.39 modified in this way. Note that the final partial remainder is the required remainder R shifted to the left, so that in Fig. 3.40, $R = 2^{-3}R_4$.

A central problem in division is determining the quotient digit q_i. If radix r numbers are being represented, then q_i must be chosen from among r possible

---

[4]R_i is also termed the partial dividend because it is used as the dividend in step $i + 1$.

values. When $r = 2$, q_i may be generated by comparing V and $2R_i$ in the ith step, as is done in Fig. 3.40. If $V > 2R_i$, then $q_i = 0$; otherwise $q_i = 1$. If V is long, a combinational comparator circuit may be impractical, in which case q_i is usually determined by subtracting V from $2R_i$ and examining the sign of $2R_i - V$. If $2R_i - V$ is negative, $q_i = 0$; otherwise $q_i = 1$.

<table>
<tr><td></td><td style="text-align:right">0111</td><td>Quotient $Q = q_0q_1q_2q_3$</td></tr>
<tr><td>Divisor V</td><td>101) 100110</td><td>Dividend $D = R_0$</td></tr>
<tr><td></td><td>000</td><td>q_0V</td></tr>
<tr><td></td><td>100110</td><td>R_1</td></tr>
<tr><td></td><td>101</td><td>$q_1 2^{-1}V$</td></tr>
<tr><td></td><td>10010</td><td>R_2</td></tr>
<tr><td></td><td>101</td><td>$q_2 2^{-2}V$</td></tr>
<tr><td></td><td>1000</td><td>R_3</td></tr>
<tr><td></td><td>101</td><td>$q_3 2^{-3}V$</td></tr>
<tr><td></td><td>011</td><td>$R_4 =$ remainder R</td></tr>
</table>

Figure 3.39 Typical pencil-and-paper method for division of positive integers.

Divisor V			Quotient Q
101	100110	Dividend $= 2R_0$	
	000	q_0V	0
	100110	R_1	
	1001100	$2R_1$	
	101	q_1V	01
	100100	R_2	
	1001000	$2R_2$	
	101	q_2V	011
	100000	R_3	
	1000000	$2R_3$	0111
	101	q_3V	
	011000	$R_4 = 2^3R$	

Figure 3.40 The division of Fig. 3.39 modified for machine implementation.

Basic dividers The circuits used for multiplication in Examples 2.1 and 2.2 can easily be modified to perform division, as shown in Fig. 3.41. The pair of n-bit shift registers A, Q is used to store the partial remainders. Initially the dividend (which may be $2n$ bits in length) is placed in these registers. The divisor V is placed in the M register where it remains throughout the division process. In each step A, Q is shifted to the left. The cells vacated at the rightmost end of the Q register can be used to store the quotient bits as they are generated.

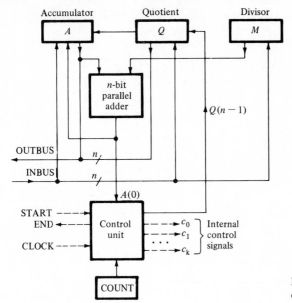

Accumulator   Quotient   Divisor

Figure 3.41 Block diagram of a sequential divider.

When the division process terminates, Q contains the quotient while A contains the (shifted) remainder.

As noted already, the quotient bit q_i may be determined by a trial subtraction of the form $2R_i - V$. This trial subtraction also yields the new partial remainder R_{i+1} when $2R_i - V$ is positive, i.e., when $q_i = 1$. Clearly, the process of determining q_i and R_{i+1} may be integrated. Two major division algorithms are distinguished by the way in which they combine the computation of q_i and R_{i+1}. If $q_i = 0$, then the result of the trial subtraction is $2R_i - V$; however, the required new partial remainder R_{i+1} is $2R_i$. R_{i+1} may be obtained by adding V back to the result of the trial subtraction. This straightforward technique is called *restoring division*. Figure 3.42 shows a restoring division algorithm for positive integers that uses the circuit of Fig. 3.41. In every step the operation

$$R_{i+1} \leftarrow 2R_i - V$$

is performed. When the result of the subtraction is negative, a restoring addition is performed as follows:

$$R_{i+1} \leftarrow R_{i+1} + V$$

If the probability of $q_i = 1$ is 1/2, then this algorithm requires n subtractions and an average of $n/2$ additions.

The restoration step of the foregoing algorithm is eliminated in a slightly different technique called *nonrestoring division*. It is based on the observation that a restoration of the form

$$R_i \leftarrow R_i + V \tag{3.15}$$

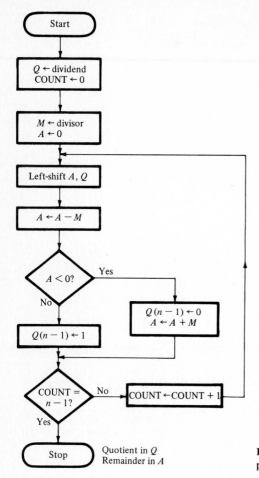

Figure 3.42 Restoring division algorithm for positive integers.

is followed in the next step by a subtraction

$$R_{i+1} \leftarrow 2R_i - V \qquad (3.16)$$

(3.15) and (3.16) can be merged into the single operation

$$R_{i+1} \leftarrow 2R_i + V \qquad (3.17)$$

Thus when $q_i = 1$, which is indicated by a positive value of R_i, R_{i+1} is computed using (3.16). When $q_i = 0$, R_{i+1} is computed using (3.17). Each quotient bit calculation requires either an addition or a subtraction but not both. Nonrestoring division therefore requires n additions and subtractions, whereas restoring division requires an average of $3n/2$ additions and subtractions. Figure 3.43 contains a flowchart for nonrestoring division using the circuit of Fig. 3.41.

The restoring and nonrestoring algorithms just described can be extended in a straightforward way to handle both positive and negative numbers. This ex-

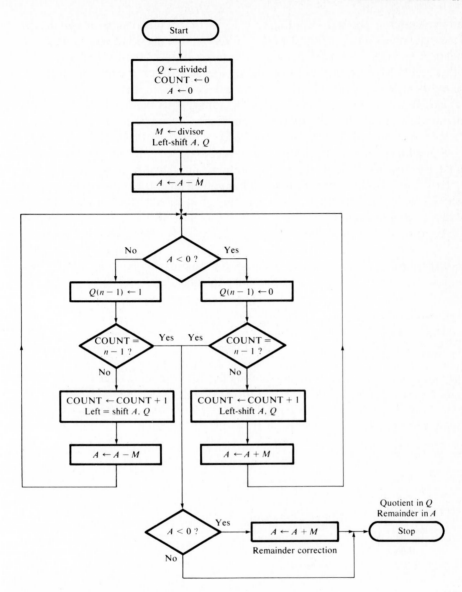

Figure 3.43 Nonrestoring division algorithm for positive integers.

tension is essentially similar to that required in the multiplication algorithms examined earlier. Sign-magnitude numbers present no difficulties since the magnitudes of the quotient and remainder can be computed as in the positive-number case, while their signs can be determined separately. The modifications required to handle division involving negative twos-complement numbers is left as an exercise (see Prob. 3.12). As in the twos-complement multiplication algorithm of Example 2.2, it may be necessary to correct the result (quotient and remainder) in the last step. Figure 3.44 illustrates the main issues involved. Here a positive dividend $D = 0.1011_2 = 0.6875_{10}$ is being divided by a negative divisor $V = 1.0001_2 = -0.9375_{10}$ using the nonrestoring algorithm of Fig. 3.43 with suitable changes. Since V is negative, a trial addition is used to determine the quotient bit q_i. If $q_i = 1$, V is subtracted from $2R_i$ in step $i + 1$. Note that it is necessary to correct the quotient by adding 1 to the least significant bit position. The final contents of the A register is the remainder multiplied by 2^4. Thus we conclude that $0.1011 \div 1.0001 = 1.0101 + 0.00001011$.

Since the length of the quotient is not necessarily bounded, division is terminated when a sufficient number of quotient bits have been generated. The quotient may then be rounded off (which involves an extra addition or subtraction) to obtain the final result. Note that the quotient is undefined when $V = 0$. Division circuits usually test the divisor at the start of the division process. If $V = 0$, no division is performed and a divide-by-zero error indication is given.

High-speed dividers The methods discussed for increasing multiplication speed can also be modified to speed up division, specifically,

1. High-speed addition and subtraction
2. High-speed shifting
3. Simultaneous division by several divider bits

The major difficulty of division is selecting the quotient bit q_i. If division is performed k bits at a time, i.e., the radix of the number system is 2^k, then q_i may have 2^k values. q_i is usually determined by a trial-and-error process, as is evident in the restoring binary division algorithm (restoration "corrects" an erro-

V	A	Q	Comments
1.0001	0.1011		
	1.0001		Add V
	1.1100	1.	
	1.1000		Shift A
	1.0001		Subtract V
	0.0111		
	0.1110	1.0	Shift A
	1.0001		Add V
	1.1111	1.01	
	1.1110		Shift A
	1.0001		Subtract V
	0.1101	1.010	
	1.1010		Shift A
	1.0001		Add V
$2^4R =$	0.1011	1.0100	
		1	Add 1 to correct Q
		1.0101	$= Q$

Figure 3.44 Example of twos-complement division using the nonrestoring approach.

neous choice of q_i) and in the usual pencil-and-paper method for decimal division.

An efficient division algorithm was devised independently by D. Sweeney, J. E. Robertson, and K. D. Tocher about 1958. It is called *SRT division* in their honor. Two of the key features of this method are

1. Normalization of the divisor and partial remainders
2. Use of a signed digit quotient representation

Assume that numbers are represented as twos-complement fractions $X = x_0.x_1x_2 \cdots x_n$, where x_0 determines the sign, as before. X is normalized when $x_0 \neq x_1$. If x is normalized, then $1/2 \leq |X| < 1$. In SRT division the divisor V is first normalized. In the basic division algorithms, the partial remainder R_i is left-shifted and compared to V in order to determine the quotient digit q_i. In SRT division, however, q_i is determined directly from the two leftmost bits of the shifted partial remainder $2R_i$ using the rules

$$q_i = 1 \qquad \text{if } 2R_i \geq 1/2$$

$$q_i = \overline{1} \qquad \text{if } -2R_i < -1/2$$

$$q_i = 0 \qquad \text{otherwise}$$

If $q_i = 1(\overline{1})$, the divisor V is added to (subtracted from) $2R_i$ to form the new partial remainder R_{i+1}. No operation is performed when $q_i = 0$. Since $q_i = 1$ or $\overline{1}$ only when $2R_i$ is normalized, the algorithm can be viewed as normalizing the partial remainder between successive addition or subtraction operations. This normalization corresponds to shifting over runs of leading 0s or 1s, an operation which can be accelerated to reduce the overall division time. The analysis of SRT division is complex, so the interested reader is referred to the Refs. 13, 15, and 25 for further details.

Combinational array dividers Combinational arrays can be used for division as well as multiplication. Figure 3.45 shows a cell D suitable for implementing a version of the restoring division algorithm. The cell is basically a full subtracter with t and u being the borrow-in and borrow-out bits, respectively. The main output z is controlled by input a. When $a = 0$, z is the difference bit defined by

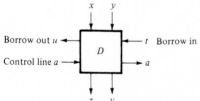

Figure 3.45 A cell for array implementation of restoring division.

the arithmetic equation $z = x - (y + t)$; when $a = 1$, $z = x$. Thus the behavior of the cell D is defined by the logic equations

$$z = x \oplus \bar{a}(y \oplus t)$$

$$u = \bar{x}y + \bar{x}t + yt$$

Figure 3.46 shows an array of D cells that divides two 3-bit positive numbers and generates a 5-bit quotient. Each row of the array subtracts the divisor V from the shifted partial remainder $2R_i$ generated by the row above it. The sign of the result, and therefore the quotient bit, is indicated by the borrow-out signal from the leftmost cell in the row. This signal u_i is connected to the control inputs a of all cells in the same row. If $u_i = 0$, then the output from the row is $2R_i - V$ and $q_i = \bar{u}_i = 1$. If $u_i = 1$, then the output from the row is restored to $2R_i$ and again $q_i = \bar{u}_i = 0$. Thus the output of each row is initially $2R_i - V$, but it is restored to $2R_i$ if required. Note that restoration is achieved by overriding the subtraction performed by the row rather than by explicitly adding back the divisor.

Let d and d' be the carry propagation and restore times of a cell, respectively. Let the divisor and dividend be n bits long. Each row of the divider array functions as an n-bit ripple borrow subtracter; hence the maximum time required to compute one quotient bit is $nd + d'$. The time required to compute

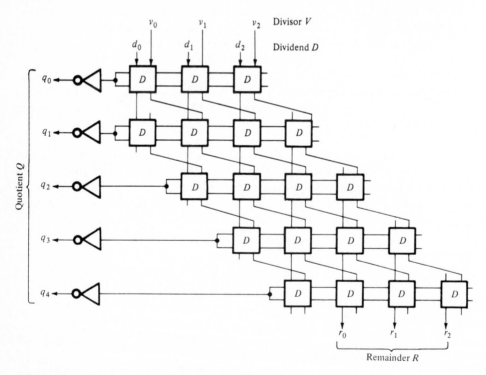

Figure 3.46 A divider array for 3-bit positive numbers using the cell of Fig. 3.45.

an m-bit quotient and the corresponding remainder is therefore $m(nd + d')$, and the number of cells required is $m(n + 1) - 1$.

Division by repeated multiplication In systems containing a high-speed multiplier, division can be performed efficiently and at low cost using repeated multiplication. In each iteration, a factor F_i is generated and used to multiply both the divisor V and the dividend D. F_i is so chosen that the sequence $V \times F_0 \times F_1 \times F_2 \cdots$ converges rapidly toward 1. This implies that $D \times F_0 \times F_1 \times F_2 \cdots$ converges toward the desired quotient Q, since

$$Q = \frac{D \times F_0 \times F_1 \times F_2 \cdots}{V \times F_0 \times F_1 \times F_2 \cdots}$$

If the denominator converges towards 1, the numerator must also converge towards Q.

The convergence of the method depends on the selection of F_i. For simplicity, assume that D and V are positive normalized fractions so that $V = 1 - x$, where $x < 1$. Set $F_0 = 1 + x$. We can now write

$$V \times F_0 = (1 - x)(1 + x) = 1 - x^2$$

Clearly $V \times F_0$ is closer to 1 than V. Next set $F_1 = 1 + x^2$. Hence

$$V \times F_0 \times F_1 = (1 - x^2)(1 + x^2) = 1 - x^4$$

and so on. Let V_i denote $V \times F_0 \times F_1 \times \cdots \times F_i$. The multiplication factor at each stage is computed as follows:

$$F_i = 2 - V_{i-1}$$

which is simply the twos-complement of V_i. It follows that $F_i = 1 + x^{2^i}$ and $V_i = 1 - x^{2^{i+1}}$. As i increases, V_i converges rapidly toward 1. The process terminates when $V_i = 0.11 \cdots 11$, the number closest to 1 for the given word size.

3.3.4 ALU Design

The various circuits used in the execution of instructions by a processor are frequently combined in a single unit called an arithmetic-logic unit, or ALU. Generally the complexity of the ALU is determined by the manner in which arithmetic instructions are executed. Extensive sharing of arithmetic circuits is possible if similar algorithms are used for the various operations, particularly for multiplication and division.

Figure 3.47 shows one of the most widely used ALU designs. (For simplicity, the relatively trivial circuits used for nonarithmetic operations are omitted.) This ALU organization is found in the IAS computer (see Fig. 1.13) and in many computers built after IAS. It is intended to implement multiplication and division using one of the sequential digit-by-digit shift and add-subtract algorithms discussed earlier. Three one-word registers are used for operand storage: the accumulator AC, the multiplier-quotient register MQ, and the data

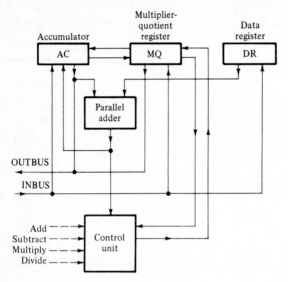

Figure 3.47 Structure of a typical fixed-point ALU.

register DR. AC and MQ are organized as a single register AC, MQ capable of left- and right-shifting. The main additional data-processing capability is provided by a parallel adder that derives its inputs from AC and DR and places its results in AC. The MQ register is so-called because it stores the multiplier during multiplication and the quotient during division. DR stores the multiplicand or divisor, while the result (product or quotient and remainder) is stored in AC, MQ. The use typically made of these registers may be defined concisely as follows:

Addition:	$AC \leftarrow AC + DR$
Subtraction:	$AC \leftarrow AC - DR$
Multiplication:	$AC, MQ \leftarrow DR \times MQ$
Division:	$AC, MQ \leftarrow MQ \div DR$

Bit-sliced ALUs It is possible to manufacture an entire fixed-point ALU on a single IC chip. Pin requirements limit such one-chip ALUs to short word sizes, e. g., 2 or 4 bits. Although these word sizes may appear too small to be of practical value, an ALU can easily be designed so that it is directly expandable to handle words of arbitrary length. Specifically, k m-bit ALUs may be combined in a simple manner to form a single ALU capable of processing km-bit words. The resulting ALU is called *bit-sliced*, since each component ALU processes an independent "slice" of m bits from each km-bit operand. The use of bit-sliced ALUs has the advantage that a user can design a general-purpose processor with any desired word size simply by choosing the appropriate number of bit slices.

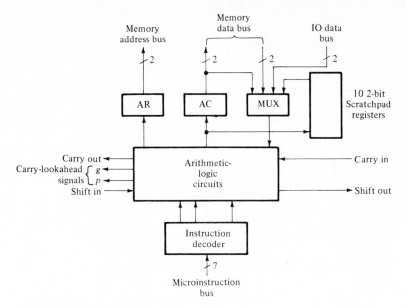

Figure 3.48 Intel 3002 2-bit ALU slice.

Example 3.2: The Intel 3002 ALU [20] Figure 3.48 shows a slightly simplified block diagram of a typical ALU bit slice, the Intel 3002 central processing element. The 3002 performs conventional arithmetic, logical, and data-transfer operations on 2-bit slices. It is designed to work with an external microprogram control unit (the 3001 chip) from which it receives microinstructions indicating the function to be performed. The 3002 can perform the Boolean operations AND, OR, EXCLUSIVE-NOR (EQUIVALENCE), and NOT. Its repertoire of arithmetic instructions comprises add, subtract, increment, and decrement using twos-complement operands. A right-shift operation can also be performed. There is a 2-bit accumulator AC, a 2-bit memory address register AR, and a set of 10 addressable scratch-pad registers.

Boolean operations involve no interaction between adjacent bits or bit slices of a word. The arithmetic and shift operations, however, require communication between adjacent bit slices, for which purpose six special data lines are included in the ALU chip. The carry-in and carry-out lines permit ripple carry propagation between adjacent slices. In order to reduce carry propagation time when long words are being processed, the 3002 also computes the g and p signals required for carry lookahead (see Sec. 3.3.2). These may be fed into a carry-lookahead circuit such as the Intel 3003 chip, which provides eight stages of carry lookahead. Finally, two lines called shift in and shift out are provided to implement right shifting. Figure 3.49 shows an 8-bit ALU constructed from four 3002 chips using the carry-lookahead facility instead of ripple carry.

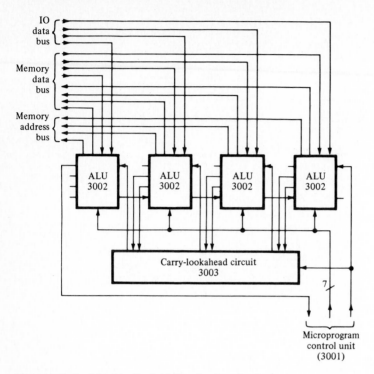

Figure 3.49 An 8-bit bit-sliced ALU using four Intel 3002's.

3.3.5 Floating-Point Arithmetic

Let (X_M, X_E) be the floating-point representation of a number X. Hence $X = X_M \times B^{X_E}$. To simplify the discussion, the following realistic assumptions are made:

1. X_M is an n_M-bit twos-complement fraction
2. X_E is an n_E-bit integer in excess -2^{n_E-1} code
3. $B = 2$

It is also assumed that floating-point numbers are stored in normalized form only; hence the results of all floating-point arithmetic operations should be normalized.

The basic formulas used to perform floating-point addition, subtraction, multiplication, and division are given in Fig. 3.50. Multiplication and division are relatively simple, since the mantissas and exponents can be processed independently. Floating-point multiplication requires a fixed-point multiplication of the mantissas and a fixed-point addition of the exponents. Floating-point division requires a fixed-point division involving the mantissas and a fixed-

Addition: $\qquad X + Y = (X_M 2^{X_E - Y_E} + Y_M) \times 2^{Y_E}$

Subtraction: $\qquad X - Y = (X_M 2^{X_E - Y_E} - Y_M) \times 2^{Y_E}$

$$\left. \right\} \quad \text{where } X_E \leq Y_E$$

Multiplication: $\quad X \times Y = (X_M \times Y_M) \times 2^{X_E + Y_E}$

Division: $\qquad X \div Y = (X_M \div Y_M) \times 2^{X_E - Y_E}$

Figure 3.50 The four basic arithmetic operations for floating-point numbers.

point subtraction involving the exponents. Thus multiplication and division are not significantly more difficult to implement than the corresponding fixed-point operations. Floating-point addition and subtraction are complicated by the fact that the exponents of the two input operands must be made equal before the corresponding mantissas can be added or subtracted. As suggested by Fig. 3.50, this can be done by right-shifting the mantissa X_M associated with the smaller exponent X_E a total of $Y_E - X_E$ positions to form a new mantissa $X_M 2^{X_E - Y_E}$ which can then be combined with Y_M. Thus addition and subtraction require the following three steps.

1. Compute $Y_E - X_E$ (a fixed-point subtraction)
2. Shift X_M $Y_E - X_E$ places to form $X_M 2^{X_E - Y_E}$
3. Compute $X_M 2^{X_E - Y_E} \pm Y_M$ (a fixed-point addition or subtraction)

An extra step is needed for each of the four floating-point arithmetic operations in order to normalize the result. A number $X = (X_M, X_E)$ is normalized by left-shifting (right-shifting) X_M and decrementing (incrementing) X_E by 1 for each one-digit shift. As noted in Sec. 3.3.1, a twos-complement fraction is normalized when the sign bit x_0 differs from the bit x_1 on its right. This fact may be used to terminate the normalization process. A sign-magnitude fraction is normalized by left-shifting the magnitude part until there are no leading 0s, that is, until $x_1 = 1$. (Note that the normalization rules are different if the base B differs from 2.)

Several minor problems are associated with the use of exponent biasing. If exponents are added or subtracted using ordinary integer arithmetic in the course of a calculation, the resulting exponent is doubly biased and must be corrected by subtracting the bias. For example, let the exponent length be 4, so that the bias is $2^{4-1} = 8$. The possible exponent values are listed in Fig. 3.10. Suppose that $X_E = +7$ and $Y_E = -3$ are to be added. If ordinary integer addition is used, we obtain the following (ignoring the sign bits).

$$
\begin{array}{rl}
& \text{Unbiased equivalent} \\
X_E = 1111 & 15 = 7 + 8 \\
X_Y = 0101 & 5 = -3 + 8 \\
\hline
10100 & 20 = 4 + 8 + 8
\end{array}
$$

The integer sum 10100 is now corrected by subtracting the bias 1000 to produce 1100, which is the correct biased representation of $X_E + Y_E = 4$. Of course, the correction step could be avoided by using an excess-eight adder. Another problem arises from the all-0 representation required of zero. If $X \times Y$ is computed as $(X_M \times Y_M) \times 2^{X_E + Y_E}$ and either X_M or Y_M is zero, the resulting product has an all-0 mantissa but may not have an all-0 exponent. A special step is then required to set the exponent bits to 0.

All the floating-point operations can lead to overflow or underflow if the result is too large or too small to be represented. Overflow or underflow resulting from mantissa operations can usually be corrected by shifting the mantissa of the result and modifying its exponent. This is done automatically during floating-point processing. If, however, the exponent ever overflows or underflows, an appropriate error indication must be generated.

Floating-point arithmetic units Floating-point arithmetic may be implemented by two loosely connected fixed-point arithmetic circuits, an exponent unit and a mantissa unit, as suggested in Fig. 3.51. The mantissa unit is required to perform all four basic operations on the mantissas; hence a general-purpose fixed-point arithmetic unit such as that of Fig. 3.47 can be used. A simpler circuit capable of only adding, subtracting, and comparing exponents suffices for the exponent unit. Exponent comparison may be performed by a comparator or else by subtracting the exponents. Figure 3.52 shows the general structure of a floating-point arithmetic unit employing the latter approach. The exponents of the input operands are placed in registers $E1$ and $E2$, which are connected to a parallel adder that permits $E1 \pm E2$ to be computed. The exponent comparison required for floating-point addition and subtraction is performed by computing $E1 - E2$ and placing it in a counter E. The larger exponent is then determined by the sign of E. Furthermore, the shifting of one mantissa required before the mantissa addition or subtraction can take place is easily controlled by E. The magnitude of E is sequentially decremented to zero. After each decrement, the appropriate mantissa (whose location in the mantissa unit varies with the operation being performed) is shifted one digit position. Once the mantissas have been aligned, they are processed in the normal manner. The exponent of the result is also computed and placed in E.

Although the scheme of Fig. 3.52 is conceptually simple, it has the disadvantage that it can be used for n-bit (one-word) floating-point operations only,

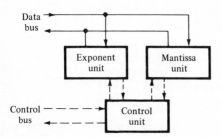

Figure 3.51 A floating-point arithmetic unit viewed as two fixed-point arithmetic units.

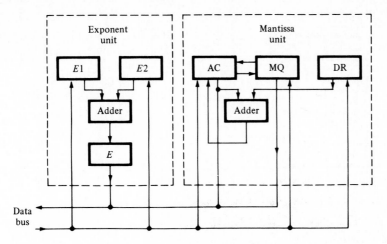

Figure 3.52 Data-processing part of a simple floating-point arithmetic unit.

even though it has most of the facilities required for n-bit fixed-point operations. Since all computers with floating-point instructions also have fixed-point instructions, it is often desirable to design a single unit for both fixed-point and floating-point instruction execution. In principle, this is not difficult, although a more complicated control unit is needed. Essentially it has the form of a one-word fixed-point arithmetic unit in which the registers and the adder can be partitioned into exponent and mantissa parts when floating-point operations are being performed. Figure 3.53 shows the main components of such a system.

Floating-point addition and subtraction We now consider the implementation of addition and subtraction in more detail. Multiplication and division are simpler to implement and so will not be considered further. Figure 3.54 contains an addition and subtraction algorithm designed for the circuit of Fig. 3.52. The mantissa is assumed to be a twos-complement fraction, and the exponent a biased

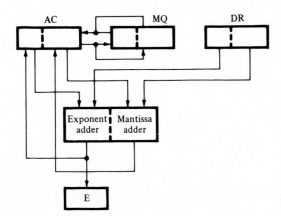

Figure 3.53 A combined fixed-point and floating-point arithmetic unit.

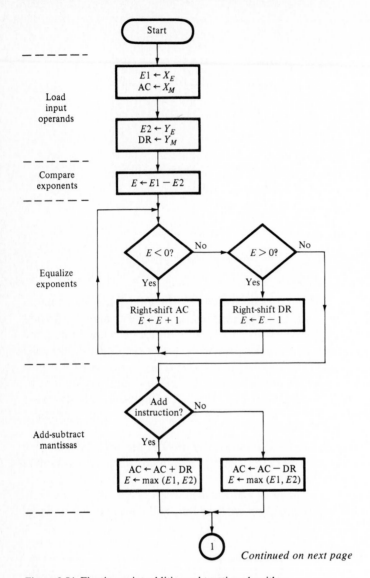

Figure 3.54 Floating-point addition-subtraction algorithm.

integer. The base B is 2. The algorithm involves four main steps:

1. Comparison of the exponents by subtraction
2. Alignment of the mantissas by shifting
3. Addition or subtraction of the mantissas
4. Normalization of the result

Tests are performed for overflow and for a zero mantissa in the result. If a zero

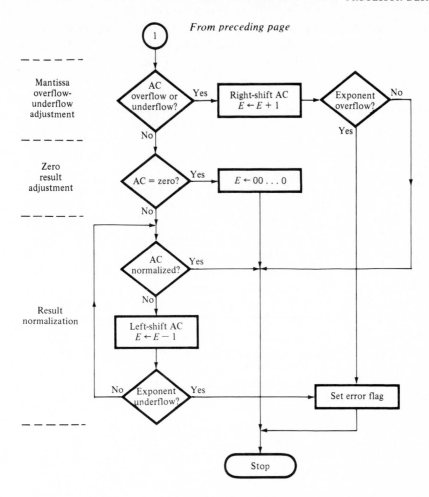

From preceding page

mantissa is detected, the exponent of the result is set to a sequence of 0s, which in biased code represents the smallest possible exponent.

Several points should be noted about the comparison of exponents and mantissa alignment. If E is no larger than $E1$ and $E2$, the initial test subtraction $E1 - E2$ can result in overflow or underflow. Even when no overflow or underflow occurs, $|E|$ may be very large, indicating that one of the two numbers is insignificant compared with the other. If $|E|$ exceeds n_M, the number of mantissa bits, the shifting process to align one mantissa, say X_M in AC, will eventually result in $AC = 0$, so that the result of the addition or subtraction will be $0 \pm Y_M$. Note also that it would be more efficient to terminate the shifting after n_M steps instead of $|E|$ steps, as is done in Fig. 3.54. A shift counter could be included in the design to implement this.

We conclude with a description of the floating-point adder used in a high-performance scientific computer, the IBM System/360 Model 91. (This machine was withdrawn by IBM shortly after its announcement in 1965). Two separate floating-point arithmetic units are employed in this machine, one for addition and subtraction (the add unit), the other for multiplication and division (the multiply-divide unit). For a description of the multiply-divide unit see Refs. 2 and 24.

Example 3.3: Floating-point adder of the IBM S/360 Model 91 computer [2] The data-processing part of the adder (with minor simplifications) is shown in Fig. 3.55. It is designed to add or subtract floating-point numbers with the 32-bit format of Fig. 3.11, and also 64-bit "long" floating-point numbers which have a 56-bit mantissa but are otherwise the same. The general algorithm of Fig. 3.54 is used with some changes to increase speed. In particular, the shifting required to align the mantissas and subsequently to normalize their sum is carried out by combinational circuits, called (*barrel*) *shifters*. These shifters allow k hexadecimal digits (recall that base 16 rather than base 2 is used in the S/360) to be shifted simultaneously. The corresponding subtraction of k from the exponent required in normalization is also achieved in one step by using an additional adder (adder 3).

The operation of this unit will now be described. The exponents of the input operands are placed in registers $E1$ and $E2$ and the corresponding mantissas are placed in $M1$ and $M2$. Next $E2$ is subtracted from $E1$ using adder 1, and the result is used to select the mantissa to be right-shifted

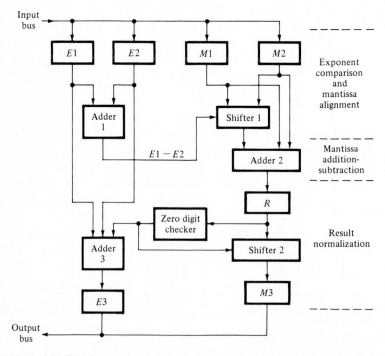

Figure 3.55 Floating-point adder of the IBM S/360 Model 91.

by shifter 1, and also to determine the length of the shift. For example, if $E1 > E2$ and $E1 - E2 = k$, $M1$ is right-shifted by k digit positions, that is, $4k$ bit positions. The shifted mantissa is then added to or subtracted from the other mantissa using adder 2, a 56-bit parallel adder with several levels of carry lookahead. The resulting sum or difference is placed in a temporary register R where it is examined by a special combinational circuit called the zero digit checker. The output z of this circuit indicates the number of leading zero digits (or leading F's in the case of negative numbers) of the number in R. z is then used to control the final normalization step. The output of R is left-shifted z digits by shifter 2 and the result is placed in register $M3$. The corresponding adjustment is made to the exponent by subtracting z using adder 3. In the event that $R = 0$ adder 3 can be used to set all bits of $E3$ to 0, which denotes an exponent of -64.

3.4 PARALLEL PROCESSING

3.4.1 Introduction

The term parallel processing is used in a very general sense to cover methods that involve a deliberate attempt to increase speed by performing computations simultaneously or in parallel. Like any type of processing, parallel processing can be viewed at various levels of complexity. At the gate level, for example, a distinction is made between serial arithmetic, which involves computing numbers one bit at a time, and parallel arithmetic, in which all bits of a number are computed simultaneously. (Compare the serial and parallel adders described in Sec. 3.3.2.) At the register level, the basic unit of information is the word, so one can distinguish serial machines which compute one word at a time from parallel machines which can compute several words simultaneously. Finally, at the processor level where the information unit is a block of words, e.g., a program or data set, a parallel machine can process several blocks of information simultaneously.

All modern computers involve some parallelism. Whether or not a computer is termed parallel is a matter of degree only, and is therefore highly subjective. Early machines such as the EDVAC (see Sec. 1.3.2), which processed bits serially at the gate level, were called serial computers. Later machines such as the IAS computer, were termed parallel computers. The introduction of IO processors added a new element of parallelism, permitting IO instructions and non-IO instructions to be executed simultaneously. Nowadays the term *parallel computer* is reserved for two types of machines:

1. Multiprocessors, i. e., computers with more than one CPU
2. Computers with a single CPU that is capable of executing several instructions or computing several distinct data items simultaneously

In this chapter, the term parallel processor will be used for a CPU or portion thereof capable of processing more than one instruction or set of operands simultaneously at the register level.

Increasing the level of parallelism in a processor increases its potential operating speed. The amount of hardware required also increases and with it the cost of the system. Since recent technological developments have reduced hardware costs to the point where it is economically feasible to build relatively large parallel processors, there is a great increase in interest in the design of such machines.

Types of parallel processors A typical processor (CPU) operates by fetching instructions and operands from main memory, executing the instructions, and placing the results in memory. The steps associated with processing the instruction form the instruction cycle (See Fig. 3.56). The instructions can be viewed as forming an *instruction stream* flowing from main memory to the processor, while the operands form another stream, the *data stream*, flowing between the processor and the memory, as depicted in Fig. 3.57.

M. J. Flynn has made an informal but useful classification of processor parallelism based on the number of simultaneous instruction and data streams seen by the processor during program execution [14]. Suppose that a processor P is operating at its maximum capacity so that its full degree of parallelism is being exhibited. Let $m_I(m_D)$ denote the minimum number of distinct instruction (data) streams which are being actively processed in any of the seven steps listed in Fig. 3.56. m_I and m_D are termed the instruction and data stream *multiplicities* of P and measure its degree of parallelism. Note that m_I and m_D are defined by the minimum number of streams at any point, since the most constrained components of the system (its bottlenecks) determine the overall parallel-processing capabilities.

Computers can be roughly divided into four major groups based on the values of m_I and m_D for their CPUs.

1. *Single instruction stream single data stream* (SISD): $m_I = m_D = 1$. Most conventional machines with one CPU containing a single arithmetic-logic unit capable only of scalar arithmetic fall into this category.

1. Generate the next instruction address.
2. Fetch the instruction.
3. Decode the instruction.
4. Generate the operand addresses.
5. Fetch the operands.
6. Execute the instruction.
7. Store the results.

Figure 3.56 Major steps in processing an instruction.

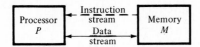

Figure 3.57 Instruction and data streams in a simple computer.

2. *Single instruction stream multiple data stream* (SIMD): $m_I = 1$, $m_D > 1$. This category includes machines with a single program control unit and multiple execution units such as ILLIAC IV. It also includes associative or content-addressable memory processors [30]. In such machines many stored data items may be accessed and processed simultaneously by a single instruction. The Goodyear STARAN is a commercially available computer designed around an associative processor.

3. *Multiple instruction stream single data stream* (MISD): $m_I > 1$, $m_D = 1$. The class of machines that can be placed in this category seems to be small. Pipeline processors may be considered to be MISD machines if the viewpoint is taken that each data item is processed by different instructions in different segments of a pipeline.

4. *Multiple instruction stream multiple data stream* (MIMD): $m_I > 1$, $m_D > 1$. This covers machines capable of executing several independent programs simultaneously. The class of MIMD machines appears to coincide with the class of multiprocessors.

It should be noted that the foregoing classification is based on a subjective distinction between control (instructions) and data, (see the discussion of these concepts in Sec. 2.1.1). The term stream is equally ill-defined. Hence it may not always be clear to which of the four classes a particular machine belongs. For a survey of other possible ways of classifying parallel processors, see Ref. 30.

Basic parallel processors A useful measure of the performance of a parallel processor is the (*data*) *bandwidth* or maximum throughput b_D measured in terms of the maximum number of results that can be generated per unit time. This is more appropriate than the instruction bandwidth or instruction execution time since it allows for the fact that one instruction may process many data streams. One measure often used for high-performance machines is the number of floating-point operations per second, or "flops". Composite terms such as megaflops (millions of floating-point operations per second) are also used.

Consider the behavior of a typical SISD processor P. For simplicity, assume that P performs a single operation I on a single input data stream D producing an output data stream D'. Furthermore let I be executed by m sequential steps (which may also be called phases, microoperations, or subprocesses) $S_1, S_2, \ldots, S_m$ depicted in Fig. 3.58. I may, for example, represent the complete processing of an instruction with the steps listed in Fig. 3.56, or it may be a single function such as floating-point addition.

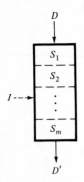

Figure 3.58 A simple *m*-stage processor *P* (SISD organization).

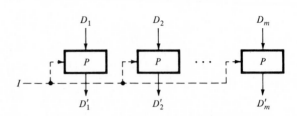

Figure 3.59 An *m*-unit processor with a single instruction stream (SIMD organization).

There are two major ways to increase the bandwidth b_D by introducing parallelism.

1. We can use *m* distinct copies of *P*, as shown in Fig. 3.59, and distribute the data operands uniformly among them. This effectively creates *m* separate data streams, so that the resulting processor has the SIMD organization. This machine will be called a *multiunit processor* with *m* units or, more simply, an *m-unit processor*. If each unit is supplied by an independent instruction stream, we obtain the more general MIMD organization shown in Fig. 3.60.

2. We can also physically separate the *m* functional stages of *P* so that each stage S_i, now called a *segment* of *P*, can operate on a distinct set of data operands. When S_i has computed its results, it passes its operands to S_{i+1} and receives a new set of operands from S_{i-1}. It is necessary to provide buffer registers between the various stages so that there is no interference between distinct sets of operands. The result is the *m-segment pipeline processor* depicted in Fig. 3.61. Pipelining increases the bandwidth by a factor of approximately *m*, since we may process up to *m* independent operand sets in the *m* segments or elements of the pipeline. The pipeline processor requires more hardware and more complex control circuitry than the original processor, but it often requires much less hardware than a comparable multiunit processor. The pipeline processor is usually consid-

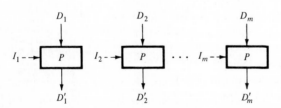

Figure 3.60 An *m*-unit processor with multiple instruction streams (MIMD organization).

ered to have the MISD organization since, as indicated in Fig. 3.61, the single data stream is acted upon by multiple (micro) instructions $i_1, i_2, \ldots, i_m$. However, it is not unreasonable to regard it as an SISD processor at the instruction I level.

In this chapter we will be mainly concerned with machines having a single CPU for which the multiunit and pipeline designs of Figs. 3.59 and 3.61 are most applicable. Multiprocessor systems having the structure depicted in Fig. 3.60 are discussed in Chap. 6.

3.4.2 Performance Considerations

It is useful to represent the behavior of a parallel processor by a *space-time diagram* which indicates hardware utilization as a function of time. Consider, for example, an m-unit processor P_1 of the type shown in Fig. 3.59, and an m-segment pipeline processor P_2 of the type shown in Fig. 3.61. Assume that P_1 and P_2 perform the same operation F and require times t_1 and t_2, respectively, to produce a result. Figure 3.62 shows space-time diagrams for these two processors, ignoring any setup time needed to initiate F. The shaded areas represent busy periods; the numbers they contain denote the particular set of operands or instructions being processed. Observe in the pipeline processor P_2 how each set of operands moves from segment to segment before emerging from the end. Figure 3.62 shows both processors operating at full capacity, which implies that there is no interaction between the operations being performed in the various elements or segments. This means that the instructions initiating these operations are independent.

Let T_1 and T_2 be the times required by P_1 and P_2, respectively, to execute n independent instructions of type F. Let $\lceil x \rceil$ denote the smallest integer

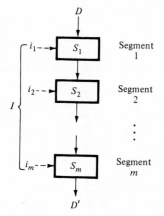

Figure 3.61 An m-segment pipeline processor (MISD organization).

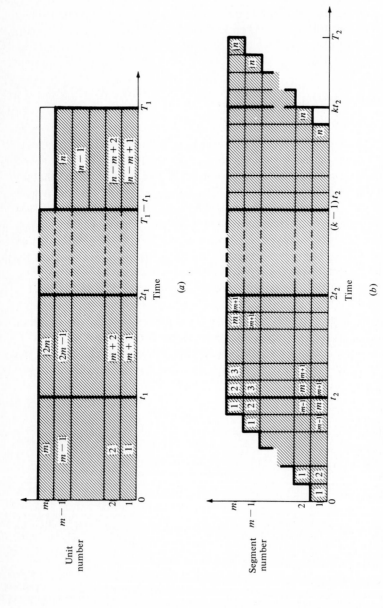

Figure 3.62 Space-time diagram for (*a*) a multiunit processor and (*b*) a pipeline processor.

greater than or equal to the number x. Clearly for the multiunit processor P_1,

$$T_1 = \left\lceil \frac{n}{m} \right\rceil t_1$$

so that its bandwidth b_{D_1} is given by

$$b_{D_1} = \frac{n}{T_1} = \frac{n}{\lceil n/m \rceil t_1}$$

which approaches m/t_1 as n increases. Now consider the pipeline processor P_2. Assume that the delay associated with each segment is t_2/m seconds. If P_2 implements the same algorithms and uses the same technologies as P_1, we can expect that $t_2 = t_1 + \delta$, where δ is a relatively small delay due primarily to the buffering between the segments of P_2. From Fig. 3.62b it can be deduced that

$$T_2 = \left\lceil \frac{n}{m} \right\rceil t_2 + \left[n - m \left(\left\lceil \frac{n}{m} \right\rceil - 1 \right) - 1 \right] \frac{t_2}{m}$$

where the second term in this expression represents the period from kt_2 to T_2 in the figure. As n increases, T_2 approaches nt_2/m; hence the bandwidth b_{D_2} approaches m/t_2. If $t_1 \approx t_2$, we conclude that $b_{D_1} \approx b_{D_2}$. Thus an m-unit processor and an m-segment pipeline processor using the same algorithms and technologies have approximately the same bandwidth. Since the cost of the pipeline is generally less when $m > 1$, the pipeline approach has been more widely used in commercial parallel computers.

Parallelism in programs The extent to which the inherent parallelism of a processor is utilized in any application depends on the independence of the items in the instruction and data streams arising from the application. Consider, for example, an instruction stream $I = I_1 I_2 \ldots I_n$ which is to be processed by a parallel processor capable of executing m instructions simultaneously. (It may be either a pipeline or a multiunit processor.) Ideally we would like to divide I into $\lceil n/m \rceil$ subsequences of m independent instructions so that all instructions in each of these subsequences can be processed concurrently. There are several factors which may prevent any two instructions, say I_1 and I_2, from being executed in parallel.

1. I_2 requires as input data a result computed by I_1—for example, if I_1 is $A \leftarrow f_1(X)$ and I_2 is $B \leftarrow f_1(A)$.
2. I_1 and I_2 both require a unique resource of the system, e. g., a memory area or a functional unit.
3. I_1 is a conditional branch instruction. The instruction required to follow I_1 (which could possibly be executed in parallel with it) is not known until I_1 has completed its execution.

The degree of parallel processing possible using ordinary computer programs has been the subject of considerable and rather inconclusive debate.

Amdahl has argued that typical programs contain too much essentially serial or irregular code for efficient parallel processing [1]. Kuck et al., on the other hand, present experimental evidence for the existence of a substantial amount of parallelism in ordinary programs [21]. There is, however, a large and important class of algorithms with a high degree of easily exploited parallelism, and parallel processors are generally designed with these algorithms in mind. Most involve vector and matrix processing of the kind associated with the solution of large sets of equations.

Consider, for example, the FORTRAN statement

$$\text{DO } 10 \text{ I} = 1, 1000$$

$$10 \quad C(I) = A(I) + B(I)$$

which represents a vector addition instruction. This statement involves 1000 independent additions, which can easily exploit any available parallel addition capability. Suppose that a four-segment floating-point pipeline adder is available with a bandwidth of $4/t$. If operand pairs $A(I)$, $B(I)$ are fed into the pipeline at the maximum possible rate, a result is obtained every $t/4$ seconds. The pipeline is then said to be in its *streaming* mode.

Now suppose that the same pipeline is to be used to compute

$$B = \sum_{I=1}^{16} A(I)$$

A FORTRAN program for this summation is

$$B = 0$$

$$\text{DO } 10 \text{ I} = 1, 16$$

$$10 \quad B = B + A(I)$$

which is equivalent to the program

$$B = 0$$

$$B = B + A(1)$$

$$B = B + A(2)$$

$$\cdots$$

$$B = B + A(16)$$

This sequence of 16 additions contains no explicit parallelism, since each addition derives its initial value of B from the preceding addition. In this form, the pipeline can perform the addition no more efficiently than a simple serial processor. However, the program can easily be restructured to take advantage of the available parallelism. The following program expressed in our informal register transfer language computes B in only five sequential steps.

t_1: $A(1) \leftarrow A(1) + A(2)$, $A(3) \leftarrow A(3) + A(4)$, $A(5) \leftarrow A(5) + A(6)$,
      $A(7) \leftarrow A(7) + A(8)$;

t_2: $A(9) \leftarrow A(9) + A(10)$, $A(11) \leftarrow A(11) + A(12)$, $A(13) \leftarrow A(13) + A(14)$,
      $A(15) \leftarrow A(15) + A(16)$;

t_3: $A(1) \leftarrow A(1) + A(3)$, $A(5) \leftarrow A(5) + A(7)$, $A(9) \leftarrow A(9) + A(11)$,
      $A(13) \leftarrow A(13) + A(15)$;

t_4: $A(1) \leftarrow A(1) + A(5)$, $A(9) \leftarrow A(9) + A(13)$;

t_5: $B \leftarrow A(1) + A(9)$;

Thus we see that parallelism can be exploited in some cases if an appropriate parallel algorithm can be found. Standard programming languages such as FORTRAN and ALGOL contain no facilities for specifying parallel operations; hence if programs in these languages are to be executed efficiently by parallel processors, compilers with the ability to detect implicit parallelism are required. Alternatively, programming languages can be developed which allow explicit specification of parallel operations. (Note that most register transfer languages allow some parallel operations to be specified. For example, in the language used in this book, parallel operations are separated by commas, whereas sequential operations are separated by semicolons.)

Vector operations Highly parallel pipelined computers like the CDC STAR-100 and the TI ASC are distinguished by the inclusion of vector operations in their instruction sets, in addition to the scalar instructions of conventional machines. A vector A of dimension n is a set of ordered words $[A(1), A(2), \ldots, A(n)]$. A typical vector instruction has the form $C \leftarrow f(A, B)$, where $C(I) \leftarrow f(A(I), B(I))$ for $I = 1$ through n. In machines with vector instructions, these n instructions are performed simultaneously or are overlapped to the extent allowed by the available parallelism.

Figure 3.63 lists some representative vector instructions from the instruction set of the ASC [27]. The characteristics of the vectors being processed are stored in a vector parameter file. These include the initial addresses of the vector operands A, B, C, that is, the addresses of $A(1)$, $B(1)$, and $C(1)$, and the dimension n, which is stored in a length field L. An instruction of the form $C \leftarrow f(A, B)$ is implemented as follows. The index I is set to 1. $A(I)$ and $B(I)$ are fetched and entered into a pipeline which computes $f(A(I), B(I))$. I is incremented, L is decremented, and the process is repeated until $L = 0$. When the result $f(A(I), B(I))$ emerges from the pipeline, it is stored in $C(I)$. The indices of A, B, and C may be incremented by different amounts if desired; the increments are specified in the vector parameter file. There are different versions of the various instructions for the four possible data formats: fixed-point, floating-point, single-precision (32 bits), double-precision (64 bits). The instructions listed in Fig. 3.63 refer to single-precision and, where applicable, fixed-point numbers only.

Mnemonic	Description
VA	Vector add: $C(I) \leftarrow A(I) + B(I)$ for $I = 1$ through n
VS	Vector subtract: $C(I) \leftarrow A(I) - B(I)$ for $I = 1$ through n
VM	Vector multiply: $C(I) \leftarrow A(I) \times B(I)$ for $I = 1$ through n
VD	Vector divide: $C(I) \leftarrow A(I) \div B(I)$ for $I = 1$ through n
VDP	Vector dot product: $C(1) = \sum_{I=1}^{n} A(I) \times B(I)$
VC	Vector arithmetic compare: compare $A(I)$ to $B(I)$ for $I = 1$ through n; set $C(I)$ to indicate greater than, less than, or equal
VAND	Vector logical AND: $C(I) \leftarrow A(I) \wedge B(I)$ for $I = 1$ through n
VMAX	Vector maximum: $C(I) \leftarrow \max(A(I), B(I))$ for $I = 1$ through n
VMG	Vector merge: $C \leftarrow [A(1), B(1), A(2), B(2), \ldots, A(n), B(n)]$
VL	Vector search for largest element; the index of the largest element in A is determined and stored at a specified address

Figure 3.63 Representative vector instructions from the TI ASC.

Additional performance measures It is of interest to determine the efficiency with which a parallel processor can be used to execute a particular program or set of programs Q. Let P_m denote a processor with instruction or data stream multiplicity m such as an m-unit processor or m-segment pipeline processor. Suppose that we can reduce Q to a sequence of operations $F_1, F_2, \ldots, F_n$ each of which exhibits the maximum degree of parallelism. Further suppose that each operation F_i can be performed in unit time provided a processor of multiplicity M_i or more is used. M_i therefore measures the inherent parallelism of F_i. Let Q be executed by P_m and let T_i^m be the time required by P_m to perform operation F_i. Assuming that F_i can be arbitrarily partitioned among the m available elements of P_m, we conclude that

$$T_i^m = 1 \qquad \text{if } m \geq M_i,$$

$$T_i^m = \left\lceil \frac{M_i}{m} \right\rceil \qquad \text{if } m < M_i$$

The improvement in processing time may be measured by the *processor speedup* s_m defined as the total execution time using the serial processor P_1 divided by the total execution time using P_m. For the program Q defined above,

$$s_m = \frac{\sum_{i=1}^{n} T_i^1}{\sum_{i=1}^{n} T_i^m} \tag{3.18}$$

The efficiency with which a program utilizes the available facilities of P_m is measured by the *processor utilization* u_m. This may be defined as the total space-time (number of processing elements multiplied by processing time) required by the program, divided by the total space-time available in P_m [7]. In terms of the program Q we have

$$u_m = \frac{\sum_{i=1}^{n} M_i}{m \sum_{i=1}^{n} T_i^m} \tag{3.19}$$

Since

$$\sum_{i=1}^{n} M_i = \sum_{i=1}^{n} T_i^1$$

(3.18) and (3.19) imply that

$$u_m = \frac{s_m}{m}$$

so that u_m can also be interpreted as the ratio of the actual speedup s_m to the maximum possible speedup m for any program. Figure 3.64 shows a representative plot of M_i for a program that exhibits modest parallelism. Figure 3.65 shows s_m and u_m plotted against m using the data provided by Fig. 3.64 and the foregoing equations. It can be seen that once m increases much beyond the average value of M_i (2.16 in this case), there is little further increase in s_m, while u_m continues to decline.

System requirements A computer using parallel processors to achieve very high throughput poses a number of special design problems. Chief among these is that of moving instructions and data to and from the processors and main memory at sufficiently high rates to keep the processors at or near their streaming modes. A possible solution is to partition main memory into indepen-

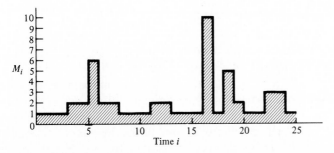

Figure 3.64 Plot of the maximum inherent parallelism of a program Q.

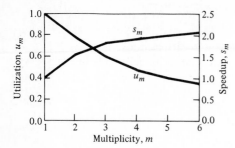

Figure 3.65 Processor utilization and speedup for the program of Fig. 3.64.

dently addressable modules or banks so that many words can be accessed simultaneously. Instruction and operand addresses should be distributed uniformly among the memory banks so that successive accesses are made to different memory modules; this is called address interleaving. A communications link of high bandwidth is also needed between the memory banks and the processors.

Just as instructions and data are carefully distributed among the memory modules, they must also be carefully distributed to the various processing elements. This requires the program control unit to schedule the tasks performed by the processing elements to minimize the number of conflicts and idle processors.

We now consider how some of these problems were tackled in the design of the CDC STAR-100, a supercomputer completed in the early 1970s. Although originally intended to be part of CDC's regular product line, only a few copies of the STAR-100 have been built to date.

Example 3.4: Information flow in the CDC STAR-100 computer [16] The STAR-100 is designed around a CPU containing two parallel pipeline processors for 64-bit floating-point operands. Processor 1 performs addition and multiplication. Processor 2 performs addition, multiplication, division, and square root extraction using pipeline circuits; it also contains a nonpipelined floating-point divider. The two 64-bit pipeline processors can each be used to process two sets of 32-bit operands simultaneously. Hence there are, in effect, four independent 32-bit pipelines. Each of these pipelines is capable of producing a new 32-bit floating-point result every 40 ns in the streaming mode of operation. The main memory has a capacity of 4M (4×2^{20}) bytes and is constructed from ferrite cores with a cycle time of 1.28 μs, i.e., it requires 1.28 μs to access a single word in main memory.

The overall performance goal of the system can be stated succinctly as follows: it should be capable of producing 10^8 32-bit floating-point results per second, that is, 100 megaflops. We now retrace the designers' steps in determining a system configuration that achieves this high level of performance [16].

In the streaming mode, results are generated at a rate of 4096 bits per memory cycle and must be stored at that rate in main memory. Most results require two 32-bit input operands; hence 2×4096 operand bits must be fetched per memory cycle. Some allowance must also be made for fetching instructions, say one 32-bit instruction per result, which is an additional 4096 bits per memory cycle. We conclude that it is necessary to fetch 3×4096 bits and store 4096 bits in main memory every 1.28 μs. Now $(3 \times 4096 + 4096) = 16{,}384 = 32 \times 512$, so it was decided to partition main memory into 32 interleaved modules and use 512-bit memory words. Each module therefore has a capacity of 2048 words.

Figure 3.66 shows the main data paths of the STAR-100. There are four data buses between the CPU and memory: one is used for transferring operands to memory, two are used for fetching operands from memory, the final bus is used for fetching instructions and for communicating with the IO system. Each of the four buses consists of 128 lines and can transmit 128 bits every 40 ns. During streaming, therefore, $128 \times 4 \times 32 = 16{,}384$ bits are being transferred over these buses each memory cycle; this exactly matches the main-memory bandwidth.

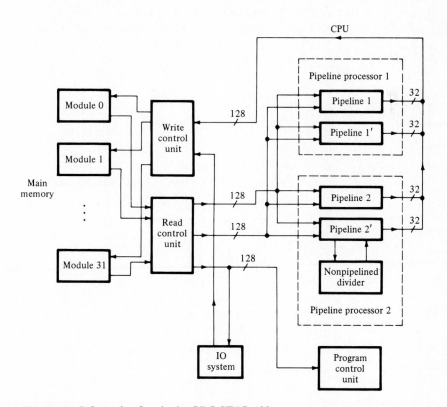

Figure 3.66 Information flow in the CDC STAR-100.

3.4.3 Pipeline Processors

A pipeline processor consists of a sequence of processing circuits, called segments, through which a data stream passes (see Fig. 3.61). Partial processing is performed by each segment, and a final result is obtained after the data has passed through all segments of the pipeline. Occasionally it may be necessary to make several passes through the pipeline in order to process a data set completely. Parallel processing is achieved by having distinct operand sets or processes in several segments at the same time. Each operand set moves from segment to segment until it has been completely processed. As demonstrated in Sec. 3.4.2, an m-segment pipeline has approximately the same throughput as a multiunit processor with m units.

Each segment S_i of a pipeline processor consists of an input register R_i and a processing circuit C_i, which is a combinational or sequential logic circuit. The output of C_i is applied to the input register R_{i+1} of the next segment S_{i+1}, as depicted in Fig. 3.67. The registers $\{R_i\}$ act as buffers between the segments. Segment-to-segment transfer should take place only when the outputs of all the processing circuits $\{C_i\}$ have stabilized at their final values. The operating speed of the pipeline is ultimately determined by its slowest segment, which implies that the segment delays should be approximately equal.

Any operation that can be decomposed into a sequence of well-defined suboperations of about the same complexity can, in principle, be realized by a pipeline processor. The resulting improvement in performance, if any, may be

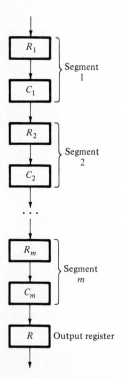

Figure 3.67 Pipeline processor structure.

estimated as follows. Let P_1 be a nonpipelined processor with total delay t_1, that is, with bandwidth t_1^{-1}. Let P_m be an m-segment pipelined version of P_1. For simplicity, assume that P_m has the structure shown in Fig. 3.67, in which each processing circuit C_i has the same delay t_C, and t_R is the delay of each segment attributable to buffer register R_i and its associated control logic. The total delay of one segment of P_m is therefore $t_C + t_R$; hence the maximum throughput of P_m is $(t_C + t_R)^{-1}$. Now if P_m is formed by partitioning P_1 into segments of approximately the same delay, then $t_1 \approx mt_C$. Hence the maximum throughput of P_1 is approximately $(mt_C)^{-1}$. We conclude that P_m has greater maximum throughput than P_1 if the following condition is satisfied

$$mt_C > t_C + t_R$$

There are two areas where pipelining appears to be particularly appropriate.

1. The transfer of instructions through the various stages in the instruction cycle of a CPU, which amounts to realizing most or all of the CPU in the form of a pipeline called an *instruction pipeline*
2. The implementation of arithmetic operations, particularly the more complex arithmetic operations such as those involving floating-point numbers; a pipeline processor for this purpose is called an *arithmetic pipeline*

Instruction pipelines The purpose of an instruction pipeline is to overlap some or all of the steps in the instruction cycle. Figure 3.68 shows the simplest instruction pipeline organization which allows instruction fetching and instruction execution to be overlapped. While the instruction I with address A_i is being executed, the instruction with the next consecutive address A_{i+1} is fetched from memory. If I happens to be a branch instruction, the next instruction to be executed may have address $A_j \neq A_{i+1}$. In that case the instruction that has been fetched must be discarded and a new fetch cycle initiated after I has been executed. Thus the two-segment pipeline is no more efficient for executing branch instructions than a nonpipelined processor. Often branch instructions form a small fraction of the total number of instructions executed, so throughput can be increased by this kind of pipelining. For example, 17 percent of the instructions in the Gibson mix (see Fig. 2.58) are branch instructions.

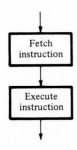

Figure 3.68 A simple two-segment instruction pipeline.

The instruction cycle can be segmented even further, as shown in Fig. 3.69. This is appropriate in machines with complex addressing methods like indexing or virtual addressing. In such machines, e. g., the Amdahl 470, a significant part of the instruction cycle is devoted to the construction of addresses for the instruction and its operands.

There is considerable variability in the execution times and execution requirements of a typical instruction set, which makes it difficult to operate an instruction pipeline at its maximum rate. The number of operand fetches required can vary from zero (for immediate instructions) to a relatively large number (for instructions with variable-length operands). The time required to fetch an operand can also vary. For example, if indirect addressing is used, two fetches are required to obtain the operand. The problem associated with branch instruction processing was noted earlier. It may be desirable to allow the structure of the pipeline to be varied by permitting instructions to bypass segments that they do not require. Simple instructions might therefore pass through a shorter pipeline than more complex ones. Instruction pipelines typically achieve their maximum throughput only when executing streams of simple instructions. A detailed description of the instruction pipeline of a powerful computer, the Manchester University MU5, can be found in Ref. 18.

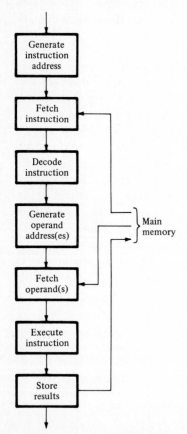

Figure 3.69 A seven-segment instruction pipeline.

Arithmetic pipelines Most arithmetic functions are easily implemented by pipelining. Arithmetic pipelines have been constructed for performing a single arithmetic function, e. g., floating-point addition, or for performing all four basic operations on both fixed-point and floating-point numbers. We now consider briefly examples of both kinds.

Floating-point addition pipeline Floating-point addition, as discussed in Sec. 3.3.5, can be implemented in four sequential steps: exponent comparison, mantissa alignment, mantissa addition, and result normalization. Figure 3.70 shows the result of modifying the adder of Fig. 3.55 to form a four-stage pipeline adder. The only significant change is in the addition of buffer registers to isolate

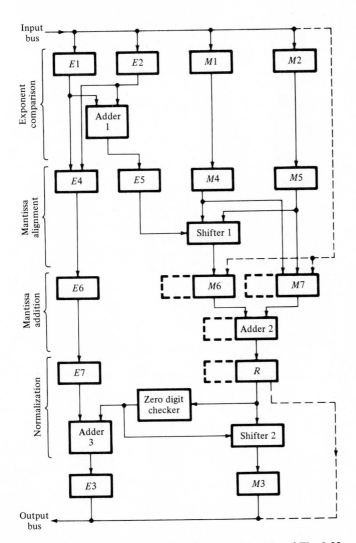

Figure 3.70 Pipelined version of the floating-point adder of Fig. 3.55.

the four segments. A further modification can be made to permit execution of fixed-point as well as floating-point addition. The circuits that perform the mantissa addition in segment 3 can be enlarged (as indicated by broken lines in Fig. 3.70) to accommodate full-word operands. The remaining three segments may be bypassed during fixed-point addition. Thus the unit can be made to appear like a one-segment pipeline for fixed-point addition.

Multiplication pipeline Pipeline multipliers generally use the carry-save approach described in Sec. 3.3.2. Figure 3.71 shows a pipelined fixed-point multi-

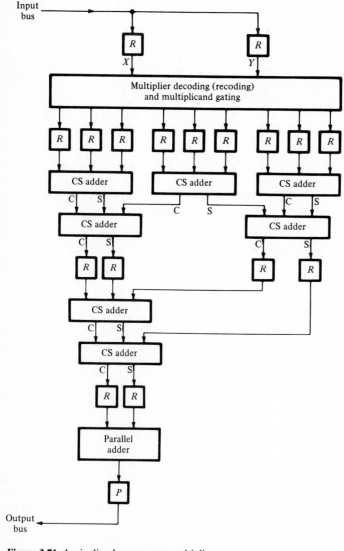

Figure 3.71 A pipelined carry-save multiplier.

plier based on the design in Fig. 3.38. This is quite similar to the pipeline multipliers of the CDC STAR-100 [16]. Four segments are used. The first segment decodes the multiplier and gates appropriately shifted copies of the multiplicands into the carry-save adder circuit. Multiplier recoding may also be done in this segment to reduce the number of additions required. The carry-save adder tree has been divided into two segments by the insertion of buffer registers denoted by R. The final parallel addition segment completes the carry assimilation. This multiplier can easily be modified to handle floating-point numbers. The input mantissas are processed using the basic fixed-point multiplication pipeline. The exponents are combined using an extra fixed-point adder, and a normalization circuit is added, if required. A detailed description of a floating-point multiplier of this general type used in the S/360 Model 91 can be found in Refs. 2 and 24.

Complex multifunction arithmetic pipelines are used in both the STAR-100 (see Example 3.4) and the Texas Instruments ASC. Instructions in the ASC are executed by an arithmetic-logic unit organized as a single pipeline of variable structure.

Example 3.5: Arithmetic-logic unit of the TI ASC [27, 32] This computer contains an eight-segment pipeline capable of executing all (fixed-point and floating-point) arithmetic and logical instructions. The eight segments are shown in Fig. 3.72. The data flow between the segments depends on the instruction and is not shown in this figure. Different instructions use different subsets of the available segments. (See Fig. 3.36 for a list of representative vector instructions in the ASC.) The pipeline is designed to process 64-bit words at a maximum rate of one result per clock period (60 ns). A brief description of the functions of the various segments will now be given.

1. The input segment acts as a receiver for all input operands.
2. The exponent subtract segment is used for mantissa comparison during floating-point addition and subtraction.
3. The align segment performs variable-length shifts. It is used to execute shift instructions and also floating-point addition and subtraction.
4. The add segment performs 64-bit fixed-point addition and is used in the execution of fixed-point and floating-point addition and subtraction, as well as certain other instructions.
5. The normalize segment is used primarily in floating-point operations to normalize results.
6. The multiply segment can perform a 32-bit fixed-point or floating-point multiplication every 60 ns. A carry-save multiplication method is used. The output of the multiply segment is two 64-bit words, a sum and a carry word. To form the final product, these two words are added by the accumulate segment.
7. The accumulate segment is basically similar to the add segment. It is

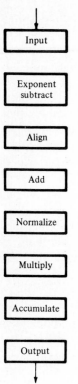

Figure 3.72 The eight segments of the TI ASC arithmetic pipeline.

used in multiplication and also for accumulation of the result in operations requiring repeated addition, e. g., in computing the dot (scalar) product of two vectors.

8. The output segment is used to execute logical instructions. All results are gated through this segment.

Figure 3.73 shows the pipeline segments used in floating-point addition and fixed-point multiplication. Several instructions require feedback paths in the pipeline, e. g., 64-bit multiplication and division. Division is performed by repeated multiplication using the algorithm described in Sec. 3.3.3.

Pipeline scheduling The discussion of performance in Sec. 3.4.2 was limited to pipeline processors in which operand sets flow linearly through the pipeline visiting each segment just once. Examination of real pipeline processors such as that of the ASC (Example 3.5) indicates that one segment may be visited many times by the same operand set. In such pipelines the possibility of a *collision* between two different operand sets exist, which is defined as the situation where both attempt to use the same segment at the same time. Collision

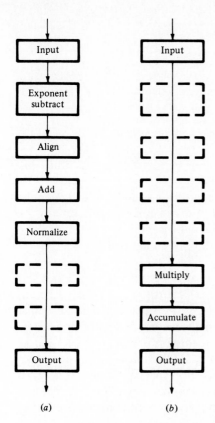

(b)

Figure 3.73 ASC pipeline data flow for (a) floating-point addition and (b) fixed-point multiplication.

can be avoided by providing an adequate delay between the initiation of consecutive processes that use the pipeline. Following the work of Davidson [10], we examine the problem of scheduling pipeline operations to avoid collisions. Consider a pipeline P consisting of m segments $S_1, S_2, \ldots, S_m$. We will restrict P to performing a single function, that is, P can execute only one type of instruction. That instruction may be a complex one such as floating-point division that requires an operand set to make several visits to certain segments. The path taken by an operand set through the pipeline is represented by a *reservation table R*, as in Fig. 3.74. Each row of R represents a segment of P, while the columns represent a sequence of time periods during which an operand set is completely processed by P. An x is placed at the intersection of row S_i and column t_j if segment S_i is required by the process at time t_j.

The collision possibilities for P can be derived from its reservation table R in the following manner. Two processes initiated k time units apart collide at segment S_i if row S_i of R contains two x's whose horizontal distance apart is k. In the case of Fig. 3.74, collision will occur at S_1 if $k = 3$, and at S_2 if $k = 5$. Let F be a set of numbers called the *forbidden list* of P whose entries are the set of

	Time						
Segment	t_1	t_2	t_3	t_4	t_5	t_6	t_7
S_1	x			x			
S_2		x					x
S_3			x				
S_4				x			
S_5					x		

Figure 3.74 Reservation table for a pipeline.

distances between all distinct pairs of x's in every row of R. The forbidden list for Fig. 3.74 is $\{3, 5\}$. The following easily-proven result characterizes the collision conditions for P. Two processes initiated k periods apart on a pipeline processor P collide if and only if k is in the forbidden list of P.

In the case of the pipeline defined by Fig. 3.74, if we initiate a process at t_1, we may immediately initiate a second process at t_2 because $t_2-t_1 = 1$ and 1 is not in F. A third process can be initiated at t_3. A fourth process cannot be initiated at t_4, however, since $t_4-t_1 = 3$, which is in F. In fact, the earliest time process 4 can be initiated without colliding with one of the preceding processes is t_9. If, however, we had initiated the first three processes at t_1, t_3, and t_5, the fourth could be initiated at t_7 rather than t_9. (If the interval between process initiations is 2, no collision can occur since F in this case contains no even numbers.) Thus to schedule the pipeline to maximize throughput or, equivalently, to minimize the overall delay between process initiations requires additional analysis.

The minimum time that must elapse between the initiation of two processes in P is called the *latency*. The latency at any time is a function of the positions of the processes currently in P. The *minimum constant latency* of P is the smallest number L such that any number of processes can be initiated L time units apart without collisions. The minimum constant latency L can be determined from the forbidden list F using the fact that L is the smallest integer $n \geq 1$ such that kn is not in F for any integer $k \geq 1$. By allowing variable periods between process initiation, it may be possible to determine a scheduling strategy which yields a lower average latency, i. e., higher throughput, than if the minimum constant latency is used. A scheduling algorithm that minimizes the average latency is described in Ref. 10.

3.4.4 Multiunit Processors

A multiunit processor consists of a set of m disjoint processing elements each of which is capable of acting on a data stream independently of the others. The CPU of the CDC STAR-100 depicted in Fig. 3.66 contains a two-unit arithmetic processor comprising pipeline processor 1 and pipeline processor 2. (Further parallelism exists within these units themselves.)

A central component of any multiunit processor system is a scheduler or control unit which coordinates activities among the various units. The scheduler must preserve the precedence among the instructions being executed and use the available processing units as efficiently as possible. It must keep track of the status (busy or idle) of each processing unit as well as any facilities such as registers or buses shared among them. This is usually done by associating a status bit or flag with each processing unit and shared facility.

The units composing a multiunit processor may be specialized to execute one instruction type, or they may be general-purpose arithmetic-logic units capable of executing a large instruction set. Two computers have been chosen to illustrate these design concepts, the CDC 6600 and ILLIAC IV. The CDC 6600 attempts to exploit the local parallelism inherent in ordinary programs using a single multiunit ALU. ILLIAC IV, on the other hand, contains 64 identical ALUs and is intended primarily for parallel computations involving vector and matrix operations. Associative processors form another important class of multiunit processors. In associative processors the data processing and storage functions are intimately related. These machines are organized around associative or content-addressable memories (examined in Chap. 5).

Example 3.6: The central processor of the CDC 6600 [29] Instructions are executed in the CPU of the 6600 by 10 separate circuits called functional units, which are shown in Fig. 3.75. The functional units communicate with a set of operand and address registers via three groups of data buses. The buses are distributed among the units in a way that attempts to equalize the amount of data they carry.

The purpose of most of the functional units is obvious from their names. The shift unit is a barrel shifter and is used to execute shift and normalize instructions. The Boolean unit executes a conventional set of logical operations. The increment units are used for address computations such as indexing; they can perform integer addition and subtraction. The branch unit (which is really part of the program control unit) executes branch instructions by modifying the address in the program counter PC.

Like the ASC described earlier, the 6600 has a 32-module interleaved main memory which permits up to 32 accesses to take place simultaneously. This allows data and instructions to be transferred between main memory and the CPU at a high rate. The selection of the registers and functional units to be used in the execution of each instruction is the responsibility of a special control unit called the "scoreboard." The scoreboard selects a functional unit and directs it to the registers containing its input operands. Once initiated by the scoreboard, the functional unit proceeds independently and signals the scoreboard when its result is ready. The scoreboard then directs the result to a CPU register from which it may be transferred to main memory. The CPU maintains a stack of up to 32 consecutive instructions which are issued by the scoreboard to the functional units as rapidly as possible. Independent instructions may be selected in

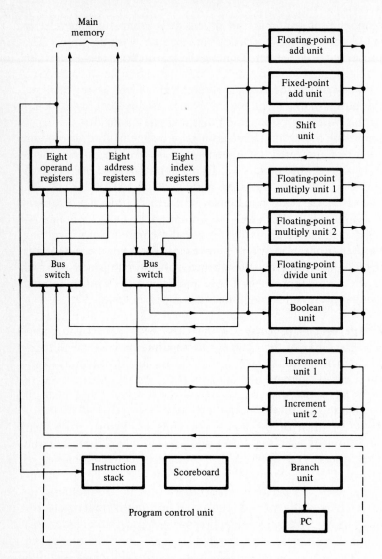

Figure 3.75 CPU data flow in the CDC 6600.

any order for execution. The execution of an instruction *I* is delayed by the scoreboard if any of the following three types of conflicts occurs.

1. *I* requires the same functional unit or result register as some instruction that is currently being executed.
2. *I* requires as an input operand the result of some instruction that has not yet been completely executed.
3. *I* requires an output register that contains an input operand for some pending instruction whose execution has not yet begun.

During execution of a typical program, at least two or three of the functional units can be expected to be in operation simultaneously.

Example 3.7: Parallel processing in ILLIAC IV [3, 26] ILLIAC IV is an experimental computer designed at the University of Illinois in the late 1960s and manufactured by Burroughs Corporation. Its architecture is derived from the SOLOMON computers designed by Westinghouse Electric Corporation in the early 1960s. The general structure of ILLIAC IV is shown in Fig. 3.76. It contains a set of 64 identical processing units (PUs) with a common external control unit CU. A PU comprises a processing element (PE) and a processing memory (PM). A PE is a general-purpose ALU capable of executing a conventional instruction set that includes 64-bit floating-point operations. Each PM has a capacity of 2048 64-bit words.

The CU plays the role of program control unit for the system. It decodes instructions and, when an instruction for the PEs is encountered, it broadcasts the instruction via control lines to all PEs simultaneously. The CU can access information randomly in all 64 PMs. Each PE has access only to its own PM. Thus a common instruction is executed by all PEs simultaneously; however, each PE uses data from its own memory. ILLIAC IV is capable of processing 64 separate data streams simultaneously under the control of a single instruction stream. A supervisory computer system

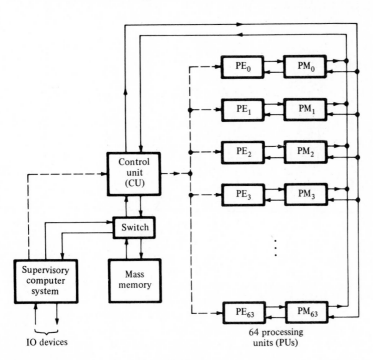

Figure 3.76 Structure of ILLIAC IV.

(a single Burroughs B6500 in the original design, but subsequently several computers) performs housekeeping functions such as program compilation and input-output management.

Consider, for example, the addition of two 64-component vectors A and B to form a result C. The CU can store the ith components of A, B, and C in locations a, b, c of PM_i. If it then broadcasts the instruction

$$c \leftarrow a + b$$

to the PEs, all 64 additions take place simultaneously. Note that careful placement of the data in the PMs is essential to correct operation.

In addition to the common data and control buses that link the PUs to the CU, there are direct data paths connecting each PU to four neighboring PUs. Specifically, PU_i is connected to PU_j if $j = i + 1$ (modulo 64), $j = i - 1$ (modulo 64), $j = i + 8$ (modulo 64), or $j = i - 8$ (modulo 64). The PUs therefore form a two-dimensional array as shown in Fig. 3.77. For this reason ILLIAC IV is often referred to as an *array processor*.

An array organization of this kind is very useful in computations involving the calculation of a function defined on a mesh or grid of points, where the value of the function at each point is influenced by the value of its neighbors. The following simple but illuminating example is given by Slotnick [26]. Suppose that we have to compute the steady-state temperature over the surface of a rectangular slab of material where the temperature at the edges is known. Let $U(x, y)$ denote the temperature over the

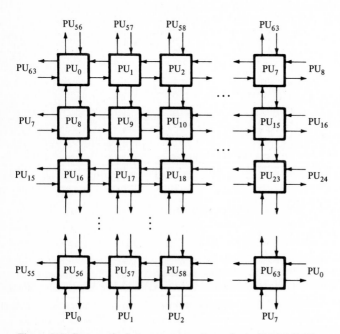

Figure 3.77 Data paths between processing units in ILLIAC IV.

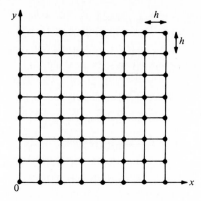

Figure 3.78 An 8 × 8 grid for the heat-flow problem.

slab. Suppose that the slab is covered by an 8 × 8 grid with vertices at the points $x = ih$ and $y = jh$, as indicated in Fig. 3.78. The temperature at (x, y) is, intuitively, the average of the temperatures at its four neighbors. This is expressed by the equation[5]

$$U(x, y) = \frac{U(x + h, y) + U(x, y + h) + U(x - h, y) + U(x, y - h)}{4} \quad (3.20)$$

A standard method of solving this equation, called the relaxation method, is to compute $U(x, y)$ repeatedly for all grid points beginning at some bounda-

---

[5]The flow of heat over a continuous surface is defined by the partial differential equation (Laplace's equation)

$$\frac{\partial^2 U}{\partial x^2} + \frac{\partial^2 U}{\partial y^2} = 0 \quad (3.21)$$

The problem amounts to solving this equation with the boundary conditions given by the temperature along the edges of the slab. The second-order derivatives of U are defined by the limit as h goes to zero of the following expressions.

$$\frac{\partial^2 U}{\partial x^2} = \frac{U(x + h, y) - 2U(x, y) + U(x - h, y)}{h^2} \quad (3.22)$$

$$\frac{\partial^2 U}{\partial y^2} = \frac{U(x, y + h) - 2U(x, y) + U(x, y - h)}{h^2} \quad (3.23)$$

For small values of h, these expressions can be used as approximations to the derivatives. Therefore, if we substitute (3.22) and (3.23) into (3.21), we obtain the following approximation to Laplace's equation:

$$\frac{1}{h^2} [U(x+h, y) + U(x-h, y) + U(x, y+h) + U(x, y-h) - 4U(x, y)] = 0 \quad (3.24)$$

which immediately reduces to (3.20). We have therefore replaced the original differential equation by a set of algebraic difference equations, one for every grid point (x, y). This is an example of Newton's method of finite differences and is of fundamental importance in applying digital computers to problems in analysis. Note that it is also the underlying technique in Babbage's Difference Engine (cf. Example 1.3).

ry point. For example, on a serial computer one might begin at the point 0 in Fig. 3.78 and traverse all 64 points in sequence moving from left to right and from bottom to top. This process is repeated many times until the difference between successive values of $U(x, y)$ at all points is very small. (The process is known to converge.) Initially only the values of $U(x, y)$ at the 28 boundary points are known; the 36 internal values may be set to zero. Successive iterations cause the internal values of $U(x, y)$ to change gradually until equilibrium is reached.

Now suppose that ILLIAC IV is applied to the solution of the foregoing problem. Each of the 64 grid points is assigned to a separate PU. ILLIAC IV can then compute $U(x, y)$ from Eq. (3.20) at all grid points simultaneously. Since the boundary values are known, only the values at the 36 internal grid points need to be computed. Note that the array organization provides each PU with direct access to the data it requires from its four neighbors. ILLIAC IV therefore solves this problem at approximately 36 times the rate of a comparable serial (SISD) computer.

3.5 SUMMARY

The primary purpose of an instruction set processor such as a CPU is to fetch instructions from an external (main) memory and execute them. The functions performed by the CPU are defined by its instruction set. An instruction specifies an operation and a set of operands or data. Usually the instruction specifies an operand by its address, which is the name of a CPU register or memory location containing the operand value. Frequently operand addresses are implicit to reduce instruction length. If m is the maximum number of explicit addresses allowed in any instruction, the processor is called an m-address machine. An address may be completely specified by an instruction, or it may be necessary to construct it from several components, e. g., a base address, an index, and a displacement. Relative addressing allows one instruction address to specify many operands, and also facilitates the relocation of information in main memory.

No precise criteria for the selection of instruction sets are known, although some informal criteria for completeness can be given. Instructions may be grouped into five major types: data transfer, arithmetic, logical, program control, and input-output. All practical computers contain at least a few instructions of each type, although in theory one or two simple instructions are sufficient to perform all operations. While many instructions imply redundancy, they also imply greater efficiency in the sense that the more well-chosen instructions available, the shorter the average program. The power of an instruction set is frequently characterized by the arithmetic instructions it contains. Simple machines may be limited to addition and subtraction of fixed-point numbers. More powerful machines are capable of multiplication and division, floating-point arithmetic, and in the case of a small number of supercomputers, vector arithmetic.

The two major number formats are fixed-point and floating-point. Fixed-point numbers may be binary or decimal, where decimal means a binary code such as BCD that preserves the decimal weights found in ordinary (radix 10) decimal numbers. The most common binary number codes are sign-magnitude, ones complement, and twos complement. Each code simplifies the implementation of certain arithmetic operations. Ones and twos complement simplify the implementation of subtraction, so they are preferred in most applications. A floating-point number comprises a pair of fixed-point numbers, a mantissa M, and an exponent E, and is used to represent numbers of the form $M \times B^E$, where B is an implicit base. Floating-point numbers greatly increase the range obtainable using a given word size but require much more complex arithmetic circuits than fixed-point numbers. In order to provide a unique representation for every number, floating-point numbers are normalized.

Arithmetic circuit design is a well-developed field. Fixed-point addition is easily implemented using a variety of circuits. One of the simplest is a ripple carry adder. High-speed adders attempt to reduce carry propagation time by techniques such as carry lookahead. Fixed-point multiplication and division are generally implemented by algorithms that are similar to manual methods. The product or quotient of two km-bit numbers may be formed in k sequential steps, where each step involves an m-bit shift and, possibly, a km-bit addition or subtraction. Multiplier recoding can be used to reduce the number of additions and subtractions required in multiplication. Division is inherently more complex than multiplication due to the problem of determining the quotient digit. Both multiplication and division can be implemented by combinational logic circuits, but at a substantial increase in the amount of hardware required. Floating-point addition and subtraction require that the input exponents be equalized before their mantissas can be added. Furthermore, it is usually necessary to normalize the result. Apart from the normalization requirement, floating-point multiplication and division are comparable in complexity to the corresponding fixed-point operations.

Processors capable of executing several instructions or processing several distinct operand sets simultaneously are called parallel processors. Parallelism may be achieved within a computer by the use of multiunit processors, pipeline processors, or a combination of both. An m-unit processor and an m-segment pipeline of similar design have approximately the same throughput.The efficiency of a parallel processor is highly dependent on the inherent parallelism of the programs it executes. Certain problems, notably those involving vector operations, e. g., the solution of large sets of equations, can be solved much more rapidly by a parallel processor than by a conventional (SISD) computer.

PROBLEMS

3.1 Developments in LSI technology have made it feasible to build computers with identical CPU and memory cycle times. Presumably this makes it also feasible to treat a large main memory as a set of CPU registers and to eliminate all the operand registers usually included in the CPU such as the accumulator. Discuss the advantages and disadvantages of doing this.

3.2 A new microprocessor is being designed with a conventional architecture employing single-address instructions and 8-bit words. Due to physical size constraints, only eight distinct 3-bit opcodes are allowed. The use of modifiers or the address field to extend the opcodes is forbidden.

(a) What eight instructions would you implement? Specify the operations performed by each instruction as well as the location of its operands.

(b) Demonstrate that your instruction set is functionally complete in some reasonable sense; or if it is not, describe an operation that cannot be programmed using your instruction set.

3.3 Many computers contain the instruction NOP, meaning no operation, which has no effect on the CPU state other than causing the program counter to be incremented. List as many uses for NOP as you can.

3.4 Consider a simple hypothetical computer with a main memory M having a capacity of 2^{n-1} n-bit words. The CPU contains an n-bit accumulator AC and an $(n-1)$-bit program counter PC. It has a repertoire of two n-bit instructions in which the leftmost bit is the opcode and the remaining bits form an address in M. The first instruction is called SUBS (subtract and store). SUBS X causes the following microoperations to take place:

$$AC \leftarrow AC - M(X);$$

$$M(X) \leftarrow AC, PC \leftarrow PC + 1;$$

The second instruction is an unconditional branch JUMP X which causes the following operation to take place

$$PC \leftarrow M(X(0:n-2));$$

A word in M may be either a instruction (SUBS or JUMP) or a fixed-point binary number in twos-complement code. Prove informally that this instruction set is complete by demonstrating that the following operations can be programmed.

(a) The memory data transfers $AC \leftarrow M(X)$ and $M(X) \leftarrow AC$
(b) The addition operation $AC \leftarrow AC + M(X)$
(c) Conditional branching
(d) The logical OR operation $AC \leftarrow AC \lor M(X)$
(e) Input-output transfers

3.5 A floating-point processor is being designed with a number format that must meet the following requirements.

1. Numbers in the range $\pm 1.0 \times 10^{\pm 50}$ must be represented.
2. The precision required is six decimal digits, i.e., the six most-significant digits of the decimal equivalent of every number in the required range must be representable.
3. The representation of each number should be unique. Zero is to be represented by a sequence of 0s.
4. Binary arithmetic is to be used throughout with $B = 2$, where B is the floating-point base to be used.

Design a number format that satisfies these requirements and uses as few bits as possible. Indicate clearly the number codes used and why they were chosen.

3.6 Discuss the advantages and disadvantages of choosing 2^k where $k > 1$ rather than 2 as the base B for floating-point number representation.

3.7 The set of real numbers R with the operations addition and multiplication form a closed algebraic system called a *field*. The axioms defining a field are listed in Fig. 3.79. (Compare the laws of Boolean algebra in Fig. 2.12.) Consider an arithmetic processor in which real numbers are represented by floating-point numbers R^* which are truncated to a fixed number of bits.

    (*a*) Prove that the addition and multiplication operations are not associative when defined on R^*.

    (*b*) Determine whether or not the commutative and distributive laws are valid for R^*.
(Note that all the field axioms are at least approximately true for R^* and the approximation improves as the precision of numbers in R^* is increased.)

3.8 Let X^* be the canonical signed-digit representation of a fixed-point n-bit number defined by Fig. 3.33. Prove each of the following.

    (*a*) Every two nonzero digits in X^* are separated by at least one zero.

    (*b*) The average number of nonzero digits in n-bit canonical signed-digit numbers is $n/3$.

3.9 Design a combinational array circuit to multiply two 4-bit positive binary numbers using the cell M of Fig. 3.36.

3.10 Figure 3.80 shows a cell M' intended for a twos-complement combinational array multiplier that implements Booth's algorithm. M' is capable of acting as a full adder or a full subtracter. The particular operation to be performed by M' is specified by the control lines a and b in the following way.

a	b	Operation
0	–	None
1	0	Addition
1	1	Subtraction

The main data inputs are x and y. During addition z is the sum bit, while t and u are the carry in and carry out, respectively. During subtraction, z is the difference bit, while t and u are the borrow in

No.	Statement of axiom	Name
1	There exist numbers $0, 1 \in R$ such that $a + 0 = a$ $a1 = a$	Existence of identity elements
2	$a + b = b + a$ $ab = ba$	Commutative laws
3	$a(b + c) = ab + ac$	Distributive law
4	For every $a \in R$ there exists $(-a) \in R$ such that $a + (-a) = 0$ For every $a \in R$ where $a \neq 0$ there exists $a^{-1} \in R$ such that $aa^{-1} = 1$	Existence of inverses
5	$a + (b + c) = (a + b) + c$ $a(bc) = (ab)c$	Associative laws

Figure 3.79 Axioms of a field.

and borrow out, respectively. The cell functions are expressed concisely by the following logic equations:

$$z = x \oplus a(y \oplus t)$$

$$u = (x \oplus b)(y + t) + yt$$

The input signals a, b, and y are connected directly to cell outputs in order to simplify interconnection of the cells.

Design a combinational array multiplier for 3-bit twos-complement numbers using these cells. (Additional elements may also be included in the circuit to generate the control signals a and b.) Estimate the multiplication time of your array assuming a gate delay of d seconds.

3.11 Describe how the adder-subtracter cell M' of Fig. 3.80 can be used to construct an array divider using the nonrestoring division principle. Give the block diagram of an array that divides 3-bit positive numbers and computes the quotient to 6 significant bits.

3.12 Modify the flowchart for restoring division given in Fig. 3.42 to handle both positive and negative integers in twos-complement code.

3.13 The CORDIC (*CO*ordinate *R*otation *D*igital *C*omputer) technique has been widely used in scientific calculators for computing trigonometric functions. It is relatively fast and can be implemented by very simple circuits. In the CORDIC system a number Z is treated as a vector represented by its cartesian coordinates (X, Y), and the required functions of Z are calculated by operations that are analogous to vector rotation. Suppose that the vector Z is rotated through an angle θ. The resulting vector $Z' = (X', Y')$ is defined by the equations

$$X' = X \cos \theta \pm Y \sin \theta$$

$$Y' = Y \cos \theta \mp X \sin \theta \tag{3.25}$$

where the upper and lower signs correspond to clockwise and counterclockwise rotation, respectively. These equations imply that

$$X'' = \frac{X'}{\cos \theta} = X \pm Y \tan \theta$$

$$Y'' = \frac{Y'}{\cos \theta} = Y \mp X \tan \theta \tag{3.26}$$

$Z'' = (X'', Y'')$ can be interpreted as the original vector Z after rotation through an angle θ and a magnitude increase by the factor $K = 1/\cos \theta$. If $\tan \theta$ is a power of 2, then the multiplication by $\tan \theta$ required in (3.26) can be realized by shifting. The essence of CORDIC is to implement the rotation described by (3.26) as a sequence of $n + 1$ rotations through angles α_i such that

$$\theta = \alpha_0 \pm \alpha_1 \pm \alpha_2 \pm \cdots \pm \alpha_n \tag{3.27}$$

and

$$\alpha_i = \tan^{-1}(2^{-i}) \tag{3.28}$$

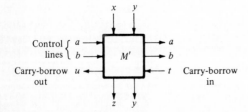

Figure 3.80 Cell M' for an array multiplier.

Then if we set $Z = (X_0, Y_0)$, each rotation through angle α_i is defined by (3.26) and (3.28) and has the form

$$X_{i+1} = X_i \pm Y_i 2^{-i}$$
$$Y_{i+1} = Y_i \mp X_i 2^{-i}$$
(3.29)

The resulting vector Z_n has magnitude $Z_n = K_n |Z_0|$, where $K_n = \prod_{i=0}^{n} (\cos \alpha_i)^{-1}$. K_n is a constant depending on n and it converges towards 1.6468. Note that the only operations required in (3.29) are addition, subtraction, and shifting.

The signs appearing in (3.27) depend on the given angle θ; these signs must be computed in order to determine the operations (addition or subtraction) needed in evaluating (3.29). The sign computation is carried out by storing the constants $\{\alpha_i\}$ in a table. In each iteration it is determined which of $+\alpha_i$ and $-\alpha_i$ causes $|\theta + (\pm \alpha_0 \pm \alpha_1 \ldots \pm \alpha_i)|$ to converge toward zero. If $+\alpha_i$ ($-\alpha_i$) is selected then the upper (lower) signs in (3.29) are used which correspond to a clockwise (counterclockwise) rotation through the angle α_i. Note that each iteration increases the accuracy of (X_i, Y_i) by approximately one bit.

The CORDIC method can be used to calculate $\sin \theta$, $\cos \theta$, and $\tan \theta$ as follows. Let $X_0 = K_n^{-1} \approx 0.6073$ and $Y_0 = 0.0$, where n has been chosen to achieve the desired accuracy. Compute (X_n, Y_n) according to (3.29). From (3.25) and (3.26) we see that $X_n = K_n X_0 \cos \theta$ and $Y_n = K_n X_0 \sin \theta$ hence X_n and Y_n are the required values of $\cos \theta$ and $\sin \theta$, respectively. $\tan \theta$ can now be computed by a single division since $\tan \theta = Y_n/X_n$.

(a) Give in tabular form all the calculations required to compute $\cos 37°$ to three decimal places using the CORDIC method.

(b) Draw a register level logic circuit for a simple CORDIC arithmetic unit that computes $\sin \theta$ and $\cos \theta$.

3.14 Describe how the CORDIC technique presented in Prob. 3.13 can be adapted to compute the inverse trigonometric functions $\sin^{-1}x$, $\cos^{-1}x$, and $\tan^{-1}x$.

3.15 Many methods of computing trigonometric functions, logarithms and the like are based on power series expansions. In Example 1.3, $\sin x$ is obtained from a power series using the method of finite differences in the manner of Babbage's Difference Engine. In modern computers the trigonometric functions are often computed by subroutines that evaluate the power series directly using addition, subtraction, multiplication and division. Let machine M_1 compute $\sin x$ using the CORDIC approach with parallel addition. Let machine M_2 compute $\sin x$ by power series evaluation. Assume that M_2 has efficient hardware implementations of the four basic arithmetic operations. If M_1 and M_2 employ the same logic technologies, estimate their relative speeds in computing $\sin x$ to 16 binary places.

3.16 In digital signal processing it is sometimes necessary to multiply a high-speed stream of numbers $Y_1, Y_2, Y_3, \ldots$ by a single number X. Design a pipeline multiplier to carry out this special type of multiplication efficiently. Assume that X and the Y_i are positive n-bit binary fractions. The output should be a stream of n-bit results $XY_1, XY_2, XY_3, \ldots$ moving at the same rate as the input stream. Assume a gate delay of d and estimate the bandwidth of your pipeline.

3.17 Consider a pipeline processor P with the reservation table given in Fig. 3.81.

(a) Calculate the minimum constant latency L of P.

(b) Find a schedule for initiating processes on P that results in an average latency that is less than L, or prove that no such schedule exists.

3.18 Write an essay comparing the efficiency with which the CDC 6600, the TI ASC and ILLIAC IV might execute programs of the following general types:

(a) A program with little or no inherent parallelism

(b) A program involving simple arithmetic operations on floating-point vectors of dimension 48

(c) A program to compute the position, speed, and bearing of several dozen airplanes in the vicinity of an airport from radar data supplied to the computers in real time

| | Time | | | | | | | | | |
Segment	t_1	t_2	t_3	t_4	t_5	t_6	t_7	t_8	t_9	t_{10}
S_1	x				x					
S_2		x				x				
S_3			x					x		
S_4				x				x		
S_5	x				x				x	
S_6						x				
S_7		x					x			
S_8										x

Figure 3.81 Reservation table for P.

3.19 Consider the performance of a pipelined supercomputer such as the STAR-100. The floating-point arithmetic operations it performs can be roughly divided into two groups: vector operations involving vector operands of length N where N is large, and scalar operations where $N = 1$. Let $f(1 - f)$ be the fraction of the floating-point operations that are executed by the computer at scalar (vector) speed. Let P be the average throughput of the machine measured in megaflops. It has been observed experimentally that P approaches its maximum value only when f is very small. Furthermore, when f is very small a slight increase in f can result in a very large decrease in P. Construct an analytic model to explain these phenomena in quantitative terms.

REFERENCES

1. Amdahl, G. M.: "Validity of the Single Processor Approach to Achieve Large Scale Computing Capabilities," *AFIPS Conf. Proc.*, vol. 30, pp. 483–485, 1967.
2. Anderson, S. F., et al.: "The IBM System/360 Model 91: Floating-Point Execution Unit," *IBM J. Res. Develop.*, vol. 11, pp. 34–53, January, 1967.
3. Barnes, G. H., et al.: "The ILLIAC IV Computer," *IEEE Trans. Comput.*, vol. C-17, pp. 746–757, August 1968. (Reprinted in Ref. 4, pp. 320–333.)
4. Bell, C. G., and A. Newell: *Computer Structures: Readings and Examples,* McGraw-Hill, New York, 1971.
5. Booth, A. D.: "A Signed Binary Multiplication Technique," *Quart J. Mech. Appl. Math.*, vol. 4, pt. 2, pp. 236–240, 1951.
6. Bucholz, W.: "Instruction Formats," in W. Bucholz (ed.): *Planning a Computer System*, pp. 122–132. McGraw-Hill, New York, 1962.
7. Chen, T. C.: "Parallelism, Pipelining and Computer Efficiency," *Comput. Des.*, vol. 10, pp. 69–74, January 1971.
8. Chu, Y. (ed.): *High-Level Language Computer Architecture*, Academic, New York, 1975.
9. Creech, B. A.: "Architecture of the Burroughs B-6500," in J. Tou (ed.), *Software Engineering*, pp. 29–43, Academic, New York, 1970.
10. Davidson, E. S.: "The Design and Control of Pipelined Function Generators," *Proc. 1971 Int. IEEE Conf. Syst., Networks Comput.*, Oaxtepec, Mexico, pp. 19–21, January 1971.
11. Digital Equipment Corp.: *Small Computer Handbook*, Maynard, Mass., 1973.
12. Feustel, E. A.: "On the Advantages of Tagged Architecture," *IEEE Trans. Comput.*, vol. C-12, pp. 644–656, July 1973.
13. Flores, I.: *The Logic of Computer Arithmetic*, Prentice-Hall, Englewood Cliffs, N. J., 1963.
14. Flynn, M. J.: "Very High-Speed Computing Systems," *Proc. IEEE*, vol. 54, pp. 1901–1909, December 1966.

15. Garner, H. L.: "Number Systems and Arithmetic," in F. Alt and M. Rubinoff (eds.): *Advances in Computers*, vol. 6, pp. 131–194, Academic, New York, 1965.
16. Hintz, R. G., and D. P. Tate: "Control Data STAR-100 Processor Design," *Proc. 6th Annu. IEEE Comput. Soc. Int. Conf. (COMPCON 72)*, San Francisco, Calif., pp. 1–4, September 1972.
17. Huffman, D. A.: "A Method for the Construction of Minimum Redundancy Codes," *Proc. IRE*, vol. 40, pp. 1098–1101, September 1952.
18. Ibbett, R. N.: "The MU5 Instruction Pipeline," *Comput. J.*, vol. 15, pp. 42–50, February 1972.
19. Iliffe, J. K.: *Basic Machine Principles*, 2d ed., Macdonald, London, 1972.
20. Intel Corp.: *Series 3000 Reference Manual,* Santa Clara, Calif., 1976.
21. Kuck, D. J., et al.: "Measurements of Parallelism in Ordinary FORTRAN Programs," *Computer*, vol. 1, no. 1, pp. 37–46, January 1974.
22. Peterson, W. W., and E. J. Weldon: *Error-correcting Codes*, 2d ed., MIT Press, Cambridge, Mass., 1972.
23. Pezaris, S. D.: "A 40-ns 17-bit by 17-bit Array Multiplier," *IEEE Trans. Comput.*, vol. C-20, pp. 442–447, April 1971.
24. Ramamoorthy, C. V., and H. F. Li: "Pipeline Architecture," *Comput. Surv.*, vol. 9, pp. 61–102, March 1977.
25. Robertson, J. E.: "A New Class of Digital Division Methods," *IEEE Trans. Electron. Comput.*, vol. EC-7, pp. 218–222, September 1958.
26. Slotnick, D. L.: "The Fastest Computer," *Sci. Amer.* vol. 224, pp. 76–88, February 1971.
27. Texas Instruments, Inc.: *The ASC System Central Processor*, Publ. H 1005P, Austin, Texas, 1973.
28. Texas Instruments, Inc.: *990 Computer Family Systems Handbook,* Manual 945250-9701, Austin, Texas, 1975.
29. Thornton, J. E.: *Design of a Computer : The Control Data 6600*, Scott, Foresman, Glenview, Ill., 1970.
30. Thurber, K. J., and L. D. Wald: "Associative and Parallel Processing." *Comput. Surv.*, vol. 7, pp. 215–255, December 1975.
31. Van der Poel, W. L.: "The Essential Types of Operations in an Automatic Computer," *Nachrichtentechnische Fachberichte*, vol. 4, pp. 144–145, 1956.
32. Watson, W. J.: "The TI ASC-A Highly Modular and Flexible Super Computer Architecture," *AFIPS Conf. Proc.*, vol. 41, pp. 221–228, 1972.
33. Wilner, W. T.: "Burroughs B1700 Memory Utilization," *AFIPS Conf. Proc.*, vol. 41, pp. 579–586, 1972.

FOUR

CONTROL DESIGN

The implementation of the control part of a processor is studied in this chapter using two basic design approaches—hardwired and microprogrammed. Hardwired control is discussed briefly, whereas microprogramming is examined in detail.

4.1 INTRODUCTION

In Sec. 2.1.1, we noted that it is generally useful to separate a digital system into two parts, a data processing unit and a control unit. The data processing unit is a network of functional units capable of performing certain operations on data. The purpose of the control unit is to issue control signals or instructions to the data processing part. These control signals select the functions to be performed at specific times and route the data through the appropriate functional units. In other words, the data processing unit is logically reconfigured by the control unit to perform certain sets of (micro) operations. The sequence in which these microoperations are performed is very important, so the control unit is intimately involved in the sequencing and timing of the data processing unit.

In this chapter we are concerned with the design of control units for digital systems. Of particular interest is the design of control units for instruction set processors such as the CPU of a computer. The function of the control unit in such cases is to fetch instructions from a memory and interpret them to determine the control signals to be sent to the data processing units. Two central aspects of this process can be identified.

1. *Instruction sequencing*, that is, the methods by which instructions are selected for execution or, equivalently, the manner in which control of the processor is transferred from one instruction to another
2. *Instruction interpretation*, or the methods used for activating the control signals that cause the data processing unit to execute the instruction.

4.1.1 Instruction Sequencing

Conceptually, the simplest method of controlling the sequence in which instructions are executed is to have each instruction specify the address of its successor (or successors, if more than one possibility exists). This was done in some early computers such as EDVAC (see Sec. 1.3.2). Explicit inclusion of instruction addresses in all instructions has the disadvantage of substantially increasing instruction length, which in turn increases the cost of the memory where the instructions are stored.

Most instructions in a typical program have a unique successor. If an instruction I is stored in memory location A, and I has a unique successor I', then it is natural to store I' in the location $A + 1$ which immediately follows A. Let PC denote a *program counter* or *instruction address register* containing the address A of instruction I. The address of I' can then be determined by incrementing PC thus

$$PC \leftarrow PC + k$$

where k is the length in words of I. A program counter therefore makes it unnecessary for I to specify the address of its successor.

In order to select one of several possible courses of action or to repeat instructions, it is necessary to provide some instructions that transfer control between instructions at nonconsecutive addresses. Such instructions, called *branch instructions*, specify implicitly or explicitly an instruction address X. An *unconditional* branch always alters the flow of program control by causing the operation

$$PC \leftarrow X$$

to take place. A *conditional* branch instruction first tests for some condition C within the processor; C is typically a property of a result generated by an earlier instruction. If C is present, then $PC \leftarrow X$, otherwise $PC \leftarrow PC + k$.

Transfer of control between programs Conditional and unconditional branch instructions are adequate to direct the flow of control within a single program or procedure. Very often it is necessary to implement a temporary transfer of control from a main program P_1 to a subprogram P_2. There are two major situations where this occurs: subroutine calls and interrupts. A *subroutine call* is a temporary transfer of control from P_1 to P_2 initiated by P_1. An *interrupt* is a temporary transfer of control from P_1 to P_2 initiated by P_2 or some device associated with P_2.

The transfer of control from P_1 to P_2 required by subroutine calls or interrupts is accomplished by a special branch instruction called a subroutine *call* or a *jump to subroutine* instruction. A typical mnemonic expression for such an instruction is

CALL X

where X (or some address computed from X) is the address of the first instruction of P_2. CALL X is executed in two steps. First the contents of PC, which is the address of the next instruction of P_1, is saved in some predetermined location S, typically a processor register or a main-memory location. Then X is loaded into PC causing P_2 to begin execution. In order for control to be transferred back to the main program P_1, the last instruction from P_2 that is executed should transfer the contents of S, called the *return address*, to PC. Special "return" instructions may be designed for this purpose.

Example 4.1: Subroutine calls in the DEC PDP-8 computer [6]. A common way of implementing subroutine calls is illustrated by the PDP-8. The instruction

JMS SUB

where JMS stands for jump to subroutine, causes the current contents of the program counter PC (the return address) to be stored in main-memory location SUB. PC is then incremented, implying that the first instruction of the subroutine SUB should have address SUB + 1. Control can be transferred from the subroutine back to the calling program by executing the statement

JMP I SUB

which is an indirect (specified by the modifier I) jump to location SUB. This method of subroutine calling has the disadvantage that a subroutine cannot be allowed to call itself, since a second call to the subroutine results in the second return address overwriting the first return address and thus destroying it. One subroutine may call another, however, and thereby permit the nesting of distinct subroutines.

Control stacks Pushdown stacks, whose use in evaluating arithmetic expressions was discussed in Sec. 3.2.1, also provide a particularly powerful mechanism for transferring control between programs [4]. In this application, a stack is used primarily to store return addresses. The stack may also be used to store variables that are local to the subroutine. Each time a subroutine call statement is executed, the return address is entered into the top of the stack and the program counter is loaded with the subroutine address. Thus the statement

CALL SUB

results in the following sequence of actions:

PUSH PC;

$$PC \leftarrow SUB;.$$

A return from the subroutine may be effected by the instruction RETURN, which is equivalent to POP PC and causes the topmost entry in the stack to be transferred to the program counter.

The last-in first-out (LIFO) organization of a pushdown stack is precisely what is required in transferring control among nested subroutines, since the last calling program is the first program to which control must be returned. Furthermore, there is no restriction on the use of recursive subroutine calls as there is in the case of the PDP-8 JMS instruction discussed above. Because the location where return addresses are saved is the top of the stack, which varies dynamically, successive PUSH operations to save return addresses do not interfere with one another. Consider, for example, the following segment of recursive code.

Begin

```
        . . .
        CALL SUB
   X:   . . .
        . . .
  SUB:  . . .           ⎫
        CALL SUB        ⎪
   Y:   . . .           ⎬   Definition of subroutine SUB
        . . .           ⎪
        RETURN          ⎭
        . . .
```

End

When SUB is first called from the main program, the return address X is saved in the stack, as shown in Fig. 4.1a. Control is then transferred to the subroutine, where the statement CALL SUB is encountered. This causes a new re-

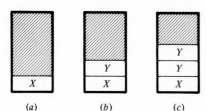

Figure 4.1 Use of a pushdown stack to control recursive subroutine calls.

(a)   (b)   (c)

turn address Y to be pushed into the stack, as shown in Fig. 4.1b. If CALL SUB is again executed, Y is pushed into the stack, as shown in Fig. 4.1c, and so on. This process continues until eventually RETURN is executed. If a total of k calls to SUB are made, then k-1 returns must be made to the instruction at location Y in SUB, with an additional RETURN transferring control back to the main program.

Stack implementation A stack with a capacity of n k-bit words is easily constructed from k n-bit shift registers having left- and right-shift capabilities. The shift registers are arranged as shown in Fig. 4.2 to form an n-word shift register. One end of this shift register, say the left end, is defined as the "top" of the stack. To perform a push operation, the word X to be written into the stack is applied to the left inputs of the shift register and the right-shift control line is activated. Conversely, a pop operation is performed by activating the left-shift control line, which transfers the word at the top of the stack to the output data bus.

Two possible error conditions may arise in stack operation. An attempt to push an additional word into a stack containing n words results in *stack overflow*. An attempt to pop a word from an empty stack results in *stack underflow*. Both the overflow and underflow conditions can be detected by including a counter in the stack circuitry to indicate the number of words currently in the stack. This counter is incremented (decremented) by each push (pop) operation. The combination of a push (pop) signal and a count of n (zero) results in an overflow (underflow) indication.

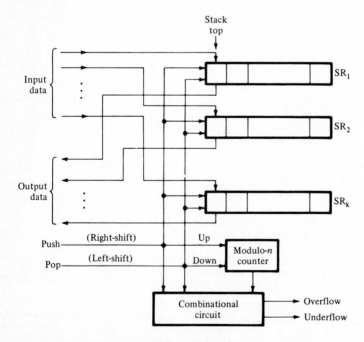

Figure 4.2 A stack constructed from shift registers.

Shift registers, which are serial access memories, are suitable for constructing stacks of limited capacity. When large stacks are required, it is generally more economical to use a contiguous region of random access memory as the main stack area. The push and pop operations are then implemented by memory write and read operations, respectively. A simple way of controlling the stack is to provide a special control register (actually a counter), called a *stack pointer* register SP. This register contains the address of the memory location that is currently acting as the top of the stack. A pop operation is performed by reading M using SP as an address register. Then SP is decremented by one to point to the new top element. Similarly, to perform a push operation, SP is first incremented by 1 and a write operation is performed using SP as an address register.

Stack overflow and underflow can be detected by including additional registers in the processor to store the highest and lowest addresses of the stack region. The register containing the highest stack address is called the *limit register* L: the register containing the lowest stack address is called the *base register* B. B, L, and SP define the boundaries of the stack, as indicated in Fig. 4.3. If an attempt is made to access a stack word whose address SP is such that SP > L (SP < B), an overflow (underflow) signal is issued.

Some computers such as the Burroughs B5000 and its successors have stacks which are partially in the CPU and partially in main memory [4]. The topmost words of the stack are stored in high-speed CPU registers, while the remaining words are in the main-memory stack region. This permits rapid access to the top of the stack while also allowing very large stacks to be implemented at reasonable hardware cost.

4.1.2 Instruction Interpretation

We turn now to the manner in which a control unit interprets an instruction in order to determine the control signals to be issued. The control signals are transmitted from the control unit to the outside world via control lines. Figure

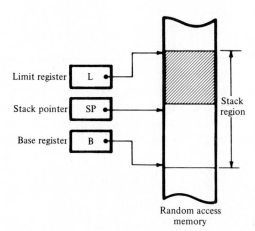

Random access
memory

Figure 4.3 A stack implemented by a random access memory.

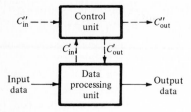

Figure 4.4 A control unit and its input-output lines.

4.4 shows the main control lines connected to a typical control unit. They are often indicated by broken lines to distinguish them from (unbroken) data lines. Again it should be emphasized that control and data are relative rather than absolute concepts; it may be convenient, therefore, to view the same physical lines as either data or control lines at different complexity levels.

The four groups of control signals distinguished in Fig. 4.4 have the following functions.

1. C'_{out}: These signals directly control the operation of the data processing unit. The main function of the control unit is to generate C'_{out}.
2. C'_{in}: These signals enable the data being processed to influence the control unit, allowing data-dependent decisions to be made. A frequent function of C'_{in} is to indicate the occurrence of unusual conditions such as errors, e.g., overflow, in the data processing unit.
3. C''_{out}: These signals are transmitted to other control units and may indicate status conditions such as "busy" or "operation completed."
4. C''_{in}: These signals are received from other control units, e.g., from a supervisory controller. They typically include start and stop signals and timing information. C''_{in} and C''_{out} are primarily used to synchronize the control unit with the operation of other control units.

Control unit specification Flowcharts and description languages, separately or in combination, appear to be the most useful formal tools for describing the behavior of a control unit. A flowchart describes the microoperations to be performed and indicates graphically the way in which they are to be sequenced. Once the data processing unit design has been completed and the control points identified, each microoperation $Z \leftarrow f(X)$ can be identified with a set of control lines $\{c_{i,j}\}$ that must be activated in order to execute that microoperation. If these control-signal sets are entered into the flowchart, then we obtain a description of the input-output behavior of the control unit. In this chapter, a flowchart description identifying the control lines to be activated will be taken as the starting point in the control-unit design process.

Implementation methods Historically, two general approaches to control-unit design have evolved. The first of these views the control unit as a sequential logic circuit to generate specific fixed sequences of control signals. As such, it is designed with the usual goals of minimizing the number of components used and maximizing the speed of operation. Once constructed, changes in behavior can be implemented only by redesigning and physically rewiring the unit. Such a circuit is therefore said to be a *hardwired control unit*.

Processor control units are among the most complex logic circuits in computers. Different instructions are executed by the activation of control-signal sequences which may have little resemblance to one another. As a result, a hardwired control unit often has little apparent structure and is frequently said to contain random logic. This lack of structure makes complex hardwired control units costly to design and debug.

Around 1950 several computer designers, notably M. V. Wilkes, observed the need for a flexible and systematic way of designing control circuits [10, 20]. The technique proposed by Wilkes, which he named *microprogramming*, treats a statement of the form

$$\text{Activate control lines } \{c_{i,\,j}\}$$

as a (micro)instruction stored in a special addressable memory called a *control memory*. The sequence of microinstructions needed to execute a particular operation constitutes a *microprogram* for that operation. The operation is performed by fetching the microinstructions one at a time from the control memory and using them to activate the control lines directly. A control unit designed around a control memory is called a *microprogrammed control unit*.

Microprogramming clearly makes control-unit design more systematic by organizing control signals into words (microinstructions) having a well-defined format. Since these signals are implemented in software rather than hardware, design changes can easily be made by altering the contents of the control memory. Furthermore, a microprogrammed CPU can, if the necessary microprograms are available, execute programs written in the machine languages of several different computers—a process called emulation. On the negative side, microprogrammed control units are often more costly than hardwired units due to the presence of the control memory and its access circuitry. They are also slower because of the extra time required to fetch microinstructions from the control memory. Microprogramming did not become widely used until its appearance in the smaller models of the IBM S/360 series in the mid-1960s. (Microprogramming was not used in the larger faster S/360 models because of the decrease in operating speed it entails.) Since then improvements in memory technology have greatly lowered the cost of control memories, and microprogramming has become a standard method of designing control units.

4.2 HARDWIRED CONTROL

4.2.1 Design Methods

In this section we consider the design of control units that use fixed logic circuits to interpret instructions and generate control signals. Three possible design approaches are discussed here.

Method 1: The standard approach to sequential circuit design of switching theory, which is called the state-table method here, since it begins with the construction of a state table for the control unit

Method 2: A method based on the use of delay elements for control-signal timing

Method 3: A related method that uses counters, which we call sequence counters, for timing purposes

Method 1, the most formal of these design approaches, incorporates systematic techniques for minimizing the number of gates and flip-flops. Methods 2 and 3, which are less formal, attempt to derive a logic circuit directly from the original (flowchart) description of the control-unit behavior. The resulting designs may not contain the minimum number of gates and flip-flops, but they are often obtained with much less effort. Furthermore, these designs are usually easier to comprehend and are therefore more likely to be free of error and easier to maintain. Our main emphasis will be on methods 2 and 3.

The foregoing design methods are by no means unrelated, nor are they the only systematic approaches to hardwired control design. In practice, control units are often so complex that no one design method by itself can yield a satisfactory circuit at an acceptable design cost. As a result, ad hoc design techniques are often used which cannot readily be formalized. However, it appears that most of these methods can be directly related to at least one of our three methods.

State-table method The behavior required of a control unit, like that of any finite-state sequential machine, can be represented by a *state table* of the type shown in Fig. 4.5. Let C_{in} and C_{out} denote the input and output variables of the control unit. The rows of the state table correspond to the set of internal states $\{S_i\}$ of the machine. An internal state is determined by the information stored in the unit at discrete points of time (clock periods). The columns correspond to the set of external signals to the control unit, that is, C_{in}. The entry in row S_i and column I_j has the form $S_{i,j}$, $z_{i,j}$, where $S_{i,j}$ denotes the next state of the control unit, and $z_{i,j}$ denotes the set of output signals $z_{i,j}$ from C_{out} that are activated by the application of I_j to the control unit when it is in state S_i.

A state-table description may be a suitable starting point for the implementation of small control units. A well-defined design methodology exists using

States	Input combinations C_{in}			
	I_1	I_2		I_m
S_1	$S_{1,1}, z_{1,1}$	$S_{1,2}, z_{1,2}$	$\cdots$	$S_{1,m}, z_{1,m}$
S_2	$S_{2,1}, z_{2,1}$	$S_{2,2}, z_{2,2}$	$\cdots$	$S_{2,m}, z_{2,m}$
	$\cdots$			
S_n	$S_{n,1}, z_{n,1}$	$S_{n,2}, z_{n,2}$	$\cdots$	$S_{n,m}, z_{n,m}$

Figure 4.5 State table for a control unit.

the state-table approach [7, 13]. This method is outlined in Sec. 2.1.4 and illustrated by an example in Sec. 4.2.2. There are several practical disadvantages to using state tables.

1. The number of states and input combinations may be so great that the state-table size and the amount of computation needed become excessive.
2. State tables tend to conceal useful information about a circuit's behavior, e.g., the existence of repeated patterns or loops.

Control circuits designed in this way tend to have a random structure, which makes design debugging and subsequent maintenance of the circuit difficult.

Delay-element method Consider the problem of generating the following sequence of control signals at times $t_1, t_2, \ldots, t_n$ using a hardwired control unit.

$$t_1: \quad \text{Activate}\{c_{1,j}\};$$

$$t_2: \quad \text{Activate}\{c_{2,j}\};$$
$$\ldots$$
$$t_n: \quad \text{Activate}\{c_{n,j}\};.$$

Suppose that an initiation signal called START(t_1) is available at t_1. START(t_1) may be fanned out to $\{c_{1,j}\}$ to perform the first microoperation. If START(t_1) is also entered into a time delay element of delay $t_2 - t_1$, the output of that circuit, START(t_2) can be used to activate $\{c_{2,j}\}$. Similarly, another delay element of delay $t_3 - t_2$ with input START(t_2) can be used to activate $\{c_{3,j}\}$, and so on. Thus a sequence of delay elements can be used to generate control signals in a very straightforward manner.

A control unit using delay elements can be constructed directly from a flowchart that specifies the control-signal sequences required. The circuit thus formed has essentially the same structure as the flowchart, a consequence of the fact that the circuit simply mirrors the flow of control through the flowchart. A few simple rules illustrated in Fig. 4.6 indicate the way in which the control circuit is derived from the flowchart.

1. Each sequence of two successive microoperations requires a delay element. The signals that activate the control lines are taken directly from the input and output lines of the delay, as shown in Fig. 4.6a. Signals that are intended to activate the same control line c_i are fed to an OR gate whose output is c_i. This line may then be connected to the control point it activates.
2. k lines in the flowchart that merge to a common line are transformed into a k-input OR gate, as shown in Fig. 4.6b.
3. A decision box (which indicates a branch in the control flow based on a condition test) can be implemented by two AND gates, as shown in Fig. 4.6c. This AND circuit forms a simple 1-bit demultiplexer controlled by

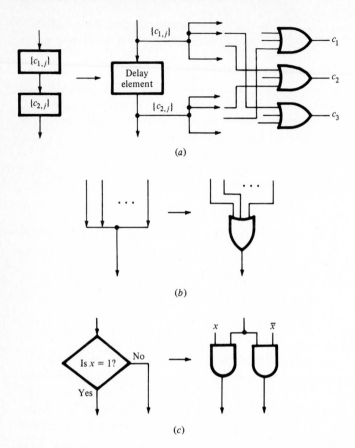

(a)

(b)

(c)

Figure 4.6 Rules for transforming a flowchart into a control circuit using delay elements.

the test variable x. Note that x may be replaced by a Boolean function $f(x)$, so that condition tests of arbitrary complexity can be used to determine the flow of control.

Figure 4.7 shows a portion of a typical flowchart indicating the control signals $\{c_{i,j}\}$ that must be activated at each step. Figure 4.8 shows the control circuit obtained using these transformation rules. Note that the AND gates derived from the two decision boxes have been merged in an obvious manner.

Delay-element structure The delay element required in control circuits of this type is more than just a passive two-terminal delay line. Its output must be a signal pulse of precise magnitude and duration that is synchronized with the main system clock. If all delays are one clock period in duration, then a clocked D-type master-slave flip-flop can be used to construct the delay element, as shown in Fig. 4.9. The control pulses are assumed to be of the same duration as the clock pulse. When an input control pulse arrives, it is stored in the D flip-

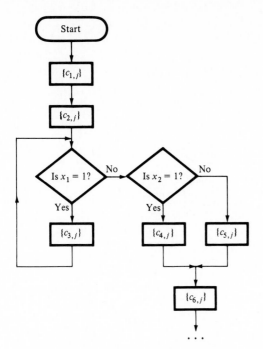

Figure 4.7 Portion of a flowchart showing the control signals to be activated.

flop and is gated out by the following clock pulse. A more complex circuit may be required if an input control pulse can become appreciably out of phase with the clock due to propagation delays between delay elements.

Some difficulties Despite the conceptually simple way that control circuits can be constructed from flowcharts using delay elements, this design method has the disadvantage that the number of delay elements needed may be very large. Roughly speaking, each delay element defines a state of the control unit. The number of delay elements is therefore approximately equal to the number of states n_s. Furthermore, each delay element is a sequential circuit of equal or greater complexity than a flip-flop [9]. Using classical state-table design methods, one can design a synchronous sequential circuit of n_s states with no more than $\lceil \log_2 n_s \rceil$ flip-flops. Thus the delay-element approach tends to produce expensive circuits in which timing is controlled by pulses traveling through cascades of delay elements. (These cascades are sometimes called *timing chains*.) Synchronization of many widely distributed delay elements may also be difficult.

Sequence counter method Consider the circuit of Fig. 4.10a, which consists basically of a modulo-k counter whose output is connected to a l/k clocked decoder. If the count enable input is connected to a clock source, the counter cycles continually through its k states. The decoder generates k pulse signals $\{\Phi_i\}$ on its output lines. Consecutive pulses are separated by one clock period,

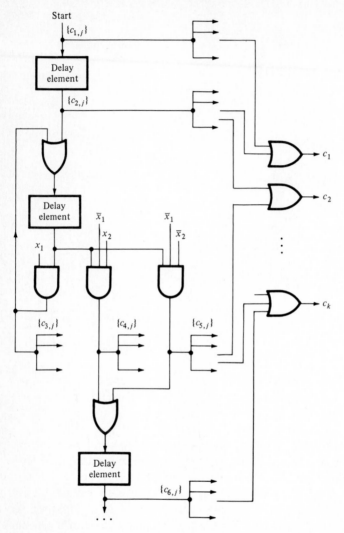

Figure 4.8 Control unit using delay elements which corresponds to the flowchart of Fig. 4.7

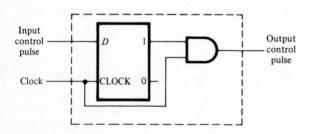

Figure 4.9 A simple delay element for synchronous control circuits.

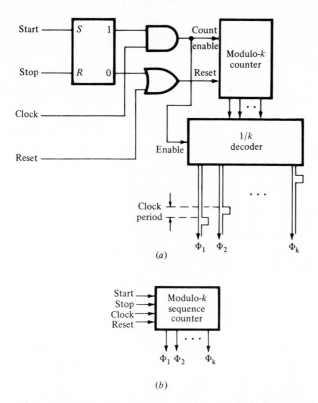

Figure 4.10 A modulo-k sequence counter: (a) logic diagram; (b) symbol.

as shown in the figure. The $\{\Phi_i\}$ effectively divide the time required for one complete cycle by the counter into k equal parts; the $\{\Phi_i\}$ may be called *phase* signals. Two additional input lines and a flip-flop are provided for turning the counter on and off. A pulse on the start line causes the counter to begin cycling through its states by logically connecting the count enable line to the clock source. A pulse on the stop line disconnects the clock and resets the counter. The circuit of Fig. 4.10a will be called a *sequence counter* and will be represented by the circuit symbol of Fig. 4.10b.

The usefulness of control counters of this type stems from the fact that many digital circuits are designed to perform a relatively small number of actions repeatedly. This type of behavior can be described (usually at a fairly high level) by a flowchart consisting of a single closed loop containing k steps. For example, Fig. 4.11 shows a one-loop flowchart containing six steps that describes the behavior of a typical CPU. Each pass through the loop constitutes an instruction cycle. Assuming that each step can be performed in an appropriately chosen clock period, one may build a control unit for this CPU around a single (modulo-6) sequence counter. Each signal Φ_i activates some set of control lines in step i of every instruction cycle. It is usually necessary to be able to vary the operations performed in step i depending on certain control sig-

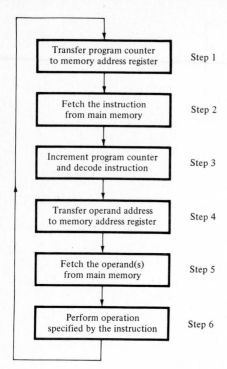

Transfer program counter to memory address register	Step 1
Fetch the instruction from main memory	Step 2
Increment program counter and decode instruction	Step 3
Transfer operand address to memory address register	Step 4
Fetch the operand(s) from main memory	Step 5
Perform operation specified by the instruction	Step 6

Figure 4.11 CPU behavior represented as a single closed loop.

nals or condition variables applied to the control unit. These are represented by the signals $C_{in} = \{C'_{in}, C''_{in}\}$ in Fig. 4.12. A logic circuit N is therefore needed which, as shown in Fig. 4.12, combines C_{in} with the timing signals $\{\Phi_i\}$ generated by the sequence counter.

Relationship to other methods Most of the state information in a control unit of the type shown in Fig. 4.12 resides in the sequence counter. If the logic circuit N is combinational, then the entire circuit has the form of the Huffman model of a sequential circuit shown in Fig. 2.16. This, of course, is also the type of circuit produced by the state-table design method.

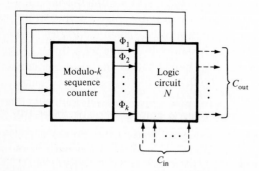

Figure 4.12 A control unit based on a sequence counter.

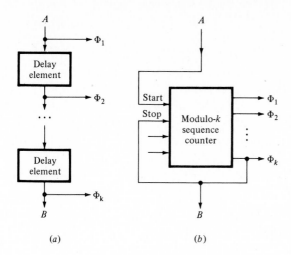

Figure 4.13 (*a*) A delay-element cascade; (*b*) the equivalent sequence counter circuit.

A strong relationship exists between the sequence counter and delay-element methods. A modulo-k sequence counter can easily be made to behave like a cascade of $k - 1$ delay elements. This is accomplished by connecting the kth output line Φ_k to the stop line, as shown in Fig. 4.13b, so that the counter shuts itself off after one complete cycle. Thus the control-unit design method with delay elements described earlier can, in principle, be directly modified to apply to sequence counters if every cascade of $k - 1$ delay elements is replaced by the circuit of Fig. 4.13b. However, the resulting design would generally be very inefficient compared with a sequence counter design of the type shown in Fig. 4.12.

Conversely, a cascade of $k - 1$ delay elements can be made to behave like a sequence counter by connecting its output to its input via an additional delay element and an OR gate, as shown in Fig. 4.14. The resulting circuit, which behaves like a free-running modulo-k sequence counter, is called a (modulo-k) *ring counter*. It is a useful component for control design. A ring counter is most easily constructed from a shift register, since a cascade of identical delay elements is essentially a shift register. A single control pulse propagates around the ring counter, so that at any time only one delay element is in the set state. No decoding circuitry is required, unlike the usual type of counter, and this is perhaps its most useful feature. On the other hand, a modulo-k ring counter requires k flip-flops, whereas an ordinary modulo-k counter requires only $\lceil \log_2 k \rceil$ flip-flops. In the sequel, sequence counters will be assumed to have the general form of Fig. 4.10. However, any such counter can be replaced by an equivalent modulo-k ring counter.

In the next two sections, some examples are presented to illustrate the foregoing methods for designing hardwired control units. Section 4.4.2 examines in detail the design of a control unit for a sequential multiplier. This can be viewed as a specialized control unit to interpret a single instruction, namely, multiply. In Sec. 4.2.3, the design of a CPU control unit which must interpret a

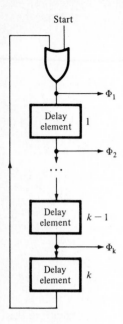

Figure 4.14 A delay-element circuit (ring counter) that behaves like a sequence counter.

variety of instructions is briefly considered. These examples will be used again in our discussions of microprogramming, thus providing some concrete comparisons between hardwired and microprogrammed control.

4.2.2 Multiplier Control Unit

In this section we examine the design of the control unit for the two-complement multiplier discussed in Example 2.2. Figure 2.45 is a block diagram of the overall system design showing in detail the data processing unit and the control points. Figure 4.15 shows the input-output connections of the control unit. (Note that the iteration counter COUNT is somewhat arbitrarily assigned to the data processing unit.) The functions of the control signals c_0 through c_{11} transmitted to the data processing unit are listed in Fig. 2.46. $Q(7)$ is the rightmost bit of the multiplier register Q. COUNT 6 is a signal derived from the iteration counter which is 1 when COUNT = 6 and 0 otherwise. Figure 4.16 repeats the algorithm of Fig. 2.44 showing the control signals that are ac-

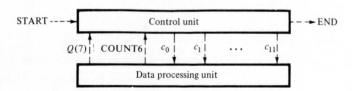

Figure 4.15 Input-output lines of the multiplier control unit.

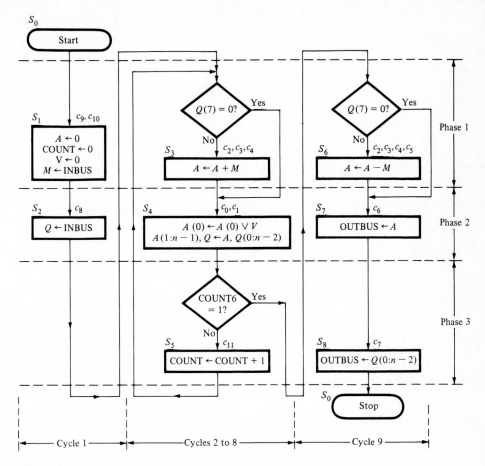

Figure 4.16 Flowchart for twos-complement multiplication.

tivated during the execution of each microoperation. We now consider how these control signals are generated.

All three techniques of hardwired control design discussed in Sec. 4.2.1 will be applied to this example, i. e., the state-table method of switching theory, the delay-element method, and the sequence counter method. In each case it is assumed that the starting point is the flowchart of Fig. 4.16.

State-table method The multiplier control unit is sufficiently small and simple so that the state-table design approach is feasible. First it is necessary to construct a state table for the control unit. We can associate a state S_i with every microoperation block in Fig. 4.16, giving eight states labeled S_1 through S_8. S_0 will denote an additional state representing the idle or waiting state of the control unit. The control unit has three external input signals START, Q(7), and COUNT6, hence there are eight possible input combinations. Figure 4.17 shows a state table for the control unit which is derived directly from the

State	\multicolumn{8}{c}{Input combination (START, Q(7), COUNT6)}							
	000	001	010	011	100	101	110	111
S_0	$S_0, \varnothing$	$S_0, \varnothing$	$S_0, \varnothing$	$S_0, \varnothing$	$S_1, \varnothing$	$S_1, \varnothing$	$S_1, \varnothing$	$S_1, \varnothing$
S_1	S_2, c_9, c_{10}	S_2, c_9, c_{10}	S_2, c_9, c_{10}	S_2, c_9, c_{10}				
S_2	S_4, c_8		S_3, c_8					
S_3			S_4, c_2, c_3, c_4	S_4, c_2, c_3, c_4				
S_4	S_5, c_0, c_1	S_7, c_0, c_1	S_5, c_0, c_1	S_6, c_0, c_1				
S_5	S_4, c_{11}	S_4, c_{11}	S_3, c_{11}	S_6, c_{11}				
S_6				S_7, c_2, c_3, c_4, c_5				
S_7		S_8, c_7		S_8, c_7				
S_8		S_0, END		S_0, END				

Figure 4.17 State table for the multiplier control unit.

flowchart. Each entry indicates the next state followed by a list of the control signals that are activated. The empty set symbol $\varnothing$ means no control line is activated in that particular state. Certain state- and input-signal combinations should not occur during normal operation, so the corresponding table entries are left unspecified (blank). For example, the START signal should assume only the 1 value when the control unit is in the idle state S_0. Similarly COUNT6 (which becomes 1 when COUNT $= 6$) is never 1 in state S_2, since COUNT is reset to zero in the preceding state S_1. Unspecified entries (which are also called "don't cares") may be used to simplify the logic design of the unit.

The techniques of switching theory can now be applied to obtain a gate-level logic design for the control unit. We outline the steps involved and refer the reader to any standard logic design text for details [13].

First an attempt is made to reduce the number of states in the state table. Let O_i and O_j be the output sequences resulting from applying any input sequence I to the control unit with S_i and S_j, respectively, as initial states. S_i and S_j are *compatible* if corresponding values of O_1 and O_2 are identical whenever both are specified. Sets of states that are pairwise compatible can be merged into a single state. In Figure 4.17, for example, S_2 and S_8 are compatible, so they can be merged to form a new state S_2' whose entries in the reduced state table are the union of rows S_2 and S_8. It is easily verified that no further reduction of the resulting eight-state table is possible. Hence to implement the control unit, $\lceil \log_2 8 \rceil = 3$ flip-flops are required.

The next step is to select the flip-flop types to be used and assign the eight possible combinations of the three state variables to the eight states that have been identified. JK flip-flops are a good choice, if available, since their tolerance of unspecified values on either the J or the K inputs often leads to simpler circuits. An arbitrary state assignment can be made because the control unit is synchronous. (In asynchronous or unclocked circuits, an improper state assignment may result in error conditions called races and hazards.) Some state-assignment methods for synchronous circuits exist which attempt to minimize the

	State variables		
States	y_1	y_2	y_3
S_0	0	0	0
S_1	0	0	1
S_2'	0	1	0
S_3	0	1	1
S_4	1	0	0
S_5	1	0	1
S_6	1	1	0
S_7	1	1	1

Figure 4.18 A state assignment for the multiplier control unit.

number of gates used; these methods are computationally complex, however. Here we arbitrarily chose the simple state assignment of Fig. 4.18.

If we use JK flip-flops to store the state variables, the control unit has the general form shown in Fig. 4.19. The remaining problem is to design the 6-input 19-output combinational logic circuit N, a straightforward but, in this case, a tedious task. The standard approach is to construct a *transition table* having the format shown in Fig. 4.20. The transition table can be regarded as a truth table which represents the various outputs of N as functions of the state variables and the other inputs to N. The entries in the output part of the transition table are determined from the state table, the state assignment, and the defin-

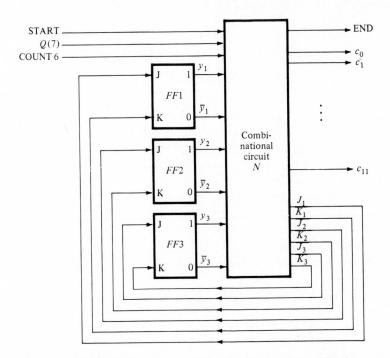

Figure 4.19 Multiplier control unit obtained by the state-table method.

	Inputs									Outputs							
START	Q(7)	COUNT6	y_1	y_2	y_3	END	c_0	c_1	$\cdots$	c_{11}	J_1	K_1	J_2	K_2	J_3	K_3
0	0	0	0	0	0	0	0	0		0	0	0	0	0	0	0
0	0	0	0	0	1	0	0	0		0	0	0	1	d	d	1
		$\cdots$								$\cdot\cdot$						
*0	0	1	1	0	0	0	1	1		0	0	0	1	d	1	d
		$\cdots$								$\cdots$						
1	1	1	1	1	1	d	d	d		d	d	d	d	d	d	d

Figure 4.20 Transition table for the multiplier control unit.

ing equations of the flip-flops. Consider, for example, the row marked by an asterisk in Fig. 4.20. This entry corresponds to column 001 and row S_4 in the state table of Fig. 4.17, since S_4 has been assigned the values $y_1 y_2 y_3 = 100$. From the state table we see that the corresponding next state is $S_7 = 111$ and that the output variables c_0 and c_1 should be activated. The output values are entered directly into the transition table as shown. The state transition $S_4 \rightarrow S_7$ implies that flip-flop $FF1$ should be left in the set state ($y_1 = 1$), while the other two flip-flops must be changed from the reset state ($y_2 = y_3 = 0$) to the set state ($y_2 = y_3 = 1$). Knowing the behavior of JK flip-flops, we can immediately specify the values required by flip-flop inputs $\{J_i, K_i\}$ to cause these state changes. $J_1 = K_1 = 0$ leaves $FF1$ unchanged, while $J_2 = J_3 = 1$ and $K_2 = K_3 = d$ (don't care) set both $FF2$ and $FF3$. These values are then entered into the transition table. Once completed, the transition table constitutes a truth table for N. A realization of N can then be obtained using any combinational circuit design method. N may be implemented with relatively few components by using PLAs (see Sec. 2.2.3).

Delay-element method We can design the multiplier control unit directly from the flowchart of Fig. 4.16 by using the transformation rules defined in Fig. 4.6. The result is shown in Fig. 4.21. Eight delay elements are required, a consequence of the approximately one-to-one correspondence between the states and the delay elements. This circuit has the advantage of closely reflecting the structure of the flowchart being implemented, a fact that greatly simplifies the design process as well as subsequent maintenance of the circuit. It is also worth noting that very few combinational components are required, fewer than can be expected using the state-table approach. This is largely due to the fact that no decoding is required to identify the control-unit state.

Sequence counter method The essence of this approach is the organization of the multiplication algorithm into cycles of k repetitive actions that can be timed by a modulo-k sequence counter. Inspection of the flowchart for the multiplication algorithm reveals that it contains a single closed loop involving three steps—add, shift, and increment. This loop is traversed seven times. (In the

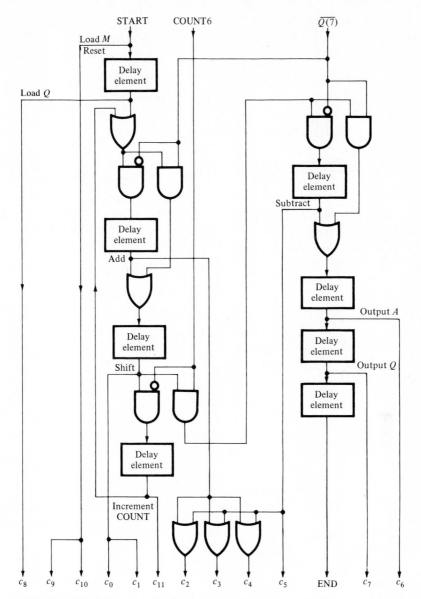

Figure 4.21 Multiplier control unit using delay elements.

general case where n-bit numbers are involved, it is traversed $n - 1$ times.) Thus we can attempt to design the control unit around a modulo-3 sequence counter.

The algorithm involves some steps which are not part of the main closed loop. Two clock periods are required at the beginning to reset the control unit and load the input operands. At the end of the algorithm, three clock periods are required for correcting the results when the multiplier is negative and for transferring the product to the output bus. These initiation and termination steps can be performed in two extra cycles of the sequence counter, as indicated in Fig. 4.16. Thus the execution of a single multiplication instruction can be performed in nine cycles organized as follows.

Step 1 (cycle 1): Initialize the control unit and load the multiplier and multiplicand.

Step 2 (cycles 2 to 8): Form the product, multiplying by one multiplier bit per cycle.

Step 3 (cycle 9): Correct the product if necessary, and output the result.

In order to distinguish these three steps, it is necessary to introduce flip-flops that can be set to identify the steps. Figure 4.22 shows a design based on the foregoing principles. The modulo-3 sequence counter provides the main timing signals. Three SR flip-flops have been included to identify the three steps of the algorithm. (Actually two flip-flops would suffice.) Each is set at the beginning of the corresponding step and reset at the end. A set of AND gates identify the particular microoperations to be performed in each clock period. The inputs to

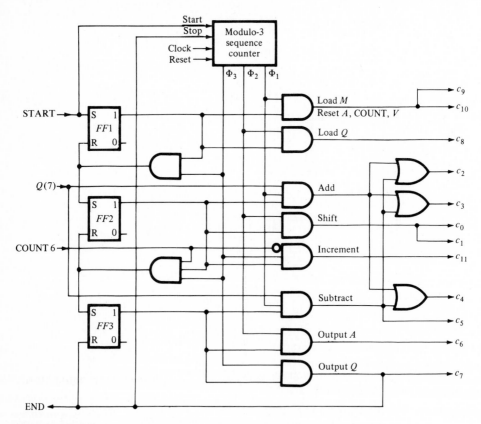

Figure 4.22 Multiplier control unit using a sequence counter.

these AND gates come from three sources:

1. The sequence counter
2. The three flip-flops
3. The external control signals to the control unit

The inputs required by each AND gate are easily determined from the flowchart. For example, to load the Q register from the input bus, the control unit must be in step 1 with $\Phi_2 = 1$. Hence, the corresponding AND gate is connected to $FF1$ and Φ_2. Finally, the control signals c_0 through c_{11} and END are derived from the AND gates outputs via OR gates when two or more distinct microoperations require the same control lines to be activated.

4.2.3 CPU Control Unit

The design of the control logic for a CPU differs in degree but not in kind from the multiplier control unit of the preceding section. A CPU may contain several hundred control lines, which makes control-unit design quite complex. In this section we briefly examine some of the design issues involved, using the simplest possible CPU as an example.

Description of CPU Consider the hypothetical CPU organization depicted in Fig. 3.2. Assume that it is required to execute the set of eight one-address instructions listed in Fig. 4.23. The algorithms needed to implement each instruction using the given hardware are easily derived. Figure 4.24 is a flowchart describing the instruction fetch cycle common to all instructions, as well as the distinct execution cycle required for each of the specified instructions. The microoperations in this flowchart determine the control signals and control points needed in the CPU. Figure 4.25 lists a suitable set of control signals and their functions, while Fig. 4.26 shows the approximate positions of the corresponding control lines in the CPU.

Implementation The microoperations performed by the CPU can be viewed as forming a six-step closed loop as depicted in Fig. 4.11. The first three steps

Mnemonic	Description
LOAD X	$AC \leftarrow M(X)$ (transfer contents of memory location X to the accumulator)
STORE X	$M(X) \leftarrow AC$
ADD X	$AC \leftarrow AC + M(X)$ (twos-complement addition)
AND X	$AC \leftarrow AC \wedge M(X)$ (logical AND)
JUMP X	$PC \leftarrow X$ (unconditional branch)
JUMPZ X	**if** $AC=0$ **then** $PC \leftarrow X$ (conditional branch)
COMP	$AC \leftarrow \overline{AC}$ (complement accumulator)
RSHIFT	Right-shift accumulator

Figure 4.23 Instruction set to be implemented.

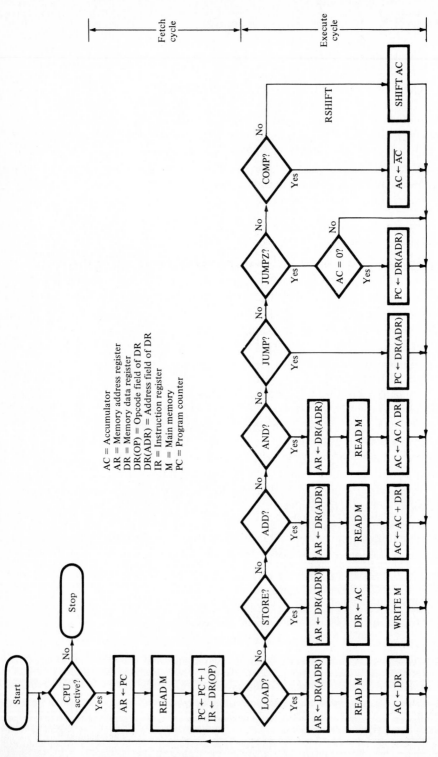

Figure 4.24 Operation of the eight-instruction CPU.

AC = Accumulator
AR = Memory address register
DR = Memory data register
DR(OP) = Opcode field of DR
DR(ADR) = Address field of DR
IR = Instruction register
M = Main memory
PC = Program counter

Control signal	Operation controlled
c_0	$AC \leftarrow AC + DR$
c_1	$AC \leftarrow AC \wedge DR$
c_2	$AC \leftarrow \overline{AC}$
c_3	$DR \leftarrow M(AR)$ (READ M)
c_4	$M(AR) \leftarrow DR$ (WRITE M)
c_5	$DR \leftarrow AC$
c_6	$AC \leftarrow DR$
c_7	$AR \leftarrow DR(ADR)$
c_8	$PC \leftarrow DR(ADR)$
c_9	$PC \leftarrow PC + 1$
c_{10}	$AR \leftarrow PC$
c_{11}	$IR \leftarrow DR(OP)$
c_{12}	RIGHT-SHIFT AC

Figure 4.25 Control signals of the simple CPU.

form the fetch cycle, and are identical for all instructions. The remaining execution steps vary with the instruction, which suggests that the control unit can be designed efficiently around a sequence counter. This is the only method we will consider here.

Let us suppose that every microoperation except READ M and WRITE M can be performed in one time unit of suitable length. Further suppose that READ M and WRITE M can be completed in two time units. Inspection of the

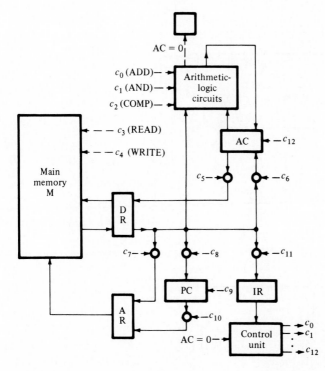

Figure 4.26 Structure of the simple CPU.

CPU flowchart reveals that a "slow" instruction such as ADD requires eight time units, which are divided evenly between the fetch and execute cycles. An instruction such as JUMP requires only five time units, four in the fetch cycle and one in the execute cycle. We will therefore use a modulo-8 sequence counter driven by a clock whose period is equal to one time unit.

Figure 4.27 shows the general structure of a simple hardwired control unit. From the CPU flowchart it is determined which control signals must be activated for each instruction at every point of time in the instruction cycle. For example, c_3, which causes a memory read operation to take place, is activated when $\Phi_2 = 1$ to fetch an instruction. It is also activated when $\Phi_6 = 1$ to fetch an operand provided that the LOAD, STORE, ADD, or AND output of the instruction decoder is 1. c_3 can therefore be defined by the following logic equation

$$c_3 = \Phi_2 + \Phi_6 \, (\text{LOAD} + \text{STORE} + \text{ADD} + \text{AND})$$

which is implemented by the combinational circuit N in Fig. 4.27. In general, each control signal c_i can be defined by a logic equation of the form

$$c_i = \sum_j \left(\Phi_j \sum_m I_m \right)$$

where I_m is an output of the instruction decoder. In the case of an instruction requiring $j < k$ steps where k is the sequence counter modulus, the sequence counter may be reset after the jth step.

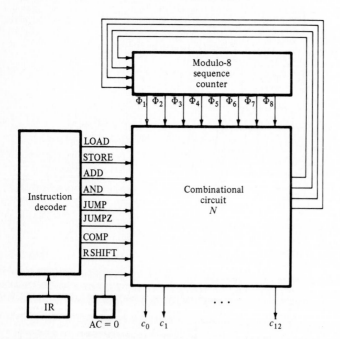

Figure 4.27 Hardwired CPU control unit using a sequence counter.

4.3 MICROPROGRAMMED CONTROL

4.3.1 Basic Concepts

Every instruction in a CPU is implemented by a sequence of one or more sets of concurrent microoperations. Each microoperation is associated with a specific set of control lines which, when activated, cause that microoperation to take place. Since the number of instructions and control lines is often in the hundreds, a hardwired control unit that selects and sequences the control signals can be exceedingly complicated. As a result, it is costly and difficult to design. Furthermore, such a control unit is inherently inflexible in that changes (e.g., to correct design errors or modify the instruction set) require that the control unit be redesigned.

Microprogramming is a method of control design in which the control-signal selection and sequencing information is stored in a random access memory called a *control memory* CM. The control signals to be activated at any time are specified by a word called a *microinstruction*, which is fetched from CM in much the same way an instruction is fetched from main memory. Each microinstruction also explicitly or implicitly specifies the next microinstruction to be used, thereby providing the necessary information for microoperation sequencing. A set of related microinstructions is called a *microprogram*. Microprograms, being software rather than hardware, can be changed relatively easily; hence microprogramming yields control units that are far more flexible than their hardwired counterparts. This flexibility is achieved at some extra hardware cost due to the control memory and its access circuitry. There is also a performance penalty due to the time required to access the microinstructions from CM. These disadvantages have been greatly diminished by the advent of low-cost high-speed memory technologies suitable for control memory applications.

In a microprogrammed CPU, each machine instruction is executed by a microprogram which acts as a real-time interpreter for the instruction. The set of microprograms that interpret a particular instruction set or language L is sometimes called an *emulator* for L. A microprogrammed computer C_1 can often be used to execute programs written in the machine language L_2 of some other computer C_2 by placing an emulator for L_2 in the control memory of C_1. C_1 is then said to be capable of emulating C_2.

Wilkes' original design A microinstruction in its simplest form has two major parts: a set of *control fields* which indicate the control lines to be activated, and an *address field* which indicates the address in the CM of the next microinstruction to be executed. In the original scheme proposed by Wilkes [20], each bit k_i of the control fields corresponds to a distinct control line c_i. When $k_i = 1$ in the current microinstruction, c_i is activated; otherwise c_i remains inactive.

Figure 4.28 shows the microprogrammed control unit design proposed by Wilkes in 1951 [10, 20]. The control memory, organized as a read-only memo-

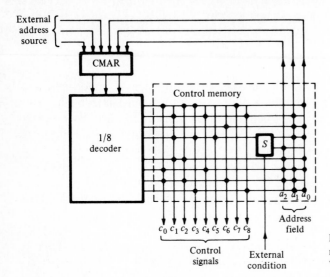

Figure 4.28 A microprogrammed control unit based on Wilkes' original design.

ry (ROM), is a diode matrix of the type discussed in Sec. 2.2.3. The left part of the ROM (called matrix A in Ref. 20) contains the control fields of every microinstruction, while the right part (matrix B) contains the (3-bit) address fields. The rows of CM represent microinstructions. The columns of CM represent either control lines or address lines. A register, called the *control memory address register* (CMAR), stores the address of the current microinstruction. This address is decoded, causing one of the horizontal lines of the diode matrix to become active. All vertical lines connected by a black dot (denoting the presence of a diode) to any given horizontal line are activated when the horizontal line becomes active. For example, when the topmost horizontal line in the CM of Fig. 4.28, which represents the microinstruction with address 000, is selected, control lines c_0, c_2, c_3, and c_7 are activated. At the same time the address field contents (001) are sent to the CMAR, where they are stored and used to address the next microinstruction.

As Fig. 4.28 indicates, the CMAR may be loaded from an external source as well as from the address field of a microinstruction. Typically this external source is used to provide the starting address of a microprogram stored in the CM. For example, in a microprogrammed CPU, each instruction is executed by (or interpreted by) a specific microprogram. The instruction opcode after suitable encoding can provide the starting address for its microprogram.

A requirement of any control unit is the ability to respond to external signals or conditions. This requirement is satisfied in the Wilkes scheme by providing a switch S controlled by an "external condition" flip-flop which allows one of two possible address fields to be selected. Thus in Figure 4.28, the fourth microinstruction may be followed by the microinstruction with address 011 or 100 as specified by the external condition. This feature makes conditional jumps within a microprogram possible.

Many modifications to this basic design have been proposed over the years. A major area of concern is the microinstruction word length, since it greatly influences the size and cost of the CM. Microinstruction length is determined by three major factors:

1. The maximum number of simultaneous microoperations that must be specified, i.e., the degree of parallelism required at the microoperation level
2. The way in which the control information is represented or encoded
3. The way in which the next microinstruction address is specified

Parallelism in microinstructions Microprogrammable processors are frequently characterized by the maximum number of microoperations that can be specified by a single microinstruction. This number can vary from one to several hundred.

Microinstructions that specify a single microoperation are quite similar to conventional machine instructions. They are relatively short, but due to the lack of parallelism, more microinstructions may be needed to perform a given operation. The format of the IBM S/370 Model 145, which is shown in Fig. 4.29, is representative of this type of microinstruction [11]. It consists of 4 bytes (32 bits). The leftmost byte (shaded) is an opcode that specifies the microoperation to be performed. The next two bytes specify operands. In most cases, these bytes are addresses of CPU registers. The rightmost byte contains information used to construct the address of the next microinstruction.

Microinstructions are often designed to take advantage of the fact that at the microprogramming level, many operations can be performed in parallel. If all useful combinations of parallel microoperations were specified by a single opcode, the number of opcodes would, in most cases, be enormous. Furthermore, a microinstruction decoder of considerable complexity would be needed. To avoid these difficulties it is usual to divide the microoperation specification part of the microinstruction into k disjoint parts called *control fields*. Each control field is associated with a set of microoperations, any one of which can be performed simultaneously with the microoperations specified by the remaining control fields. A control field usually specifies the control-line values for a single device such as an adder, a register, or a bus. In the extreme case represented by Fig. 4.28, there may be a 1-bit control field for every control line in the system.

A more typical example is shown in Fig. 4.30, which is the microinstruc-

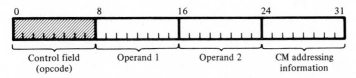

Figure 4.29 Microinstruction format at the IBM S/370 Model 145.

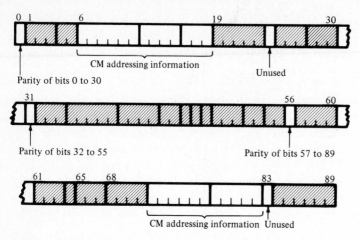

Figure 4.30 90-bit microinstruction format of the IBM S/360 Model 50 (shaded areas are control fields).

tion format used in the IBM S/360 Model 50 [10]. A total of 90 bits are used which are partitioned into separate fields for various purposes. There are 21 fields, shown shaded in Fig. 4.30, which constitute the control fields. The remaining fields are used for generating the next microinstruction address and for error detection by means of parity bits. For example, the 3-bit control field consisting of bits 65 to 67 controls the right input to the main CPU adder. This field indicates which of several possible registers should be connected to the right input of the adder. The control field comprising bits 68 to 71 identifies the particular function to be performed by the adder. The possible functions include binary addition and decimal addition with various ways of handling input and output carry bits. (For further details, see Husson [10].)

Encoding the control information The scheme of Fig. 4.28, in which there is a control field for every control line, is usually wasteful of CM space, since many combinations of control signals that can be specified by the microinstruction are never used. Consider, for instance, the register R of Fig. 4.31 which may be loaded from one of four independent sources using the control lines c_0, c_1, c_2, c_3. Suppose that there is 1 bit for each of these control lines in a microinstruction

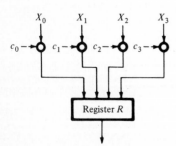

Figure 4.31 A register that can be loaded from four independent sources.

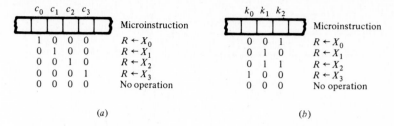

Figure 4.32 Control field for the circuit of Fig. 4.31: (*a*) unencoded format; (*b*) encoded format.

control field. Only the 5 bit patterns shown in Fig. 4.32*a* are valid, since any other patterns will cause an erroneous attempt to load R from two independent sources simultaneously. These five patterns can be encoded into a field of width $\lceil \log_2 5 \rceil = 3$ bits, as shown in Fig. 4.32*b*. In general, any n independent control signals or microoperations can be encoded in a control field of $\lceil \log_2(n + 1) \rceil$ bits, assuming that it is necessary to be able to specify a no-operation condition when no control signals are to be activated.

The unencoded format of Fig. 4.32*a* has the advantage that the control signals may be derived directly from the microinstruction. Suppose that the microinstruction is loaded into a register, e. g., the CM data register. The outputs of the control part of this register are the control lines, as shown in Fig. 4.33*a*. When encoded control fields are used, each control field must be connected to a decoder from which the control signals are derived, as shown in Fig. 4.33*b* and *c*.

Horizontal and vertical classification Microinstructions are commonly classified as horizontal or vertical. Unfortunately, there is no agreement about the precise meaning of these terms. *Horizontal* microinstructions have the following attributes:

1. Long formats
2. Ability to express a high degree of parallelism
3. Little encoding of the control information

Vertical microinstructions, on the other hand, are characterized by

1. Short formats
2. Limited ability to express parallel microoperations
3. Considerable encoding of the control information

The format of the IBM S/360 Model 50 shown in Fig. 4.30 is representative of horizontal microinstructions, while that of the S/370 Model 145 shown in Fig. 4.29 is representative of vertical microinstructions.

The reader will encounter more rigid definitions of horizontal and vertical in the literature on microprogramming than those given above. One definition is

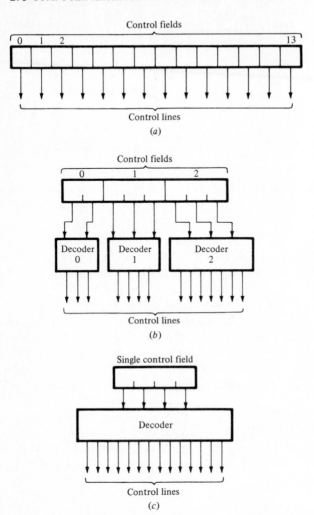

Figure 4.33 Control field formats: (*a*) no encoding; (*b*) some encoding; (*c*) complete encoding.

based entirely on the degree of encoding. A horizontal microinstruction format allows no encoding of control information, whereas a vertical format does. An alternative definition is based on the degree of parallelism possible. A vertical microinstruction can specify only one microoperation (no parallelism), while a horizontal microinstruction can specify many microoperations. These definitions are not entirely independent, since a large amount of parallelism implies little encoding, and vice versa. Thus the format of Fig. 4.33*a* is horizontal and that of Fig. 4.33*c* is vertical under both definitions. The intermediate case represented by Fig. 4.33*b* may be called horizontal by some authors and vertical by others. Many microprogrammed processors use formats that are difficult to classify as horizontal or vertical under any definition of the terms. For example, Agrawala and Rauscher [3] define horizontal and vertical precisely in terms of parallelism but find it necessary to introduce a third type of microinstruction called "diagonal." In view of these difficulties, we will use the terms vertical and horizontal only in the foregoing informal sense.

Microinstruction address specification In the Wilkes design of Fig. 4.28, each microinstruction contains the CM address of the next microinstruction to be executed. In the case of branch microinstructions, two possible next addresses are included. This explicit address specification has the advantage that no time is lost in microinstruction address generation, but it is wasteful of CM space.

The address fields can be eliminated from all but branch instructions by using a *microprogram counter* μPC as the primary source of microinstruction addresses. Its role is analogous to that of the program counter PC at the instruction level. Since only instructions have to be fetched from CM, the μPC is also used as the CM address register. (The main-memory address register must store both instruction and data addresses and therefore must be distinct from PC.)

Conditional branching, clearly a desirable feature in microprograms, is implemented in a variety of ways. The condition which is to be tested is generally an (*external*) *condition variable* generated by the data processing unit. If several such conditions exist, a *condition select* subfield is often included in the microinstruction to indicate which of the possible condition variables is to be tested. The branch address may be contained in the microinstruction itself, in which case it is loaded into the CM address register when a branch condition is satisfied. CM space can be conserved by not storing a complete address field in the microinstruction, but by storing instead, say, some low-order bits of the address. This restricts the range of branch instructions to a small region of the CM, and may increase the difficulty of writing some microprograms.

An alternative approach to branching is to allow the condition variables to modify the contents of the CM address register directly, thus eliminating wholly or in part the need for branch addresses in microinstructions. For example, let the condition variable v indicate an overflow condition when $v = 1$, and the normal condition when $v = 0$. Suppose that we want to execute a SKIP ON OVERFLOW microinstruction. This can be done by logically connecting v to the count enable input of μPC at an appropriate point in the microinstruction cycle. This allows the overflow condition to increment μPC an extra time, thus performing the desired skip operation.

Microoperation timing So far we have assumed that each microinstruction generates a set of control signals which are active for the duration of the microinstruction's execution cycle. A single clock pulse therefore synchronizes all the control signals; the clock period can be the same as the microinstruction cycle period. This mode of control has been termed *monophase* [15]. The number of microinstructions needed to specify a particular operation can often be reduced by dividing the microinstruction cycle into several *phases*, where each phase corresponds to a single clock period. Each control signal is typically active during only one of the phases. This mode of operation, which is called *polyphase*, permits a single microinstruction to specify a sequence of microoperations. An increase in the complexity of the microinstruction format can be expected, since it is necessary to specify the phases during which a control signal is to be activated.

Consider a microinstruction that implements the register transfer operation

$$R \leftarrow f(R_1, R_2)$$

where R can be R_1 or R_2. Depending on the implementation, this operation might be performed in several phases. The following four-phase interpretation is common [10].

Phase 1: Transfer the contents of registers R_1 and R_2 to the inputs of the f unit.
Phase 2: Store the result generated by the f unit in a temporary register or latch L.
Phase 3: Transfer the contents of L to the destination register R.
Phase 4: Fetch the next microinstruction from CM.

Figure 4.34 shows the timing signals associated with the four phases.

The time required to fetch a microinstruction from CM is often a significant portion of the total microinstruction cycle time. The microinstruction fetch and execute steps can be overlapped in much the same way that the instruction fetch and execute steps are overlapped at the machine-language level. A fairly simple way of doing this is to replace the control memory data register CMDR by a pair of registers forming a two-segment pipeline, as shown in Fig. 4.35. While one microinstruction in CMDR1 is being executed, the next microinstruction can be fetched and placed in CMDR0. The equivalent behavior may also be achieved by using a single register composed of master-slave flip-flops.

So far we have assumed that the influence of a microinstruction control field is limited to the period during which the microinstruction is executed. This

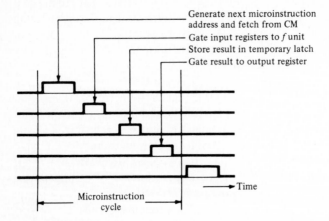

Figure 4.34 Timing diagram for a typical four-phase microinstruction.

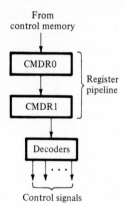

From
control memory

CMDR0

} Register
pipeline

CMDR1

Decoders

· · ·

Control signals

Figure 4.35 A register pipeline allowing overlap of microinstruction fetching and execution.

restriction can be lifted by storing the control field in a register which continues to exercise control until it is modified by a subsequent microinstruction. This technique is called *residual control* and is particularly useful when microinstructions are used to allocate the resources of a system. For example, a connection between two units may be established by a microinstruction and maintained for an arbitrarily long period of time via residual control.

Microprogrammed control-unit organization We now consider the structure of a typical modern microprogrammed control unit. Suppose that the microinstruction format shown in Fig. 4.36 is used. Each microinstruction has three main parts.

1. A condition select field is used to specify the external condition to be tested in the case of conditional branch microinstructions.
2. An address field contains the next address field to be used when a branch condition is satisfied. It is assumed that a microprogram counter μPC is used to provide the next microinstruction address when no branching is required.
3. The rest of the microinstruction specifies in encoded or unencoded format the control signals that must be activated to perform the desired microoperations.

Figure 4.37 shows a control unit designed around this microinstruction format. The counter μPC is the address register for the control memory CM. The

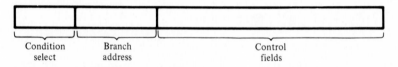

Condition   Branch   Control
select   address   fields

Figure 4.36 Typical microinstruction format.

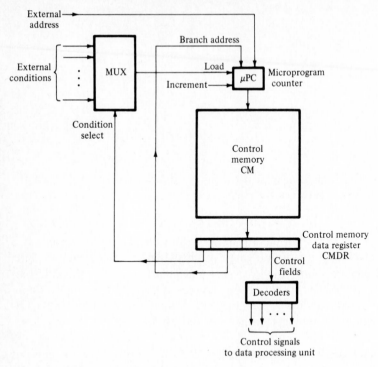

Figure 4.37 Typical microprogrammed control unit.

contents of the addressed word in CM are transferred to the control memory data register CMDR. The control fields are decoded (if necessary) and used to generate control signals for the data processing unit. μPC is then incremented. If a branch is specified by the microinstruction in CMDR, the contents of the microinstruction address field are loaded in μPC.

In the scheme of Fig. 4.37, the microinstruction condition select field is used to control a multiplexer which activates the parallel-load control input of μPC based on the status of external condition variables. Suppose, for example, that two condition variables v_1, v_2 must be tested. A condition select field $s_0 s_1$ of 2 bits suffices, with the following interpretation.

s_0	s_1	Meaning
0	0	No branching
0	1	Branch if $v_1 = 1$
1	0	Branch if $v_2 = 1$
1	1	Unconditional branch

The multiplexer has four inputs x_0, x_1, x_2, x_3, where x_i is routed to the multiplexer output when $s_0 s_1 = i$. Hence we require $x_0 = 0$, $x_1 = v_1$, $x_2 = v_2$, and

$x_3 = 1$ to control the loading of microinstruction branch addresses into μPC in this case.

Finally, a provision is also made for loading μPC with an address from an external source. This is used for loading the starting address of the desired microprogram in cases where CM contains more than one microprogram.

Writable control memory In the early years, control memories were read-only devices, i.e., their contents could not be altered on-line. Indeed the terms read-only memory (ROM) and read-only store (ROS) were synonymous with control memory. Among the reasons for this is the fact that read-only memory technologies such as diode matrices provide faster access rates than read-write memories such as ferrite cores. Furthermore, the instruction set of a microprogrammed processor was viewed as permanent, implying no need to alter the CM except for the correction of design errors or minor enhancements to the system.

It was recognized from the beginning that the CM could be a read-write memory. Wilkes observed that such a device, usually called a *writable control memory* (WCM), would have a number of "fascinating possibilities," but doubted that its cost could be justified [20]. The most interesting feature of a WCM is that it allows the instruction set of a machine to be changed, simply by changing the microprograms that interpret the instruction opcodes. Thus we can provide the same machine with different instruction sets which may be tailored to specific applications. Computers with WCMs are often considered to have no instruction set in the usual sense. A computer with a WCM is called *dynamically microprogrammable* because the control memory contents can be altered under program control.

Writing microprograms Microprogramming is the process of writing microprograms for a microprogrammable processor. As an activity it can be compared with assembly-language programming; however, the microprogrammer requires a more detailed knowledge of the processor hardware than the assembly-language programmer. Symbolic languages similar to assembly languages are normally used to write microprograms: these are referred to as *microassembly languages*. A *microassembler* is required to translate such microprograms into executable programs that can be stored in the control memory.

4.3.2 Minimizing Microinstruction Size

Problem definition As noted in the preceding section, the control fields of a microinstruction may be encoded in order to reduce the size of the microinstruction. This has the advantage of reducing the width and therefore the cost of the control memory where the microinstructions are stored. In this section we examine the problem of encoding the control fields so that the absolute minimum number of bits are used. Although its practical value is limited, this problem is one of the few general problems in the microprogramming area that can be precisely stated and solved. Several solution methods have been proposed [2]. The one described here is due to Das, Banerji, and Chattopadhyay [5].

Suppose that a set of microinstructions $I_1, I_2, \ldots, I_m$ has been defined for a given processor. Each microinstruction specifies a subset of the available control lines $c_1, c_2, \ldots, c_n$ which must be activated. Our objective is to derive a format for the microinstruction control fields of the type depicted in Fig. 4.33 such that the total number of bits in the control fields is a minimum. In other words, we want a control-field encoding method that uses as few bits as possible.

An encoded control field can activate only one control signal at a time. Two control signals can be included in the same control field only if they are never simultaneously activated by a microinstruction; such control signals are said to be *compatible*. More formally, let $c_i \in I_j$ denote that control signal c_i is to be activated by microinstruction I_j. Two control signals c_1 and c_2 are *compatible* if $c_1 \in I_j$ implies that $c_2 \notin I_j$, and vice versa. A *compatibility class* is a set of control signals that are pairwise compatible. Clearly the control signals included in any one control field must form a compatibility class. The minimum number of bits needed to encode a compatibility class C_i is $\lceil \log_2(|C_i| + 1) \rceil$. We will assume that the control field decoder must produce $|C_i| + 1$ distinct outputs, including the no-operation case where no control line is activated.

The minimization problem can now be defined formally as follows. Find a set of compatibility classes $\{C_i\}$ such that

1. Every control signal is contained in at least one member of $\{C_i\}$
2. The width cost function $w = \sum_i \lceil \log_2(|C_i| + 1) \rceil$ is a minimum

Note that only the microinstruction control field width is being minimized. Other fields such as the next address or condition select fields are not considered.

Outline of the algorithm A useful starting point is to find the *maximal compatibility classes* (MCCs), which are defined as compatibility classes to which no control signals can be added without introducing a pair of incompatible control signals. Clearly the compatibility classes that minimize w are subsets of the MCCs.

The algorithm described in Ref. 5 involves three major steps.

Step 1: Determine the set of MCCs.
Step 2: Determine all minimal sets of MCCs that include each control signal. Each of these sets is called a *minimal MCC cover*. (Note that a minimal MCC cover does not in general yield a minimum value of the cost function w.)

Step 3: Inspect each minimal MCC cover $\{C_i\}$ in turn and determine all ways of including each control signal in exactly one subset of some C_i. Calculate the cost w of the resulting solutions and select one with the minimum cost.

It is interesting to note that the first two steps are closely related to well-known procedures in switching theory [13]. The problem of minimizing the number of states in an incompletely specified sequential machine involves finding maximal compatibility classes among the states (see Sec. 4.2.2). Step 2 requires solving a covering problem similar to the prime implicant covering problem which forms part of most two-level gate minimization methods. The MCCs correspond to prime implicants and the control signals correspond to minterms. Many of the methods developed for simplifying the prime-implicant covering problem may be used in step 2. Step 3 also involves a similar covering problem.

Determining the MCCs The MCCs may be derived systematically by first determining all compatibility classes containing two control signals, then determining all compatibility classes containing three control signals, and so on. Let S_i denote the set of compatibility classes $\{C_{ij}\}$ such that C_{ij} contains i control signals and $i \geq 1$. The members of S_1 are simply the n original control signals. S_{i+1} is constructed from S_i as follows. Consider each member C_{ij} of S_i in turn. Add a new control signal to C_{ij} to form C. Test C to determine if it is a compatibility class. If it is, add C to S_{i+1} and delete C_{ij} and any other subsets of C from S_i. Form all possible $(i + 1)$-member compatibility classes in this way, then move on to S_{i+2}. The process terminates when no new compatibility classes can be formed, i.e., when $S_k = \emptyset$, the empty set, for some $k \leq n + 1$. The compatibility classes that have not been deleted from the list $S_1, S_2, \ldots, S_k$ are the MCCs. Figure 4.39 shows the computation of the MCCs for the four microinstructions defined in Fig. 4.38.

Microinstruction	Control signals
I_1	a, b, c, g
I_2	a, c, e, h
I_3	a, d, f
I_4	b, c, f

Figure 4.38 A set of microinstructions and the control signals they activate.

S_1: $a, \not{b}, \not{c}, \not{d}, \not{e}, \not{f}, \not{g}, \not{h}$

S_2: $\not{bd}, \not{be}, \not{bh}, cd, \not{de}, \not{dg}, \not{dh}, \not{ef}, \not{eg}, \not{fg}, \not{fh}, gh$

S_3: $bde, bdh, deg, dgh, efg, fgh$

S_4: $\emptyset$

Figure 4.39 Computation of the MCC's for the microinstructions of Figure 4.38.

For brevity, a compatibility class $\{a, b, c, \ldots\}$ is denoted by abc. . . . It can be seen that there are eight MCCs in this case: a, cd, bde, bdh, deg, dgh, efg, and fgh.

Determining the minimal MCC covers The minimal MCC covers are most easily obtained by constructing a *cover table* containing a row for each MCC C_i and a column for each control signal c_j. An x is placed at the intersection of the ith row and jth column if $c_j \in C_i$ or, in other words, if C_i *covers* c_j. Figure 4.40 shows the cover table corresponding to the microinstruction set of the running example (Fig. 4.38).

Certain rows and columns can be deleted from a cover table to simplify determination of the minimal MCC covers.

1. Suppose that column c_j contains only one x, which occurs in row C_i. C_i is said to be an *essential MCC* and must appear in every minimal MCC cover, since it is the only MCC that covers c_j. All rows corresponding to essential MCCs can be deleted from the cover table. In the case of Fig. 4.40, C_1 and C_2 are the essential MCCs and can be deleted. Furthermore, all columns with x's in essential rows can be deleted. This implies that the columns a, c, and d can be deleted from Fig. 4.40.
2. If the cover table contains two or more identical columns, then all but one of those columns can be deleted.
3. Column c_i is said to *dominate* column c_j if c_i contains an x in every row where c_j contains an x, and c_i contains more x's than c_j. The dominating column c_i can be deleted since every MCC that covers c_j automatically covers c_i. In Fig. 4.40, d dominates b and c, while g dominates f.
4. Row C_i is said to dominate row C_j if C_i contains an x in every column where C_j contains an x, and C_i contains more x's than C_j. In this case, the dominated row C_j can be deleted, since C_i covers all the control signals that are covered by C_j. Figure 4.40 contains no row domination.

Figure 4.41 shows the result of deleting essential rows, the columns cov-

MCCs	Control signals							
	a	b	c	d	e	f	g	h
$C_1 = a$	x							
$C_2 = cd$			x	x				
$C_3 = bde$		x		x	x			
$C_4 = bdh$		x		x				x
$C_5 = deg$				x	x		x	
$C_6 = dgh$				x			x	x
$C_7 = efg$					x	x	x	
$C_8 = fgh$						x	x	x

Figure 4.40 Cover table for the microinstructions of Figure 4.38.

MCCs	Control signals			
	b	e	f	h
$C_3 = bde$	x	x		
$C_4 = bdh$	x			x
$C_5 = deg$		x		
$C_6 = dgh$				x
$C_7 = efg$		x	x	
$C_8 = fgh$			x	x

Figure 4.41 Reduced cover table obtained from Figure 4.40.

ered by essential rows, and dominating columns from the example cover table. It can be seen immediately that a minimal cover for this table contains two MCCs, and the possible choices are $\{C_3, C_8\}$ and $\{C_4, C_7\}$. Combining these with the essential MCCs C_1 and C_2, we conclude that the desired MCC solutions are $\{C_1, C_2, C_3, C_8\}$ and $\{C_1, C_2, C_4, C_7\}$.

While minimal MCC covers can be obtained by inspection from very small cover tables, more formal methods are needed for large tables. A conceptually simple approach is to derive the minimal MCC cover from a logical expression that embodies the covering conditions. This is known as *Petrick's method* [13]. Let C_i be a Boolean variable which is 1 if C_i is selected for inclusion in a set of MCCs that cover all columns of a cover table; C_i is 0 otherwise. Let $C_{j1}, C_{j2}, \ldots, C_{jn_j}$ be the MCCs that cover column f_j. To ensure that f_j is covered, the Boolean equation

$$\mathbf{C}_{j1} + \mathbf{C}_{j2} + \ldots + \mathbf{C}_{jn_j} = 1$$

must be satisfied. This equation says, in effect, that C_{j1} must be selected or C_{j2} must be selected or C_{j3} must be selected, etc. In order that every column be covered, the expression $\mathbf{C}_{j1} + \mathbf{C}_{j2} + \ldots + \mathbf{C}_{jn_j}$ must be 1 for $j = 1, 2, \ldots, n$. In other words, the Boolean equation

$$\prod_{j=1}^{n} (\mathbf{C}_{j1} + \mathbf{C}_{j2} + \ldots + \mathbf{C}_{jn_j}) = 1 \tag{4.1}$$

must be satisfied. Every solution to (4.1) defines a cover for the original cover table.

To solve (4.1) we can simply multiply it out, using the distributive laws of Boolean algebra to convert it to a sum-of-products expression of the form

$$\sum_{k=1}^{p} (\mathbf{C}_{k1} \mathbf{C}_{k2} \cdots \mathbf{C}_{kn_k}) = 1 \tag{4.2}$$

Every product term $\mathbf{C}_{k1} \mathbf{C}_{k2} \cdots \mathbf{C}_{kn_k}$ in (4.2) implies that $\{C_{k1}, C_{k2}, \ldots, C_{kn_k}\}$ is a distinct solution to the covering problem. The product terms containing the fewest $\mathbf{C}_i$ variables define the minimal MCC covers.

Let us apply Petrick's method to the reduced cover table of Fig. 4.41. The initial product-of-sums expression is

$$(C_3 + C_4)(C_3 + C_5 + C_7)(C_7 + C_8)(C_4 + C_6 + C_8) = 1 \qquad (4.3)$$

This expression is reduced to a sum-of-products by applying the two distributive laws from Fig. 2.12:

$$a(b + c) = ab + ac \qquad (4.4)$$

$$(a + b)(a + c) = a + bc \qquad (4.5)$$

in any order. It is desirable to apply (4.5) as often as possible, since it eliminates an a term, whereas (4.4) adds an a term. Applying (4.5) twice to (4.3) yields

$$(C_3 + C_4(C_5 + C_7))(C_8 + C_7(C_4 + C_6)) = 1$$

Two applications of (4.4) yield

$$(C_3 + C_4C_5 + C_4C_7)(C_8 + C_4C_7 + C_6C_7) = 1$$

Using (4.5) again we obtain

$$C_4C_7 + (C_3 + C_4C_5)(C_8 + C_6C_7) = 1$$

and finally

$$C_4C_7 + C_3C_8 + C_3C_6C_7 + C_4C_5C_8 + C_4C_5C_6C_7 = 1 \qquad (4.6)$$

From inspection of (4.6) it can be seen that the only minimal MCC covers for the reduced cover table are $\{C_4, C_7\}$ and $\{C_3, C_8\}$. Combining these with the essential MCCs C_1 and C_2, we conclude that $\{C_1, C_2, C_4, C_7\}$ and $\{C_1, C_2, C_3, C_8\}$ are the minimal MCC covers for the original cover table.

The amount of computation required by Petrick's method for large tables is substantial. It may be more efficient to derive the minimum covers using integer linear programming or similar techniques [12]. (See also Prob. 4.7.)

Determining covers that minimize w The number of MCCs in each minimal MCC cover is the minimum number of control fields required to encode the given microinstructions. If control signal c_i is covered by two MCCs C_1 and C_2, then c_i can be deleted from C_1 or C_2 to yield a new non-MCC cover of potentially lower cost. In the final step of the algorithm, we consider all possible ways of deleting control signals from the MCC covers so that in the resulting cover each control signal is covered once, i.e., the cover is a partition of the set of control signals. The final solution is obtained by computing w for each partition and selecting one with the minimum value of w.

The partitions may be derived manually from each minimal MCC cover by setting up a cover table whose rows are the members of the MCC cover. Then for each control signal c_i, select a row C_j containing c_i and delete c_i from the covers defining the remaining rows. (Note that if C_j is an essential row it is the only possible cover for c_i.) The process is repeated until all control signals have been covered. The resulting compatibility classes form a partition. All possible partitions of the set of microoperations are obtained and their cost functions w are calculated. This procedure is repeated for every MCC solution, and a partition with the minimum value of w is selected.

	a	b	c	d	e	f	g	h
$C_1 = a$	x							
$C_2 = cd$			x	x				
$C_3 = bde$		x		x	x			
$C_8 = fgh$						x	x	x

Figure 4.42 Cover table for the minimal MCC cover $\{C_1, C_2, C_3, C_8\}$.

Consider one of the two minimal MCC covers $\{C_1, C_2, C_3, C_8\}$ obtained for the running example. Figure 4.42 shows the corresponding cover table. There is only one way in which a, b, c, e, f, g, and h can be covered. d may be covered by either C_2 or C_3. If we decide to cover it by C_2, we delete d from C_3 obtaining the partition $\{a, cd, be, fgh\}$ for which $w = 7$. If, however, we cover d using C_3, we obtain the partition $\{a, c, bde, fgh\}$ for which $w = 6$. Similarly, the other minimal MCC cover $\{C_1, C_2, C_4, C_7\}$ yields the two partitions $\{a, cd, bh, efg\}$ and $\{a, c, bdh, efg\}$, for which $w = 7$ and 6, respectively. Hence there are two possible assignments of the control signals to four control fields yielding the minimum cost of $w = 6$ bits. Figure 4.43 shows one of the many possible ways of coding the control fields using the minimum-cost partition $\{a, c, bde, fgh\}$. Figure 4.44 gives the corresponding control bit patterns for the four original microinstructions.

Control field	Bits used	Code	Control signal activated
0	0	0	No operation
		1	a
1	1	0	No operation
		1	c
2	2, 3	00	No operation
		01	b
		10	d
		11	e
3	4, 5	00	No operation
		01	f
		10	g
		11	h

Figure 4.43 Optimal encoding scheme for the microinstructions of Figure 4.38.

	Control bits
Microinstruction	0	1	2	3	4	5
I_1	1	1	0	1	1	0
I_2	1	1	1	1	1	1
I_3	1	0	1	0	0	1
I_4	0	1	0	1	0	1

Figure 4.44 Control field codes for the microinstructions of Figure 4.38.

4.3.3 Multiplier Control Unit

Consider once more the twos-complement multiplication circuit defined in Example 2.2 (Sec. 2.2.5). Several hardwired control-unit designs for this circuit were presented in Sec. 4.2.2. We now turn to the design of a microprogrammed control unit. Again our starting point is the flowchart in Fig. 4.16, which defines the flow of control and identifies the control signals to be activated at specific times during the multiplication process.

As a first attack we shall employ the straightforward microinstruction format of Fig. 4.36 consisting of three parts: a condition select field, a branch address, and a set of control fields. Initially, no encoding will be used, so that there are thirteen 1-bit control fields, one for each of the control lines $c_0, c_1, \ldots, c_{11}$ and one for the END signal. The control unit will have the general organization of Fig. 4.37, which uses a microprogram counter μPC as the control memory address register. During each microinstruction cycle, μPC is incremented to form the address of the next microinstruction. In the case of a branch microinstruction, the address stored in the microinstruction itself is used as the next address. The need for an external address input will be eliminated by storing the first microinstruction in CM address zero and simply resetting μPC to zero at the start of every multiplication.

It may be helpful to rewrite the flowchart of Fig. 4.16 using our formal description language, since the resulting description is essentially the microprogram we require in abstract symbolic form. This description is given in Fig. 4.45. (Compare the flowchart and the formal language description for Example 2.1.) Each nonbranching statement in Fig. 4.45 or, equivalently, each microoperation box in the flowchart, requires a distinct microinstruction. Hence we conclude that a microprogram of approximately 10 microinstructions is required. An address field of 4 bits should therefore suffice.

Every microinstruction may contain a branch address if desired and thus implement a conditional or unconditional **go to**. The condition select field is

```
   START:  [Initialize the microprogrammed control unit];
           A ← 0, COUNT ← 0, V ← 0, M ← INBUS;
           Q ← INBUS;
   TEST1:  if Q(7) = 0 then go to RSHIFT;
           A ← A + M;
  RSHIFT:  A(1:n−1), Q ← A, Q(0:n−2), A(0) ← A(0) ∨ V;
           if COUNT6 = 1 then go to TEST2;
           COUNT ← COUNT + 1;
           go to TEST1;
   TEST2:  if Q(7) = 0 then go to FINISH;
           A ← A − M;
  FINISH:  OUTBUS ← A;
           OUTBUS ← Q(0:n−2);
           STOP;
```

Figure 4.45 A formal language description of the twos-complement multiplier.

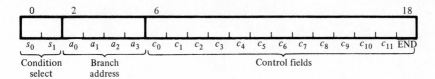

Figure 4.46 An unencoded (horizontal) microinstruction format for the twos-complement multiplier.

required to indicate four conditions:

1. No branching
2. Branch if $Q(7) = 0$
3. Branch if COUNT6 $= 1$
4. Unconditional branch

Hence a 2-bit condition select field suffices. We conclude that a 19-bit microinstruction having the horizontal format shown in Fig. 4.46 is to be used.

It is now quite easy to write the microprogram that implements multiplication. The symbolic microprogram of Fig. 4.45 is converted line by line into the bit patterns shown in Fig. 4.47. Consecutive microinstructions are assigned to consecutive addresses, and the appropriate condition select bits are inserted (00 denotes no branching; the remaining condition codes can easily be deduced from Fig. 4.47). When the multiplication is completed, the microprogram enters a waiting state by repeatedly executing the no-operation microinstruction in CM location 1011. It remains in this state until μPC is reset by the arrival of a new external START signal. Alternatively, we could introduce a flip-flop to enable CM operation, which is set (reset) by the START (END) control signal. The structure of the control unit is shown in Fig. 4.48.

Very few of the 2^{13} possible control-field patterns allowed by the microinstruction format of Fig. 4.46 are actually needed. From Fig. 4.47 it can be seen that several sets of control signals are always activated simultaneously; hence it suffices to reserve a single 1-bit control field for these signals. Thus the 7 bits reserved for the three sets $\{c_0, c_1\}$, $\{c_2, c_3, c_4\}$, and $\{c_9, c_{10}\}$ can be replaced by 3 bits yielding the shorter microinstruction shown in Fig. 4.49.

Control-field encoding A further reduction in control-field size can be achieved by encoding the control fields. Since there are 12 distinct microinstructions in the multiplication microprogram, we can encode the control information in a single 4-bit control field or opcode yielding a purely vertical microinstruction format. However, this severely limits our ability to modify the microinstruction set. Let us suppose that the microinstruction format we are designing will be used for more applications than the control of multiplication. (Note that the multiplier circuit being controlled has all the essential components of a general purpose arithmetic-logic unit.) Thus it is of interest to encode the microinstruc-

Microinstruction

Address in CM	Condition select	Branch address	c_0	c_1	c_2	c_3	c_4	c_5	c_6	c_7	c_8	c_9	c_{10}	c_{11}	E N D	Comments
0000	00	0000	0	0	0	0	0	0	0	0	0	1	1	0	0	$A \leftarrow 0$, COUNT $\leftarrow 0$, $V \leftarrow 0$, $M \leftarrow$ INBUS;
0001	00	0000	0	0	0	0	0	0	0	0	1	0	0	0	0	$Q \leftarrow$ INBUS;
0010	01	0100	0	0	0	0	0	0	0	0	0	0	0	0	0	**if** $Q(7) = 0$ **then go to 4;**
0011	00	0000	0	0	0	1	1	0	0	0	0	0	0	0	0	$A \leftarrow A + M$;
0100	10	0110	1	1	0	0	0	0	0	0	0	0	0	0	0	$A(1:n-1)$, $Q \leftarrow A$, $Q(0:n-2)$, $A(0) \leftarrow A(0) \lor V$, **if** COUNT6 $= 1$ **then go to 6;**
0101	11	0010	0	0	0	0	0	0	0	0	0	0	0	1	1	COUNT $\leftarrow$ COUNT $+ 1$, **go to 2;**
0110	01	1000	0	0	0	0	0	0	0	0	0	0	0	0	0	**If** $Q(7) = 0$ **then go to 8;**
0111	00	0000	0	0	1	1	1	0	1	0	0	0	0	0	0	$A \leftarrow A - M$;
1000	00	0000	0	0	0	0	0	0	1	0	0	0	0	0	0	OUTBUS $\leftarrow A$;
1001	00	0000	0	0	0	0	0	0	0	1	0	0	0	0	0	OUTBUS $\leftarrow Q(0:n-2)$;
1010	00	0000	0	0	0	0	0	0	0	0	0	0	0	0	1	Issue completion signal;
1011	11	1011	0	0	0	0	0	0	0	0	0	0	0	0	0	Halt;

Figure 4.47 Multiplication microprogram using the microinstruction format of Figure 4.46.

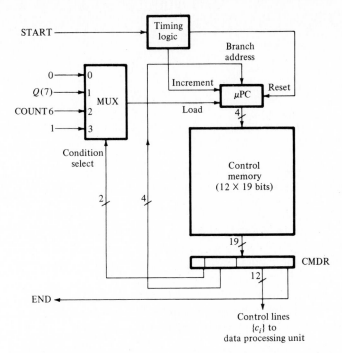

Figure 4.48. Microprogrammed control unit for the twos-complement multiplier.

tions in such a way that microinstructions as yet unspecified can readily be accommodated.

One possible approach is to divide the control information into compatible control fields using the method of Sec. 4.3.2. This method minimizes the number of control bits while maintaining the maximum degree of parallelism inherent in the original microinstruction set. Let $\{I_j\}$ denote the microinstructions in the multiplication microprogram, where j is the CM address of I_j. After the elimination of redundant bits from the control field, we are left with nine microoperations to be specified; these can be represented by the control signals c_0, c_2, c_5, c_6, c_7, c_8, c_9, c_{11}, and END. Figure 4.50 lists the 12 microinstructions and the control signals they specify.

The first step is to determine the MCCs. This is easy because there are

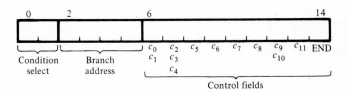

Figure 4.49 Unencoded microinstruction format for the twos-complement multiplier after removal of redundant control fields.

Microinstruction	Control signals
I_0	c_9
I_1	c_8
I_2	
I_3	c_2
I_4	c_0
I_5	c_{11}
I_6	
I_7	c_2, c_5
I_8	c_6
I_9	c_7
I_{10}	END
I_{11}	

Figure 4.50 Microinstructions for the twos-complement multiplier and the control signals they specify.

only two incompatible microoperations c_2 and c_5. The only two MCCs are $C_0 = c_0c_2c_6c_7c_8c_9c_{11}$ END and $C_1 = c_0c_5c_6c_7c_8c_9c_{11}$ END, each containing eight members. C_0 and C_1 are also the minimal MCC covers, so a format containing two encoded control fields suffices. Since there are nine control signals to be specified as well as the no-operation condition, at least $\lceil \log_2 10 \rceil = 4$ control bits are needed. There exist several ways of choosing subsets of C_0 and C_1 that cover all control signals and yield a value of 5 for the cost function

$$w = \sum_{i=1}^{2} \lceil \log_2 (|C_i| + 1) \rceil$$

which is clearly the minimum cost. For example, we can set $C_0' = c_0c_2c_6$ and $C_1' = c_5c_7c_8c_9c_{11}$ END. The resulting microinstruction has the format shown in Fig. 4.51 and requires a pair of decoders to generate the control signals. The fact that there are only two control fields indicates that there is very little inherent parallelism in the multiplication algorithm.

Encoding control fields by function A disadvantage of the minimum-bit control format of Fig. 4.51 is that functionally unrelated control signals are combined

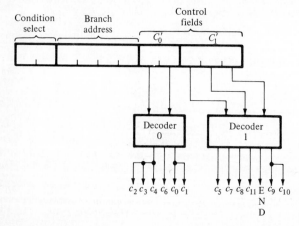

Figure 4.51 Encoded microinstruction format with maximum parallelism and the minimum number of control bits.

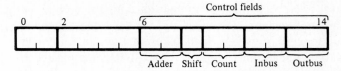

Figure 4.52 Microinstruction format with control fields encoded by function.

in the same control field, while related signals are derived from different control fields. For example, both C_0' and C_1' control the transfer of information to OUTBUS. This lack of functional separation makes the writing of microprograms more difficult, since the microprogrammer must associate several unrelated opcodes with each control field. An encoded format in which each control field specifies the control signals for one component or for a related set of operations of the system is usually preferred, even though more control bits may be needed.

On examining the multiplier design, we see that there are five major components to be controlled: the adder, the A, Q register combination, the external iteration counter COUNT, and the two data buses INBUS and OUTBUS; this suggests the encoded microinstruction format of Fig. 4.52. Figure 4.53 in-

Control field	Bits used	Code	Microoperations specified	Control signals activated
ADDER	6, 7	00	No operation	
		01	$A \leftarrow A + M$	c_2, c_3, c_4
		10	$A \leftarrow A - M$	c_2, c_3, c_4, c_5
		11	Unused	
SHIFT	8	0	No operation	
		1	Right-shift A, Q and load $A(0)$	c_0, c_1
COUNT	9, 10	00	No operation	
		01	Clear COUNT, A, V	c_{10}
		10	COUNT $\leftarrow$ COUNT + 1	c_{11}
		11	Unused	
INBUS	11, 12	00	No operation	
		01	$Q \leftarrow$ INBUS	c_8
		10	$M \leftarrow$ INBUS	c_9
		11	Unused	
OUTBUS	13, 14	00	No operation	
		01	OUTBUS $\leftarrow A$	c_6
		10	OUTBUS $\leftarrow Q(0{:}n-2)$	c_7
		11	Unused	

Figure 4.53 Interpretation of the microinstruction control fields with encoding by function.

dicates possible control-field bit assignments and their interpretation. Note that this ad hoc encoding has combined the "incompatible" control signals c_2 and c_5; this is unlikely to be of concern, however, if the microinstruction set is later enlarged, since there is no obvious functional advantage in keeping these control signals in separate fields. The assignment of a separate control field to INBUS is of questionable wisdom. It prevents INBUS from transferring data to two or more destinations, for example, Q and M, simultaneously. This capability could be useful, for example, to clear both registers at once. Thus it might be better to associate a control field with each register that is a potential destination of INBUS rather than with INBUS itself.

Multiple microinstruction formats In the original multiplication microprogram of Fig. 4.47, several microinstructions are used only for next-address generation and do not activate any control lines. This suggests that microinstruction size could be reduced by using a single field to contain either control information or address information. This results in two distinct microinstructions types—branch microinstructions, which specify no control information, and "operate" microinstructions, which activate control lines but have no branching capability. Note that this approach is almost always used at the instruction level. The division of microinstructions into the branch and operate types is a rather natural one, since the branch instructions directly control the internal operations of the control unit, while the operate instructions directly control the external data processing unit.

Suppose that we wish to use unencoded control fields for the multiplier, since that allows a maximum of flexibility. Nine control bits are required, as demonstrated in Fig. 4.49. Now let us define a microinstruction format consisting of two parts, a 2-bit condition select field with the same meaning as before, and a 9-bit field which can contain either a branch address or control information. The condition select code 00 which means no branching serves to identify the operate microinstructions. The remaining three select field codes identify conditional and unconditional branches. We thus obtain the 11-bit microinstruction formats of Fig. 4.54. Note that the additional address bits make it possible to write microprograms containing up to $2^9 = 512$ instructions. Because we have destroyed the ability of every microinstruction to implement a two-way branch, more microinstructions may be needed to perform certain functions.

Figure 4.55 shows a microprogram for twos-complement multiplication using the formats of Fig. 4.54. This microprogram is somewhat easier to derive from the flowchart (Fig. 4.16) than the earlier microprogram (Fig. 4.47), since we can now transform decision blocks directly into branch microinstructions, while activity boxes are transformed into operate microinstructions. There is also a one-to-one correspondence between the microinstructions and statements in the formal-language description given in Fig. 4.45.

The control-unit design of Fig. 4.48 is easily modified to handle these new microinstruction formats. The condition select field can be used to control a

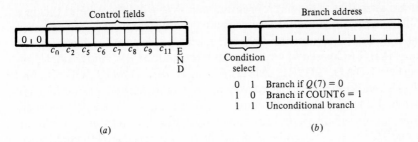

Figure 4.54 Example of multiple microinstruction formats: (*a*) operate microinstruction; (*b*) branch microinstruction.

demultiplexer which routes bits 2 to 10 either to external control lines (operate microinstructions) or to the branch address loading circuitry (branch microinstructions).

4.4 MICROPROGRAMMED COMPUTERS

4.4.1 CPU Control Unit

A simple CPU Consider again the hypothetical CPU discussed in Sec. 4.2.3. Assume that the 13 control signals listed in Fig. 4.25 define the microopera-

Address in CM	Condition select 0 1	Branch address or control bits 2 3 4 5 6 7 8 9 10	Comments
		Microinstruction	
0000	0 0	0 0 0 0 0 0 1 0 0	$A \leftarrow 0$, COUNT $\leftarrow 0$, $V \leftarrow 0$, $M \leftarrow$ INBUS;
0001	0 0	0 0 0 0 0 1 0 0 0	$Q \leftarrow$ INBUS;
0010	0 1	0 0 0 0 0 0 1 0 0	**if** $Q(7) = 0$ **then go to** 4;
0011	0 0	0 1 0 0 0 0 0 0 0	$A \leftarrow A + M$;
0100	0 0	1 0 0 0 0 0 0 0 0	$A(1{:}n{-}1)$, $Q \leftarrow A$, $Q(0{:}n{-}2)$, $A(0) \leftarrow A(0) \vee V$;
0101	1 0	0 0 0 0 0 0 1 1 1	**if** COUNT6 $= 1$ **then go to** 8;
0110	0 0	0 0 0 0 0 0 0 1 0	COUNT $\leftarrow$ COUNT $+ 1$;
0111	1 1	0 0 0 0 0 0 0 1 0	**go to** 2;
1000	0 1	0 0 0 0 0 1 0 1 0	**if** $Q(7) = 0$ **then go to** 10;
1001	0 0	0 1 1 0 0 0 0 0 0	$A \leftarrow A - M$;
1010	0 0	0 0 0 1 0 0 0 0 0	OUTBUS $\leftarrow A$;
1011	0 0	0 0 0 0 1 0 0 0 0	OUTBUS $\leftarrow Q(0{:}n{-}2)$;
1100	0 0	0 0 0 0 0 0 0 0 1	Issue completion signal;
1101	1 1	0 0 0 0 0 1 1 0 1	Halt;

Figure 4.55 Multiplication microprogram using the microinstruction formats of Fig. 4.54.

tions that are available to the microprogrammer. (We will later extend this to a more realistic set.) To simplify the discussion, we will represent the microinstructions in symbolic form using only our hardware description language.

Suppose that it is desired to write an emulator for the eight instructions considered earlier: LOAD, STORE, ADD, AND, JUMP, JUMPZ, COMP, and RSHIFT. The microoperations needed to interpret the various instructions are shown in Fig. 4.24, from which the required microprograms are easily derived. The microprogram to be selected for each instruction is determined by the instruction opcode; hence the contents of the instruction register IR can be used to determine the microprogram starting address. We will use the unmodified contents of IR as the microprogram address. We will further assume that each microinstruction can specify a branch condition, a branch address used only if the branch condition is satisfied, and a set of control fields defining the microoperations to be performed.

Figure 4.56 shows a complete emulator for the given instruction set in symbolic form; the conversion of each microinstruction to binary form is easy. The emulator contains a distinct microprogram for each of the eight instruction execution cycles and a microprogram called FETCH which implements the instruction fetch cycle. The **go to** IR statement can be implemented as μPC $\leftarrow$ IR, which transfers control to the first microinstruction in the microprogram that interprets the current instruction.

```
FETCH:     AR ← PC;
           READ M;
           PC ← PC + 1, IR ← DR(OP);
           go to IR;

LOAD:      AR ← DR(ADR);
           READ M;
           AC ← DR, go to FETCH;

STORE:     AR ← DR(ADR);
           DR ← AC;
           WRITE M, go to FETCH;

ADD:       AR ← DR(ADR);
           READ M;
           AC ← AC + DR, go to FETCH;

AND:       AR ← DR(ADR);
           READ M;
           AC ← AC ∧ DR, go to FETCH;

JUMP:      PC ← DR(ADR), go to FETCH;

JUMPZ:     if AC ≠ 0 then go to FETCH;
           PC ← DR(ADR), go to FETCH;

COMP:      AC ← AC̄, go to FETCH;

RSHIFT:    RIGHT-SHIFT(AC), go to FETCH;
```

Figure 4.56 A microprogrammed emulator in symbolic form for a small instruction set.

Suppose that because of design error, we have forgotten to implement a required instruction called CLEAR whose function is to reset all bits of the accumulator AC to zero. Although no control line to clear AC was included in the CPU, we can still write a microprogram to implement the CLEAR instruction as follows

CLEAR: $DR \leftarrow AC$;
                $AC \leftarrow \overline{AC}$;
                $AC \leftarrow AC \wedge DR$, **go to** FETCH;

Thus by adding this microprogram to CM, CLEAR can be added to the instruction set without changing any hardware. This flexibility is the main advantage of microprogramming.

An extended CPU We will now add to the basic CPU structure of Fig. 4.26 the necessary circuits to implement fixed-point multiplication and division using iterative algorithms of the type discussed in Chap. 3. Two new registers are required, a multiplier-quotient register MQ and a counter called COUNT, which can be used for counting the number of shift operations used during multiplication or division. The memory data register DR will be assigned the role of multiplicand or divisor register when required.

Figure 4.57 shows the extended CPU in which the number of control lines has been approximately doubled. The complete set of control lines defined for this unit is given in Fig. 4.58. Note that lines c_0 through c_{12} are the control lines defined for the original circuit of Fig. 4.26.

Figure 4.59 lists the microprogram used to implement twos-complement multiplication using the algorithm first given in Example 2.2. A special-purpose microprogrammed controller for this type of multiplication was developed in Sec. 4.2.3. The microprogram given here is essentially the same as the one defined previously (Fig. 4.45). It is assumed that before the microprogram MULT is executed, the multiplier is in MQ and the multiplicand is in DR. Each statement in Fig. 4.59 corresponds to a single microinstruction.

The control unit The general three-part microinstruction format comprising a condition select field, a branch address field, and a set of control fields will be used. Five conditions to be tested are identified in Fig. 4.57, specifically $AC = 0$, $AC < 0$, $MQ(n-1)$, $COUNT = n - 2$ and V, the overflow-underflow indicator. Adding the possibilities of an unconditional branch and no branching, we obtain seven branch condition codes which can be represented by a 3-bit condition select field.

Various control signals can be grouped together in common encoded fields to reduce microinstruction size. Many of these can be identified from the list of control signals, without reference to the actual microinstructions that are to be implemented. For example, there are three control signals c_3, c_5, and c_{19} that transfer data to DR. Since they are mutually exclusive (compatible), we can encode them in a 2-bit field. (Note that one bit pattern must be reserved for the

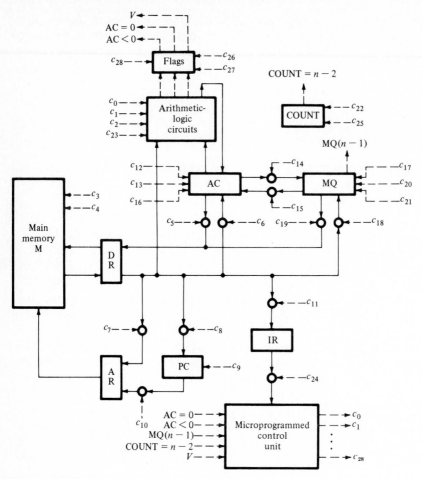

Figure 4.57 Structure of the extended CPU.

no-operation case.) Similarly, the many control signals that alter the contents of AC can be combined.

Let us suppose that it has been decided not to encode the control signals. This implies that the condition select and control fields occupy 28 bits of each microinstruction. Let us further suppose that an 8-bit branch address representing a complete CM address is included in each microinstruction. A CM with a capacity of 256 36-bit words is therefore to be used.

Figure 4.60 shows a possible organization for the CPU control unit with the foregoing design assumptions. As in our previous designs, external conditions are used to load branch addresses into the μPC. In addition, the μPC may be loaded from the instruction register IR via a logic circuit K (possibly a ROM) which maps instruction opcodes onto microinstruction addresses.

Control signal	Operation controlled
c_0	$AC \leftarrow AC + DR$
c_1	$AC \leftarrow AC \wedge DR$
c_2	$AC \leftarrow \overline{AC}$
c_3	$DR \leftarrow M(AR)$
c_4	$M(AR) \leftarrow DR$
c_5	$DR \leftarrow AC$
c_6	$AC \leftarrow DR$
c_7	$AR \leftarrow DR(ADR)$
c_8	$PC \leftarrow DR(ADR)$
c_9	$PC \leftarrow PC + 1$
c_{10}	$AR \leftarrow PC$
c_{11}	$IR \leftarrow DR(OP)$
c_{12}	RIGHT-SHIFT AC
c_{13}	LEFT-SHIFT AC
c_{14}	RIGHT-SHIFT (AC, MQ)
c_{15}	LEFT-SHIFT (AC, MQ)
c_{16}	$AC \leftarrow 0$
c_{17}	$AC(0) \leftarrow AC(0) \vee V$
c_{18}	$MQ \leftarrow DR$
c_{19}	$DR \leftarrow MQ$
c_{20}	$MQ(n-1) \leftarrow 1$
c_{21}	$MQ(n-1) \leftarrow 0$
c_{22}	$COUNT \leftarrow COUNT + 1$
c_{23}	$AC \leftarrow AC - DR$
c_{24}	$\mu PC \leftarrow IR$
c_{25}	$COUNT \leftarrow 0$
c_{26}	$V \leftarrow 0$
c_{27}	$V \leftarrow 1$
c_{28}	$FLAGS \leftarrow 0$

Figure 4.58 Control signals of the extended CPU.

Microprogram sequencers Recent developments in integrated circuit technology have resulted in components which allow a microprogrammed control unit for a CPU to be designed using a very small number of IC chips. In particular, all the circuitry required to generate microinstruction addresses can be placed in a single package called a *microprogram sequencer* (also called a micropro-

```
MULT: AC ←0, COUNT  ←0, V ←0;
TEST1: if MQ(n−1) = 0 then go to SHIFT;
       AC ← AC + DR;
SHIFT: AC, MQ ← RIGHT-SHIFT (AC, MQ), AC(0) ← AC(0) ∨ V,
          if COUNT = n − 2 then go to TEST2;
       COUNT ← COUNT + 1, go to TEST1;
TEST2: if MQ(n−1) = 0 then go to FETCH;
       AC ← AC − DR, go to FETCH;
```

Figure 4.59 Twos-complement multiplication microprogram for the extended CPU.

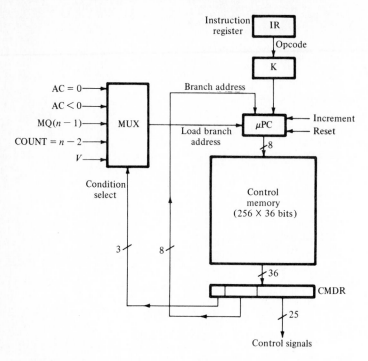

Figure 4.60 Microprogrammed CPU control unit.

gram control unit by some manufacturers). A microprogram sequencer typically contains a microprogram counter as well as the logic required for conditional branching and the transfer of control between microprograms. A microprogrammed control unit can be constructed from two major components: a RAM or ROM used as the control memory, and a microprogram sequencer. Figure 4.61 shows a microprogrammed CPU designed in this way. As indicated, facilities may be provided for inserting a pipeline register between the control memory and the ALU to allow microinstruction fetching and execution to be overlapped.

Microprogram sequencers are primarily an outgrowth of microprocessor technology. Again note that in current usage the terms microprogramming and microprocessor are unrelated. Some, but by no means all, microprocessors have microprogrammed control units. Many microprogrammed microprocessors employ bit-sliced ALUs of the type discussed in Sec. 3.3.4. Bit-sliced ALU components allow a designer to construct a CPU with any desired word length. The addition of a microprogrammed control unit adds further flexibility by allowing the designer to specify instruction types and formats. The bit-slicing concept can readily be extended to the control unit by designing microprogram sequencers that can be cascaded to handle microinstruction addresses of arbitrary length. The following example describes a representative microprogram sequencer chip from the Advanced Micro Devices Am2900 series of bit-sliced microprocessor components.

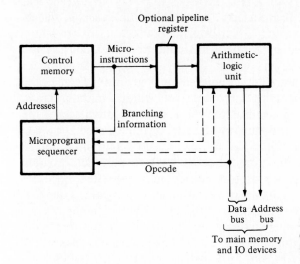

Figure 4.61 A microprogrammed CPU containing a microprogram sequencer.

Example 4.2: The Advanced Micro Devices Am2909 microprogram sequencer [1] Figure 4.62 shows a slightly simplified version of this microprogram sequencer which was designed to process a 4-bit address slice. k of these devices can be cascaded to form a microprogram sequencer for $4k$-bit addresses. The 4-bit addresses generated by the Am2909 are derived from four sources:

1. A microprogram counter μPC
2. A set of four external lines
3. A register R which can be loaded from an external source
4. A set of four registers in the Am2909 that form a pushdown stack

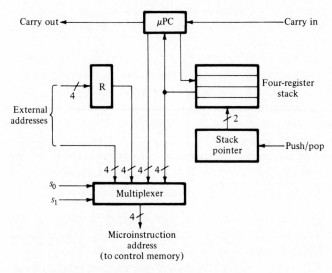

Figure 4.62 The Am2909 microprogram sequencer.

Two external control signals are used to control a multiplexer that selects the address to be used.

The stack is controlled by external push and pop lines and a stack pointer which is a 2-bit up-down counter. The contents of the stack pointer indicate the position of the last address entered (pushed) into the stack. The stack is intended for implementing subroutine calls within a microprogram. A push signal in response to a subroutine call microinstruction causes the microprogram counter contents (the return address) to be stored at the top of the stack. A subsequent pop signal in response to a subroutine return microinstruction transfers the stored address back to the microprogram counter. In this way, up to four subroutine calls may be nested.

The connections required to form a $4k$-bit microprogram sequencer using k copies of the Am2909 chip are very simple. Corresponding control lines such as s_0, s_1 and the push and pop lines in different chips are joined. The μPC of each chip is provided with carry in and carry out lines which are used to cascade the k μPCs to form a single $4k$-bit μPC. No connections are required between the remaining address sources.

4.4.2 A Conventional Computer

Introduction We conclude this chapter by presenting descriptions of some commercially available microprogrammed computers. There is remarkable diversity to be found in such machines, as can be seen from some recently published surveys [3, 18]. Every family of computers uses microinstruction formats and microoperation types that are largely unique to that family. Even within the same family, different models, e.g., the microprogrammed CPUs of different models in the IBM S/360 series [10, 19], may be programmed in an entirely different manner. It is therefore difficult if not impossible to select a microprogrammed computer that is typical in any general sense. Two machines have been chosen which serve to indicate the range and complexity of microprogrammed processors available.

The first of these is the Hewlett-Packard 21MX, a recent general-purpose minicomputer that is microprogrammed in a conventional way. The second example, the Nanodata QM-1, has been chosen for its unique architecture, which employs two levels of microprogramming. A microinstruction is not executed directly by the QM-1 but is instead interpreted by a lower-level program, called a nanoprogram, which is stored in a second control memory. As might be expected, this additional level of control greatly increases the flexibility of the machine. For example, the bus interconnections of the QM-1 can be altered under program control.

Structure of the HP 21MX The HP 21MX is a minicomputer of 1974 vintage employing a microprogrammable CPU [8]. It is designed to implement a specific machine language that is upward compatible with the machine language of its predecessor, the HP 2100. The HP 21MX is also intended to execute user-defined microprograms and therefore contains a writeable control memory. (Although compatible at the instruction level, the HP 2100 and HP 21MX are incompatible and quite different at the microinstruction level.)

The architecture of the HP 21MX is shown in Fig. 4.63. The main-memory word size is 16 bits. The CPU is organized around two 16-bit buses: the S bus, which is connected to main memory and the input side of the ALU; and the T bus, which is connected to the output side of the ALU. The two registers A and B fill the role of main accumulators in the HP 21MX. The L (latch) register is used to store one ALU operand; the other is obtained directly from the S bus. Sixteen additional registers are connected to the S and T buses. Thirteen of

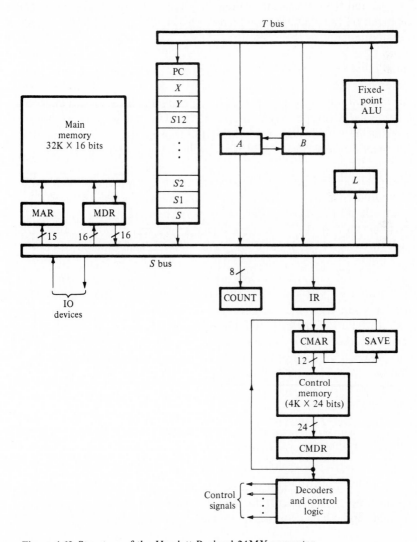

Figure 4.63 Structure of the Hewlett-Packard 21MX computer.

these registers, designated $S, S1, S2, \ldots, S12$, are general-purpose or scratch-pad registers. The X and Y registers are used as index registers, while PC is a standard program counter. The 8-bit counter COUNT is intended for controlling loops within a microprogram, e.g., counting the number of iterations performed during multiplication. The arithmetic-logic unit ALU directly implements a set of fixed-point operations including add, subtract, increment, shift, NAND, and EXCLUSIVE-OR, which is typical of a small computer. More complex functions such as fixed-point multiply and divide and floating-point arithmetic operations are implemented by microprograms.

Information is processed in the HP 21MX in the following way. Operands are transferred from the memory data register, IO devices, or the CPU registers to the S bus, and from there they enter the ALU. The result generated by the ALU is placed on the T bus from which it may be loaded into any of the 18 CPU registers connected to the T bus.

Microinstruction types Microinstructions in the HP 21MX are 24 bits long, and the control memory CM has a capacity of 4K (2^{12}) microinstructions. A conventional control unit organization is used. A special 12-bit SAVE register is used, as its name indicates, to save a microinstruction address. This permits a one-level subroutine call capability within microprograms. Semiconductor memories are used for both M and CM with cycle times of 650 and 140 ns, respectively.

The microinstructions of the HP 21MX are relatively short and highly encoded and have limited ability to define parallel microoperations. As such, they are usually considered to be of the vertical type. (They are, however, considered as "diagonal" in Ref. 3.) Four main formats, illustrated in Fig. 4.64, are used. They are designated common, immediate, conditional jump, and unconditional jump.

The common format is used mainly to specify data transfers and arithmetic-logic operations. The opcode field specifies the general type of the microinstruction, while the ALU field indicates the operation, if any, to be performed by the arithmetic-logic circuits. The source and destination fields contain the names of registers that store the operands to be used. The "special" field performs a variety of control functions, including specification of the next microinstruction address. Consider, for example, the following microinstruction whose control fields are defined symbolically in the manner of the HP 21MX microassembly language.

Opcode	ALU function	Source register	Destination register	Special field
NOP	INC	T	A	RTN

This microinstruction takes the contents of the memory data register (called T in HP 21MX terminology), passes it through the arithmetic-logic circuits where it is incremented, and places the result in the A register. The opcode NOP

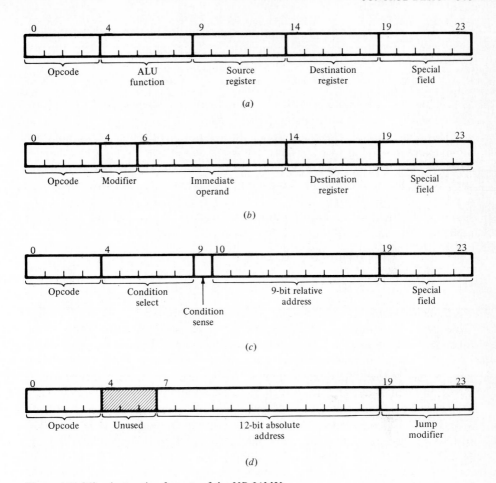

Figure 4.64 Microinstruction formats of the HP 21MX.

means no operation, indicating that no additional function is specified by this field. The code RTN in the special field means return, indicating that this is the last microinstruction in a subroutine and that the next microinstruction address should be taken from the SAVE register. In terms of our description language, the foregoing microinstruction corresponds to

$$A \leftarrow T + 1, \textbf{go to } \text{SAVE};$$

Note that the opcode, ALU function, and special fields are largely independent and permit up to three microoperations to be specified.

    The second format is used to load immediate operands into registers. The opcode field is (in symbolic form) IMM, while two modifier bits indicate which half of the destination register is to be used, and whether the immediate operand is to be stored in true or complemented form. For example, the microinstruction

Opcode	Modifier	Immediate operand	Destination field	Special field
IMM	CMLO	8	S4	

causes the logical complement (CM) of the number 8 to be placed in the low-order (LO) half of the scratch-pad register $S4$.

The remaining two formats are used for jump instructions. A conditional jump instruction (Fig. 4.64c) can test for a variety of conditions such as overflow resulting from the preceding ALU operation, or external conditions such as pending interrupts. Bit 9 indicates if the jump is to take place when the condition is true or when the condition is false. Only 9 address bits are specified, restricting conditional jumps to a 512-word "page" within the control memory. An example of a conditional jump is

Opcode	Condition select	Condition sense	Address	Special field
JMP	OVFL	RJS	200	CNDX

which means branch to address 200 within the current page if the overflow flag OVFL = 0. Omitting the RJS (*Reverse Jump Sense*) term causes the jump to take place only if OVFL = 1, that is, when the selected condition is satisfied.

The final instruction format is the unconditional branch which can specify a jump to any of the 4096 control memory addresses. There are two types of instructions which use this format: a simple unconditional jump with opcode JMP, and an unconditional jump to subroutine or subroutine call with opcode JSB. JSB causes the contents of the microprogram counter μPC to be placed in the SAVE register. The jump modifier field can be used to indicate that the branch address is to be taken from the microinstruction address field (bits 7 to 18), the instruction register IR, or the SAVE register. The jump modifier field therefore acts as a condition select field. The microinstruction

Opcode	Address	Jump modifier
JSB	SUB1	UNCD

causes a jump to the subroutine with starting address SUB1, while the return address (the address of the JSB instruction plus one) is placed in the SAVE register.

The multiple microinstruction formats of the HP 21MX require a two-level process to decode each microinstruction. First the opcode field is decoded to identify the instruction type. This determines the meaning of the remaining fields, which can then be decoded. Microinstructions of this kind, in which the meaning of a field depends on another field, are said to have *two-level encoding*. This is to be contrasted with the *single-level encoding* schemes depicted in Fig. 4.33b and c.

Microprogramming the HP 21MX Microprograms for the 21MX can be written using a microassembly language whose structure is fairly typical [8]. Mnemonics are provided for specifying the control fields, and symbolic names may be used for operands and addresses. A statement in the 21MX microprogramming language defines one microinstruction. Each statement is divided into seven fields, organized as shown in Fig. 4.65. Field 1 is used to specify an optional label, which is the symbolic address to be assigned to the microinstruction; field 2 specifies the opcode. In all cases except the common format, only one or two opcodes are defined. The remaining fields are self-explanatory. Note that while there is a one-to-one correspondence between fields 2 to 6 in the microassembly-language format and the binary formats given in Fig. 4.64, the positions of the corresponding fields are not the same.

Figure 4.66 shows a HP 21MX microassembly-language version of the simple emulator described in Fig. 4.56. (Some minor liberties have been taken with the microassembly language in order to simplify this example.) As before, the emulator comprises an instruction fetch routine called FETCH and a separate routine for each of the eight instructions to be emulated. The FETCH routine in this case also fetches the operand for all memory reference instructions. The special field command JTAB used in the last microinstruction of FETCH causes the control memory address register to be loaded with an address obtained from a special "jump table" using the opcode part of the current instruction IR(OP) to address that table. JTAB also causes the SAVE register to be set to zero. It is assumed that the instruction labeled FETCH is in control memory location zero, that is, FETCH = 0. Hence after the specific operations required by each instruction have been performed, another FETCH cycle can be initiated by giving the return-from-subroutine command RTN.

Consider, for example, execution of the ADD instruction. JTAB causes a branch to the microinstruction labeled ADD which transfers the contents of the memory data register T (containing the prefetched ADD operand) to the L register. The command PASS in this microinstruction indicates that no function is to be performed by the ALU. The next instruction contains the com-

Microinstruction type	Field 1	Field 2	Field 3	Field 4	Field 5	Field 6	Field 7
Common		Opcode	Special	ALU function	Destination register	Source register	
Immediate	Label (address in CM)	IMM	Special	Modifiers	Destination register	Operand	Comment
Conditional jump		JMP	CNDX	Condition select	Condition sense	Branch address	
Unconditional jump		JMP or JSB	Jump modifier	Unused	Unused	Branch address	

Figure 4.65 Format used for microinstructions in the HP 21MX microassembly language.

* HP 21MX Emulator for a Simple Computer
* A = Accumulator
* L = ALU latch
* M = Memory address register
* P = Program counter
* T = Memory data register
*

1	2	3	4	5	6	7 (Comments)
FETCH	READ		INC	PNM	P	$M \leftarrow P$. Read instruction into T. $P \leftarrow P + 1$.
				IR	T	$IR \leftarrow T$
	READ	JTAB	PASS	CM	ADR	If IR contains a memory reference instruction, $M \leftarrow IR(ADR)$ and read data into T. Jump to CM address specified by IR(OP) and jump table. Clear SAVE register.
*						
LOAD		RTN	PASS	A	T	$A \leftarrow T$. Return.
*						
STORE	WRITE	RTN	PASS	T	A	$T \leftarrow A$. Write T into memory. Return.
ADD			PASS	L	T	$L \leftarrow T$.
	ENV	RTN	ADD	A	A	Enable overflow flag. $A \leftarrow A + L$. Return.
*						
AND			PASS	L	T	$L \leftarrow T$.
		RTN	AND	A	A	$L \leftarrow A \wedge L$. Return.
*						
JUMP		RTN	PASS	P	ADR	$P \leftarrow IR(ADR)$. Return.
*						
JUMPZ			PASS	S1	A	Set test for $A = 0$.
	JMP	CNDX	TBZ	RJS	FETCH	If $A \neq 0$ then go to FETCH.
		RTN	PASS	P	ADR	$P \leftarrow IR(ADR)$. Return.
*						
COMP		RTN	CMPS	A	A	$A \leftarrow \bar{A}$. Return.
*						
RSHIFT	ARS	RTN	PASS	B	B	Right-shift (A, B) register pair. Return.

Figure 4.66 Emulator for a simple computer in HP 21MX microassembly language.

mand ENV, which enables the overflow indication flip-flop and specifies the addition $A \leftarrow A + L$. Note that L is an implicit operand register for this microinstruction. The addition is carried out and the overflow flip-flop is set if overflow occurs. Finally, the RTN statement transfers the SAVE register contents to the microprogram counter, which results in another FETCH cycle being executed.

4.4.3 An Unconventional Computer

Our final example is the Nanodata QM-1 [14, 17]. This machine which was designed around 1970 is remarkable for its use of two levels of microprogram control. In conventional microprogrammed computers, each instruction fetched from main memory is interpreted by a microprogram stored in control memory. The microprogram exercises direct control over the hardware by activating control lines. In the QM-1, these microprograms do not directly control the hardware. Instead, each microinstruction is interpreted by a nanoprogram stored in a second control memory, called the nanostore. It is the nanoinstructions that directly control the hardware.

An important advantage of this two-level control technique is that a high degree of parallelism can be achieved using a relatively small amount of control memory space. Microprograms, which may be very long, are encoded in a vertical format allowing them to be stored in a control memory of small word size. Nanoprograms, on the other hand, use a highly parallel horizontal format. The nanostore therefore has a very long word size, but it stores relatively few words since nanoprograms are usually quite short. The main disadvantages of two microprogramming levels are the extra delay required to fetch nanoinstructions and the increased complexity of the CPU.

The operations performed by the nanoinstructions of the QM-1 are at a somewhat lower level than normal for microprogrammed machines. As a result, the (nano) programmer can exercise more than usual control over the operation of the computer. In particular, the source and destination points of the major buses can be altered by nanoinstructions, thus making the logical structure of the QM-1 variable. The QM-1 has no machine language of its own at the instruction level. It was designed to emulate other computers and is capable of concurrent emulation of more than one machine.

Structure of the QM-1 Figure 4.67 shows the main components of the QM-1. The standard word size used is 18 bits, but the QM-1 can also be operated in a 16-bit mode in which two bits are not used. The CPU is designed around a set of 32 registers called the *local store*. Most of these are general purpose. Four of the registers are implemented as counters so that they can be used as program counters at the instruction or microinstruction levels. One local store register is used exclusively as a microinstruction register, i. e., as a data register for control memory 1.

The unit designated the main ALU in Fig. 4.67 is the major data processing

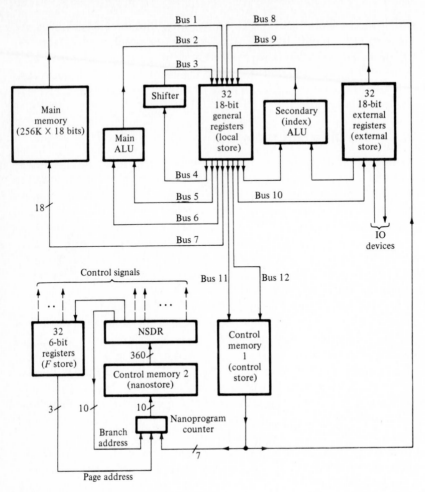

Figure 4.67 Structure of the Nanodata QM-1.

component of the system. It is a fixed-point ALU capable of performing addition, subtraction, and standard logic operations. Operations requiring shifting are performed in a special shift circuit which may, if required, be integrated with the main ALU. The second ALU, called the index ALU, is used primarily for high-speed indexing and similar address-manipulation functions. A second set of 32 registers, called the *external store*, contains index registers and buffer registers for IO operations.

The QM-1 contains three large memories designated main memory, control store CS, and nanostore NS. These memories store programs, microprograms, and nanoprograms, respectively. Main memory and CS accommodate 18-bit words and use registers in the local store as address and data registers. A single bus (BUS 7) is used to transfer addresses and data to main memory, while separate buses (BUS 11 and BUS 12) convey addresses and data to CS. The nanostore NS is designed to store up to 1024 360-bit words. It is organized in the manner of a conventional microprogrammed control unit, deriving addresses from a 10-bit address register (the nanoprogram counter) and transferring instructions to a 360-bit data register NSDR where they are decoded and used to activate control signals.

The QM-1 makes extensive use of the residual control concept. Residual control information is stored in a special set of 32 6-bit registers called the *F store*. These registers, which are under nanoprogram control, specify the way in which certain resources are to be allocated. For example, the name of the local store register to be used as the microprogram counter is stored in the *F* register FMPC. A major function of the *F* registers is to specify the local stores that are currently connected to the main QM-1 buses. There are 12 such buses labeled BUS 1 through BUS 12 in Fig. 4.67. At any time only one local store register is connected to each bus as determined by the *F* store. The 12 buses are quite independent, so up to 12 data transfers can take place simultaneously.

Microprogram control The microprogram control unit is composed of the control memory CS and the local store registers used as its microprogram counter and data register. The high-order 7 bits of each microinstruction form an opcode which is used to address NS. This means that a total of $2^7 = 128$ distinct microinstructions can be defined. When a microinstruction is fetched from CS, it is placed in a specific local store register $R31$. $R31$ has three accessible fields called the C, A, and B fields consisting of 7, 5, and 6 bits, respectively. The C field stores the opcode, while the A and B fields can be used to indicate operands. For example, the A and B fields can be used to identify local store registers containing operands or the addresses of operands in main memory. Microinstructions of this type are clearly vertical rather than horizontal. Thus the "natural" microinstruction of the QM-1 is an 18-bit word containing an opcode and two addresses. However, the user can define other microinstruction formats, e. g., multiword microinstructions.

Nanoprogram control The nanostore NS has a capacity of 1024 nanoinstructions. The nanoinstructions are 360 bits long and take full advantage of the considerable inherent parallelism of the QM-1; they can therefore be called horizontal. NS is divided into eight 128-word pages, each of which may, if desired, contain a distinct emulator. As can be seen from Fig. 4.67, the nanoprogram control unit has a conventional organization. 10-bit nanoinstruction addresses are generated by a nanoprogram counter and nanoinstructions are placed in a register NSDR from which control signals are directly obtained. The next address is generated by either incrementing the nanoprogram counter or loading it from an external source such as the branch field within the current nanoinstruction or an address derived from a microinstruction opcode.

Each microinstruction is interpreted by a nanoprogram stored in the nanostore. The 7-bit opcode of the microinstruction is used as the nanoprogram starting address relative to some page. The 3-bit page address needed to form an absolute address for the nanostore is obtained from one of the *F* registers.

The general format of a QM-1 nanoinstruction is shown in Fig. 4.68. It consists of five major fields, each containing 72 bits. The leftmost field is called the K field. The remaining four fields are called T fields. The K field contains a 10-bit branch address, condition select fields, and some control fields. Most of the specific control functions to be performed are specified by the T fields. Detailed specifications of the K and T fields may be found in the Refs. 3, 14, and 18. The T fields have a common format consisting of 41 separate control fields. Most of the control fields contain 1 bit, implying that very little encoding is used.

A nanoinstruction is executed in four phases, where each phase is normally one machine clock cycle (80 ns) in duration. The K field is active during all four phases, but only one T field is active during each phase. Thus during the first phase of executing a nanoinstruction, K and T_1 control the machine, during the second phase K and T_2 control it, and so on. Each 360-bit nanostore word can be thought of either as a single polyphase nanoinstruction or else as four distinct nanoinstructions $(K, T_1), (K, T_2), (K, T_3)$, and (K, T_4) which are executed in sequence.

In the assembly language defined for QM-1 nanoinstructions [14], each nanoinstruction is specified by five statements which define the K field and the four T fields as follows.

Statement identifier	Operations
. . . .	K field
x . . .	T_1 field
. x . .	T_2 field
. . x .	T_3 field
. . . x	T_4 field

A simple nanoprogram As an example we will now describe a nanoprogram consisting of a single nanoinstruction that interprets the microinstruction

ADD R3, R6

which adds the contents of local store registers $R3$ and $R6$ and places the result in $R3$. The microinstruction is assumed to be in the microinstruction register $R31$, with the operands $R3$ and $R6$ in the A- and B- fields of $R31$, respectively. As noted earlier, these fields may be accessed by nanoprograms. The following nanoinstruction, written in the QM-1 nanoassembly language [14], implements ADD.

0	72	144	216	288	359
K	T_1	T_2	T_3	T_4	

Figure 4.68 Nanoinstruction format of the QM-1.

. . . .   KALC = ADD

x . . .   A → FAIR, B → FAIL, A → FAOD, MPC PLUS 1

. *x* . .   GATE ALU, READ CS(MPC)

. . *x* .   READ NS(CS)

. . . *x*   GATE NS

The first statement specifies that the control field called KALC in the nanoin-struction *K* field be set to indicate the ADD operation. The second statement causes the registers *R*3 and *R*6 identified by the microinstruction *A* and *B* fields to be connected to the ALU. This is done by loading *A* and *B* into the three *F* registers FAIR, FAIL, and FAOD that control the input and output buses of the ALU. For example, the contents of FAIR controls BUS 5 (*A*LU *i*nput *r*ight AIR), FAIL controls BUS 6 (*A*LU *i*nput *l*eft AIL), while FAOD controls BUS 2 (*A*LU *o*utput *d*ata AOD). Thus the microoperation A → FAIR effec-tively causes BUS 5 to connect local store register *R*3 to the rightmost input of the ALU. Figure 4.69 shows the bus connections produced by the ADD R3, R6 microinstruction. At this point the sum is computed and placed on BUS 2. The final microoperation MPC PLUS 1 in T_1 increments the local store regis-ter being used as the microprogram counter MPC.

Moving to T_2, the microoperation GATE ALU causes the result on BUS 2 to be loaded into the local store register currently connected to BUS 2, that is, *R*3. This completes the addition operation. The remaining parts of the

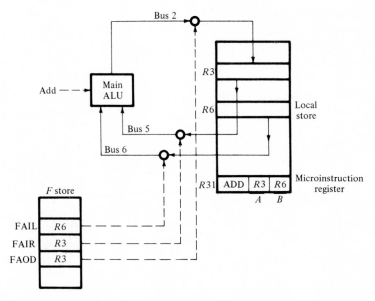

Figure 4.69 Effective QM-1 bus connections during execution of the microinstruction ADD R3,R6.

nanoinstruction cause the next microinstruction to be fetched and decoded. The statement READ CS(MPC) in T_2 causes the control store CS to be read using the address in MPC. This results in a new microinstruction being placed on BUS 8. T_3 then causes the opcode part of the microinstruction (7 bits) to be loaded into the nanoprogram counter NPC; the remaining 3 bits of the 10-bit nanostore address are obtained from F register FIDX. The final statement GATE NS causes the nanostore to be read using the address in NPC. The nanoinstruction obtained is placed in the nanostore data register where it is decoded and executed.

Remarks For many applications, the QM-1 may be programmed directly at the microprogram or nanoprogram level. If programmed at the microinstruction level (bypassing the usual instruction level), the QM-1 takes on the appearance of a conventional computer with one level of microprogramming. In this case the control store and nanostore of the QM-1 correspond to the main and control memories, respectively, of the conventional machine. The main memory of the QM-1 is then treated as large data store by the microinstructions. This view of the QM-1 may be encouraged by the fact that the QM-1 microinstructions strongly resemble conventional machine instructions.

4.5 SUMMARY

A digital system can be partitioned into control and data processing units. The function of the control unit is to issue to the data processing unit control signals that select and sequence the data processing operations. Processors such as a computer's CPU are controlled by instructions obtained from an external program memory. In such cases the control unit has two main functions, instruction sequencing and instruction interpretation.

Instructions are normally obtained from consecutive locations in the program memory, and a program counter is used to generate instruction addresses. Deviations from the normal instruction sequence within a program are indicated by conditional and unconditional branch instructions. Two methods are used for temporary transfer of control between distinct programs—subroutine calls and interrupts. A pushdown stack is a particularly convenient mechanism for controlling subroutines and interrupts.

Two general techniques for interpreting instructions have been identified: hardwired control and microprogrammed control. Hardwired control units employ fixed special-purpose logic circuits to generate control signals. In a microprogrammed control unit, control signals are stored in the form of microinstructions in a special addressable memory called the control memory. Microprogramming has two major advantages:

1. It provides a systematic method for control unit design.
2. Since instructions are interpreted by microprograms, an instruction set can easily be changed by changing the microprograms.

Thus the behavior of a microprogrammed control unit can be altered by software rather than by hardware changes. On the other hand, microprogrammed control units are generally slower than the corresponding hardwired units.

Hardwired control units are often designed using unsystematic or ad hoc methods, resulting in control circuits whose logical structure may be called random. We have attempted to define three systematic approaches to this design problem which we term the state-table, delay-element, and sequence-counter methods. The state-table method, the formal-design approach derived from switching theory, attempts to minimize the number of gates and flip-flops used. It is computationally very difficult, thereby limiting its usefulness to small control units. The delay-element method yields a circuit whose structure mirrors the flow of control in a flowchart specification of the control-unit behavior. Delay elements are used for timing purposes and constitute the memory part of the control unit. While this design approach is relatively simple to use, it may yield circuits containing an excessive number of delay elements. The third method uses a counter as a centralized source of timing signals. It is particularly useful for implementing control in processors whose behavior is cyclic in nature. Most processors within a computer appear to have such behavior and can be controlled efficiently by sequence counters.

A microprogrammed control unit is designed around a control memory which stores microprograms. It contains logic for generating microinstruction addresses, fetching microinstructions, and decoding them to determine the control signals to be activated. These control signals are specified by the control fields of the microinstructions. Microinstructions also contain control memory addresses which allow branches within a microprogram to be implemented. Branching may be made dependent on an external condition specified in a condition select field. All the methods used for program control at the instruction level, e.g., subroutine calls, can also be implemented at the microinstruction level.

The formats used for microinstructions vary greatly from computer to computer. These formats may be divided into two groups, horizontal and vertical. Horizontal microinstructions are typically characterized by long formats, little encoding of the control fields, and the ability to control many microoperations in parallel. Vertical microinstructions have short formats, considerable encoding of the control fields, and limited ability to control parallel microoperations. Formal methods exist for designing microinstructions which contain as few bits as possible. One such method discussed here minimizes the number of bits used in the control fields, while still preserving the parallelism inherent in a given instruction set. In practice, control fields are often identified with specific data paths or components of the system being controlled.

A much greater variability exists among computers at the microinstruction level than at the instruction level. Some microprogrammed machines use a read-only memory as the control memory and thus execute a fixed-set of microprograms. This is usually the case in a microprogrammed CPU with a fixed instruction set. The microprograms then constitute an emulator for that instruction set. If a writeable control store is employed, many emulators may be used, thus enabling the computer to interpret dynamically a variety of instruction sets. The HP 21MX is a conventional microprogrammed computer using vertical microinstructions. It is designed to implement a specific instruction set (the HP 21MX machine language), but it can also execute user-written microprograms. The QM-1 is an unconventional machine which uses two levels of microprogramming; microinstructions are interpreted by nanoinstructions which directly control the hardware.

PROBLEMS

4.1 Programming languages like ALGOL and PL/1 allow variables to be defined as local to a particular block of instructions such as a subroutine. The local variables are only required to exist, i.e., to have memory space allocated to them, when the block in question is actually being executed. Describe how a stack organization that is embedded in a random access memory can be used

(*a*) To allow storage space for the local variables of a subroutine to be allocated when the subroutine is entered, and be deallocated when the subroutine is left

(*b*) To allow a subroutine S to have access to the local variables of another subroutine when those variables are global variables of S

4.2 Write an essay comparing the three hardwired control design approaches (state table, delay element, sequence counter) discussed in this chapter, paying particular attention to component cost and design difficulty.

4.3 A hardwired control unit is to be designed for a 32-bit fixed-point multiplier that implements the version of Booth's algorithm given in Fig. 3.31.

(*a*) Select what you think is the most appropriate design method for the control unit, when the major design objective is to specify a complete correctly functioning logic circuit in the shortest possible time. (Component cost and complexity are secondary considerations.) Give the reasons for your choice.

(*b*) Using the method you have selected, construct a logic circuit for this control unit. Use the control signal names given in Fig. 2.46, making any necessary modifications.

4.4 Let $\{C_i\}$ be a compatibility class cover for a set of microinstructions. $\{C_i\}$ is called a *minimum-cost cover* if

$$w = \sum_i \lceil \log_2(|C_i| + 1) \rceil$$

is a minimum. A compatibility class C_i is called a *principal* compatibility class if $|C_i| \neq 2^j$ for every integer $j \geq 1$. Prove that for any set of microinstructions there exists a minimum-cost cover whose members are principal compatibility classes. (This means that only principal compatibility classes need be considered when constructing a minimum-cost cover.)

4.5 A compatibility class C_i is called *prime* if it satisfies either of the following conditions:

1. C_i is nonmaximal and $|C_i| = 2^h - 1$ for some integer $h \geq 1$.
2. C_i maximal, that is, C_i is an MCC, and $|C_i| \neq 2^h$ for any integer $h \geq 1$.

Prove that for any set of microinstructions there exists a minimum-cost cover whose members are prime compatibility classes.

4.6 Find a method of encoding the microinstructions described by Fig. 4.70 so that the minimum number of control bits is used and all inherent parallelism among the microoperations is preserved.

4.7 Integer linear programming is a useful mathematical technique for solving many optimization problems. An *integer linear program* is defined as follows. Find a set of values of the n integer vari-

Microinstruction	Control signals activated
I_1	a, b, c, d, e
I_2	a, d, f, g
I_3	b, h
I_4	c
I_5	c, e, g, i
I_6	a, h, j
I_7	c, d, h
I_8	a, b, i

Figure 4.70 A set of microinstructions for Prob. 4.6.

ables $x_1, x_2, \ldots, x_n$ which maximizes or minimizes a linear expression (called the objective function) of the form

$$\sum_{i=1}^{n} c_i x_i$$

while satisfying a set of m linear inequalities of the form

$$\sum_{i=1}^{n} a_{i,j} x_i \approx b_j \quad j = 1, 2, \ldots, m$$

where the quantities $a_{i,j}$, b_j, and c_i are constant real numbers and $\approx$ denotes either $\leq$ or $\geq$. Although the term programming in this context has nothing to do with computer programming, efficient computer routines are commercially available for solving integer linear programs.

Consider the problem of determining a minimal MCC cover, which forms part of the microinstruction size minimization technique discussed in Sec. 4.3.2. Show how this covering problem can be formulated as an integer linear program.

4.8 A number of practical considerations severely limit the applicability of control-field minimization algorithms of the type discussed in Sec. 4.3.2. Analyze these considerations in detail.

4.9 Design a microprogrammed control unit for the Booth multiplier specified in Prob. 4.3. Draw a block diagram of the control unit and give a binary listing (with suitable comments) of the multiplication microprogram to be used.

4.10 A microprogrammed control unit is to be designed for a floating-point adder with the general structure shown in Fig. 3.55. A number of the form $M \times B^E$ is represented by a 32-bit word comprising a 24-bit mantissa, which is a twos-complement fraction, and an 8-bit exponent, which is a biased integer. The base B is 2.

(*a*) Using our description language, give a complete listing of a symbolic microprogram to control this adder.

(*b*) Derive a suitable microinstruction format that uses unencoded control fields.

4.11 A microprogrammed emulator is required for the CPU of Fig. 4.57. It should implement the eight instructions defined in Fig. 4.23 as well as the instructions SUB and MULT which perform fixed-point subtraction and multiplication respectively.

(*a*) Give in symbolic form a complete listing of a suitable emulator.

(*b*) Design a microinstruction format for the emulator with control fields encoded by function. Use the control signals listed in Fig. 4.58, making any necessary modifications.

4.12 Modify the CPU design of Fig. 4.26 to allow dynamic microprogramming using a writable control memory. Draw a block diagram showing the structure of the microprogrammed control unit and all changes made to the original design.

4.13 A number of computers have microinstructions containing an "emit" field, in which the microprogrammer can place an arbitrary constant for use as an immediate operand. Give some general reasons for including an emit field in microinstructions.

4.14 A computer manufacturer is planning to introduce a new series of scientific computers covering a wide range of cost and performance. Give the arguments for and against using microprogrammed CPUs in the various models of the series.

4.15 An important aspect of the operation of any digital computer is *fault diagnosis*, which is the process of identifying or locating faulty components. Fault diagnosis is accomplished by applying input sequences (test sequences) to the unit under test and observing the resulting output responses at appropriate observation points. When an observed response differs from the known correct response, a fault has been detected in the unit in question. By applying many test sequences, one can usually isolate faults to the smallest replaceable components. Fault diagnosis is generally implemented by diagnostic (micro) programs which carry out the necessary test generation and response analysis in a systematic manner.

Consider the problem of diagnosing faults in the CPU of a computer where it is desired to isolate faulty components at the register level. Discuss the relative merits of hardwired and microprogrammed control for the CPU from the viewpoint of implementing on-line fault-diagnosis procedures.

4.16 Analyze in terms of hardware cost, computational speed, and microprogramming complexity the advantages and disadvantages of using two levels of microprogramming in the manner of the QM-1.

REFERENCES

1. Advanced Micro Devices Inc.: *The Am2900 Family Data Book,* Sunnyvale, Calif. 1976.
2. Agerwala, T.: "Microprogram Optimization: A Survey," *IEEE Trans. Comput.,* vol. C-25, pp. 962–973, October 1976.
3. Agrawala, A. K., and T. G. Rauscher: *Foundations of Microprogramming: Architecture, Software, and Applications,* Academic, New York, 1976.
4. Carlson, C. B.: "The Mechanization of a Push-down Stack," *AFIPS Conf. Proc.,* vol. 24, pp. 243–250, 1963.
5. Das, S. R., D. K. Banerji, and A. Chattopadhyay: "On Control Memory Minimization in Microprogrammed Computers," *IEEE Trans. Comput.* vol. C-23, pp. 845–848, September 1973.
6. Digital Equipment Corp.: *Small Computer Handbook,* Maynard, Mass., 1973.
7. Gerace, G. B.: "Digital System Design Automation—A Method for Designing a Digital System as a Sequential Network System," *IEEE Trans. Comput.,* vol. C-17, pp. 1044–1061, November 1968.
8. Hewlett-Packard Co.: *Microprogramming 21MX Computers: Operating and Reference Manual,* Manual 02102-90008, Cupertino, Calif., 1974.
9. Hill, F. J., and G. R. Peterson: *Digital Systems: Hardware Organization and Design,* Wiley, New York, 1973.
10. Husson, S. S.: *Microprogramming: Principles and Practices,* Prentice-Hall, Englewood Cliffs, N. J., 1970.
11. International Business Machines Corp.: *An Introduction to Microprogramming,* Publ. GF20-0385-0, White Plains, N. Y., 1971.
12. Jayasri, T., and D. Basu: "An Approach to Organizing Microinstructions which Minimizes the Width of Control Storage Words," *IEEE Trans. Comput.,* vol. C-25, pp. 514–521, May 1976.
13. McCluskey, E. J.: *Theory and Design of Switching Circuits,* McGraw-Hill, New York, 1965.
14. Nanodata Corp.: *QM-1 Hardware Level Users Manual,* 2d ed., Williamsville, N. Y., 1972.
15. Redfield, S. R.: A Study of Microprogrammed Processors: A Medium Sized Microprogrammed Processor," *IEEE Trans. Comput.,* vol. C-20, pp. 743–750, July 1971.

16. Rosin, R. F.: "Contemporary Concepts of Microprogramming and Emulation," *Comput. Surv.*, vol. 1, pp. 197–212, December 1969.
17. Rosin, R. F., G. Frieder, and R. H. Eckhouse: "An Environment for Research in Microprogramming and Emulation," *Commun. ACM*, vol. 15, pp. 748–760, August, 1972.
18. Salisbury, A. B.: *Microprogrammable Computer Architectures*, Elsevier, New York, 1976.
19. Tucker, S. G.: "Microprogram Control for System/360," *IBM Syst. J.*, vol. 6, pp. 222–241, 1967.
20. Wilkes, M. V.: "The Best Way to Design an Automatic Calculating Machine," Rept. Manchester University Computer Inaugural Conf., pp. 16–18, 1951 (Reprinted in E. E. Swartzlander (ed.): *Computer Design Development: Principal Papers*, pp. 266–270, Hayden, Rochelle Park, N. J., 1976.)

FIVE

MEMORY ORGANIZATION

This chapter considers the architecture of a computer's memory system. The characteristics of the most important storage-device technologies are surveyed. Hierarchical memory systems including virtual memory are studied, as well as some high-speed memory organizations.

5.1 MEMORY TECHNOLOGY

Every computer system contains a variety of devices to store the instructions and data required for its operation. These storage devices plus the algorithms (either implemented by hardware or software) needed to control or manage the stored information constitute the memory system of the computer. In general, it is desirable that processors should have immediate and uninterrupted access to memory, so the time required to transfer information between a processor and memory should be such that the processor can operate at, or close to, its maximum speed. Unfortunately, memories that operate at speeds comparable to processor speeds are very costly. It is not feasible (except for very small systems) to employ a single memory using just one type of technology. Instead the stored information is distributed in complex fashion over a variety of different memory units with very different physical characteristics.

The memory components of a computer system can be divided into three main groups:

1. *Internal processor memory*. This usually comprises a small set of high-

speed registers used as working registers for temporary storage of instructions and data.

2. *Main memory* (also called primary memory). This is a relatively large fast memory used for program and data storage during computer operation. It is characterized by the fact that locations in main memory can be directly accessed by the CPU instruction set. The principal technologies used for main memory are semiconductor integrated circuits (ICs) and ferrite cores.

3. *Secondary memory* (also called auxiliary or backing memory). This is generally much larger in capacity but also much slower than main memory. It is used for storing system programs and large data files and the like which are not continually required by the CPU; it also serves as an "overflow" memory when the capacity of the main memory is exceeded. Information in secondary storage is usually accessed indirectly via special programs that first transfer the required information to main memory. Representative technologies used for secondary memory are magnetic disks and tapes.

The major objective in designing any memory system is to provide adequate storage capacity with an acceptable level of performance at a reasonable cost. Four important interrelated ways of approaching this goal can be identified.

1. The use of a number of different memory devices with different cost/performance ratios organized to provide a high average performance at a low average cost per bit. The individual memories form a hierarchy of storage devices.

2. The development of automatic space-allocation methods to make more efficient use of the available memory space.

3. The development of virtual-memory concepts to free the ordinary user from memory management and make programs largely independent of the physical memory configurations used.

4. The design of communication links to the memory system so that all processors connected to it can operate at or near their maximum rates. This involves increasing the effective memory processor bandwidth and also providing protection mechanisms to prevent programs from accessing or altering one another's storage areas.

5.1.1 Memory-Device Characteristics

The computer architect is faced with a bewildering variety of different memory devices to use. However, all memories are based on a relatively small number of physical phenomena and employ relatively few organizational principles. In this section we examine the functional characteristics that are common to the devices used to build main and secondary computer memories. A knowledge of these general properties is essential in evaluating any memory technology. The characteristics and underlying physical principles of some specific representative technologies are also discussed.

Cost The cost of a memory unit is most meaningfully measured by the purchase or lease price to the user of the complete unit. The price should include not only the cost of the information storage cells themselves but also the cost of the peripheral equipment or access circuitry essential to the operation of the memory. Let C be the price in dollars of a complete memory system with S bits of storage capacity. We define the *cost* c of the memory as follows:

$$c = \frac{C}{S} \text{ dollars/bit}$$

Access time and access rate The performance of a memory device is primarily determined by the rate at which information can be read from or written into the memory. A convenient performance measure is the average time required to read a fixed amount of information, e. g., one word, from the memory. This is termed the *read access time* or, more commonly, the *access time* of the memory and is denoted by t_A. (The write access time is defined similarly; it is typically, but not always, equal to the read access time.) Access time depends on the physical characteristics of the storage medium, and also on the type of access mechanism used; a precise general definition of t_A is difficult. It is usually calculated from the time a read request is received by the memory unit to the time at which all the requested information has been made available at the memory output terminals. The *access rate* b_A of the memory defined as t_A^{-1} and measured in words per second is another widely used performance measure for memory devices.

Clearly low cost and high access rates are desirable memory characteristics; unfortunately they appear to be largely incompatible. Memory units with high access rates are generally expensive, while low-cost memories are relatively slow. Figure 5.1 shows the relation between cost c and access rate b_A for some representative current (1977) technologies. This relation can be approximated by the straight line AB. If we write $b_A = 10^y$ and $c = 10^x$, then $y \approx mx + k'$, where m denotes the slope of AB. Hence $b_A = 10^{mx + k'}$ and $b_A = kc^m$, where k, k' are constants. From the data provided in Fig. 5.1, it can be concluded that $m \approx 2$; hence $b_A \approx kc^2$.

Improvements in manufacturing techniques are continually reducing c and increasing b_A for almost all memory technologies. Most forecasters expect the parameter m to remain fairly constant [25]. Note that the technologies shown on Fig. 5.1 fall into two groups, with a significant gap between them. Several recent technologies, notably magnetic-bubble memories and memories built from charge-coupled devices (CCDs), appear likely to fill this gap.

Access modes: random and serial An important property of a memory device is the order or sequence in which information can be accessed. If locations may be accessed in any order and access time is independent of the location being accessed, the memory is termed a *random access memory*. Ferrite-core and

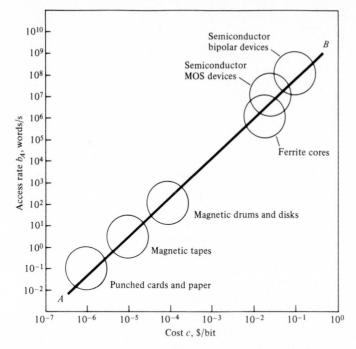

Figure 5.1 Access rate versus cost for various memory technologies.

semiconductor memories are usually of this type. Memories where storage locations can be accessed only in certain predetermined sequences are called *serial access memories*. Magnetic-tape units and magnetic-bubble memories employ serial access methods.

In a random access memory each storage location can be accessed independently of the other locations. There is, in effect, a separate access mechanism, or read-write head, for every location, as illustrated in Fig. 5.2. In serial memories, on the other hand, the access mechanism is shared among different locations. It must be assigned to different locations at different times. This is accomplished by moving the stored information, the read-write head, or both. Many serial access memories operate by continually moving the storage loca-

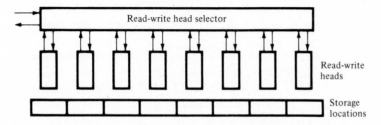

Figure 5.2 Conceptual model of a random access memory.

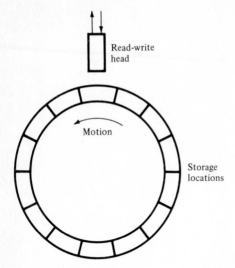

Figure 5.3 Conceptual model of a serial access memory.

tions around a closed path or track, as shown in Fig. 5.3. A particular location can be accessed only when it passes the fixed read-write head; thus the time required to access a particular location depends on its position relative to the read-write head when the access request is received.

Since every location has its own addressing mechanism, random access memories tend to be more costly than the serial type. In serial access memories, however, the time required to bring the desired location into correspondence with a read-write head increases the effective access time, so serial access tends to be slower than random access. Thus the access mode employed contributes significantly to the inverse relation between cost and access time. In Fig. 5.1, for example, random access and serial access technologies are clearly separated into two groups.

Some memory devices such as magnetic disks and drums contain a large number of independent rotating tracks. If each track has its own read-write head, the tracks may be accessed randomly, although access within each track is serial. In such cases the access mode is sometimes called *semirandom* or, rather misleadingly, *direct access*. It should be noted that access mode is a function of memory organization as well as the inherent characteristics of the storage technology used. Memory technologies, e. g., semiconductor, that are primarily used to construct random access memories can also be used to construct serial access memories. The converse is not usually true, however.

Alterability; ROMs The method used to write information into a memory may be irreversible, in that once information has been written, it cannot be altered while the memory is in use, i. e., on-line. Punching holes in cards and printing on paper are examples of essentially permanent storage techniques. Memories whose contents cannot be altered on-line (if they can be altered at all) are called *read-only memories* (ROMs). A ROM is therefore a nonerasable storage

device. ROMs are widely used for storing control programs such as microprograms. ROMs whose contents can be changed (usually off-line and with some
difficulty) are called *programmable read-only memories* (PROMs).

Memories in which reading or writing can be done with impunity on-line
are sometimes called *read-write* memories (RWMs) to constrast them with
ROMs. All memories used for temporary storage purposes are RWMs. Unless
otherwise specified, we will generally use the term memory to mean a read-
write memory.

Permanence of storage The physical processes involved in storage are sometimes inherently unstable, so that the stored information may be lost over a
period of time unless appropriate action is taken. There are three important
memory characteristics that can destroy information:

1. Destructive readout
2. Dynamic storage
3. Volatility

Ferrite-core memories have the property that the method of reading the
memory alters, i.e., destroys, the stored information; this phenomenon is called
destructive readout (DRO). Memories in which reading does not affect the
stored data are said to have *nondestructive readout* (NDRO). In DRO memories, each read operation must be followed by a write operation that restores
the original state of the memory. This restoration is usually carried out automatically using a buffer register, as shown in Fig. 5.4. The word at the
addressed location is transferred to the buffer register where it is available to
external devices. The contents of the buffer are automatically written back into
the location originally addressed.

Certain memory devices have the property that a stored 1 tends to become
a 0, or vice versa, due to some physical decay process. For example, in the now
obsolete Williams tube memories and in many recent MOS devices, a stored
1 is represented by an electric charge in a capacitor; the absence of a stored

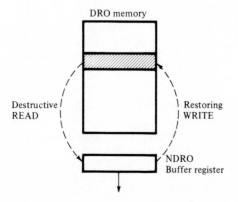

Figure 5.4 Memory restoration in a destructive
readout (DRO) memory.

charge represents a 0. Over a period of time, a stored charge tends to leak away, causing a loss of information unless the charge is restored. The process of restoring is called *refreshing*. Memories which require periodic refreshing are called *dynamic* memories, as opposed to *static* memories, which require no refreshing. (Note that the terms dynamic and static in this context do not refer to the presence or absence of physical motion in the storage device.) Most memories using magnetic storage techniques are static. Refreshing in dynamic memories can be carried out in the same way data is restored in a DRO memory. The contents of every location are transferred systematically to buffer registers and then returned, in suitably amplified form, to their original locations.

Another physical process that can destroy the contents of a memory is the failure of its power supply. A memory is said to be *volatile* if the stored information can be destroyed by a power failure. Most semiconductor memories are volatile, while most magnetic memories are nonvolatile.

Cycle time and data-transfer rate We defined the access time t_A of a memory as the time between the receipt of a read request by the memory and the delivery of the requested information to its external output terminals. In DRO and dynamic memories, it may not be possible to initiate another memory access until a restore or refresh operation has been carried out. This means that the minimum time that must elapse between the initiation of two different accesses by the memory can be greater than t_A; this rather loosely defined time is called the *cycle time* t_M of the memory.

It is generally convenient to assume that t_M is the time needed to complete any read or write operation in the memory. Hence the maximum amount of information that can be transferred to or from the memory every second is $1/t_M$; this quantity is called the *data-transfer rate* or *bandwidth* b_M. The data-transfer rate is frequently measured in bits per second (bauds) or words per second. A factor limiting memory bandwidth is the *memory bus width* w, which is the number of bits that can be transferred simultaneously over the memory bus. w is generally, but not necessarily, the same as the standard memory word size. Clearly $b_M = wt_M^{-1}$ bauds.

In cases where $t_A \neq t_M$, both are used to measure memory performance. The access time may be more important in measuring overall computer-system performance since it determines the length of time a processor must wait after initiating a memory access request; during the remainder of the memory cycle, both processor and memory can operate simultaneously. On the other hand, if $t_A \neq t_M$, then $b_A \neq b_M$ and b_A does not represent the actual number of accesses that can be carried out per second, whereas b_M does.

Physical storage media Many different physical properties of matter are used for information storage. The more important properties used for this purpose can be classified as electronic, magnetic, mechanical, and optical. A basic requirement for a storage medium is that it have two well-defined physical states that can be used to represent the logical 0 and 1 values. The access rate of a particular memory device depends on the rate at which its physical states can be measured and altered.

If a memory and the processor connected to it use the same physical storage media, they are said to be *compatible*. If they are not compatible, special interface devices, called *transducers*, are needed; they can add significantly to both memory cost and access time. Most processors employ electronic (semiconductor) technologies; hence only memories using similar technologies are compatible.

Figure 5.5 contains a table showing representative physical characteristics of some major modern memory technologies.

Miscellaneous physical characteristics There are several other attributes of memories that do not directly involve functional behavior but nevertheless significantly affect the cost of a memory technology in a particular application.

A factor determining the physical size of a memory unit is the *storage density* measured, perhaps, in bits per unit volume. The physical size also determines the *portability* of the memory. The *energy consumption* of the memory units may contribute significantly to the running costs of a computer system. Large energy consumption combined with high storage density may require expensive cooling equipment.

Finally, some mention should be made of *reliability*. This can be measured

Technology	Cost c, $/bit	Access time t_A, s	Access mode	Alterability	Permanence	Physical storage medium
Bipolar semiconductor	10^{-1}	10^{-8}	Random	Read/write	NDRO, volatile	Electronic
Metal-oxide-semiconductor (MOS)	10^{-2}	10^{-7}	Random	Read/write	DRO or NDRO, volatile	Electronic
Ferrite cores	10^{-2}	10^{-6}	Random	Read/write	DRO, nonvolatile	Magnetic
Magnetic disks and drums	10^{-4}	10^{-2}	Random or semi-random	Read/write	NDRO, nonvolatile	Magnetic
Magnetic tapes	10^{-5}	10^{-1}	Serial	Read/write	NDRO, nonvolatile	Magnetic
Punched cards and paper tape	10^{-6}	10	Serial	Read only	NDRO, nonvolatile	Mechanical

Figure 5.5 Characteristics of representative memory technologies.

by the mean time before failure (MTBF). In general, memories with no moving parts have much higher reliability than memories such as magnetic disks which involve considerable mechanical motion. Even in memories that involve no moving parts, reliability problems arise, particularly when very high storage densities or high data-transfer rates are used. The reliability of any memory can be increased by using error-detecting and error-correcting codes (see Sec. 3.1.2).

5.1.2 Random Access Memories

Random access memories are characterized by the fact that every location can be accessed independently. The access and cycle times for every location are constant and independent of its position. Figure 5.6 shows the main components of a random access memory unit. The storage cell unit comprises N cells each of which can store one bit of information. The memory operates as follows. The address of the required location (a set of $w \geq 1$ cells) is transferred via the address bus to the memory address register. The address is then processed by the address decoder which selects the required location in the storage cell unit. A read-write select control line specifies the type of access to be performed. If read is requested, the contents of the selected location is transferred to the output data register. If write is requested, the word to be written is first placed in the memory input data register and then transferred to the selected cell. Since it is not usually desirable to permit simultaneous reading and writing, the input and output data registers are frequently combined to form a single data register (also called the memory buffer register).

Each storage cell has a number of lines connected to it. Figure 5.7 shows an idealized model of a cell and its external connections. The address lines are used to select the cell for either reading or writing, as determined by the read-write control lines. A set of data lines is used for transferring data to and from the memory. The actual number of physical lines connected to a storage cell is

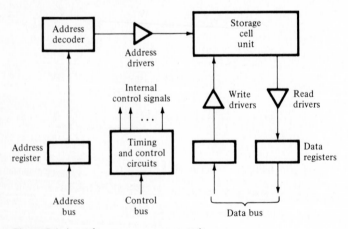

Figure 5.6 A random access memory unit.

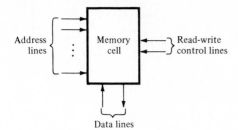

Figure 5.7 General model of a random access memory cell.

very much a function of the technology being used. Frequently one physical line has several functions, e.g., it may be used as both an address and a data line. Thus the cell connections depicted in Fig. 5.7 should be viewed as logical rather than physical. In each line connected to the storage cell unit one can expect to find a driver which acts as either an amplifier or a transducer of physical signals. Thus we find in Fig. 5.6 a set of address line drivers and a set of data line drivers. The various drivers, decoders, and control circuits are collectively referred to as the *access circuitry* of the memory unit.

Array organization The access circuitry needed has a very significant effect on the total cost of any memory unit. A general approach to reducing the access circuitry cost in random access memories is called *matrix*, or *array*, *organization* [18]. It has two essential features:

1. The storage cells are physically arranged in space as rectangular arrays of cells. This is primarily to facilitate layout of the connections between the cells and the access circuitry. Such arrays are also particularly suitable for LSI manufacturing techniques.
2. The memory address is partitioned into d components so that the address A_i of Cell C_i becomes a d-dimensional vector $(A_{i,1}, A_{i,2}, \ldots, A_{i,d}) = A_i$. Each of the d parts of an address word goes to a different address decoder and a different set of address drivers. A particular cell is selected by simultaneously activating all d of its address lines, i. e., by the *coincidence* of d address signals. A memory unit with this kind of addressing is said to be a *d-dimensional memory* [18]. (The reader is cautioned, however, that the term d-dimensional is frequently used in a loose sense to describe both the addressing scheme and the physical layout of the memory unit.) The main reason for using more than one address line per cell is to reduce the size of the address decoders and the number of address drivers required.

A major advantage of array memories lies in the fact that their symmetry makes them easily extensible. Array memory devices are often available in standard-sized modules designed so they can be easily interconnected to form larger array memories. Thus two modules organized as 1024 4-bit words can be connected to form a memory of 2048 4-bit words or 1024 8-bit words. (A specific example of this is given later.)

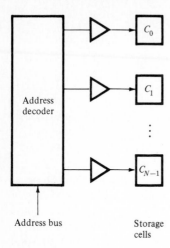

Address bus

Storage cells

Figure 5.8 One-dimensional addressing scheme.

1-D organization The simplest array organizations have $d = 1$ and are called *one-dimensional*, or 1-D, memories. Each cell is connected to one address line, as shown in Fig. 5.8. If the storage capacity of the unit is N bits, then the access circuitry typically contains a one-out-of-N address decoder and N address drivers.

2-D organization In the *two-dimensional* (2-D) organization shown in Fig. 5.9, the address field is divided into two components, called X and Y, which consist

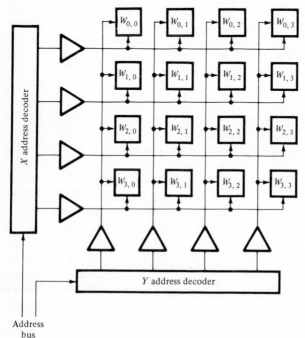

Y address decoder

Address bus

Figure 5.9 Two-dimensional addressing scheme.

of a_x and a_y bits, respectively. The cells are arranged in a rectangular array of $N_x \le 2^{a_x}$ rows and $N_y \le 2^{a_y}$ columns so that the total number of cells is $N = N_x N_y$. A cell is selected by the coincidence of signals on its X and Y address lines. The 2-D organization requires substantially less access circuitry than the 1-D. For example, if $N_x = N_y = \sqrt{N}$, the number of address drivers needed is $2\sqrt{N}$. Instead of one one-out-of-N address decoder, two one-out-of-$\sqrt{N}$ address decoders are required.

Random access memories frequently use a word of length w bits as the unit of storage; hence w cells must be selected in each memory access. Such memories are conveniently implemented in the form of an $N \times w$ array of 1-bit cells, where N is the word capacity of the memory. Each row of w cells is then addressed by a single address line. This type of *word-organized* memory is commonly called two-dimensional, although it may be regarded as one-dimensional from the addressing viewpoint taken here.

Dimensions greater than 2 The foregoing addressing schemes can in principle be extended to higher values of d. In a 3-D memory, three address lines per cell would be expected. In practice, values of d greater than 3 are not used. One reason for this is that as d increases, it becomes more difficult to distinguish a cell with d active address lines (which should be accessed) from one with $d - 1$ active address lines (which should not be accessed). Large values of d also make manufacture of the cell matrix more difficult.

Semiconductor memories Semiconductor devices in which the basic storage cells are transistor circuits have been used for high-speed processor (CPU) registers since the early 1950s. It was not until the advent of integrated circuit (IC) manufacturing techniques in the late 1960s that it became economical to produce high-capacity semiconductor memories suitable for main-memory applications. Such memories can now be fabricated in the form of IC chips using either bipolar or MOS technology (see Sec. 1.5.3) with storage capacities of 16K bits or higher. The chips are then incorporated into standard dual in-line packages. The present limitations of IC circuit manufacturing methods make it impossible to manufacture, say, a 10^9-bit memory on a single chip. Thus large memories must be formed by interconnecting a number of memory ICs.

Types of semiconductor memory Semiconductor memory cells fall into two main categories:

1. Flip-flops
2. Charge storage devices

The flip-flops used for random access memories are essentially similar in operation to the flip-flops long used to make processor registers. They differ primarily in the methods used for addressing a cell and transferring data to and from the cell. Multifunction lines are used to minimize the number of external connections to each cell and so facilitate the manufacture of large planar arrays. The charge storage devices are typically integrated circuits in which the 1 and 0 states correspond to the presence or absence of a charge stored in a capacitor. Since the charge in a capacitor tends to decay with time, charge storage devices are almost always dynamic and need refreshing. Refreshing circuitry can be included as part of the timing and control logic on each chip. Almost all semiconductor memory devices, unlike ferrite cores, are volatile.

A bipolar flip-flop cell Bipolar storage cells are usually of the flip-flop type. Figure 5.10 shows an example. The two bipolar transistors T_0 and T_1 function as cross-coupled NAND gates (or NOR gates, depending on whether the logic convention used is positive or negative). At any time exactly one transistor is switched on, i. e., conducting current, while its companion is switched off.

The cell is selected for either the read or write operation by changing the voltage on the address line from low to high. The data line can be considered to have three distinct states represented by three voltage levels V_0, $V_{1/2}$, and V_1. V_0 and V_1 are used for writing, while the intermediate voltage level $V_{1/2}$ is used in reading. V_a and V_b are the circuit power lines. V_b is held at the voltage level $V_{1/2}$. To read the cell, the data line is held at $V_{1/2}$ and the address line voltage is raised. This causes the current flowing through the on transistor to transfer from its lower emitter to its upper emitter. The resulting signal indicating the state of the cell is detected by a sense amplifier connected to the data line. A 0 (1) is written into the cell by again activating its address line and applying V_0 (V_1) to its data line.

An MOS charge-storage cell MOS storage cells may be either of the flip-flop or charge-storage type. Figure 5.11 shows a particularly simple MOS cell based on the charge-storage concept. It comprises a field-effect MOS transistor T,

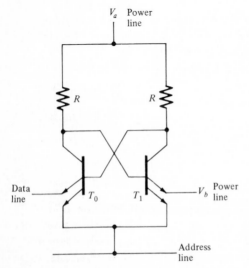

Figure 5.10 A bipolar flip-flop memory cell.

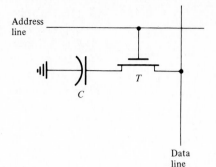

Address
line

T

C

Data
line

Figure 5.11 A dynamic MOS memory cell using charge storage.

which acts as a switch, and a capacitor C, which stores the data. It has only two external connections: a data line and an address line. To write information into the cell, a voltage (either high or low, representing 1 and 0, respectively) is placed on the data line. A voltage is then applied to the address line to switch T on. This causes a charge to be transferred to C if the data line is in the 1 state; no charge is transferred otherwise. To read the cell, the address line is again activated, causing the charge stored in C, if any, to be transferred to the data line where it is detected by a sensitive sense amplifier. The readout process is destructive. The information read out is amplified and subsequently rewritten into the cell; this may be combined with the periodic refreshing operation required by dynamic memories of this type. The advantages of this memory cell are its simplicity, which means that ICs with very high cell density can be built, and its low power consumption.

Memory array design A semiconductor memory IC is a self-contained random access memory. It typically has a word-organized matrix structure and contains all required access circuitry including address decoders, drivers, and control circuits. A memory with a capacity of n w-bit words is called an $n \times w$ *bit memory*. Figure 5.12 shows a simple 4×2 bit array that incorporates eight bipolar flip-flop cells of the type shown in Fig. 5.10. The more important access circuitry is also shown. WE is the *write enable* line; a write (read) operation can take place only if WE = 1 (0). A second control line, the *address enable* or *chip enable* line AE, is also needed. A word can be accessed for either reading or writing only if AE = 1. The behavior of the bidirectional data lines connected to each cell is determined by the underlying device physics.

A memory design problem that the computer architect may encounter is the following: given that certain $m \times n$ bit memory ICs, denoted $M_{m \times n}$, are available, design an $m' \times n'$ bit random access memory where $m' \geq m$ and/or $n' \geq n$. A general approach is to construct a $p \times q$ array of the $M_{m \times n}$ modules where $p = \lceil m'/m \rceil$ and $q = \lceil n'/n \rceil$, and $\lceil x \rceil$ denotes the smallest integer greater than or equal to x. In this modular array, each row stores m words (except possibly the last row), while each column stores a fixed set of n bits from every word (except possibly the last column). When $m' \geq m$, additional

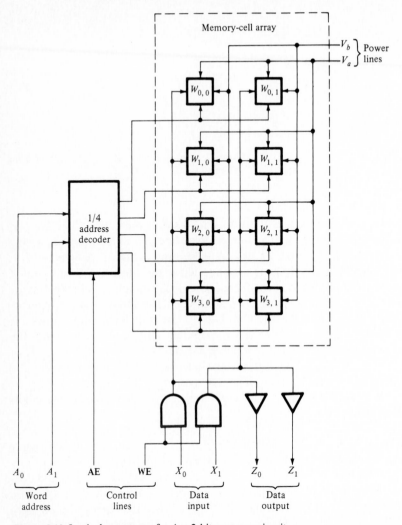

Figure 5.12 Logical structure of a 4×2 bit memory circuit.

external address decoding circuitry will be required. We now present an example illustrating this rather straightforward technique.

Example 5.1: Design a 16x4 bit memory using 4x2 bit ICs of the type shown in Fig. 5.12 It is convenient to represent each IC by a single block with its external connections labeled as in Fig. 5.13. Clearly eight of these ICs are needed. They can be arranged as a 4×2 array as shown in Fig. 5.14. The left column of ICs stores the two low-order data bits, while the right column stores the two high-order data bits. Since there are four address lines, some additional decoding circuitry is needed. We therefore introduce a one-out-of-four decoder with an address enable input similar to the decoder shown in Fig. 5.12. Two of the incoming address lines are connected to

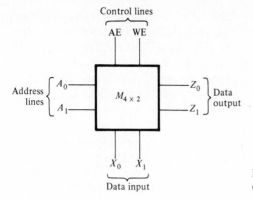

Figure 5.13 Symbol for the 4×2 bit memory circuit of Fig. 5.12.

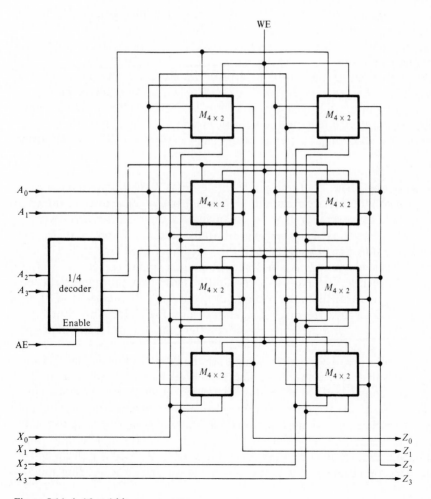

Figure 5.14 A 16×4 bit memory array.

every IC; the remaining two address lines are inputs to the external decoder. Each of the output lines of this decoder is connected to the address enable inputs of the ICs in the same row. Thus each row of cells in the resulting array has a unique address. The output data lines of all cells in the same column are connected together under the assumption (which is valid for many semiconductor technologies) that this connection forms a wired-OR.

Ferrite-core memories Until the advent of high-capacity semiconductor memory ICs, most main memories in computers employed ferrite cores. The basic storage cell in this technology is a tiny doughnut-shaped piece of ferrite material called a *core* through which several wires are threaded. By passing an electric current called a *drive current* through these wires, the core can be magnetized in either a clockwise or counterclockwise direction; these two directions of magnetization represent the logical 0 and 1 states. The direction of the drive current determines the direction of magnetization. The properties of the ferrite material are such that when this current is reduced to zero, the core retains its previous magnetized state. This implies that ferrite cores can be used to build nonvolatile memories.

While ferrite-core memories have been widely used, they have several disadvantages. They are basically incompatible with processor technologies. They are also difficult to manufacture due to the complex wiring patterns needed. The memory cycle time achievable is primarily a function of core size; the smaller the core, the shorter the cycle time but the more difficult the wiring problem.

Principles of operation To employ a ferrite core as a read-write memory cell at least two conductors are required, a drive line and a sense line, as shown in Fig. 5.15. The drive line is used for changing the state of the core (writing) and the sense line is used for sensing the state (reading). Suppose that a current of magnitude I is passed through the drive line, as shown in Fig. 5.15a. This produces a magnetic flux φ in the direction indicated which can be taken to represent the 0 state. If I exceeds a certain threshold or saturation level and is then reduced to zero, the core remains in the 0 state. If a current of $-I$ amperes is passed through the drive line, as shown in Fig. 5.15b, the direction of the magnetic flux is reversed and the core enters the 1 state. Again this state remains if the drive current is switched off.

The readout process requires using both the drive and sense lines. A current I is passed through the drive line in a fixed direction, say that of Fig. 5.15a. If the core is in the 0 state, there is no change in its direction of magnetization. If, however, the core is in the 1 state, the magnetic flux in the core reverses direction and, as described by Faraday's law, a voltage pulse is induced in the sense line. This pulse is detected by a sense amplifier and transferred to the memory data register. Thus the state of the cell is determined by the presence or absence of a signal on the sense line. The reading method

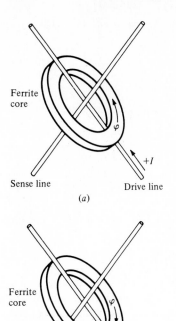

Ferrite
core

Sense line

Drive line
+*I*

(*a*)

Ferrite
core

Sense line

Drive line
−*I*

(*b*)

Figure 5.15 Switching a ferrite core to (*a*) the 0 state and (*b*) the 1 state.

used is clearly destructive (DRO), so the cell state must be restored before a second read operation can take place.

The memory cycle In order to streamline the operation of a ferrite-core memory, both read and write requests are carried out in two steps, or "cycles," which together form one memory cycle.

1. *The read cycle*: A 0 is written into every core of the addressed location, as in Fig. 5.15*a*. If the requested operation is read, the output of the sense lines is transferred to the memory data register, at which point the memory unit indicates that the requested data is available. If the requested operation is write, the sense signals are ignored and this step serves to clear the addressed location.
2. *The write cycle*: The cores of the addressed location which should be in the 1 state are set to 1. This either completes a write operation or else restores the original state in the case of a read operation.

3-D organization Ferrite-core memories are generally organized as arrays of the type discussed earlier. One of the most economical and widely used organizations, called the 3-D organization, will now be described. The term 3-D

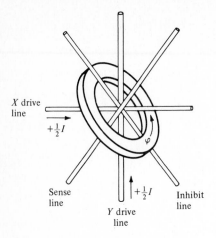

X drive line

$+\frac{1}{2}I$

φ

Sense line

$+\frac{1}{2}I$

Y drive line

Inhibit line

Figure 5.16 The storage cell in a 3-D ferrite-core memory.

derives mainly from the fact that three drive (address) lines, called the X, Y, and inhibit lines, are needed, as illustrated in Fig. 5.16. The effective drive current is the algebraic sum of the currents on the three drive lines. The state of the core can therefore be changed to 0 by applying a "half-current" $+\frac{1}{2}I$ to both the X and Y drive lines, as shown in Fig. 5.16. It is changed to 1 by applying $-\frac{1}{2}I$ to both the X and Y drive lines. The inhibit drive line is connected to the output of the memory buffer register and is used only during the write cycle.

The operation of a 3-D ferrite-core memory is as follows: The addressed cells are switched to the 0 state in the read cycle by applying $+\frac{1}{2}I$ to the X and Y drive line exactly as in Fig. 5.16. In the write cycle the currents in the X and Y lines are reversed. No current is passed through the inhibit lines of those cores whose final state is to be 1. If the final state of a core is to be 0, a current of $+\frac{1}{2}I$ is applied to its inhibit line. The net drive current is thereby reduced to $-\frac{1}{2}I$, and the core remains in the 0 state. Thus the inhibit line is used to inhibit the writing of 1 into selected cells during the write cycle.

Figure 5.17 shows a 3-D ferrite-core memory that stores eight 3-bit words. It comprises three 4×2 submatrices M_0, M_1, and M_2 each of which is a two-dimensional array of ferrite cores and stores a specific bit of every word. There are three sense and three inhibit lines, one for each submatrix M_0, M_1, and M_2. It will be observed that the sense and inhibit lines are threaded through all the cores in the corresponding submatrix. When a word is being accessed, currents are generated on the X and Y address lines which select one core in each of M_0, M_1, and M_2. A core in the same row or column as a selected core will receive a half-current of magnitude $\frac{1}{2}I$ on its X or Y drive lines; this is insufficient to cause it to switch states. Cells that receive half-currents do experience small changes in flux which can result in spurious signals ("noise") on the sense line. The rather complicated pattern of wires shown in Fig. 5.17 is intended to minimize this noise. In comparing the ferrite-core cell of Fig. 5.16 to the general model shown in Fig. 5.7 it will be observed that the wires threading the core have multiple functions. The sense line is a clearly defined data-output line, but the drive lines are used for both addressing and data-input purposes.

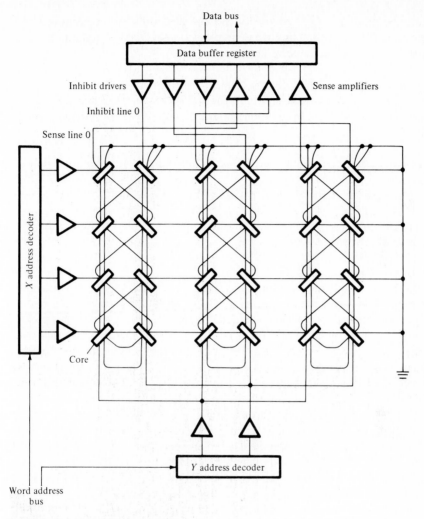

Figure 5.17 A 3-D ferrite-core memory.

5.1.3 Serial Access Memories

Serial access memories are characterized by the fact that the read-write circuitry is shared among different storage locations. Large serial memories are
usually designed so that the stored information moves continuously along a set
of fixed paths or tracks. A track consists of a sequence of cells each capable of
storing one bit of information. Each track has a number of fixed access points at
which a read-write "head" may transfer information to or from the track. A
specific stored item is accessed by moving either the stored information, the
read-write heads, or both. From a functional point of view, the storage tracks in
serial memories are shift registers with a limited number of input-output points.
Thus the transfer of information to and from any one track is essentially serial.

Serial access memories find their main application as secondary or bulk on-line computer memories. They have low cost per bit and low access rates. Low cost per bit is obtained by using very simple and very small storage cells. The low access rate is due to several factors:

1. The read-write head positioning time
2. The relatively slow speed at which the tracks move
3. The fact that data transfer to and from the memory is serial rather than parallel

Because access rate is so important, we now consider this factor in more detail.

Access rate Serial memories may be divided into two types:

1. Memories where each track has one or more fixed read-write heads
2. Memories whose read-write heads are shared among different tracks

In memories that share read-write heads, a delay is introduced by the need to move read-write heads between different tracks. The average time required to move a head from one track to another is called the *seek time* t_S of the memory unit. Once the head is in position, the desired cell may be in the wrong part of the moving storage track. Some time is required for this cell to reach the read-write head so that data transfer can begin. The average time needed for this movement to take place is called the *latency* t_L of the memory. In memories where information rotates around a closed track, t_L is also called the *rotational delay*.

Each storage cell in a track stores a single bit. A w-bit word may be stored in two different ways. A word may consist of w consecutive bits along a single track. Alternatively, w tracks may be used to store a word, with each track storing a different bit. By synchronizing the w tracks and providing a separate read-write head for each track, all w bits can be accessed simultaneously. In either case it may be inefficient to access just one word per access since so much time is consumed by the seek time and latency. Words are frequently grouped into larger units called *blocks*. All the words in a block are stored in consecutive locations, so that the time required to access an entire block includes only one seek and one latency period.

Once the read-write head is positioned at the start of the requested word or block, data may be transferred at a rate which depends primarily on the speed at which the stored information is moving and the storage density along the track. The amount of information that can be transferred continuously to or from the track under these circumstances is called the *data-transfer rate*. If a track has a storage density of T bits per centimeter and moves at a velocity of V centimeters per second past the read-write head, the data-transfer rate is TV bits per second. (Note that this definition of data-transfer rate is consistent with the general definition given in Sec. 5.1.1 if t_S and t_L are ignored.)

Example 5.2: Estimation of the time t_B required to access a block of information in a serial access memory Assume that the memory has closed rotating tracks of the type shown in Fig. 5.3. Let each track have a capacity of N words and rotate at a rate of r revolutions per second. Let n be the number of words per block. The data rate of the memory is rN words per second. Hence once the read-write head is positioned at the start of the desired block, it can be transferred in approximately $n(rN)^{-1}$ seconds. The average latency is $(2r)^{-1}$ seconds, which is the time needed for half a revolution. If t_S is the average seek time, an appropriate formula for t_B is

$$t_B = t_S + (2r)^{-1} + n(rN)^{-1}$$

Memory-unit organization Figure 5.18 shows the general organization of a serial memory unit. Assume that each word is stored along a single track and that each access results in transfer of a block of $n \geq 1$ words. The address of the information to be accessed is loaded into the memory address register. The output of the address decoder determines the track to be used (the track address) and the location of the desired block of information within the track (the block address). The track address determines the particular read-write head to be selected. Then, if necessary, the selected head is moved into position to transfer data to or from the target track. The desired block cannot be accessed until it reaches the selected head. To determine when this occurs, some type of track position indicator is needed which generates the address of the

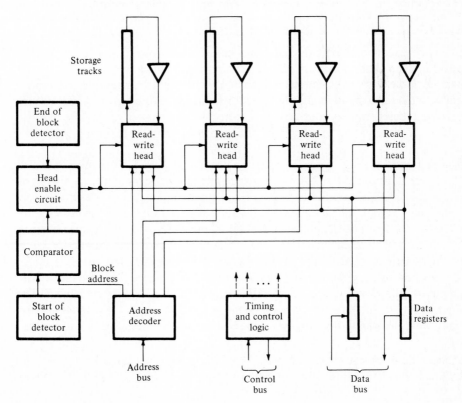

Figure 5.18 A serial access memory unit.

block that is currently passing the read-write head. The generated address is compared with the block address produced by the address decoder. When they match, the selected head is enabled and data transfer between the storage track and the memory data buffer registers begins. The read-write head is disabled when a complete block of information has been transferred. The memory input and output data registers are generally shift registers of the parallel-in/series-out and series-in/parallel-out types, respectively.

Classification by physical access mechanism The number of different types of storage media and access mechanisms used to construct serial access memories is very large; they can be classified in many ways. A possible classification, which we will use here, distinguishes memories on the basis of type of physical access mechanism used.

1. *Memories with dynamic access mechanisms.* The read-write heads and/or the storage locations are moved through space, usually by electromechanical devices such as electric motors, in order to perform an access. The most widely used group of secondary memory devices, magnetic-disk and -tape units, fall into this category.
2. *Memories with static access mechanisms.* No mechanical motion is required to access the memory. The now obsolete mercury delay line memory was of this type, as are magnetic bubble and CCD memories.

Magnetic memories with electromechanical access have had many years of development. The storage media (disks and tapes) used are inexpensive and also portable. However, electromechanical equipment is inherently unreliable and a major source of computer-system failures. Memories with no moving parts are therefore very attractive from the point of view of reliability. We will discuss representative examples of both types of serial access memory.

Magnetic-surface recording In magnetic-drum, -disk, and -tape memories, information is stored in tracks on the surface of a magnetic medium, usually ferric oxide. Each cell in a track has two stable magnetic states that represent the logical 0 and 1 values. The magnetic states are typically defined by the direction or magnitude of the magnetic flux in the cell (many different methods of encoding information in magnetic states are used). Each cell is therefore similar in principle to a ferrite core. As in the case of ferrite cores, electric currents are used for altering and sensing the magnetic state. In surface magnetic storage, however, an external read-write head of the type shown in Fig. 5.19 is employed. The read and write currents pass through coils around a ring of soft magnetic material. There is a gap in this ring which permits magnetic flux to pass into the surrounding air. A very narrow space separates the ring gap from a cell on the storage track, so that their respective magnetic fields can interact. This interaction permits information transfer between the read-write head and the storage medium.

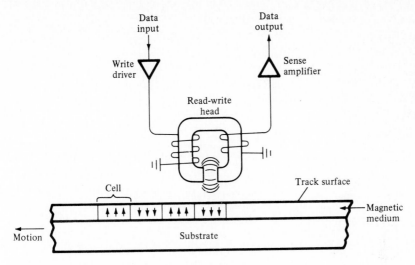

Figure 5.19 Magnetic-surface recording mechanism.

In order to write information, the addressed cell is moved under the read-write gap. A pulse of current is then transmitted through the write coil which alters the magnetic field at the ring gap; this in turn alters the state of magnetization of the cell under the gap. The direction or magnitude of the write current determines the resulting cell state. To read a cell, it is moved past the read-write head. The magnetic field of the cell induces a magnetic field in the core material of the read-write head. Since the cell is in motion, this magnetic field varies and so induces an electric voltage pulse in the read coil. This voltage which is then fed to a sense amplifier identifies the state of the cell. The readout process is nondestructive. In addition, magnetic-surface storage is nonvolatile.

Electromechanically accessed magnetic memories are distinguished by the shapes of the surfaces in which the storage tracks are embedded. In drum memories, the tracks are parallel circular paths around the surface of a cylindrical drum. In disk memories, the tracks form concentric circles on the surface of a disk. In tape memories, the tracks form parallel lines on the surface of a long narrow plastic tape. Magnetic drums will not be discussed explicitly, since they are seldom used nowadays and their operation resembles that of magnetic disks.

Magnetic-disk memories A magnetic disk is similar in size and appearance to a phonograph record. It may be made of aluminum or plastic with a thin coating of magnetic material on its surface. On each surface of the disk there are up to several hundred tracks which are arranged in concentric circles as shown in Fig. 5.20a. Typically several disks are attached to a common spindle to form a disk pack that can be easily removed. During operation of a disk memory, the disks are rotated continuously at a constant speed. In modern disk units, each recording surface is supplied with at least one read-write head. The read-write

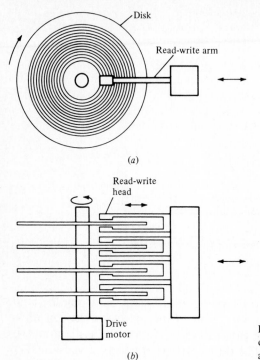

Figure 5.20 (a) Top view and (b) side view of a magnetic disk pack and its read-write arm.

heads may be connected to form a read-write "arm," as shown in Fig. 5.20*b*, so that all heads move in unison. This arm may then be moved in a fixed linear path to select a particular set of tracks. Disk memories have also been designed with one head per track, thus eliminating the need for a moving read-write arm and effectively reducing the seek time to zero.

Example 5.3: The IBM 3330 disk storage unit This is a moving-arm disk memory designed for the IBM System/370 computer series. Each disk drive accommodates a removable disk pack, the IBM 3336. Figure 5.21 shows some of the principal characteristics of this device. The basic unit of storage used is 1 byte = 8 bits.

Number of disks per disk pack	12
Number of recording surfaces	19
Number of tracks per surface	404
Track storage capacity	13, 030 bytes
Disk pack storage capacity	Approximately 10^8 bytes
Disk rotation speed	3600 r/min
Average seek time	30 ms
Average latency	8.4 ms
Data transfer rate	Approximately 8×10^5 bytes/s

Figure 5.21 Characteristics of the IBM 3330 disk storage unit.

Magnetic-tape memories Magnetic-tape memories are essentially similar to domestic tape recorders; instead of storing analog information, they store binary digital information. The storage medium has as its substrate a flexible plastic tape. Information is generally stored in nine parallel longitudinal tracks. A read-write head that can simultaneously access all nine tracks is used; hence the basic memory "word" is 9 bits. This usually comprises 8 bits (1 byte) of information and 1 parity check bit. Magnetic tapes are stored on reels and provide a compact, inexpensive, and portable medium for storing large information files.

Figure 5.22 shows the main components of a tape drive unit. Two reels are used to store the tape. Unlike disk or drum memories, the storage medium is not in continuous motion. When an access request is received, the tape is moved forward or backward to the desired location; it is stopped at the end of the data transfer. In order to permit rapid starting and stopping, two large loops of tape are permitted to hang freely on each side of the read-write head. The rotating drums (called capstans) that pull the tape past the read-write head are here only to accelerate the tape in these loops while the reels themselves are brought up to speed. This procedure reduces the influence of the inertia of the reels. After its initial acceleration, the tape moves at a constant velocity, called the *tape speed*.

Data transfer takes place only when the tape is moving at constant velocity; hence the data-transfer rate of a particular tape unit is determined by the storage density and the tape speed. For example, if the tape storage density is 1600 bytes/in and the tape speed is 18.75 in/s (these figures are representative of commonly used low-speed tape systems), the data-transfer rate is $1600 \times 18.75 = 30,000$ bytes/s. Information stored on magnetic tapes is organized into blocks of various sizes. Relatively large gaps must be inserted at the end of each block to permit the tape to start and stop between blocks. Note that the time required to rewind an entire tape is of the order of 1 min.

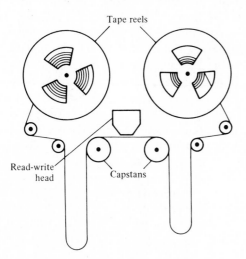

Figure 5.22 A magnetic-tape drive unit.

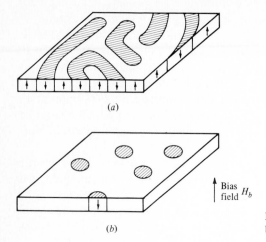

(a)

(b)

↑ Bias field H_b

Figure 5.23 The formation of magnetic bubbles.

Magnetic-bubble memories In thin plates of certain materials, e.g., orthoferrites and garnets, the natural directions of magnetization are perpendicular to the surface of the plates. When no external magnetic field is present, serpentine areas called *domains* form spontaneously in the plate; see Fig. 5.23a. The material within each domain is magnetized in one of the two possible directions, and adjacent domains are magnetized in opposite directions. Suppose that an external magnetic field H_b, called a *bias field*, is applied perpendicular to the plate surface, as shown in Fig. 5.23b. As the magnitude of H_b is increased, the domains whose direction of magnetization is opposite to that of H_b contract in size until eventually they are cylindrical in shape. These cylindrical domains are called *magnetic bubbles*. Typical bubble diameters are 1 to 10 μm.

Bubbles can be moved at high velocity through the plate if an additional external magnetic field called a *drive field H_d* is applied whose direction is parallel to the plate surface. Usually the drive field is rotated at a fixed rate. This rotating field is generated by an electromagnet, so no mechanical motion is involved. By depositing linear tracks of a soft magnetic material (*permalloy*) on the plate surface, the bubbles can be moved along predetermined paths. The permalloy tracks are designed so that they constrain the bubbles to remain under the tracks. They also convert the drive field into magnetic fields that force the bubbles trapped under the track to move continuously in a fixed direction.

Figure 5.24 shows a *T-bar* track, which consists of T- and bar-shaped permalloy elements in an alternating linear sequence. The rotating drive field H_d induces a magnetic field in the permalloy elements parallel to H_d. Thus, depending on the orientation of H_d, the extremities of the T's and bars and the junctions of the T's become north (N) or south (S) magnetic poles at various times. Each magnetic bubble is like a small magnet, one of whose poles (the S pole in Fig. 5.24) is at the surface on which the permalloy track has been laid. According to the classic law of magnetism (like poles attract, unlike poles repel), a bubble is attracted to the nearest N pole in either a T or a bar. Figure

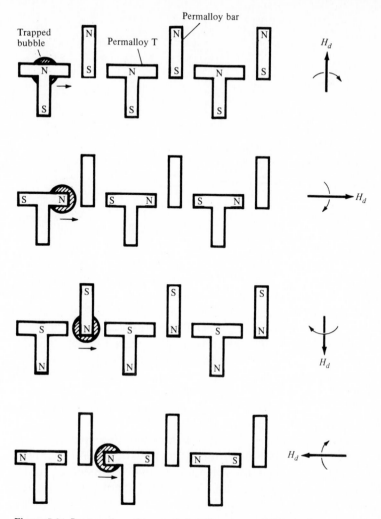

Figure 5.24 Propagation of magnetic bubbles along a T-bar track.

5.24 shows how one revolution of H_d causes a bubble to move in a straight line from one T to the corresponding position under a neighboring T. Many other equally ingenious permalloy track designs exist for bubble propagation [3, 18].

Bubble-memory devices are constructed by forming closed tracks around which bubbles can be circulated continuously at a fixed rate. Each track is then a shift register. In the case of the T-bar track of Fig. 5.24, each pair of adjacent T's and bars constitutes a cell. The presence (absence) of a bubble in a cell denotes the logical 1 (0) state. In order to be able to write data into a cell, two special devices are needed; a *bubble generator* to introduce bubbles into a track and a *bubble annihilator* to remove bubbles. These devices also act as transducers, since the input data is invariably in the form of electrical pulses.

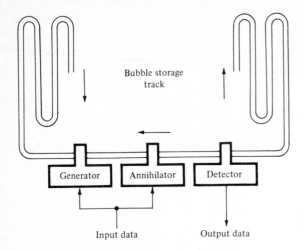

Bubble storage
track

Generator | Annihilator | Detector

Input data

Output data

Figure 5.25 Basic bubble-memory organization.

For reading purposes, a *bubble detector* is required that can produce an electrical signal indicating the presence or absence of a bubble.

The structure of a bubble memory chip organized as a single N-bit shift register is shown in Fig. 5.25. The average access time for 1 bit (which in this case is the same as the latency) is the time required to propagate a bubble through $N/2$ cells. The access time can be decreased by a factor of k by the common stratagem of using k independent bubble shift registers that can be accessed in parallel.

An example of a relatively fast bubble-memory system is the *major-minor loop* organization shown in Fig. 5.26. Data is stored in k bubble shift registers called the minor loops, which are rotated in synchronism by a common magnetic-drive field. Data is transferred to or from the minor loops via another bubble shift register called the major loop. Each minor loop is connected to the major loop by a device called a transfer gate. An external control signal applied to the transfer gates causes one bit of information to be transferred between the major loop and each of the minor loops. The major loop is attached to the input-output circuitry (bubble annihilators, generators, and detectors) and acts as a communication link between the minor storage loops and the outside world.

Magnetic bubble memories have only recently become available; they are not yet widely used in computer systems. Integrated-circuit manufacturing techniques are used that require few steps, which should eventually lead to very low cost per bit. Storage capacities of 10^6 bits per chip have been reported. The lack of moving parts promises high reliability and suggests that bubble memories may ultimately replace "those marvelous mechanical whirling dervishes" [3], magnetic disk and tape memories, as the main technology for secondary or low-speed computer memories. Nonvolatility is achieved in bubble memories by using a permanent magnet to generate the bias field. On the negative side, bubble devices are incompatible with processor technologies so that interfacing can be difficult. However, it is possible to design

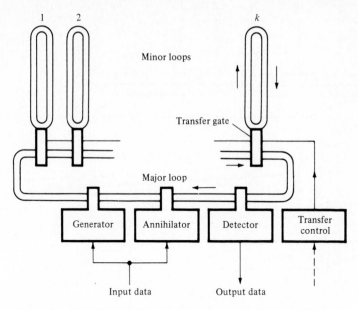

Figure 5.26 A major-minor loop bubble-memory organization.

bubble circuits that perform logic functions, which may minimize this difficulty. Indeed the construction of an entire computer using magnetic bubble technology has been suggested [19].

CCD memories The charged-coupled device (CCD) announced by Bell Telephone Laboratories in 1970 is a shift register whose cells are constructed from MOS capacitors [8, 18]. Information is represented by packets of electrically charged particles, e.g., electrons, which circulate continuously through the shift register under the influence of an electric "drive" field. The presence (absence) of a charge packet in a cell denotes a logical 1 (0). A CCD memory is in many ways analogous to a magnetic bubble memory with charge packets replacing magnetic bubbles. The small size of the MOS capacitors makes it possible to manufacture one-chip memories with very large storage capacity, e.g., 64K bits.

Figure 5.27a shows the structure of a representative CCD. It consists of a linear array of closely-spaced MOS capacitors which form the basic memory cells. The drive field is provided by a three-phase voltage source. Every third cell in the array is connected to the same phase. The waveforms of the drive voltages are shown in Fig. 5.27b.

Figure 5.28 illustrates the charge-transfer process. When a nonzero voltage is applied to any cell, a potential well forms in the cell substrate which can store a charge packet whose sign (positive or negative) is opposite to that of the applied voltage. The well "depth" is determined by the voltage magnitude. Figure 5.28 shows the potential well shape at the three points of time defined in

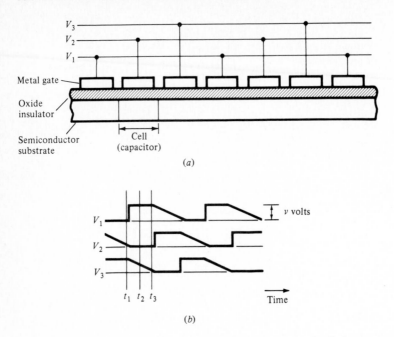

(a)

(b)

Figure 5.27 A charge-coupled device (CCD) shift register: (a) physical structure; (b) three-phase drive-field waveforms.

Fig. 5.27b. At t_1 a potential well is associated with the V_3 gates only. A charge packet previously injected from an external source can be stored in any of these wells; one such packet is shown in the figure. At t_2 a potential well forms under the V_1 gates, while the wells under the V_3 gates begin to shrink. As a result, the charge packet begins to flow from the V_3 gate to the neighboring V_1 gate. At time t_3 the charge transfer is complete. It is easily seen that the three voltages interact in such a way that they effectively cause the potential well containing the charge packet to move linearly along the cell array. The period of the drive

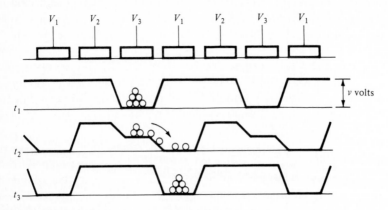

Figure 5.28 Charge-packet transfer in a CCD memory.

voltages determines the basic shift period and hence the speed of operation of the CCD memory. Three adjacent cells are needed to store one bit of information because the charge packet in any cell must be isolated from other charge packets by its two neighboring cells.

CCDs may be organized to form computer memory units in various ways. The simplest organization is that of a single closed shift register around which charge packets circulate continuously. Refresh amplifiers must be included to regenerate the charge packets periodically. Access time can be decreased by using organizations similar to the major-minor loop organization for bubble memories shown in Fig. 5.26. Unlike bubble devices, CCDs are volatile. On the other hand, CCDs can be more easily interfaced with conventional semiconductor logic circuits.

5.2 VIRTUAL MEMORY

Virtual memory loosely describes a hierarchical storage system of at least two levels, which is managed by an operating system to appear to a user like a single large directly addressable main memory. There are three main reasons for using virtual memory.

1. To free users from the need to carry out storage allocation
2. To make programs independent of the configuration and capacity of the memory systems used during their execution
3. To permit efficient sharing of memory space among different users and achieve the high access rates and low cost per bit that is possible with a memory hierarchy

Most virtual memory systems employ a two-level hierarchy comprising a main memory M_1 of relatively small capacity S_1 and a much larger secondary memory M_2 of capacity S_2. The ordinary user, who may program in high-level languages only, views the system as a single virtual or logical memory of unlimited capacity (in fact, its capacity is bounded by $S_1 + S_2$). The virtual memory is addressed by the set L of logical addresses or identifiers explicitly or implicitly specified in the user's program. The fixed physical storage locations in the memory units are identified by a set of physical addresses P. Virtual memory systems are implemented by providing an automatic mechanism for the address mapping $f:L \rightarrow P$.

5.2.1 Memory Hierarchies

The various major units in a typical memory system can be viewed as forming a hierarchy of memories $(M_1, M_2, \ldots, M_n)$ in which each member M_i is in some sense subordinate to the next highest member M_{i-1} of the hierarchy. The CPU and other processors communicate directly with the first member of the hierar-

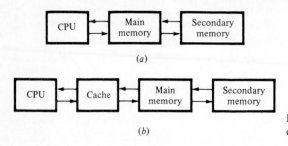

(a)

(b)

Figure 5.29 Common memory hierarchies: (a) two-level; (b) three-level.

chy M_1, M_1 can communicate directly with M_2, and so on. Let c_i, t_{A_i}, and S_i denote the cost per bit, access time, and storage capacity, respectively, of M_i. The following relations normally hold between the memory levels M_i and M_{i+1}:

$$c_i > c_{i+1}$$

$$t_{A_i} < t_{A_{i+1}}$$

$$S_i < S_{i+1}$$

Figure 5.29 shows two of the most common memory hierarchies.

During the execution of programs, the CPU generates a continuous stream of logical memory addresses. At any time these addresses are distributed in some fashion throughout the memory hierarchy. If an address is generated which is currently assigned to M_i where $i \neq 1$, the address must be reassigned to M_1, the only level of the memory hierarchy that the CPU can access directly. This relocation of logical addresses generally requires the transfer of information between levels M_i and M_1, a relatively slow process. In order for a memory hierarchy to work efficiently, the addresses generated by the CPU should be found in M_1 as often as possible. This requires that future addresses be to some extent predictable, so that information can be transferred to M_1 before it is actually referenced by the CPU. If the desired information cannot be found in M_1, then execution of the program originating the memory request must be suspended until an appropriate reallocation of storage is made.

Locality of reference The predictability of logical memory addresses which is essential to the successful operation of a memory hierarchy is based on a common characteristic of computer programs called locality of reference. This describes the fact that over the short term, the addresses generated by a typical program tend to be confined to small regions of its logical address space, as illustrated in Fig. 5.30. The items of information whose addresses are referenced during the time interval from $t - T$ to t, denoted $(t-T, t)$, constitute the *working set* $W(t, T)$ [10]. It has been found that $W(t, T)$ tends to change rather slowly; hence by maintaining all of $W(t, T)$ in the fastest level of memory M_1, the number of references to M_1 can be made considerably greater than the number of references made to the other levels of the memory hierarchy.

One reason for locality of reference is that instructions and, to a lesser extent, data are written down and subsequently stored in the computer's memory in approximately the order in which they are needed during program execution.

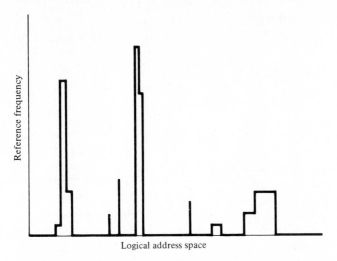

Figure 5.30 Typical nonuniform distribution of address references.

Suppose that a request is made for an address A containing an instruction I, and this address is currently assigned to $M_i \neq M_1$. The next most likely instruction to be required by the CPU is the instruction immediately following I whose address is $A + 1$. Thus instead of simply transferring the instruction I to M_1, it is desirable to transfer a block of consecutive words containing I. A common way of implementing this is by subdividing the information stored in M_i into pages, each containing S_{p_i} consecutive words. Information is then transferred one page or S_{p_i} words at a time between levels M_i and M_{i+1}. Thus if the CPU requests word I in level M_i, the page of length $S_{p_{i-1}}$ in M_i containing I is transferred to M_{i-1}, then the page of length $S_{p_{i-2}}$ containing I is transferred to M_{i-2}, and so on. Finally the page P of length S_{p_1} containing I is transferred to M_1 where it can be accessed by the CPU. Subsequent memory references are likely to refer to addresses in P, so that the single page transfer to M_1 anticipates future memory requests by the CPU.

A second factor in locality of reference is the presence of program loops. Statements within a loop may be executed repeatedly, resulting in a high frequency of reference to their addresses. When a loop is being executed, it is clearly desirable to store the entire loop in M_1 if possible.

Design objectives The goal in memory hierarchy design is to achieve a performance close to that of the fastest device M_1 and a cost per bit close to that of the cheapest device M_n. The performance of a memory hierarchy depends on a variety of factors, which are related in a complex manner. The more important of these are the following.

1. The address reference statistics, i.e., the order and frequency of the logical addresses generated by programs that use the memory hierarchy
2. The access time t_{A_i} of each level M_i relative to the CPU

3. The storage capacity of each level
4. The size of the blocks of information transferred between successive levels
5. The strategy, called the allocation algorithm, used for determining the regions of memory to which blocks of information are transferred by the swapping process

These design factors interact in a complex manner which is by no means fully understood. A number of simple analytic models exist, however, which reveal the general way in which some of these factors are related. Some representative models of this kind are discussed in the present chapter. It should be emphasized that simulation is still the major tool for memory-system design. Simulation is used for determining such program-dependent design parameters as address reference frequencies. It is also the main technique for evaluating memory-system performance.

Cost and performance For simplicity we restrict our attention to the most common form of memory hierarchy, a two-level hierarchy (M_1, M_2). It is not difficult to generalize the cost and performance measures discussed here to n-level hierarchies.

Cost The average cost per bit of memory is given by

$$c = \frac{c_1 S_1 + c_2 S_2}{S_1 + S_2} \tag{5.1}$$

where c_i denotes the cost per bit of M_i and S_i denotes the storage capacity in bits of M_i. To achieve the goal of making c approach c_2, S_1 must be very small compared with S_2.

Hit ratio The performance of a two-level memory hierarchy is frequently measured in terms of the *hit ratio* H, which is defined as the probability that a logical address generated by the CPU refers to information stored in M_1. Hit ratios are generally determined experimentally as follows. A set of representative programs is executed or simulated. The number of address references to M_1 and M_2, denoted by N_1 and N_2, respectively, are recorded. H is then given by the equation

$$H = \frac{N_1}{N_1 + N_2} \tag{5.2}$$

Clearly H is highly program dependent. The quantity $1 - H$ is called the *miss ratio*.

Access time Let t_{A_1} and t_{A_2} denote the access times of M_1 and M_2, respectively, relative to the CPU. The average time t_A for the CPU to access a word in the memory system is given by the equation

$$t_A = Ht_{A_1} + (1 - H)t_{A_2} \tag{5.3}$$

In most two-level hierarchies, a request for a word not in main memory causes a block of information containing the requested word to be transferred to main memory. When the block transfer has been completed, the requested word is accessed in main memory. The time t_B required for the block transfer is called the *block-replacement*, or *block-transfer*, time. Hence we have $t_{A_2} = t_B + t_{A_1}$. Substituting into Eq. (5.3) yields

$$t_A = t_{A_1} + (1 - H)t_B \tag{5.4}$$

Block transfer usually requires a relatively slow IO operation; therefore t_B is usually much greater then t_{A_1}. Hence $t_{A_2} \gg t_{A_1}$ and $t_{A_2} \approx t_B$.

Let $r = t_{A_2}/t_{A_1}$ denote the access-time ratio of the two levels of memory. Let $e = t_{A_1}/t_A$, which is the factor by which t_A differs from its minimum possible value; e is called the *access efficiency* of the virtual memory. From Eq. (5.3) we obtain

$$e = \frac{1}{r + (1 - r)H} \tag{5.5}$$

In Fig. 5.31, e is plotted as a function of H. This graph shows the importance of achieving high values of H in order to make $e \approx 1$, that is, $t_A \approx t_{A_1}$. For ex-

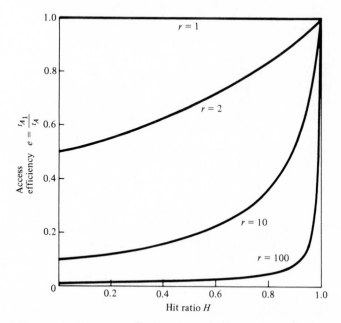

Figure 5.31 The access efficiency e of a two-level memory as a function of hit ratio H for various values of $r = t_{A_2}/t_{A_1}$.

ample, suppose that $r = 100$. In order to make $e > 0.9$, we must have $H > 0.998$.

Memory utilization Memory capacity is limited by cost considerations; it is therefore desirable that as little memory space as possible be wasted. The efficiency with which space is being used at any time can be loosely defined as the ratio of the memory space S_u occupied by "active" parts of user programs to the total amount of memory space available S. We call this the *space utilization u* and write

$$u = \frac{S_u}{S}$$

Since main-memory space is more valuable than secondary-memory space, it is useful to restrict u to measuring main-memory space utilization. In that case, the $S - S_u$ words of M_1 which represent "wasted" space can be attributed to several sources.

1. Empty regions. The blocks of instructions and data occupying M_1 at any time are generally of different lengths. As the contents of M_1 are changed, unoccupied regions or holes of various sizes tend to appear between successive blocks. This phenomenon is called *fragmentation*.
2. Regions occupied by the memory management system. A certain amount of main-memory space is required to store memory management routines and memory maps.
3. Regions occupied by inactive user information. Certain words may be transferred to M_1, for example, as part of a page, and may be subsequently transferred back to M_2 without ever being referenced by a processor. Some superfluous transfers of this kind are unavoidable, since exact address references are unpredictable. However, superfluous transfers can also be caused by an inefficient memory-allocation strategy.

The efficiency with which a given program Q utilizes main memory can be measured by its *memory space-time* function defined as

$$q = \int_0^T S(t) \, dt$$

where $(0, T)$ is a real-time interval and $S(t)$ is the amount of main-memory space assigned to Q at time t. $(0, T)$ includes time spent actively executing Q, as well as waiting time while memory swapping and other IO operations take place.

Address mapping The set of all abstract locations that can be referenced by a program is loosely defined as its logical address space L. Logical addresses may be explicitly named by identifiers assigned by the programmer. Many addresses are implicit or relative to other addresses. In order to execute the program on a particular machine, the logical addresses must be mapped onto the physical address space *P* of the machine's main memory. This process is called *address mapping* or, occasionally, *address binding*. The physical address space is represented by a linear sequence of numbers $0, 1, 2, \ldots, n-1$. Main memory is therefore a one-dimensional array of word locations. The mathematical structure of a program represented by *L* is usually more complex; it can include multidimensional arrays, trees, and other nonlinear structures. Before the program can be executed, it and its data sets must be "linearized," which means, in effect, transforming them into a set of contiguous word sequences, each of which can fit in main memory.

Address mapping can be viewed abstractly as a function $f: L \rightarrow P$. This function is not easily determined, since address mapping can be carried out wholly or in part at various stages in the life of a program, specifically:

1. By the programmer while writing the program
2. By the compiler during program compilation
3. By the loader at initial program load time
4. By the operating system while the program is being executed

Specification of physical addresses by the user was necessary in the earliest computers which had neither operating systems nor the facilities to support any programming languages except machine language. It is rarely used nowadays. It is generally not permitted in systems where memory space is shared by different users. In modern computer systems, the user is limited to specifying relative addresses within the program. The final physical addresses are determined by the compiler, the loader, or the operating system.

The compiler transforms all user identifiers into binary addresses. If the program is sufficiently simple, the compiler may be able to make a complete transformation of logical to physical addresses, especially if the program in question contains no concurrent or recursive procedures, i.e., it is strictly sequential and nonrecursive. In general, the output of the compiler is a set of program and data *blocks* each of which is a sequence of contiguous words. (Pages and segments are special types of blocks, which are discussed in more detail later.) Each word within a block can be identified by a logical address which comprises a *base address* and *relative address* (also called a displacement or index), as shown in Fig. 5.32.

Address mapping can be completed when the program is first loaded by assigning fixed values to the base address of each block. This is called *static allocation*, since the physical address space of the program is fixed for the duration of its execution.

In systems that support recursive or concurrent procedures, the logical space of a program may vary dynamically during execution. For example, a recursive procedure is typically controlled by a stack containing the linkage between successive calls to the procedure. The size of this stack cannot be predicted before execution, because it depends on the number of times the

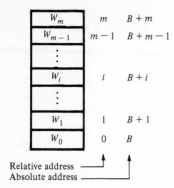

Relative address
Absolute address

Figure 5.32 A block of information with base address B.

procedure is invoked. In such cases it is desirable to be able to allocate storage during execution. In multiprogramming systems where a common store is shared by many programs, it is also useful to be able to alter storage allocation, i.e., vary f, while programs are being executed. The ability to do this is called *dynamic allocation*.

Relocation mechanisms The fundamental method of implementing both static and dynamic storage allocation is by giving the operating system control over the addresses assigned to each program and data block. This can be accomplished by storing base addresses in a special *memory map* or *memory address table* in main memory or a set of high-speed CPU registers. In the latter case, the registers are called *base*, or *relocation*, registers. The address generation circuitry of the CPU computes relative addresses within a block from the specifications contained in a program. Each relative address A_r is converted to a physical address A_p by adding A_r to the contents of the corresponding base register B_i. Often B_i contains only the high-order bits of A_p, while A_r contains the low-order bits. A_p can then be formed by concatenating B_i and A_r, as shown in Fig. 5.33, a process that does not significantly increase the time required for address generation.

Blocks are relocated in main memory by altering their base addresses. Base-address modification may therefore be a privileged operation that is restricted to the operating system. Figure 5.34 illustrates block relocations using base-address modification. Suppose that two blocks are allocated to main memory M as shown in Fig. 5.34a. It is desired to load a third block K_3 into M; however, a contiguous empty space, or "hole," of sufficient size is not available. A solution to this problem is to move block K_2, as shown in Fig. 5.34b, by assigning it a new base address B_2' and reloading it into memory. This creates a gap into which block K_3 can be loaded by assigning to it an appropriate base address.

In systems with dynamic memory allocation, it is necessary to control the references made by a block to locations outside the memory area currently assigned to it. (The block may be permitted to read from certain locations, but writing outside its assigned area must be prevented.) A common way of

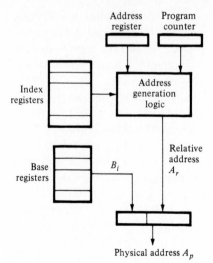

Figure **5.33** Physical address generation using base registers.

implementing this is by specifying the highest address, L_i, called the *limit address*, that the block may access. Equivalently, the size of the block may be specified. The base address B_i and the limit address L_i are stored in the memory map. Every physical address A_p generated by the block is compared to B_i and L_i; the memory access is completed only if

$$B_i \le A_p \le L_i$$

Design problems The major operation involved in any virtual memory system is the swapping of blocks of information between the levels of memory in accordance with processing demands. There are three central questions to be answered.

1. When should swapping take place?
2. Where should the block being transferred into main memory be placed?
3. How many words are transferred during each swap, i.e., what is the block size to be used?

The first question is usually answered by *demand swapping*, which means initiating a swap when the requested item is not currently in main memory. The

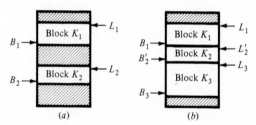

Figure **5.34** Dynamic memory relocation using base and limit registers.

alternative is some kind of *anticipatory swapping*, which implies transferring blocks to main memory in anticipation that they will be required in the future by the CPU. This is not easily implemented, since it requires relatively long range predictions of memory access requests. Short-range prediction is possible because of the locality of reference property of programs.

The method used to determine the part of main memory where an incoming block is to be placed is called the *allocation policy*. In systems with static memory allocation, each block of information is bound to a fixed region of main memory. When dynamic allocation is used, the region to which a block K is assigned is variable: it depends on the manner in which main memory is occupied by other blocks when K is to be placed in main memory. Two methods of dynamic allocation may be distinguished: preemptive and nonpreemptive. An allocation strategy is *preemptive* if an incoming block can be assigned to a region occupied by another block required by a currently executing program. This entails either moving the preempted block to another part of main memory or else expelling it entirely from main memory. Preemptive allocation techniques are often called *replacement* techniques. In *nonpreemptive* allocation, an incoming block can be placed only in an unoccupied region that is large enough to accommodate it. A successful allocation algorithm results in a high hit ratio and a high average access rate. If the hit ratio is very low, an excessive amount of swapping occurs; this phenomenon is called *thrashing*.

Figure 5.35 shows the main components of a virtual memory system and their logical interconnections. The physical addresses assigned to each block of information are stored in a set of tables called the memory map. This map is used to translate logical (virtual) block addresses into physical addresses and to maintain priority information for the blocks if preemptive allocation is used.

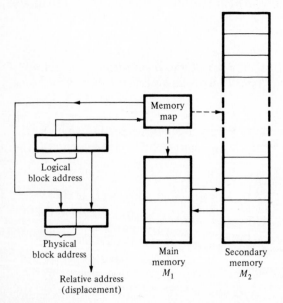

Figure 5.35 Structure of a virtual memory system.

5.2.2 Main-Memory Allocation

It is convenient to view main memory as divided into sets of contiguous word locations called *regions*, each of which can store a block of information. In a paging system, the regions are nonoverlapping page frames, and each region has a base address which is a multiple of the page size. The process of determining the region to which a particular block is to be assigned is called *main-memory allocation*. The information needed for memory allocation is maintained by the operating system in the memory map. The memory map may be stored in high-speed registers, in main memory, or in both. It can be expected to contain the following information.

1. An *occupied space list*, each entry of which specifies a block name, the (base) address of the region it occupies, and the block size. The block size may be omitted if a fixed block size is used. In systems using preemptive allocation, additional information is associated with each block to determine when and how it may be preempted.
2. An *available space list*, each entry of which specifies the address of an unoccupied region and, if necessary, its size.
3. A secondary-memory *directory* or a list specifying the secondary-memory devices which contain the directories for all the blocks associated with currently executing programs. These directories define the regions of the secondary-memory space to which each block is assigned.

When a block is transferred from secondary to main memory, the operating system makes an appropriate entry in the occupied space list. When a block is no longer required in main memory, it is *deallocated*, and the region it occupies is transferred from the occupied space list to the available space list. A block is deallocated when the programs using it terminate execution, or when it is replaced to make room for a block with higher priority.

A variety of preemptive and nonpreemptive algorithms have been developed for dynamic memory allocations. The mathematical analysis of the performance of these algorithms is generally very difficult. Monte Carlo simulation is the most widely used performance evaluation tool. The performance of an allocation algorithm can be measured by the various parameters introduced in Sec. 5.2.1; specifically, hit ratio H, memory access time t_A, and space utilization u.

Nonpreemptive allocation Suppose that a block K_i of n_i words is to be transferred from secondary to main memory. If none of the blocks already occupying main memory may be preempted (overwritten or moved) by K_i, then it is necessary to find or create an unoccupied "available" region of n_i or more words to accommodate K_i. This process is termed nonpreemptive allocation. The problem is trivial in a paging system where all blocks (pages) comprise S_p words, and main store is divided into fixed S_p-word regions (page frames). The memory map (page table) is searched for an available page frame; if one is found, it is assigned to the incoming block K_i. This ease of space allocation is one of the primary reasons for using paging. If memory space is divisible into regions of variable length, however, then it becomes much more difficult to allocate incoming blocks efficiently.

Best fit and first fit There are two algorithms for nonpreemptive allocation of variable-length blocks that have been widely used: first fit and best fit. The *first-fit* method merely scans the memory map sequentially until an available region R_j of n_i or more words is found, where n_i is the number of words in the incoming block K_i. It then allocates K_i to R_j. The *best-fit* approach requires searching the memory map sequentially and then assigning K_i to a region of $n_j \geq n_i$ words such that $n_j - n_i$ is minimized.

> **Example 5.4: Comparison of first-fit and best-fit allocation** Suppose that at some time main memory is storing three blocks, as illustrated in Fig. 5.36a. There are three available regions, and the available space list might have the form:
>
> | Region address | Size (words) |
> |:---:|:---:|
> | 0 | 50 |
> | 300 | 400 |
> | 800 | 200 |

Suppose that two additional blocks K_4 and K_5 whose sizes are 100 and 250 words, respectively, are to be assigned to main memory. Figure 5.36b and c, show the results obtained using the first-fit and best-fit methods, respectively, when the memory scan starts at address 0.

The first-fit algorithm has the advantage that it requires less time to execute than the best-fit approach. If the best-fitting available region can be found by

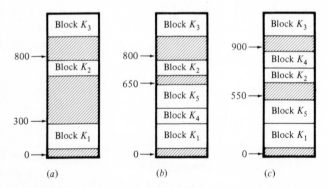

Figure 5.36 (a) Initial state of main memory. (b) Allocation of K_4 and K_5 by the first-fit method. (c) Allocation of K_4 and K_5 by the best-fit method.

scanning k entries of the available space list, the first fit can always be found by scanning k or fewer entries. The relative efficiency of the two techniques has been a subject of debate, since both have been implemented with satisfactory results [14, 24]. The performance obtained in a given environment depends on the distribution of the sizes of the blocks being allocated. Based on simulation studies, Knuth has concluded that in practice, first fit outperforms best fit [14]. Shore suggests that this results from the tendency of first fit to allocate blocks to one end of the memory, so that large regions of available space are likely to be present at the other end of the memory to accommodate large incoming blocks [24]. This indicates that first fit is likely to be superior to best fit when there is a high frequency of requests for memory allocation by blocks of longer than average size. For other types of request distributions, best fit has been shown to be superior. Example 5.4 illustrates some of these issues.

Suppose that a request is received to allocate space to a sixth block K_6 of 200 words. The available space lists corresponding to Fig. 5.36b and c. are, respectively,

Region address	Size (words)
0	50
650	50
800	200

and

Region address	Size (words)
0	50
550	150
900	100

Using the first-fit algorithm, we have an available 200-word region which can accommodate K_6. If the best-fit method is used, however, K_6 cannot be placed in memory, so overflow occurs. First fit seems to be generally preferred to best fit. It is used, for example, in the operating system of the Burroughs B5500 computer.

Preemptive allocation Nonpreemptive allocation techniques cannot make efficient use of memory in all situations; overflow can be expected to occur with main memory only partially full. Much more efficient use of the available memory space is possible if the occupied space can be reallocated to make room for incoming blocks. This may be done in two ways:

1. The blocks already in main memory can be relocated in main memory to make a "hole" large enough for the incoming information; this is illustrated in Fig. 5.34.
2. One or more occupied regions can be made available by deallocating or ex-

pelling the blocks they contain. This requires a rule for selecting blocks to be replaced. A distinction must also be made between "dirty" blocks, which have been modified since being loaded into main memory, and "clean" blocks, which have not been modified. Blocks of instructions generally remain clean, whereas blocks of data generally become dirty. To replace a clean block, the operating system can simply overwrite it with the new block, and update its entry in the memory map. Before a dirty block can be overwritten, it must be copied onto secondary memory, which usually involves a time-consuming IO operation.

Memory compaction The relocation of the blocks already occupying main memory can be accomplished by a technique called *compacting*, which is illustrated in Fig. 5.37. The blocks currently in memory are combined into a single block placed at one end of the memory. This creates a single available region of the maximum possible size. The main disadvantage of this technique is the time required for compacting. If t_M is the cycle time of main memory, then the time required to compact an S-word memory is at least $2uSt_M$, where u is the fraction of the memory that is occupied.

A simple allocation technique can be based on compacting alone [14]. After each compaction, incoming blocks are assigned to contiguous regions at the unoccupied end of the memory. The memory is therefore viewed as having a single available region; new available regions due to freed blocks are ignored. When the hole at the end of the memory is filled, compaction is again carried out. The advantage of this scheme is that it eliminates the problem of selecting an available region; it may, however, result in the system's spending an excessive amount of time compacting memory. Compacting may also be combined with a nonpreemptive allocation strategy such as first fit. When the allocation strategy results in overflow, the memory is compacted. If the allocation strategy achieves a high level of storage utilization, then little may be gained by compaction.

5.2.3 Replacement Policies

The second major approach to preemptive allocation involves preempting a region R occupied by block K and allocating it to an incoming block K'. The

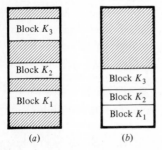

Figure 5.37 Main-memory allocation (*a*) before compacting and (*b*) after compacting.

criteria used for selecting K as the block to be replaced constitute the *replacement policy*. The major objective in choosing a replacement policy is to maximize the hit ratio or, equivalently, minimize the number of times a referenced block is not in main memory, a condition called a *memory fault*.

It is generally believed that the hit ratio tends to a maximum if the time intervals between successive memory faults are maximized. An *optimal replacement strategy* would therefore at time t_i determine the time $t_j > t_i$ at which the next reference to block K is to occur; the K to be replaced is the one for which $t_j - t_i$ has the maximum value t_K. This ideal strategy has been called OPT [17]. OPT can be implemented by making two passes through the program. The first is a simulation run to determine the sequence S_B of distinct logical block addresses generated by the program; the sequence is called the *block address stream* or *block address trace*. The values of t_K at each point in time can be computed from S_B and used to construct the optimal sequence S_B^{OPT} of blocks to be replaced. The second run is the execution run which uses S_B^{OPT} to specify the blocks to be replaced. OPT is not a practical replacement policy because of the cost of the simulation run and the fact that S_B may be extremely long, making S_B^{OPT} very expensive to compute. A practical replacement policy attempts to estimate t_K using statistics it gathers on the past references to all blocks currently in main memory.

Two of the most commonly implemented replacement policies are *first-in first-out* (FIFO) and *least recently used* (LRU). FIFO selects for replacement the block least recently loaded into main memory. FIFO has the advantage that it is easily implemented. A loading sequence number is associated with each block in the occupied space list. Each time a block is transferred to or from main memory, the loading sequence numbers are updated. By inspecting these numbers, the operating system can easily determine the oldest (first-in) block. FIFO has the defect, however, that a frequently used block, e.g. one containing a program loop, may be replaced because it is the oldest block.

The LRU policy selects for replacement the block that was least recently accessed by the processor. It is based on the very reasonable assumption that the least recently used block is the one least likely to be referenced in the future. The LRU policy avoids the replacement of frequently used blocks which can occur with FIFO. It is more difficult to implement than FIFO, however, since the operating system must maintain statistics on the number of references to all blocks in main memory. LRU can be implemented by associating a hardware or software counter, called an *age register*, with every block in main memory. Whenever a block is referenced, its age register is set to a predetermined positive number. At fixed intervals of time, the age registers of all the blocks are decremented by a fixed amount. The least recently used block at any time is the one whose age register contains the smallest number.

Block hit ratio The performance of a replacement policy in a given memory organization can be analyzed using the block address stream generated by a set of representative computations. Let N_1^* and N_2^* denote the number of references to M_1 and M_2, respectively, in the block address stream. The *block hit ratio H** is defined by

$$H^* = \frac{N_1^*}{N_1^* + N_2^*}$$

which is analogous to the (word) hit ratio H defined by Eq. (5.2). Let n^* denote the average number of consecutive word address references within each block. H can be estimated from H^* using the following relation:

$$H = 1 - \frac{1 - H^*}{n^*}$$

In a paging system, H^* is the page hit ratio. $1 - H^*$, the page miss ratio, is usually called the *page fault probability*.

Example 5.5: Comparison of replacement policies Consider a paging system in which main memory has a capacity of three pages. The execution of a program Q requires reference to five distinct pages P_i where $i = 1, 2, 3, 4, 5$, and i is the page address. The page address stream formed by executing Q is

$$2 \quad 3 \quad 2 \quad 1 \quad 5 \quad 2 \quad 4 \quad 5 \quad 3 \quad 2 \quad 5 \quad 2$$

which means that the first page referenced is P_2, the second is P_3, etc. Figure 5.38 shows the manner in which the pages are assigned to main memory using FIFO, LRU, and the ideal OPT replacement policies. The next block to be selected for replacement is marked by an asterisk in the FIFO and LRU cases. It will be observed that LRU recognizes that P_2 and P_5 are referenced more frequently than other pages, whereas FIFO does not. Thus FIFO replaces P_2 twice but LRU does so only once. The highest page hit ratio is achieved by OPT, the lowest by FIFO. The page hit ratio of LRU is quite close to that of OPT, a property which seems to be generally true.

Stack replacement policies As discussed in Sec. 5.2.1, the cost and performance of a memory hierarchy can be measured by average cost per bit c and average access time t_A. Equations (5.1) and (5.4) are convenient expressions for c and t_A:

$$c = \frac{c_1 S_1 + c_2 S_2}{S_1 + S_2} \tag{5.1}$$

$$t_A = t_{A_1} + (1 - H)t_B \tag{5.4}$$

The quantities c, t_{A_1}, and t_B are determined primarily by the memory-device technologies used for M_1 and M_2. Once these have been chosen, the hit ratio H must be computed for various possible system configurations. The major variables on which H depends are

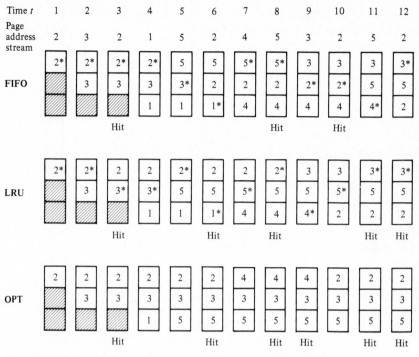

Figure 5.38 Action of three replacement policies on a common address stream.

1. The types of address streams encountered
2. The average block size
3. The capacity of main memory
4. The replacement policy used

Simulation is perhaps the most practical technique used for evaluating different memory system designs. H is determined for a representative sample of address streams, memory technologies, block sizes, memory capacities, and replacement policies. Figure 5.38 shows a sample point in this simulation process. In this example, the block address stream, block size, and main-memory capacity are fixed, and three different replacement strategies are being tested.

Due to the large number of alternatives that exist, the amount of simulation required to optimize the design of a virtual memory system can be very great. A number of analytic models for optimizing memory design have been proposed. Notable among these is a technique called *stack processing*, which is applicable to paging systems that use a class of replacement algorithms called stack algorithms [17].

Let A be any page address stream of length L to be processed using a replacement policy R. Let t denote the point in time when the first $t - 1$ pages of A have been processed. Let n be a variable denoting the page capacity of M_1.

$B_t(n)$ denotes the set of pages in M_1 at time t, and L_t denotes the number of distinct pages that have been encountered at time t. R is called a *stack algorithm* if it has the following *inclusion property*:

$$B_t(n) \subset B_t(n+1) \qquad \text{if } n < L_t$$

$$B_t(n) = B_t(n+1) \qquad \text{if } n \geq L_t$$

LRU retains in M_1 the n most recently used pages. Since these are always included in the $n+1$ most recently used pages, it can be immediately concluded that LRU is a stack algorithm. Many other replacement policies are also of this type. FIFO is a notable exception, however. Consider the following page address stream:

$$A = 1 \quad 2 \quad 3 \quad 4 \quad 1 \quad 2 \quad 5 \quad 1 \quad 2 \quad 3 \quad 4 \quad 5$$

Figure 5.39 shows how this address stream is processed using FIFO and main-memory capacities of three and four pages. It can be seen that at various points of time the conditions for the inclusion property are not satisfied. For example, when $t = 7$, $B_7(3) = \{1, 2, 5\}$ and $B_7(4) = \{2, 3, 4, 5\}$; therefore $B_7(3) \not\subset B_7(4)$. Hence FIFO is not a stack replacement algorithm.

The usefulness of stack algorithms lies in the fact that the hit ratios for different capacities of M_1 can be easily determined by processing the address stream once, and representing M_1 by a list, or "stack." The stack S_t at time t is an ordered set of L_t distinct pages $S_t(1), S_t(2), \ldots, S_t(L_t)$; $S_t(1)$ is referred to as the top of the stack at time t. The inclusion property of stack algorithms implies that the stack can always be generated so that

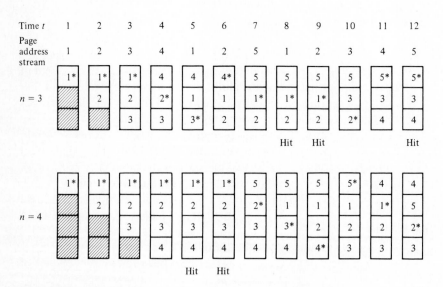

Time t 1 2 3 4 5 6 7 8 9 10 11 12

Page address stream 1 2 3 4 1 2 5 1 2 3 4 5

Figure 5.39 FIFO replacement with two different M_1 capacities.

$$B_t(n) = \{S_t(1), S_t(2), \ldots, S_t(n)\} \qquad \text{for } n < L_t$$
$$B_t(n) = \{S_t(1), S_t(2), \ldots, S_t(L_t)\} \qquad \text{for } n \geq L_t$$

In other words, the behavior of a system in which M_1 has capacity n is determined by the top n entries of the stack. By scanning S_t, we can easily determine whether or not a hit occurs for all possible values of n. This type of analysis therefore permits the simultaneous determination of hit ratios for various main-memory capacities.

The procedures for updating the stack depend on the particular stack algorithm R being used. There may be little resemblance between the order of the elements in S_t and S_{t+1}; the stack should not be confused with simple LIFO pushdown stacks. We now describe the stack updating process for LRU replacement.

Example 5.6: Determination of hit ratios using stack processing with LRU replacement Let $S_t = S_t(1), S_t(2), \ldots, S_t(k)$ denote the stack contents at time t. The strategy used is to place the most recently used page addresses in the top of stack so that the least recently used page gets pushed to the bottom. More formally, let x be the new page reference at time t. If $x \notin S_t$, x is pushed into the stack, so that x becomes $S_{t+1}(1)$; $S_t(1)$ becomes $S_{t+1}(2)$; and so on. If $x \in S_t$, x is removed from S_t and then pushed into the top of the stack to form S_{t+1}. Figure 5.40 illustrates this for the address stream used in Fig. 5.38. To determine if a hit occurs at time t for memory page capacity n, it is necessary only to check if the new page reference x is one of

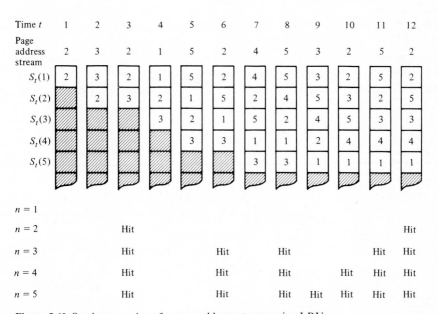

Figure 5.40 Stack processing of a page address stream using LRU.

the top n entries of S_t; if it is, a hit occurs. The hit occurrences for all values of $n \le 5$ are also shown in Fig. 5.40. The values for the various page hit ratios H^* are seen to be as follows:

$n =$	1	2	3	4	5	> 5
$H^* =$	0.00	0.17	0.42	0.50	0.58	0.58

Figure 5.41 shows a plot of H^* against n.

It is a general characteristic of stack-replacement algorithms that the hit ratio increases monotonically with the available capacity n of M_1. This is a direct consequence of the inclusion property. If the next page address x is in $B_t(n)$, it must also be in $B_t(n+1)$, since $B_t(n) \subseteq B_t(n+1)$. Hence if a hit occurs with M_1 of capacity n, a hit also occurs when the capacity is increased to $n+1$. It might be expected that this is true for all replacement policies, but such is not the case. As the example in Fig. 5.39 shows, increasing n from three to four pages in a system using FIFO replacement actually reduces the page hit ratio in this particular case from 0.25 to 0.17. This appears to be a relatively rare phenomenon, not occurring for most address streams.

5.2.4 Segments and Pages

Segments The smallest or most primitive elements of a computation are instruction and data words. A well-written program, however, exhibits a substantial amount of high-level structure. A sequence of instructions may thus be defined as a subroutine or procedure and be given an appropriate name. Similarly, primitive data items may be grouped into lists, arrays, and the like. We will refer to groups of instructions and data of this general type as *modules*. A well-structured program has clearly defined modules whose relations with one another are also clearly defined. Programming languages such as ALGOL which are "block-structured" have a syntax that yields a high degree of modularity.

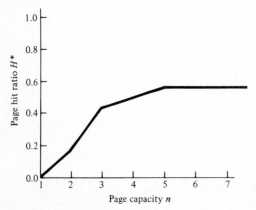

Figure 5.41 Page hit ratio versus page capacity for Example 5.6.

A module may be loosely regarded as a named sequence of statements that are usually processed in the sequence in which they are written by the programmer. Compilation transforms this into a machine-executable module with essentially the same sequential ordering as the original module; this type of module is termed a segment. Formally, a *segment* is a set of logically related contiguous words generated by a compiler or a programmer. It is therefore a special type of block in the sense defined in Sec. 5.2.1. A word in a segment is referred to by specifying a base address (the segment address) and a relative address or displacement within the segment. The relative addresses are derived from program identifiers at compilation time. Segment addresses may be assigned during program execution by the operating system.

Segmentation A program and its data sets can be viewed as a collection of linked segments. The links arise from the fact that a program segment may use, or "call," another program or data segment. Since segments contain logically related words, it seems reasonable to maintain complete segments in main memory. A memory management technique that allocates main memory by segments is called *segmentation*. When a segment not currently resident in main memory is required, the entire segment is transferred from secondary memory. The physical addresses assigned to the segments are maintained in a memory map called a *segment table*, which may itself be a relocatable segment.

Example 5.7: Segmentation in the Burroughs B5500 [5] The B5000 family of computers uses segmentation extensively. Each main program has associated with it a segment called its *program reference table* (PRT). The PRT is used in part as a segment table. Each segment associated with a program is defined by a word called a descriptor in the corresponding PRT. A descriptor contains the following information:

1. A "presence" bit P which is set to 1 if the segment in question is currently assigned to main memory, and to 0 otherwise
2. A size field Z, which is the number of words in the segment
3. An address field S, which is the segment address in main memory if $P = 1$, or in secondary memory if $P = 0$

A program refers to a word within a segment by specifying the segment descriptor word W in its PRT and the displacement D (called an index in Burroughs literature). W is fetched and examined by the central processor. If the presence bit $P = 0$, then an interrupt occurs, and execution of the requesting program is suspended while the operating system transfers the required segment from secondary to main memory. If $P = 1$, the CPU compares the displacement D to the segment size field Z in the descriptor. If $D \geq Z$, D is invalid and an interrupt occurs. If $D < Z$, the address field S of the descriptor is added to the displacement D. The result, $S + D$, is the absolute address of the required word in main memory which may then be accessed.

The main advantage of segmentation is the fact that segment boundaries correspond to natural program boundaries. Because of their logical independence, a segment can be changed and recompiled at any time without affecting other segments. Certain properties of programs such as the scope (range of definition) of a variable and the access rights to a program are specified by segment. These properties require that accesses to segments be checked to protect against unauthorized use; this protection is most easily implemented when the units of allocation are segments. Certain segment types, most notably stacks and queues, can vary in length during program execution. A segmentation system can vary the region assigned to such a segment as it expands and contracts, thus efficiently using the available memory space. On the other hand, the fact that segments can be of different length requires a relatively complex main-memory allocation method to avoid excessive fragmentation of main-memory space. This problem can be alleviated by combining segmentation with paging, as discussed later.

Paging Paging systems use fixed-length blocks called pages and assign them to fixed regions of physical memory called page frames. The flowchart of a typical demand paging system can be found in Fig. 1.28. The main advantage of paging is that memory allocation is greatly simplified, since an incoming page can be assigned to any available page frame. Each logical address consists of two parts: a *page address* and a displacement (often called a *line address*). The memory map, now called a *page table*, contains the information shown in Fig. 5.42. When the presence bit P is 1, the page in question is present in main memory, and the page table contains the base address of the page frame to which the page has been assigned. If $P = 0$, a memory fault called a *page fault* occurs, and a page swap ensues. The change bit C is used to specify whether or not the page has been changed since being loaded into main memory. If a change has occurred, indicated by $C = 1$, the page must be copied onto secondary memory when it is preempted. The page table also contains priority information R used to select the page to be replaced. Note that unlike a segment table, a page table contains no block size information.

As noted earlier, paging requires a simpler memory allocation system than

Page name	Page frame	P	C	R
A	0	1	0	
C		0		
F	2	1	1	
B	1	1	0	

Replacement priority, Change bit, Presence bit

Figure 5.42 A page table.

segmentation, since block size is not a factor in paging. On the other hand, pages have no logical significance; they do not correspond to program elements. It can be useful to regard segmentation as partitioning the logical address space, while paging partitions the physical address space [26]. The two techniques can also be compared from the point of view of memory fragmentation. In systems with segmentation, holes of different sizes tend to proliferate throughout main memory; they can be eliminated only by the time-consuming process of memory compaction (see Sec. 5.2.2). Unusable space between occupied regions is called *external fragmentation*. Since page frames are contiguous, no external fragmentation occurs in paged systems. However, if k words are divided into p n-word pages, and k is not a multiple of n, the last page will not be filled. When this page is assigned to a page frame, part of the page frame is empty; this is called *internal fragmentation*.

Paged segments Paging and segmentation can be combined in an attempt to gain the advantages of both. This is done by dividing each segment into pages. A word then has a logical address with three components:

1. A segment address
2. A page address
3. A line address

The memory map may then consist of a segment table and a set of page tables, one for each segment. The segment table contains for each segment address a pointer to the base of the corresponding page table. The page table is then used in the usual way to determine the required physical address. This technique is used in the IBM S/360 Model 67.

Page size The page size S_p has a significant impact on both storage utilization and the memory-access rate. Let us first consider the influence of S_p on the space-utilization factor u introduced in Sec. 5.2.1. If S_p is too large, excessive internal fragmentation results; if it is too small, the page tables become very large and tend to reduce space utilization. A good value of S_p should achieve a balance between these two difficulties. Let S_s denote the average segment size in words. If $S_s \gg S_p$, it can be expected that the last page assigned to a segment contains, on the average, $S_p/2$ words. The size of the page table associated with each segment is approximately S_s/S_p words, assuming each entry in the table is a word. Hence the memory space overhead associated with each segment is

$$ S = \frac{S_p}{2} + \frac{S_s}{S_p} $$

The physical memory space utilization u can be defined as

$$ u = \frac{S_s}{S_s + S} = \frac{2S_s S_p}{S_p^2 + 2S_s(1 + S_p)} \tag{5.6} $$

The optimum page size S_p^{OPT} may be defined as the value of S_p which maximizes u or, equivalently, which minimizes S. Differentiating S with respect to S_p, we obtain

$$\frac{dS}{dS_p} = \frac{1}{2} - \frac{S_s}{S_p^2}$$

S is a minimum when $dS/dS_p = 0$, from which it follows that

$$S_p^{\text{OPT}} = \sqrt{2S_s} \qquad (5.7)$$

The optimum space utilization u^{OPT} is given by

$$u^{\text{OPT}} = \frac{1}{1 + \sqrt{2/S_s}}$$

Figure 5.43 shows the space utilization u defined by Eq. (5.6) plotted against S_s for representative values of S_p.

The influence of page size on hit ratio is complex, depending on the program reference stream and the amount of main-memory space available. Let the logical address space of a program be a sequence of numbers $A_0, A_1, \ldots, A_{L-1}$. Let A_i be the logical address referenced at some point in time; and let A_{i+d} be the next address generated, where d is the "distance" between A_i and A_{i+d}. For example, if both addresses point to instructions, A_{i+d} points to the $(d+1)$st instruction either preceding or following the instruction whose logical address is A_i. Let S_p be the page size, and suppose that an efficient replacement policy such as LRU is being used. The probability of A_{i+d} being in M_1 is high if one of the following conditions is satisfied.

1. d is small compared with S_p, so that A_i and A_{i+d} are in the same page P. The probability of this being true increases with the page size.
2. d is large relative to S_p, but A_{i+d} is associated with a set of words that are frequently referenced. A_{i+d} is therefore likely to be in a page $P' \neq P$ which is also in M_1. The probability of this being true tends to increase with the

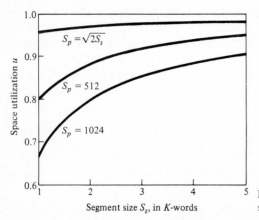

Figure 5.43 Influence of page size S_p and segment size S_s on space utilization u.

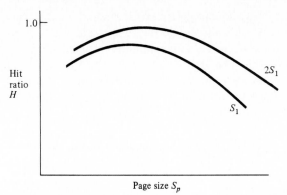

Figure 5.44 Influence of page size S_p on hit ratio H.

number of pages that can be stored in M_1; it therefore tends to decrease with the size of S_p.

Thus H is influenced by two opposing forces as S_p is varied. The result is that when S_p is small, H increases with S_p. However, when S_p exceeds a certain value, H begins to decrease. Figure 5.44 shows some typical curves relating H and S_p for various main-memory capacities. Simulation studies indicate that in large systems, the values of S_p yielding the maximum hit ratios can be as large as 1024 words, which may be much greater than the "optimum" page size given by Eq. (5.7). Since high H is important in achieving small t_A (due to the relatively slow rates at which page swapping takes place), values of S_p that maximize H are preferred. The first computer with a paging system (the ATLAS) used a 512-word page. The IBM S/360 Model 67 uses pages of 1024 words.

5.2.5 File Organization

Introduction We now consider the manner in which information is stored in the secondary-memory system of a computer [16]. Secondary-memory devices are characterized by very large storage capacities and relatively slow access rates. The slow access rates reflect the fact that, in general, the access modes of these devices are serial or else semirandom direct access (which might also be called semiserial). The information stored in secondary memory is usually grouped into large sets of related items called *files*. For example, the payroll file of an organization contains information about all the employees of the organization; their names, addresses, wage rates, etc. Because they are usually very large, files must be carefully organized so that they can be efficiently accessed or modified. Rapid access methods such as random or associative addressing are precluded by the essentially serial access modes of most secondary storage units. The individual items in a file are often of varying length; hence such files may not have a simple word-organized structure.

A file can be viewed as a set of smaller addressable units called *records*. A record can, in turn, be further subdivided into *fields*. Thus in a payroll file, the information about each employee may constitute a record. The individual items of information about the employee—his name, address, wage rate, etc.—form the fields. Every item that has to be accessed independently—the entire file, a record, or a field within a record—must be identified by means of a name called a *key*. The key therefore constitutes the logical address of the item in question. As in an associative memory, the keys are stored with the data they specify. There are three general ways in which the data can be accessed.

1. The file can be searched sequentially comparing the given key to the stored keys until the desired one is found. This is normally done with tape files which can only be accessed serially.
2. A memory address map, usually called a directory, can be used to map the key onto a physical storage address. This may be used when the memory permits random or semirandom access.
3. The physical address is generated by a simple transformation of keys according to some algorithm. Again this is suitable only for random or semirandom access memories.

At the present time the most important secondary storage device is probably the magnetic-disk unit. As discussed in Sec. 5.1.3, information is stored in a disk memory by means of circular tracks on a set of concentric rotating disks. A set of tracks with the same radius is referred to as a cylinder. The smallest addressable unit of storage will be assumed to be a record. The length of a record may be fixed or variable. A track may therefore store a fixed or variable number of records. Each record contains a key which is its logical address. It is convenient to view a disk unit as a two-dimensional storage device with the structure suggested by Fig. 5.45. A particular track may be accessed randomly by specifying a cylinder and a track number. The required record is then accessed serially by scanning the track until a record whose key matches the given key is found.

Sequential files The simplest type of file organization requires storing records in some sequence and performing all access and modification operations by serial processing. The record sequence may be arbitrary, in which case the organization is called *unordered sequential*. More commonly, the records are or-

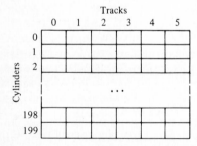

Figure 5.45 Storage organization in a magnetic-disk memory.

dered by a key and stored in that order; this is called *(ordered) sequential organization.* This type of organization therefore has the structure of a linear list.

Since records cannot be randomly accessed in most secondary-memory devices, the access time of any specific record is relatively long. Sequential files are most useful when all records must be accessed in sequence and processed. For example, a payroll file is typically processed in this manner to produce employees' paychecks. More generally, records that are processed in batch mode may be organized sequentially. If real-time access to any record is required, then other file organizations with shorter access time are more suitable. A second disadvantage of sequential organization is that it is necessary to move large amounts of data in order to make insertions or deletions. This organization is therefore inefficient if the file must be updated frequently. Updating can be simplified by leaving gaps between records or groups of records into which insertions can be made.

Magnetic-tape files are invariably organized sequentially. Magnetic-disk files are frequently sequential also. Figure 5.46a shows a possible file organization of this kind. The file consists of fixed-length records with the format

key, data

stored in ascending numerical order determined by the keys. The file is filled cylinder by cylinder and track by track. Changes are made by transferring an

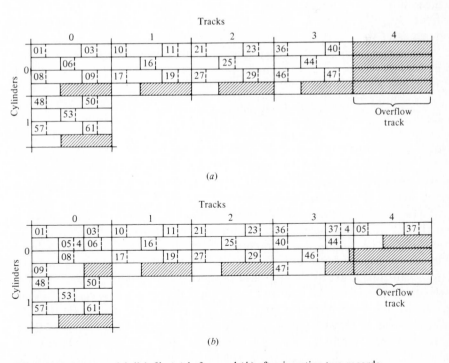

(a)

(b)

Figure 5.46 A sequential disk file (a) before and (b) after inserting two records.

entire track into main memory, making the required changes, and then writing the information back onto the same track. To facilitate the insertion of new records, overflow areas are included in every track, and an overflow track is included in every cylinder. New records may be inserted directly into a track until its overflow area is filled. Further insertions can be made using the overflow track. Instead of inserting an entire record into a track, a short pointer of the form

key, overflow track

is inserted in the correct position in the logical sequence of records. Figure 5.46b shows how the records with keys 05 and 37 are placed on the disk file when pointers and the overflow track are used. The use of overflow areas permits insertions and deletions to be made rapidly without moving large amounts of data. Note that when pointers are introduced, the physical sequence of the records is no longer the same as the logical sequence. The file must be processed from time to time to eliminate the pointers and restore the records to their proper physical sequence.

Indexed sequential files A popular method for organizing disk files so that individual items can be accessed rapidly is called the indexed sequential organization. It is characterized by the use of directories or indexes which specify the location of each record. The records are ordered sequentially by key as in sequential file organization, so that records can also be accessed sequentially without using the directories. The directories, however, permit rapid semirandom access.

The simplest kind of directory stores the entire physical address, specified by a disk-unit number, a cylinder number, and a track number for every record. It thus consists of a list of items of the form

record key, physical address

A record is located by sequentially searching the directory until a matching key is found. If the number of records is very large, this type of directory is impractical due to both its size and the time required to search it. In such cases, several levels of directories are employed where each directory provides a part of the physical address.

Figure 5.47 shows a typical three-level directory system. The first directory, called the unit directory, indicates the disk unit where each record can be found. Each disk unit stores a cylinder directory that specifies the cylinder address of every record in the unit. Finally, each cylinder contains a track directory indicating the track addresses of every record in the cylinder. The size of the directories can be minimized by storing only the highest record key associated with each level of storage (unit, cylinder, or track). This is done in Fig. 5.47. The unit directory contains one entry for each unit. It specifies, for example, that unit 0 stores all records with keys between 0 and 9999, while unit 1 stores all records with keys between 10,000 and 17,426. The structure of the

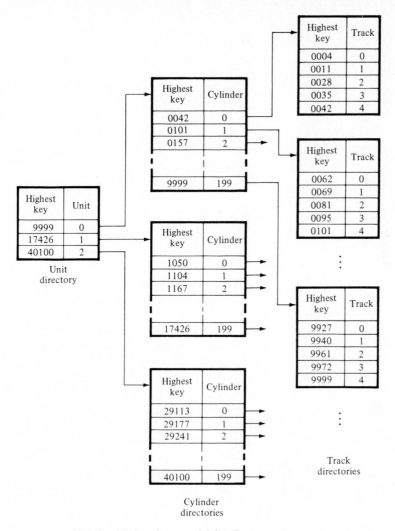

Figure 5.47 Multilevel indexed sequential file directory.

cylinder and track directories is similar. The physical address of a given record is found by first examining the unit directory. This points to the appropriate cylinder directory, which in turn points to a track directory. For example, suppose that record 0087 is to be accessed. The unit directory indicates that it can be found in unit 0. The cylinder directory for unit 0 indicates that the record is in cylinder 1. Finally, a search through the track directory for cylinder 1 of unit 0 reveals that the desired record is in track 3.

Let n_u, n_c, and n_t denote the number of units, the number of cylinders per unit, and the number of tracks per cylinder, respectively. The number of possible physical (track) addresses is $n_u n_c n_t$. Using the three-level directory of Fig.

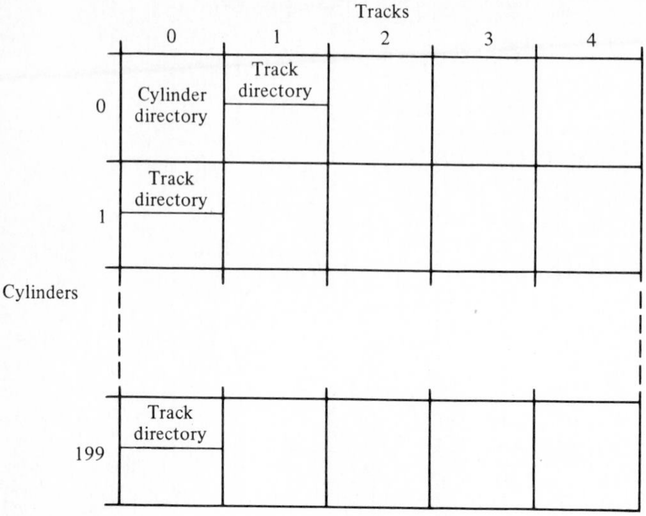

Figure 5.48 Storage of file directories in a disk memory unit.

5.47, we see that the maximum number of directory entries that must be scanned to locate a record is $n_u + n_c + n_t$. The various directories are generally stored along with the data they define. Figure 5.48 shows how directories are often stored within a disk unit. The first track of cylinder 0 contains the cylinder directory for that unit. The first item stored in each cylinder is its track directory. Information in the disk unit is typically processed in the following way:

1. The required cylinder directory is read into main memory and searched to identify the cylinder storing the desired information.
2. The track directory stored in this cylinder is transferred to main memory and searched to determine the required track.
3. The contents of this track are read into main memory where they are searched to obtain the required records. The records can then be processed. If records are inserted or deleted, the cylinder and track directories are also updated.
4. All modified records and directories are transferred from main memory back to the disk unit.

Linked list files A linked list is a set of items of information each of which has an address field called a *link* appended to it. The link contains the address of the next item in the list. By using linked lists a sequence of items can be stored in nonconsecutive physical locations. The logical sequence or order of the items is specified by the links. Figure 5.49a shows an example of a linked list in which the logical sequence of the items is A, B, D, and E. A file organization in which the records form a linked list is called a linked-list file.

Links greatly simplify the problem of making insertions and deletions in a

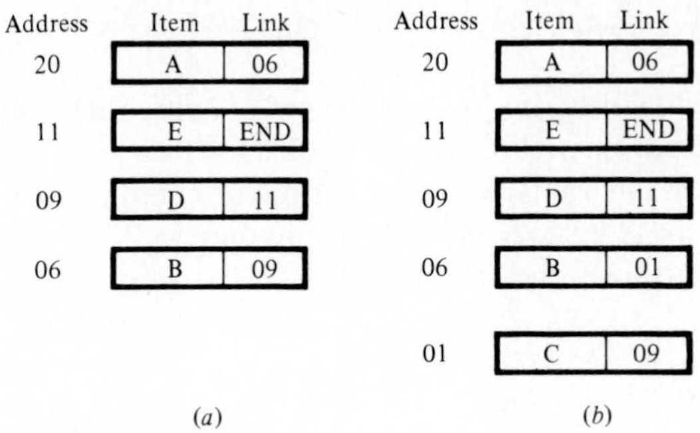

Address	Item	Link
20	A	06
11	E	END
09	D	11
06	B	09

(a)

Address	Item	Link
20	A	06
11	E	END
09	D	11
06	B	01
01	C	09

(b)

Figure 5.49 A linked-list file (a) before and (b) after inserting item C.

list. Figure 5.49b shows how a new item C can be inserted into the list of Fig. 5.49a so that C is logically positioned between B and D. Only item B in the original list has to be accessed in order to alter its link. Thus it is not necessary to move large amounts of data to make insertions and deletions. On the other hand, extra memory space is needed to store the links. A further disadvantage of linked-list files is the difficulty of accessing a batch of records that are logically but not physically contiguous.

Random file organizations Many so-called random file organizations have been devised, where the word random refers to the fact that there is no apparent logical connection between records. Records with consecutive keys are not necessarily in consecutive physical locations, nor are there links between the records. The physical address $f(X)$ of record X is determined by processing its key X using some well-defined algorithm. Two techniques for doing this have been distinguished [22]:

1. *Compression.* The physical address is formed by selecting a subset of the characters forming the key and (possibly) rearranging them. An example of this approach is truncation of the key. Compression is particularly suitable for processing nonnumerical keys. It can be designed to produce physical addresses that resemble the keys.
2. *Hashing.* The key X is treated as a number and an arithmetic function f, called a *hash function*, is used to compute the physical address $f(X)$. Many hash functions have been devised [12]. One technique is to divide X by a constant n and use the remainder as the address, i. e.,

$$f(X) = \text{remainder}(X) \quad \text{modulo } n$$

The number of possible valid record keys is generally much larger than the number of physical addresses available. Thus two distinct keys may yield the same value of $f(X)$. A good choice of f should generate addresses that are distributed uniformly over the available file storage area. If each addressable unit of storage, e. g., a track, can accommodate several records, then records with the same address are assigned sequentially to consecutive locations within the track. Once the track is filled, subsequent items with the same address must be assigned to an overflow area.

The function f which is used to determine where a record is written in a file is also used to retrieve that record, thus eliminating the need for directories. This type of addressing is very suitable for large files that must be accessed randomly in real time. Because there is no logical sequence among the records, batch processing of randomly organized files is difficult.

5.3 HIGH-SPEED MEMORIES

A major problem in achieving high-speed computation is the disparity in operating speeds between processors (CPUs, IOPs, etc.) and main memory M. Typically the cycle time of M is greater by a factor of 5 or so than the cycle time of a processor. Furthermore, several memory words may be required during a processor cycle. To eliminate processor idle time while waiting for memory accesses to be completed, special measures may be taken to increase the effective processor-memory interface bandwidth. Several methods are possible:

1. Decrease the memory access time by using a faster (and more expensive) technology for main memory.
2. Use a longer memory word.
3. Insert a fast cache memory between the processor and main memory to reduce access time.
4. Access more than one word during each memory cycle.

The design of cache memories is the topic of Sec. 5.3.2. We first describe a memory organization that permits more than one word to be accessed per memory cycle.

5.3.1 Interleaved Memories

In order to carry out m independent accesses simultaneously, main memory must be partitioned into m separate *modules* or *memory banks* $M_0, M_1, \ldots, M_{m-1}$, as shown in Fig. 5.50. Each module must be provided with its own addressing circuitry. If the physical buses between the processors and memory must be shared by the modules, an appropriate bus-control mechanism must also be introduced. Finally, sufficient buffer storage must be included in the processors to accommodate the increased flow of information. A modular memory organization is particularly useful in systems where several processors require access to a common memory, e. g., in the Burroughs B5000 system shown in Fig. 1.26. Different processors can access memory simultaneously provided that they reference separate modules.

In order for this memory organization to be utilized efficiently, the memory references generated by the processors should be distributed evenly among the

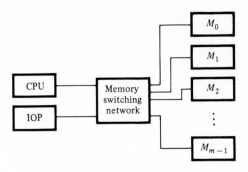

Figure 5.50 A modular memory organization.

m modules. Ideally, every member of a set of m consecutive memory references should address a separate module. Any set of m or fewer memory accesses, no two of which refer to the same module, can be carried out simultaneously. The processor-memory interface bandwidth is then m words per memory cycle.

Address interleaving Let $X_0, X_1, \ldots, X_{k-1}$ be k words that are known (or expected) to be required in sequence by a processor, for example, k consecutive instructions in a program. They will normally be assigned k consecutive physical addresses $A_0, A_1, \ldots, A_{k-1}$ in main memory. The following rule can be employed to distribute these addresses among the memory modules.

Interleaving rule. Assign address A_i to module M_j if $j = i$ (modulo m).

Thus $A_0, A_m, A_{2m}, \ldots$ are assigned to M_0; $A_1, A_{m+1}, A_{2m+1}, \ldots$ are assigned to M_1, etc. This technique for distributing addresses among memory modules is termed *interleaving*. The interleaving of addresses among m modules is called *m-way* interleaving. It is convenient to make m, the number of modules, a power of 2, say $m = 2^p$. Then the least significant p bits of every (binary) address immediately identify the module to which the address belongs.

The efficiency with which any interleaved memory system can be used is highly dependent on the order in which memory addresses are generated; this order is clearly determined by the programs being executed. If two or more addresses require simultaneous access to the same module, then there is said to be memory *interference* or *contention*. The memory accesses in question cannot be executed simultaneously. In the worst case, if all addresses refer to the same module, the advantages of memory modularity are entirely lost.

Interleaving is frequently applied to program addresses in order to increase the rate at which instructions can be fetched from memory. The instructions of a program are normally assigned consecutive addresses and executed in the sequence in which they are written. Only program control instructions such as branch instructions cause a deviation in the execution sequence. Since the proportion of instructions that result in branching is often small, the CPU can reasonably assume that the current instruction will be followed by the instructions in the next consecutive instruction addresses. Thus the CPU can fetch instructions in advance and store them in an instruction buffer. With m-way interleaving m consecutive instructions can be fetched during one memory cycle.

A performance model A model for measuring the efficiency of interleaved memory systems has been studied by Burnett and Coffman [4] based on earlier work by Hellerman [11]. It is assumed that there are m independent memory modules and that the CPU maintains a "request queue" of addresses A_1, $A_2, \ldots, A_q$ that it needs to access. Before each memory cycle, the request queue is scanned and a sequence called the *request sequence* $A_1, A_2, \ldots, A_k$ of $k \leq m$ addresses is selected from the head of the queue. $A_1, A_2, \ldots, A_k$ is the longest sequence with the property that no two of its members are in the same module. During the next memory cycle, these addresses are used to carry out k simultaneous memory accesses.

The efficiency of this system clearly depends on the average length of the request sequences, the closer to m the better. Following Ref. 4, let $p(k)$ denote the probability density function of the request sequence lengths, where $k = 1$, $2, \ldots, m$. The mean value of k is denoted by b_m and is given by the equation

$$b_m = \sum_{k=1}^{m} kp(k) \tag{5.8}$$

b_m is the average number of words that can be accessed per cycle and therefore represents the memory bandwidth.

Since $p(k)$ depends on the programs being executed, $p(k)$ and b_m may be difficult to determine. Consider the case where the request queue contains only instruction addresses. An instruction request queue can be characterized by the *branching probability* λ, defined as the probability that any given instruction causes a jump to a nonconsecutive address. $p(k)$ can then be defined as follows:

$$p(1) = \lambda$$

$$p(k) = (1-\lambda)^{k-1}\lambda \qquad \text{for } 1 < k < m$$

$$p(m) = (1 - \lambda)^{m-1}$$

Substituting into Eq. (5.8), we obtain

$$b_m = \lambda + 2(1-\lambda)\lambda + 3(1-\lambda)^2\lambda + \ldots + m(1-\lambda)^{m-1} \tag{5.9}$$

It can easily be shown by induction on m, that (5.9) implies that

$$b_m = \sum_{i=0}^{m-1} (1-\lambda)^i$$

which is a simple geometric progression. Hence

$$b_m = \frac{1 - (1 - \lambda)^m}{\lambda} \tag{5.10}$$

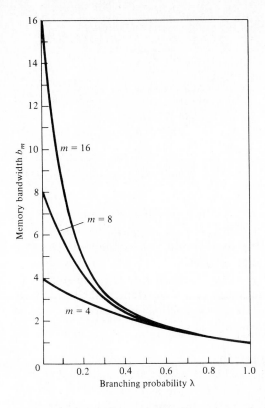

Figure 5.51 Memory bandwidth b_m as a function of branching probability λ in an m-way interleaved memory.

It can be seen from (5.10) that $b_m = 1$ when $\lambda = 1$, while $b_m = m$, its maximum value, when $\lambda = 0$. Figure 5.51 shows b_m plotted as a function of λ for several values of m. These curves indicate that λ must be close to zero for b_m to approach its maximum value.

5.3.2 Cache Memories

A cache is a small fast memory placed between a processor and main memory as illustrated in Fig. 5.29b. The cache is then the fastest component in the memory hierarchy. It can be viewed as a buffer memory for the main memory, so that the cache M_1 and main memory M_2 form a two-level hierarchy. It is common to manage the three-level system of Fig. 5.29b as two largely independent two-level hierarchies (M_1, M_2) and (M_2, M_3). The main–secondary system (M_2, M_3) may be organized as a virtual memory system of the type examined in Sec. 5.2. The cache–main-memory system (M_1, M_2) is organized along essentially similar lines; hence (M_1, M_2) has many of the properties of a virtual memory system.

The performance goal of adding a cache memory to a computer is to make the average memory access time t_A seen by the processor as close as possible to that of the cache t_{A_1}. To achieve this, a high percentage of all memory refer-

Two-level hierarchy (M_{i-1}, M_i)	Cache–main memory (M_1, M_2)	Main–secondary memory (M_2, M_3)
Typical access time ratios $t_{A_i}/t_{A_{i-1}}$	5/1	1000/1
Memory management system	Implemented by special hardware	Mainly implemented by software
Typical page size	1 to 16 words	16 to 1024 words
Access of processor to second level M_i	Usually has direct access to M_2	All access to M_3 is via M_2

Figure 5.52 Main differences between cache–main-memory and main–secondary-memory hierarchies.

ences should be satisfied by the cache, i. e., the cache hit ratio should be close to 1. This is possible because of the locality of reference property of programs. Although small buffer memories were used to prefetch instructions in some early machines, cache memories did not become economically feasible until the advent of LSI semiconductor memories in the late 1960s. Historically, therefore, virtual memories preceded cache memories. Many of the techniques designed for virtual memory management have been applied to cache systems and have stimulated their development.

Distinctive features of cache memories There are some important differences between the cache–main-memory hierarchy (M_1, M_2) and the main–secondary-memory hierarchy (M_2, M_3); these differences are summarized in Fig. 5.52. Because it is higher in the memory hierarchy, the pair (M_1, M_2) functions at a higher speed than (M_2, M_3). The access time ratio t_{A_2}/t_{A_1} is typically 10 or less, while t_{A_3}/t_{A_2} is typically 100 or more. These differences in operating speed require (M_1, M_2) to be managed by high-speed logic circuits rather than software routines. (M_2, M_3), on the other hand, is controlled mainly by programs within the operating system. Thus while the (M_2, M_3) hierarchy may be transparent to the applications programmer but visible to the systems programmer, (M_1, M_2) is transparent to both. Another important difference is in the block size used. Communication within (M_1, M_2) is invariably paged, and the page size is much smaller than that used in (M_2, M_3). Finally, we note that the processor generally has direct access to both M_1 and M_2, so that Fig. 5.53 is a more accurate representation of the logical data paths in a cache system. For this reason, cache memories have also been called "look-aside" memories.

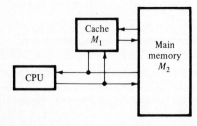

Figure 5.53 Data flow in a cache-based system.

Example 5.8: The cache system of the Data General Corporation ECLIPSE computer ECLIPSE is a general-purpose machine with a 16-bit word size which was introduced in the early 1970s. It contains a cache memory that uses bipolar semiconductor technology with an access time of 200 ns. Main memory uses MOS technology with a 700-ns access time. The memory system is modular; each 8K module M_2 of main memory has a 16-word cache M_1 associated with it, as depicted in Fig. 5.54. The cache is divided into four pages of four words each. The addresses assigned to the cache are stored in an associative or content-addressable memory CAM. When a memory request is generated by the CPU, the address of the required word is sent to the CAM. If the CAM indicates that the requested word W is in the cache, W is transmitted from the cache to the CPU. If W is not in M_1, its address is sent to M_2 from which W is transmitted to the CPU. At the same time, a page of four consecutive words that includes W is sent to M_1, where it replaces the least recently used page in M_1. The LRU algorithm is implemented by special circuits which constantly monitor the cache usage.

Address mapping methods The addresses assigned to a cache are maintained in a hardware-implemented memory map. The fastest and most general type of map uses an associative memory which permits any word in main memory to be assigned to any location in the cache. Associative memories are expensive, so that a number of more economical memory mapping methods have been proposed and implemented [2, 6].

One of the simplest memory mapping techniques is called *direct mapping*. Let M_1 be divided into $S_1 = 2^k$ regions $M_1(0), M_1(1), \ldots, M_1(S_1-1)$, each of which stores a block of n consecutive words. Main memory M_2 is similarly divided into one-block regions $M_2(0), M_2(1), \ldots, M_2(S_2-1)$. Each region $M_2(i)$ in M_2 is mapped onto a fixed region $M_1(j)$ in M_1. The address j is determined from i by the rule

$$j = i \quad (\text{modulo } S_1)$$

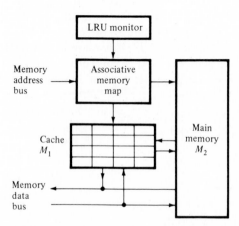

Figure 5.54 Cache system of the ECLIPSE computer.

For example, if $S_1 = 2$, every even block in M_2 is mapped onto $M_1(0)$, while every odd block in M_2 is mapped onto $M_1(1)$. The hardware needed to implement direct mapping is very simple. The low-order k bits of each block address identify the cache region that may contain the block. These k bits therefore constitute the cache address. If there are 2^p words per block, then the low-order $k+p$ bits of each effective address generated by the CPU constitute the cache address of the word in question. Thus unlike associative mapping, there is no need to store the addresses of items in the cache. A disadvantage of direct mapping is that the cache hit ratio drops sharply if two or more frequently used blocks happen to map onto the same region in the cache. This possibility is minimized by the fact that such blocks are relatively far apart in the logical address space.

There is a more general mapping method called *set associative* which includes pure associative and direct maping as special cases. As in direct mapping, blocks in main memory are grouped into equivalence classes determined by their addresses. $M_2(i)$ and $M_2(j)$ are in the same equivalence class E if $i=j$ (modulo S_1'). The cache is divided into S_1' regions $M_1'(0)$, $M_1'(1)$, ..., $M_1'(S_1'-1)$ called *sets*, each of which accommodates 2^s blocks. A block $M_2(i)$ in M_2 is mapped into the set $M_1'(h)$ satisfying $i = h$ (modulo S_1'). Each set $M_1'(h)$ is controlled by a small associative memory, so that mapping within each set is associative. This permits several members of the same equivalence class E to be stored in the cache simultaneously, which is not possible with direct mapping. Set associative mapping reduces to direct mapping when the set size $2^s = 1$; it reduces to pure associative when $2^s = S_1$, the number of blocks in the cache. Intermediate set sizes lead to mapping methods requiring an intermediate amount of associative hardware.

Updating main memory As noted earlier, the CPU generally has direct physical access to main memory, so that when a required item is not found in the cache, the CPU can access it in main memory with minimal delay. The existence of direct communication links between the CPU and M_2 permits some different schemes for updating M_2 when information in M_1 is altered. The same swapping approach used in virtual memory sytems can be employed. An altered "dirty" block in the cache is tagged; when the block is to be replaced, it is first copied into main memory. A different approach is to write all information into both M_1 and M_2 even when the address in question is currently assigned to M_1. This policy, called *write through*, is easily implemented and ensures that M_2 never contains obsolete information. This is a useful feature when M_2 is being shared by several independent processors. On the other hand, write through results in many "unnecessary" writes to M_2 when the information in question is also written into M_1.

5.3.3 Associative Memories

Introduction Consider the table shown in Fig. 5.55 which is to be stored in a computer's memory. It consists of a list of records, each containing three

Name	ID number	Age
J. Smith	124	24
J. Bond	007	40
A. Jones	106	50
R. Roe	002	19
J. Doe	009	28

Figure 5.55 A table to be stored in a computer's memory.

(major) subfields: a person's name, an identification number, and an age. Most information storage and retrieval problems involve accessing certain subfields within a set of one or more records in answer to questions such as: "What are A. Jones's ID number and age?" If a conventional random access memory is being used, it is necessary to specify exactly the physical address of the Jones entry in the table, e. g., by the instruction

READ ROW 3

The address ROW 3 has no logical relationship to Jones; hence it can be viewed as an artificial construct which adds to programming complexity.

An alternative approach is to search the entire table using the name field as an address. In such a system, the request for the Jones data would be in the form of an instruction such as

READ NAME = A. JONES

The conventional method of implementing this approach involves scanning all entries in the table sequentially and comparing their NAME fields to the given address, A. JONES, until a match is found. Sequential searching of this type is easily implemented with serial-access memories, but it is very slow. An associative memory eliminates this difficulty by simultaneously examining all entries in the table and selecting the one that matches the given address. It is clearly useful to be able to select other fields of the record to use as an address. For example,

READ ID = 106

uses the ID number field as an address and also accesses the Jones entry in the table.

In general, an *associative memory* is one in which any stored item can be accessed directly by using the contents of the item in question, generally some specified subfield, as an address. Associative memories are also commonly known as *content addressable memories*. The subfield chosen to address the memory is called the *key*. Items stored in an associative memory can be viewed as having the format

KEY, DATA

where KEY is address and DATA is the information to be accessed. For example, if a page table of the kind shown in Fig. 5.42 is placed in an associative

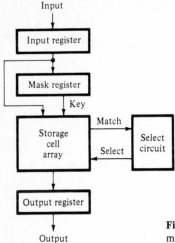

Input

Output

Figure 5.56 The structure of a word-organized associative memory.

memory, the page name forms the key; and the page frame, presence bit, etc., form the data.

Word-organized associative memory Figure 5.56 shows the structure of a simple associative memory. Each unit of stored information is a fixed-length word. Any subfield of the word may be chosen as the key. The desired key is specified by the *mask register*. The key is compared simultaneously with all stored words; those which match the key emit a match signal which enters a *select circuit*. The select circuit enables the data field to be accessed. If several entries have the same key, then the select circuit determines which data field is to be read out; it may, for example, read out all matching entries in some predetermined order. Since all words in the memory are required to compare their keys with the input key simultaneously, each must have its own *match circuit*. The match and select circuits make associative memories much more complex and expensive than conventional memories. The advent of LSI techniques has made associative memories economically feasible. However, cost considerations still limit them to applications where a relatively small amount of information must be accessed very rapidly, e. g., memory address mapping.

The logic circuit for a 1-bit associative memory cell is shown in Fig. 5.57 [1]. It comprises a flip-flop, a match circuit for comparing the flip-flop contents to an external data bit, and circuits for reading from and writing into the cell. The output match line M is normally 1. When the input enable line IE is set to 1, the input data bit ID is compared with the bit stored in the cell; if they agree, M remains at 1, otherwise M becomes 0. The bit on ID can be written into the flip-flop by applying 1 to both IE and the write enable line WE. The select line (address line) S is used to select the cell for either reading or writing. Cells of this type can easily be assembled into arrays. Figure 5.58 shows an associative memory with a capacity of two 2-bit words which is constructed from four such

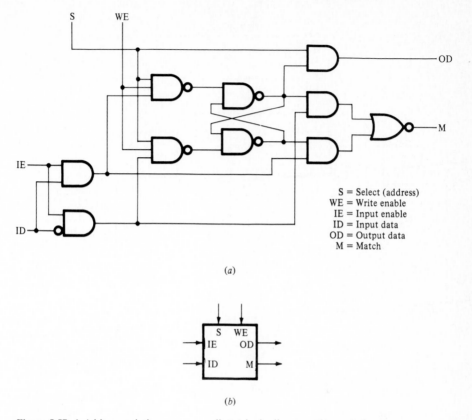

S = Select (address)
WE = Write enable
IE = Input enable
ID = Input data
OD = Output data
M = Match

(a)

(b)

Figure 5.57 A 1-bit associative memory cell: (a) logic diagram; (b) symbol.

cells. Note that each column of this array represents a word, and that the M lines of all cells in the same word are connected by a wired-AND gate.

In many applications, the key assigned to every word is unique. Any attempt to address the memory results in either no match or a single match indicated by a single M line in the 1 state. If the keys are not unique, then a *multiple match* may occur. Note that a multiple match could result from an error in the system, even when all keys are intended to be unique. An important function of the select circuit of Fig. 5.56 is to resolve multiple matches. It can do so by storing all match signals in a register, then scanning this register to access the matching words one by one.

Associative memory for variable-length data We now describe a hypothetical memory organization for associative storage and retrieval of variable-length data based on a design by Lee and Paull [15]. The memory can be viewed as a one-dimensional array of complex associative storage cells as shown in Fig. 5.59. Each cell is connected to a common set of data and control lines. In addition, a cell can communicate with its left and right neighbors. Information is stored in key-data form, where both the key and its associated data are of vari-

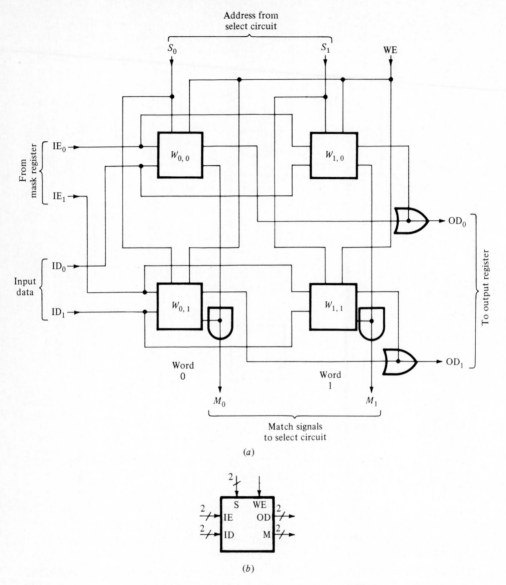

Figure 5.58 A 2×2 bit associative memory array: (*a*) logic diagram; (*b*) symbol.

able length and can be positioned anywhere within the cellular array. Each cell is capable of transferring data to and from the data bus in response to external control signals placed on the common control bus. The source of these control signals is a small processor which executes (micro) programs that specify the desired storage or retrieval operation.

The cell array may be of arbitrary length; hence it is not possible to provide individual match lines which would immediately pinpoint matching cells. All

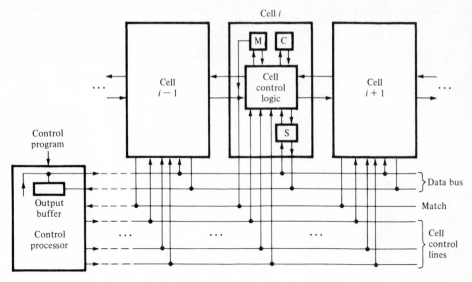

Figure 5.59 Associative memory for variable-length strings.

cell match lines are combined into a single line which tells the processor when, but not where, a match occurs. Two special flip-flops M and C are included in each cell. They are used to mark cells so that read and write operations can be localized within the memory array. In addition, every cell contains a data register S used to store a single alphanumeric symbol.

The instructions executed by the control processor have the format

operation (condition)

The condition field of an instruction specifies the values that C and M must have in order for the operation to be performed. For example,

write A $(C = 1)$

instructs all cells having $C = 1$ to store A in their S registers. An unconditional instruction such as

write A

is executed by every cell in the memory. Figure 5.60 lists the operations performed by the cells and the control processor. The "specified cells" are those that satisfy the condition, if any, appended to the operation.

In order to store or retrieve data, an appropriate program for the control processor must be written. Consider the problem of reading a specific data item from the memory. Assume that information is stored in the format

$\dots \# KEY1\$DATA1\#KEY2\$DATA2\# \dots$

where the symbols $\#$ and $\$$ act as delimiters. The given key is applied character by character to the input data bus and the match instruction as issued. The C

Instruction type	Operation	Description
Input-output	**write** X	Transfer symbol X to S registers of the specified cells.
	writeb	Transfer contents of output buffer to S registers of the specified cells
	read	Transfer S register contents of the specified cells to output buffer. (A meaningful instruction only if all specified S registers store the same data)
Cell marking	**match** X	Place symbol X on input data bus; set $M = 1$ in every specified cell where $S = X$
	$C \leftarrow a$	Set C to a in every specified cell
	$M \leftarrow a$	Set M to a in every specified cell
	rightc $\leftarrow a$	Set C to a in cell to right of every specified cell
	leftc $\leftarrow a$	Set C to a in cell to left of every specified cell
	rightm $\leftarrow a$	Set M to a in cell to right of every specified cell
	leftm $\leftarrow a$	Set M to a in cell to left of every specified cell
Program control	**go to** LABEL	Unconditional branch to instruction LABEL
	if X **then go to** LABEL	Conditional branch; compare symbol X to output buffer contents: if they match go to LABEL, otherwise go to next consecutive instruction
	if MATCH then go to LABEL	Conditional branch; if $M = 1$ in some cell go to LABEL, otherwise go to next consecutive instruction
	halt	Stop program execution

Figure 5.60 Instruction set for the associative memory of Fig. 5.59.

flip-flop in the cell to the right of each matching cell is marked using the instruction

$$\textbf{rightc} \leftarrow 1 \ (M = 1)$$

The next match instruction has the condition $C = 1$ appended to it, which restricts matching cells to those that lie on the right of a previous match. In this way a complete key can be matched and its data field uniquely marked. Figure 5.61 shows a program implementing this approach where the key is AZ. The frequently used sequence of three instructions that sets C to 1 in the right neighbor of a matching cell has been defined to be the macroinstruction MARKRIGHTC. The state of the memory after the execution of the first few instructions in this program is shown in Fig. 5.62. For clarity, M and C cells in the 0 state are shown blank. It will be observed that initially many cells are marked by the presence of 1 in their M or C flip-flops. The number of marked cells diminishes rapidly as the key is read in. Ultimately, if the key is unique, only one cell is marked and readout can commence.

A number of practical limitations of this system can readily be discerned. The very great cell complexity probably makes its cost prohibitive. The management of space in such a memory is also difficult. For example, items no longer needed result in gaps of varying lengths appearing in the memory. Locating such gaps for reuse is not easy. An obvious solution is to eliminate gaps by

Location	Instruction	Comment
SEARCH:	**match #**	Mark beginning of key
	$C \leftarrow 0$	⎫ Macroinstruction MARKRIGHTC
	rightc $\leftarrow 1\ (M{=}1)$	⎬ which sets $C = 1$ in cell to right
	$M \leftarrow 0$	⎭ of cell with $M = 1$
	match $A\ (C{=}1)$	
	MARKRIGHTC	
	match $Z\ (C{=}1)$	
	MARKRIGHTC	
	match $\$\ (C{=}1)$	
	MARKRIGHTC	Mark beginning of data
READ:	**read** $(C{=}1)$	
	if # then go to END	If output buffer contains #, go to END
	$M \leftarrow 1\ (C{=}1)$	
	MARKRIGHTC	
	go to READ	
END:	**halt**	

Figure 5.61 Program to read data with key AZ from the associative memory of Fig. 5.59.

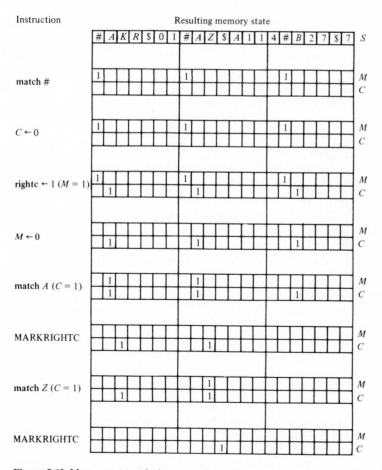

Figure 5.62 Memory states during execution of part of the program in Fig. 5.61.

periodic compaction (see Prob. 5.17). Further refinements in the design may be needed to solve the multiple match problem.

Remarks The storage cells of associative memories have certain logical capabilities, so that "distributed logic memory" is yet another term for an associative memory. By providing additional logical functions within each cell, it is possible to perform many standard arithmetic and nonnumerical operations in the memory [7, 20]. In such cases it is more appropriate to refer to the system as an associative processor. An associative processor called ALAP (*A*ssociative *L*inear *A*rray *P*rocessor), with a one-dimensional organization resembling that of Fig. 5.59, has recently been built by Hughes Aircraft Co. [9].

While associative memories allow very fast access to large information files, it should be noted that fast access methods also exist for conventional nonassociative memories. In particular, if the hash addressing method defined in Sec. 5.2.5 is used, access times close to that of an associative memory can be achieved at a much lower cost.

5.4 SUMMARY

No one technology can be used to supply all the memory needs within a computer system. This is mainly because the cost per bit of storage increases as the access rate is increased. As a result, several different memory technologies with widely varying characteristics can be found in a typical computer system. Besides cost per bit and access rate, important properties of storage devices are: alterability, storage permanence, reliability, and compatibility with processor technologies.

Main memories are usually of the random access type wherein the access time of every location is constant. Such memories are organized as multidimensional arrays to reduce the cost of their access circuitry and facilitate manufacture. The dominant technologies for this application are ferrite-core and semiconductor devices. In secondary memories, lower cost per bit and higher storage density are required. These are frequently achieved by using serial access memories, which are characterized by the use of shared access mechanisms, serial data transfer, and an access time that varies with location. Serial access memories store information on tracks which behave like shift registers. The most widely used technologies in this group are magnetic-surface memories with electromechanical access mechanisms, e.g., magnetic disk, and tape units. Serial access memories with static access mechanisms include magnetic-bubble and charge-coupled devices.

The memory units of a computer are generally organized as a multilevel hierarchy $(M_1, M_2, \ldots, M_n)$ in which M_1 is connected to the CPU and other processors, M_2 is connected to M_1, and so on. M_i has less capacity, higher cost, and a shorter access time than M_{i+1}. The objective of using a hierarchical memory is to achieve a cost per bit close to that of the least expensive memory M_n

and an access rate close to that of the fastest memory M_1. A virtual memory is a hierarchical memory, generally of two levels, which is managed by an operating system to appear like a single large memory to the applications programmer. This is achieved by automatically transferring blocks of information between M_1 and the other levels of the hierarchy. The locality of reference property of programs makes it possible to ensure that data is generally in M_1 when referenced by a processor. A fundamental measure of the performance of a virtual memory system is the hit ratio, the fraction of all memory references that are satisfied by M_1. The performance of a virtual memory is highly program-dependent; hence simulation is the principal design tool.

Memory space is generally a limited resource of a computer and therefore must usually be shared by different programs. Dynamic allocation means varying the regions of memory assigned to programs while they are being executed. Main-memory space is allocated in contiguous blocks. Two allocation techniques have been distinguished: nonpreemptive and preemptive. Nonpreemptive methods assign space to incoming blocks only if an available region of sufficient size exists. Best-fit and first-fit are two possible allocation methods of this type. Preemptive methods can assign incoming blocks to occupied regions of M_1 and thereby permit more efficient use of memory space. Blocks to be preempted are selected according to a replacement policy. Least recently used (LRU) and first-in first-out (FIFO) are perhaps the most widely used replacement policies. LRU is an example of a stack replacement algorithm. Stack algorithms permit rapid analysis of the effect of varying the capacity of M_1 on memory performance.

The block sizes used in memory allocation are also important. Segments are blocks of arbitrary size which correspond to logical units of a program. Pages are fixed-sized blocks with no logical significance. Memory space may be allocated by segments (segmentation) or pages (paging) or a combination of both, e.g., by using paged segments. Because of their fixed size, pages greatly simplify memory management.

Several methods for increasing the average access rate of main memory have been discussed. Main memory can be divided into a number of independently addressable modules to permit simultaneous access to several words. Efficient use of a modular memory requires addresses to be distributed throughout the modules in an interleaved fashion. Another approach is to insert a high-speed buffer memory or cache between the processors and main memory. The cache–main-memory pair approximates a two-level hierarchy, and many of the techniques used to manage a virtual memory are applicable to cache-based systems. Yet another approach to high-speed storage and retrieval is associative or content addressing. In an associative memory, data is accessed by comparing the logical address or key of the required item to the keys of all stored items. Data and their keys are stored together in the memory. Very fast access is achieved by comparing the input key to all stored keys simultaneously. Associative memories require complex storage cells and therefore tend to be relatively expensive.

PROBLEMS

5.1 A 2-D random access memory has N cells organized as N_x rows and N_y columns. The number of address drivers needed is $N_x + N_y$.

(a) If $N = M^2$ where M is an integer, that is, N is a perfect square, show that the number of address drivers needed is a minimum if and only if $N_x = N_y = M$.

(b) If N is not a perfect square, provide an algorithm for determining values of N_x and N_y that minimize the number of address drivers.

5.2 A 3-D ferrite-core memory stores 4K words of length 16 bits. The cost of the access circuitry is computed as $C = D_a + D_i + D_s$, where D_a is the number of X and Y line drivers, D_i is the number of inhibit line drivers, and D_s is the number of sense amplifiers. Calculate the value of C.

5.3 Using 4×2 bit semiconductor ICs of the type shown in Fig. 5.13, design an 8×6 bit random access memory.

5.4 A certain moving-arm disk-storage device has the following specifications:

Number of tracks per recording surface	200
Disk rotation speed	2400 r/min
Track storage capacity	62,500 bits

Estimate the average latency and the data-transfer rate of this device.

5.5 A high-speed magnetic-tape system accommodates 2400-ft reels of standard nine-track tape. The tape is moved past the recording head at a rate of 200 in/s.

(a) What must the linear tape-recording density be in order to achieve a data-transfer rate of 10^7 bits/s?

(b) Suppose that the data on the tape is organized into blocks each containing 32K bytes. A gap of 0.3 in separates each block. How many bytes may be stored on the tape?

5.6 A computer has a two-level virtual memory system. The main memory M_1 and the secondary memory M_2 have average access times of 10^{-6} and 10^{-3} s, respectively. It is found by measurement that the average access time for the memory hierarchy is 10^{-4} s, which is considered unacceptably high. Describe two ways in which this memory access time could be reduced from 10^{-4} to 10^{-5} s and discuss the hardware and software costs involved.

5.7 Generalize the expressions for cost per bit c and access time t_A given by Eqs. (5.1) and (5.4), respectively, to n-level memory hierarchies.

5.8 In a two-level virtual memory, $t_{A_1} = 10^{-7}$ s and $t_{A_2} = 10^{-2}$ s. What must the hit ratio H be in order for the access efficiency to be within 80 percent of its maximum possible value?

5.9 The available space list of a 1K-word memory has the following entries at time t.

Region address	Size (words)
0	200
250	150
450	100
700	185
999	25

The following sequence of allocation and deallocation requests is then received.

Time	$t + 1$	$t + 2$	$t + 3$	$t + 4$	$t + 5$
Size of block to be allocated	135	25		170	100
Address of block to be deallocated			400		

Determine the available space list after all these requests have been serviced using (a) best-fit and (b) first-fit allocation. Assume that the memory is searched in ascending address sequence.

5.10 A replacement policy that has been proposed is *least frequently used* (LFU). Under LFU the page from M_1 to be replaced at time t is the one that has had the fewest references made to it during the interval $(t - T, t)$, where T is fixed and $0 < T \leq t$. Determine whether or not LFU is a stack algorithm.

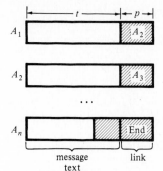

message   link
text

Figure 5.63 Message format for Prob. 5.13.

5.11 The following page address stream is representative for a particular two-level virtual memory system that uses demand paging and LRU replacement

$$3 \quad 4 \quad 2 \quad 6 \quad 4 \quad 7 \quad 1 \quad 3 \quad 2 \quad 6 \quad 3 \quad 5 \quad 1 \quad 2 \quad 3$$

Plot a graph of page hit ratio as a function of main-memory page capacity n for $1 \leq n \leq 8$. Assume that main memory is empty initially.

5.12 Assuming page size to be a function of average segment size only, determine the page size 2^k that maximizes memory space utilization when the average segment size is 1100 words and k is required to be an integer.

5.13 A word-organized random access memory is used to store messages of varying length. Each message is stored as a linked list with the format shown in Fig. 5.63. Each item in the list contains $t + p$ words, where t is the number of words of message text and p is the number of words in the link. The storage space (shown shaded) not used in the last list item A_n and the space occupied by the links is regarded as overhead, or "waste," space. Assume that the message lengths are randomly distributed with mean value L. Show that the fraction of memory space that is wasted is a minimum when t is chosen to be approximately $\sqrt{2pL}$

5.14 A 32-way interleaved memory is used for program storage. It is found that the branching probability λ of the memory-request queue is 0.25. What is the average number of words accessed per memory cycle?

5.15 In a cache-based memory system using FIFO for cache page replacement, it is found that the cache hit ratio H is unacceptably low. The following proposals are made for increasing H.
(*a*) Increase the cache page size.
(*b*) Increase the cache storage capacity.
(*c*) Increase the main-memory capacity.
(*d*) Replace the FIFO replacement policy by LRU.
Analyze each proposal to determine its probable impact on H.

5.16 It is desired to build a small word-organized associative memory using the 2×2 bit memory circuit of Fig. 5.58 as the basic building block. The memory is to store four 8-bit words having the format shown in Fig. 5.64. Any one of the fields A, B, and C may be selected as the key. Assume that all stored keys are unique. When a match occurs, the entire matching word is to be fetched (read operation) or replaced (write operation). Draw a logic diagram for the memory including all access circuitry.

5.17 Consider the associative memory system in Fig. 5.59. Using the instruction set of Fig. 5.60, write a program to compact the memory by transferring all stored character strings to the left end of

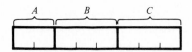

A   *B*   *C*

Figure 5.64 Associative memory word format for Prob. 5.16.

the cell array, thus eliminating all gaps between records. Assume that an unused cell stores b (blank) in its S register. Suggest some additions to the given instruction set that would simplify compaction.

REFERENCES

1. Bartlett, J., et. al.: "Associative Memory Chips—Fast, Versatile and Here," *Electronics*, pp. 96–100, August 17, 1970.
2. Bell, J., D. Casasent, and C. G. Bell: "An Investigation of Alternative Cache Organizations," *IEEE Trans. Comput.*, vol. C-23, pp. 346–351, April 1974.
3. Bobeck, A. H., P. I. Bonyhard, and J. E. Geusic: "Magnetic Bubbles—An Emerging Storage Technology," *Proc. IEEE*, vol. 63, pp. 1176–1195, August 1975.
4. Burnett, G. J., and E. G. Coffman: "A Study of Interleaved Memory Systems," *AFIPS Conf. Proc.*, vol. 36, pp. 467–474, 1970.
5. Burroughs Corp.: *Burroughs B5500 Information Processing Systems Reference Manual*, Detroit, 1964.
6. Conti, C. J.: "Concepts for Buffer Storage," *IEEE Comput. Group News*, vol. 2, pp. 9–13, March 1969.
7. Crane, B. A., and J. A. Githens: "Bulk Processing in Distributed Logic Memory," *IEEE Trans. Electron. Comput.*, vol. EC-14, pp. 186–196, April 1965.
8. Crouch, H. R., J. B. Cornett, and R. S. Eward: "CCDs in Memory Systems Move into Sight," *Comput. Des.*, vol. 15, pp. 75–80, September 1976.
9. Finnila, C. A., and H. H. Love: "The Associative Linear Array Processor," *IEEE Trans. Comput.*, vol. C-26, pp. 112–125, February 1977.
10. Denning, P. J.: "Virtual Memory," *Comput. Surv.*, vol. 2, pp. 153–187, September 1970.
11. Hellerman, H.: *Digital Computer System Principles*, McGraw-Hill, New York, 1967.
12. Horowitz, E., and S. Sahni: *Fundamentals of Data Structures*, Computer Science Press, Woodland Hills, Calif., 1976.
13. Katzan, H.: "Storage Hierarchy Systems," *AFIPS Conf. Proc.*, vol. 38, pp. 325–336, 1971.
14. Knuth, D. E.: *The Art of Computer Programming*, vol. 1, *Fundamental Algorithms*, 2d ed., Addison-Wesley, Reading, Mass., 1973.
15. Lee, C. Y., and M. C. Paull: "A Content Addressable Distributed Logic Memory with Applications to Information Retrieval," *Proc. IEEE*, vol. 51, pp. 924–932, June 1963.
16. London, K. R.: *Techniques for Direct Access*, Auerbach, Philadelphia, 1973.
17. Mattson, R. L., et. al.: "Evaluation Techniques for Storage Hierarchies," *IBM Syst. J.*, vol. 9, pp. 78–117, 1970.
18. Middelhoek, S., P. K. George, and P. Dekker: *Physics of Computer Memory Devices*, Academic, London, 1976.
19. Minnick, R. C., et. al.: "Magnetic Bubble Computer Systems," *AFIPS Conf. Proc.*, vol. 41, pp. 1279–1298, December 1972.
20. Parhami, B.: "Associative Memories and Processors: An Overview and Selected Bibliography," *Proc. IEEE*, vol. 61, pp. 722–730, June 1973.
21. Randall, B. and C. J. Kuehner: "Dynamic Storage Allocation Systems," *Commun. ACM*, vol. 11, pp. 297–306, May 1968.
22. Roberts, D. C.: "File Organization Techniques," in M. Rubinoff (ed.), *Advances in Computers*, vol. 12, pp. 115–174, Academic, New York, 1972.
23. Rodriguez, J. A.: "An Analysis of Tape Drive Technology," *Proc. IEEE*, vol. 63, pp. 1153–1157, August 1975.
24. Shore, J. E.: "On the External Fragmentation Produced by First-Fit and Best-Fit Allocation Strategies," *Commun. ACM*, vol. 18, pp. 433–440, August 1975.
25. Turn, R.: *Computers in the 1980s*, Columbia University Press, New York, 1974.
26. Watson, R. W.: *Timesharing System Design Concepts*, McGraw-Hill, New York, 1970.

SIX

SYSTEM ORGANIZATION

This chapter is mainly concerned with the way computers are interconnected and communicate at the processor level. The methods used to implement input-output operations are examined. Systems using more than one CPU to improve performance and/or reliability are discussed.

6.1 COMMUNICATION

The difficulty of connecting two components of a computer system is in part dependent on the physical distance between the components. We can distinguish three cases.

1. Communication within a single unit such as a CPU where the distances involved are less than a meter.
2. Communication within a single room or building where the distances involved are less than a kilometer, e. g., between a CPU and its IO devices. We will refer to this as *local communication*.
3. Communications over greater distances, e.g., between computers in different cities. We will refer to this as *long-distance communication*.

Internal communications between different components of the same processor present few design difficulties. A common control unit normally supervises both components. Furthermore, a common clock signal can be used to synchronize all activities within the processor, so that these activities never get out of step with one another. The design of the communication circuits at this level can be viewed as simply an aspect of gate-level or register-level logic design, and so will not be considered further.

6.1.1 Local Communication

The various processor level components (CPUs, IOPs, main memory, IO or peripheral devices) of a computer system are interconnected by switching networks, often referred to as *buses*. The term bus in this context refers not only to communication paths between the system components but also to mechanisms for controlling access to these paths and supervising the exchange of signals that provide the communication. Many bus organizations are possible. Two very common types are depicted in Fig. 6.1. In Fig. 6.1a a single bus is shared by all components. At any time only two units can communicate via the bus. Large computer systems with separate IO processors frequently employ the dual bus system of Fig. 6.1b. In most computers, communication with IO devices is a major source of difficulty due to the wide variety of operating characteristics exhibited by these devices. In contrast, communication between processors and main memory is relatively simple.

Communication between different processor-level components presents several problems. The distances involved frequently make it impractical to use

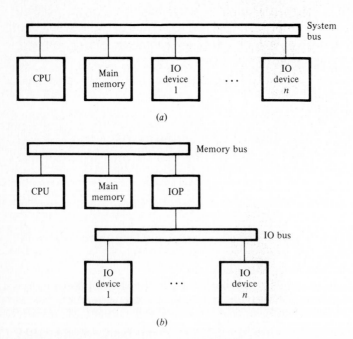

(a)

(b)

Figure 6.1 Communication methods within a computer: (a) single shared bus; (b) separate memory and IO buses.

a common clock for synchronization. For example, if a clock signal with a period of 100ns is transmitted to a device 100m away, that signal will not be received until about 330ns (3.3 clock periods) later, assuming it travels at the speed of light (300,000 km/s). Furthermore, several signals which are transmitted simultaneously over such distances are likely to arrive slightly out of phase or "skewed" at the destination. For instance, if the 100-m path by which signal *A* travels has a delay differing by 10 percent from the delay of the path traveled by signal *B*, the two signals will arrive about 33ns out of phase. The fact that the various processor-level components process data at widely different rates further suggests that their timing circuits be independent.

A second problem is determining the number and type of signals to be used during intrasystem communication. A system component presents to the outside world a set of data and control lines which are used to connect it to other components. The specifications of these lines or buses and the signals they carry constitute the device's *interface*. The interface of a device depends on its function and its manufacturer. In order to simplify communication within a computer system, a standard interface is usually defined for that computer. Figure 6.2 shows how such an interface is typically used. Special interface circuits may be needed to adapt the "natural" interface of a particular device to the standard interface which is standard only for that family. Few industry-wide interface standards exist, and they are often limited to special applications, e.g., the CAMAC (*C*omputer *A*utomated *M*easurement *a*nd *C*ontrol) interface system for digital instrumentation [8, 17].

6.1.2 Long-Distance Communication

Many computer systems have been designed in which the component parts are separated by large distances. An example is a time-sharing network of the type depicted in Fig. 6.3, which connects many user terminals, e.g., teletypes, to a remotely located computer via the public telephone system. Time-sharing networks may be for general-purpose computing services or for specialized applications such as airlines reservations. The device called a *concentrator* in Fig. 6.3 is a small computer designed to connect the users to the remote com-

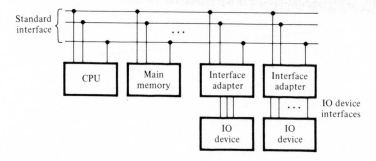

Figure 6.2 Typical use of a standard interface in a computer.

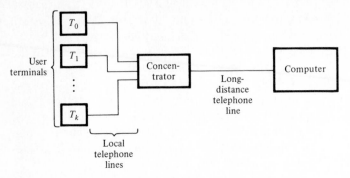

Figure 6.3 A remote time-sharing network.

puter via a single long-distance path. It permits users to gain access to the computer using a local telephone call to the concentrator rather than a more costly long-distance call directly to the central computer. Many computers and terminals can be linked together in this general way to form a computer network.

Local communication in a computer system is implemented by means of rectangular pulses traveling along lines (wires). This is referred to as direct current (DC) signaling. As the pulses are transmitted, they become distorted due to line capacitance, external interference (noise), and other phenomena. The amount of distortion increases with the length of the lines and the frequency of the pulses. Beyond a certain point the pulses become unrecognizable and errors in transmission result. Over long distances, therefore, it is more efficient to use alternating current (AC) for data transmission. An appropriate AC signal called the *carrier* is generated and is *modulated* in some manner to produce two distinct types of AC signals that represent the binary values 0 and 1. A device called a *modulator-demodulator*, or *modem*, is required to convert ordinary (DC) binary pulses to and from the modulated form used for long-distance communication.

Figure 6.4 illustrates a common modulation technique called *frequency modulation* (FM). The carrier is a sinusoidal signal (sine wave) which can have two frequencies—f_0 representing the bit 0 and f_1 representing 1. If an ordinary "voice-grade" telephone line is being used, f_0 and f_1 might be chosen as 1500 and 2000 Hz, respectively. Sine waves of these frequencies can be heard as pure tones of different pitch. A sequence of binary pulses is therefore transmitted as a sequence of "beeps" using two beep frequencies.

Long-distance communication is further complicated by the fact that it is

Figure 6.4 Long-distance transmission of binary information using frequency-modulated (FM) signals.

almost always necessary to use equipment and facilities provided by others, partly because the right to provide long-distance communications is usually severely restricted by law. In many countries a government-controlled monopoly, for example, the General Post Office in Great Britain, provides such services. In the United States, telecommunications services are provided by a number of private telephone and telegraph corporations. In all cases, the telephone network is the basic network used for long-distance communication. This is augmented by networks designed especially for data transmission such as the telex system. A variety of physical transmission media are used in these networks including telephone wires, coaxial cables, radio (microwave) links between ground stations, and radio links via orbiting satellites.

Several other important differences between local and long-distance communication methods should be noted. Whereas local communication is often serial by word, long-distance communication is usually serial by bit. This, of course, is to reduce the cost of the communication equipment used. Every long-distance data transfer requires a substantial amount of time to establish the communication path to be used, e. g., the time associated with dialing a telephone number. In order to reduce this overhead, a sequence of many bits called a *message* is usually transmitted at one time.

In a large computer network, two computers may be connected by several different paths. This increases the flexibility and reliability of the system by allowing busy or faulty links to be bypassed. If a choice of paths exists, or if a single path is shared by many unrelated users, the time required to transmit information between two points becomes variable. Thus the transmission delays of such networks are unpredictable and must usually be analyzed in probabilistic terms.

6.1.3 Interconnection Structure

In this section we consider some of the possible ways the components of a computer system can be interconnected. Many different interconnection structures have been used both for local and long-distance communication, but as yet no generally accepted classification or terminology for such systems exists [1, 33]. The *interconnection structure* of a system may be defined as a graph whose nodes represent components of the system such as processors, memories, etc., and whose edges represent physical communication paths such as buses or long-distance transmission lines. A path used to link only two devices is said to be *dedicated*. A path used to transfer information between different devices at different times is said to be (*time-*) *shared*. Sharing of communications paths is implemented by means of switching units such as the concentrator of Fig. 6.3. The shared buses of Fig. 6.1 should also be regarded as switching units. Such buses are best represented by explicit nodes of the system graph as is done in Fig. 6.1.

We now consider some common interconnection structures for computer systems. We will refer to the edges of the system graph as (communication)

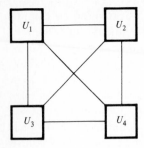

Figure 6.5 System of four units connected by dedicated links.

links. The nodes of the graph represent processor-level units such as computers, IO terminals, or switching units.

Dedicated links A conceptually simple way of connecting the components of a system is to provide dedicated links between all pairs of components that need to communicate with one another. In the most general case where n units must be connected in all possible ways, $n(n - 1)/2$ dedicated paths are needed. The interconnection structure is that of the complete graph of order n [14]. Figure 6.5 shows such a system when $n = 4$.

Dedicated links allow very fast transfer of information through the system. All n devices may send or receive information simultaneously, and there is no delay due to busy connections. Furthermore, systems with dedicated links are inherently reliable, since the failure of any link affects communication only between the two units connected to that link. Communication between these units may still be possible if they can send information to each other via other units of the system. For example, if the bus linking U_1 and U_4 in Fig. 6.5 fails, U_1 and U_4 may still be able to communicate via U_2 or U_3. The main disadvantage of dedicated paths is their high cost. The number of links needed increases approximately with the square of the number of units. Adding a new unit to the system is difficult, since the new unit must be physically connected to each of the existing units.

Shared links At the other end of the spectrum, a single path may be used for all communications among n devices, as illustrated in Fig. 6.6. At any time, only two units can communicate with each other via the shared link; the remaining units are effectively disconnected from one another. A control mechanism is required to supervise sharing of the link among the n devices. This control can be centralized in a special control unit (which may be one of the n units U_i, for

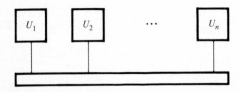

Figure 6.6 System connected by a common shared link.

example, a CPU), or several units may be capable of controlling the link (decentralized control).

In general, connection to the link can be established in two ways.

1. A unit U_i capable of acting as link controller initiates the connection of two units to the link, perhaps in response to an instruction in a program being executed by U_i.
2. A unit which is not itself a link controller sends a request to the link controller for access to the common link. The link controller then connects the requesting device to the link if it is not in use. If the link is busy, the requesting unit must wait until it becomes available. If several conflicting requests for access to the link are received simultaneously, the link controller uses some predetermined priority scheme to decide which request is granted first.

The shared communication link is perhaps the most widely used connection method in computer systems. Many computers, particularly smaller ones, are designed around a single shared bus, as in Fig. 6.1a. Other systems contain a small number of relatively independent shared buses, as in Fig. 6.1b. Figure 6.3 illustrates the use of a single shared link in long-distance communications. The main attraction of the shared link is its low cost. It is also very flexible in that new units can easily be added without altering the system structure or the connections to the old units. However, shared links are relatively slow, since units are forced to wait when the link is busy. A slow and perhaps complex process is needed to control access to the link. Finally, the system is sensitive to failure of the shared link, which can destroy all communication in the system.

Other interconnection structures A complete system of dedicated links and a single shared link represent extreme cases. Between these extremes lie various structures which involve some sharing of data paths but permit more than one data transfer at a time. A *crossbar* connection of the kind shown in Fig. 6.7 is typical. It is used to connect two groups of units $G_1 = \{U_1, U_2, \ldots, U_m\}$ and $G_2 = \{U_1', U_2', \ldots, U_n'\}$, so that any unit of G_1 can be connected to any unit of G_2, but two units in the same group need never be connected. This type of dichotomy exists in several places in computer systems. For example, G_1 could be a set of main-memory modules and G_2 a set of processors. Crossbar connections have also been used to connect IO processors to IO devices.

As shown in Fig. 6.7, each unit in G_1 (G_2) is connected to a horizontal (vertical) path. The horizontal and vertical paths are in turn connected via a switching network called a *crossbar switch*. This consists of $n \times m$ circuits called *switchpoints* which can logically connect any horizontal path to any vertical path. At any time, only one switchpoint can be activated in each row and column. If $k = \min\{m, n\}$, then any k distinct units in G_1 can be simultaneously connected to any k distinct units in G_2. Hence this crossbar connection allows up to k data transfers to take place simultaneously. Conflict and

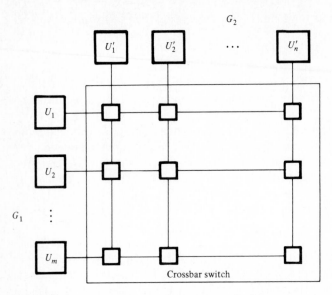

Figure 6.7 Crossbar connection of two groups of units.

delays occur only when two units in G_1 attempt to communicate with the same unit in G_2, or vice versa, at the same time.

Although the crossbar connection allows several simultaneous data transfers, there is only one path connecting each pair of communicating units. This is a common characteristic of local bus organizations, as a result of which most computers have interconnection structures which are *trees*, i. e., loop-free graphs. The structures of Figs. 6.1 and 6.3 are representative. Tree-structured systems are relatively easy to control, since no decision must be made about the routes used for data transfer. They are, however, vulnerable to failures in communication paths, because alternate paths do not exist. Long-distance communication networks often contain many alternative paths, so the overall reliability of the system is increased.

Figure 6.8 shows a basic organization called a *ring* or *mesh network* that is used in long-distance (and occasionally in local) communication. The main communication path is a closed loop to which units $\{U_i\}$ are connected via special interface switching units. It provides two distinct paths between every pair of users, so that the failure of any link in the main communication loop can be tolerated. Computer networks often take the form of a set of interconnected ring networks.

6.1.4 Bus Control

In this section we will examine the methods that are used to establish and control communication via local buses. There are two major difficulties in this type

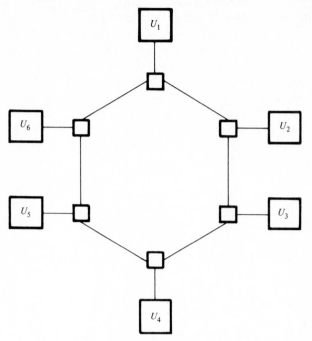

Figure 6.8 A ring-structured communication network.

of communication:

1. The timing of information transfers over the bus
2. The selection process by which a device gains access to the bus

For simplicity we will restrict our attention to the single shared bus organization of Fig. 6.6. We will also assume that one particular unit acts as the bus-control unit and supervises the selection of devices to be connected to the bus. In many computer systems, the CPU is also the bus-control unit. Systems with decentralized control, i. e., in which several devices can act as bus controller, are similar [33].

The timing of information transfers through the bus system is quite significant. We distinguish two cases, synchronous and asynchronous communication. *Synchronous communication* implies that each item of information is transferred across the bus during a time period (or time slot) which is known in advance by both the source and the destination units. This implies that the timing mechanisms of both units are synchronized. Synchronization can be achieved by driving each unit from a common clock source, a method that is feasible over short distances. Alternatively, each unit may be driven by a separate clock of approximately the same frequency. Synchronization signals must then be transmitted periodically between the communicating devices in order to keep their clocks in step with each other.

Synchronous communication has the disadvantage that the time slots used for information transfer are largely determined by the slowest units in the system. Thus fast devices may not be able to communicate at their maximum rate. An alternative approach widely used in local bus communications is *asynchronous communication*, in which each item being transferred is accompanied by a separate control signal to indicate its presence to the destination unit. The destination unit may respond with another control signal to acknowledge receipt of the information. Because each device can generate these control signals at its own rate, data-transmission rates can vary with the inherent speed of the communicating devices. This flexibility in transmission rates is achieved at the cost of more complex bus-control circuitry.

A device can be selected for connection to the main bus in two ways. The bus-control unit may initiate the selection of device U in response to an instruction in a program or a condition occurring in the system that requires the services of U. Alternatively, U itself may request access to the shared bus by sending an appropriate signal to the bus controller. In each case, specific actions must be performed by the bus-control unit in order to establish the logical connection between U and the bus. If several units can generate requests for bus access simultaneously, the bus controller must have a method for selecting the unit with the highest priority.

The lines that constitute a communication bus can usually be divided into three functional groups:

1. Data lines
2. Address lines
3. Control lines

The data lines are designed to transmit all bits of an n-bit word in parallel; they therefore consist of either two sets of n unidirectional lines or a single set of n bidirectional lines. Address lines are used to identify a unit or part of a unit to be used in a data transfer and therefore to be connected to the bus. It is possible to use the data lines for transferring addresses as well as data. This may be done to decrease the cost of the bus; or to decrease the number of external connections (pins) of the units served by the bus. Memory buses usually contain separate address lines, but IO buses usually do not (see Fig. 6.1*b*). This is because every word transfer to main memory must be accompanied by an address, whereas data transfers via an IO bus are usually in long blocks of words, which require only the address of the start of the block. Finally, the control lines are used to transfer timing signals and status information about the units in the system. They may also be used to indicate the type of information present on the data lines.

Example 6.1: The DEC PDP-11 system bus [11] The PDP-11 computer contains a single shared bus called the UNIBUS to which the CPU, main memory, and all IO devices are connected as in Fig. 6.1*a*. The UNIBUS contains 56 mostly bidirectional lines including 16 data lines, 18 address

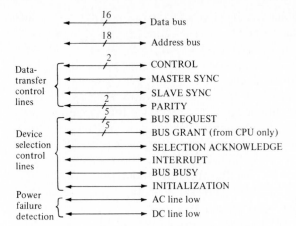

Figure 6.9 The lines of the PDP-11 system bus (UNIBUS).

lines, and 22 control lines. At any time only two devices may communicate with each other via the UNIBUS. One of these devices called the *master* acts as the bus controller; the other device is called the *slave*. The master-slave relationship is dynamic. For example, the CPU acts as master and the main memory as slave during the normal fetching and execution of instructions by the CPU. During an IO operation between, say, a disk unit and main memory, the CPU can transfer control of the bus to the disk unit which then becomes the master. Requests for control of the bus are handled by the CPU which assigns control to requesting devices based on their priority.

Figure 6.9 lists the names of the 56 lines that make up the UNIBUS. The control lines contain two major groups: lines for device selection and lines for data-transfer control. All communication via the UNIBUS is asynchronous and is completely interlocked by handshaking control signals.

Figure 6.10 shows the exchange of signals that accompanies the transfer of a data word from a slave to a master, e. g., a memory read operation. First the master places the slave's address on the address bus and

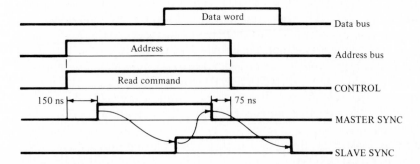

Figure 6.10 Timing diagram for data transfer from slave to master unit via the PDP-11 UNIBUS.

places signals on the two lines called CONTROL to indicate that a data transfer from slave to master is required. The signals on these lines can be viewed as forming a read or write command. All potential slave units connected to the UNIBUS then attempt to decode the contents of the address bus. After a delay of 150 ns to allow for worst-case signal propagation delays and address decoding time, the master activates MASTER SYNC to signal that data transfer should begin. On receiving this signal the slave proceeds to fetch the data to be transferred. (If the slave is main memory, a memory read cycle is performed.) The slave then places the data on the data bus and activates SLAVE SYNC. After it receives the SLAVE SYNC signal, the master copies the data from the data bus and deactivates MASTER SYNC. It then waits for at least 75 ns and clears the address and CONTROL lines. The slave responds to the deactivation of MASTER SYNC by clearing the data bus and deactivating SLAVE SYNC. This completes the data transfer and frees the UNIBUS.

An IO device may request control of the UNIBUS via the BUS REQUEST lines. There are generally two situations where this occurs.

1. The IO device wishes to transfer data to or from main memory.
2. The IO device wishes to send an interrupt command to the CPU causing the latter to begin execution of an interrupt routine (usually to service the requesting IO device).

Each IO device that is capable of being a master is connected to one of the five BUS REQUEST lines and one of the five BUS GRANT lines. Each BUS REQUEST line has a predetermined priority. If two units request bus control at the same time, the CPU gives control to the one with the higher priority.

Figure 6.11 is a timing diagram for the signals associated with the transfer of bus control from one unit to another on the UNIBUS. It is assumed that control is granted to the device that activates BUS REQUEST line *i*. The CPU acknowledges this request by activating the corresponding BUS GRANT line. When the requesting device receives the BUS GRANT signal, it responds by deactivating BUS REQUEST and activating SELECTION ACKNOWLEDGE. The CPU responds by deactivating BUS GRANT. When any ongoing data transfers are completed, the selected unit takes control of the UNIBUS by activating BUS BUSY. The selected unit is now master and can initiate data transfers via the UNIBUS in the manner previously described. It can also initiate an interrupt sequence by activating the INTERRUPT control line, which returns control to the CPU. The device relinquishes control of the UNIBUS after a data transfer by deactivating the BUS BUSY and SELECTION ACKNOWLEDGE lines, as shown in Fig. 6.11. If another unit has been selected as master by the CPU, it may now take control by activating SELECTION ACKNOWLEDGE. In this way control of the UNIBUS

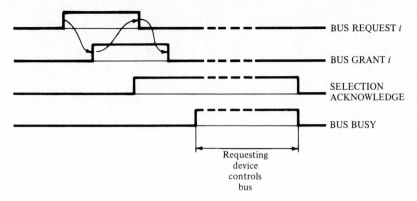

BUS REQUEST *i*

BUS GRANT *i*

SELECTION
ACKNOWLEDGE

BUS BUSY

Requesting
device
controls
bus

Figure 6.11 Timing diagram for a transfer of bus control in the PDP-11.

can be transferred from unit to unit. Note that only the CPU can activate the BUS GRANT lines. The CPU therefore retains ultimate control of the UNIBUS, since only the CPU can determine which device is master.

Priority Control An important function of any bus-control unit is to select the unit with the highest priority when several units request access to the bus at the same time. Following Thurber et al. [33], we distinguish three methods for establishing selection priority;

1. Daisy-chaining
2. Polling
3. Independent requesting

These methods differ in the number of control lines they require and in the speed with which the bus control unit can select devices with different priorities. Some bus systems such as the UNIBUS combine several distinct methods.

Daisy-chaining The *daisy-chaining* method of priority selection is depicted in Fig. 6.12. Three control signals are involved in the selection process to which we assign the generic names BUS REQUEST, BUS GRANT, and BUS BUSY. (These lines are assigned essentially the same meaning that they have in the PDP-11 UNIBUS.) All the devices are connected to a single BUS REQUEST line. When activated it merely serves to indicate that one or more units request connection to the bus. Once connected to the bus, a unit activates BUS BUSY for the duration of its bus transactions. The bus-control unit responds to a BUS REQUEST signal only if BUS BUSY is inactive. This response takes the form of a signal placed on the BUS GRANT line.

The main distinguishing feature of the daisy-chaining technique is the manner in which the BUS GRANT signal is distributed. The BUS GRANT line is not connected directly to each unit, but serially from unit to unit. When

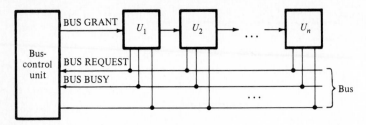

Figure 6.12 Bus control using daisy-chaining.

the first unit that is requesting access to the bus receives the **BUS GRANT** signal, it blocks further propagation of that signal, activates **BUS BUSY**, and begins to use the bus. When a nonrequesting unit receives the **BUS GRANT** signal, it forwards it to the next unit. Thus if two units are requesting bus access, the one closest to the bus-control unit, i. e., the one that receives the **BUS GRANT** signal first, gains control of the bus. Selection priority is therefore completely determined by the order in which the units are linked together (chained) by the **BUS GRANT** lines.

Daisy-chaining requires very few control lines and uses a very simple selection algorithm. It can be used with an essentially unlimited number of devices. Since priority is wired in, the priority of each device cannot be changed under program control. If it generates bus requests at a sufficiently high rate, a high priority device like U_1 can lock out a low priority device like U_n. A further difficulty with daisy-chaining is its susceptibility to failures involving the **BUS GRANT** line and its associated circuitry. If unit U_i is unable to propagate the **BUS GRANT** signal, then all $\{U_j\}$ where $j > i$ cannot gain access to the bus.

Polling In a bus-control system that uses polling, the **BUS GRANT** line of the daisy-chain method is replaced by a set of lines called *poll count* lines which are connected directly to all units on the bus, as depicted in Fig. 6.13. As before, the units request access to the bus via a common **BUS REQUEST** line. In re-

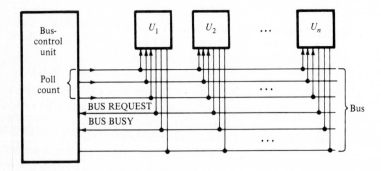

Figure 6.13 Bus control using polling.

sponse to a signal on **BUS REQUEST**, the bus controller proceeds to generate a sequence of numbers on the poll count lines. These numbers, which may be thought of as unit addresses, are compared by each unit with a unique address permanently assigned to that unit. When a requesting unit U_i finds that its address matches the number on the poll count lines, it activates **BUS BUSY**. The bus controller responds by terminating the polling process, and U_i gains control of the bus.

Clearly, the priority of a unit is determined by the position of its address in the polling sequence. The polling sequence is normally programmable (the poll count lines are connected to a programmable register); hence selection priority can be altered under program control. A further advantage of polling over daisy-chaining is that a failure in one unit need not affect any of the other units. This flexibility is achieved at the cost of more control lines (k poll count lines instead of one **BUS GRANT** line). Also, the number of units that can share the bus is limited by the addressing capability of the poll count lines.

Independent requesting The third priority selection method uses separate **BUS REQUEST** and **BUS GRANT** lines for each unit sharing the bus. This approach, which is depicted in Fig. 6.14, provides the bus-control unit with immediate identification of all requesting units and enables it to respond very rapidly to requests for bus access. Priority is determined by the bus-control unit and may be programmable. The main drawback of bus control by independent requesting is the fact that $2n$ **BUS REQUEST** and **BUS GRANT** lines must be connected to the bus-control unit in order to control n devices. In contrast, daisy-chaining requires two such lines, while polling requires approximately $\log_2 n$ lines.

The PDP-11 UNIBUS system introduced earlier combines the independent requesting and daisy-chaining approaches. There are five **BUS REQUEST** lines in the UNIBUS, each of which is assigned to a fixed priority

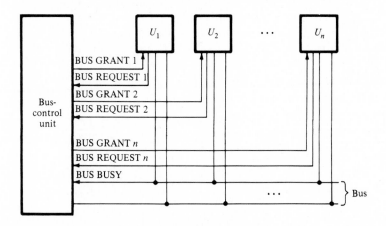

Figure 6.14 Bus control using independent requesting.

level. A distinct **BUS GRANT** line is associated with each **BUS REQUEST** line. If there are five or fewer units (excluding the **CPU**, which is the bus controller) connected to the **UNIBUS**, each may thus use the independent requesting method. If several units are connected to the same **BUS REQUEST** line, then the corresponding **BUS GRANT** line is connected in daisy-chain fashion to those units. Thus daisy-chaining determines the priority of devices connected to the same **BUS REQUEST** line. The PDP-11 CPU also has a priority level for access to the **UNIBUS**. The CPU priority is stored in a CPU status word and is under program control.

Timing signals A typical bus is shared by many devices with different data transmission speeds; hence asynchronous communication is usually employed. This requires that control signals be transmitted between the communicating devices to indicate the times at which data is being transmitted. Following Ref. 33, we distinguish two cases:

1. *One-way control,* in which timing signals are supplied by one of the two communicating devices
2. *Two-way,* or *interlocked, control,* in which both devices generate timing signals

If one-way control is employed, a single control line is used to time each data transfer. This control line may be activated by either the source or destination device. Figure 6.15a shows a source-initiated transfer. The source unit places the data word on the data lines. After a brief delay it then activates the control line to which we have assigned the generic name DATA READY. (The delay is necessary to prevent the DATA READY signal from reaching the destination before the data word.) Both the data lines and the DATA READY control line must be held in the active state for a sufficiently long period to allow the destination device to copy the data from the data bus. Figure 6.15b shows a data transfer initiated by the destination device. In this case the destination device initiates the data transfer by activating the control line called DATA REQUEST. The source device responds by placing the required word on the data lines. It must remain there long enough for the destination device to read it.

Often the DATA READY/REQUEST signals are used to gate the data from the source unit to the data bus. Such control signals are called *strobe* sig-

Figure 6.15 One-way data transfer timing: (*a*) source-initiated; (*b*) destination-initiated.

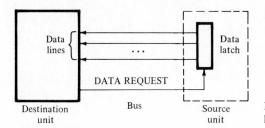

Figure 6.16 Use of a DATA REQUEST line to strobe data.

nals and are said to strobe the data onto the bus. For example, the source device, e. g., a keyboard, may generate a data word asynchronously and place it in a latch connected to the bus data lines. A signal on the DATA REQUEST line can be used to activate the clock input line of the latch and thereby strobe the data onto the bus. Figure 6.16 illustrates this.

The disadvantage of one-way control is that no verification is provided that the data transfer has been completed. For example, in a source-initiated transfer, the source unit receives no indication that the destination unit has actually received the data transmitted to it. If the destination unit is unexpectedly slow in responding to a DATA READY signal, the data may be lost. This problem can be eliminated by introducing a second control line that allows the destination unit to send a reply signal to the source when it receives a DATA READY signal. This control line is given the generic name DATA ACKNOWLEDGE. Figure 6.17*a* shows the exchange of signals often called handshaking that accompanies a source-controlled transfer in this case. The source device maintains the data on the bus until it receives the DATA ACKNOWLEDGE signal. DATA ACKNOWLEDGE is not activated by the

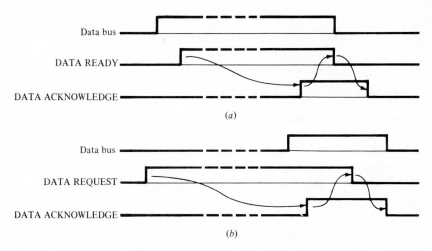

Figure 6.17 A synchronous data transmission using two-way control (handshaking): (*a*) source-initiated; (*b*) destination-initiated.

destination device until after it has copied the data from the bus. This scheme allows delays of arbitrary length to occur during the data transfer.

A similar technique depicted in Fig. 6.17b is used for destination-initiated transfers. The source unit activates DATA ACKNOWLEDGE to indicate that the requested data is available on the bus. It maintains the data on the bus until the destination unit deactivates DATA REQUEST, an action that serves to verify receipt of the data by the destination unit. In the case of the destination-controlled data transfer over the PDP-11 UNIBUS shown in Fig. 6.10, the control lines called MASTER SYNC and SLAVE SYNC are assigned the roles of DATA REQUEST and DATA ACKNOWLEDGE, respectively.

6.2 INPUT-OUTPUT SYSTEMS

The main computing function of a computer involves only two of its components, the CPU and main memory. The CPU fetches instructions and data from main memory, processes them, and stores results in main memory. The other components of the computer may be loosely called the input-output (IO) system, since their purpose is to transfer information between main memory or the CPU and the outside world. The IO system includes IO devices (peripherals), control units for these devices, and the software designed specifically for IO operations.

IO systems may be distinguished by the extent to which the CPU is involved in the execution of IO operations. Unless otherwise stated, IO operation will mean a data transfer between an IO device and main memory, or between an IO device and the CPU. If IO operations are completely controlled by the CPU, i.e., the CPU executes programs that initiate, direct, and terminate the IO operations, the computer is said to be using *programmed IO*. Programmed IO is an option in almost all computers. It can be implemented with very little special IO hardware, but can result in the CPU spending a great deal of time performing relatively trivial IO control functions. One such function is testing the status of IO devices to determine if they require servicing by the CPU.

With a fairly modest increase in hardware complexity the IO device can be provided with the ability to transfer a block of information to or from main memory without CPU intervention. This requires that the IO device (or its controller) be capable of generating memory addresses and transferring data to or from the main-memory bus. It must also be provided with a bus request and selection mechanism of the type discussed in Sec. 6.1.3. The CPU is still responsible for initiating each block transfer. The IO device can then carry out the transfer without further program execution by the CPU. The CPU and IO device interact only when the CPU must yield control of the memory bus to the IO device in response to requests from the latter. This type of IO capability is called *direct memory access* (DMA).

The IO device can also be provided with circuits enabling it to request service from the CPU, i.e., execution of a specific program to service the IO device. This type of request is called an *interrupt*. An interrupt capability frees the CPU from the task of periodically testing IO device status. Unlike a DMA request, an interrupt causes the CPU to switch programs by saving its previous program state and transferring control to a new interrupt-handling program. When the interrupt has been serviced, the CPU can resume execution of the interrupted program. Most computers nowadays have DMA and interrupt facilities, which may require that the CPU be augmented by special DMA control and interrupt control units.

A DMA facility yields partial control of IO operations to the IO system. Essentially complete control of IO operations can be relinquished by the CPU if a special unit, called an *IO processor* (IOP) or *channel*, is introduced. An IOP has direct access to main memory; it can interrupt the CPU, but it can also execute programs directly. These programs, called IO programs, may employ an instruction set different from that of the CPU—one which is oriented toward IO operations. It is not uncommon for large systems to use small computers as IOPs. An IOP can perform several independent data transfers between main memory and one or more IO devices, without recourse to the CPU. Usually an IOP is connected to the devices it controls by a separate bus system, called the IO bus or IO interface, as illustrated in Fig. 6.1*b*.

6.2.1 Programmed IO

First we examine programmed IO, a method for controlling IO operations, which is included in most computers. It requires that all IO operations be executed under the direct control of the CPU, i.e., every data-transfer operation involving an IO device requires the execution of an instruction by the CPU. Typically the transfer is between a CPU register (e.g., the main CPU accumulator) and a buffer register connected to the IO device. The IO device does not have direct access to main memory. A data transfer from an IO device to main memory requires the execution of two instructions by the CPU: an INPUT instruction to transfer a word from the IO device to the CPU and a STORE instruction to transfer the word from the CPU to main memory.

IO addressing In systems with programmed IO, IO devices, main memory, and the CPU communicate via a common shared bus. The address lines of that bus which are used to select main-memory locations can also be used to select IO devices. Each junction between the main bus and the IO device is called an *IO port* and is assigned a unique address. The IO port may include a data buffer register, thus making it little different from a main-memory location with respect to the CPU.

A strategy used in some machines such as the Motorola M6800 microprocessor [29] is to assign part of the main-memory address space to IO ports. This is called *memory-mapped* IO. A memory reference instruction that causes data to be fetched from or stored at address X becomes an IO instruction if X is made the address of an IO port. The usual memory FETCH and STORE instructions can be used to transfer a word of data to or from an IO port; no

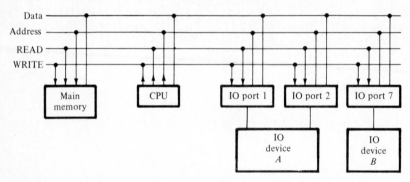

Figure 6.18 Programmed IO with shared memory and IO address space (memory-mapped IO).

special IO instructions are needed. Figure 6.18 shows the essential structure of a computer with this kind of IO programming. The control lines READ and WRITE, which are activated by the CPU on decoding a memory reference instruction, are used to initiate either a memory access cycle or an IO transfer.

In the organization shown in Fig. 6.19, the memory and IO address spaces are kept separate. A memory reference instruction activates the READ M or WRITE M control line and does not affect the IO devices. Separate IO instructions are required to activate the READ IO and WRITE IO lines which cause a word to be transferred between the addressed IO port and the CPU. An IO device and a main-memory location may have the same address. This scheme is used, for example, in the Intel 8080 microprocessor [19]. A minor modification of the circuit of Fig. 6.19 can combine the memory and IO address spaces if desired. All that is necessary is to disconnect the READ IO and WRITE IO lines from the CPU and reconnect them to the READ M and WRITE M outputs of the CPU.

Basic IO instructions Programmed IO can be implemented by as few as two IO instructions. For example, the Intel 8080 microprocessor [19] has only two explicit IO instructions. The instruction IN X causes a word to be transferred from IO port X to the 8080 accumulator. The instruction OUT X transfers a

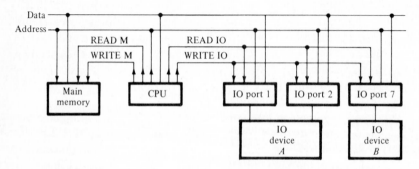

Figure 6.19 Programmed IO with separate memory and IO address spaces.

word from the accumulator to IO port X. The CPU assigns no meaning to the words transferred to IO devices. The programmer may assign special meanings to them, however. Some words may indicate IO device status and others may be special instructions to the IO device.

When an IO instruction such as IN or OUT is encountered by the CPU, the addressed IO port is expected to be ready to respond to the instruction. If handshaking is not used, i.e., the IO device does not generate an acknowledgement signal, the IO device must transfer data to or from the data bus within a specified period. To prevent loss of information or an indefinitely long IO instruction execution time, it is thus desirable that the CPU know the IO device status, so that a data transfer is carried out when the device is in a known ready state. In programmed IO systems the CPU is usually programmed to test the IO device status before initiating a data transfer. Often the status can be specified by a single bit of information that the IO device can make available on a continuous basis, e. g., by setting a flip-flop connected to the data lines at some IO port.

The determination of IO device status by the CPU requires the following steps.

Step 1: Read the status information.
Step 2: Test the status to determine if the device is ready to begin data transfer.
Step 3: If not ready, return to step 1; otherwise proceed with the data transfer.

Figure 6.20 shows a program written for the Intel 8080 microprocessor that transfers a word of data from an IO device to the CPU accumulator. It is assumed that the device is connected to ports 1 and 2 like device *A* in Fig. 6.18. The IO device status is assumed to be continuously available at port 1, while the required data is available at port 2 when the status word has the value READY.

Additional IO instructions If programmed IO is the primary method of controlling IO devices in a computer, additional IO instructions may be provided to augment the simple IN and OUT instructions discussed so far. For example, the IO instruction format of the PDP-8 shown in Fig. 3.16*c* allows eight dis-

Instruction	Comment
WAIT: IN 1	Read IO device status into accumulator
CPI READY	Compare immediate word READY to accumulator: if equal, set flag $Z = 1$, otherwise set $Z = 0$
JNZ WAIT	If $Z \neq 1$ (IO device not ready) jump to WAIT
IN 2	Read data word into accumulator

Figure 6.20 Intel 8080 program to read one word from an IO device.

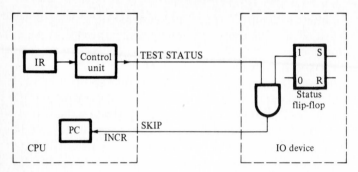

Figure 6.21 Implementation of the test status and skip (TSK) IO instruction.

tinct IO operations to be specified. The meaning attached to the three IO operation bits is determined by the circuitry connected to the IO port addressed by the instruction. IO instructions may be used to start, stop, or otherwise control the behavior of an IO device.

A useful IO instruction is one which tests the status of the IO device and modifies the CPU program counter based on the test outcome. For example, the PDP-8 is commonly used with an IO instruction TSK, meaning test IO device status flag and skip the next instruction if the status flag is set. This can be implemented by two control lines between the CPU and the IO device, as shown in Fig. 6.21. On decoding TSK, a signal called TEST STATUS is sent by the CPU to the IO device. If the device status flag is set, a return pulse is sent on the SKIP line which is used to increment the program counter, thereby skipping the next instruction. Given an instruction of this type, the IO program of Fig. 6.20 could be simplified as follows:

$$\text{WAIT: TSK} \quad 1$$
$$\text{JMP} \quad \text{WAIT}$$
$$\text{IN} \quad 2$$

A common IO programming task is the transfer of a block of words between an IO device and a contiguous region of main memory. Figure 6.22 shows an input block-transfer program written in Intel 8080 assembly language. (It is assumed that the input device generates data at the rate required by the 8080, so that no status testing is needed.) The Zilog Z80, a microprocessor announced in 1976 [34] that is software compatible with the 8080, provides a single instruction INIR (*i*nput, *i*ndex, and *r*epeat) which performs essentially all the functions specified by the last five instructions in Fig. 6.22. Specifically, INIR inputs a word from the IO port addressed by the C register and transfers it to the memory location addressed by the HL register. It then increments HL, decrements B (which is used as a word count register) and repeats the transfer, increment and decrement steps until B = 0. Thus, ignoring differences between 8080 and Z80 instruction names, the 8080/Z80

Instruction			Comments
	LXI	H, 10	Load memory address register HL with 10
	MVI	B, 100	Load (move immediate) register B with 100
LOOP:	IN	7	Read word from input port 7 into accumulator A
	MOV	M, A	Store contents of A in memory location M(HL)
	INX	H	Increment memory address register HL
	DCR	B	Decrement register B (used as a byte counter)
	JNZ	LOOP	If B $\neq$ 0, jump to LOOP

Figure 6.22 An 8080 assembly language program to input a block of data.

program of Fig. 6.22 is equivalent to the following Z80 program:

LXI   H, 10
MVI   B, 100
MVI   C, 7
INIR

It is interesting to compare these instructions to the INPUT and OUTPUT instructions of the IAS computer described in Sec. 1.3.3.

IO interface circuits The connection of IO devices to a computer system is greatly facilitated by the use of standard circuit packages variously known as IO interface circuits, IO ports, interface adapters, etc. These circuits allow devices of widely different characteristics to be connected to a common bus with a minimum of special-purpose hardware. The simplest interface circuit is a one-word buffer register that acts as a "mailbox" during IO operations. It is assigned a unique address and is accessed in essentially the same way as a main-memory location. This circuit is particularly useful for parallel (word by word) IO communication. Another useful class of interface circuits called UARTs (*u*niversal *a*synchronous *r*eceiver-*t*ransmitters) allow easy connection to the computer of IO devices that employ serial (bit-by-bit) communication, for example, a CRT terminal or a telephone line. A UART is basically a shift register that transforms serial data streams into parallel data streams, and vice versa.

The advent of microprocessors has greatly stimulated the design of powerful general-purpose interface circuits. Some of them are termed programmable, because they can be modified under program control to match the characteristics of many different IO devices. A description of a representative circuit of this type follows.

Example 6.2: The Intel 8255 programmable peripheral interface circuit [19] This circuit whose general structure is shown in Fig. 6.23 is designed for interfacing IO devices with the Intel 8080 microprocessor. It is fabricated as a single integrated circuit in a 40-pin package: 8 pins serve to

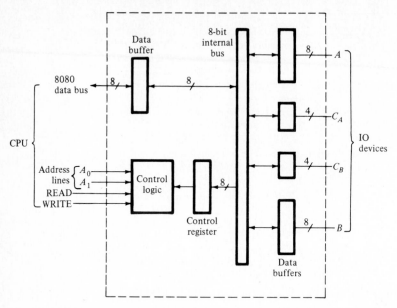

Figure 6.23 The Intel 8255 programmable peripheral interface circuit.

connect the 8255 to the 8-bit bidirectional data bus of the 8080; 24 IO pins can be connected to one or more IO devices. These IO pins are programmable in that the functions they perform are determined by a control word issued by the 8080 and stored internally in the 8255. This control word can be used to specify a variety of operating modes.

The 24 IO pins of the 8255 are divided into 8-bit groups designated A, B, and C, each of which may be treated as an independent IO port. The C lines are further subdivided into two 4-bit groups C_A and C_B. They are commonly used as control lines, e.g., status lines, in conjunction with the A and B IO ports. Two address lines A_0 and A_1 are used to select one of the three ports A, B, and C for use in an IO operation. The fourth address combination is used in conjunction with an output instruction OUT CW to store an 8-bit user-specified control word CW in the internal control register of the 8255. This control word has two major functions:

1. It is used to specify whether the A, B, and C ports are to be used as input, output, or (in the case of A and B only) as bidirectional IO ports.
2. It is used to program certain C lines to generate handshaking and interrupt signals automatically in response to actions by an IO device.

Figure 6.24 shows two of the many possible configurations in which the A, B, and C lines are programmed as simple IO ports with no handshaking or interrupt capability. Figure 6.25 shows a configuration in which the A port is programmed to be an input port with timing signals

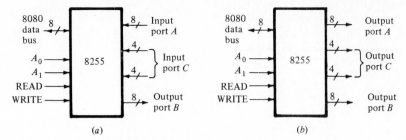

Figure 6.24 Two possible configurations of the Intel 8255 programmable peripheral interface circuit.

generated by the C lines. The line called DATA READY is used by the IO device to strobe a word into the buffer register at port A. The 8255 then automatically generates a response signal on another C line which can be sent to the IO device as a DATA ACKNOWLEDGE signal if two-way control is required by the IO device. A third C line generates an interrupt signal which can be sent to the 8080 to indicate the presence of data at IO port A.

6.2.2 DMA and Interrupts

The programmed IO method discussed in the preceding section has two drawbacks.

1. IO transfer rates are limited by the speed with which the CPU can test and service an IO device.
2. The time that the CPU spends testing IO device status and executing IO data transfers can often be better spent on other processing tasks.

The influence of the CPU on IO transfer rates is twofold. First, a delay may occur while an IO device that requires service waits to be tested by the CPU. If there are many IO devices in the system, each device may be tested relatively infrequently. Second, programmed IO transmits data through the

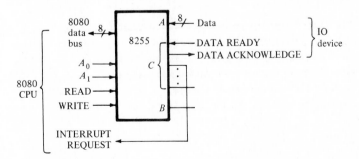

Figure 6.25 Configuration of the Intel 8255 to generate handshaking signals and interrupt requests.

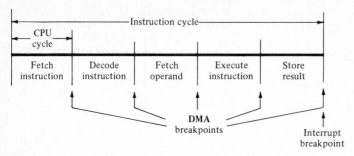

Figure 6.26 DMA and interrupt breakpoints during an instruction cycle.

CPU rather than allowing it to be passed directly from main memory to the IO device, and vice versa.

DMA and interrupt circuits are used to increase the speed of IO operations and eliminate most of the role played by the CPU in such operations. In each case special control lines to which we assign the generic names DMA REQUEST and INTERRUPT REQUEST go from the IO devices to the CPU. Signals on these lines cause the CPU to suspend its current activities at an appropriate breakpoint and attend to the DMA or interrupt request. Thus the need for the CPU to execute routines that determine IO device status is eliminated. DMA further allows IO data transfers to take place without the execution of IO instructions by the CPU.

A DMA request by an IO device requires the CPU only to yield control of the main-memory bus to the requesting device. The CPU can yield control at the end of any transactions involving use of this bus. Figure 6.26 shows a typical sequence of CPU actions during an instruction cycle. The instruction cycle is divided into a number of CPU (or machine) cycles, several of which require use of the main-memory bus. A common technique is to allow the machine to respond to a DMA request at the end of any CPU cycle. Thus during the instruction cycle of Fig. 6.26, there are five points in time (breakpoints) when the CPU can respond to a DMA request. When such a request is received by the CPU, it waits until the next breakpoint, releases control of the memory bus, and signals the requesting IO device by activating a DMA ACKNOWLEDGE control line.

Interrupts are requested and acknowledged in much the same way as DMA requests. However, an interrupt is not a request for bus control; rather, it asks the CPU to begin executing a program called an interrupt program. The interrupt program may perform a variety of tasks, such as initiating an IO data transfer, responding to an error encountered by the IO device, etc. The CPU transfers control to this program in essentially the same way it transfers control to a subroutine. The CPU responds to interrupts only between instruction cycles, as indicated in Fig. 6.26.

Direct memory access (DMA) The essential elements of a DMA system are shown in Fig. 6.27. The IO device interface contains a data buffer register

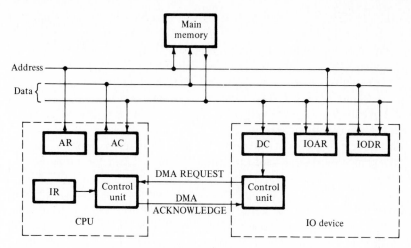

Figure 6.27 Circuitry required for direct memory access (DMA).

IODR as in the programmed IO case; but in addition there is an address register IOAR and a data count register DC. These registers allow the IO device to
transfer data to or from a contiguous region of main memory. IOAR is used to
store the address of the next word to be transferred. It is automatically
incremented after each word transfer. The data count register DC stores the
number of words that remain to be transferred. It is automatically decremented
after each transfer and tested for zero. When it reaches zero, the IO device
halts. The IO device is normally provided with an interrupt capability, in which
case it sends an interrupt to the CPU to signal the end of the data transfer.
The logic necessary to control DMA can easily be placed in a single integrated circuit. ICs called *DMA control units* are available that can supervise
DMA transfers involving several IO devices, each with a different priority of
access to the memory bus.

An IO device with DMA capability can transfer a long block of words in
one continuous operation; this is called *DMA block transfer*. Alternatively,
the IO device may transfer only one or two words before returning control of
the memory bus to the CPU; this is called *cycle stealing*. The cycles used for
DMA transfers can be interleaved with CPU cycles in an arbitrary way.
Since not all CPU cycles require use of the memory bus, the CPU may be
able to continue instruction execution after it relinquishes control of the memory bus to an IO device. Thus some overlap of CPU operations and DMA
transfers is possible.

DMA transfers proceed as follows for the system depicted in Fig. 6.27.

1. The CPU executes two IO instructions which load the IO device registers
   IOAR and DC with their initial values. IOAR should contain the base
   address of the main-memory region to be used in the data transfer. DC
   should contain the number of words to be transferred to or from that
   region.

2. When the IO device is ready to transmit or receive data, it activates the DMA REQUEST line to the CPU. The CPU waits for the next DMA breakpoint. It then relinquishes control of the memory data and address buses and activates DMA ACKNOWLEDGE. Note that DMA REQUEST and DMA ACKNOWLEDGE are essentially BUS REQUEST and BUS GRANT lines for the memory bus. Simultaneous DMA requests can be resolved by using one of the bus priority control techniques discussed earlier.
3. The IO device now transfers data directly to or from main memory. After a word is transferred, IOAR and DC are incremented and decremented, respectively.
4. If DC is not decremented to zero but the IO device is not ready to send or receive the next batch of data, it returns control to the CPU by releasing the memory buses and deactivating the DMA REQUEST line. The CPU responds by deactivating DMA ACKNOWLEDGE and resuming normal operation.
5. If DC is decremented to zero, the IO device again relinquishes control of the memory bus. It may also send an interrupt signal to the CPU. The CPU responds by halting the IO device or by initiating a new DMA transfer.

Interrupts The term interrupt is used in a loose sense for any infrequent or unexpected event that causes a CPU to make a temporary transfer of control from its current program to another program that services the interrupt. Interrupts may be generated by a variety of sources internal and external to the CPU. Interrupts are the primary means by which IO devices can obtain the services of the CPU. They greatly increase the performance of the computer by allowing the IO devices direct and rapid access to the CPU and by freeing the CPU from the task of continually testing the status of its IO devices. Interrupts are used primarily to request the CPU to initiate a new IO operation, to signal the completion of an IO operation, and to signal the occurrence of hardware or software errors affecting the IO system.

The basic method of interrupting the CPU is by activating an INTERRUPT REQUEST control line that connects the interrupting device to the CPU. The interrupt signal is then stored in a CPU register which is tested periodically by the CPU, usually at the end of every instruction cycle. On recognizing the presence of the interrupt, the CPU must execute a specific interrupt servicing program. Normally each interrupt source will require execution of a different program; the CPU must therefore determine or be given the address in main memory of the specific interrupt program to be used. A further problem is caused by the presence of two or more interrupt requests at the same time. Priorities must be assigned to the interrupts and the interrupt with the highest priority selected for service.

The CPU responds to an interrupt request by a transfer of control to another program in a manner similar to a subroutine call. The following specific steps are taken.

1. The CPU identifies the source of the interrupt. This may require polling the IO devices.
2. The CPU obtains the memory address of the required interrupt servicing program. This address may be provided by the interrupting device along with its interrupt request.
3. The program counter and other CPU status information are saved as in a subroutine call.
4. The program counter is loaded with the address of the interrupt servicing program. Execution proceeds until a RETURN instruction is encountered which transfers control back to the interrupted program.

Instructions are usually included in the CPU instruction set for *disabling* or *masking* interrupt requests. Such instructions allow a programmer to effectively disconnect some or all of the interrupt request lines causing the CPU to ignore certain interrupts. Without such control, an IO device that can generate interrupts rapidly might require too much of the CPU's time and interfere with the CPU's other tasks. When a high-priority interrupt is being serviced, it is desirable that all interrupts of lower priority be disabled. An interrupt enable instruction must subsequently be executed to give the lower-priority interrupts access to the CPU.

Interrupt selection The problem of selecting one IO device to service from several that have generated interrupts bears a strong resemblance to the selection process for bus control discussed in Sec. 6.1.3. Indeed, some interrupt methods require that the interrupting device be given control of the system bus. The various methods used for establishing bus-control priority, daisy-chaining, polling, and independent requesting can all be readily adapted to interrupt processing. These techniques can be implemented by software, hardware, or a combination of both.

The interrupt selection method requiring the least hardware is the *single-line* method illustrated in Fig. 6.28. A single INTERRUPT REQUEST line is shared by all IO ports. On responding to an interrupt, the CPU must scan all the IO devices to determine the source of the interrupt. This may be done by activating an INTERRUPT ACKNOWLEDGE line (corresponding to BUS

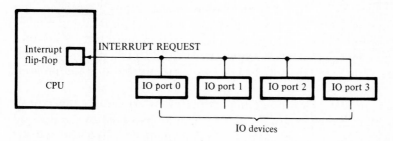

Figure 6.28 Single-line interrupt system.

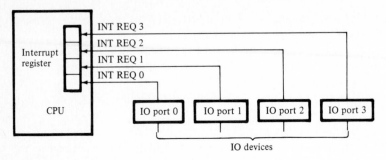

Figure 6.29 Multiple-line interrupt system.

GRANT) connected in daisy-chain fashion to all IO devices. The connection sequence of this line then determines the interrupt priority of each device. Alternatively, the CPU can execute a program that scans each IO device in turn requesting interrupt status information. This approach is often used in single-line interrupt schemes, since it allows interrupt priority to be programmed.

Figure 6.29 depicts another widely used method called *multiple-line* or *multilevel* interrupts, which corresponds to independent requesting of interrupts. Each interrupt request line may be assigned a unique priority. The source of the interrupt is immediately known to the CPU, thus eliminating the need for a hardware or software scan of the IO ports. Unless further measures are taken, the CPU must still execute a program that fetches the address of the service program to be used from the interrupting device. This step can be eliminated by a technique called vectoring of interrupts.

Vectored interrupts The fastest response to interrupts is obtained when an interrupt request from a particular device causes a direct hardware-implemented transition to the correct interrupt-handling program. This requires that the interrupting device supply the CPU with the starting address or *transfer vector* of that program. This technique, called *vectoring*, is implemented in a number of ways.

Figure 6.30 shows a widely used technique for deriving the transfer vector from multiple interrupt request lines. Each interrupt request line is used to generate a unique fixed address which in turn is used to modify the program counter. Interrupt request signals are stored in the interrupt register. The programmable mask register is used to disable any or all of the interrupt request lines. By setting bit i of this register to 1 (0), interrupt request line i is disabled (enabled). The k masked interrupt signals are then fed into a priority encoder that produces a $\lceil \log_2 k \rceil$-bit address which is then inserted into the program counter.

Figure 6.31 indicates how program control is transferred using this type of vectored interrupt. Suppose that three devices are connected to the four IO ports as shown in Fig. 6.31a. Assume that when an interrupt request from IO port i is accepted, the 2-bit address i is generated by the priority encoder and

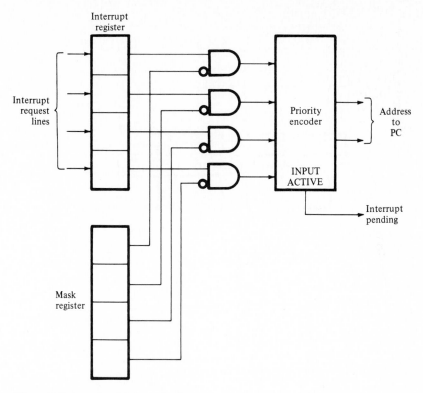

Figure 6.30 A vectored interrupt scheme.

this becomes the new contents of the program counter. Thus the four programs that can be invoked by interrupts must have their first instructions at memory addresses 0, 1, 2, and 3. As shown in Fig. 6.31*b*, branch instructions are placed in these locations, which point to the service routines proper. These routines are of arbitrary length and may be located anywhere in memory.

In the foregoing scheme there is a one-to-one correspondence between interrupt request lines and interrupt servicing programs. Hence if an IO device requires the services of *k* distinct programs, it must have *k* distinct interrupt request lines. Figure 6.32 shows another vectored interrupt scheme which does not have this restriction. Each IO port may request the services of many different programs. Again multiple interrupt request lines are used. Each IO port also has an interrupt acknowledge line. When this is activated by the CPU in response to an interrupt request signal, the IO port in question places the address of the desired interrupt program on the main data bus from which it is transferred to the CPU. The address is then used to modify the program counter. This approach requires the IO port to be capable of generating at least a partial memory address and of taking temporary control of the data bus.

Another possibility is for an IO device to send the CPU a transfer vector in the form of a CPU instruction. The CPU takes this instruction from the

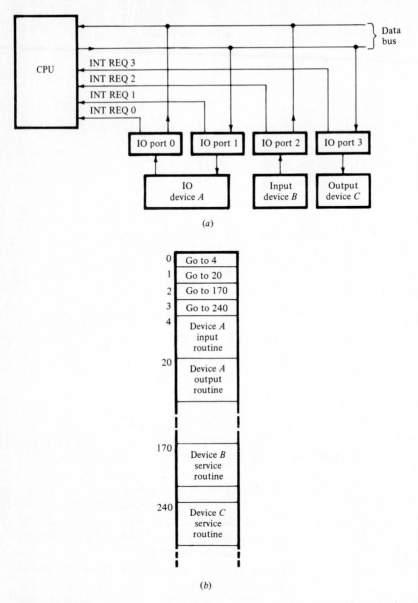

Figure 6.31 (*a*) A system with vectored IO interrupts. (*b*) Location of the interrupt servicing programs in main memory.

data bus and executes it in the normal manner. Thus if the IO device sends the instruction CALL X to the CPU, execution of this instruction saves essential CPU information such as the program counter, and transfers control to an interrupt-handling routine named X. Vectored interrupts are implemented in this manner in 8080-based microcomputers [19].

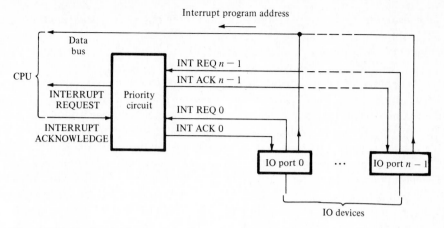

Figure 6.32 Another implementation of vectored interrupts.

In order to reduce the number of external connections to the CPU—an important consideration in the case of microprocessors—the interrupt priority selection circuit may be external to the CPU, as in Fig. 6.32. The priority of an interrupt request is determined by the priority circuit input line to which it is connected. An interrupt acknowledge signal from the CPU is transmitted to the highest-priority IO port whose interrupt request line is active.

6.2.3 IO Processors

The IO processor (IOP) is a logical extension of the IO control methods considered so far. In systems with programmed IO, IO devices are controlled directly by the CPU. The DMA concept extends to the IO devices limited control over data transfers to and from main memory. An IOP has the additional ability to execute certain instructions, called IO instructions, which give it rather complete control over IO operations. An IOP, like a CPU, is an instruction set processor, but it usually has a more restricted instruction set than the CPU. IOPs are primarily communications links between IO devices and main memory—hence the widespread use of the term "channel" for IOP. IOPs are sometimes called peripheral processing units (PPUs) to emphasize their subsidiary role with respect to the central processing unit (CPU). An early (but still representative) IOP, that of the IBM 7094 computer system, was described in Sec. 1.4.3. Because of their cost, the use of IOPs is generally limited to large high-performance computer systems.

IO instructions In a computer system with IOPs, the CPU does not normally execute IO data-transfer instructions. Such instructions are contained in IO programs stored in main memory and are fetched and executed by the IOPs. The CPU executes a small number of IO instructions which allow it to initiate and terminate the execution of IO programs via the IOP and also to test the status of the IO system. For example, in the IBM System/360-370 computer, which is examined in detail later, the CPU has three main IO instruction types: START IO, HALT IO, and TEST IO.

The IO instructions executed by the IOP are primarily associated with data transfer. A typical data-transfer instruction has the form: READ (WRITE) a block of n words from (to) device X to (from) memory location Y. The IOP is usually provided with direct access to main memory (DMA). The IOP can control the memory bus when that bus is not required by the CPU. Unlike a simple DMA controller of the kind examined in the preceding section, an IOP can execute a sequence of data-transfer instructions involving different regions of main memory and different IO devices, without CPU intervention. Other instruction types such as arithmetic, logical, and branch may be included in the IOP's instruction set to facilitate the calculation of complex addresses, IO device priorities, etc. When it requires the services of the CPU, the IOP sends it an (IO) interrupt signal.

A third category of IO instructions includes those executed by specific IO devices. These instructions control functions such as REWIND (for a magnetic-tape unit), SEEK ADDRESS (for a magnetic-disk unit), or PRINT LINE (for a printer). Instructions of this type are fetched by the IOP and transmitted as data to the appropriate IO device.

IO bus structures IO devices communicate with main memory via the IOPs. A special bus structure called the IO bus system is used for communication between the IOPs and IO devices. A separate bus system, the memory bus, links the IOPs and other processors to main memory. The IOPs and IO devices may be linked by a variety of dedicated or shared bus structures. Two common IO bus types are depicted in Fig. 6.33. The single shared bus organization is used, for example, in the IBM 7094 and in the System/360-370 [21]. Each IOP controls a fixed set of IO devices. The more complex crossbar bus organization depicted in Fig. 6.33b allows each IO device to be controlled by any of the available IOPs. This type of IO organization is used, for example, in the Burroughs B5000 and its successors [25].

> **Example 6.3: The IBM System/360-370 IO system [20, 21, 30]** The overall architecture and design philosophy of the S/360-370 series was examined in Sec. 1.6.3. Several IOPs (channels) may be used, each of which supervises a set of IO devices via a single shared bus (the IO interface). Several IO devices may be connected to the IO bus via a common control unit. However, from a logical point of view the IOP and IO devices communicate directly.
>
> The general structure of the S/360-370 IO bus is shown in Fig. 6.34. In its basic (unextended) form it contains 34 unidirectional lines [21]. Two 8-bit data buses are used for transmitting data, IO device addresses, and status information. Each IO device is assigned a unique 8-bit address, so the maximum number of devices that can be connected to the IOP is 256.

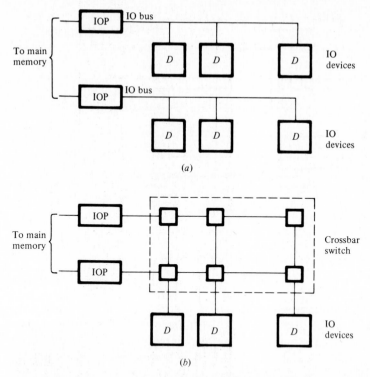

Figure 6.33 IO bus organizations using (*a*) single shared buses and (*b*) a crossbar switch.

An additional 18 control lines perform a variety of control functions. The line SELECT OUT shown in Fig. 6.34 is a daisy-chained BUS GRANT line designed to give control of the IO bus to the requesting device with the highest hardwired priority. Note that the SELECT OUT signal is returned to the IOP from the lowest-priority IO device via the line called SELECT IN.

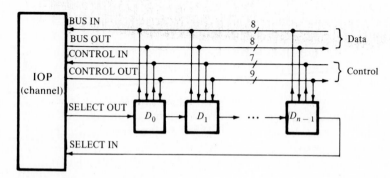

Figure 6.34 System/360-370 IO bus.

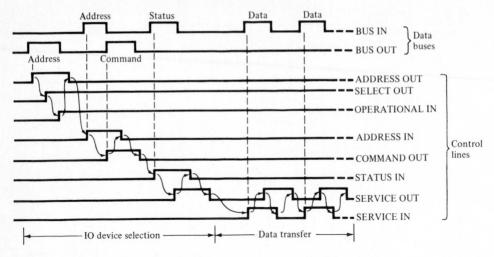

Figure 6.35 Initiation of an input operation over the S/360-370 IO interface.

The control lines have two major functions: they identify the bus transaction being performed and they time the transmission of information via the data buses. All communication is asynchronous and is interlocked using two-way control (handshaking). The details of the IO interface operation are complex [21], so we restrict ourselves to one example—the exchange of signals associated with an IOP-initiated input operation.

Figure 6.35 is a timing diagram showing all control signals involved in this operation. The IOP begins by placing the address of the required device on the data bus BUS OUT and activating the control line ADDRESS OUT. All IO devices compare their addresses to the byte on BUS OUT. The IOP then activates SELECT OUT, which propagates through the IO devices until the one with the matching address is reached. (If no such device is present, that fact is indicated by a signal on SELECT IN.) The matching IO device now activates OPERATIONAL IN. The IOP responds by deactivating ADDRESS OUT. The IO device then sends its address to the IOP for checking via BUS IN and activates ADDRESS IN. The IOP checks the returned address and, if it is correct, places a "command" byte (in this case an input instruction to the IO device) on BUS OUT and activates COMMAND OUT. ADDRESS IN is deactivated in response, which in turn causes the IOP to deactivate COMMAND OUT. The IO device now places a byte containing its status on BUS IN and activates STATUS IN. If the device status is acceptable, the IOP responds by activating SERVICE OUT. STATUS IN is deactivated and data transfer can begin. The transmission of each byte of data is controlled by the SERVICE IN and SERVICE OUT lines which act as DATA READY and DATA ACKNOWLEDGE lines, respectively.

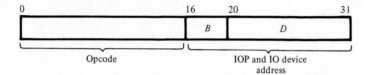

Figure 6.36 Format of S/360-370 IO instructions executed by the CPU.

IO programming The CPU supervises the operations of the IO system via a small set of privileged IO instructions [20]. The format of these instructions is shown in Fig. 6.36. An address field comprising a base register field *B* and a relative address field *D* identifies both the IO device to be used and the IOP to which it is attached. There are three major instructions of this type: START IO, HALT IO, and TEST IO. START IO is used to initiate an IO operation. It provides the IOP it names with the main-memory address of the IO program to be executed by the IOP. HALT IO causes the IOP to terminate IO program execution. TEST IO allows the CPU to determine the status of the named IO device and IOP. Status conditions of interest include available, busy, not operational, and (masked) interrupt pending.

The IO instructions executed by the IOP are called *channel command words* (CCWs) and have the format shown in Fig. 6.37. There are three main types.

1. Data-transfer instructions including input (read), output (write), and sense (read status information). These CCWs cause the number of bytes specified in the data count field to be transferred between the specified main-memory area and the previously selected IO device.
2. Branch instructions (called "transfer-in-channel"), which cause the IOP to fetch the next CCW from the specified memory address rather than the next sequential location. This is a simple unconditional jump within an IO program.
3. IO device control instructions. These instructions are transmitted directly to the IO device and are used to specify functions peculiar to that device which do not involve data transfers. For example, a magnetic-tape unit could be instructed to rewind or write a standard tape mark; a printer could be instructed to print a line or eject a page.

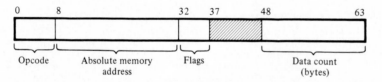

Figure 6.37 Format of S/360-370 IO instructions (CCWs) executed by the IOPs.

Note that the S/360-370 IOP has no significant arithmetic ability.

The opcode of a data-transfer instruction may be transmitted directly to the IO device as the "command" byte during the device selection process shown in Fig. 6.35. If the IO device requires additional control information, it can be supplied with it via an output data transfer. The flags field of the CCW is used to modify or extend the operation specified by the opcode. For example, a program control interrupt flag PCI can be set to instruct the IOP to generate an IO interrupt and make the current IOP status available to the CPU. Another flag specifies "command chaining," which means that the current CCW is followed by another CCW which is to be executed immediately. If this flag is not set, the IOP ceases IO program execution after executing the current CCW.

Figure 6.38 lists an IO program written in S/360-370 assembly language that writes a record on a magnetic tape. The record contains 100 bytes. The tape is assumed to contain two records, the second of which is being replaced. Every CCW contains four fields separated by commas which correspond to the opcode, memory address, flags, and data count fields of Fig. 6.37. The program contains only one data-transfer instruction which transfers 100 bytes to the tape from the memory region called BUFFER1. The other CCWs control operations that are peculiar to magnetic tapes and do not use the memory address or data count fields. In all CCWs the opcode and flags have been defined by hexadecimal numbers indicated by the prefix X. The flag field X'40' causes the command chaining flag to be set. In the last CCW no flags are set, so the IOP stops after execution of this CCW.

CPU-IOP Communication The CPU and an IOP in the S/360-370 communicate directly via dedicated control lines and indirectly via reserved storage areas in main memory. The CPU and IOP although logically separate may be physically integrated so that they share data paths and registers; the degree of sharing depends on the particular model number [18]. The IOP normally contains the following components.

1. A data buffer register in which bytes received from an IO device are reorganized into words for transmission to main memory, and vice versa

Instruction			Comments
CCW X'07',		, X'40',	Rewind tape
CCW X'37',		, X'40',	Skip first record
CCW X'01',	BUFFER1	, X'40', 100	Write second record from BUFFER1
CCW X'1F',		, X'40',	Write tape mark
CCW X'07',		, X'00',	Rewind tape and stop

Figure 6.38 An S/360-370 IO program to write a record on a magnetic tape.

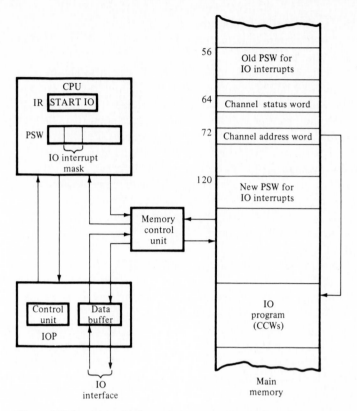

Figure 6.39 Location of information used to control S/360-370 IO operations.

2. Circuitry for fetching and decoding CCWs, maintaining the status of IO operations, and controlling the IO interface

An IOP that can control several different IO operations simultaneously (where data transfers are time-multiplexed over the IO interface) is called a *multiplexer* channel. A *selector* channel is an IOP designed to handle one IO operation at a time; it is normally used to control high-speed IO devices.

Figure 6.39 depicts the main control information associated with an IO operation. The operation begins when the CPU encounters a START IO instruction. The CPU transmits the IO device address and a start signal directly to the IOP in question. The IOP then fetches a word called the *channel address word* CAW from memory location 72. This word (which must be stored by the CPU prior to execution of the START IO instruction) contains the absolute starting address of the IO program to be executed by the IOP. The IOP now initiates an IO device selection process of the kind illustrated in Fig. 6.35. If the required IO device is available, the IOP proceeds to execute the IO program specified by the CAW. If the IO device is unavailable for some reason, the IO operation is aborted and an IO interrupt is generated.

The CPU can maintain direct control over the IO operation by periodically executing TEST IO. This causes the IOP to construct a channel status word CSW which it stores at memory location 64. The CPU can then fetch the CSW and examine it. This type of programmed IO is an inefficent way for the CPU to monitor IO operations, so the IOPs are provided with the ability to send interrupt requests to the CPU. The CPU tests for interrupts once during each CPU instruction cycle. Interrupt requests can be masked by an interrupt mask register which forms part of the CPU's program status word register PSW.

When the CPU responds to an IO interrupt, it automatically stores the current PSW as the old PSW at memory location 56 and fetches a new PSW from location 120. The new PSW contains a program counter field pointing to the interrupt service routine to be used. If it is desired to save the CPU general registers, explicit instructions for this purpose must be included in the interrupt service program. The interrupting IOP updates the channel status word at location 64 which provides the CPU with further information on the source and nature of the interrupt. In general, it may be necessary to execute several instructions and access main memory a number of times in order to complete the transfer of control to the interrupt service program. This implies that interrupt response time may be relatively slow. The interrupt request lines from the IOPs to the CPU partially identify the interrupting channel and so form a type of multiple line interrupt system.

Microprocessors in IO systems It appears that a great deal of IO processing can be performed efficiently and inexpensively by microprocessors. A microprocessor can be used as an IOP to supervise the operation of a set of IO devices. Microprocessors are general-purpose instruction set processors and have much more powerful instruction sets than a typical special-purpose IOP such as that of the S/360-370. Microprocessors can also be incorporated into the design of individual IO devices to provide them with "intelligence," and thus decrease their dependence on supervisory processors such as CPUs and IOPs. For example, an interactive terminal with keyboard and video display can be endowed with the ability to perform (simple) computations and thereby decrease the terminal user's need for access to the main computing facilities. The user might thus be able to enter several lines of text into the terminal and then edit them, e. g., correct errors, using a text editing program that is implemented in a local microcomputer. After processing in the terminal, the edited text is transferred to the main memory of the system. The full impact of microprocessors on IO system design remains to be seen.

6.2.4 CPU-IO Interaction

IOPs allow CPU and IO operations to proceed simultaneously with very infrequent interaction. The execution of a typical program in a large computer system involves an alternating sequence of CPU processing and IO operations. For example, in a system using paged virtual memory, CPU execution can proceed until a page fault occurs. Then execution of the program must be suspended until an IO page transfer operation is completed. In the meantime, the CPU may switch to another program. The concurrent execution of several distinct programs (multiprogramming) requires the supervision of an operating system to distribute the required tasks efficiently among the available processors.

Scheduling IO operations In a multiprogrammed computer the operating system distributes the available resources such as main-memory space and processing time among a set of competing programs. The memory scheduling function was examined in Sec. 5.2. We now consider how CPU time and IOP time are scheduled.

A program can access an IO device and commence IO processing if the device is not busy, i. e., if it is not being used by another program, and if the IOP controlling the device can provide the necessary access channel between the IO device and main memory. Similarly, the CPU must be available before the program can begin CPU processing. Thus each program can be viewed as being in one of four states:

S_0: engaged in CPU processing
S_1: awaiting CPU processing
S_2: engaged in IO processing
S_3: awaiting IO processing

When the CPU or an IO device becomes available, a waiting program is selected on some priority basis and assigned to the resource in question.

We now describe a straightforward scheduling technique designed to provide rapid response to requests for IO processing [9]. It is assumed that a single CPU and a set of n IO devices $\{D_i\}$ are available. At any time each IO device can be used by only one program. A batch of m programs $\{Q_i\}$ is available for execution. Each program Q_i is assigned a priority $p(Q_i)$ $\epsilon\{p_0, p_1, p_2, \ldots\}$, where $p_i > p_j$ if $i < j$. Once a program gains access to the CPU, it is not replaced until one of the following events occurs.

1. An IO instruction is encountered by the CPU
2. An (unmasked) IO interrupt is received by the CPU
3. The CPU terminates execution of the current program due to encountering a HALT instruction or an error condition

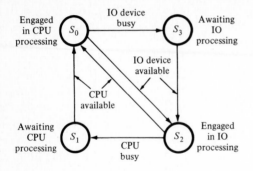

Figure 6.40 States of a program in a multiprogramming system.

Figure 6.40 shows the possible state transitions for a program in this system. The CPU can keep track of the states of all the programs by maintaining four tables of the type shown in Fig. 6.41. The tables T_0, T_1, T_2, and T_3 list the programs in states S_0, S_1, S_2, and S_3, respectively. Also listed for each program Q_i is its priority $p(Q_i)$ (in T_1, T_2, and T_3 only) and the IO device $D(Q_i)$ it requires (in T_2 and T_3 only).

Suppose, for example, that the IO operation involving program Q_2 terminates and an IO interrupt is generated. From T_2 in Fig. 6.41 we see that this frees IO device D_1. The CPU responds to the interrupt by transferring control to the operating system, which then searches T_3 to find the highest-priority program, if any, awaiting access to D_1. In this case both Q_0 and Q_8 are waiting. Q_8 has the higher priority; the IO operation it requires is therefore initiated. The Q_8 entry is deleted from T_3 and inserted in T_2. The Q_2 entry is deleted from T_2. If Q_2 requires further processing by the CPU, it is entered into T_1. Figure 6.42 is a flowchart showing the detailed operation of this straightforward scheduling scheme. It can be called *IO driven*, since it can be expected that in most cases a change in state is caused by the initiation or termination of an IO operation.

Calculating the performance of a system with overlapped CPU and IO processing is quite difficult. Simulation is often the most practical approach using models like that of Example 2.3. Analytic performance evaluation is pos-

Q_i		Q_i	$p(Q_i)$		Q_i	$p(Q_i)$	$D(Q_i)$		Q_i	$p(Q_i)$	$D(Q_i)$
Q_5		Q_1	p_0		Q_2	p_1	D_1		Q_0	p_7	D_1
		Q_3	p_5		Q_4	p_3	D_3		Q_8	p_6	D_1
		Q_7	p_0		Q_9	p_2	D_4				
					Q_6	p_9	D_6				
T_0		T_1			T_2				T_3		
Engaged in CPU processing		Awaiting CPU processing			Engaged in IO processing				Awaiting IO processing		

Figure 6.41 Tables used by the operating system to record program states.

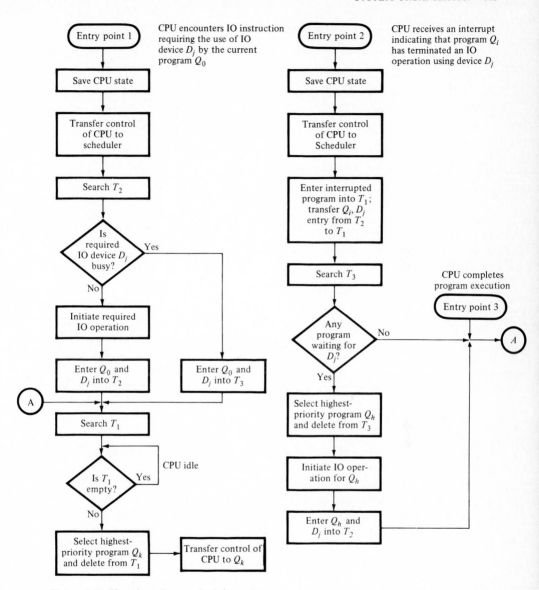

Figure 6.42 Flowchart for a scheduler program.

sible if a sufficiently simple model of the system can be constructed. We now describe a queueing system model due to Boyse and Warn [6] that can be solved analytically.

Example 6.4: Performance evaluation of an interactive computer [6] The structure of the system is shown in Fig. 6.43. The computer is designed for interactive support of a set of n users at input-output terminals. The

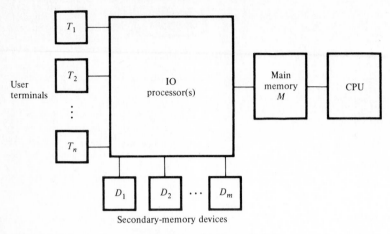

Figure 6.43 Interactive system structure for Example 6.4.

operating system supervises multiprogramming and a virtual memory system with demand paging. The IO system has m independent logical channels to the secondary memory devices used for paging. The number of programs that can occupy main memory at one time cannot exceed a certain value, called the multiprogramming level.

The system operates as follows. A user enters a request via a terminal for a job involving some program P to be performed. If space is available, P is loaded into main memory M, otherwise the request is entered into a queue for main memory. Once loaded, P competes for access to the CPU with the other programs currently available for execution in M. When it gains access to the CPU, P is executed until an IO operation is encountered, e.g., due to a page fault. When an IO operation is required, P relinquishes the CPU which can then begin executing another program. (In this model, P may not perform both CPU and IO operations simultaneously.) After the IO operation terminates, P again seeks access to the CPU. The cycle of CPU and IO operations continues until the job in question has been completed. An appropriate response can then be sent to the user. A delay, the user "think" time, can be expected before the user enters a new request. To simplify the problem further, it is assumed that the only IO operation of interest is paging, that each program is associated with a different IO channel, and that the number of IO channels equals the multiprogramming level m. Hence there is no contention for IO channels.

From the foregoing description, we can conclude that the job in this system may be in any one of four states:

1. Waiting for access to M
2. Waiting for access to the CPU
3. Busy with a CPU operation
4. Busy with an IO operation

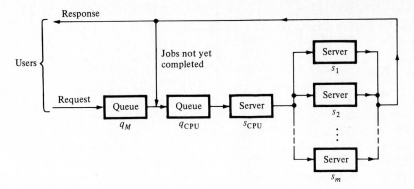

Figure 6.44 Queueing model for the interactive system example.

These states suggest that a queuing model for the system should include the following components:

1. A queue q_M for access to M
2. A queue q_{CPU} for access to the CPU
3. A single server s_{CPU} representing the CPU
4. A set of m parallel servers $s_1, s_2, \ldots, s_m$ representing the m IO channels used for paging

Figure 6.44 shows the structure of the queuing model to be used.

We will now use this model to compute the following important performance measures:

1. The CPU utilization u_{CPU}, defined as the mean fraction of time the CPU is busy
2. The system throughput v, defined as the mean number of jobs completed per unit time
3. The system response time t_R, defined as the mean time between the entry of a job request by a user and his receipt of a response from the computer

The input parameters needed for these calculations are listed in Fig. 6.45.

Let $\bar{t}_E$, $\bar{t}_{CPU}$, and $\bar{t}_{IO}$ denote the mean values of t_E, t_{CPU}, and t_{IO}, respectively. Since all IO operations are assumed to be page transfers, $\bar{t}_{CPU}$ and $\bar{t}_E$ are related by

$$\bar{t}_{CPU} = \frac{\bar{t}_E}{f}$$

where f is the average number of page faults per job, an easily measured quantity. It therefore suffices to specify the probability distributions associated with the two parameters t_{CPU} and t_{IO} only. The service rates for the

Parameter	Meaning
t_E	The total CPU time required by a job
t_{CPU}	The CPU time from the start or restart of execution of the job by the CPU until the start of an IO operation
t_{IO}	The time to complete an IO operation
t_Z	The average user think time
m	The number of logical IO channels available (assumed equal to the multiprogramming level)
n	The number of users

Figure 6.45 Input parameters for the interactive system model.

CPU and IO servers are

$$\mu_{CPU} = \frac{1}{\bar{t}_{CPU}}$$

and

$$\mu_{IO} = \frac{1}{\bar{t}_{IO}}$$

respectively. The arrival rate of jobs entering the CPU queue q_{CPU} can be assumed to be proportional to μ_{IO}, since the CPU-IO interactions tend to dominate new job arrivals. The arrival rate of jobs entering the memory queue depends on the system response time and so cannot be determined a priori.

First, we examine the case where t_{CPU} and t_{IO} are assumed to have the constant values $\bar{t}_{CPU}$ and $\bar{t}_{IO}$, respectively. Figure 6.46 shows how the execution of m jobs is overlapped by the CPU in this case. From this diagram we see immediately that

$$u_{CPU} = \frac{m\bar{t}_{CPU}}{\bar{t}_{CPU} + \bar{t}_{IO}}$$

provided that $m\bar{t}_{CPU} \leq \bar{t}_{CPU} + \bar{t}_{IO}$; otherwise $u_{CPU} = 1$ and the system is CPU bound. The system throughput v is given by

$$v = \frac{u_{CPU}}{\bar{t}_{CPU}}$$

so that when $m\bar{t}_{CPU} \leq \bar{t}_{CPU} + \bar{t}_{IO}$,

$$v = \frac{m}{\bar{t}_{CPU} + \bar{t}_{IO}}$$

To calculate the response time t_R, note that the computer must process an average of n jobs during the period $t_R + t_Z$. The time required to complete n jobs is n/v; hence

$$t_R = \frac{n}{v} - t_Z$$

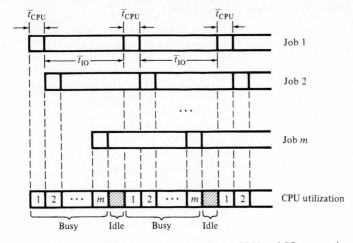

Figure 6.46 CPU utilization assuming constant CPU and IO processing time distributions.

If $m\bar{t}_{CPU} \leq \bar{t}_{CPU} + \bar{t}_{IO}$, then

$$t_R = \left(\frac{n}{m}\right)(\bar{t}_{CPU} + \bar{t}_{IO}) - t_Z$$

A somewhat more accurate model is obtained if t_{CPU} and t_{IO} are assumed to be exponentially distributed with the mean values $\bar{t}_{CPU}$ and $\bar{t}_{IO}$, respectively. The probability that t_{CPU} is less than or equal to t is defined by an expression of the form

$$p_{CPU}(t) = 1 - e^{-t/\bar{t}_{CPU}}$$

Similarly,

$$p_{IO}(t) = 1 - e^{-t/\bar{t}_{IO}}$$

Using these exponential distributions, it can be shown [6] that the CPU utilization is now given by

$$u_{CPU} = 1 - \left[m! \sum_{k=0}^{m} \frac{1}{(m-k)!} \left(\frac{\bar{t}_{CPU}}{\bar{t}_{IO}}\right)^k \right]^{-1}$$

Although the actual distributions of t_{CPU} and t_{IO} are neither constant nor exponential, these models give useful results and have been validated experimentally [6]. Figure 6.47 shows a graph of u_{CPU} as a function of $\bar{t}_{CPU}/\bar{t}_{IO}$ for both models when $m = 4$.

6.3 MULTIPLE CPU SYSTEMS

Thus far we have been mainly concerned with uniprocessors, i.e. computers with a single CPU. We turn now to consider systems containing more than one CPU. We make a broad division into two groups: multiprocessors and com-

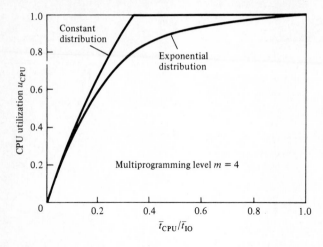

Figure 6.47 CPU utilization as a function of $\bar{t}_{CPU}/\bar{t}_{IO}$.

puter networks. A *multiprocessor* may be defined as an integrated computer system containing two or more CPUs. The qualification "integrated" implies that the CPUs cooperate in the execution of programs. Baer requires that the CPUs in a multiprocessor be capable of simultaneous execution of two or more portions of the same program [3]. Enslow adds the further requirements that the CPUs share common main memory and IO subsystems and that a single operating system be in overall control [10]. A *computer network*, on the other hand, is a collection of independent computers connected by a communications network. Each computer has its own operating system and there is no direct cooperation between the computers in the execution of programs. Multiprocessors and computer networks both belong to the general category of MIMD (multiple instruction stream multiple data stream) systems defined in Sec. 3.4.1.

6.3.1 Multiprocessors

Rationale There are two main reasons for including multiple CPUs in a single computer system:

1. To improve the system's performance
2. To increase its reliability

Performance improvement is obtained by having several CPUs executing the same program or several different programs simultaneously. This can result in a significant reduction in the total execution time for the programs involved. System reliability is improved by the fact that the failure of one CPU does not necessarily cause the entire system to fail. The functions of the faulty CPU can be taken over by one of the other CPUs.

The use of multiprocessors in reducing the execution time of an individual program is limited by the inherent parallelism of the program. As discussed in

Sec. 3.4.2, many programs contain little parallelism, so that little if any speedup is obtainable by providing multiple processors for their execution. Programs that are amenable to parallel processing often require highly specialized processor organizations such as pipelining or the array organization of ILLIAC IV. In order for a program to be executed more efficiently by a k-CPU multiprocessor than by a uniprocessor, it must be possible to divide the program into k segments that can be executed simultaneously.

The situation changes when a set of k independent programs are to be processed. This is the case, for example, in a computer center where many unrelated programs by different users are available for execution. These programs can be distributed among the k available CPUs, since little interaction between the programs occurs. (Such interaction is largely confined to competition for systems resources other than the CPUs, such as main-memory space and IO channels.) Thus multiprocessing finds its main application as a method of performance enhancement in computers designed to process many programs simultaneously at rates faster than are economically obtainable with a single CPU.

Multiprocessors are inherently more reliable than uniprocessors. If a fault causes one CPU to fail, its duties can be taken over by some other CPU. The system as a whole can thus continue to function correctly with, perhaps, some loss in throughput. Multiprocessors can be characterized by the degree of communication or coupling that exists between the various CPUs. We distinguish three cases:

1. *Stand-alone* computers in which there is no physical connection between the CPUs
2. *Indirectly coupled* CPUs which communicate via a shared IO system
3. *Directly coupled* CPUs which have direct access to a common main memory

Stand-alone systems A multiprocessor organization with a minimum of integration is a set of stand-alone computers with no direct physical connection between the computers. Cooperation among the machines exists only to the extent to which jobs are transferred manually from one machine to another. This type of organization is used when there is a subdivision of tasks among the computers. For example, one machine, the *main* computer, may be used for executing user programs, while the remaining machines, the *peripheral* computers, may be used primarily to prepare the programs for execution by the main computer and print its results. Unlike IOPs, the peripheral computers are not controlled by the main computer. They may also be used to execute user programs if, for example, the available load exceeds the capacity of the main computer.

Figure 6.48 shows a system widely used in the 1950s and 1960s employing one or more peripheral computers such as the IBM 1401. A larger machine, e.g., the IBM 7094, is the main computer. A peripheral computer is used to read jobs from a card reader and organize them into a queue on a magnetic tape.

Punched cards

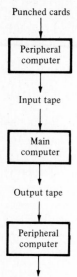

Paper printout   **Figure 6.48** A computer system with stand-alone peripheral processors.

This tape (the input tape) is then transferred manually to the main computer, which executes the batch of programs and places the results on an output magnetic tape. Finally, the output tape is moved to a peripheral computer, which transfers its contents to a line printer.

Indirectly coupled systems A higher degree of integration is achieved by providing direct communication paths between the IO systems of a set of computers. This allows one computer to treat another as an IO device, i.e., a source or sink for data, so that IO operations can be used to transfer information between the main memories of the two computers. In this way programs and data sets can be shared among the various CPUs. Main memory is not shared, however, so that the concurrent execution of the same program by several CPUs may not be feasible. Each CPU is supervised by its own operating system.

Computers in the IBM S/360-370 series can be indirectly or loosely coupled by means of a special IO device called a *channel-to-channel* adapter CTC [5]. A CTC is used to link two IOPs (channels) associated with two different computers, as depicted in Fig. 6.49. Each computer has its own separate main memory and operating system. The CTC allows each computer to regard the other as an IO device so that a data transfer between the two main memories can be accomplished. A data transfer from M_1 to M_2 requires the following actions.

1. CPU_1 initiates execution of an output (write) IO program addressed to the CTC.
2. In response to the first write command, the CTC sends an interrupt signal to CPU_2 via IOP_2.

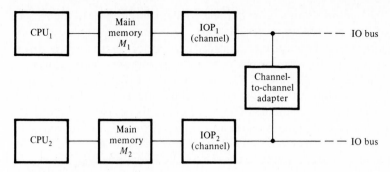

Figure 6.49 Indirectly coupled system of two S/360-370 computers.

3. CPU_2 responds to the interrupt by initiating execution of an input (read) IO program addressed to the CTC.
4. Data transfer can now proceed asynchronously from M_1 to M_2 via the CTC. When the data transfer is completed, both CPUs are interrupted.

Directly coupled systems The highest degree of cooperation between several CPUs requires that they all have direct access to a common main memory and be controlled by a single operating system. A switching network or bus system must be provided for connecting the CPUs to main memory. In order that the CPUs can access memory simultaneously, it is desirable that it be partitioned into independently addressable modules. A crossbar switching network of the type shown in Fig. 6.50 provides an efficient method of interconnecting the CPUs and the memory modules. IOPs may also be provided with direct memory access via the crossbar switch. The crossbar switching network must resolve conflicts between processor requests. Such conflicts, i.e., two processors attempting to address the same module simultaneously, can be reduced by the address interleaving technique discussed in Chap. 5. It should be noted that in a

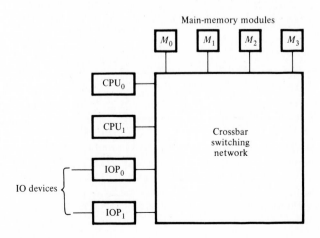

Figure 6.50 Directly coupled multiprocessor system.

large system the complexity and cost of the crossbar switching network may be comparable to that of several processors [10].

The operating system for a directly coupled multiprocessor resembles that of a uniprocessor with multiprogramming capability. It is more complex, however, since the programs requesting CPU processing can be assigned to more than one CPU. A further problem is ensuring that the key supervisory programs, which each CPU is capable of executing, are used in a consistent and uniform manner. For example, the situation where two CPUs simultaneously attempt to use the same resource in incompatible ways must be avoided. This requires that at any time the supervisory role of the operating system over the allocation of any given resource in the computer should be exercised by only one CPU. There are three general ways in which this objective can be achieved.

1. Each CPU has equal access to the operating system which contains appropriate mechanisms to prevent conflicts such as deadlock and to ensure that the system resources are protected.
2. A single CPU is designated the *master* CPU and execution of all operating system supervisory routines are restricted to that processor. The other CPUs are then termed *slaves*. The relation between the slaves and the master CPU is similar to the relation between the IOPs and the CPU in a uniprocessor.
3. Each CPU is assigned its own set of system resources such as IO devices, which are not shared with the other CPUs. Furthermore, each CPU executes the operating system routines to manage its own resources only.

The first of these systems clearly provides the greatest flexibility but also requires the most complex operating system. For example, since several CPUs may wish to use the same operating system routine simultaneously, that routine must be reentrant.[1] In multiprocessors with a unique master CPU, the operating system routines need not be reentrant, but the system is vulnerable to failure of the master CPU. The third approach mentioned above limits the sharing of resources among the CPUs. Further analysis of these methods is left as an exercise (Prob. 6.9).

Example 6.5: The Control Data CYBER-70 Model 74 [10] The CYBER-70 series introduced in 1972 includes several multiprocessor models. The Model 74 contains two CPUs which are essentially the same as that of the CDC 6600 described in Example 3.6. The system organization of the Model 74, which is directly descended from that of the CDC 6600 [32], is shown in Fig. 6.51. Two CPUs are directly coupled via main memory and are supervised by a common operating system called SCOPE (*Supervisory*

---

[1]A *reentrant program* is one that can be executed by several different users concurrently, which means that the program should not modify its own instructions and that it should have separate data-storage areas for each user.

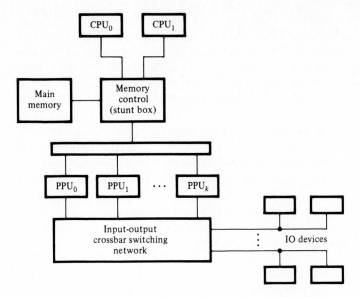

Figure 6.51 The control data CYBER-70 Model 74 multiprocessor.

Control of Program Execution). The system also accommodates up to 20 peripheral processing units (PPUs), most of which are used as IO processors. One PPU, however, is devoted to executing operating system programs and thus functions as a system monitor.

The various processors communicate with one another via main memory. Access to main memory is controlled by a special unit called the "stunt box." Address interleaving is used to minimize memory conflicts. Requests to the same memory module are queued by the stunt box. The peripheral processors communicate with main memory via a single shared bus. They communicate with a set of 12 independent IO buses via a crossbar switch. Each IO bus is, in turn, connected to one or more IO devices.

The operating system distributes tasks on a priority basis to the various CPUs and PPUs as they become available. Up to 15 independent programs may be executed concurrently in overlapped (multiprogramming) fashion. The presence of two CPUs allows two different programs to be executed simultaneously. Rapid transfer of control from one CPU program to another is accomplished by the 6600 "exchange jump" instruction [32]. This one instruction causes the contents of all significant CPU registers to be exchanged for the contents of a specified 16-word area of main memory.

Performance The inclusion of $n > 1$ CPUs in a computer clearly improves its performance as measured, say, by the effective instruction execution rate I_n. It might be expected that performance increases linearly with the number of CPUs present, that is, $I_n \approx nI_1$. However, experimental evidence indicates that the performance improvement is much less than nI_1 and that the rate of improvement diminishes with each additional CPU. For example, Enslow states that I_2 can be expected to range from 1.3 I_1 to 1.8 I_1, while I_3 can be expected to range from 1.9 I_1 to 2.3 I_1 [10]. These less than ideal performance figures can be attributed to contention for system resources. In directly coupled multiprocessors, the principal shared item is main memory. The manner in which resource sharing is accomplished depends on both the operating system and the workloads being processed.

A rough indication of the influence of the number of processors on computer performance can be obtained by considering the interaction of the processors with a set of memory modules. Consider a multiprocessor containing n processors $P_1, P_2, \ldots, P_n$ connected to m interleaved memory modules $M_1, M_2, \ldots, M_m$ via a crossbar switch as in Fig. 6.50. The instruction execution rate is roughly proportional to the rate at which memory accesses are being performed. The latter is in turn proportional to the average number of busy memory modules B. We now derive a simple expression for B due to Strecker [4].

Assume that the probability that any processor P_j generates a request for memory module M_i is $1/m$. Hence the probability that M_i is idle is $(1 - 1/m)^n$. This implies that the probability p_i that M_i is busy is $1 - (1 - 1/m)^n$. The average number of busy memory modules B is therefore given by

$$B = \sum_{i=1}^{m} p_i = m\left(1 - \left(1 - \frac{1}{m} \right)^n \right)$$

As might be expected, if m is fixed and $n \to \infty$, $B \to m$. Similarly if n is fixed and $m \to \infty$, $B \to n$, that is, all processors are kept busy. Figure 6.52 shows a plot of B against m for several values of n. A somewhat more accurate model for B using the Markov chain theory can be found in Ref. 4.

Considerable reliance is placed on simulation in the evaluation of multiprocessor systems due to the difficulty of constructing useful analytic models. We conclude our discussion with a model of a representative system due to MacDougall [26]. The model is intended for simulation using the ASPOL simulator which was described in Sec. 2.3.5.

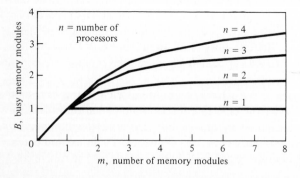

Figure 6.52 The multiprocessor performance function B.

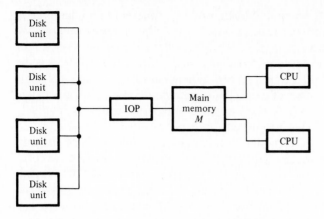

Figure 6.53 Multiprocessor system structure for Example 6.6.

Example 6.6: Simulation model of a multiprocessor [26] The structure of the multiprocessor is sketched in Fig. 6.53. It comprises two CPUs sharing a main memory M, and a single IOP to which four disk units are attached. Jobs are assumed to enter the system at an average rate of five per minute with a Poisson arrival distribution. Jobs then alternate between CPU and IO operations as in Example 6.4. It is assumed that IO operations are uniformly distributed among the available IO devices, in this case disk units; and that when a job completes an IO operation, it is assigned to the first available CPU. To simplify the model further, all IO operations are assumed to consist of reading a fixed-length record from a disk unit, an operation that is typical of paging.

The input parameters for the simulation model are listed in Fig. 6.54. Note that the CPU and IO execution times t_E, t_{CPU}, and t_{IO} have the same meaning as in Example 6.4. t_E and t_{CPU} are defined by appropriate probabil-

Parameter	Meaning	Distribution function
λ_{job}	Job arrival rate	Poisson with mean $= 5/60$ s
t_E	Job CPU time	Erlang with mean $= 10$ and variance $= 8$
t_{CPU}	CPU time between IO operations	Exponential with mean $= t_E/\text{records}$
t_{IO}	IO operation time	Computed as $t_S + t_L + t_D +$ waiting time in queues
t_S	Disk seek time	Uniform from 0 to 75×10^{-3} s
t_L	Disk latency	Uniform from 0 to 25×10^{-3} s
t_D	Record transfer time	Constant $= 2.5 \times 10^{-3}$ s
Space	Job memory space requirements	Uniform from 20 to 60 pages
Records	Number of IO operations per job	Computed as $x t_E$ where x is a uniform distribution from 2 to 10

Figure 6.54 Input parameters for the multiprocessor system model.

ity distributions. t_{io} is computed using three parameters that characterize disk unit operation: the seek time t_S, which is the time required to move the read-write heads into position; the latency t_L, which is the time required for the desired disk record to rotate to the read-write head; and t_D, which is the time required to read the desired record. When a job enters the system, it is assigned a random number of pages in main memory; this number is called the job "space." The job is also assigned a priority which is inversely related to its memory space requirements.

The complete ASPOL model with explanatory comments is given in Fig. 6.55. It consists of three parts: the main "program" **sim** and two processes named cp and io. The function of **sim** is to define the system resources via **facility** and **storage** declarations, and to create new jobs at the specified rate of $\lambda_{job} = 5$ per minute. Since the arrival distribution is Poisson, the interarrival time t_{job}, which **sim** computes, has a negative exponential distribution with mean $1/\lambda_{job} = 12$ s. The process cp simulates the processing of jobs by a CPU. Each incoming job is randomly assigned memory space and a total CPU time requirement t_{CPU}. The job is assigned to a CPU in randomly chosen segments of t_{CPU} seconds duration. After t_{CPU} seconds of execution [specified by **hold**(t_{CPU})], process cp randomly selects a disk unit and calls process io to simulate an IO operation using the current job and the chosen disk unit. Process io then simulates the three operations (seek, latency, record fetch) composing an IO operation. At the end of process io is the statement **set** (flag) with flag = ioend; this reactivates process cp, which had suspended execution on encountering the statement **wait** (ioend).

6.3.2 Fault-Tolerant Computers

Fault tolerance has been defined as "the ability of a system to execute specified algorithms correctly regardless of hardware failures and program errors" [2]. It is of concern in most computer systems, while in some applications, e.g., spacecraft control and telephone switching, fault tolerance is a major design goal. Most hardware failures have physical causes such as component wear and electromagnetic interference. The nature and frequency of hardware failures can often be determined experimentally, which makes it possible to analyze the faults and their consequences using probabilistic models. Software faults, on the other hand, are primarily due to design errors and are much more difficult to model.

Fault tolerance is intimately associated with the concept of *redundancy*. When a component fails, its duties must be taken over by other fault-free components of the system. If those components are used to improve only the reliability of the system and do not affect its computing performance, they are termed redundant. Redundancy may be introduced

1. By including multiple copies of critical hardware components (hardware redundancy)

ASPOL statement	Comments
sim multiprocessor;	
real tjob;	tjob = time between job arrivals
facility cpu (2), iop, disk (4);	Declares two CPUs, one IOP, and four disk units
storage m; **size** (m) 128;	Defines main memory *m* with capacity of 128 pages
monitor (cpu);	Requests report on CPU queue statistics
while (time .**le**. 20. *60.) **do**	Requests termination after 20 min of simulation time
begin	
initiate cp;	Calls the process cp
tjob = **expntl** (12.);	Selects random value for tjob
hold (tjob);	Waits tjob seconds before next job initiation
end;	
end sim;	
process cp;	
integer space, unit;	
real tcpu, records, tcav, te;	
event ioend;	ioend is used to communicate with process io
te = **erlang** (10., 8.);	te = total CPU time requirements of job
records = te * **random** (2., 10.);	records = number of IO operations required
tcav = te/records;	tcav = average CPU time between IO operations
space = **irandom** (20, 60);	space = job's main-memory space requirements
priority = 60 − space;	Defines job's priority in all queues
allocate (m) space;	Requests space in main memory
while (te. **gt**. 0.) **do**	
begin	
reserve (cpu);	Requests access to any available CPU
tcpu = **expntl** (tcav);	tcpu = CPU time between IO operations
te = te − tcpu	te = remaining CPU time needed by job
hold (tcpu);	Simulates CPU activities
unit = **irandom** (1, 4);	Selects disk unit for IO operation
initiate io (unit, ioend);	Transfers control to process io
release (cpu);	Releases CPU
wait (ioend);	Suspends job CPU activity until ioend occurs
end;	
deallocate (m) space;	Releases main-memory space
end process;	
process io (unit, flag);	
integer unit;	
real, ts, t*l*, td, tc;	
event flag;	
reserve (disk (unit));	Requests access to specified disk unit
ts = **random** (0., 75.) *.001;	ts = disk seek time
hold (ts);	Simulates seek operation
reserve (iop);	Requests access to any available IOP
t*l* = **random** (0., 25.) *.001;	t*l* = disk latency
td = 2.5 *.001;	td = record transfer time
tc = t*l* + td;	
hold (tc);	Simulates reading record from disk
release (iop);	Releases IOP
release (disk (unit));	Releases disk unit
set (flag);	Communicates end of IO operation to process cp
end process;	

Figure 6.55 ASPOL model of the multiprocessor.

2. By including several alternative programs for critical operations (software redundancy)
3. By using error-correcting or error-detecting codes for information representation (information redundancy)
4. By repeating critical operations several times (time redundancy)

Only hardware redundancy is examined in this section. Information redundancy was briefly discussed in Sec. 3.1.2.

Design techniques Two major approaches to fault-tolerant design have been identified which are termed static and dynamic redundancy. *Static* redundancy refers to the use of redundant components which form a permanent part of the system and serve to *mask* the erroneous signals generated by failures. An example of static redundancy is the use of error-correcting codes. In general, static redundancy is achieved by using $n \geq 3$ elements to generate a signal X and by using a *decision element* (also called a voter or restoring organ) to examine the n values of X (some of which may be erroneous), determine which is the correct value, and propagate that value to succeeding circuits. A system of this type with n identical units and a decision element is said to use *n-modular redundancy* (*n*MR). Figure 6.56 shows a frequently used version called *triple modular redundancy* (TMR) in which $n = 3$. In this case, the behavior of the decision element is defined by the logic equation

$$X = X_1 X_2 + X_1 X_3 + X_2 X_3$$

which is the well-known majority function. X has the correct value if no more than one of the signals X_1, X_2, X_3 is incorrect. Thus the TMR system is capable of tolerating faulty behavior by any one of the triplicated units.

Static redundancy may be implemented at any complexity level. *Interwoven logic* is a technique for fault-tolerant design at the gate level which has been thoroughly analyzed by Pierce [31]. In practice, hardware redundancy is normally used at the processor level where the replicated elements are CPUs, memory modules, switching networks, or entire computers. This type of high-level redundancy is sometimes called "massive" redundancy.

A system with *dynamic* redundancy tolerates faults by actively reorganiz-

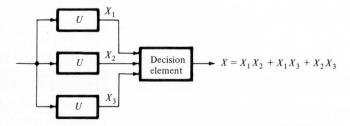

Figure 6.56 Example of triple modular redundancy (TMR).

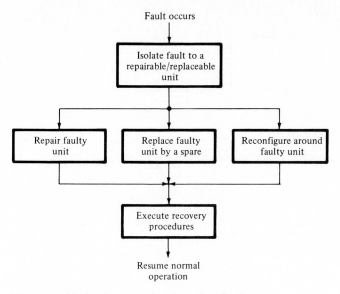

Figure 6.57 Fault tolerance using dynamic redundancy.

ing the system so that the faulty component is effectively replaced by a fault-free component. This is usually achieved in three major steps, as illustrated in Fig. 6.57.

Step 1 (fault diagnosis): Test procedures are carried out to detect the fault and isolate it to a replaceable or repairable unit.

Step 2 (fault elimination): The fault is effectively removed either by repairing the faulty unit, replacing it with a spare unit, or logically reconfiguring the system around the fault.

Step 3 (recovery): Procedures are executed to restore the system to a state that existed before the fault occurred. Normal system operation is then resumed from that point.

Although more complex than static redundancy, dynamic redundancy has the advantage that faulty units are rapidly located and eliminated. In the static case, faults can accumulate undetected until the entire system breaks down.

Figure 6.58 shows the structure of a system employing dynamic redundancy. This is sometimes called a *duplex* system, since it contains two identical copies of the basic (simplex) system which is to be made fault tolerant. The two systems operate in tandem, with both performing the same operation at the same time. A circuit called the *match detector* does a continuous comparison of the results generated by the duplicated units. When a mismatch is detected, indicating the presence of a fault in the system, normal operation is temporarily halted and diagnostic routines are executed which attempt to identify the faulty unit. Once the faulty unit is identified, it is disconnected from the system, which

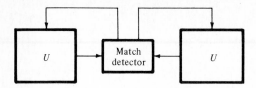

Figure 6.58 A fault-tolerant duplex system.

is then restarted as a simplex system using only the fault-free unit. The failed unit is repaired off-line and is eventually restored to the system.

Example 6.7: The Bell System No. 1 ESS (*Electronic Switching System*) [12] No. 1 ESS is a computer-controlled telephone exchange introduced in 1964 to replace the electromechanical (relay) switching networks long used in this application. A primary design goal of this system is that its down time should not exceed 2 hours over its projected 40-year life. Furthermore, the system must function unattended for very long periods. These very stringent reliability goals are achieved by a number of techniques. Circuits with extremely high intrinsic reliability are used. All critical parts of the system are duplicated, including the CPUs, memory modules, and major buses. Special checking circuits are included to detect faults when they occur. The circuits are augmented by extensive diagnostic programs used to detect and locate faults within the system.

Figure 6.59 indicates the general structure of No. 1 ESS. It consists of a programmable digital computer of fairly conventional design which controls a large telephone switching network. This switching network appears as a special IO device to the computer. Telephone calls arriving at the switching network are processed by programs stored in a read-only memory called the program store. A second read-write memory named the call store is used for storage of temporary information, e.g., the digits dialed, associated with processing a telephone call. The program and call stores form the main-memory system. To achieve the desired fault tolerance, the CPU, program store, call store, and three main bus subsystems are duplicated, as depicted in Fig. 6.59. The telephone switching network (which resembles a crossbar switch) is not replicated, since it inherently provides several alternate paths between pairs of lines.

At any time the No. 1 ESS is configured to look like two identical disjoint computers, each with its own CPU, buses, and memory modules. Only one of these computers, the "active computer," actually controls the telephone switching network. The other computer, called the standby system, operates in parallel with the active system. Their results are continually compared by match circuits. When a fault is detected, an interrupt is generated and both computers begin executing a "fault-recognition program." Thus each computer tests itself. The fault-recognition program exercises the hardware where the mismatch occurred in an attempt to reproduce the fault conditions. The object of this is, of course, to identify

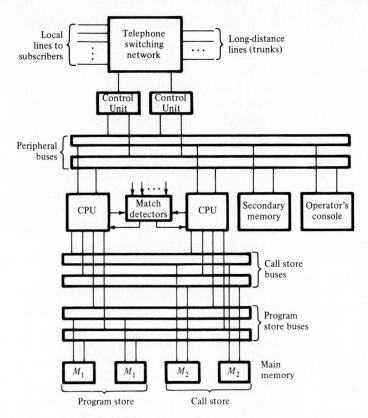

Figure 6.59 The Bell No. 1 ESS.

the faulty computer. If the active computer detects the fault, it deactivates itself and transfers control to the standby computer, which then becomes the active computer. If the standby computer fails, it is disconnected from the system by the active computer. The possibility of a faulty active computer's being unable to disconnect itself from the system is guarded against by special "emergency" circuits. The simultaneous presence of faults in both the active and standby computers can cause a total system failure. The possibility of this happening is slight; it is, however, included in the 2-hour downtime estimate.

The checking circuits and the fault-recognition program are designed to localize a fault very rapidly to one of the two computers. Once a faulty computer has been identified, it is switched out of its normal processing mode. It then proceeds to execute a series of diagnostic programs that attempt to isolate the fault to the smallest replaceable component (a circuit package). In the meantime, the other computer continues to process telephone calls. Once the fault has been located, a message is sent to a human operator, who replaces the circuit packages specified by the diagnostic programs with spare circuits. Normal duplex operation of the system is then resumed.

Cost and performance In a system with static redundancy, the extra cost to achieve fault tolerance can be attributed almost exclusively to the extra hardware used, specifically, the additional functional units and decision circuitry. When dynamic redundancy is used, the cost of the software needed for fault diagnosis, reconfiguration, and recovery must also be considered. This cost can be very substantial. For example, in order to obtain test patterns to detect and locate faults within the system, extensive gate-level simulation may be necessary [7].

The performance of a fault-tolerant system has two aspects: computational efficiency and reliability. Computation speed can be influenced by fault-tolerance requirements. For example, it may be necessary to devote a substantial amount of processing time to the execution of test and maintenance programs. Furthermore, the occurrence of one or more failures may cause a reduction in processing performance. A multiprocessor with one nonfunctioning CPU can usually continue to operate with a smaller throughput. The ability of a faulty system to continue to operate at an acceptable but lower level of performance is referred to as *graceful degradation*.

The ability of a system to tolerate faults can be measured in many ways. A useful fault-tolerance measure is *availability*, defined as the percentage of its operational life during which the system is not disabled by faults. Thus the desired availability of No. 1 ESS is 99.9994 percent based on 2 hours of downtime in 40 years. (The actual availability of No. 1 ESS measured to date is close to this figure.) A more widely used performance measure is the *reliability* $r(t)$, which is defined as the probability of the system's surviving (functioning correctly) for a period of length t. From $r(t)$ we can obtain a single number MTBF called the *mean time before failure*, which is a common measure of the average working life of the system. MTBF is defined formally as follows

$$\text{MTBF} = \int_0^\infty F(t)t \, dt \quad \text{where } F(t) = \frac{d}{dt}[1 - r(t)] \qquad (6.1)$$

The rest of Sec. 6.3.2 deals with the calculation of reliability measures, mainly involving the function $r(t)$.

Failure rates All physical units are subject to failures. These failures have many causes, not all of which may be understood. The *failure rate* is the fraction of units that fail per unit time. For many components, the failure rate as a function of time is represented by a graph of the kind shown in Fig. 6.60. During the early life of the component (the "burn-in" period), a high failure rate is experienced, reflecting faults occurring during manufacture or installation. A high rate again occurs toward the end of the component's life (the "wear-out" period). However, during most of the component's operating life, the failure

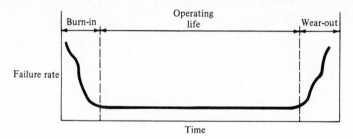

Figure 6.60 Typical variation of failure rate with time.

rate is approximately constant. During this period, failures occur randomly and at a low rate.

Suppose that $n(0)$ copies of a unit, e.g., a CPU, begin their working life (after the burn-in period) at time $t = 0$. Let $f(t)$ be the number that have failed after time t. The number surviving, denoted by $n(t)$, is $n(0) - f(t)$. The *reliability* $r(t)$ of the unit is defined to be the fraction of surviving units at time t, that is,

$$r(t) = \frac{n(t)}{n(0)} \tag{6.2}$$

(This reliability function can clearly be interpreted as the probability of any unit surviving to time t.) Let λ denote the failure rate which, in accordance with Fig. 6.60, is assumed to be constant. This means that the number of units df that fail during the small interval from t to $t + dt$ is given by

$$df = \lambda n(t)\, dt \tag{6.3}$$

Now $n(t) = n(0) - f(t)$ and $n(0)$ is independent of t; hence $dn = -df$. Substituting into (6.3), we obtain

$$dn = -\lambda n(t)\, dt$$

Now (6.2) implies that $dr = dn/n(0)$, hence $dr = -\lambda n(t)\, dt/n(0)$. Using (6.2) again to replace $n(t)/n(0)$ by $r(t)$ we obtain

$$\frac{dr}{dt} = -\lambda r(t)$$

Integration with the boundary value $r(0) = 1$ yields

$$r(t) = e^{-\lambda t}$$

This is the classic *exponential law* of failure. The corresponding mean time before failure defined by (6.1) is

$$\mathrm{MTBF} = \int_0^\infty \lambda e^{-\lambda t} t\, dt$$

which on integrating by parts immediately yields $\mathrm{MTBF} = 1/\lambda$.

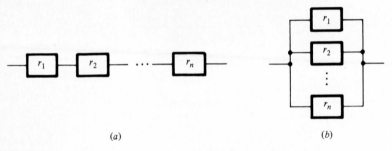

Figure 6.61 Two basic reliability structures: (a) series and (b) parallel.

System reliability Once the failure rates of the individual components of a system are known or can be estimated, it becomes possible to calculate the reliability of the entire system. Two basic systems structures from a reliability point of view are the series and parallel structures appearing in Fig. 6.61. In a series system it is assumed that if any component fails, the system fails. Hence the system reliability r is the product of the component reliabilities, i.e.,

$$r = \prod_{i=1}^{n} r_i$$

In a parallel system, on the other hand, all components must fail in order for the system to fail. Hence the system *unreliability* $1 - r$ is the product of the component unreliabilities $1 - r_i$, from which it follows that

$$r = 1 - \prod_{i=1}^{n} (1 - r_i)$$

Many systems can be decomposed into a sequence of series and parallel systems and the overall reliability can be calculated using the equations above. For example, the series-parallel system S in Fig. 6.62 can be decomposed into two subsystems S_1 and S_2 which are connected in series. S_1 and S_2 are themselves purely parallel systems. Assuming that each individual unit has reliability r, the

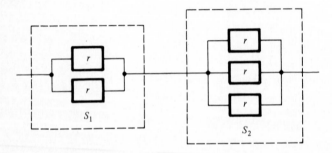

Figure 6.62 Example of a series-parallel system.

system reliability $r(S)$ is given by

$$r(S) = [1 - (1 - r)^2] [1 - (1 - r)^3]$$
$$= 6r^2 - 9r^3 + 5r^4 - r^5$$

Let us now apply the foregoing analytic tools to the TMR system of Fig. 6.56. Assume that each of the triplicated units has reliability $r_1 = e^{-\lambda t}$ and that the voter has reliability $r_v = e^{-\lambda_v t}$. Let $p_i(t)$ denote the probability of any i of the triplicated units surviving to time t. The system reliability $r_3(t)$ is given by

$$r_3(t) = [p_2(t) + p_3(t)] r_v$$

Now $p_2(t) = \begin{pmatrix} 3 \\ 2 \end{pmatrix} (e^{-\lambda t})^2 (1 - e^{-\lambda t})$, while $p_3(t) = (e^{-\lambda t})^3$; hence

$$r_3(t) = (3e^{-2\lambda t} - 2e^{-3\lambda t}) e^{-\lambda_v t} \qquad (6.4)$$

The voter is usually much simpler than the functional units; its reliability is therefore usually very high. If we assume $r_v = 1$, that is, if we ignore the possibility of a voter failure, (6.4) reduces to

$$r_3(t) = 3e^{-2\lambda t} - 2e^{-3\lambda t}$$

Figure 6.63 shows a plot of this equation for $\lambda = 0.01$. The reliability of a single unit $r_1(t) = e^{-\lambda t}$ is also shown for comparison. It can be seen that for values of t less than about $0.7/\lambda$, the reliability of the TMR system is greater than that of the simplex system; however, beyond this point its reliability is less. The reliability of a TMR system is usually better than the foregoing model suggests, since the system may continue to function correctly even if two units fail. For example, if the two failed units never generate incorrect output signals at the same time, then the decision element always produces the correct output.

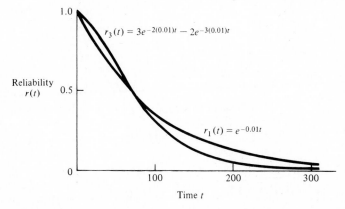

Figure 6.63 Reliability $r_1(t)$ of a single unit and reliability $r_3(t)$ of a TMR system using the same units.

System model with repair We now consider a queueing theoretic model that is appropriate in a multiprocessor or multicomputer system where faulty units are continuously repaired and replaced [16, 28]. The system is viewed as containing a total of n units, of which $n - i \leq n$ are working at any time while the remaining i units are being repaired. The repair facility is modeled by a queue of items waiting for repair and a server representing the repair process. The arrival rate at the repair facility is denoted by λ_i and is assumed to be the same as the failure rate. The service rate is denoted by μ_i. Note that λ_i and μ_i are functions of i, the number of failed units. All failures and repair operations are assumed to be independent.

Let p_i denote the probability that i units are not working. Our first goal is to derive an expression for p_i in terms of λ_i, μ_i, and n. Let h denote a short time interval. The probability of one unit failing in the period h is $\lambda_i h$. Similarly the probability of the repair of a failed unit being completed in the interval h is $\mu_i h$. h is assumed to be sufficiently small that the probability of more than one unit failing or completing repair is negligible. We can therefore express p_i as follows

$$p_i = p_{i-1} p_A + p_i (p_B + p_C) + p_{i+1} p_D \tag{6.5}$$

where p_A = probability that one unit fails and none completes repair
$\quad\ p_B$ = probability that no units fail or complete repair
$\quad\ p_C$ = probability that one unit fails and one completes repair
$\quad\ p_D$ = probability that no unit fails but one completes repair

The following expressions for p_A, p_B, p_C, and p_D are implied by these definitions:

$$p_A = \lambda_{i-1} h (1 - \mu_{i-1} h)$$

$$p_B = (1 - \lambda_i h)(1 - \mu_i h)$$

$$p_C = \lambda_i h \mu_i h$$

$$p_D = (1 - \lambda_{i+1} h) \mu_{i+1} h$$

Substituting into (6.5) and neglecting h^2 terms, we obtain

$$p_i = p_{i-1} \lambda_{i-1} h + p_i (1 - \lambda_i h - \mu_i h) + p_{i+1} \mu_{i+1} h$$

This immediately simplifies to

$$p_{i+1} = \frac{p_i(\lambda_i + \mu_i) - p_{i-1}\lambda_{i-1}}{\mu_{i+1}} \tag{6.6}$$

Now when $i = 0$, no units are awaiting repair; therefore $\mu_0 = 0$. Substituting 0 for i in (6.6) and noting that $p_{-1} = 0$, we obtain

$$p_1 = p_0 \frac{\lambda_0}{\mu_1} \tag{6.7}$$

Setting $i = 1$ in (6.6) and substituting for p_1 using (6.7) yields

$$p_2 = p_0 \frac{\lambda_0 \lambda_1}{\mu_1 \mu_2}$$

Continuing in this way we can deduce the following expression for p_i in terms of p_0:

$$p_i = p_0 \prod_{j=0}^{i-1} \left(\frac{\lambda_j}{\mu_{j+1}} \right) \tag{6.8}$$

The reliability r of the system, defined as the probability that at least one unit is working, is given by

$$r = 1 - p_n$$

where p_n can be deduced from (6.8).

In order to simplify the problem further, we assume that both λ_i and μ_i are constants, that is, $\lambda_i = \lambda$ and $\mu_i = \mu$. (For more realistic assumptions, see Refs. 16 and 28.) Equation (6.8) then reduces to

$$p_i = p_0 \rho^i \tag{6.9}$$

where, as in Sec. 2.3.4, $\rho = \lambda / \mu$. Now

$$\sum_{i=0}^{n} p_i = 1$$

therefore

$$p_0 = 1 - \sum_{i=1}^{n} p_i$$

hence

$$p_0 = 1 - p_0 \sum_{i=1}^{n} \rho^i$$

whence

$$p_0 = \left[1 + \sum_{i=1}^{n} \rho^i \right]^{-1}$$

Now by (6.9) $p_n = p_0 \rho^n$; therefore

$$p_n = \rho^n \left[1 + \sum_{i=1}^{n} \rho^i \right]^{-1}$$

Hence the system reliability is given by

$$r = 1 - \rho^n \left[1 + \sum_{i=1}^{n} \rho^i \right]^{-1}$$

Figure 6.64 shows a plot of r against ρ for several values of n.

6.3.3 Computer Networks

A computer network is a collection of computers and other system components that are linked together usually over long physical distances. The rationale for

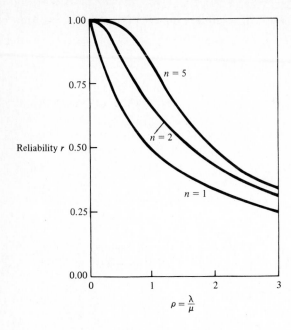

Figure 6.64 Reliability of an n-unit system with failure rate λ and repair rate μ.

such a system is to permit sharing of computing resources that are widely separated. Interaction between the various computers generally takes the form of data transfers via their IO systems; a computer network can therefore be called an indirectly coupled multiprocessing system.

The origin of computer networks can be traced to the SAGE (*S*emi-*A*utomatic *G*round *E*nvironment) air defense system built by the U.S. Air Force in the early 1950s [27]. An early nonmilitary network was the American Airlines SABRE (*S*ales *a*nd *B*usiness *R*eservations done *E*lectronically) reservation system which linked over a thousand reservation terminals distributed throughout the United States to a central computer system. SABRE was required to provide a response to a reservation inquiry in less than 3 s. Both SAGE and SABRE used duplex computers to provide a high level of fault tolerance. Another significant development of the early 1960s was the advent of time-sharing systems to provide many remote users with interactive access to a general-purpose computer with a variety of resources. An experimental computer network sponsored by the U.S. Department of Defense Advanced Research Projects Agency (ARPA), known as the ARPANET, links several dozen computer centers in the United States. This influential network, which began operating in 1969, is examined later in this section.

Most nonmilitary networks rely on an existing communication network, the worldwide telephone system, to provide the necessary communication links. When short response times are required, as in airlines reservation systems, private lines called leased lines may be obtained from the telephone companies. A set of leased lines often forms the basis of a computer network. In recent years the traditional voice-grade telephone channels which have relatively low data-transfer capacity have been augmented by high-capacity channels designed specifically for digital data transmission.

Design criteria Computer networks are generally designed to provide a user at an IO terminal with access to the computing resources of a remotely located computer. The computer may provide an immediate response to user requests (real-time processing) or it may execute jobs from remote users in batches (remote batch processing). In each case communication is accomplished by the transmission of blocks of digital information referred to as *messages* through the network.

The following parameters are of importance in evaluating a communication network.

1. The delay associated with transmitting messages through the network
2. The maximum throughput or bandwidth of the communication links
3. The reliability or fault tolerance of the network
4. The communication costs, which may be measured in dollars per bit transmitted

Network sharing In order to reduce transmission costs (which can be very high for long-distance communication), it is necessary to be able to share the available transmission paths. This may require some form of *time-sharing* or *multiplexing* that permits several users to use the same data path concurrently. A switching network may then be used to select the user to be connected to the shared line. The concentrator shown in Fig. 6.3 serves in this capacity.

The establishment of a dedicated transmission path from source to destination for each information exchange is called *line switching* or *circuit switching*. It is the usual mode of communication that is used in the public telephone network. Line switching is initiated by dialing and implemented by telephone exchanges. It has the disadvantage that once a path is established between two locations, it cannot be used by other potential users along the path, even if the utilization of that path is very low.

This problem can be overcome by a technique called *message switching* whereby intermediate switching centers on a long communication path are used to store messages temporarily and subsequently forward them to the next destination, a process called *store-and-forward*. Messages are collected at each switching center where they are organized, e.g., grouped into batches, in a manner that makes efficient use of the data paths connected to that center. An analogy can be drawn between message switching and the transmission of mail through the postal system. Compared with line switching, message switching can provide a substantial increase in circuit utilization.

Messages can vary greatly in length, so that short messages can be significantly delayed while longer messages are being transmitted. This problem can be minimized in a message-switching system by dividing all messages into short *packets* of fixed length and format and transmitting packets from long messages interspersed with packets from short messages. The store-and-forward switching centers are responsible for sorting the packets from the various messages and transmitting them to their proper next destinations. At the final destination of a message it must be reassembled from its constituent packets. This form of communication, called *packet-switching*, is used when very fast communication is required. In a packet-switching network, leased (i.e., privately operated) communication links are normally used, with small computers acting as the store-and-forward switching centers.

Example 6.8: The ARPANET computer network [13, 15] The ARPANET is a large experimental computer network which currently links over 50 research institutions in the United States via leased lines that have a bandwidth of 50,000 bits/s or more. Several satellite links to locations outside the continental United States also exist. Figure 6.65 shows the structure of the ARPANET at an intermediate stage in its evolution (1972) when it linked 24 locations. The ARPANET uses packet switching in order to achieve a low average transmission time at reasonable cost. Each node in the network contains a small computer called an *interface message processor* (IMP) which performs the store-and-forward functions required for packet switching. An IMP is used to connect one or more computers, called *hosts*, at the same location as the IMP to the ARPANET. Since many different types of computers are used as hosts, the IMP acts as a standard interface device between its hosts and the main long-distance communication network. Each host usually supports a set of interactive IO terminals by which a user gains access to the ARPANET. A special type of IMP, called a *terminal IMP* or a TIP, allows IO terminals to be connected directly to the ARPANET without a host computer.

A message is transmitted from a source host computer C_1 to a destination host C_2 in the following way. C_1 sends the message to its IMP, which breaks it into packets of approximately 1000 bits. The IMP then transmits the packets to one or more of the IMPs to which it is directly connected. These IMPs in turn forward the packets toward C_2. The IMPs attempt to choose fast routes through the network based on current traffic conditions which they continually monitor. Eventually the packets reach the IMP associated with C_2, where the original message is reassembled and sent to C_2.

Some of the important design objectives of the ARPANET are listed below [13].

1. The average packet transmission delay through the network should be less than 0.2 s.
2. The maximum bandwidth for IMP-to-IMP communication should be 85K bits/s.
3. At least two disjoint communication paths should exist between every pair of IMPs.

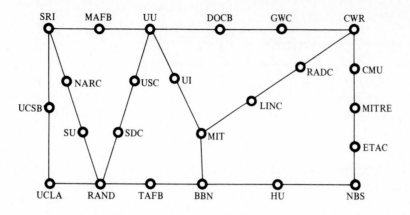

Figure 6.65 Structure of the ARPANET, circa 1972.

4. Transmission errors should occur at a rate of 1 bit in 10^{12} or less.
5. The cost of transmitting 1000 packets (about 10^6 bits) should be less than 30 cents.

Figure 6.66 shows the main features of a packet in the ARPANET. The data to be transmitted, which is part of a host-generated message, forms the text field of the packet. The IMP attaches a header field to the text that identifies the packet and specifies its source and destination. Transmission errors are detected by error-detecting codes. Before it forwards a packet, each IMP generates a sequence of check bits which it attaches to the end of the packet. These check bits can detect any error involving at most 4 bits or a continuous sequence (burst) of up to 24 erroneous bits. An IMP retains a copy of each packet it forwards until it receives

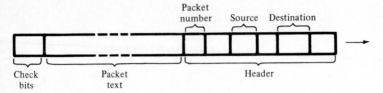

Figure 6.66 The ARPANET packet format.

an acknowledgement signal from the next IMP. If such an acknowledgement is not received, due to detection of a transmission error or because the destination IMP is busy, for example, the source IMP retransmits the packet, perhaps to a different IMP. When an IMP receives a packet from another IMP, it checks the packet for errors. If the packet is found to be error-free, it is stored and an acknowledgement signal is transmitted to the source IMP. The latter may then release the storage area containing its copy of the packet.

Network delay Probably the single most useful measure of communication network performance is the average delay t_D encountered by a message in traveling through the network from its source to its destination. t_D and related parameters can be effectively analyzed using queueing theory [23, 24]. Useful results can be obtained using the single-queue single-server model introduced in Sec. 2.3.4.

First consider a network consisting of a single link or channel L that connects two computers. The computers are viewed as generating messages which request service in the form of data transmission through L. The message arrival rate at L can reasonably be assumed to follow a Poisson distribution with exponential interarrival times. The service (transmission) time depends on many factors, including message length and the bandwidth of the transmission medium. If an exponential service time distribution is assumed, then the network delay is defined by Eq. (2.18) as follows:

$$t_D = \frac{1}{\mu - \lambda}$$

where λ is the mean message arrival rate, μ is the mean service rate, and $\mu > \lambda$. The message length can be treated as an independent random variable with a mean value of m bits. The link L is characterized by its bandwidth or channel capacity c bits per second. The mean service time $1/\mu$ can therefore be taken as m/c. Hence the delay t_D can be rewritten as

$$t_D = \frac{1}{c/m - \lambda} \tag{6.10}$$

The average message delay t_D in a network containing n links $\{L_i\}$ can be modeled by treating each link as a queue with a single server. t_D can be expressed in the form

$$t_D = \sum_i \frac{\lambda_i t_i}{\gamma} \tag{6.11}$$

where t_i is the average message waiting time in link L_i, λ_i is its average traffic in messages per second, and γ is the total (Poisson) arrival rate of messages to the network from external sources [23]. Let c_i be the bandwidth of L_i in bits per second and let m be the average length of a message. The mean time taken by L_i to service a message is $m/c_i = 1/\mu$. If we assume that the service time of L_i is exponential, then t_i is defined by (6.10) so that (6.11) can be rewritten as

$$t_D = \sum_i \frac{\lambda_i}{\gamma(c_i/m - \lambda_i)}$$

While Poisson arrival distributions or, equivalently, exponential interarrival time distributions model the arrival process fairly accurately, the service process is often far from exponential. Consider a single-queue single-server model with Poisson arrivals and an arbitrary service-time distribution characterized by a mean value of $1/\mu$ and a standard deviation of σ. Any queueing discipline that is independent of service time may be used. Under steady-state conditions, the mean queue length l_Q is defined by the *Khinchin-Pollaczek equation* [16, 24]

$$l_Q = \rho + \rho^2 \frac{1 + \sigma^2 \mu^2}{2(1 - \rho)} \tag{6.12}$$

This is considered to be the fundamental equation for analyzing single-server systems. Note that with exponential service times, $\sigma = 1/\mu$ and (6.12) reduces to (2.16). The mean waiting time or delay t_D follows from (6.12) by Little's equation $t_D = l_Q/\lambda$. No corresponding expressions for l_Q or t_Q are known when the arrival distribution is arbitrary, i.e., non-Poisson. The parameter $\rho = \lambda/\mu$ measures the utilization of the communication links—hence its name "traffic intensity."

Reliability Let G be a graph with n nodes V and m edges E representing a computer network. The nodes V represent computers or IO terminals, while the edges E represent communication links. For simplicity it will be assumed that these links are bidirectional (half or full duplex) and that G is an undirected graph. Two nodes v_i and v_j are connected if there exists at least one path between v_i and v_j; otherwise they are disconnected. Of prime interest is the possibility of failures that disconnect any two nodes of G. Such failures can be modeled by the removal of nodes or edges from G. We assume that when a node is removed, all edges connected to that node are also removed.

Two simple nonprobabilistic measures of network reliability are the node and edge connectivity of G. The *node connectivity* (or simply the *connectivity*) $c_N(G)$ is defined as the smallest number of nodes whose removal disconnects G, that is, eliminates all paths between at least two nodes, or else reduces G to the trivial 1-node 0-edge graph G_T. Similarly, the *edge connectivity* (or *cohesion*) $c_E(G)$ is the smallest number of edges whose removal disconnects G or reduces it to G_T. The complete graph K_n with n nodes, such as that of Fig. 6.5, cannot be disconnected by node removal. It can be reduced to G_T, however, by removing $n-1$ nodes; hence $c_N(K_n) = n-1$. K_n can be disconnected by removing the $n-1$ edges connected to any one node; hence $c_E(K_n) = n-1$. It can be shown [14] that for any graph G, edge and node connectivity are related by the inequality $c_N(G) \leq c_E(G)$. Unfortunately, it is very difficult to compute the connectivity of an arbitrary graph. In the worst case, it may be necessary to consider all possible ways of disconnecting every pair of nodes.

A frequent assumption made in the analysis of faults in computers is that only single faults, i. e., the failure of just one component, need be considered. This assumes that a fault can be detected and repaired before another occurs. The class of networks that can tolerate a single fault represented by the removal of a node or edge can be characterized by the following result, which is proven in Ref. 14: $c_N(G) \geq 2$ if and only if every pair of nodes in G lie on a common closed loop (cycle). Tolerance of a single failure of this type is a design requirement of the ARPANET. Clearly the foregoing condition is satisfied by the graph in Fig. 6.65.

Thus a single node removal cannot destroy communication in a network if and only if every pair of nodes lie on a closed loop. Since $c_N(G) \leq c_E(G)$, this condition is also sufficient (but not necessary) for a network to remain connected after the removal of a single edge. Figure 6.67 shows a graph G with $c_N(G) = 1$ but $c_E(G) = 2$. The single node v_3, whose removal disconnects G, is called a *cutpoint*; it represents the most "sensitive" node in the graph.

Suppose that in a network containing n links, each link has a probability p of failing. A natural question is: What is the probability $f(p)$ of the network becoming disconnected, so that communication between at least two nodes becomes impossible? The failure probability $f(p)$ may be expressed as

$$f(p) = \sum_{i=0}^{n} C(i) p^i (1-p)^{n-i} \qquad (6.13)$$

where $C(i)$ is the number of sets of i links called *cutsets* whose failure disconnects the original network, and all link failures are assumed to be independent. A measure of the network reliability is $r(p) = 1 - f(p)$. The main difficulty in

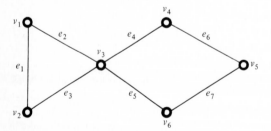

Figure 6.67 A graph G with $c_N(G) = 1$ and $c_E(G) = 2$.

using $f(p)$ and $r(p)$ is computing $C(i)$. $C(i)$ can be determined by enumeration if n is reasonably small. In the case of very large networks, it may be necessary to use approximate methods such as simulation to compute $C(i)$.

6.4 SUMMARY

The nature of the communication methods used in a computer system depends on the physical distances involved. Over short distances, system components are connected by buses which transmit binary (DC) pulses. Long-distance communication generally requires the use of telephone lines or similar facilities, as well as signal transmission by AC carrier modulation. The interconnection structures used differ in the degree to which physical communication links are shared. The extreme cases are dedicated links, which involve no sharing, and a single shared link, which is used for all communication. Intermediate structures include crossbar and ring connections.

Two basic problems in bus communication are the timing of information transfers and the control of access to the bus. In a computer with a single shared bus such as the PDP-11 UNIBUS, information is transferred asynchronously, and special control lines are used for timing and access control. Three methods were discussed for establishing a unit's priority for access to the bus: daisy-chaining, polling, and independent requesting. Two methods for generating timing control signals exist: one-way control, in which only one of the communicating devices provides timing signals; and two-way control, in which both devices provide timing signals. The latter method is often called interlocked control or handshaking.

An important aspect of every computer is its IO system. IO systems are characterized by the extent of CPU involvement in IO operations. The use of CPU programs to control all phases of an IO operation is called programmed IO, a standard feature of most computers. It is inefficient in that it requires the CPU to devote a large amount of time to very simple tasks such as IO data transfers. By providing the IO devices with direct memory access (DMA) capability, simple data transfers can be implemented independently of the CPU. The need for the CPU to test an IO device continually to determine its status can be eliminated by providing IO interrupts. An IO interrupt causes the CPU to transfer control from its current program to an interrupt servicing program. Three kinds of interrupts were identified: single-line, multiple-line, and vectored interrupts, which differ in the amount of information transmitted to the CPU by the interrupt signals.

The maximum amount of independence between CPU and IO operations is achieved by providing IO processors (IOPs). An IOP is capable of executing IO programs that perform complex IO operations. The CPU communicates with the IOP by means of a small number of instructions, e. g., start, stop, and test, while the IOP communicates with the CPU by means of interrupts. If an operating system with multiprogramming ability is employed, a high level of

CPU utilization can be maintained, while individual programs alternate between periods of CPU and IOP processing.

An integrated computer system containing more than one CPU is called a multiprocessor. A multiprocessor has higher potential throughput and reliability than the corresponding uniprocessor. Multiprocessors are distinguished by the way in which their CPUs communicate with one another. In indirectly coupled multiprocessors, the CPUs communicate via the IO system; whereas in directly coupled multiprocessors, they communicate via a common main memory. Multiprocessors such as No. 1 ESS have fault tolerance as their primary design goal. This goal is achieved by the systematic use of redundant components. Fault tolerance can be implemented by static redundancy, e. g., triple modular redundancy (TMR), or by dynamic redundancy, e. g., duplex systems capable of self-diagnosis and repair.

A computer network is a collection of computers and IO terminals separated by long physical distances; it can be regarded as a form of loosely coupled multiprocessor. A computer network gives users access to remote computing resources. Communication is typically via the telephone network using public or private (leased) lines. The communication paths are shared by line-switching, message-switching, or packet-switching; the latter two methods require the network nodes to have a message store-and-forward ability. The ARPANET is an example of a nationwide computer network using packet-switching. The performance of a network can be measured by the mean delay of messages traversing it and by its reliability in the event of failures in communication links.

PROBLEMS

6.1 Consider the timing diagram for a data transfer via the PDP-11 UNIBUS which appears in Fig. 6.10. Explain why a delay of at least 75 ns is allowed by the master unit between deactivating MASTER SYNC and clearing the address bus and CONTROL lines.

6.2 Analyze the three bus-control methods daisy-chaining, polling, and independent requesting with respect to communication reliability in the event of hardware failures.

6.3 Using register-level components carry out the logic design for the interrupt priority circuit shown in Fig. 6.32. Assume that $n = 8$.

6.4 A computer consists of a CPU and an IO device D connected to main memory M via a one-word shared bus. The CPU can execute a maximum of 10^5 instructions per second. An average instruction requires five machine cycles, three of which use the memory bus. A memory read or write operation uses one machine cycle. Suppose that the CPU is continuously executing "background" programs that require 95 percent of its instruction execution rate but not any IO instructions. Now the IO device is to be used to transfer very large blocks of data to and from main memory M.

(a) If programmed IO is used and each one-word IO transfer requires the CPU to execute two instructions, estimate the maximum IO data-transfer rate r_{MAX} possible through D.

(b) Estimate r_{MAX} if DMA transfer is used.

6.5 An IOP controls data transfers between main memory and a set of IO devices with widely differing data-transfer rates. The IOP can interleave (multiplex) transfers involving several IO devices provided that their combined effect does not exceed the data-transfer capacity of the system. Data transfers are initiated by requests from the IO devices. A request is accepted by the IOP only if it has sufficient spare capacity to service the requesting device. Devise an easily implemented algorithm for use by the IOP to determine whether or not it can accept a service request from an IO device. State all assumptions you make.

6.6 A new computer intended to have very fast and efficient IO processing abilities is being designed. List all the features of the IBM S/360-370 IO system that you would *not* include in the new computer. In each case give your reasons for rejecting the S/360-370 approach and define your alternative approach.

6.7 Consider a multiprocessor in which n processors are connected to n interleaved memory units via a crossbar switching network. Let u, the system utilization, be defined as the average fraction of the memory units that are busy, i.e., communicating with processors. Thus u is also a measure of processor utilization. Assuming that memory accesses are distributed randomly among the memory units, show that u is approximately 0.6. Hence it can be expected that on the average 60 percent of the processors and memory units will be busy.

6.8 Because of the low cost of microprocessors and related components, several proposals have been made to build very powerful multiprocessors containing hundreds of thousands of microprocessors. Analyze the feasibility, usefulness and cost of such multimicroprocessor systems, addressing each of the following issues:

(a) The interconnection structure of the system

(b) The methods used for interprocessor communication

(c) The types of computing problems for which the system is suited

6.9 Analyze in detail the relative merits of the following three approaches to supervising the operation of a directly coupled multiprocessor:

(a) Allowing only one fixed processor (the master) to execute the supervisory program or operating system; all other processors are treated as slaves

(b) Allowing all processors equal access to the supervisory program, so that any processor can be master at any time

(c) Assigning each processor its own supervisory program with control over a distinct set of system resources

6.10 Calculate the mean time before failure MTBF of a TMR system of the kind shown in Fig. 6.56 whose reliability is defined by

$$r_3(t) = 3e^{-2\lambda t} - 2e^{-3\lambda t}$$

Discuss the significance of the fact that the MTBF of the TMR system is less than that of the corresponding simplex system.

6.11 A variation of TMR called TMR/Simplex uses a disagreement detector to identify the failed unit when the first failure occurs. At that time the TMR system is changed to a simplex system using one of the two correctly working units. Normal operation continues until the simplex system fails. If the reliability of each unit is $e^{-\lambda t}$, calculate the reliability and MTBF of the TMR/Simplex system.

6.12 Identify the types of failures that interrupt telephone-call processing by the No. 1 ESS, i.e., the failures that are not tolerated by the system.

6.13 In the single-queue single-server model of a system with repair considered in Sec. 6.3.2 it was shown [Eq. (6.9)] that $p_i = p_0 \rho^i$, where p_i is the probability of i items being either in the queue or being serviced. Show that if $\rho < 1$ and $n \to \infty$, then $p_i = \rho^i(1 - \rho)$, thus demonstrating the validity of Eq. (2.15).

6.14 A single communication line transmits messages from A to B. The line has a capacity (bandwidth) of c bits per second. Messages arrive at A with Poisson distribution and a mean rate of λ messages per second. The message length measured in bits is an independent random variable with mean value m and second moment s. The mean time to service a message is assumed to be m/c. Derive an expression for the mean message delay t_D in terms of c, λ, m, and s.

6.15 Let G be a graph with n nodes, m edges, and edge connectivity $c_E(G)$. Prove that $c_E(G) \leq \lfloor 2m/n \rfloor$.

6.16 Consider a computer network whose structure is represented by the graph in Fig. 6.67. Let 0.01 be the failure probability of each link in the network. Calculate the probability of the entire network failing, i.e., becoming disconnected.

REFERENCES

1. Anderson, G. A., and E. D. Jensen: "Computer Interconnection: Taxonomy, Characteristics, and Examples," *Comput. Surv.*, vol. 7, pp. 197–213, December 1975.
2. Avizienis, A.: "Fault Tolerant Computing—An Overview," *Computer*, vol. 4, pp. 5–8, January/February 1971.
3. Baer, J. L.: "A Survey of Some Theoretical Aspects of Multiprocessing," *Comput. Surv.*, vol. 5, pp. 31–80, March 1973.
4. Bhandarkar, D. P.: "Analysis of Memory Interference in Multiprocessors," *IEEE Trans. Comput.*, vol. C-24, pp. 897–908, September 1975.
5. Blaauw, G. A.: "The Structure of System/360: Part V—Multisystem Organization," *IBM Syst. J.*, vol. 3, pp. 181–195, 1964.
6. Boyse, J. W., and D. R. Warn: "A Straightforward Model for Computer Performance Prediction," *Comput. Surv.*, vol. 7, pp. 73–93, June 1975.
7. Breuer, M. A., and A. D. Friedman: *Diagnosis and Reliable Design of Digital Systems*, Computer Science Press, Woodland Hills, Calif., 1976.
8. Cluley, J. C.: *Computer Interfacing and On-line Operation*, Crane Russak, New York, 1975.
9. Cohen, L. J.: *Operating System Analysis and Design*, Spartan Books, Rochelle Park, N. J., 1970.
10. Comptre Corp. [P. H. Enslow (ed.)]: *Multiprocessors and Parallel Processing*, Wiley-Interscience, New York, 1974.
11. Digital Equipment Corp.: *PDP-11 Interface Manual*, 2d ed., Maynard, Mass., 1971.
12. Downing, R. W., J. S. Novak, and L. S. Tuomenoksa: "No. 1 ESS Maintenance Plan," *Bell System Tech. J.*, vol. 43, pp. 1961–2019, September 1964.
13. Frank, H., R. E. Kahn, and L. Kleinrock: "Computer Communication Network Design—Experience with Theory and Practice," *AFIPS Conf. Proc.*, vol. 40, pp. 255–270, 1972.
14. Harary, F.: *Graph Theory*, Addison-Wesley, Reading, Mass., 1969.
15. Heart, F. E., et al.: "The Interface Message Processor for the ARPA Computer Network," *AFIPS Conf. Proc.*, vol. 36, pp. 551–567, 1970.
16. Hellerman, H., and T. E. Conroy: *Computer System Performance*, McGraw-Hill, New York, 1975.
17. Horelick, D., and R. S. Larsen: "CAMAC: A Modular Standard," *IEEE Spectrum*, vol. 13, pp. 50–55, April 1976.
18. Husson, S. S.: *Microprogramming: Principles and Practices*, Prentice-Hall, Englewood Cliffs, N. J., 1970.
19. Intel Corp.: *Intel 8080 Microcomputer System Manual*, Santa Clara, Calif., 1975.
20. IBM Corp.: *IBM System/370 Principles of Operation*, Publ. GA22-7000-4. White Plains, N. Y., 1974.
21 IBM Corp.: *IBM System/360 and System/370 I/O Interface Channel to Control Unit: Original Equipment Manufacturers' Information*, Publ. GA22-6974-3, Poughkeepsie, N. Y., 1976.
22. Kimbleton, S. R. and G. M. Schneider: "Computer Communication Networks: Approaches, Objectives, and Performance Considerations," *Comput. Surv.*, vol. 7, pp. 129–173, September 1975.
23. Kleinrock, L.: *Communication Nets: Stochastic Message Flow and Delay*, McGraw-Hill, New York, 1964. (Reprinted by Dover Publications, New York, 1972.)
24. Kleinrock, L.: *Queueing Systems*, vol. I, *Theory*, vol. II, *Computer Applications*, Wiley, New York, 1975 (vol. I) and 1976 (vol. II).
25. Lonergan, W., and P. King: "Design of the B5000 System," *Datamation*, vol. 7, pp. 28–32,

May 1961. (Reprinted in C. G. Bell and A. Newell, *Computer Structures: Readings and Examples*, pp. 267–273. McGraw-Hill, New York, 1971.)

26. MacDougall, M. H.: "System Level Simulation," in M. A. Breuer (ed.): *Digital System Design Automation: Languages, Simulation, and Data Base*, pp. 1–115, Computer Science Press, Woodland Hills, Calif., 1975.

27. Martin, J.: *Telecommunications and the Computer*, 2d ed., Prentice-Hall, Englewood Cliffs, N. J., 1976.

28. Miller, J. S., et al.: *Multiprocessor Computer System Study*, Final Report NASA Contract 9-9763, Intrametrics Inc., Cambridge, Mass., March 1970.

29. Motorola, Inc.: *M6800 Microprocessor Applications Manual*, Phoenix, Arizona, 1975.

30. Padegs, A.: "The Structure of System/360: Part IV—Channel Design Considerations," *IBM Syst. J.*, vol. 3, pp. 165–180, 1964.

31. Pierce, W. H.: *Failure-tolerant Computer Design*, Academic, New York, 1965.

32. Thornton, J. E.: *Design of a Computer: the Control Data 6600*, Scott Foresman, Glenview, Ill., 1970.

33. Thurber, K. J., et. al.: "A Systematic Approach to the Design of Digital Bussing Structures," *AFIPS Conf. Proc.*, vol. 41, pp. 719–740, 1972.

34. Zilog Corp.: *Z80-CPU Product Specification*, Los Altos, Calif., 1976.

INDEX

INDEX